TENTH EDITION

ORAL

Speaking
Across
Cultures

Communication

LARRY A. SAMOVAR
San Diego State University

JACK MILLS

Boston, Massachusetts   Burr Ridge, Illinois   Dubuque, Iowa
Madison, Wisconsin   New York, New York   San Francisco, California   St. Louis, Missouri

McGraw-Hill

*A Division of The **McGraw·Hill** Companies*

ORAL COMMUNICATION: SPEAKING ACROSS CULTURES

 This book is printed on recycled, acid-free paper containing 10% postcomsumer waste.

1 2 3 4 5 7 8 9 0 QPD/QPD 9 0 9 8 7
ISBN 0–697–29909–0

Publisher: *Phil Butcher*
Sponsoring editor: *Marge Byers*
Project manager: *Jane C. Morgan*
Cover and interior design: *Kristyn A. Kalnes*
Cover image: *© Jose Ortega/SIS*
Photo credits: Page 329 *© James L. Schaffer;* All others unless otherwise indicated by *© Lisa Stefani*
Compositor: *Carlisle Communications, LTD.*
Typeface: *10/12 Goudy*
Printer: *Quebecor Printing Dubuque, Inc.*

Library of Congress Catalog Card Number: 96–86800

http://www.mhcollege.com

Brief Contents

Contents

Part II

YOUR IDEAS   125

Chapter 6

Evidence   *The Foundation of Your Ideas*   127

Chapter 7

Visual Aids   *Displaying Your Ideas*   155

Chapter 8

Research   *The Content of Your Ideas*   176

Chapter 9

Critical Thinking   *The Appraisal of Your Ideas*   197

Chapter 10

Organization   *Assembling Your Ideas*   216

Chapter 11

Introductions and Conclusions   *Connecting Your Ideas*   238

Chapter 12

Language   *The Medium of Your Ideas*   254

Part III
HAVING AN INFLUENCE   279

Chapter 13
Informative Speaking   *Being Understood*   281

Chapter 14
Persuasive Speaking
Changing Beliefs, Attitudes, Values, and Behavior   316

Part IV
CHANGING ENVIRONMENTS   357

Chapter 15
Special Occasions
The Unique Communication Situation   359

Chapter 16
Discussion   *Group Communication*   389

To Jack Mills

My friend and mentor for thirty years.

Memory is the treasure-house of the mind wherein the monuments thereof are kept and preserved.   Thomas Fuller

Preface

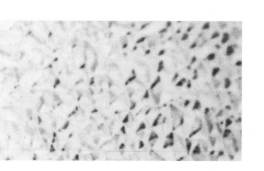

> Today is not yesterday. We ourselves change. How then can our words and thoughts, if they are always to be the fittest, continue always the same? *Thomas Carlyle*

In a culture that is so very fond of novelty, it is indeed rewarding to be asked to prepare a tenth edition of this text. The message of this longevity, at least as read by our pride and egos, is that we have had something basic and worthwhile to say for the last thirty years. However, our feelings of exhilaration are tempered by the realization that we have survived not only because we have always preserved some fundamental precepts from previous editions, but because we welcomed alterations when we believed change would assist us in our efforts. In approaching this current edition, we have once again endeavored to retain the basic framework and philosophy that sustained prior editions, while at the same time offering new materials to help readers improve their communication skills in a changing society.

As you would suspect, tampering with a book that apparently has met the needs of students for such a long period of time is not an easy assignment. We know we need to strike a balance between what represents the core of the discipline and what is new and innovative. Accordingly, we have tried in this edition to make changes that, we think, take into account the new complexities of communicating in the 1990s and into the next century. It is our contention that it will be an era that will be marked by two significant developments—*the first involving new technological advancements that affect communication, and the second the shifting ethnic and cultural composition of our communication partners.* While both of these "revolutions" are commonplace and well documented by the media, their specific impact on public speaking may not be as transparent. Yet these two phenomena serve as the major motivation for most of the significant changes in this current edition. Therefore, throughout this book, we will offer advice as to how you can adapt your communication behavior to the electronic age and to people from diverse cultural backgrounds.

Rationale

The freedom to speak, and the ability to speak effectively, has long been recognized as an asset to the citizens of a democracy. The utility of this skill is seen in both our personal and professional lives. In the United States, even the success and failure of our relationships and careers are often linked with our ability to speak well. In this book, we hope to present material that will assist you in understanding communication principles and in mastering the techniques of speaking that are instrumental to the achievement of success in our society.

Philosophy

A dual philosophy has guided us in the preparation of every edition of this book: first, a recognition of the individual's need to know how to speak well, and second, a conviction that a person's speaking ability is something that can always be developed and improved. We maintain that speech improvement does not begin and end with a single course or with the reading of one textbook. It is the study of a lifetime. Each attempt at sharing an idea or feeling with another person offers us yet another new learning experience, the result of which can teach us something about the principles of social adaptation. Your course, and this book, represent a first step in that adaptation process. As you complete the course and the book we would urge you to seek out as many of these experiences as possible.

Approach

Fundamental to our approach to communication is the belief that communication is a social activity; *it is something we do with and to other people*. Since it is a behavior, we feel it can be approached from a practical viewpoint. Therefore, we have put into this book information and advice that we feel will be usable—*ideas that can be translated into action*.

Organization

Determining the sequence of chapters for our book might well have been one of our most difficult assignments, for any arrangement we selected would have been linear. The nature of language forces us to employ words and ideas one at a time. However, the act of communicating, because it is a dynamic, holistic process, has many things going on at the same time. For example, you are using evidence, vivid language, interesting material, and clear organization while you are talking, looking at your audience, and moving. Ideally, we would offer advice on these six or seven concepts all at the same time. But we cannot. Again, we cite the dilemma. Which of these many skills do we treat first? Which second? Which last? Forced to make the choice of which skills to discuss first and which to discuss later, we based our decisions on one of the philosophies behind this book—students need information that meets their current stage of communication development. That development, like most evolutionary stages or learning processes, reflects movement from the simple to the complex. In short, as you progress from the first simple speeches to the later complex presentations, you will experience a need for a steadily growing supply of information. This book is organized with that need in mind. Acquiring information in manageable increments enables you to move smoothly from simple to more advanced principles, taking along the accumulated learning from one experience to the next. Each chapter builds upon the preceding chapter.

The book is divided into four major parts, each part encompassing a group of closely related chapters. Part I, "Preliminary Considerations," encompasses chapters 1 through 5, which collectively introduce you to some of the basic concepts of oral communication. Chapter 1 looks at the communication process in general, then focuses on public speaking, comparing it to writing and to conversation. This chapter also offers the reader a model of communication that helps explain the role of culture in human interaction. The ethical responsibilities of both the speaker and listener, although treated throughout the book, are introduced and described in this first chapter. Some rudimentary skills and techniques are offered at the conclusion of the chapter so that you can begin speaking during the first days of your class. Chapter 2 further develops the principles already set forth and adds information about selecting a speech topic, formulating a general and a specific speech purpose, choosing a method of presentation, using notecards, and practicing the speech. Some guidelines for gaining confidence and reducing apprehension are also in this early chapter. Chapter 3 examines the process of audience analysis. The advice offered here focuses on individual, group, and cultural differences. Methods of analyzing the occasion and developing empathy are also presented in chapter 3. Chapter 4 deals with speech delivery. Suggestions for improving both the visual and aural dimensions of communication are offered. Chapter 5 examines ways to improve both informative and critical listening.

Part II, "Your Ideas," moves to more advanced principles. It begins with chapter 6, which offers explanations and suggestions regarding the various forms of evidence needed to prove and clarify your ideas. A discussion of the ethical uses of evidence is also included in this chapter. In chapter 7, the focus is on visual aids: how to gather, prepare, and use them. Gathering speech materials from personal, written, and electronic sources are some of the topics in chapter 8. Ethical considerations in collecting data are also covered in this chapter. Ways to critically evaluate your speech materials are treated in chapter 9. In chapter 10, the discussion is primarily concerned with the proper ways of organizing materials for oral presentation. The subject of speech introductions and conclusions occupies chapter 11. Chapter 12, the final chapter in Part II, examines the details of language usage. Various devices for making words clear and vivid are presented. The ethics of appropriate word choice are also discussed in this chapter.

Part III, "Having an Influence," shows you how to move on to more complicated speech forms. Advice on how to prepare and deliver a speech to inform is offered in chapter 13. Advice regarding persuasive speaking is set forth in chapter 14.

The last section, Part IV, "Changing Environments," is composed of two chapters dealing with unique communication situations. Chapter 15 examines impromptu speeches, manuscript speeches, entertaining speeches, television speeches, speeches of introduction, and answering questions. Chapter 16 deals with communication in small groups. This chapter also includes a section on teleconferencing (or videoconferencing) as a potential small-group context.

New Features

Perhaps the most obvious new feature of the tenth edition, at least for those who are not familiar with the previous editions, is the new design of the book. The book has been visually altered with the addition of color, new display type, and fifty-three new photographs. The new material on ethics, cultural considerations, and electronic technology has also increased the amount of text.

Because of the requests of our readers and reviewers, we have added material on ethics throughout the book. Rather than having a single chapter on this important topic, we have included material on ethics in nearly every phase of the communication process. We have examined the appropriate ethical considerations in each chapter, ranging from gathering material, to using material, to listening, and to appearing on television.

A far more detailed analysis that directly relates to the two revolutionary changes we alluded to earlier in the preface—electronic technology and cultural composition—has been added. Guidance in dealing with the link between the new electronic technology and speech communication is found throughout the book. For example, Chapter 7 has current information concerning the use of audiovisual aids such as computer graphics and video equipment. In Chapter 8, there is an expanded section on employing new technology to aid you in your research. Conducting computer searches and using microfilms, microfiche, and ultramicrofiche are included in this chapter. Chapters 15 and 16 have been enlarged to include new information on television speaking (Chapter 15) and teleconferencing (Chapter 16). Throughout the book, we have offered advice and encouragement intended to stimulate you to use personal video equipment to practice, gather information, and present information.

New material in the area of intercultural communication is so infused into the book that it would be impossible to indicate each and every place the concept of cultural adaptation appears. Instead of designating one chapter to look at culture, we have woven this topic into all aspects of communication. For example, the role of culture as it relates to communication models, ethics, feedback, ethnocentrism, empathy, language, small groups, stereotyping, listening, credibility, humor, forms of reasoning, conflict, audience analysis, delivery, and persuasion are just a few of the places where this component is discussed. It is not our intent to write a book on intercultural communication, but rather to raise your consciousness of the place of culture in human interaction. As we will stress in each chapter, we are now in a period of history that sees us doing business, going to school, socializing, and giving speeches to people from cultures other than our own. We simply want you to be aware of and adapt to those differences when you are engaged in a communication event.

Other *features that have been added or expanded* upon include the following:

- An analysis of *inappropriate and offensive words as they relate to culture and gender*.
- A detailed listing of new *computerized reference works* to assist research.
- Much more detail on *taking notes*.
- Expanded section on gaining *confidence*.
- An enlarged section on *credibility*.
- Additional *proverbs from a variety of cultures* to stimulate interest and discussion.

As with prior editions, we have fresh new examples throughout the book. In addition, we have increased the number of examples as a way of responding to some of the feedback we received from past readers.

Supplementary Materials

Instructor's Manual

An enlarged *Instructor's Manual* is available with *Oral Communication: Speaking Across Cultures* that offers guidelines for organizing the structure of the course while providing goals, overviews, classroom activities, and examination questions for each text chapter.

The MicroTest is a computerized system that enables the instructor to make up cus- **MicroTest**
tomized exams quickly and easily. Test questions can be found in the Test Item File,
which is printed in the Instructor's Manual or as a separate packet. For each exam, the
instructor may select up to 250 questions from the file and either print the test or have
McGraw-Hill (formerly Brown & Benchmark) print it. Printing the exam requires access to a personal computer—an IBM that uses 5.25- or 3.5-inch diskettes, an Apple IIe
or IIc, or a Macintosh. MicroTest requires two disk drives and will work with any
printer. Diskettes are available through the local McGraw-Hill Higher Education Sales
Representative. Call 1-800-338-3987 to secure the name and phone number for your
local representative.

A new student workbook is now available for *Oral Communication: Speaking Across* **Student**
Cultures. The workbook includes activities, assignments, sample outlines, speech eval- **Workbook**
uation forms, and other items to help improve basic communication skills.

Acknowledgments

A number of individuals have helped us with this project. In particular, we want
to thank our editors, Eric Ziegler and Kassi Radomski. They have, as in the past,
offered us support, sound advice, and most importantly, freedom to stake out new territory. We cannot hope to list all the reviewers and other people who have provided invaluable insights and suggestions over the nine previous editions of the book. Their
feedback has made each edition a more useful teaching and learning tool than its predecessor.

      We would like to thank the reviewers of this tenth edition: Denise M. Casey, San
Diego City College; Janice R. Courtney, University of Texas-Pan American; Francis
L.M. Daub, St. Louis University; Risa Dickson, California State University, San
Bernardino; Jullia Fennell, Community College of Allegheny County; Patricia Milford,
California University of Pennsylvania; and Jill Schmid, Willamette University.

      Finally, we thank the nearly 650,000 users of prior editions of *Oral
Communication*. They are the ones who have given us a chance to "talk to them" about
communication. While it may have been a rather intangible link, we have greatly appreciated it.

Larry A. Samovar

Part I

PRELIMINARY CONSIDERATIONS

Chapter 1

Communication

Overview and Preview

The seeds of knowledge may
be planted in
solitude, but must
be cultivated in public.

Edgar Johnson

3

Talkativeness is one thing, speaking well another.

Sophocles

I f you are even remotely like the millions of other students who have had to register for a required course in oral communication, we are convinced that you have already asked yourself or your instructor the following question: "Why do I have to take this course?" As a history, chemistry, computer science, art, or engineering major, you are justly concerned with the question of taking a course "outside" your special major. In this age of specialization most college students, regardless of their major, realize the vast amount of knowledge they need to master in their selected area of study. So the query remains: "Why a speech class?" The answer, at least in its stating, is quite simple: *We are born into and live in a society that we share with other people, and it is communication that enables us to function in that society.* We are social creatures who operate in a social world, and communication links us to that world. We need to add at this point that one of the major themes of this book is that, while we may be in contact with many people who share a somewhat similar view of that world, today, more than ever before, we are communicating with people from cultures that do not perceive the world or interact with it the same way we do. International business, global conflicts, worldwide pollution, new immigration patterns, affirmative action rulings, and calls for "equal justice" have put us in contact with a great number of new people who communicate differently than do members of the dominant culture of the United States.

Importance of Communication

We begin our discussion on the significance of communication by making two significant points that underscore the importance of communication as an integral part of every person's life. First, *our communication behavior has an influence on other people.* Put in slightly different terms, *communication is an activity that produces a result.* Although this activity may originate in the mind, communication is first and foremost something people do with and to each other. When you smile and someone sees your smile, you have done something to that person. If your best friend is smoking and you suggest that she terminate this habit, you have done something to her—whether or not she discontinues smoking. If you are successful in getting an audience of three hundred people to sign a petition opposing the use of animals for testing cosmetics, you have done something to that audience. As you can see from these three simple examples, *communication has a consequence*—sometimes subtle, sometimes powerful, but a consequence. Second, *because communication is something we do (an activity), we can alter the way we engage in that activity; we can improve.* Thus, *this book can help you improve your communication ability*—your ability to influence your environment in a way that benefits both you and the people you come in contact with.

You need only take stock of your waking hours to see the importance of communication in both your professional and private life. Reflect on what you consider a normal day, and you will discover that you spend most of that day in communication.

In the workplace you may use communication in a host of different ways.

Studies estimate that humans spend up to 80 percent of their waking hours engaged in communication. Let us pause for a moment and discuss how some of those hours are spent and how, with practice, you can improve the quality of those hours.

Communication and Democracy

For anyone who has ever studied government the link between communication and democracy is crucial and clear. Thomas Jefferson eloquently told us of this link when he wrote, "Democracy is cumbersome, slow and inefficient, but in due time, *the voice of the people* will be heard and their latent wisdom will prevail." The key words in Jefferson's dictum are "the voice of the people." What he was telling us is that the people must be heard if democracy is to succeed. And to be heard *we must speak*. However, our gift of speech cannot benefit us unless we have the ability to speak effectively. For democracy to work each citizen must take part in the process of governing. A philosopher once said that democracy is the only form of government in which the free are rulers. To help "rule," you need to speak in a lucid manner, you need to put words in their proper place, and you need to promote and defend your ideas in a clear and persuasive fashion. It is not enough to simply imagine that you do not want a trailer park built in a surrounding wilderness area; you must *speak* before the County Board of Supervisors and articulate your position clearly and concisely. Although it may sound hackneyed and simplistic, that is the way democracy works.

Communication and Careers

Communication is an important part of nearly all your professional life. In the workplace you may use communication in many different ways. You may need to complete a sale, take part in an important meeting, negotiate a contract, demonstrate a product, be a participant of an international teleconference, teach a lesson in a class, appear before a judge and jury, or explain company procedures to a new employee. In each of these instances, and we could cite countless others, communication is crucial. And as more and more careers focus on "service industries" instead of manufacturing, the importance of effective communication skills for job success will become even more evident.

Communication and Social Relationships

The personal uses for communication can range from the therapeutic to the pragmatic. You might tell a friend how much you are suffering because you failed an important examination, knowing full well your friend cannot change the results of the test. Nevertheless, sharing the information about the examination seems to have a therapeutic effect. As trite as it sounds, talking usually makes us feel better. Whether that talk is about our spiritual life or our social life, using communication to make contact with other people seems to be a basic human drive. Much of what we know about chronic depression suggests that it is often caused by a lack of human contact. We also know that our relational contacts are also more profitable if we understand the communication process. Knowing how to listen and how to talk in a sincere and competent manner to a family member or a close friend can offer a great deal of satisfaction to both parties.

Communication and Culture

As indicated earlier, being able to communicate effectively with people from different cultures has taken on added significance during the past few decades. Events both abroad and at home have radically changed intercultural communication. At one time, the international arena was reserved for a small proportion of the world populace. Government officials, selected merchants, missionaries, and a few tourists were primarily the people who visited with "strangers." Today, this is not the case. A combination of circumstances has created a world in which we are constantly meeting with people from diverse backgrounds. These people may live and work thousands of miles away or right next door. What is certain is that Marshall McLuhan's global village prophecy has become a reality. The causes of this increased contact are almost as divergent as the contacts themselves. Knowing what has brought about the increase in intercultural contact might well be the first step in arousing interest in this important development. Hence, to better understand the role of intercultural communication in all of our lives, let us look at some of these new "contact points" on the international as well as the domestic level.

International Contacts

Internationally, there are a number of reasons why we find ourselves communicating with people from various cultures. First, new technology in transportation and information systems places us in instant and constant contact with people all over the world. Air travel to "foreign" places is now relatively inexpensive and rapid. Through communication satellites, sophisticated television transmission equipment, and digital switching networks, we are now sharing information and ideas with people whose cultures are far removed from our own.

Second, intercultural "conversations" have increased because people all over the world have started to realize that the earth cannot continue to yield its current bounty unless all people work together. People now realize we need to talk to each other so that we can avoid world hunger, learn to share natural resources, and combat global pollution. As simplistic as it sounds, intercultural communication is being used to deal with these and other universal problems.

Third, the past few decades have given credence to the axiom that violence and conflict in one part of the world influences the entire planet. Staying aloof from global disorder is no longer an alternative. From the Middle East to Eastern Europe, from southern Lebanon to South America, we are learning that distant places can be as troublesome as next-door neighbors.

Finally, shifts in the international business community, coupled with new problems of supply and demand, have forced us to rethink our relationships with import and export cultures. At one time, the United States was the only military superpower, as well as the dominant economic force in the world. The world's economy danced to the U.S. financial tune. Only 5 percent of all American businesses faced international competition. In the 1990s, however, 75 percent of all North American industries face international competition. To deal with this new situation, American companies have internationalized their operations. Today, nearly all major U.S. companies have offices in foreign countries. More than a third of the profits of U.S. companies is generated by overseas operations. Millions of Americans are finding that they are communicating with people from other cultures on a daily basis. The foreign presence in the United States has also increased; more than 6,500 foreign firms now operate in the United States. Foreigners have invested billions of dollars in the U.S. and own nearly $1.5 trillion in U.S. assets. Joint ventures, such as those found in the Maquilador plants along the Mexican-American border, often have three different cultures working in the same factory. In short, whether we stay home or leave the country, we are doing business with, working for, or sharing work space with someone from another culture.

As changes throughout the world began to alter our communication patterns and even reconstruct life in the United States, a kind of cultural revolution was also affecting our need to interact with people who had, until this time, remained silent and/or invisible. It seemed that the word "American" could no longer be used to describe a single group of people. Americans were now coming in different colors and from different ethnic backgrounds. Alterations in birth rates and legal and illegal immigrations into the United States have significantly transformed the demographics of this country. The United States permits more legal immigration than the rest of the world combined. This fact is clearly reflected in the following set of numbers: the population of this country annually increases by a net figure of 3 million people. Of these, between 1.2 million and 1.9 million are immigrants—both legal and illegal. These figures only confirm what we can all observe—ethnic groups are the fastest growing segment of the population. All these groups have cultural characteristics that they are proud of and that influence the way they communicate with the European American dominant culture. When we add groups such as Native Americans, homosexuals, the disabled, and the elderly to the dominant culture, we can see that members of the dominant culture are interacting with people from different cultures with greater regularity and in a variety of settings. For example, the workplace in the United States is experiencing a dramatic increase in cultural diversity. By the year 2000, women and people of color will account for 92 percent of the growth in the American workforce and approximately 84 percent of new workers. Foreign-born workers constitute nearly 20 percent of the workforce in California.

Domestic Contacts

Recent immigration patterns have also increased the cultural diversity of students participating in the American educational system. In many cities nonwhite students outnumber whites in public schools. By some estimates 30–40 percent of the students now entering public schools represent ethnically diverse populations. So here again we observe examples of how schoolteachers, parents, and students are having daily interactions with people, who, because of their backgrounds, often communicate in a manner that is different from the dominant culture of the U.S. This book seeks to increase your understanding of those interactions so that your encounters, whether one-to-one or in the public-speaking setting, will be more rewarding and more successful.

From all the instances cited in the previous pages, it should be clear that your chances for success as a speaker are greatly increased if you have acquired some specialized skills in communication. These skills are so essential in today's society that most universities and corporations offer courses in effective communication to their students and personnel. The assumption behind this training is that, by learning about communication, you will be able to acquire the skills necessary to think critically, solve problems, manifest high levels of personal credibility, adapt to social changes, develop self-confidence and poise, present creative and important ideas, and communicate interculturally. The main point should be clear: *without communication skills, we are isolated from one another, unable to share thoughts and feelings with family, friends, and foes*.

Because of the significance of communication and because communication can be improved, this book is about how to communicate. It is primarily concerned with the efficiency with which you share your opinions and ideas with other people. However, understanding the processes in which you are involved is the first step toward improvement. Therefore, this chapter is based on the assumption that understanding and doing are two sides of the same coin. In this chapter, we seek to discover that interrelationship by examining what communication is and how it works. We will also discuss the ways in which communication and public speaking are both alike and different.

Communication Process

To understand the nature and function of speech, we must examine the process of communication, of which speech is but one manifestation. This text uses the terms *communication, speech communication, public speaking, oral communication,* and *speech* synonymously, simply because a speaker is primarily engaged in communication whenever he or she is, consciously or unconsciously, affecting the behavior of others. We ask and answer questions, we take part in conversation, we exchange ideas in committees, we take part in class discussions, we deliver formal speeches, and we participate in situations for which we are prepared and in some for which we are not prepared. In short, we use communication and speech interchangeably because, in most instances, the same principles and concepts apply to both. In fact, someone once referred to public speaking as a kind of expanded conversation; the components of communication are essentially the components of public speaking. In both cases, factors such as credibility, culture, interest, motivation, organization, clarity, feedback, and delivery come into play. Even the differences we will discuss later can be taken into account in nearly all instances. For example, although usually only one person talks during public speaking, the "other person" is still sending messages. Nonverbal communication is present in all public-speaking situations. The way the audience responds is a type of message. There is even commonality in preconceived purposes. In both public and private interaction, we have a purpose that has triggered our role in the communication process; we seldom engage in random behavior. Thus, although the number of people involved may vary and the time allowed for preparation may differ from occasion to occasion, public speaking and communication basically include the same elements. As already stated, this text should help you improve your use of those elements, both on and off the public platform. In short, you will find it useful if throughout this book you can transfer your newly acquired public-speaking skills to various situations and settings. To help you understand the relationship between the general concept of communication and the public-speaking setting, the next few pages will (1) define communication, (2) discuss the ingredients of communication, (3) offer a model of communication, and (4) explain in what specific ways public speaking and communication are both alike and different.

Defining communication is one of those assignments in life that is analogous to having to explain to someone why you love him or her. In both instances, it is often easier to remain silent and hope that you and your partner have similar meanings. The difficulty in both instances is that definitions of concepts as complex as love and communication are bound to be incomplete. The reason, of course, is that both can take so many different forms. With regard to communication, actors, artists, writers, and musicians communicate with their audiences by diverse methods, including spoken and written words, sounds, actions, forms, and colors. Audiences participate in the communication process by responding to the contrasting symbols sent by each communication source. Not only are the sources and symbols different, but so are the messages. A tired student who yawns in an early morning class communicates something to the professor and to those who sit around her. A smile is a communication act, and so is a frown. The term communication is enigmatic; although it is something we all do, communication is so capacious that it is difficult to define. An article in the *Journal of Communication* presented no less than fifteen working definitions of human communication.

The problem of defining communication becomes even more difficult when we realize that, in one sense, inanimate as well as animate objects can communicate. Therefore, in any definition, we must allow sufficient latitude to include the processes as well as the functions of the act. One such definition suggests that communication is the process of verbally and nonverbally sharing with another person or persons one's knowledge, interests, attitudes, opinions, feelings, and ideas. Perhaps the most useful of all definitions is that *the term communication includes all methods of conveying any kind of thought or feeling between people.*

What Is Communication?

Although each communication event differs in some ways from every other one, we can isolate certain elements that all communication situations have in common. Every time you talk to your neighbor, deliver a speech, or act as a member of a group composed of people from various cultures, certain ingredients of communication are present. What are they?

Ingredients of Communication

The communication act has to originate from a **source.** You, as the source, want to express yourself—to pass on your feelings, to convey information, to give directions, to obtain agreement, to get something done, or to relate an idea. You have something that you want to share with others.

Your idea, which to this point you have held privately, must now be put into a code, a systematic set of **symbols** that can be transferred from person to person. While symbols can take the form of art, dance, and even architecture, in most human interaction we think of symbols as being either verbal (words) or nonverbal (actions). The procedure of translating ideas, feelings, and information into a verbal or nonverbal code is called **encoding.**

Your original idea, now represented by a set of symbols, is the **message.** This is the essential part of the communication process—the subject matter to be communicated. Your message, in written or spoken language or in nonverbal actions, is the symbolic representation of your idea. Regardless of the language system employed or the meaning given to various nonverbal actions, all of us use symbols as the primary means of sharing our internal states.

You send your message through a carrier, or medium, called a **channel.** Channels take various forms, such as wires, graphic signs, light vibrations, and air vibrations. Channels should be thought of as the vehicles that carry the message.

Even though you have sent your message, communication has not yet taken place, for there must be another ingredient, someone to whom your message is directed—a **receiver.** For the receiver to understand and react to your message, he or she must engage in **decoding** your message—translating it into a code that he or she can use. This operation (the converting of external energies to meaningful experiences) is once again a private matter—the initial response to the message happens inside the receiver.

Communication takes place within a particular **context,** or setting. As you know from personal experience, the place of an act controls many aspects of that act. The same words spoken at a party may take on different meanings if uttered in a classroom. The locale of communication, whether in a classroom, large auditorium, television studio, hallway, or church, influences the channels we use (speaking, writing), our purpose for communicating (persuasion, information, enjoyment), and the roles we play (student at school, nurse at hospital, boss at work).

The number of people receiving the speaker's message is also an issue when considering the subject of context. The four most common contexts we find ourselves in are dyadic, small group, mass (often referred to as mediated) and public. *Dyads* are those situations that place us in a communication encounter with one other person. These events are usually more intimate than the other three settings and, because we are close to our communication partner, allow us an opportunity to monitor their response to us and our message.

The *small group* context, because we are sharing ideas and information with six to ten other people, influences everything from the amount of time we get to talk to the type of feedback we receive and send. The popularity of this context demands that we treat it in detail in chapter 16. In fact, that entire chapter examines how communication can be improved in a group situation.

Mass communication represents those situations when we communicate via some electronic device. As is the case in all four settings, adjustments are required when we engage in mediated communication. Television, for example, will influence everything from the feedback we receive to the clothes we wear. In chapter 15 we spend some time discussing how you tailor your presentation when you are confronted with a mass communication context.

Public speaking is yet another context that makes specific demands on the speaker. However, what is important to keep in mind is that you do not have to develop an entirely different set of skills to speak in public, but rather have to adapt the ones you learned in other settings to the public arena. Throughout this book we will offer specific advice that will allow you to expand and develop those basic skills.

As senders of messages, we usually perceive the response people make to our messages. The response may be words, silent actions, or both. It matters little; what is important is that our message, as a stimulus, produces a response that we take into account. Our perception of the response created by our message is called **feedback.**

The term *feedback* applies directly to (1) the reactions you obtain from your listeners and (2) your efforts to adapt yourself to these perceived reactions. The term was originally used only in the literature of engineering and cybernetics to designate the return of information to a machine so that the machine could adjust itself to changing conditions. A thermostat is an example of a device that uses feedback. As information related to the original message (heat) is returned to the machine, the machine readjusts—it shuts off the heater when the air is hot and turns it on when the air is cold. The source makes adjustments because of the information it receives.

Feedback provides a communicator with essential information concerning his or her success in accomplishing desired objectives. In so doing, feedback controls future messages. Whether talking to one or one hundred, a speaker has the twofold task of (1) observing and interpreting audience reactions and (2) readjusting the next message in light of his or her observations and interpretations.

The source is not the only one sending messages to the receiver. Each situation is also characterized by **competing stimuli,** all those other messages vying for the listener's attention. Noise or talk coming from another source are examples of competing stimuli. Listeners "talking to themselves" are also a form of competing stimuli. In short, remember that most listeners are constantly attending to many messages at the same time. A successful communicator realizes that he or she is competing with other stimuli and works to overcome this obstacle.

An accurate description of human communication must allow for the fact that the responses people make to messages do not occur as single, one-dimensional acts. There are *levels of responses;* people usually respond in more than one way. Let us assume that someone tells you that driving a motorcycle is dangerous and that you should not purchase one. At one level—the cognitive level—you agree with the person, yet, while that person is talking, you discover that you have some bad feelings about him or her, which you keep to yourself. This is a type of conscious unstated response. When the person is finished speaking, you reply that perhaps you should think over the entire issue—a verbally expressed response. A few weeks later, you find that you have still other feelings about motorcycles. This is another level of response—your subconscious is reacting.

Let us construct a very transparent situation and observe all the ingredients of communication in operation. Suppose you (source) enter a professor's office (context) and attempt to persuade her that you should have received a higher grade on your last examination. (You have a reason for engaging in communication.) Your nervous system orders your speech mechanism to construct a message to gain the support you want. At the same time that the professor's phone rings (competing stimuli), your speech mechanism, serving as part of the encoding process, produces the following message: "If you have some free time, I would like to talk to you about my last examination." The message is transmitted via sound waves through the air so the receiver can hear it. The sound waves constitute the channel. Your professor hears your message and, using her nervous system, tries to find meaning in what you have said (decoding). She responds to you by saying, "Please come in and sit down." (She gives feedback based on your message.)

Two more important points should be made before we temporarily leave the topic of the ingredients of communication. First, *our enumeration of these ingredients could extend for the remainder of this book, for communication is highly complex and multidimensional—it is not subject to simple analysis.* Factors such as perception, gender, culture, motivation, communication skills, knowledge level, and social systems all play a role in the process. We have merely isolated the factors that are common and dominant in the final response made by the receiver of the message. We will return to these elements and others as we weave our way through the skills needed in successful communication.

Second, *although at times it may have appeared that the text describes a linear process by placing one item ahead of another, communication is not linear, but language is.* Hence, only one element can be discussed at a time, even though this distorts the way communication actually operates. In "real life," things happen all at once, not one after another. In most communication encounters, both parties simultaneously are using feedback, are encoding and decoding, and are aware of the context and the relationship.

Communication Model

The Greek historian Herodotus remarked that "we are all less convinced by what we hear than by what we see." Many scholars in the field of speech communication would agree. They maintain that the ingredients we have just examined, plus some additional considerations, can be understood best if they are placed within the context of *a communication model that is both verbal and visual.* Illustrating a complex concept in the form of a model can make it more intelligible.

As you know, a **model** is simply a representation or an analogue of an object or a phenomenon. You have used models in a variety of ways—airplane models, models of the human body, and even dolls. Models are all partial replicas of the real thing. Models are useful in communication for two reasons. First, they help us understand and make predictions about communication by reducing some of the complexities of this highly intricate process to a form that can be visualized as well as described with words. Second, many communication models are useful because they can abstract from the total phenomenon those features that the model maker wishes to highlight. That is, because we believe that culture greatly influences communication, we can include this variable in our model.

Having briefly established the utility of models, let us now examine a model that will help you understand how communication works. Keep in mind as you move through this model that communication is a complex activity; thus, we must limit the number of factors included in the model (see figure 1.1).

At the outset, you will notice that the model is divided into three large sections. Two of the sections are labeled WHAT WE BRING TO COMMUNICATION and are intended to represent the experiences of two speakers who are about to begin a communication act. The section labeled TAKING PART IN COMMUNICATION denotes the two parties are together in a time-space continuum. Although these portions of the model are interrelated, it might be useful to examine them as separate units.

What We Bring

Each portion of the WHAT WE BRING TO COMMUNICATION section shows two communication participants (Persons A and B) *before* the communication act occurs. You will notice that under each participant is an arrow labeled TIME with points on both ends. One of the points of the arrows is headed in the direction of TAKING PART. This point is used to call your attention to the notion that, in this section of the model, the participants are moving toward the communication event. The precommunication stage is important in that it reminds us that both Person A and Person B were engaged in another activity just before they came in contact with each other. In fact, in a very real sense they have been involved in millions of other communication events before the specific encounter, and as we shall see, each of these events can influence how both parties respond to the immediate situation. The points of the arrows moving away from TAKING PART indicate that, once Persons A and B finish communicating with each other, they will move on to other events and other people, taking new ideas and information they gathered from the specific encounter.

Starting our model with WHAT WE BRING allows us to focus on the impact of past experiences on each new moment in our lives. That is to say, *if we are going to understand what is happening during an encounter, we must appreciate what has happened*

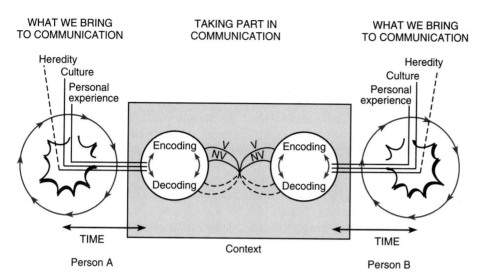

WHAT WE BRING
TO COMMUNICATION

TAKING PART IN
COMMUNICATION

WHAT WE BRING
TO COMMUNICATION

Figure 1.1
Model of
Communication

Person A

Context

Person B

before the meeting. All of us have accumulated a vast history of events and circumstances that find their way out when we communicate. Hence, our model begins by pointing out some aspects of human behavior that are reflected in how we send and receive messages. Let us look at a few of the most important of these aspects.

In the beginning stages of the model, Persons A and B are represented by *irregularly shaped circles with light and dark shading.* These markings, in combination with the *arrows surrounding the circles,* symbolize four important ideas concerning human communication. First, *the circle itself represents the individual's personality.* This is the life space one occupies—the total of one's personal history.

Second, *the irregular shape is to call your attention to the idea that all of us are capable of numerous moods and dispositions.* The peaks and valleys demonstrate, for instance, that we are apt to feel happy after receiving an "A" on an examination and, in the next instant, experience sadness as our best friend tells us he has failed it and must withdraw from school. Like communication, our moods are dynamic and always in a state of flux. When another person arrives in your life, you might not know what mood he or she was in just prior to your visit. State of mind and our moods even shift during the communication encounter.

Third, *the lines surrounding each person also have shades of lightness and darkness, symbolizing the many attitudes and beliefs we hold before, during, and after each communication event.* We arbitrarily use the dark lines to denote strongly held attitudes and beliefs, while the light lines signify attitudes and beliefs that are not firmly held. The open spaces in the circle illustrate the areas that find us without any attitudes or opinions.

Finally, *the arrows surrounding each person suggest motion.* They tell us that the participants, like every other aspect of nature, are in a state of flux. This action is yet another sign of the dynamic nature of communication.

Although we are still in the early portion of this book, we have already discussed the fact that both people and communication are composites of many factors. As we have repeatedly pointed out, human beings are complicated creatures. For thousands of years religious leaders, philosophers, psychologists, and scientists have been trying to understand what factors make us act one way or another. The results of their findings, and common sense, tell us that there is no simple answer to why we behave as we do. Yet, to understand human communication, we must attempt to learn about some of the forces that drive and motivate our behavior. Although there is no magic formula for discovering why people act as they do, most experts agree that, in very general terms, the personal attributes we bring to a communication event have their origins in (1) heredity (biological past), (2) cultural background, and (3) personal experiences. Our communication model shows these three factors with lines entering and leaving the life space of Persons A and B. These three factors, working in combination with the situation we are in at the moment, greatly determine how we send and receive messages.

Heredity   The Roman poet Horace once observed, "Deep in the cavern of the infant's breast / nature lurks, and lives anew." Even though Horace wrote those words over two thousand years ago, they are still true today. He was referring to the power of our biological and evolutionary past (heredity), the traits and characteristics that, through millions of years of evolution, are found in the genes. Many of these characteristics directly relate to how we communicate. These include, among many others, our natural tendency to fear the unknown, our use of eye contact, our drive for self-preservation, our need to be touched, and our attraction to other human beings. Our demands for space and propensity for shyness are also rooted in the genes. The list of genetic and evolutionary traits that affect communication is long, and it continues to grow as we learn about the brain and body chemistry. However, it is not the specific items on the list that are important for our analysis but, rather, the central assertion that much of our behavior is innate and that you need to appreciate these inborn properties if you are going to understand human communication.

Culture   One group of people eats with wooden chopsticks, another uses metal utensils shaped like miniature farm implements, and still another simply uses their hands. Why? One group puts dogs on their plates while another lets them on their couches. Why? One group talks to God, while another sits quietly and lets God talk to them. Why? One group knows about remote control boxes, pocket phones, cash-machine cards, mineral water from the Alps, beepers, and rollerblades, while another group has never seen or heard of these items. Why? The answer rests in culture. Simply put, *our culture, by placing us, at the moment of birth, in a specific geographic area, offers us some experiences and denies us others*. Hence, our culture teaches us everything from what language to speak to what life is and how to live it. So powerful is the pull of culture that anthropologist Edward T. Hall wrote, "There is no aspect of human life that is not touched and altered by culture."

Once we begin to realize that culture is learned, we can start to acknowledge its impact on communication, for, not only does culture teach us what utensils to use and what foods to eat, but culture and communication also work in tandem. Each culture teaches its members ways of perceiving the world and patterns for communicating with that world. These perceptions and patterns are seen in literally thousands of ways. Cultures use space differently, have contrasting norms for the use of eye contact, treat language in unique ways, solve problems differently, vary in their view of who is a credible source, and even have conflicting perceptions of silence and the use of time. If a person's cultural experiences have stressed the importance of talking, as is the case in the United States, Mexico, and the Middle East, he or she will find it normal to talk a great deal to friends and strangers. However, if the tradition of the culture emphasizes silence, as is the case of the Japanese, Chinese, and Korean cultures, people raised in these cultures have a different

view of public speaking. Let us be more specific. Most Western cultures are influenced by the Greco-Roman rhetorical tradition that emphasizes the link between democracy and one's obligation to speak well and often. In the Confucian, Buddhist, and Taoist heritages, people learn to be restrained, controlled, subtle, implicit, and indirect.

Throughout this book, you will encounter the idea that, *as cultures vary, so does the manner in which people communicate*. For now, however, it is important to remember that one of the major influences on what we bring to communication is our culture.

Personal Experience   Our personal experiences, when combined with our cultural learning, have helped shape many of our views about issues such as the death penalty, the use of drugs, sexual freedom, animal rights, the environment, and abortion. For example, let us assume that your personal history has given you a bad experience with marijuana (arrow entering your personality, marked "personal experiences"). This would, of course, influence your response to speakers who attempt to persuade you that marijuana should be legalized. It would, of course, be impossible to catalogue all the personal experiences any one individual has had in their lifetime. But here again our purpose for mentioning "personal experiences" as a communication variable is to simply make you aware of some of the forces that drive our behavior.

A number of observations are in order before we move on to the next phase of the model. First, *the role of heredity (biology, evolution, etc.) in human communication is shown with a broken line instead of a solid line because its influence and impact are much harder to calculate than are cultural and personal experiences.* For example, culture influences the pace at which people solve problems. North Americans tend to be impulsive, while East Asians are reflective. However, we do not know the exact impact of heredity on leadership or aggression. Second, *the precise effect of the three elements we have been discussing is almost impossible to appraise with perfect accuracy.* Each of us is unique and the product of literally millions of experiences. Third, *although we have discussed each of the three factors one at a time, in reality they work together and are interrelated.* Fourth, *notice that the lines carrying heredity, culture, and personal experience from the WHAT WE BRING segment eventually end up in the TAKING PART section of the model.* This visual representation is to call your attention to the idea that who we are, what we know, and what we think and feel get acted out when we interact with other people. Finally, *in chapter 3, when we discuss audience analysis, we will once again return to these three factors and examine them in detail as part of speech preparation.*

Taking Part in Communication

In the middle section of the model, *the participants are together—sharing a common environment.* Although the middle section is called TAKING PART IN COMMUNICATION, from our earlier analysis you should be able to see how all the ingredients and phases of communication are interdependent. This relationship is noted by the arrows that link preencounter activities (WHAT WE BRING) with the portion labeled TAKING PART. With this idea in mind, let us look at some of the elements of interaction.

We talked about encoding and decoding earlier in the chapter during our discussion on the ingredients of communication. We noted that *encoding puts feeling and ideas into a code that can be transmitted and that decoding gives meaning to that code once it has been received.* In the model we are examining now, these two operations (E and D) are linked by the two arrows that run through both processes. They point to the fact that *we are usually encoding and decoding at the same time: we are receiving and formulating simultaneously.* Next, you should notice that the messages being sent are both verbal (V) and nonverbal (NV). For instance, we may smile and move as we talk. The model shows both parties sending and receiving messages; *communication is a circular process*—as we talk to people, they produce responses (words or actions) that become the messages they send to us. It is also important to recognize in this model that *the messages begin as solid lines but eventually become broken lines.* This shift of line structure is used to call attention to a very important axiom of communication: *the message sent is not the message that produces the response or action within the other person.* There is not a direct stimulus-response relationship between what is sent and what is received. *Meaning is what happens inside of people—messages are only sounds or marks on a paper that represent meaning.* For example, if a speaker said, "Freedom is more important as one gets older," he or she had a specific idea when selecting those eight symbols. However, when you decode the symbols, you will, because of your history and culture (what you bring to communication), have different meanings for and responses to the words. If you, as the recipient of the words, are from a culture that has a different definition of "freedom" and "older," the meaning would be even harder to assess. Hence, *the broken line should tell you that what is finally decoded and responded to is only an individual approximation of the original concept.*

Finally, *our model points out that interaction does not occur in a vacuum.* The rectangle marked CONTEXT portrays the idea that communication takes place within a context—a setting that must be considered if you are to adapt your message to people and places. As noted earlier, the location of an act often controls many communication variables. We use different words in a classroom than we do at a party. We dress one way for a job interview and another for a dance. Even the number of people present in the communication environment can have an effect. We talk differently to one person than to a crowd of people gathering to hear a speech. Later in the book, we will look at a number of settings such as small groups, mass media, and public platforms. In each instance, our purpose will be to discover how to adapt communication behavior to the environment.

Communication and Public Speaking

Thus far, we have talked about communication in general terms, lumping together all the ways we share ideas and feelings into a few broad categories. This view, although useful as an introduction, does not make important distinctions that you should be aware of as you begin your training in public speaking. Consequently, we will now turn our attention to the differences between public speaking and other forms of communication. We will then conclude this section by examining a number of ways in which public speaking resembles other forms of communication. An awareness of these differences and similarities will help you adapt your message to the unique situation you find yourself in.

Public Speaking and Writing

Although oral and written discourse have a great deal in common (they both employ symbols), and have the same primary goal—to assist us in sharing internal states with others—they have some obvious differences that affect all phases of the communication process. Let us look at some of the most obvious distinctions and briefly discuss how these differences influence the way you prepare and present your message.

The most obvious difference between oral and written discourse is that they use *different channels*. You will recall that a channel is a carrier, or medium, for moving the message from person to person. For example, an essay requires writing devices (paper, computer keyboard and screen, blackboard), while a speech uses aural (hearing), oral (speaking), and visual (seeing) channels.

Another major difference between written and oral channels is *personal contact*. Because of the face-to-face nature of oral communication, the entire personality comes into play. This, of course, makes oral communication more informal than written communication. You are being heard and seen at the same moment. Not only is everything about you being evaluated on the spot, but you often have to adapt to this live setting. If people begin to show a lack of interest or ask a question you did not expect, you may find yourself altering your planned presentation. Although at times personal contact may be unnerving, it gives oral discourse a greater sense of reality than written communication has.

The differences we have described often require the speaker to make a series of adjustments to both the content and presentation of the message. For example, if a writer makes a point that a reader does not immediately understand, the reader can go back and reread that section. With oral communication, the participants are not afforded that luxury. Hence, the speaker has the added burden of being clear at the first hearing. This difference in the two styles often means that *oral language demands more elaboration*. Successful speakers learn how to orally develop, underscore, and repeat key and/or potentially confusing ideas and information. It is also important for you to learn an entirely different set of organizational and "punctuational" devices. As a speaker, you do not have paragraphs, bold print, quotation marks, underlining, and other devices. This fact, then, requires you to replace these writing or printing devices with vocal nuances, body movements, glances, and other nonverbal substitutes. It also means using a series of verbal transitions to replace paragraphs, periods, and the like. Throughout this book, we will discuss specific speech techniques that can be used as public speaking "punctuation" devices.

Other alterations need to be made when you move from written to spoken discourse. For instance, oral style asks for a greater variety in sentence length, sentences that are less involved, more personal pronouns (I, we, you), and more use of rhythmic phrasing. Once again, remember that all these techniques that involve changing your style will be expanded upon later in the book.

Public Speaking and Conversation

Although public speaking and conversation are basically both concerned with sharing information, ideas, and feelings, they are not identical. There are some major differences that help explain why an effective public speaker does not simply "talk as usual" when thrust into a speech-making situation. To be successful, he or she must take the following ten differences into account.

First, public speaking, as the words suggest, is *public*, while everyday conversation is often private. This difference has a number of spin-off effects that help define the boundaries of public speaking. In a one-to-one situation, you have to interest only *one* other person. In the public context, the need to be interesting and relevant is much more complicated. Not only are there more people, but they are apt to come from a variety of backgrounds and cultures. As you might suspect, the more heterogeneous your audience, the more difficult is your task of locating a "general level" on which to speak. For example, there are major cultural differences in what constitutes humor. In cultures that value the elderly, humor that makes old people the brunt of a joke is in poor taste. Because this need to adapt to an audience instead of to an individual is of such importance, an entire chapter is needed to treat this topic (chapter 3).

Second, in the public-speaking context, *feedback* from the listener is primarily nonverbal. Although on some occasions your listeners will ask questions, in most instances feedback comes from nonverbal actions such as head nods, smiles, yawns, aimless movement, and even observing someone falling asleep. In face-to-face meetings, your partner sends both words and nonverbal codes in response to your message.

Third, in the public-speaking situation, *roles* are clearly defined and are not subject to the shifting patterns found in conversation. The speaker realizes his or her responsibility to do the talking, and the audience members are aware that they are the listeners. In conversation, roles usually change each moment and with each topic.

Fourth, one of the most important differences between conversation and public speaking is in the area of *purpose*. For example, the purpose and content of conversation grows out of what is going on at that instant. This often contributes to a constant shifting of purpose. However, in public speaking you know in advance what you want to accomplish and how you plan to accomplish it. Whether you decide on your purpose or someone selects it for you is not important at this point. What is important is your realizing that public speaking is not aimless chatter; it is goal directed. Even impromptu speaking, or getting up before a group to speak with little or no preparation, has a specific purpose. In chapter 2, we will discuss in detail the various types of speech purposes and how to select them.

Fifth, because public speaking is purposeful, it is characterized by *preparation* before the communication begins. Your plan to influence your listeners demands that you prepare your material before you see them. Conversation is usually spontaneous—with both people responding to what is happening. The topic of how to prepare for a public-speaking situation will be examined in nearly every chapter of this book.

Sixth, public speaking is bound by *time and space*, but conversation is not thus constrained. For example, as a speaker, you have a set amount of time to accomplish your purpose. It matters little whether you or someone else sets the time limit, because in either case the clock must be taken into account. Being aware of the time constraints imposed by public speaking means that you must be cognizant of the need for your speech to be structured and well planned. In addition, you must keep the time limit in mind because you may lose the attention of some or all of your audience. In conversation, as you know from experience, people can engage in communication acts for long periods of time. Most of us like to talk, but we are less than enthusiastic about just sitting and listening. This book will offer information that will make it easier for you to gain and hold the attention of an audience. When we speak of being space bound, we are not talking about science fiction but are referring to the idea that a public speaker is confined to a location. It can be a conference room, a television studio, a classroom, or an auditorium. When we take part in a conversation, we can walk on the street or move from room to room. As you would suspect, this lack of mobility is yet another reason why successful speakers strive to be interesting and to motivate their listeners.

Seventh, both conversation and public speaking involve sending messages to other people, but the *delivery* of those messages is influenced by the setting. For example, in conversation, you have eye contact with just one person; in public speaking, you need to look at many more people. In conversation, your voice level may be low when someone is sitting or standing next to you. In public speaking, your voice level must be adjusted to the context. Are you in a large hall, a small room, or using a microphone? The answer to these questions affects your volume, rate, and pitch. Because your physical presentation is under greater scrutiny during public speaking, you must also try to avoid vocal distractions such as "uh," "er," and "um." Even your body must reflect the differences between conversation and public speaking. The added distance between you and your listeners demands that your gestures be clearer and larger. Posture and movement must also be tailored to the situation. The adjustments necessary for successful public speaking are important enough to occupy an entire chapter (chapter 4).

Eighth, as you move from conversation to public speaking, you also modify your *language*. With one person, you can be very personal in your use of language. Slang and jargon might be appropriate. In the public-speaking context, however, you should be flexible in your language use. A speech before the county board of supervisors might require you to be formal, yet a speech to your peers explaining a new piece of office equipment would require less formality. The requirements of language for public speaking will be treated in chapter 12.

Ninth, public speaking differs from conversation in regard to the *amount and control of distraction* found in each. When you talk with one person, the two of you are focused on each other, sharing a common topic, and taking turns as speaker and listener. Conversation tends to produce very few distractions, and, if they do arise, the two of you can probably reduce them. If the distractions are serious, you can even change the location. In the public-speaking setting, there is a greater chance for distractions—there are more people to create "noise." These distractions are also harder to overcome. In most cases, you cannot tell someone to stop talking or move the entire audience to another location.

Tenth, the *potential for influence* is greater for public speaking than for conversation. We are not diminishing the power of face-to-face persuasion but are only pointing out that in public discourse you reach more people and, hence, affect more lives. Telling one person the dangers of driving without wearing a seat belt does not have the same impact as giving this message to sixty or six thousand people. The ethical responsibility that this places on the speaker is important enough to make it a topic of discussion later in this chapter.

Although we have just spent some time differentiating public speaking from conversation, we need to end this section by noting that in most instances the skills that mark a successful communicator are the same skills that distinguish the person who is a good conversationalist. Reflect for a moment on the people who are most captivating and persuasive even in a one-to-one situation. They are people who are organized; who tailor their message to a person or setting; who adapt to what is going on at the moment (using feedback); who are interesting, attentive, credible, and knowledgeable; and who use language effectively. These, and other traits, represent the major components of this book. Hence, as noted earlier, becoming a good public speaker also means becoming a good communicator.

Ethical Responsibilities of Communication

We now come to one of the most important topics in this entire book—**ethics.** It is a subject that, for all of us, is often easier to talk about than to put into practice. For when we speak of ethics we are talking about the standards we employ to judge the rightness or wrongness of our behavior. Because all culture and societies need ethical standards, philosophers and religious leaders have, for thousands of years, been trying to offer us guidelines by which we can evaluate our actions and the actions of others. Nowhere are these actions more profound than in the public-speaking arena. When you occupy the role of the "speaker," you are asking other people to believe you, trust you, and to adopt the actions you are recommending. These are indeed ethical issues. As George Horne reminds us, "Words may safely guide us in the direction of truth or they may lead us into swamps where there is no solid footing."

Some Working Principles

The entire topic of ethics is of such great importance that we will discuss it in nearly every chapter of this book. However, because you are preparing to give your first speeches, we need to introduce you to some of the issues related to ethics and to provide you with some guidelines for judging your own actions and the actions of others.

We have, earlier in the book, alluded to three principles of human communication that directly related to this important section on ethics. Let us crystalize these three ideas so that we can use them as the basis for our analysis of the ethical dimensions of human communication.

First, early in the chapter we noted that, regardless of our culture, *we are all social creatures.* The society in which we live depends on communication to pass on the past, live in the present, and prepare for the future. We need others for reasons as basic as receiving love and as pragmatic as gathering material comforts. English essayist Samuel Johnson expressed the same idea in a rather impassioned way when he observed, "In civilized society we all depend upon each other, and our very happiness is owing to the rest of mankind." Hence, our first point is that there is a symbiotic relationship existing between all people, and that this relationship and interdependence is negotiated through communication.

Second, even at this early stage of the book, you have seen how you can select material that enables you to adapt to both person and place. Embedded in this idea is a fact about human life that is both elementary and profound: *we have free choice*. From selecting a mate to deciding on a specific word when we talk, in most instances we exercise our free will. Even though many of our actions are habitual, when we greet a stranger we can still decide to smile, frown, look the other person in the eye, or glance down. The choice, like thousands of others we make each day, is ours. As a philosopher once remarked, "The difficulty in life is the choice."

Third, from our first two points, it should be evident that our choices influence other people—the very people we need so that we can accomplish our physical and social goals. Put in slightly different terms, *communication is something that persons do with each other, and this behavior produces a response that has an effect*. Because of the nature of our complex nervous system, the perception of any message involves varying degrees of behavioral change in both sender and receiver. Each party gains entry into the other's life. This entry may only alter body chemistry or may change the person forever. In either case, the link between communication and ethics should be clear. Whether we accept the responsibility or not, we are invading the personality of our communication partners. Remember, we have free choice, and therefore in nearly all instances have made the decision to influence another person. The significance of affecting another person's personality is clearly confirmed by Ordway Tead in his book *Administration: Its Purpose and Performance* (p. 52). He observes

> Tampering with personal drives and desires is a moral act even if its upshot is not a far-reaching one, or is a beneficial result. To seek to persuade behavior into a new direction may be wholly justifiable, and the result in terms of behavior consequences may be salutary. But the judgment of benefit or detriment is not for the communicator safely to reach by himself. He is assuming a moral responsibility. And he had better be aware of the area with which he concerns himself and the responsibility he assumes. He should be willing to assert as to any given new policy, "I stand behind this as having good personal consequences for the individuals whom it will affect." That judgment speaks a moral concern and desired moral outcome.

Tead is talking about ethical standards related to the production of messages that influence other people. Ethics, as we noted earlier, is a mode of conduct based on high moral standards. As members of a culture that has given us various moral values and principles, most of us are aware of the constituents of these high standards and of our moral responsibilities to our fellow humans. These responsibilities are compounded as the group we are addressing grows in size. Our audience may range from a handful of friends to a large conference or convention. This social responsibility has never been more important than it is today, when television and radio make it possible for a single speaker to influence the actions and thinking of millions of persons.

For centuries, the power of speech to influence minds has caused grave apprehensions. The crux of the fear is this: the means of changing behavior are so potent that a malicious person may use them to induce an audience to act unwisely or unjustly. One of the most astute rebuttals to this position was written by Aristotle over two thousand years ago. In *The Rhetoric*, Aristotle asserted that the art of persuasion (changing behavior) is good in itself but can be used either for good or bad ends:

If it is urged that an abuse of the rhetorical faculty can work great mischief, the same charge can be brought against all good things (save virtue itself), and especially against the most useful things such as strength, health, wealth, and military skill. Rightly employed, they work the greatest blessings; and wrongly employed, they work the utmost harm.

Because communication is so powerful, we must consider the ethical implications of our messages on other people. In the communication context, the study of ethics embraces an analysis of the conscious choices we make about our intentions toward and strategies for influencing other people. To better appreciate the need to consider our motives and tactics, we should examine our role as the sender of messages, as well as our responsibilities as the recipient of messages. In addition, because culture greatly influences our view of ethics, we should also examine cultural differences in perceiving ethical behavior.

Sender

Recall the quotation from Aristotle. Understand that the evils, if they occur, are brought forth by humans, not by the processes of communication. The devices and means used by speakers are indeed their own responsibility. The issue is one of speakers realizing that they have an obligation to their listeners as well as to themselves. In short, all of us need to be aware of the potential power of our communication behavior. It is imperative that we think about this power *before* we speak, before we modify another person. As noted in a Chinese proverb, "A harsh word once dropped from the tongue cannot be brought back again by a coach and six horses." Accordingly, you should consider the following seven questions each time you initiate a communication act.

1. *Have you investigated the subject fully before expressing opinions about it?* In your speech class and in this textbook, you will discover that serious research and analysis are important parts of successful, effective, and ethical speaking. Anyone can "make up" facts and figures, but common sense and good judgment tell you that is not proper behavior. Because you should speak only from a sound background, you have a obligation to be silent if you do not understand what you are called on to discuss. "I don't know" is a valuable and too rarely used phrase. When you do speak, you have a duty to be morally thoughtful—to know what you are talking about before you try to influence the thinking of your associates. The idea of investigation is of such importance that chapters 6, 8, and 9 are set aside to assist you in developing the skills necessary to inquire into any topic.

2. *Once you have gathered and analyzed the "facts," can you present your material in an accurate and ethical manner?* This means avoiding half-truths, outdated information, lies, and unsupported assertions.

As you would suspect, there are vast cultural differences in how information and ideas are presented. In East Asian cultures, concepts are understated, and at times very few words are used to express important ideas. In most Arab cultures, however, where language use is highly valued, speakers embellish, exaggerate, and use very ornate language. This does not mean that they are unethical; rather, they have a different cultural orientation toward communication than do American speakers. Knowing these and other cultural differences will enable you to judge carefully the remarks of others.

Following ethical guidelines also demands that any type of plagiarism be avoided. Presenting information that is not your own or repeating entire paragraphs without citing sources are just two of the ways plagiarism occurs. We show respect for our listeners when we share the origins of our material. This same respect is buttressed when an ethical speaker acknowledges that some of the information may be incomplete.

3. *Do you respect the intelligence of the people to whom you are speaking?* You should never amplify, oversimplify, or "adjust" the truth because you think the listeners will not notice the distortion because they are not knowledgeable on the topic. You must not also assume that listeners are not capable of understanding your message as a justification for withholding or altering information. This lack of respect for people is insulting and unethical. Respect the worth of each individual and allow each person to think for themselves.

When speaking to members of cultures other than your own, it is important to guard against this tendency to make decisions without respecting their point of view. It is wrong to assume that, because they are unacquainted with the material, you can leave things out and alter the truth. Any misrepresentation is unethical and can easily lead an audience to reject you and your cause; once audience members perceive you as being a dishonorable person, it will be nearly impossible to recapture their confidence. An Ashanti proverb admonishes us with the following warning: "One falsehood spoils a thousand truths."

The audience's perception of you as a good person greatly influences the success of your communication act. Volumes of research indicate that what the audience thinks of you as a person can either hinder or aid your cause. Aristotle, Quintilian, and Cicero, the great speech theorists of classical Greece and Rome, agree—a speaker whose prestige is high in the eyes of the audience has a better chance of gaining acceptance for ideas presented than does a speaker whose credibility is low.

4. *Are you continuously aware that what you say will influence others?* Do you realize that you are altering the attitudes, the feelings, and even the health of others? A constant awareness of this fact allows you to reevaluate your content and your intent. Realizing you are altering the thinking and behavior of other people compels you to continuously ask yourself if your purpose is responsible, reasonable, and honorable. Are you advocating ideas that will benefit others or only yourself? Always being aware of the notion of speech consequences also reminds you of the power of a single word and impact of your overall message. When you think of this power, consider both the short- and long-range effects of your speech. For example, the short-range purpose of a persuasive speech on the advantages of vegetarianism may be ethically sound, but, if you fail to inform your listeners about the need to supplement their diets with foods high in protein, you are ignoring the long-range effects.

Being conscious of your responsibilities should also encourage you to make sure that all sides of the issues are heard. Notice in our example on vegetarianism how important it is for the speaker to identify some of the other issues involved with this subject. Although none of us has the duty to solicit contradictory arguments on every idea we express, to suppress essential information diminishes us and our listeners.

5. *Have you tried to be interesting and enthusiastic?* Not all speakers, at all times, need to be humorous and entertaining, but all attempts at communication should be worthy of the receiver's time and energy. It is important to remember always that you are asking others to stop whatever they are doing to give you one second or one hour of their time. Try to deserve that time.

It should be noted that this advice regarding interest and attention greatly reflects the Western orientation of this book. In many parts of the world, speakers feel they are under no obligation to be interesting or to hold attention. In fact, in countries such as China and Japan, people who speak too well are often perceived as low-credibility sources. There is even a proverb in Japan that states, "He who has no knowledge speaks; he who has knowledge is silent." What this proverb tells us is that being a dynamic speaker has unique implications in every part of the world. Hence, be careful when you apply North American standards to people from other cultures.

6. *Is the material clearly presented?* As a speaker, you have the obligation to make your speech understandable to your listeners. It is an unethical practice to intentionally use words your audience does not understand or to advance ideas you do not fully explain. In addition, you need to avoid using motive appeals that are intended only to frighten your audience. For example, recently a speaker stated that if people who have tested positive for the HIV virus were allowed to enter the United States it would cause a major AIDS epidemic. This is a vivid example of using hysteria to accomplish a purpose.

7. *Is the speech free from personal attacks?* To slander another person or culture is yet another example of poor ethical behavior. If you opposed the North American Free Trade Agreement, it would have been far more ethical to point out the weakness of the treaty than to attack the people involved with it, the people of Canada and Mexico. Also avoid "name calling" and other forms of demagoguery. The word is a commanding instrument and should be used with great care. A Native American proverb can remind us of the power of communication: "Talk is but wind, but wind can break a tree."

At times the issue of right and wrong speech may seem complex and difficult, but for most of us common sense is often the best guide. We all know deep down, because of the way we feel, if we have been ethical or unethical in our actions. Although he was talking about morality, the American author Ernest Hemingway said much the same thing when he wrote, "I know only what is moral is what you feel good after and what is immoral is what you feel bad after."

Receiver   Ethical responsibility in the communication situation is not borne by the speaker alone. The listener also shares the moral issues of the speech act. Much ethical responsibility lies in listening itself. If one is to evaluate, accept, and respond to the remarks of others, one must first hear and understand those remarks. It is unfair, as well as unethical, for us, as listeners, to act on a message to which we have not fully attended. Therefore, *a listener's first commitment is to offer full attention to the speaker*. Each communication act is characterized by countless distractions, but the listener must overcome them to analyze fairly what is said. We will discuss much more about listening in chapter 5.

In addition to paying attention, *ethical listeners create a listening atmosphere that encourages speakers to do their best job*. As a listener, if you send speakers negative feedback (looking out the window, doodling, or yawning), they are bound to be tense when delivering their talks. By sending positive feedback (leaning forward, smiling, making eye contact) and being attentive, you help speakers relax. It follows that their speeches will be better delivered and much more accurate. In short, remember the circular nature of the communication act. Speaker and listener are interdependent—touch one and you touch the other.

Ethical listeners are discriminating and suspend conclusions. Since listeners are influenced, in one form or another, by the speaker, they must *not* accept everything that is said without questioning key assertions. There is nothing wrong with some degree of measured skepticism when someone is asking you to behave in one way or another. Your ethical obligation is to question, reason, and hold off your conclusions until all the evidence has been presented.

To this point, we have talked about the role of ethics in human communication and how each of us must be aware of the ethical decisions inherent in asking someone to think, feel, or respond according to *your* wishes. We are now ready to talk about how those decisions transcend a single culture. The need for this discussion should not surprise you, for it is evident even at this early juncture of the book that we will be talking about the role of culture in nearly every phase of the communication process. Therefore, we need to pause for a moment to discuss how ethics and culture are linked. When we examine ethical issues in intercultural communication, we are immediately confronted with a dilemma: cultures, when compared with one another, are like people; they differ on some characteristics and share others. The members of one culture may believe in animal sacrifice as a religious ritual, while the members of another bury their pets in animal cemeteries. The people of one culture may believe in multiple spouses, while those of another believe in monogamy. Thousands of other examples demonstrate that cultures differ from one another. As you would suspect, many of these differences make it difficult to arrive at a universal set of truisms or a metaethic. However, ethical speakers can take two courses of action. One deals with cultural differences, the other with cultural similarities.

First, *it is crucial to learn all you can about the cultures of the people you will be addressing.* You need to discover if the changes you are requesting are consistent with the values and norms pervasive in that culture. From judgments of beauty to attitudes about birth control, to dietary habits, to the perception of women, cultural variations need to be taken into account.

Second, *an ethical speaker respects diversity.* There is a natural tendency among all of us to believe that "our way is the best way." In fact, in intercultural matters, this penchant to judge all other cultures through the perceptual lens of one's own culture, and to conclude that one culture is superior to another, is called **ethnocentrism.** This is an orientation that maintains that cultural differences are neither right or wrong, but simply different. This sort of cultural sensitivity and intercultural ethic not only respects the rights of others, but is also a first step toward overcoming racism and prejudice.

Finally, although differences exist between cultures, *people of all cultures share many characteristics that help determine and define an ethic for intercultural communication.* As famous photographer Edward Steichen noted, "I believe that in all the things that are important, in all of these we are alike." Reflect for a moment about just a few of the universal characteristics that unite people. We all sense the thrill of a new birth, crave freedom, desire a mate, and love our families. People of all cultures enjoy music, art, and humor and believe in being civil to each other. Finally, all of us must face old age, death, and the suffering that can go with both.

Our list of commonalities could fill the remainder of this book. However, the point is not to document specific cultural likenesses but, rather, to suggest that, because we are alike in so many ways, we can be guided by an ethical code. That code, as simple as it sounds, is the Golden Rule. Although many Westerners have been exposed to the phrase "Do to others what you would have them do to you" through Christianity, the same concept is found

Culture and Ethics

Learn all you can about the people you will be addressing.

in the writings of the Buddha, in the Koran, and in every other religious and philosophical tradition. When applied to speech making, the canon reminds us that it is unethical to send messages that demean or belittle another person if we would not welcome the same messages to be directed at us. The canon also tells us something we discussed earlier in this section—that all of us, regardless of our culture, are linked together. The great humanitarian Albert Schweitzer made this same point when he wrote, "The first step in the evolution of ethics is a sense of solidarity with other humans." We urge you to take that step and to appreciate the fact that while each of us is unique, we also share a common humanity.

We conclude this section on the ethics of communication by once again exhorting you to think about your intentions and your actions. Once you send a message to someone, it will have an effect, and it is almost impossible to undo that effect. An Arab proverb captures this idea in a more poetic manner: "It is with a word as with an arrow—once let loose it does not return."

Preview of Principles

Although it may appear that we are making a rather sudden shift in emphasis as we now move from theory to practice, it is important to remember we are still talking about communication. Up to this point, we have examined some of the theory behind human communication—what communication is and how it works. On the other hand, *communication is an activity that persons engage in; it is something we do.* Because communication "is something we do," theory and practice can never be separated. Therefore, we shall now focus our attention on the "doing." We shall look at the aspects of communication concerned with the practical phases of human communication. Everything we have discussed thus far about communication and ethics leads to the conclusion that becoming a more effective communicator should be the goal of everyone who shares ideas and information. In short, we take part in communication so that we can have an influence. Let us now talk about how you can develop the skills that will contribute to your greater efficiency in carrying out that influence.

We want to introduce some of these skills in chapter 1 so that you can start to practice them early in your training. In every instance, what is canvassed in the next few pages will be expanded in subsequent chapters; however, it is important that you begin at once. What follows is some advice to assist you in your initial efforts.

In your speech class, you may face the issue of having to give speeches in the first few days of the semester before you have had an opportunity to study all the principles treated in this book. For this reason, we shall briefly look at some steps you should take in preparing your first speeches. The order of the steps is not nearly as rigid as the list might suggest. For example, you may discover situations in which audience analysis precedes the analysis of the purpose of the speech. Regardless of the order in which you consider the six items, however, a thorough preparation should include them all.

Organizing Ideas

1. *Determine the purpose of your speech.* Nearly all communication is purposeful—it seeks to elicit a response from the person receiving the message. We smile at someone because we are glad to see them. We give someone specific directions on how to find the library so that they will not get lost. We tell a good friend to stop eating so many potato chips because we are concerned about their health. As you can see, the reaction we want from the other person can range from enjoyment (the warmth of a smile being returned) to direct, specific action (stop eating those potato chips). So ask yourself, do you want your listeners to understand how to select the best methods for preparing a term paper? Do you want them to sign a petition outlawing the sale of cigarettes in the college cafeteria? Do you want them to believe that teenage suicide is a serious problem? Think of your speech as an instrument of utility—a means of getting a reaction—and think of that reaction as your first step of speech preparation.

When analyzing the reaction you want from your audience, you should begin with your **general purpose.** The next chapter will introduce three kinds of general purposes and discuss each of them in greater detail; however, for now it is important for you to know that these purposes are: *to inform* (increasing your listeners' fund of knowledge), *to persuade* (changing the thinking and/or behavior of your listeners), and *to entertain* (eliciting a pleasurable response from your listeners). Although these purposes often overlap each other, you nevertheless need to decide on the *general* response you hope to elicit. You should also think about the *specific* reaction you hope to produce. For a speech to inform, your specific purpose might be to have your listeners understand the operation of the campus general store. A speech to persuade could have the specific purpose of asking the audience to support a law to make it illegal for anyone to transport a dog unattended in the back of an open pickup truck. A specific purpose for a speech to entertain might be to have the audience laugh while you explain how to pick a winning horse at the racetrack simply by examining the horses in the paddock.

2. *Choose and limit the topic.* In speech class, you may be assigned a subject area, but in most cases your instructor will let you make your own selections. You will find that, in speaking situations outside the class, circumstances are much the same.

Observing a few basic principles will enable you to choose the proper subject and to limit its scope to meet the demands of the audience, the occasion, and your purpose.

    a.   *Select a topic worthy of your time and the time of your audience.* No listener enjoys hearing about a subject that is insignificant. Although it might make an excellent humorous speech, very few college students would like to hear you give a ten-minute speech to inform on how to sew a button on a shirt, yet that group might find a speech on using campus health services very informative. In short, talk about subjects, issues, and controversies that affect the lives of your listeners.

    b.   *Select a topic that interests you.* Unless you are interested, you will not be sufficiently motivated to accomplish your purpose. Pick a topic in which you are or can become interested, and you may find that your enthusiasm is contagious.

    c.   *Select a topic you can deal with adequately in the time at your disposal.* It is apparent that subject areas such as "Peace in the World" or "The Meaning of Life: Part II" cannot be intelligently discussed in a five-minute speech.

    3. *Analyze the location of your speech, the occasion of your speech, and your audience.* By knowing the impact of these three factors, you will be able to adapt your material and your preparation to the situation you meet.

The process of analyzing the audience and the occasion is discussed more thoroughly in chapter 3. However, following are a few guidelines to assist you in your early speeches.

    a.   *Learn all you can about the place where the communication will occur.* Interaction is influenced by the position you take in regard to the other members of the gathering, the size of the room, its shape, and other physical conditions. If you are being interviewed by the school newspaper regarding your position on the use of animals in research and later will talk on the same subject on television, you would need to adjust to these two very different locations.

    b.   *Learn the occasion for the gathering.* Is it a regular weekly meeting, is it a special meeting, or is it a spontaneous gathering? Are the people going to listen to you because they are interested in the topic, or are they meeting for another purpose? If the occasion is a festive celebration and you talk about the menacing effects of acid rain, the audience is apt to find your observation rather inappropriate.

    c.   *Learn as much as you can about the people to whom you will speak.* Knowing their age, gender, educational background, occupation, interests, ethnic and cultural background, values, and attitudes will enable you to adapt your remarks to the needs of the listeners you will face. For example, an audience of Chinese and Native American students, who have learned to value harmony in interpersonal relationships, might not be receptive to your speech on the advantages of being assertive unless you were to adapt your message to point out the benefits of being assertive while maintaining or promoting harmony in relationships.

4. *Find the material for your speech.* There are basically two places to look for materials: within yourself for what you already know and outside yourself to discover what you do not know. Start your preparation by looking in your private, internal "library." What you already know, however, may not be enough to accomplish your objective. In most instances, it is necessary to augment your observations and opinions with those from other sources. In chapter 8, we will talk about finding materials in books, magazines, newspapers, through computer searches, and other storehouses of information. At this point, it is important to remember that successful speakers are seldom the ones who think they know everything there is to know on all subjects.

5. *Organize and arrange the speech.* Now that you have the ingredients of your message—the materials—you must arrange them so that they make sense to your listeners. In chapter 10 we will present a number of organizational sequences, but for now you should arrange your material around the following three parts of a speech—introduction, body, and conclusion.

The main purpose of the *introduction* is to gain the attention and interest of the listeners, to put them at ease, to help them focus their attention on your speech, and to begin to establish your credibility. The material you select should accomplish those objectives.

It is the *body* of your talk that contains the majority of your message. The body of the speech should be planned first. This includes marshalling all the supporting material designed to establish the central idea of the speech. You also need to think about keeping your material interesting if you expect to hold the audience's attention for any period of time.

The *conclusion* ends the speech gracefully and in a compelling manner. It may take the form of a summary, an illustration, an appeal, a challenge, or several other endings that we will discuss later in chapter 11. As you might suspect, issues such as your specific purpose and the amount of time at your disposal will influence the concluding device you select.

An outline is one of the chief organizational aids. It enables you to see what materials you have and assists you in sorting the relevant from the irrelevant. An outline helps you avoid the aimless, disorganized thinking characteristic of many speeches.

6. *Practice your speech aloud.* If you hope to have your message understood, to accomplish your purpose, and to feel relaxed, you must practice aloud. You should deliver your speech three or four times before you present it to the audience. In the next chapter, we will examine some ways to make your practice session more productive. For now, try to keep these few ideas in mind as you prepare and practice.

   a.   Avoid memorizing while you practice.

   b.   Learn the main ideas of the speech, rather than trying to memorize every word.

   c.   Practice your speech aloud and allow time for changes if, after hearing it, you decide that you need to make alterations.

Of all the aspects of public speaking, it is delivery that makes people most anxious. Although delivery is important, it certainly does not warrant the amount of energy we give it or the degree of stress it produces. An entire chapter will deal with the topic of

Presenting Ideas

speech delivery (chapter 4); however, you will need a few general suggestions at this time so that you can present your first speeches in a natural, relaxed manner.

   1. *Have a good mental attitude.* A good mental attitude toward the presentation of your ideas will make the job of delivering your speech much simpler and much more pleasurable for you and your audience. Do not be unduly alarmed about stage fright. The following suggestions may help allay your apprehensions.

   a. *Realize that some nervousness is normal.* This realization may, in itself, help reduce your nervousness. You are not odd because your body is not enjoying the prospect of having to talk in front of a group of strangers.

   b. *Recognize that, in most instances, the audience is your friend, not your enemy.* This is particularly true of your speech class, where you can be assured that everyone is wishing you well. Your classmates will also get a turn in front of the class and will welcome the same support.

   c. *Come before your audience fully prepared.* If you have doubts about your speech and your preparation, you will likely appear nervous.

   d. *Try to feel confident.* Your attitude toward yourself is the single most important variable in successful communication. Do not rush through your speech; remember that you are talking with your audience. Feel free to pause whenever you desire. Do not be embarrassed if you find that some of your words are not coming out as you wish. In many instances, you may be the only one to realize what is happening. There are even occasions when acknowledging a "flub" will relax you and your audience.

   e. *Nervous tension can be reduced by having some meaningful physical action in your speech.* Try walking during your talk as a method of relaxing and releasing nervous strain.

   f. *Remember, even if you are nervous, you will be able to finish your speech.* Everything in life has a beginning and an end. Whether it is sitting in the dentist's chair, reading this sentence, or giving a speech, eventually it will be over. Too many speakers tell themselves during their speech that they are just too nervous to go on, only to find out at the conclusion of their talk that the presentation went very well, so keep going.

   g. *Take comfort in the fact that there is a relationship among improvement, practice, and nervousness.* Students say that, as they become more proficient in speech making, their nervousness and all its outward manifestations seem to lessen. In short, the more you speak, the less you will be nervous.

   2. *Be direct.* Looking directly at your audience serves two vital functions. First, directness adds to a lively sense of communication. It tells your listeners that you care about accomplishing your purpose and that you are interested in them. Second, by looking directly at the audience, you gain valuable insight into how your message is being received. Successful communicators use the information they receive by observing their audience and making adjustments based on audience reactions.

3. *Be physically animated.* Try to avoid a rigid appearance. Your posture should be comfortable and natural. Gestures are quite useful in conveying thought or emotion or in reinforcing oral expression. They increase your self-confidence, ease nervousness, aid in the communication of ideas, and help hold attention. Relax and be yourself, and you will learn that gesturing comes naturally.

4. *Use vocal variety.* Just as movement and gesture help reinforce ideas, so does an animated voice. If there is a sameness of rate, pitch, loudness, and quality, there is monotony. Vary as many of these elements of voice as you can, consonant with conveying the full meaning of your ideas and emotions.

Avoid unpleasant and distracting vocalizations such as "and a," "like," "ya know," "well," and "uh," which call attention to themselves and detract from your message.

Competent delivery is simply direct, friendly, natural, conversational, animated, and enthusiastic. Good luck with your first few speeches.

Summary

This chapter introduced the fields of communication and public speaking and presented a few elementary principles, the essential tools of effective speech making.

In its broadest sense, communication is the process of sending and receiving messages. All communication involves the following ingredients: a source, encoding, a message, a channel, a receiver, and decoding. To better understand these ingredients, we examined a model of communication that included what people bring to a communication event and how they send, receive, and respond to messages during and after that event. We also looked at the similarities and differences between public speaking and other forms of communication.

The responsibility and seriousness of communication are so great that communicators must be of the highest ethical character. They should know their subject, respect the intelligence of their listeners, treat their content honestly, and realize that they are changing behavior—both theirs and the receivers'.

In preparing early speeches, remember to determine the purpose of the speech, choose and limit the topic, analyze the audience and the speaking occasion, gather material, organize and arrange the material, and practice aloud.

In delivering speeches, it is essential that you have a good mental attitude, that you be direct, that you be physically animated, and that you use vocal variety.

The beginning is
the most
important part
of the work.

Plato

Chapter 2

Your First Speeches

Getting Started

Meet the first beginnings; look to the budding mischief before it has time to ripen to maturity.

William Shakespeare

I n Aesop's fable "The Crow and the Pitcher," the reader is offered the following advice: "Little by little does the trick." We begin this chapter with that same counsel. That is to say, start the process of improving your communication little by little. One of the philosophies driving this book maintains that *communication is something we do.* Although it takes shape in our minds, the act of communicating demands some outward behavior. This book is organized so that you can start working on that behavior *now* instead of having to wait until you have turned the last page of the final chapter. In short, now that you have encountered a preview of the basic principles of oral communication, you can begin to apply those principles in an actual speech.

You probably have questions running through your mind such as, Where do I go from here? and How do I get started? Answering those questions is the principal objective of this chapter. Nearly all the ideas offered in this preliminary chapter will be developed in much more detail later in this book, but for now you should begin practicing so that, "little by little," you will become a more effective communicator.

We noted in chapter 1 that most communication is initiated because someone wants to fulfill a purpose. In the specialized form of human communication called public speaking, the speaker wants a *specific response* from the audience and communicates in order to secure that response. The speaker has a *preconceived purpose,* which the speaker has chosen *before* the talk. In fact, that characteristic often distinguishes public speaking from other, more random communication activities. Trying to talk to an audience without having a clear idea of what you want them to hear and learn would be an unnerving experience, to say the least. The audience (and you) would be frustrated and confused as you drifted aimlessly from point to point. What is needed, then, is a unifying thread to weave all the pieces together, and that thread is the preconceived purpose. By deciding on the response you want from your audience, you can more wisely select the materials, organizational patterns, language, and delivery methods that will enable you to reach your goal.

Let us turn our attention to the initial stages of speech preparation and look at the processes of (1) deciding on a topic, (2) narrowing the topic, (3) formulating a general purpose, (4) formulating a specific purpose, (5) choosing a title, (6) choosing a method of delivery, (7) using notecards, (8) practicing the speech, and (9) methods of gaining confidence and overcoming nervousness.

Selecting a Topic

An inevitable question facing the speaker is, What shall I talk about? There are, of course, several ways of answering this question. First, in many instances, *you are asked to speak on a particular subject.* On those occasions, subject selection has been done for you. If your professor says to you, "Please give a talk on the history of rhetoric," or your

There will be speaking situations when the occasion dictates the subject area.

employer tells you, "Explain the company's new computer billing system to the rest of your department," your questions regarding subject selection are answered—someone has told you what to talk about. Your job, then, is to narrow the subject to fit the specific audience and the various constraints imposed by time.

There will also be speaking situations *when the occasion dictates the subject area*. A political rally for a specific candidate, a eulogy, or a graduation ceremony are such instances.

In most instances *you must select the subject*. You should screen potential subjects with an eye to their value and interest to the audience and their appropriateness for the occasion. Specific time limits should also be kept in mind. Where do you locate those potential subjects in the first place? Many beginning speakers are overwhelmed at the prospect of talking on any subject they want. Most speech instructors spend many office hours trying to help students pick a topic, yet, if students would not panic, would slow down, and would reflect for a little while, the task of topic selection would not be such a drudgery. Let us suggest a few procedures to follow that will help you make intelligent choices regarding the general subject of your talks.

Begin your search for a topic by reviewing what you already know. Examine your personal interests, experiences, and convictions. Consider any special knowledge you have acquired, places you have traveled, or jobs you have held. Many students find it helpful to start the process of topic selection by taking an inventory of their fund of knowledge and personal beliefs. When students make their inventories early in the semester, they develop a list of possible topics to draw on for future speeches. An inventory works best when it is developed in a systematic manner. A sample inventory follows.

Begin with Yourself

Personal Experiences
cultural background
favorite vacations
summer jobs
interesting elective classes

Abilities
artistic
athletic
intellectual
educational

Hobbies
tennis
politics
sculpture
rock hunting
computer graphics
sport cars
skydiving
cooking
musical instruments
hot-air balloons
hang gliding
writing
gardening
sports cars
astrology
rodeos
camping
drama
horse racing
calligraphy

Beliefs and Attitudes
student loans
value of health food
funding the arts
health care costs
crime victims' rights
insurance rates
housing the homeless
pollution control
judicial caseloads
sex and violence on TV
private education
military reduction
future of the family
new European alliances
welfare
animal rights
public transportation
underage drinking
gun control
trade investments
drug abuse
immigration quotas
advertising abuses
beauty contests
gangs
labor unions
vegetarianism

Personal Knowledge
animal handling
appliance repair
fitness equipment
foreign languages
automotive upkeep
Native American folklore

In addition to your personal inventory, you can probe other sources for possible speech topics. Newsmagazines, newspapers, reference books, computer searches, and newscasts can enable you to assess current events. Questioning your friends and professors can also yield useful topics. Most college campuses have a variety of activities

Looking Elsewhere

In addition to your personal inventory, you can probe other sources for possible speech topics.

that can help generate still other topics: guest speakers, controversial debates, and career opportunity lectures are just a few events that can produce subjects. However, in the final analysis, it is usually *your personal decision and your perception of your audience* that serves as the stimulus for your talk. You must determine, and eventually formulate, your reason and purpose for engaging in communication.

There are five categories of topics that normally *do not* lend themselves well to the public-speaking situation. First, some topics are *too technical* for your audience. A speech dealing with the stress requirements of materials used in fashioning artificial knee joints might be appropriate for a group of orthopedic surgeons, but most other audiences would find it boring and confusing. Second, some topics are *too broad* to be covered adequately in a single speech. Trying to offer a detailed explanation of the social and economic causes of the collapse of Communist rule in Eastern Europe is too ambitious an objective for a single speech. Third, subjects that are *trivial* are risky material for a speech because the listeners may feel that the speaker is insulting their intelligence. Shallow topics can be used in some humorous speeches, but in most cases you should not ask adults to listen to a speech, for example, on how to heat a frozen TV dinner in a microwave oven or how to wind a watch. Fourth, there are topics *too personal* to be suitable for public airing. For example, confidential and intimate self-disclosure is ordinarily out of place in speaking to anyone other than a group of very close friends. Most audiences would be embarrassed if you were to offer intimate details regarding how your father's bout with alcoholism caused you great mental anguish. Finally, you need to decide if there will be *adequate material* available on your subject. Too often, speakers select topics that cannot be researched and developed because there is not adequate

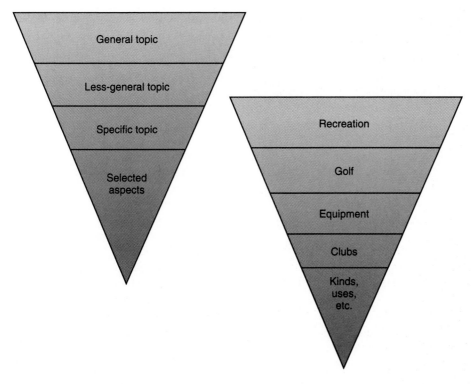

Figure 2.1
Narrowing a Topic

information on the subject. Although it might be interesting to look at the behind-the-scenes operation of the United States Supreme Court, if that information were not available it would not make much of a speech.

Once you have completed your personal inventory, you are in a much better position to narrow your focus and start the process of speech preparation. The steps of preparation were briefly introduced in the last chapter; now we will return to those preparatory phases and examine them in much more detail.

Narrowing a Topic

After you have chosen your general subject area, you must determine what aspects of that subject will be relevant to your audience, will offer them something new, and be of greatest interest to you. Some serious paring of the subject is necessary if you are to accomplish your goal. Most subjects need to be limited to meet the demands imposed by both time and purpose. Try to visualize the narrowing stage as an inverted pyramid—wide (general) at the top and narrow (specific) at the bottom (see figure 2.1).

As you can see from the pyramid, the scope of the subject is reduced so that it can be researched in a specific amount of time and presented in an intelligent manner. Regardless of the subject, you must concentrate your focus. It is best to remember that you are treating only part of the whole. An audience doesn't expect you to cover a broad subject in its entirety. Consider, for example, how much more manageable the following subjects are after they have been narrowed:

General Topic	Narrowed Topic
Environmental issues	Home recycling procedures
Gambling	Native American gaming casinos
Cambodian culture	Games Cambodian children play
Japanese management practices	Treatment of American workers in Japanese-managed automobile plants
Health	Finding meat substitutes
Consumer electronics	How high-definition television will affect your viewing habits
Professional athletes	Basketball's greatest star
Nuclear energy	Problems in nuclear waste disposal
Native Americans	Native American medicine
Advertising	Subliminal advertising
Weight loss	Fat reduction in diets
Animal rights	Animal testing for cosmetics
Folk art	Handmade African masks
Education	Teaching English as a second language
Current events	Balancing the national budget
Court reform	Eliminating trial by jury
Financial planning	Establishing a trust fund
The elderly	Elderly parents living with their children

In many instances, these topics could be narrowed even further. The time spent in thoughtful consideration of the many aspects of a subject will pay dividends when it comes to selecting the approach that will be most stimulating to you and your audience.

Formulating a General Purpose

The next step of preparation is perhaps the most crucial phase of all, for it is in this stage that you determine your *general purpose*—why are you speaking? The classification of speech purposes has long been a subject of controversy among rhetorical scholars and teachers of communication. Since ancient times, disagreements have arisen over the number and nature of these purposes. However, critical study of the historical arguments indicates that there are three general speech purposes—*to inform, to persuade,* and *to entertain.* These three purposes apply equally to public and private communication.

You should remember as we discuss these speech purposes that in reality we are talking about *responses* you desire from your audience. You must take into account the obvious fact that individuals are all different and, therefore, what is intended by the speaker as a speech to inform may well persuade or entertain certain audience members. For example, it is possible that, while you are "informing" an audience about the hiking trails within the Grand Canyon, someone might be "persuaded" to go camping there. This does not mean your general purpose was altered but, rather, that there were multiple responses to that purpose. Once again, *general purposes are simply targets that you aim at so that your arrow will have some direction and purpose.*

Although all three types of speeches will be treated in later chapters, they are introduced now to offer you some working principles early in your speech training. Remember that you need some information and skills now so that you can start practicing the art of speech making without delay. As William Shakespeare said so eloquently, "In delay we waste our lights in vain, like lamps by day."

The purpose of informative communication is to increase a receiver's knowledge and understanding of a subject. As already indicated, it is possible that a speech to inform may also entertain or change listeners' beliefs. A speaker whose immediate purpose is to impart information may use amusing or dramatic illustrations to entertain the audience members, thus holding their attention. Moreover, information may lead to changes of belief and eventually to physical action, although such results may not be a part of the speaker's purpose.

Informative Speeches

An informative speaker's main concern is to have the audience understand, learn, and remember the information presented. A librarian leading a group of students on an orientation tour of the library, a teacher demonstrating how to study for an examination, and a personnel officer explaining the duties of a job to new staff members are all engaged in informative speaking. How much the listeners know at the conclusion of a talk is the test of the speech to inform.

Following are some examples of informative subjects:

1. Gender differences in ways of speaking.
2. An explanation of Canada's health care system.
3. Unusual uses for a microwave oven.
4. How to use a videocassette recorder to tape FM musical programs.
5. The workings of a pollution-free engine.
6. An analysis of the federal drug interdiction program.
7. A description of a proposed student activity center.
8. The major causes of crime in the downtown area.
9. Cures for a computer virus.
10. How to install a simple home security system.

In all of these examples, the apparent aim is to have the listeners acquire or improve on a skill or gain new knowledge. In short, after the speech, the listeners would know something they did not know before the speech.

A persuasive speech seeks to induce the audience to believe, feel, or act in a manner selected by the speaker. Perhaps you want your listeners to discard old beliefs or form new ones, or perhaps you just want to strengthen opinions that they already hold. You may even want them to take an action. A salesperson uses a speech to persuade as a means of getting a customer to buy a word processor. A worker asking for a raise, a college student asking a professor to extend a deadline for submitting an assignment, a parent trying to get a child to practice the piano, a motorist asking a traffic officer for leniency, and a telephone solicitor asking a homeowner to subscribe to a magazine are all attempting to persuade someone to do something. Your own daily routine probably requires you to use persuasion from time to time.

Persuasive Speeches

The following are examples of persuasive subjects:

1. Newspaper recycling bins should be placed on campus.
2. Library hours should be extended to ten o'clock on weekend evenings.
3. High school students possessing knives on campus should be expelled immediately.
4. The city should rent vacant commercial buildings for use as temporary shelters for the homeless.
5. The police department should double its staff of multilingual patrol officers.
6. All new-car dealerships should be required to provide on-site air bag installation.
7. The use of wooden shingles on residences in drought-prone areas should be prohibited by law.
8. Women should be allowed to join military units that might be involved in combat.
9. You should reduce your intake of fat.
10. All cigarette advertising should be prohibited.

In each of these examples, a persuasive purpose is apparent. The speaker wants the audience to modify a behavior, attitude, or opinion.

Entertaining Speeches

The third major type of speech has the purpose of entertaining the audience. We are using the word "entertainment" in its broadest sense to include anything that stimulates a pleasurable response, whether humorous or dramatic.

The speaker's objective is simply to have the listeners enjoy themselves. There is no concern that they learn a great deal or that they change their minds in one direction or another. Many after-dinner speeches have entertainment as the principal aim, and it goes without saying that the speech to entertain is a comedian's favorite type of speech.

Following are some subjects that lend themselves to humorous treatment:

1. Popular alibis for being late to work.
2. Trying to order a meal in a foreign restaurant.
3. How to occupy your time when waiting in a line.
4. Cloning as a way of life.
5. The case for procrastination.
6. Twenty-four hours in a shopping mall.
7. How to keep smiling when the computer erases your term paper.
8. Proven methods to fall asleep easily at night.
9. How I live with a talking dog.
10. Backpacking through the university library.

The speaker's goal in all these instances is to provide a view of the subject that the listener will find amusing and pleasurable.

Formulating a Specific Purpose

Whereas the general purpose of a speech may be stated in terms of informing, persuading, or entertaining, *the specific purpose describes the exact nature of the response you want from your audience.* The specific purpose is a one-sentence summary of what you want your audience to know, feel, believe, or do by the end of your talk. Some speakers even find it useful to use the phrase "At the end of my speech my audience will . . ." as a means of visualizing their specific purpose. In this way the specific purpose becomes the *precise* spot on the target they are aiming at.

In selecting and wording your specific purpose, you should remember that a well-phrased specific purpose contains *one* central and distinct idea; begins with an *infinitive* (To explain, To inform,); is *clear and concise*; shows speaker *intent*; and, most important, is worded in terms of the *audience response desired* at the end of the speech.

When your general purpose is to *inform*, your specific purpose might be

1. To have the audience understand how the magnitude of earthquakes is measured.
2. To have the audience understand the tutorial services available on campus.
3. To have the audience understand how to find the best air travel bargains.
4. To have the audience understand the dietary habits of vegetarians.
5. To have the audience understand the economic impact of military base closures on the local economy.
6. To have the audience understand the procedure for applying for student loans.
7. To have the audience understand the concept of "saving face" in the Chinese culture.
8. To have the audience understand how to protect themselves from the harmful rays of the sun.

If your general purpose is to *persuade*, your specific purpose might be

1. To get the audience to contribute money to the Special Olympics Fund.
2. To get the audience to believe that caller-identification devices should be prohibited in all telephone systems in the United States.
3. To get the audience to sign a petition calling for a mandatory ceiling on student activity fees.
4. To get the audience to support a ban on the possession of alcoholic beverages on public beaches.
5. To get the audience to register for a course in cardiopulmonary resuscitation.
6. To get the audience to request that their supermarket purchases be placed in paper bags rather than plastic bags.
7. To get the audience to support a federal bill that outlaws the sport of boxing.
8. To get the audience to support a plan to keep the campus tennis courts open at night.

If your general purpose is to *entertain*, your specific purpose might be

1. To have the audience enjoy, vicariously, your tour through a merchants' bazaar in Tunisia.
2. To have the audience enjoy your predicament in finding yourself going the wrong direction when on a nonstop high-speed train trip.
3. To have the audience enjoy the absurdities of manufacturers' claims for their products.
4. To have the audience enjoy hearing about your experience in trying to crash closed classes.
5. To have the audience enjoy your account of a day in traffic court.
6. To have the audience enjoy hearing about the hazards of caring for your vacationing neighbor's pets.
7. To have the audience enjoy the thrills associated with a day of hang gliding.
8. To have the audience enjoy hearing about the first time you went skiing.

Very early in your preparation process you should write down your specific purpose. This will give you a constant target at which to aim. It allows you to see, at a glance, if the material you have gathered and its organization relate directly to your specific purpose.

Choosing a Title

On certain occasions, you may be asked to provide a title for your speech. Ideally, a speech title should be (a) short, (b) provocative, (c) suggestive of your purpose, and (d) appropriate to the target audience and occasion.

A few examples might illustrate how these characteristics can be brought into play in phrasing a speech title. A student speech reviewing the growth of credit card buying and high interest rates in the United States was entitled "Credit Cards: Bankruptcy Made Easy." The title stimulated interest in the talk even before the presentation began. A student giving a talk on world religions used the following title: "God Comes in Various Shapes and Colors." Titles such as "Killer Bees: Is the Name Justified?," "Are Headphones Music to Your Ears?," and "Term Papers: A Growth Industry" are others that capture attention and steer the listener toward the content of the speech.

Choosing a Method of Speaking

Regardless of your background, knowledge, and skill, each time you speak is a unique experience. An effective communicator recognizes this fact and prepares specifically for each occasion. Included in his or her thought and preparation is an analysis of the type of delivery best suited for the subject, audience, and occasion.

There are four fundamental ways of presenting a speech: (1) reading it from a *manuscript*, (2) reciting it from *memory*, (3) giving it in an *impromptu* manner, and (4) delivering it *extemporaneously*. Three observations are in order before we examine each of these methods of speaking. First, many speaking situations call for a combination of two or three of these types. You might begin by reading your introduction from a manuscript and then move to notecards as you use an extemporaneous style. Second, because all four of the methods are concerned with the act of communicating, you will find that they have a great deal in common. For example, in each instance, issues such as credibility, interest and attention, eye contact, vocal variety, posture, and organization need to be taken into consideration. Finally, because our focus at this point is on *delivery*, we will only discuss the presentational aspects of these four methods of speaking. Other considerations, such as organization, content, and the like, will be reserved for later chapters.

Speaking from Manuscript

In the manuscript form of delivery, you read your speech directly from a manuscript. In some instances, this type of delivery is essential and appropriate. For example, on radio and television, and at conferences and conventions, speakers are often accountable for their remarks and must be extremely accurate in what they say. Indeed, all speakers should be accountable and accurate, but a mass media speaker has to be able to make instant referrals to sources and materials. At conventions and business meetings, a manuscript is helpful for a speaker who would like a speech to be circulated.

There are certain advantages to manuscript speaking in addition to those just cited. The obvious advantage is that it puts no strain on your memory. Your speech is before you and you need only read it. A second advantage is that the manuscript, having been written well in advance of the speech situation, enables you to be very selective in your choice of materials and equally meticulous in your style of delivery. Hence, a manuscript speech should be free of vague phrases, rambling sentences, and inappropriate colloquialisms.

Third, the manuscript mode of delivery and preparation is also useful for situations in which time constraints demand that your speech fit into a specific time period. Using a manuscript allows you the luxury of keeping your speech within the assigned limits. The importance of staying within time limitations is perhaps best illustrated by the demands of television. If allotted ten minutes on television, you usually cannot take eleven. If you attempt to take the extra time, you are apt to be cut off the air. Therefore, a manuscript speech, because it is prepared, practiced, and timed in advance, can easily meet time requirements.

This type of delivery also has serious disadvantages. One marked disadvantage is that you can easily lose sight of the importance of communication. You read your remarks and may fail to establish rapport with your listeners. The manuscript becomes more significant than the audience. When this happens, you forget eye contact and lose all sense of spontaneity. Because each word and phrase is decided on in advance, a manuscript speech does not allow for immediate and specific adaptation of its content to the changing moods and needs of the audience. About all you do is modify an aspect of delivery. For example, if someone in the audience appears bored or disinterested, you cannot make major changes in the content of your speech; you can only speak louder, pause in a dramatic way, or intensify your gaze.

For a beginning speech student trying to acquire the ability of sharing personal ideas and feelings, the manuscript type of delivery is not nearly as helpful—nor is it likely to be as effective—as the impromptu and extemporaneous methods. However, if you find occasions for manuscript delivery, remember to (1) write your speech for listeners and not for readers, (2) practice reading aloud, (3) use eye contact and other techniques of effective delivery, and (4) concentrate on getting your ideas across, not just the words.

A memorized speech, much like a manuscript speech, provides you with the advantage of a carefully thought-out and well-worded speech. Every word is committed to memory and this, of course, frees you from the manuscript. One problem of the memorized speech is that this "freedom" often leads to a mechanical delivery, the presentation of a so-called canned speech.

Speaking from Memory

A memorized speech is also dangerous because you are apt to forget the entire speech. It is often difficult to recall the exact wording, and, if you forget one word, you may forget the entire speech. As Thomas Fuller warned, "We have all forgot more than we remember."

Even though a memorized speech permits a careful ordering of your thoughts and materials, you should avoid it. Training in the other methods will offer you and other beginning students practice in speech situations that more closely resemble real-life occasions.

We should discuss two important points before we conclude our treatment of the memorized speech. First, the phrase "speaking from memory" refers to word-for-word memorization, not remembering key ideas and phrases. That is to say, a vast difference exists between word-for-word memorization and knowing in advance what points you want to cover and the general phraseology you want to use. We will examine this distinction in more detail when we discuss extemporaneous delivery. Second, many cultures prefer the memorized speech. For example, in Korea, Japan, and China, students study and learn by memorizing. People in these cultures also feel uncomfortable with direct eye contact. Hence, it is logical and comfortable for them to use a memorized or manuscript speech.

Impromptu Delivery

When you speak on the spur of the moment, without advance notice or time for preparation, you are engaging in impromptu speaking. Much of your daily conversation is nothing more than a series of short, impromptu talks.

In facing an impromptu situation, a speaker must quickly tie together all of his or her thoughts in a few seconds or minutes. The best preparation for impromptu speaking is being well informed and having practice in the prepared speaking situations. A speaker who knows how to prepare a speech when time is not a factor in preparation will have little trouble in making the transition to the spur-of-the-moment occasion. Chapter 15 will examine the problems, principles, and skills of impromptu speaking. However, because many speech classes start with some impromptu speaking, you may need to turn to that chapter early in the semester.

Extemporaneous Delivery

Extemporaneous delivery is often referred to as the "middle course." This speech form is by far the most desirable of the four. Therefore, we will examine it in the most detail.

Extemporaneous speaking has a number of characteristics that help explain both its uniqueness and its attractiveness. Extemporaneous speaking calls for a speech to be (1) researched, (2) outlined, (3) practiced, and (4) delivered in a conversational manner.

When you choose the extemporaneous method, you are also making a decision concerning **research** and **preparation.** Because you know about your speaking assignment beforehand, you have time to gather the necessary information. This investigation should be thorough. Remember, you do not have to spend time memorizing or writing out your speech word for word.

After you have gathered the data, you must **organize** and **outline** the material into a clear and systematic pattern. A major advantage of an extemporaneous speech is that it is prepared in advance and, therefore, can be well organized. You are not asked to speak "off the top of your head" but, instead, are usually granted ample time to prepare and make adjustments in your talk. This time factor not only gives you an opportunity for research and organization, but it means that you can **practice** the speech and clarify your analysis.

Keep three points in mind as you practice your talk. First, read over your complete outline a number of times so that you become familiar with your material. Do not memorize the exact language for delivery; instead, learn your organizational pattern, main points, subpoints, opening, and closing. The focus during practice is on ideas, not specific words. Too much practice can give your speech the appearance of a formal stage performance rather than a conversation with your audience. "Canned" speeches lack sincerity, and often the artificiality detracts from the content of the speech. Again, learning your outline does not mean memorizing your speech.

Second, when you think you have learned your outline, you are ready to determine the approximate amount of time needed to deliver your speech. This can be accomplished by putting aside your outline and timing your talk as you deliver it aloud. Timing your speech will help you decide how much material to delete or how much more detail to add.

The delivery style of the extemporaneous approach is conversational.

Third, after you have made the necessary adjustments to your outline, you are ready to determine what notes to write down on the cards that you will use when you present the talk. You will learn more about notecards in the next section of this chapter but, for now, try to remember that you should learn your outline, not memorize it.

The delivery style of the extemporaneous approach is conversational, and it is this characteristic that is one of its most attractive features. Because preparation stops short of memorization and because notecards may be used, you do not have to worry about forgetting key sections of the talk. Instead, you can give attention to establishing rapport with the audience, directness, eye contact, spontaneity, and a general conversational tone. If you think of extemporaneous delivery as *expanded conversation,* you can develop delivery techniques (chapter 4) while still being relaxed, friendly, and natural.

Extemporaneous delivery also enables you to make maximum use of feedback. That is, the flexibility of this method lets you adapt to the responses being produced by your talk. If you observe some confusion on the faces of your listeners while you are offering your statistics, the extemporaneous style will let you deviate from your outline and explain the statistics in a slightly different manner. For example, the extemporaneous method would allow you to say, "If these comparisons seem to be a little bewildering, I can explain them in yet another way." Memorizing or reading does not allow for this sort of adaptation to feedback.

The shortcomings of the extemporaneous method are probably obvious to you now that we have discussed three other styles. The extemporaneous method takes time— research, outlining, and practice cannot be done in haste. Also, because the speech is not written out word for word or memorized, the beginning speaker often becomes careless in his or her choice of language—there is a tendency to rely completely on inspiration for one's vocabulary. This indictment is really directed more at the misapplication of the method than at an inherent weakness in the method itself. There is, after all, nothing in the explanation of this form of speaking to suggest that language is unimportant. In fact, the notion of preparation and practice implies that all phases of the communication process are of equal significance.

We conclude this section on the four methods of delivery with two final thoughts. First, although we have treated the four methods of speaking independently, in most instances you will find yourself using more than one at a time. For example, following this advice, you decide to deliver your talk by means of the extemporaneous method. However, because you wish to quote some very important expert testimony, you write down the complete quotation on a card, expecting to read from it when you deliver the speech. In addition, you are so pleased with your clever introduction and conclusion that you decide to commit them both to memory. Now you are ready to give your speech—a speech that combines bits and pieces of the extemporaneous, memorized, and manuscript methods. However, once you start giving your talk, you find that you are momentarily thrust into an impromptu situation—someone stops you to ask a question. You now prepare and respond on the spur of the moment.

Second, throughout this book, we will continuously look at the link between culture and communication; much of what we will discuss about speech making has a North American tone. The area of speaking methods is an excellent illustration of these two points. For instance, not all cultures would agree about the advantages of the extemporaneous style. In cultures such as the Japanese and the Chinese, in which there is a lack of a rhetorical tradition and direct eye contact often makes people feel uncomfortable, the manuscript speech is usually the preferred method of delivery. However, in the Arab and Mexican cultures, in which rhetorical artistry is admired, most people enjoy speaking and are not the least bit bothered by the impromptu situation.

Although these two concluding comments might be somewhat overstated, they do illustrate one of the major themes of this book—that a successful speaker does not get locked into any single technique but, instead, is able to adapt his or her preparation and presentation to a variety of topics and situations.

Using Notecards

"When out of sight, quickly also out of mind." Why is it we all know those famous few words written over five hundred years ago by German philosopher Thomas à Kempis? The reason is obvious—our memories cannot be trusted. It is very easy to forget something, even if we concentrate and are motivated to remember. Hence, this is one reason why people use notecards—but there are other reasons as well. Cards serve at least two purposes. First, they assist you in recalling what you want to talk about in your speech. Second, they also have the advantage of offering a sense of security. It is reassuring to know that, if you draw a mental blank during a speech, your notecards are there to rescue you. You can pause, look at your cards, and quickly resume speaking. Moreover, the audience doesn't have to worry about the embarrassment of seeing a speaker flounder because of memory failure. One additional advantage of notecards is that they are more effective than entire sheets of $8\frac{1}{2}$-by-11-inch paper. When using sheets of paper, speakers often have a tendency to include too much information. Large sheets of paper can also cause a speaker to read his or her speech instead of trying to deliver it in an extemporaneous manner. And finally, if you bring sheets of paper to a particular room, and find that a lectern is not available, then you are forced to juggle the papers from hand to hand.

Although most people like the idea of using notecards, they often have difficulty in both constructing and utilizing their cards. Let us therefore offer some guidelines that will help you use notecards to the best advantage.

First, *put your notes on stiff cards, preferably the three-by-five-inch size.* Cards this size fit in the palm of your hand and do not impede your gestures. Larger cards, or sheets of paper, can be rather clumsy to handle, thus causing a distraction.

Second, *you should keep in mind that you are preparing notes, not a manuscript.* You should not write the entire speech on your cards. A good rule of thumb is to write down only what it takes to remind you of your main points and subpoints. For example, if your topic is recycling, one of your notecards on the need for recycling might read

RECYCLING—NEED FOR

1. Conserve limited resources
   a. Minerals
   b. Forestry
2. Avoid waste build-up consequences
   a. Limited landfill space
   b. Costly disposal methods

In the sample notecard, notice that an outline is used. In fact, it should be the same outline form and structure as the larger speech outline. However, now the outline is only highlighting key points that will trigger your memory. Notecards are based on the premise that you have practiced your speech and that certain words and phrases will serve as a stimulus for what you have stored in your head.

Third, *you might want to completely write out any long quotations, expert testimony, and statistics you might be using in your talk.* This will relieve you of having to memorize long and complex portions of your speech. It will enable you to be more accurate when presenting these three types of support. If you try to remember long passages or series of numbers, you may present them in a confusing or misleading fashion. It is always a good idea to write down completely anything you deem too crucial to be left to memory. This rule applies to your introduction and conclusion as well. At the very least, you should consider writing out the first sentence of each of these two crucial sections of your speech.

Fourth, *the printing or writing on your notecards should be clear, easy to read, and confined to only one side of the card.* Many speakers have found themselves unable to use their cards simply because their writing was illegible. Some speakers have also made the mistake of writing on both sides of their cards, which requires flipping cards in a distracting manner during their presentation.

Fifth, *it is also distracting if you happen to get your notecards out of their correct sequence.* Therefore, number your cards in the upper right-hand corner.

Sixth, *you may find it useful to insert a card containing a helpful hint or an important reminder.* For example, speakers who talk too fast might include a card that says SLOW DOWN!!!

Seventh, *while practicing your speech, you should use your notecards in the same way you intend to use them during the actual speech.* This means placing them on a table if one will be available when you talk or holding them in your hand if the room does not have a table or speaker's stand. Practicing with your cards will help you keep them from becoming a distraction to you or the audience. As noted earlier, you might have a tendency to spend too much time looking at your notes. You should also avoid randomly shuffling cards or moving them from hand to hand in a purposeless manner. Remember, your cards should aid communication, not hinder it.

Finally, *when using your notecards, do not try to hide them from your audience.* With practice, you will learn to strike the balance between the cards being a distraction and the fear that the audience will see them. There is nothing wrong with using notecards. What is most important is that you remember to speak directly to your audience while still having the security of using notecards. In time, you will gain the confidence and poise to use your cards in a variety of ways. You will be able to glance at them, pause, read from them when appropriate, walk around with them, set them down on a table, use them as cues, and still not have them inhibit your delivery.

Although we primarily concentrated on notecards to help you remember your talk, we need to add one additional note system that is often used by some speakers. This technique uses the speaker's visual aids as a prompting device. For example, if you are using transparencies (which will be discussed in detail in chapter 7) you might find it helpful to let each aid contain some of speech content. As you move from aid to aid you are automatically being reminded of the points you plan to cover.

Practicing the Speech

Although it might be somewhat of a cliche, and it might be an overstatement, but practice does makes perfect. It would be great folly not to believe that practice is essential for successful public speaking. To help with that practice, let us offer a few suggestions as you move into these final stages of your speech preparation.

Have a systematic sequence for practicing well in mind. You should start by taking your complete-sentence outline and talking from it two or three times. This will help you think about transitions and also identify difficult passages. You should then abridge the outline to a smaller version that you will eventually place onto your notecards. You are now ready to start practicing your speech.

Have a positive attitude toward practice. The preceding sentence is easier to write and read than it is to put into action. We all know from personal experience that, whether it is baseball or the piano, it is more fun to play than to practice. This analogy is also true of speech making. Just as a professional baseball player and a concert performer have accomplished their goals through study and training, you, too, must practice if you want to deliver a successful speech. Seeing the bond between practice and achievement should help you develop a positive attitude. In short, see your practice sessions as times to sharpen your skills so that the actual speaking event will be smooth and free from tension.

Practice early and often. Author Henry Miller was talking about all of us when he wrote, "Life for most of us is one long postponement." We are all victims of procrastination from time to time. This can be a great hindrance, however, when it comes to developing your proficiency as a speaker. You can reap a number of benefits from avoiding this fault and starting your practice sessions early. First of all, the extra time spent in practice will help you master your ideas. It takes time to secure the delicate balance between knowing what you want to say and falling into a pattern of memorization. Trying to accomplish this balance in only one or two sessions is nearly impossible, particularly if your only rehearsal is behind the steering wheel of your car as you drive to class to present your speech. This will most likely make you a candidate for failure and, perhaps, for an accident as well.

Second, by allowing yourself ample time for practice sessions, you will reduce your chances of forgetting the speech once it comes time to deliver it before an audience. These practice sessions should also help you build confidence. Sometimes a nervous presentation signals a lack of preparation, a fear of forgetting parts of the speech. By starting practice early, you will have one less thing to worry about.

Third, by starting your practice sessions early, you will allow yourself sufficient time to identify and correct any flaws in your speech content or delivery. In addition, if the speech is too long, you will have time to do some editing and, if it is too short, you can add some material.

Fourth, start by practicing with your main outline. Once you learn the key points of your outline, it will be easy to move to your notecards. This weaning process will lead you smoothly from your detailed outline to your notecards, to the words and phrases you use during your talk.

Fifth, work to remember ideas, not words. Your practice sessions—and you should try for five to seven of them—should focus on your learning the main points of your speech, the ideas and sequence. Again, do not try to remember exact words.

Make your practice sessions as realistic as possible. Practicing your speech by "running it through your head" as you lie flat on your back in bed may not be much help when you face the actual speaking situation. Experience has shown that practice sessions should be as realistic as possible. What follows are a few suggestions to increase the realism.

First, practice the speech standing up. You will not deliver the speech from your bed or your desk at home, so do not practice at those places. Instead, try to get your body and mind accustomed to the position and posture that you will use when you deliver the speech before an audience. If at all possible, try to rehearse in a room that approximates the type of room in which you will present your talk. Ideally, you should rehearse in the room, studio, or auditorium where you will give the speech.

Second, practice the speech in a realistic manner. Visualizing your speech in your head can create a false feeling of security. Silently responding to thoughts is not the same thing as actually producing the sounds. You need to speak many, but not all, of the same words you plan to use in the talk.

Third, practice using whatever memory aids (cards, outline, cue cards, TelePrompTer) and audiovisuals (posters, models, films, tapes) that you will use in your final presentation. Many public speakers have spoiled all their research and preparation by not having practiced with their aids prior to their speech.

Fourth, develop the habit of not stopping your speech when you are saying it aloud. The reason behind this suggestion should be clear—when you give the speech, you will not be able to stop every time you select the wrong word or make a mistake. In addition, too much stopping during your rehearsals works against the impression that your speech is a smooth, continuous flow from start to finish.

Finally, if possible, rehearse your speech before an audience. That audience can be your roommate, parents, fellow class members, or secretary. Talking to people is a very different matter from talking to tables, chairs, or pets. Not only will you get the "live" feeling, but you will be able to solicit suggestions from those present at your practice sessions. Depending on their qualifications as critics, they can comment on content and delivery.

Try to locate a videocassette recorder and camera. A speaker makes a big mistake if he or she does not take advantage of all available electronic equipment. Most campuses have media centers that provide students with video equipment that enables them to record and play back speech assignments. Seeing and hearing yourself enables you to make adjustments to your presentation and content.

Allow time for one final run-through. We have already mentioned the importance of budgeting your time; allow yourself a few quiet minutes before the speech has to be delivered. This private time can serve two purposes. First, you can practice your speech one final time. Second, you can put your mind and body into a relaxed mood. If you have taken time to prepare and practice, you should have little trouble with your mental attitude—your confidence should be high. If your body has not gotten the message and you seem physically nervous, you can try some of the following tension-relieving techniques: (1) walk around (it releases nervous energy), (2) take deep breaths or yawn (it increases your supply of oxygen), and (3) take a drink of water (it keeps your mouth from going dry).

Gaining Confidence

Ralph Waldo Emerson noted that "all the great speakers were bad speakers at first." He might have also added that all speakers, regardless of their ability, have experienced at least some of the conditions associated with stage fright. It is because a fear of public speaking is so common that we have decided to examine the issue of stage fright during the early stages of this book.

Picture the following scene:

> The voice quavers or becomes very tense. The rate of speaking becomes unusually rapid or agonizingly slow. The voice lapses into a monotone and emphasis is neglected. Breathing becomes labored. There is an urge to swallow or clear the throat frequently. Stammering sets in. Every pause is vocalized with an "um" or "er" or other meaningless sound. There is a fumbling for words. Eye contact with the audience is lost. The face becomes expressionless. The hands and arms become rigid and start to tremble uncontrollably. The body begins to sway back and forth and the feet begin to shuffle restlessly.

According to communication researchers Anthony Mulac and Robert Sherman, the conditions just described are those typically associated with speech fright. Although as a whole they may sound frightening, they are experienced by nearly everyone who speaks before a group. In short, whether we call it speech fright, stage fright, communication apprehension, or speech anxiety, it is well known to anyone who has been at a party composed of strangers, had a "blind date," attended a crucial job interview, appeared before the public, whether as a theatrical performer, a product demonstrator, a teacher, or a student in a speech class. Even the most experienced platform artists are not totally immune to stage fright, although some hide its effects more skillfully than do others. You can take comfort from The Bruskin Report, which claims to have discovered that Americans fear speaking before a group more than they fear flying, deep water, snakes, height, and even death.

We begin our discussion of speech anxiety with these two key questions: *What is speech anxiety and why is it so prevalent?* Basically, speech anxiety is your body reacting to a fear-producing situation. In many ways, it is no different than the feelings you would experience if you were to see a car coming directly at you as you were driving on the freeway—your body would want to flee the situation. In speech anxiety, it is not an approaching car that your body is responding to but, rather, the idea of having other people evaluate you and your message. However, just as you can control the situation of the advancing automobile by manipulating your car, so can you control speech anxiety.

Just as some eating and sleeping disorders can be controlled, so can speech anxiety be kept from paralyzing you during your public presentations. In this final section of the chapter, we shall (1) attempt to explain speech anxiety and (2) suggest ways to deal with it.

Speech anxiety is but one of a number of related conditions that are referred to collectively as **communication apprehension.** A person suffering the most severe degree of communication apprehension may try to avoid communicating with anyone other than relatives and close friends. He or she may even seek out an occupation that does not require much interaction with other people or may find housing that is remote from others.

Speech anxiety may be generalized—that is, experienced in any or all public-speaking situations—or it may be situational—that is, experienced to a greater degree in certain public-speaking contexts than in others. For example, one might experience very little anxiety when contemplating or presenting a speech before friends, but a great deal of anxiety when faced with the prospect of appearing before an audience of total strangers. At any rate, this mild form of communication apprehension—speech anxiety—is what the majority of us experience.

The causes of communication apprehension are not clearly established. Some scholars theorize that a genetic predisposition to shyness might be operative. Others see communication apprehension as essentially a learned behavior, perhaps stemming from childhood communication experiences that had negative outcomes. For example, a child might have been punished for talking too much or rewarded for staying quiet. Perhaps the child chose to imitate the quiet behavior of an adult role model. We shall not debate the merits of these theories but shall deal, instead, with the reality of the anxiety that is clearly present.

What is there about the public-speaking situation that might trigger an attack of anxiety? For one thing, it may be the *sheer strangeness* of suddenly being thrust into the spotlight. After all, giving a public speech is not an everyday activity for most of us, so it is natural for us to experience anxiety about the unfamiliar role we are being called on to play.

Understanding Communication Apprehension

Sometimes the *physical setting* can be intimidating. If the speaker's platform is elevated several feet above the seated spectators, we may feel vulnerable and ill at ease. If we are obliged to use a microphone, stand in a spotlight, or face a television camera, we may be unnerved. The strangeness of the physical environment can induce anxiety.

The very fact that *many eyes are staring* at us can make us feel terribly uncomfortable. This seems to be entirely normal behavior in both humans and animals. Most of us do not like to be conspicuous, and we may actually fear being stared at.

Having a *strict time limit* placed on our presentation can cause anxiety. This is apt to be the case in a speech class, where the instructor may limit us to, say, five minutes for our presentation. Worrying about finishing on time or, conversely, about not talking long enough, can aggravate our anxiety.

Then there is the sheer *uncertainty of how our listeners will perceive us and our ideas*. This is especially true when we feel we are being evaluated: I wonder if they will like me? Will they notice my knees shaking? What will they think if I forget part of my speech? Suppose they disagree with my arguments? What if they misinterpret my meaning? What if they think I'm being presumptuous? What if my voice fails me? These are all questions that can flash through our minds when we face an audience, particularly an audience of strangers. Our anxiety seems to grow or diminish, depending on the degree to which we think we are being evaluated.

For people who have *English as their second language*, anxiety might be aroused by having to speak in a language that they are not yet comfortable with. Imagine for a moment how any of us would feel if, wanting to do a good job with our speech, we were asked to deliver that speech in a language that was not the one we normally spoke. We would, indeed, be very nervous. Later in this chapter we promise to talk to you about ways of overcoming these feelings of apprehension.

All of these conditions—unfamiliar role, strange environment, time constraints, uncertain reception, English as a second language—are potentially anxiety arousing. It is understandable that we react to them as we would to any unnerving stimulus. Now the question is, How shall we deal with our anxieties?

Dealing with Communication Apprehension

With this background in the symptoms and causes of speech anxiety, you can begin to understand the problem. Actually, you are already on the road to coping with speech anxiety if you have read and followed the advice provided in chapter 1. Let us remind you of a few of the principles that can help build your confidence. First, we will talk about some things you can do before the speech and then what you can do during the actual presentation. Finally, we will examine some measures to be taken in the future that can help you maintain control over those natural anxieties that arise whenever you face the prospect of speaking in public.

Before the Speech

The measures to combat speech anxiety should be set into motion well before the time the actual speech is presented. In the following paragraphs, we will discuss some of the most important things you can do prior to your talk.

Although it seems somewhat apparent, you need to develop a positive attitude. If you dread the speaking experience too much, you will find that it can develop into a minor phobia and you will never enjoy the public-speaking arena. Shakespeare said much the same thing when he told us "In time we hate that which we often fear." To keep you from abhorring public speaking, let us suggest some ways to promote a positive attitude.

One way to develop a positive attitude is by selecting a subject that interests you. If you have strong feelings about your subject and you want others to feel the same way about it, you are apt to commence your preparation with a greater sense of confidence. Since fear and confidence can hardly be experienced at the same time, you have put fear on the back burner right at the outset. If a condition in your community makes you indignant, talk about it. If you are interested in necromancy, talk about it. Feeling strongly about something—whether the feeling is anger, indignation, love, pity, or mirth—can help you forget about being frightened, so give careful thought to your subject selection. Being preoccupied by your topic will keep you from being preoccupied by speech anxiety.

A confident point of view can be accomplished if you openly discuss the upcoming speech with *yourself*. Tell yourself such things as "These are my classmates, they want me to do well," "Countless other students have given speeches and managed to get an "A" in the course," and "The speech will eventually end and I will be able to sit down." Although these three examples may at first blush appear frivolous, years of experience and countless student observations have taught that they do work.

A positive attitude can also be encouraged by visualizing the communication experience in an optimistic and upbeat manner. Run a movie in your head that shows you being calm, relaxed, and successful. There is evidence that this sort of positive image making can be helpful.

Finally, you might find that wearing one of your favorite outfits can also help build your confidence. Although it is somewhat of a cliche, when we think we look good we tend to feel good.

Be thorough in your audience analysis. By taking more-than-ordinary pains to find out who your listeners will be, what their probable attitudes will be toward you as an individual and as an authority on the subject matter, what their beliefs are on your topic of discussion, and what their expectations are likely to be, you can dispel some of the mystery surrounding the reception you are likely to get from your audience. You can use that information to plan and prepare your speech more intelligently.

As noted in the first suggestion, *think of speech anxiety as short-lived.* The degrees of anxiety experienced by the average speaker tend to vary greatly. Anxiety is probably at its highest level in the moments before one stands up to speak. If one gets through the speech opening satisfactorily, anxiety usually starts to dissipate. By the time the speech is in full swing, the last traces of anxiety may be gone. In certain cases, the anxiety is connected with a controversial point the speaker must address. Once that point is successfully concluded, the anxiety subsides.

Knowing that speech anxiety is usually short-lived not only serves as a source of comfort, but it also enables you to pay particular attention to the preparation of the materials you will present during your most anxious moments.

Start your preparation early. Although we have stressed this idea elsewhere, it is worth repeating, for to start preparing your speech the night before you have to give it is inviting trouble. By starting earlier and making yourself really knowledgeable about your subject, you can tell yourself, "I know what I'm talking about." By making yourself more expert than your listeners, you are less likely to feel intimidated by them.

Rehearse your speech, but do not memorize it unless the situation demands it. Beginning speakers often make the mistake of writing down their speeches and attempting to commit them to memory. If anything can contribute to speech anxiety, it is the fear of forgetting words that have been memorized. It is a better idea to rehearse your speech extemporaneously, varying your word choice from rehearsal to rehearsal. In that way, you are focusing on the ideas, not the words. Prepare your speaking notes on small, stiff cards, as suggested earlier in the chapter.

Inspect the physical environment in which you will be speaking. By knowing in advance the peculiarities of the physical environment and its limitations, you can make necessary adjustments and, thus, remove another uncertainty from the speaking situation. Perhaps you will be afforded the luxury of controlling the seating arrangements, placement of the speaker's stand, adjustment of the microphone, and so on. Control over these variables helps build your confidence.

Finally, *try to engage in some relaxing behaviors just before your speech.* Let us suggest some common relaxing techniques that have proven to be effective when applied to speech anxiety. Some of these techniques can slow breathing, lower your pulse rate, ease muscle tension, and help you focus on your speech, not your nervousness. First, excessively yawn a minute or two before you begin. This not only gives you more oxygen, but it relaxes your throat muscles. Second, try stretching as many parts of your body as you can without calling attention to your strange acrobatics. This stretching relaxes the muscles that are apt to be tensing up as you wait for your speech to begin. Third, if time allows, you might also try to sit quietly, close your eyes, concentrate on relaxing your entire body, take slow deep breaths and imagine oxygen slowly flowing throughout your entire body. Finally, take a small drink of water so you can avoid the "dry mouth" feeling that makes talking seem impossible. A word of warning—be careful of too much water; we remind you of the results of consuming too much liquid in a short period of time.

During the Speech

When it is finally time to give the speech, you can adopt some behaviors that should help you maintain good control over your anxieties about speaking. Let us examine these behaviors.

Use relaxation techniques. We have already mentioned the value of deep breathing on nervousness, now we simply urge you to take some final breaths before you utter your first words. In order to benefit from deep breathing, you should position yourself so that you can make full use of your diaphragm, the muscle that separates your chest cavity from your abdominal cavity. You should be able to feel your waistline expand as you inhale and contract as you exhale. Deep, regular diaphragmatic breathing will soon make you feel more relaxed. You might even pause one final time and take one last breath just a few seconds before you begin. If you feel some tension in your upper torso, let your shoulders slump down and allow your arms to hang loosely at your sides. This will help further promote the feeling of relaxation induced by your deep breathing.

Adopt behaviors associated with confidence. Before you rise to speak, sit "tall," with your shoulders relaxed, and lean slightly forward. After rising, walk with a confident stride to the podium. Do not be in a hurry to start. Arrange your notes on the lectern. If you choose, let your hands rest lightly on the lectern, but do not grip the lectern; you may let your arms hang comfortably at your sides. Now look at your audience for a moment and then commence. Once you begin speaking it is important to speak slowly and to remember to pause from time to time. Both of these activities will help your overall delivery at the same time they are helping you relax.

Focus your mind on your audience and your speech. Are my knees shaking? Is my face red? Am I making a spectacle of myself? are thoughts that can serve no useful purpose. If your mind does drift to self-evaluation while you are talking, simply remind yourself that the audience is there to hear what you have to say, not to see you fail or to ridicule you. You might also, during the "visit" with yourself, offer a short "pep talk" and tell yourself how well you are doing.

Use message-related bodily actions. Hand gestures, bodily movement, and walking ought to be used as fully as possible. They will help dissipate the natural tension that you are feeling and will reinforce your verbal message at the same time. If you have an opportunity to use visual aids, the movements involved in manipulating the aids can give a healthy outlet to the nervous energy crying for release.

Seek out receptive faces and talk to them. Once you establish one-to-one eye contact with friendly persons, you may soon stop thinking of your listeners as a mysterious crowd and start treating them as friends engaging in a one-sided conversation with you. After all, a public speech is essentially an enlarged conversation, with you doing all the talking.

If you should make a mistake, do not apologize, simply go on with your speech. In most instances the audience will not even know that you made a minor error or left out one of your illustrations. We should add, however, if the mistake involves a major distortion of the facts, you ethically must pause and correct the misunderstanding.

After the Speech

Once you have completed your speech, and gained your composure, you should congratulate yourself for a job well done. You will also find that each time you talk, the task gets easier and easier. To alter an old expression, "familiarity breeds confidence." Look for further opportunities to speak in public, thus changing an unfamiliar role into a familiar one by sheer repetition of, and exposure to, the act of speaking. As we have already indicated, experiencing the act of speaking over and over again is one of the best ways to calm needless fears. You will probably find that, in your classroom speeches, you will experience a lessening degree of anxiety with each successive speech, especially if you maintain a consistent level of preparation.

Perhaps the single most important key to reducing speech anxiety is remembering the words of poet T. S. Eliot: "Every beginning has an end." This applies to both your speech and your anxiety.

Summary

Communication normally takes place because the speaker wants to achieve a preconceived purpose. Thus, the purpose must be clear in the speaker's mind. Public speakers usually prepare and give speeches that fulfill three general speech purposes—to inform, to persuade, and to entertain. In addition to selecting a general purpose, a speaker must formulate a specific purpose that describes the immediate and exact nature of the response wanted from the audience.

Speakers may encounter situations that make it necessary for them to provide titles for their speeches. In these cases, it is important to remember that a good title is brief, is appropriate, is provocative, and suggests the purpose of the speech.

In deciding on a method of preparation and delivery, a speaker can use any one of the following procedures: (1) speaking from a manuscript, (2) speaking from memory, (3) speaking impromptu, and (4) speaking extemporaneously. The extemporaneous method is recommended for beginning speakers.

When using notecards, it is important to (1) use stiff cards, (2) keep notes brief, (3) write out direct quotations, expert testimony, and statistics, (4) write clearly, (5) write yourself personal reminders, and (6) practice with the cards.

When practicing, speakers should start early, make practice sessions realistic, use video equipment, and allow time for one final run-through.

Fear of speaking, or communication apprehension, is a common condition experienced even by seasoned speakers. While its causes are not fully understood, it seems to surface particularly when a speaker is faced with an unfamiliar role in an unfamiliar environment before an unfamiliar audience. The control of communication apprehension lies in removing as many of the areas of uncertainty and unfamiliarity as possible. Thorough preparation and practice, coupled with a good mental attitude, will help guard against the disabling effects of communication apprehension.

Chapter 3

Audience Analysis

Understanding Your Listeners

There were never in the world two opinions alike, any more than two hairs or two grains. Their most universal quality is diversity.

Michel Eyquem de Montaigne

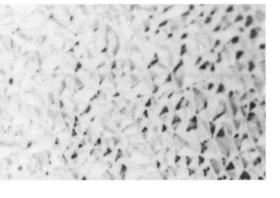

If we would consider not so much wherein we differ, as wherein we agree, there would be far less of uncharitableness and angry feeling in the world.

Joseph Addison

T he lyrics of a song by Scottish poet Thomas Campbell lament

Oh, how hard it is to find
The one just suited to our mind!

These words could easily apply to a speaker in search of a sympathetic audience. Trying to get a diverse group of people just to listen may seem to be an impossible task at times; what interests one individual may not interest another. Also, when it comes to persuading such a group, the problem is further complicated. Any individual's reasons for believing or acting in a certain way are the product of many and varied influences. From the neighborhoods we grew up in to the groups we hold allegiance to, we are the product of countless affiliations. Yet in spite of the problems we face when trying to adjust to the people around us, we have all, very early in life, learned to adapt our messages to these diverse populations. Think back to your own childhood, when you had to convince several people—perhaps family members—to let you do something. Maybe you wanted to go to the video arcade with a friend, buy a certain car, or get a special kind of haircut. Chances are you had to use a variety of approaches. The arguments you used with one individual were not precisely the same as those you used with another. Experience had taught you that there were vulnerable spots in each person's makeup, so you tailored your arguments accordingly. You knew your mother's first concern was with your personal safety, so when you asked to go to the video arcade you stressed the fact that the arcade had a security guard, who does not allow any "rough stuff" in the place. You knew your dad was concerned with how you spent his money, so you told him about the "every fifth game is free" policy at the arcade and added that you would not waste money on frivolous junk food. You knew your success depended on how accurately you had forecast the responses of your listeners and how well you could adapt your message to meet those potential responses. This chapter, in principle, is about your adapting not to a single person such as your mother or father, but rather how you can tailor your message to an entire audience composed of many individuals. These individuals might even be from a variety of cultures.

Importance of Audience Analysis

The interrelated concepts of prediction and adaptation are perhaps two of the most basic principles of human communication. In nearly all of your communication experiences, you take the other person into account, make some predictions about who he or she is, and adapt your behavior accordingly. Even in your initial encounters with strangers, you note some features that affect the image you form of each person. You know rather quickly if that person is old or young, attractive or unattractive, African American or Caucasian, male or female, neat or sloppy. You know if he or she is wearing a uniform, western clothing, or a three-piece business suit. Once you make these observations, you automatically begin to adapt your messages to this individualized data. As you get more information about your communication partner, you make further adjustments to your message. You are using **predictions** about how your receivers are going to respond to you and your ideas. When your predictions and resultant adaptation involve a collection of people, you are engaging in audience analysis. **Audience analysis** means *finding out all you can about the people you are talking to or will be talking to so that you can adapt your material to their interests, needs, attitudes, fund of knowledge, beliefs, values, and backgrounds.*

If you present a speech without considering the audience, you have very little chance of being understood or gaining support. On the other hand, if you ask and answer questions such as Who are they? What are they like? and What will they think of me and my message? you can make the necessary adjustments in language, arguments, emotional appeal, evidence, explanations, and the like.

Audience analysis also enables you to promote rapport among the listeners and to establish your own rapport with them. You do this by discovering some common denominators that exist in spite of individual, cultural, and group differences. For example, if you were to talk to a group of Japanese businesspersons and you knew that the Japanese like a patient, calm communication style, you could adapt your speaking to fit that specific audience.

Central to this idea of adaptation, and to the entire process of communication, is the concept of identification. In *Rhetoric of Motives*, Kenneth Burke suggests, "You persuade a man only insofar as you can talk his language by speech, gesture, tonality, order, image, attitude, idea, identifying your ways with his." Successful communication must ask the speaker to "talk the language" of those he or she hopes to influence. Audience analysis allows you an opportunity to learn the "history" and current language of your receivers so that you can fuse your goals and purposes with theirs.

The importance of audience analysis should be clear. Information about your audience can help you forecast how that audience is likely to perceive you and your topic. For example, prior to your speech, if the audience does not feel compatible with you (you are a young male speaking about preventing sexually transmitted diseases to an audience composed of older women in the morning and a group of sixth-grade students in the afternoon), it is important to have that information in advance of your talk. The arguments you use, the evidence to support those arguments, the language of those arguments, the amount of time you spend establishing rapport, the content of your emotional appeals, and the ways in which you define new concepts are all touched by what the audience members believe before you begin. Likewise, if they have little or no information about your subject, or if they are opposed to the stand you will be taking, then knowing that in advance will enable you to cope with the situation more intelligently. Such knowledge helps you control future events. As philosopher Eric Hoffer wrote, "The only way to predict the future is to have the power to shape the future." Audience analysis enables you to shape your speech.

Types of Audiences

There are very few pages in this text that do not contain a reference to "the audience." However, remember that the concept of "the audience" is an abstraction. No such creature exists. When you present a speech, you are facing a group of individuals, who together make up an audience. Most classifications of audiences include those situations when you are in a dyad, small group, public-speaking situation, or mediated event. A more specific description was offered by H. L. Hollingsworth, in his book *The Psychology of the Audience*. He classified audiences into six groups: pedestrian, passive, selected, concerted, organized, and absent.

An audience made up of persons having no obvious common ties to one another is called a **pedestrian audience.** These are people who have temporarily gathered and are now about to listen to the speech. An example of this kind of audience is a chance gathering of people at a park or on a street corner. Capturing their attention is the first problem the speaker must solve. We should add that in most instances you will not be confronted with very many pedestrian audiences, but because this type of audience does exist we believe you should be aware of this specific configuration.

A group that is initially attentive to the speaker, but not necessarily interested in what is to come, is termed a **passive audience.** In most instances these are individuals who have been thrust into the audience for reasons other than their own choosing. For example, an employer or a teacher may ask the audience to listen to a specific speech. The members of such an audience must be shown that it is worthwhile to continue giving their attention to the speaker.

A **selected audience** is characterized by members who share a common purpose, but who lack a plan for working in concert with one another. With such an audience, the speaker must promote feelings of cohesion and direction.

A **concerted audience** consists of members who are ready to achieve their common goal but need to be satisfied that any recommendations the speaker makes are logically defensible. Therefore, the speaker must exert every effort to convince the audience of the soundness of the measures he or she advocates.

An **organized audience** is one so unified in purpose and in loyalty to the speaker that it needs only to be told what to do. With such audiences, no persuasion is necessary, only directions or instructions.

An **absent audience** is physically separated from the speaker. These audiences are very common when mediated equipment such as a video camera, television, radio, or audiotape is used. In most cases, these audiences have made a conscious effort to hear the speaker's presentation.

Assessing the Audience

Since no two audiences are exactly alike, you need to ask yourself a series of questions at the beginning of your audience analysis. Although our list

An organized audience is one so unified in purpose and in loyalty to the speaker that it needs only to be told what to do.

of questions is by no means exhaustive, it does represent a general sampling of the type of questions that will help point you toward your specific audience:

1. What is the attitude of the audience toward my purpose?
2. What is the attitude of the audience toward me?
3. What do my listeners have in common?
4. What are their differences?
5. What does my audience already know about my subject?
6. Do they have the power and/or authority to respond to my specific request?
7. Will the audience come to the speech already interested in the topic?

Your answer to each question will have greater utility if you visualize a point on a continuum where you think your audience is to be found. A sample scale is shown below:

Knowledgeable ....Not knowledgeable
Favorable ....Unfavorable
Willing...Unwilling
Interested..Uninterested

You will notice that each end of a continuum demands a different level of preparation if the speaker's purpose is to be attained. Let us examine three brief examples that will demonstrate this link between preparation and audience analysis.

A student from San Francisco who was attending a university in San Diego was so enamored of San Diego that he decided to give a speech to inform about the sightseeing attractions within reach of the university. However, he failed to take into account the knowledge level of his potential audience. The majority of his classmates were local residents. Although his speech provided interesting and useful information to the handful of nonresidents in the class, the rest of his classmates were bored by hearing information about places they had already visited.

Time is well spent in trying to determine how favorably your listeners are apt to look on you and your purpose. For example, residents of Oregon who live in communities where the lumber industry flourishes are inclined to take a dim view of a speech calling for a halt in the cutting of timber in order to preserve certain species of owls. A speech on that same theme designed for an audience of Sierra Club members would require an entirely different set of arguments and appeals. Knowing the type of audience helps in selecting your means of persuasion.

There are times when listeners are enthusiastic about listening to a speech and are willing to lend their time and attention to it. For example, a group of tax accountants might pay to hear a speech describing new tax laws. There are also occasions when the audience is less willing to take part and may even resent having to be present—for example, a group of senior honor students having to attend a mandatory lecture reviewing some elementary methods of studying for an objective examination.

What Listeners Bring to Communication

The American playwright Eugene O'Neill was right when he wrote, "The past is the present, isn't it? It's the future too." What O'Neill was telling us is that our past experiences, to a large extent, determine our response to the present and the future. Yet deciding on the impact of past experiences is a very difficult task. That is to say, there is no escaping the fact that it is at times very puzzling to investigate the impact and influence of what each of us brings to a communication experience. For example, a person receiving bad news just before entering a classroom will react to a classmate's speech differently than will those who are untroubled. This "mood of the moment," as well as what happened to the person ten years ago, could affect his or her reaction to the speech.

We need to focus our discussion of audience analysis on two rather obvious points. First, it is impossible to know everything about each audience member. All of us are extremely complex individuals. We have had millions of experiences that have shaped our character and personality. It would be impossible for any speaker to know even a small fraction of those specific experiences. Second, because each of us is unique, a speaker's conclusions about an audience might not apply to every member of that audience. Therefore, what we have gathered at the end of an audience analysis is some general information about cultural background, group affiliation, educational level, occupation, gender, age, and the like. If we know how to use it, this general information can tell us a great deal about the people we will be addressing. The usefulness of this information is based on the assumption that, *as members of a culture or group, listeners share a set of norms, perceptions, attitudes, motives, needs, values, and interests.* As speakers, our job is to discover the affiliations of our listeners, to make some valid generalizations about those affiliations, and to adapt our material to accommodate those generalizations.

What do listeners bring to a speech that will influence how they respond to the speaker and the specific purpose? As we have seen, this is a rather difficult question to answer, for, in essence, what listeners bring is both general and specific and falls into four broad categories: (1) a fund of knowledge (what they know about a countless number of subjects), (2) attitudes (their feelings about a topic), (3) beliefs (what they believe to be true or false about the world), and (4) values (how they believe they should act in the world). As you would suspect, each of these denominations has countless subsets that influence the manner in which people respond to the outside world. In subsequent chapters, we will examine these categories in more detail, but for now you need to understand how those four elements influence listeners' responses to your ideas and information. Your understanding can be increased if you discover what is often called the demographics of your audience, the *salient characteristics of the people you will be addressing.* The study of these characteristics, be it age, gender, or culture, is based on two simple assumptions. First, although we are all unique individuals, we are also members of countless groups that supply us with our fund of knowledge, attitudes, beliefs, and values. Second, if you know something about the group and cultural affiliations, you can make some important choices about your speech content and delivery.

Throughout this book, we have discussed the idea that, during the past twenty years, the world has undergone a series of cultural changes. In fact, the phrase "cultural diversity" has now become a common term. We, too, will use this phrase as a part of the unavoidable truism that on most occasions you will be communicating with people from many cultural backgrounds. In the United States, large populations of people are from various ethnic and cultural groups, whose experiences make them perceive the world very differently than do members of the dominant culture. Also, if you leave the United States, you will interact with people whose cultural composition may not be the same as your own. It is because of this increase in cross-cultural contact that we begin our discussion of audience analysis with the topic of culture.

Cultural Characteristics

Culture has been described as the totality of learned and accumulated experience that is socially transmitted from generation to generation. Our culture gives each of us, in both conscious and subconscious ways, modes of behavior, patterns of thought, beliefs, attitudes, ideas, values, and many of our habits. To understand those with whom we attempt to communicate, we must know something about the culture that they bring to a communication event.

A word of caution before we proceed with our examination of culture. We must be careful not to rely too heavily on preconceived notions about another's culture. All too often, those notions are based on limited experiences and unrealistic images of a culture as portrayed in movies, novels, and the remarks of biased observers. Moreover, we must remember that our perceptions of other cultures might be influenced by a feeling of **ethnocentrism.** As mentioned in the first chapter, ethnocentrism is a tendency to judge all other cultures by the standards set by one's own culture. The danger of ethnocentrism is that it usually adds a dimension that can obstruct our perceptions of another culture.

It might be helpful if we begin our discussion of cultural influences on communication by briefly summarizing some key values as they apply to the dominant North American culture. A list of these values will not only help you understand members of the dominant culture but will serve as a backdrop and reference point for looking at how values function in other cultures.

North American Values

1. The value of *individuality* is perhaps the most sacred of all values in the United States. This key value manifests itself in a variety of ways. It stresses individual initiative ("Pull yourself up by your own bootstraps"), independence ("Rules are for fools"), individual self-expression ("The squeaky wheel gets the grease"), and even privacy ("A man's home is his castle"). Each of these beliefs needs to be considered when trying to persuade people who value individualism.

2. People in the United States *value materialism and material comforts;* they tend to evaluate people and even set goals in light of material and monetary results. There is even a popular bumper sticker that proclaims, "The person with the most toys wins."

3. *Activity and work* are important values in the United States, a fast-paced society composed of people who "like doing things." They perceive work as a virtue and a means to accomplish material success.

4. People in the United States have a long history of being highly *humanitarian*. They give more to charity, both at home and abroad, than any other country in the world. Americans act swiftly, both as individuals and as a government, to help those in need.

5. People in the United States believe in *efficiency and practicality*. In the name of efficiency, Americans emphasize adaptability, technological innovation, economic expansion, currency, practicality, expediency, and effectiveness.

6. In the United States, *progress and change* are valued. Almost since the founding of the country, people have railed against stagnation and the status quo. From conquering the land, seas, airways, and finally space, progress and change have been prime articles of faith for most Americans. They enjoy what is new and different. It is also important to remember that each generation seeks to stake out new territory and contribute to change.

7. *Democracy*, while perhaps closely linked with the value of individual freedom, is important enough to have its own enumeration. Since the founding of the United States, Americans have rejected aristocracy and authoritarianism. From the Declaration of Independence to an insistence on majority rule, Americans pride themselves on being the most democratic people in the world.

8. Americans' valuing of *science and rationality* is reflected in an interest in objectivity over faith, the scientific method over magic, and rationality over intuition. Americans desire an ordered universe, one over which they have control.

9. In the United States, the high value placed on *success* manifests itself in many ways. Americans have long respected high achievers and self-made persons. This value is so important that people are even encouraged to try to succeed after a number of failures. Think for a moment about the latent message in the proverb "If at first you do not succeed, try, try again."

10. The culture of the United States is marked by *competitiveness*. Whether in sports, business, or personal life, Americans are taught to strive to be "number one." The U.S. economic and social systems thrive on perceiving life as a contest that categorizes people as winners or losers.

Obviously, the foregoing values are not held by all people who live in the United States; however, as indicated earlier, they do represent values that permeate much of U.S. middle-class culture.

The sway of cultural attitudes, beliefs, and values on communication is of immense importance. A culture gives its members a worldview that enables them to deal with the large issues of life and death, suffering and happiness, heaven and hell. It also provides them with certain ways of perceiving and responding to events and ideas such as work, leisure, violence, change, conflict, sex rules, the elderly, and self-worth. The cataloging of cultural values and characteristics could, of course, fill an entire book. Therefore what we offer in the next few pages are some important cultural values and characteristics that need to be considered when speaking to diverse audiences.

Cross-Cultural Values

Centuries ago, Aristotle wrote in *The Rhetoric* that a speaker needs to know the audience members' conceptions of happiness, because that is the "object at which they aim in whatever they choose and whatever they reject." If you know that your audience belongs to an East Asian culture or is composed of many Native Americans, who believe that living in harmony with nature leads to happiness, you can be cautious about recommending measures that exploit nature. The Western view that it is both a right and a mandate for human beings to control nature is an unsuitable premise on which to base arguments for that audience.

A speaker can profit from knowing how the Asian and Latin outlook on individualism versus collectivism differs from the view found in the dominant North American culture. Whereas North Americans tend toward individualism, stressing self-motivation and competition with others, Eastern cultures give primacy to the group. Hence, a speaker addressing Japanese business executives might say, "This product will benefit all the members of your firm."

In the Middle East and Latin America, the family is seen as the most important social unit. Middle Easterners are so protective of their families that they would never berate a family member, even in jest, in the presence of an outsider. Moreover, if one were to boast of being a "self-made man," it would be seen as an affront to the family—that the family had been derelict in its responsibility to the man.

A culture's attitude toward work is also important for a speaker to know. In most Asian cultures, for example, hard work is highly valued, and at times employees must be forced to take their vacations. Think what is being said in the Chinese proverb "It might take a thousand battles to win a single victory."

Cultures also differ in the degree to which they tolerate ambiguity. That is to say, people from cultures such as the Greek, Japanese, French, and Portuguese do not like the unknown and function much more efficiently when the uncertainties they face are reduced. However, some cultures have a very high tolerance for the ambiguous nature of life. People from the United States, Denmark, Sweden, Ireland, and Great Britain do not suffer great feelings of stress when some issues are left unresolved. Knowing a culture's view of ambiguity can enable you to decide how specific your proposals must be.

Part of your audience analysis should include a consideration of a culture's value of formality or informality. This issue has an impact on issues such as language, content, and delivery. For instance, the United States is a rather informal culture, while Germany, Japan, Egypt, and Great Britain are cultures in which correct protocol and conventional behavior are appreciated. The manifestations of formality are seen in many ways. For instance, in most formal cultures last names are used instead of first, dress style is conservative, and correct language is stressed. A violation of these norms might keep you from accomplishing your specific speech purpose.

Cultures also perceive time differently. A speaker should know, for example, if the people he or she will be addressing are past, present, or future oriented. For North Americans, what is yet to happen—the future—is of great importance. Buddhists believe in "mindfulness"—the complete focus of all senses on the present. Each view influences how people respond to messages and how they concentrate.

Although we will have much more to discuss about credibility in chapter 14, it is important at this juncture that you understand that cultural influences play an important part in shaping an audience's view of the speaker's credibility. A speaker who is perceived as dynamic by an American audience is apt to be viewed as aggressive or presumptuous by a Japanese audience more accustomed to a quiet, reserved approach. American diplomats and executives dealing with the Japanese can attest to the advisability of downplaying the demonstrations of enthusiasm and persuasiveness so admired by many Western audiences. On the other hand, for an Arab audience, signs of ebullience and energy in both content and delivery add to a person's credibility.

Language use is also a reflection of culture. Many cocultures evolve language codes that are part of their cultural experience. Some African Americans, for example, have an entire glossary of terms unique to their coculture. "Bad" may mean the opposite of "good" to most Americans, but to some African Americans it means "good" when used in certain contexts. "Jive" may mean a way of dancing to a person raised in the 1950s, but to certain African Americans, it means "phony." In similar fashion, other cocultures in our society have their special ways of using words. Although the speaker may not speak or even understand the language of a coculture, he or she should be aware of it. The need to understand variations in the use of language is even more acute when the person is from a culture in which English is the second language. Imagine if you did not fully understand English and you heard a speaker say, "All I want to do today is give you a ballpark figure as to what this entire ball of wax is going to run," or reflect on how difficult it would be for someone for whom English is a second language to decide what a speaker means when she says, "Now that we know the bottom line, we need to go for broke and stop this beating around the bush." There will be much more to discuss about language and culture in chapter 12, but for now simply remember to tailor your words to your audience.

There are also major cultural differences in the perception of age. It does not take a great deal of documentation to justify the assertion that the dominant American culture prefers youth to old age. This condition does not exist in all cultures. In the Arab culture, for example, children kiss the hands of older people and respect their views and opinions. We find this same view in most of the cultures of Asia. Both the Japanese and Chinese show great respect to the elderly. The Filipino and Native American Indians are two additional cultures that greatly value old people. Knowing this type of information might prevent you from telling your audience, if it was composed of members of these five cultures, that something should be rejected just because "it is old."

Our final value deals with cultural differences as they apply to assertiveness versus interpersonal harmony. Because we value individualism and freedom of expression, American culture is known for its assertiveness and aggressive style. We are expected to "stand up for our rights" and even be confrontational should the situation call for such action. The Thais, Filipinos, Chinese, and Japanese stress harmony and a lack of direct confrontation instead of assertiveness. Staying calm is valued, not outward aggressive action. There is even a Chinese proverb that states "The first man to raise his voice loses the argument." And for the Japanese the same view toward "speaking up" is expressed in the saying, "It is the quacking duck that gets shot."

Our mission to this point has been clear: to explore the role of culture in human communication. What we have discovered is that cultural and ethnic affiliations influence how members of a particular audience will respond to you and your ideas. Although there are individual differences among the people within each culture, it would not be surprising to learn that an audience of Jewish Americans is pro-Israel, that Native American listeners do not view Christopher Columbus as a great hero, or that most Hispanic Americans support bilingual education.

Let us add a cautionary note at this point. One must be careful in generalizing about foreign nationals now residing in the United States. Some are more assimilated into the dominant North American culture than are others. Some still observe the traditions of their homeland, while others have adopted the ways of their new land. The more heterogeneous a group is, the more difficult it is for a speaker to make reliable assumptions about the viewpoints and probable reactions of the individuals within that group.

Considerations of culture, then, should constitute a portion of the data we gather as part of our audience analysis. Each item we collect can aid us in accomplishing our speech purpose.

Religious Characteristics

Religious orientations, much like culture, have a strong influence on how people perceive the world and live in the world. Former Supreme Court Justice Oliver Wendell Holmes, Jr. said much the same thing when he noted that "religion is at work on those things that matter most." For thousands of years people have turned to religion for guidance as to how they should conduct their lives. Therefore, knowing the religious views of your audience is an essential part of any audience analysis. Whether it be beliefs about vegetarianism (some Hindus don't eat meat and most members of the Islamic faith don't eat pork) or attitudes toward nature (the Shinto religion has a strong emphasis on nature), you need to examine how religion gets translated into one's value system. Knowing the ethical underpinnings of Karma would enable you to discuss the consequences of your proposal as it applies to the notion of "good deeds."

Religious alliances can influence one's thinking on a number of matters. We are all more than our religion, but, all things considered, you can expect Quakers to oppose all types of violent activity and be in favor of human rights. Someone who is Catholic is likely to oppose abortion and most types of birth control. Jews, for thousands of years, have historically valued education, and are more inclined than others to support a tax increase if the money is earmarked for colleges and universities. Mormons have a strong commitment to self-help and the church being part of the family. They believe these two institutions, church and family, not the government, should take care of individuals who have financial problems. Therefore, they are not strong supporters of the current welfare system. And Hindus, with their strong belief in reincarnation, are most likely not to feel rushed in making a decision.

Age-Level Characteristics

Spanish writer Baltasar Gracian once noted that "at twenty the will rules, at thirty the intellect, at forty judgment." Although this commentary is a generalization, it nevertheless calls our attention to the notion that, at different stages of life, we are apt to have different concerns and interests. As we accumulate a personal history, naturally we

The age of an audience will help determine what subjects it is interested in.

change. Knowing about those changes, and how they influence listeners, should be part of audience analysis.

A great number of studies and public opinion polls have revealed the impact of age level on a number of issues. That is to say, studies confirm that older people are more inclined to become entrenched in their opinions and, hence, are much harder to persuade, while younger people are much more open to persuasion. Growing older also tends to make one more conservative. Hence, it is not surprising that many older people differ with the younger generation on subjects such as Social Security, pornography, censorship, and prayer in school.

The age of an audience will also help determine their fund of knowledge and what subjects they are interested in. An older audience will know more about John Wayne, Frank Sinatra, "Howdy Doody," "Watergate," and "boat people" than will a group of high school students. Therefore, in selecting examples you need to take the age of the audience into consideration. References to MTV, and the people who appear on that channel, might well be confusing to older adults who seldom watch that channel.

The age level of your audience can be an important determinant of the kind of language that would be most appropriate to use in your speech. The meanings attributed to words such as "chill out," "blast," "cool," "stoned," "pits," "awesome," and "wasted" are clearly related to age.

Needless to say, there can be many exceptions to any generalization about a given age group. By and large, however, a group of older persons differs in attitudes and experiences from a group of young persons. After all, there is an old saying that a forty-year-old has been sixteen, but a sixteen-year-old has not been forty. Put in slightly different terms, someone who served in the military in World War II might have a difficult time understanding why some young people refuse to "serve their country."

In recent years, regardless of the culture, there has been a growing awareness that gender plays a key role in how we perceive the world and interact in the world. While men and women share many common experiences, goals, values, and the like, they are different in many ways. This condition has important implications for public speaking. A speaker who fails to consider the ratio of males to females in the audience when preparing and presenting a speech may not succeed in achieving his or her purpose. Thus, it is crucial to ask yourself these questions: Will my audience be an all-male or an all-female group? Will it be made up of mostly one sex, or will it be equally divided between the sexes?

The answers to these questions govern everything from your choice of a subject to the examples you decide to place in your speech. As we have indicated, the two sexes, while living in the same country, are often socialized in different ways. Our particular gender propels us, in both subtle and manifest ways, to behave according to certain cultural patterns. A few examples will emphasize this idea. On certain topics, women appear to be easier to persuade than are men. This might be related to the fact that, because of the manner in which they are socialized, women are generally more cooperative and less dogmatic and assertive. Studies also show that the sexes differ in how they rank certain cultural values. For example, women hold more traditional values regarding family and religion. Polls show that women often hold different attitudes than do men on social issues such as the homeless, rape, defense spending, poverty, unwed mothers, child care, the death penalty, contraception, equal rights, affirmative action, and sexual harassment.

Even though a speaker must be aware of differences in experiences imposed by our culture, he or she must also be aware of similarities and try to avoid stereotyping. In recent years, the behaviors and attitudes of women have undergone a major transformation. In areas of sexual relations, education, and employment, the sexes have grown closer together. They now share a number of common experiences in sports, language, occupations, and politics.

These changes in our culture have not only enabled women to share a wider range of experiences but have made many women highly conscious of the problems inherent in our culture's perception and treatment of women. For example, most women would be offended by a male speaker who referred to them as "girls." A speaker's credibility could also suffer if, by his or her examples and illustrations, female roles were portrayed in a demeaning light. To speak as if only men were governors, judges, engineers, or corporation heads, while only women were schoolteachers, nurses, or homemakers, is an example of insensitivity that could lower a speaker's credibility. Also, humor that returns to old stereotypes that characterized women as vain and "empty headed" is insulting and must be avoided.

Gender Characteristics

Not only does the socialization process influence culture and gender, but we can often gain clues to a listener's values, attitudes, and even sense of humor from what he or she does for a living. The rationale behind the importance of occupation is based on two closely related assumptions. First, people have certain personality characteristics that draw them to one career over another. The traits that make someone a good engineer are different from the attributes associated with being a divorce attorney or welfare worker. Second, part of being a member of an occupational group usually means adopting, either consciously or unconsciously, many of the values associated with that profession.

Occupational Characteristics

Remember, most people spend eight to ten hours a day on the job. Someone who is a teacher might see things differently than a doctor, professor, steelworker, restaurant owner, rancher, computer programmer, or fashion designer.

Whether you are preparing an informative or a persuasive speech, you should ask yourself this question: Is the occupation of my audience related in any way to what I am going to talk about? For example, a construction worker would most likely know about framing a house, while a genetic engineer might have little experience with the terms, tools, and mechanics of construction. It should be remembered that occupation often influences much more than a listener's fund of knowledge. Polls show that there is a direct link between occupation and current events. Business executives are apt to be concerned with tax regulations, government controls, and unemployment. Schoolteachers are interested in issues related to class loads, community funding, academic freedom, literacy, and multicultural education.

In many instances, audiences are made up of people from a variety of occupational backgrounds. Knowing those backgrounds enables a speaker to locate the points shared by the majority of the listeners. Remember, however, that in times of national economic distress many people are not fortunate enough to work at the job for which they were trained. Making generalizations about them based on their temporary jobs, or jobs they have been forced to take, may be misleading.

Educational Characteristics

Suppose you were invited to talk about your college or university at an assembly of "students." Very likely, you would ask, What is meant by "students"? First graders? Seventh graders? Graduating seniors? Graduate students? Their educational level would dictate your approach to language, examples, evidence, interest factors, and the like.

Like so much of the demographic data we have discussed in this chapter, the educational level of your potential audience can be reflected in a number of ways. First, polls have demonstrated a link between an interest in current events and high education. For example, well-educated people tend to be more health conscious and more interested in environmental issues than are people who have not gone to college. Second, the educational level of your listeners might also influence how much they know about your topic. In most instances, the more education one has, the larger is one's fund of knowledge. You know from your own experience that the more you go to school the more you learn. Finally, your choice of ideas, concepts, and people you allude to must be modified according to your listeners' education. Nearly everyone has heard of poet Bob Dylan, but recognizing poet Dylan Thomas may take some formal education. The same can be true with regard to countless other specific references. We all know that for Muslims God is Allah, yet it is only through education that we learn the importance of the Five Pillars of Islam and the specific role Muhammad plays in this religion. In short, with education comes information.

The *type* of education your audience has should also be considered. Someone with a Ph.D. in physics has a different pool of information than does an individual with a degree in English literature. This type of data will help you decide what words need defining and which words the audience will automatically understand.

Educational levels might also influence the types of arguments you present to support your assertions. For example, there is some evidence that suggests that for highly educated people it is best to offer both sides of the argument when delivering a persuasive speech.

It is important not to overestimate or underestimate the education of your listeners. In either case, the cycle of communication can be broken if there is a lack of understanding. Moreover, it is good to remember that education acquired through practical experience, as well as through formal schooling, helps determine what your audience members think about and how they tend to react.

Before we close this section on education we need to note the link between culture and education. For instance, when compared with students in the United States, students in Korea, Japan, and Germany have almost three more years of education by the time they graduate from high school. In addition, cultures often stress different subjects as part of their educational curriculum. In much of Europe, the emphasis is on history, language, and literature. In Japan, China, and other Asian cultures, the accent is on science. In Mexico, education focuses on folklore and the arts. In short, knowing what your audience knows, and does not know, needs to be part of your audience analysis.

A Spanish proverb notes, "Tell me with whom you live and I will tell you who you are." We might alter this maxim to read "Tell me with whom you associate and I will tell you who you are." The point is obvious, the people with whom we affiliate, be they family members or fellow members of a group, can be a reflection of who we are, what we believe in, and what interests us. Hence, part of audience analysis should include an examination of the civic, social, political, and professional groups that hold sway over listeners. We see ourselves and others in terms of the roles we play, and the groups to which we belong contribute to the creation of these roles. As indicated, group membership suggests, in a general way, types of people, their points of view, their interests, their attitudes, and even their vocabulary.

The information you secure about your listeners' group affiliations has important implications for both informative and persuasive speeches. A member of Greenpeace might know more about the harmful consequences of using driftnets than would a person belonging only to the Radio Amateur's League. Our general fund of knowledge seems to be directly related to how we spend our time. Whether we belong to the American Society of Mechanical Engineers, the National Organization for Women, the Sierra Club, the National Rifle Association, the International Backpackers' Association, or the Young Republicans, our group affiliation tells other people something about us and what we deem to be important.

In your class, you must also attempt to discover the groups that your colleagues affiliate with. You might try to determine what clubs they belong to (Ski Club, Debate Team, International Students Society, etc.) and what college majors are represented in class (psychology, education, computer science, etc.).

Group Characteristics

Where people have been raised and where they live can help mold their beliefs and actions. Whether you live in a location by design or by chance, the place of your residence will expose you to certain topics and deny you others. A small rural high school, with its 4-H programs and agricultural classes, offers experiences quite different from the situations faced by students attending a large high school in a densely populated urban area. Interests and attitudes and what you know and do not know, are partly shaped by these geographic experiences. A person from a fishing village in Maine, who makes a living by catching fish, might well have a different concept of the ocean than a person

Geographical Characteristics

who rides a surfboard in Malibu Beach in southern California. When an Oklahoma rancher refers to "my neighbors," he or she may be thinking of distances that would seem anything but neighborly to a person living in the middle of Manhattan Island. The notions of gun control and farm supports certainly have different meanings in Texas than in Beverly Hills. People in San Diego, California, have a different view of military base closures than does someone from an area that does not have a military garrison. And if you are from a small town in Indiana your view of unemployment might be significantly different than someone from a much larger city.

Special Characteristics

You might face some occasions when your listeners are homogeneous. They might all be the same age, gender, college major, vocational background, religion, and the like. In these instances, the content of your speech might be accepted by the majority of your audience. You could also find yourself in situations in which one common interest unites the audience. That shared special interest may be a passing one (wanting to learn about treating snake bites prior to a camping trip), or it may be something permanent (wanting to know the best ways to maintain good health). In any case, as part of your audience analysis, you should locate that area and adapt your speech to it. The audience may consist entirely of disabled students or residents of the same dormitory. To disregard this type of information—especially if the audience deems the affiliation to be important—might be perceived as an insult to the group.

Gathering Information About Your Audience

Now that you are alerted to some of the factors that influence an audience, factors that you need to consider before you make your predictions about how the audience will respond to you and your message, you are probably wondering, how do I gather the information to make those predictions? Before we explore some sources of information, we should examine two factors that will direct the way you gather data. First, there are time constraints that limit your efforts to identify your audience's beliefs and values. The amount of time you are given to prepare your talk—whether one minute or one month—is often out of your control. Second, the availability of information obviously has an impact on your investigation. At times data about your audience will be available from a number of sources, yet on other occasions you might be talking to complete strangers. When information is not accessible you might have to rely heavily on educated guesses, common sense, and speculation. If you are fortunate enough to have sufficient time to conduct your analysis, some of the following sources will help you discover the composition of your audience.

Before the Speech

Shared Affiliations

If you share membership in some of the same groups as the audience, you can gather information directly. For instance, if you are active in environmental issues, you can understand some of the topics that interest an audience of the college recycling club. If you are talking to members of your class, you also share common experiences that you can call on. Being a member of a specific ethnic group also enables you to understand the backgrounds of an audience should the majority of your listeners be from this same group. Speakers addressing members of their company or organization are yet another example of sharing mutual interests and experiences that can help in the construction of the audience profile.

Published opinion polls yield information about your audience's interests, beliefs, attitudes, values, needs, motives, and the like. Polls such as the Gallup Report, CBS/New York Times, Harris, CNN/USA Today, and Roper appear regularly on television and in newspapers and magazines. They offer information regarding specific groups' views on issues such as inflation, welfare, race relations, military spending, capital punishment, federal aid to education, term limits, gun control, drugs, and teenage pregnancy. These polls are often categorized by specific affiliations such as education, race, gender, age and the like. By using these polls, you can learn a great deal about prospective audiences.

Opinion Polls

Almanacs, statistical digests, computer searches, all of which will be discussed in detail in chapter 8, *represent excellent sources that offer facts to help you construct a profile of your prospective audience.*

General Reference Material

There might be some special occasions when you can find out about your listeners by giving them an information or attitude pretest. This is a questionnaire or attitude scale that tries to determine what an audience knows and/or believes *before* you start your speech. These tests and scales can be administered minutes, hours, or even days before you give your speech. In most cases, the tests can tell you a great deal about your audience, making adaptation much easier.

Attitude Scales

An interview can produce valuable information concerning your audience. Information-gathering interviews are useful because you can directly question the people to whom you will be talking. You can ask individual members or a group of members about their views on various topics. You can also interview various individuals who may not be potential audience members, but are familiar with the audience. Their observations could help you harmonize your information with the audience's fund of knowledge and belief system. We will, in the chapter on conducting research (chapter 8), offer you some specific advice on how to conduct effective information-gathering interviews.

Interviews

You will notice that all the methods just described deal with gathering information before the speech begins. However, *there are many instances when you can collect information about the audience during the speech.* For example, you can ask for a show of hands as a means of detecting audience attitudes. A question as simple as, "How many of you believe admission requirements at this university are too restrictive?" would reveal how some members of your audience feel about this issue. You could also ask for verbal responses to the same question. This information, whether through raised hands or verbal answers, lets you tailor your talk to the group.

During the Speech

Experienced speakers also use very subtle nonverbal messages during the speech to help them with their audience analysis. They interpret listeners' eye contact, facial expressions, restless movement, and the like and can decide if these behaviors are indicating confusion, disinterest, lack of understanding, anger, frustration, or some other emotion. Sensitivity to the mood of the audience gives experienced speakers the information to make the necessary changes in their speech. They might employ some of the following techniques when trying to adapt to their "on the spot" audience analysis: adding additional interesting examples and stories, directly arousing the listless members of the audience, altering their rate of delivery, using more humor, walking toward the audience, pausing in a dramatic way, personalizing their information, or changing their organizational sequence during the speech.

We conclude this section by once again thinking about the potential pitfalls associated with conducting an audience analysis. Speakers must be vigilant when making demographic generalizations. People are complex and unique. We are all much more than our gender, race, age, culture, profession, religion, education, and the like. Thus, although speakers can benefit from doing a detailed audience analysis, they must also remember that a single characteristic does not define who and what we are.

Analyzing the Speaking Occasion

In our attempt to discover as much information as possible about our listeners, we must not lose sight of the fact that the circumstances under which we will be presenting the speech will play a vital role in determining its outcome. As was pointed out in chapter 1, communication does not take place in a vacuum. The place, setting, occasion, and the time of the day all influence the entire communication event. Common sense tells you that your attire, topic selection, language, and overall demeanor are partially controlled by the occasion in which you share a time-space continuum with other people. For this reason, the speaking occasion also demands a careful analysis.

In isolating some of the key factors of the speaking environment, you should give careful thought to the following questions:

1. *What kind of occasion will it be?* The answer to this question affects the tone and purpose of the meeting and, hence, the speech itself. Your initial concern should be to discover why the meeting is being held. Have the people gathered only to hear your speech, or do they meet on a regular basis? Is it a spontaneous gathering? You should also know whether the procedure will follow certain well-established traditions. Will these traditions be ritualistic? Will they be formal or informal? Will the occasion be a panel discussion or a "stand up" speech? You also need to ask yourself if the occasion will put certain constraints on the audience's ability to respond to you.

2. *What will the physical surroundings be?* The physical setting in which a speech is delivered often contributes considerably to the success or failure of the speaker's attempt to get a message across. Analyzing the physical setting involves being able to answer the following questions:

   a. Is the speech being delivered indoors or outside?
   b. Will I need an extension cord for my slide projector, VCR, or other electronic visual aids?
   c. Will there be a table and/or a podium?
   d. Will the speech be in a very large auditorium or a small room? In a television studio or before a "live" audience?
   e. Will people be sitting in circles or in rows?
   f. How effective are the acoustics of the room or hall?
   g. Will there be a public-address system?
   h. What will the lighting arrangements be like if I want to use a VCR, transparency projector, or other visual tool?

    i. Will there be noises or outside distractions that might disturb my audience?

    j. How many people will be in attendance?

All of the questions govern issues ranging from the mood and attention span of the audience to the number of handouts you might need to bring to the speech.

The questions we just presented also influence the way you deliver your talk. For example, if there are only a few people in the audience and it is an informal gathering, you do not need to use the same volume level as if it were a large room with many people. Even your gestures and movements have to be adjusted to the physical surroundings. Also, if you use a microphone to amplify your voice, it will restrict your ability to move around the room or the platform. (In later chapters, we will discuss the constraints imposed by microphones and television cameras.)

3. *What will precede and follow your speech?* Your message is never sent to passive minds. You must always remember, whether on or off the speaker's platform, that your listeners have a "state of mind" before you send your first sound. They are thinking about something before you enter their lives and ask for attention—what they are doing is important. You should also know whether your speech comes before or after dinner, whether other speakers will precede you, and other factors related to the mental state of the listeners.

4. *What time of the day or night will the speech be delivered?* Personal experience tells you that most people are more vigorous and energetic in the day than they are at night. Hence, ask yourself if the listeners will be tired or alert because of the clock.

The audience's culture might also impact the occasion and setting. For example, people from cultures that are very ritualistic and formal, such as the Japanese and German, perceive a business meeting very differently than does someone from the United States. Mixing business and pleasure is the exception, not the rule, in formal cultures. Knowing these, and other cultural differences, will enable you to make the necessary adjustments to your delivery and content should you be speaking to an audience composed of people from these cultures.

Achieving Empathy

Plato once wrote that "No law or ordinance is mightier than understanding." He, of course, was talking about understanding other people. This same point has been weaved in and out of every chapter to this point and will continue to be a major theme of this book. The idea is a simple one: human communication demands that the sender of a message knows the other person so that he or she can predict how that person will respond to a particular message. All of us carry around in our minds images of other persons, and we take these images into account whenever we speak. A successful communicator is accurate in his or her predictions and fully understands the message receiver. When you make accurate predictions, you have skill in **empathy**—the process of projecting ourselves into others' personalities. If you can understand the ideas and feelings of your listeners, you greatly increase the chance that you will be able to find out their attitudes, desires, backgrounds, interests, and goals. It is only through empathy—the sharing of another's personality—that you can hope to draw accurate profiles.

Sources of Information

As mentioned previously, to project yourself into another's personality requires having a correct image of that person. Who is he or she? What are they like? What are they feeling? How can I better understand them? To answer these types of questions you need to gather data about the other person or persons. In most instances, we assemble information about another person in four closely related phases.

Often, the first bits of information that begin to shape your image of another person comes before the communication encounter. Maybe you are planning to welcome a new person to your neighborhood and a friend tells you, "I just met our new neighbor. He's a French Canadian named Claude. He has a great sense of humor, but he's really agitated about the no-pets clause in his rental agreement." This **preencounter** information helps you form an image and helps you predict what message and behavior will be appropriate when you meet the man. You may find out from someone else that Claude is a doctor, plumber, or bus driver. This information gives you data for your prediction. Perhaps you observed Claude's car and noticed that it was very dirty and in desperate need of a major cleaning. This information might also give you a partial picture of Claude. What applies to one individual can often be transferred to a larger group as we make empathetic predictions before the encounter. Knowing that you are going to speak before a group of MADD (Mothers Against Drunk Drivers) members that have all had children killed by drunk drivers can offer you useful information about some of their feelings on drinking and driving.

The second source of information regarding the other person often arrives quickly and before any words pass between the two parties. This **nonverbal (preverbal)** information comes in a variety of forms. For example, research suggests that some of our image and impressions come from our first eye contact with another person. How many times have you looked someone in the eye, before a word was ever spoken, and felt you liked this person and knew something about him or her? Your image of another person is shaped by such nonverbal cues as dress, manner, and stature. In all instances, you use this information to construct a profile of the person with whom you will communicate.

The third body of information comes from the **verbal messages** you get from other persons. What you hear others say gives you a great deal of insight into what they are like. If someone tells you, "I always vote against bond issues because my taxes are already too high," you use this comment to infer other things about the person who said it. The topics of a person's conversation and what he or she says on that topic can offer you valuable data for constructing an image of that person.

A fourth area of image building comes to you by means of **extraneous messages,** information apart from the person. For example, do you not make judgments and generalizations about persons when you discover what cars they drive and what restaurants they frequent? Even where people live and the clubs they belong to offer you insight into their personalities. Once you know these personalities you can begin to imagine how they respond to this or that idea.

Developing Empathy

Developing empathy toward one person or a group of individuals is no easy assignment. However, there are a few behaviors that will enable you to better use the material you have gathered about your communication partners. First, learn to focus on the other person. This means both watching them and listening to them. Second, suspend your conclusions until you have more than one or two pieces of data concerning the other person. Finally, ask for feedback regarding your assumptions. This will enable you to confirm or reject some of the impressions you have of the other person.

It is wise for a speaker to be sensitive to the factors that can interfere with the achievement of empathy. If you are thinking constantly about yourself, it is difficult to concentrate on cues from other persons. A successful communicator is aware of others, cares about them, and is not preoccupied with thoughts about himself or herself. This is indeed a very difficult assignment, for as the German proverb states, "Everyone thinks that all the bells echo his own thoughts." In short, *constant self-focus hinders empathy.*

Another interference is our common *tendency to note only some features of behavior to the exclusion of others.* We notice when someone does not smile and at once draw a conclusion about that person—a conclusion based on only one bit of information. Individuals are complex, and it is an error in communication to let one act represent the entire person.

Although there are many other hindrances to empathy, we will look at only one more, which is perhaps the most common: *the tendency to react to stereotyped notions about the meaning of physical features, gender, race, religion, and nationality.* In committing this error, we automatically assume that all people of the same group are alike. We forget the uniqueness of individuals.

Empathy flows in both directions. Your audience also experiences a kind of empathy during your speech. As you are making your presentation, the audience is feeling (sharing) the experiences along with you. Therefore, if you appear tense, your listeners will very likely feel uncomfortable and strained. If you display genuine enthusiasm, the audience will probably experience a similar sensation. It pays to be aware of this reciprocal feeling between speaker and listener and behave in ways that will put your audience at ease.

The process of adapting one's speech purpose to a particular group of people calls for very careful analysis of the target audience. Such an analysis will help a speaker make reasonable predictions about how the audience will respond both to the speaker as a person and to the speaker's message. Valuable insight into the audience's values, beliefs, attitudes, needs, wants, and desires can be gained from information about the listener's cultural background, religious characteristics, age, gender, occupation, education, group affiliations, geographical experiences, and special interests. Information about these matters can be derived from such sources as published opinion polls, reference books, computer searches, information and attitude pretests, and interviews. Interviews are especially useful for yielding crucial information. Useful information about the audience can also be gathered while the speech is being given.

An experienced speaker should also take time to analyze the speaking occasion. This investigation consists of questions related to the kind of occasion the speaker will be facing, what the physical surroundings will be, and what will precede and follow the speech.

By implementing the material gathered through an analysis of the audience and the occasion, a speaker can use empathy—the projecting of oneself into the personalities of one's listeners. Knowing what the listeners are like enables a communicator "to speak their language."

Factors Interfering with Empathy

Empathy and the Audience

Summary

There is no index
of character so sure
as the voice.

Tancred

Chapter 4

Sound and Action

Presenting the Message

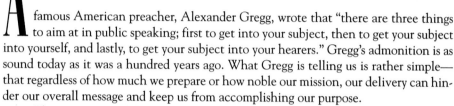

Suit the action to the word,
the word to the action;
with this special observance,
that you o'erstep not the modesty of nature.

William Shakespeare

A famous American preacher, Alexander Gregg, wrote that "there are three things to aim at in public speaking; first to get into your subject, then to get your subject into yourself, and lastly, to get your subject into your hearers." Gregg's admonition is as sound today as it was a hundred years ago. What Gregg is telling us is rather simple—that regardless of how much we prepare or how noble our mission, our delivery can hinder our overall message and keep us from accomplishing our purpose.

The importance of skillful delivery is manifested in a number of ways. First, and perhaps most obvious, *the components of voice and body carry your ideas to your listeners.* As we noted in chapter 1 when we described the process of communication, your voice and your actions are the channels that move your thoughts to another human being. Second, *the manner in which you use the nonverbal elements of voice and body influences the audience's perception of you as a credible person as well as an effective speaker.* As we will point out in detail in chapter 14 when discussing credibility, personal image and delivery are directly linked. Third, delivery is also important because it *helps capture and control the audience's interest and attention.* Nothing hurts a speaker more than a dull voice and listless bodily activity. Finally, *your nonverbal behavior carries a strong emotional message.* Your face, body, voice, and the like are perhaps better indicators of your emotional state than are your words. Even cultural barriers are crossed with universal actions such as smiling, pointing, waving, and the like.

Because language is linear, we are forced in this chapter to treat the elements of delivery as separate entities. This, of course, is very misleading, for in reality your ideas are expressed by all parts of your body *at the same time.* That is to say, your tone of voice, volume, pitch, and rate are in operation at the same time you are moving, gesturing, using eye contact, and using many other nonverbal elements. Therefore, even though we discuss the variables of delivery one at a time, it behooves you as a speaker to see to it that these elements blend harmoniously.

When we talk about nonverbal behavior, we are referring to what is communicated beyond what is contained in the meaning of your words. These behaviors include everything from your tone of voice to your selection of jewelry.

We will be talking about the speaker's nonverbal behavior and the messages such behavior conveys largely from a North American point of view. Nonverbal behaviors carry different meanings for different cultures. This is especially true of learned behaviors such as gazing, gesturing, moving, using space, and manipulating the voice. We learn when, where, and before whom we can show certain emotions according to the rules of our culture. The meanings we assign to another person's nonverbal behavior are influenced by what our culture says that behavior means. It is easy to see that misunderstandings can arise when people from different cultures interact in a communication situation. Therefore, be aware that we are going to talk about nonverbal behaviors as they tend to be viewed from a North American perspective. During the course of this chapter, we will explore some cultural variations that apply to nonverbal communication. This information will serve two purposes. First, it will allow you the option of adapting your delivery to culturally diverse audiences. Second, having a fund of knowledge on cultural differences in nonverbal communication will enable you to appreciate these differences when you are a member of the audience.

Let us turn now to an examination of the visual and aural dimensions of speech delivery.

Visual Dimensions of Presentation

As you give voice to your words, you also send a number of visual signals to your audience that may profoundly affect the way they react to your words. Your (1) general appearance, (2) facial expression, (3) eye contact, (4) movement, and (5) use of space all play key roles in determining the quality of the message the audience receives. Your awareness of each element's unique role in influencing listener reaction to your verbal message may help you avoid placing barriers in your path to effective communication.

General Appearance

Remember that, in most instances, the audience will see you before they hear you. The way you are standing, the clothing you are wearing, the jewelry and accessories you are displaying, and your general grooming all contribute to that vital first impression. Let us examine some of the ways in which these elements of general appearance exert an influence.

Posture

Perhaps you have seen speakers who fit into the following categories. One speaker looks like a soldier standing rigidly at attention; another slouches as though all the burdens of the world have fallen on her shoulders; still another stands with feet placed comfortably apart, shoulders held straight (but not rigidly so). The first speaker's posture probably communicates tension, anxiety, and uncertainty; the slumping posture of the second speaker probably suggests resignation or a woeful lack of enthusiasm or energy; the posture of the third speaker may suggest a comfortable alertness. North American audiences are likely to react most favorably to the third posture, at least at the moment before the speaker utters the opening words of the speech. However, before we render a final judgment on what is the "right" posture, we need to account for the circumstances prompting the speech, the audience being addressed, the speaker's purpose, and the verbal message that accompanies the unspoken message of the speaker's posture. There is no single posture that is always right for all speakers on all subjects on all occasions.

Later we will explore the topic of posture when we discuss its relationship to the speaker's movements, but for now it is important to keep in mind that whatever posture you assume should be comfortable and natural without being too nonchalant. As noted earlier in the book, public speaking is "extended conversation." Even though you are "only talking" to your audience, nevertheless you have to make some alterations because of the situation—posture is one of those alterations.

Benjamin Franklin once offered the following advice: "Eat to please thyself, but dress to please others." Although this caveat might be a slight overstatement, nevertheless it indicates the importance of apparel in human interaction. In fact, in every culture, the way we dress plays a role in how people perceive us. The reason is obvious; we all make generalizations about speakers from the clothes they wear, the objects they keep on their person, and their general grooming habits. Rightly or wrongly, we judge people by their appearance. "His head's shaved and he's wearing heavy boots; he must be one of those skinheads we've been reading about." "That guy wearing the Brooks Brothers suit must be an executive." "Guess she's really into fitness; she's wearing a health club sweatshirt." "Did you see that huge diamond? I'll bet she's from Beverly Hills." Then the speaker commences talking and we reexamine the tentative label we have imposed. Perhaps we find out that the label doesn't fit after all. "Well, I'll be darned! She doesn't look like a ship's captain." "He's a college president? You've got to be kidding. He's wearing an old T-shirt, ragged jeans, and sandals." We are not so much concerned with the validity of generalizations drawn by listeners on the basis of the speaker's apparel and grooming as we are with emphasizing the point that generalizations are drawn, and the speaker should be ready to accept the consequences.

Throughout this book we have stressed, and will continue to stress, the idea that a successful communicator is able to adapt to the audience, the occasion for the speaking event, and the particular setting. Therefore, it is difficult to prescribe appropriate dress or appropriate grooming for all situations. Common sense, however, tells you that in general terms you should be well groomed and neat. For specific canons of appearance it is up to you to become familiar with the audience's standards and expectations. Remember that the standards the audience sets, and the judgments it makes about the speaker's compliance with those standards, are subject to cultural variations. In one culture, robes and a veil might be the correct attire, while in another a black formal suit would be considered proper dress. In short, your grooming and apparel, like your posture, should be compatible with your subject, purpose, audience, and occasion.

Apparel

Some of the most revealing visual signals come from the face. From a speaker's facial expression, we form impressions of the speaker's attitude toward us, toward himself or herself, and toward the subject matter. The expression may tell us, "I like you people," "I'm really enthusiastic about my topic," and "I believe what I'm saying," or it may tell us just the opposite. It may depict a wide range of emotions from fear to confidence, from joy to sadness. Tiny subtleties of expression, of which we may be unaware, tell us that one speaker's animation is sincerely motivated but that another's is feigned. It is probably no coincidence that a speaker who lacks facial expression generally lacks all visual and vocal animation. If this paucity of animation stems from apathy toward the ideas being expressed, the solution would seem to be to abandon the speech rather than to fake a display of animation or other artificial facial expressions. For although the affected or counterfeited animation might temporarily gain the listeners' attention, they would probably become conscious of the affectation rather than the ideas of the speech. On the other hand, if the lack of animation results from inhibition rather than from apathy, then the answer lies essentially in placing oneself in the proper psychological attitude.

Facial Expression

Eye Contact

The importance of eye contact was eloquently captured by Ralph Waldo Emerson when he wrote, "One of the most wonderful things in nature is a glance of the eye; it transcends speech; it is the bodily symbol of identity." Some writers in the area of human communication maintain that eye contact with our communication partners is the single most significant of all the components of delivery. Their rationale is a simple one. *Our eyes are capable of sending innumerable messages.* They tell others when our communication channels are open and when we wish to terminate or avoid communication. They say something of our emotional state, be it elation or depression, interest or boredom, trust or suspicion, love or hatred. The quality of interpersonal relationships is often signaled by the kind of eye contact taking place. It reveals information concerning status, relationships, interest, motivation, anxiety, and many other factors that are in operation during communication.

In using eye contact you should try to keep three simple ideas in mind. First, establish eye contact with your audience *before* you begin talking. Second, look at *everybody*. Finally, *sustain your eye contact* for a few seconds before you move on to another member of the audience.

We conclude our discussion of eye contact by once again reminding you to "keep in touch" with your listeners by looking at them. As indicated, this allows you to show interest and enthusiasm while you monitor their reaction to your message.

Movement

As an introduction to the study of movement, we need to remind you of two important yet often overlooked points regarding our use of nonverbal communication. First, we all engage in bodily actions that are *intentional* and some that are *unintentional*. Intentional movements are those that we use consciously and with purpose. A gesture that sees you pointing your arm and finger toward the window in your classroom, while you say, "I ask you to notice how polluted the sky over our city looks at this time," is an example of intentional movement. Playing with an object on the table or random pacing are examples of unintentional movements. In this next section we will be talking about both types of movements. Second, we need to once again alert you to the notion that, although we often discuss one movement or gesture at a time in this chapter, they usually work in combination, not in isolation. Therefore, as we discuss movement in the next few pages, try to think of your entire body, including your voice and your words, working as a single integrated unit.

Movement and Meaning

Any movement a speaker makes, *whether intended or not*, may be assigned meaning by an observer. For example, let us say that, during a pause in his speech, Bill takes a step toward the audience. What does that step imply to the audience? Does it mean "I want to take you into my confidence," or "I'm about to say something important"? It could be saying either of these things, or neither of them, depending on the circumstances. The movement may even be aimless as Bill uses up some excess energy. Because movement can have a variety of meanings, you need to take a number of factors into consideration. Who is the audience? What is their relationship to me? What is my topic? What meaning will my movements convey? The entire context in which the movement takes place is an important determinant of the meaning that will be assigned to the movement.

Movement and Attention

Imagine that you are gazing at a serene lake somewhere far from civilization. Your eyes take in the glassy smoothness of the lake but do not focus on any particular object. Suddenly, the placid surface of the lake is broken by a leaping fish. Instantly, your eyes are

Bodily movement during the communication act is a natural, spontaneous response to our uttered thought, the reactions of the listener, and the impact of the occasion.

riveted on the spot. The motion of the fish and the splashing of the water have captured your complete attention. Now try an experiment. Look up from this page for a moment. Is there anything in particular that immediately seizes your attention, or does your gaze rove about at random? There is a good chance that, if something in your field of vision were to move, you would notice it, and you would probably continue to look at it until a more powerful stimulus drew your attention elsewhere. The point is simple—movement draws and holds attention.

Many applications of this attention factor are obvious. A motion picture attracts attention more quickly than a still picture. A still picture that depicts action attracts attention more quickly than one that depicts a static situation. A flashing neon sign attracts us more quickly than a steadily glowing sign. The movement causes us to focus our eyes and, thus, our attention on the object.

Given the power to intensify listener attention through appropriate bodily action, we are unwise not to use it. In fact, our natural impulse is to use it. Bodily movement during the communicative act is a natural, spontaneous response to our own uttered thoughts, the reactions of the listener, and the impact of the occasion. In most informal, unstructured communication situations, we use movement freely, without inhibition. We are not even conscious of using it because it accompanies our utterances so naturally. Public-speaking situations, on the other hand, frequently impose restraints that inhibit us from our natural impulse to move. We root ourselves in one spot (usually behind a lectern) and remain there for the duration of the speech. We grip the lectern or thrust our hands in our pockets or otherwise immobilize them so that they cannot be used for meaningful, spontaneous gestures. Thus, we deprive ourselves of the use of an important means of reinforcing our verbal message and of successfully competing with the other stimuli fighting to gain the listeners' attention.

Unfortunately, there is no sure cure for the paralysis that can beset us in a formal, structured communication situation. Perhaps the adoption of a healthy mental attitude—a genuine desire to share ideas with others—is the best course to follow. The more we concentrate on our ideas and our listeners' responses to those ideas, the less we will be concerned with the inhibiting formalities of the public-speaking occasion.

Facilitating Movement

When circumstances suggest that meaningful bodily action will add impact to your verbal message, you should adopt a bodily position that encourages (or at least does not inhibit) easy, spontaneous movement. If the occasion does not call for a formal stand-up speech, your movements are likely to be largely gestural. When you and your audience are in very close proximity, changes in your facial expression may be the only movements that are needed. Whatever the case, you would do well to place yourself in a position that does not immobilize the muscles you need for easy use of your hands, arms, and facial expressions.

Perhaps we can determine the characteristics of an appropriate stance for a stand-up speech if we reexamine the postures we discussed earlier. A slouch tends to inhibit movement of the entire body from one location to another within the speaking area, because you must first return to a position of equilibrium before you can move easily to the right or left, toward or away from the listeners. Thus, you take the path of least resistance and remain in the slouch. The "soldier at attention" posture encourages movement but of the wrong kind, a nervous, rocking motion that can call so much attention to itself that it overrides the verbal message. The last posture we discussed, the alert posture, probably provides the best starting point for meaningful movement. Many speakers find it easier to move from that posture when they feel it necessary. However, the best advice is to experiment with a variety of positions and make an honest appraisal of each.

Kinds of Movement

The number of movements involved in nonverbal communication can be staggering. It has been estimated that we are capable of using over half a million physical signs. To examine each of them individually in this book is an obvious impossibility, so we have to talk about them in terms of major groups. For purposes of analysis, we are going to group them into (1) those that involve movements of the whole body from one location to another on the speaking platform and (2) those that involve motions of the arms, head, and shoulders.

Movement of the Entire Body   Have you noticed that, when speakers make a verbal transition from one point to another in a speech, they often move from one location on the platform to another? Picture yourself saying, "Now that we've examined the causes of the problem, let's take a look at some of the possible solutions." Doesn't such a statement beg for an accompanying movement of the body to reinforce what is being said? Very likely, such a transitional movement would be to your left or right because, in the North American culture, lateral movements tend to be associated with a change from one group of related ideas to another. Sometimes, this transitional movement is as subtle as a shift of weight from one foot to the other.

When you move toward the audience, you seem to be suggesting (nonverbally) that you want to emphasize what you are saying or that you wish to take the listeners into your confidence. "Now listen to this," you say as you lean toward a companion in conversation or as you take a step toward the audience in a public-speaking situation. Feelings of warmth, friendship, and rapport tend to be suggested by such actions, especially when the speaker appears to be relaxed rather than tense or stiff.

Movements of the Upper Body   Almost daily, we make use of hand gestures, sweeping movements of the arms, shoulder thrusts, and head nods, which carry standardized meanings for the majority of our population. A wave of the hand substitutes for "hello" or "good-bye." We signal disapproval by folding our arms across our chest and shaking our head from side to side. We shrug our shoulders while we turn our palms upward to communicate "I don't know." Such conventionalized behaviors, called **emblems,** are a part of our everyday interactions with others of our culture. However, although they are common to our culture, they may carry different meanings (or no meanings) for other cultures. One study revealed that twenty common hand gestures carried different meanings for each of forty cultures. The gesture made in the United States to signal "everything is fine" or "OK" is likely to be interpreted as a sign of hostility in the Arab world, as a vulgar expression in Mexico, as an indication of monetary significance in the Far East, and as a way of saying "I'll kill you" in Tunisia. Even the simple gesture of the pursed hand can change meaning from culture to culture. In Italy it means a question, "good" in Greece, and "fear" in northern Europe. Sensitivity to cultural variations in the interpretation of gestures is important as we move into speaking situations involving audiences of mixed cultures.

It is reassuring to note that there are thousands of gestures and movements that hold a common meaning for all people. The simple fact that we can usually understand the behaviors of the actors in a foreign film shows the extent to which body language is universal; it has the power to heighten attention and to intensify the meaning conveyed by the spoken word.

When a speech teacher suggests that a student try to use more gestures in a public speech, the all too familiar retort is, "But it doesn't feel natural to gesture." Why is it, then, that the objector can be seen carrying on an animated conversation with another student in the corridor, using dozens of gestures in the process? Why does gesturing become "unnatural" when one faces an audience?

Most of us acquire a number of inhibitions when we have to appear before an audience. These inhibitions are simply the manifestation of a response to a strange situation. We become tense, as we do in any fearful situation. The same hands that move about so freely and effortlessly when we converse with a friend suddenly are bound by an invisible force. Our first impulse is to get them out of sight, so we thrust them into our pockets (where they will probably jingle coins and keys), we lock them behind our backs, we clasp them together in front of us in the so-called fig-leaf position, or we grip a lectern until our knuckles whiten. This may well be one reason why it does not feel natural to gesture at such times: we have placed our hands and ourselves in a position that inhibits free, spontaneous movement.

Just as it is wise to adopt a posture, or stance, that will not inhibit you from moving from one location to another on the platform, it is also wise to adopt a "starting position" for your hands and arms that does not inhibit their movement. The best thing to do is to keep your hands and arms unencumbered. Then, when you feel a spontaneous urge to gesture, your hands and arms can move naturally into motion.

Bodily action should
be sincerely
motivated.

Some Guidelines for the Use of Movement

It would now be beneficial to examine a few guidelines for using movement in public speaking.

1. *Bodily action should be sincerely motivated.* To gesture effectively, we must feel like gesturing. If we force ourselves into action, the listener can usually detect the artifice, equating it with insincerity. If we perform planned actions, we run the risk of concentrating on the actions rather than on the ideas we are explaining. The conscious use of movements, gestures, and facial expressions should be reserved for practice sessions.

2. *Bodily action should not be overused.* Most of us habitually use certain actions for emphasis, but, if we are not careful, we overwork those actions to the point that the listener begins to notice the actions rather than the ideas they are supposed to emphasize. By cultivating a greater variety of actions during practice sessions, we will be less likely to overwork any one spontaneous action.

3. *Bodily action should be appropriate for the occasion.* A speech can be delivered in several ways, depending on the circumstances. For example, if we are speaking in a large room where there is some distance between the speaker and the most remote section of the audience, we will have to make actions more pronounced so that they can be seen clearly. If we speak in a small, intimate room, our actions will be subtler (and probably fewer in number).

4. *Bodily action should be appropriate to the audience.* Later in this chapter we will talk about cultural differences as they relate to all aspects of nonverbal communication, but for now it is important that you appreciate the idea that not all cultures use and interpret movement in the same manner. Therefore, you need to return to your audience analysis when you think about using movement. For example, if you know that a culture values a calm demeanor then it would behoove you to show some constraint when gesturing.

5. *Bodily action should not be random*. The wrong kind of movement may impair the effectiveness of your verbal message. If you continually tap your pencil or drum your fingers on the speaker's stand, tug at your sleeve or collar frequently, rub your nose, or stroke your hair very often, these movements may eventually call attention to themselves and away from what you are saying. It is probably better to have no movement at all than to have such distracting movements. They are, after all, manifestations of nervous tension seeking release. The best way to avoid the buildup of this tension may be to use message-related movements, thus giving the tension a constructive outlet.

6. *Bodily action should not be one-dimensional*. You need to strive for variety in your movement. This means you attempt to vary your gestures and that you try to alternate between walking and standing still.

7. *Bodily action should be natural*. Although we have mentioned this idea elsewhere in the chapter, it is worth using as a final summary to our section on movement. Remember communication is contagious; if you are relaxed your audience will feel relaxed.

Use of Space

The silent messages conveyed by the physical distances separating communication partners are many and varied. As onlookers, we make judgments about the quality of a communication encounter partially on the basis of spatial cues. We surmise that there is cordiality or hostility, interest or disinterest, acceptance or rejection, depending on how close one person is to the other. We judge that people are lovers, enemies, close friends, strangers, bosses, or workers by the way they use space.

The study of using personal space as a means of communication is often referred to as **proxemics.** Proxemics is primarily concerned with how the distances between people send various messages. The distance you set up between you and your audience is contingent on a number of factors. For example, if you find yourself in a very small room, you might be much closer to your listeners than if you were in a large auditorium. It is important to remember that formality and "coldness" increase as you get farther away from your audience. On the other hand, getting too close to your listeners could make them feel uncomfortable. We all have personal space that surrounds us like an invisible bubble. If someone gets inside that bubble, we feel uneasy and even hostile.

We are primarily concerned with how considerations of space affect public-speaking situations. The physical distance that separates you from your audience affects you in several ways. First, *it has an impact on your use of movements, hand gestures, and facial expressions*. If these nonverbal elements are to serve you properly, they must be seen. Therefore, the greater the distance between you and your listeners, the more exaggerated these visual factors must be. Second, *physical distance affects your use of voice*. If there is no public-address system available, you will probably have to talk louder and enunciate more distinctly as the distance increases between you and your audience. Third, *physical distance may affect your feeling of mental proximity to the audience*. It is more difficult to get mentally close to your listeners when a large space looms between you and them. Imagine trying to get an audience to enjoy your favorite joke when twenty rows of empty seats separate you and them. The audience also may feel alienated if too much distance separates them from you. Rapport, then, can be affected by spatial relationships. Remember that your management of spatial cues provides the audience with information by which to judge how you feel, your degree of confidence and authority, and your sincerity and enthusiasm.

Visual Dimensions and Culture

We once again remind you that culture is all-pervasive. It influences our behavior in both obvious and subtle ways. The same is true of the nonverbal influences that are part of our cultural heritage. Let us pause at this time and observe how some of those influences can be reflected in the public-speaking arena.

Posture

The effect of culture on posture during communication can be seen in a variety of ways. In North America, being spontaneous and casual is highly valued. It is not uncommon to see speakers reflecting these values in the way they stand. However, in cultures that are more formal (German, English, Japanese), being too fortuitous and incidental can resonate an attitude of disrespect and even lower one's credibility.

Cultures also differ in the body orientations they assume during communication. Anyone who has interacted with Arabs realizes that they use a very direct body orientation when communicating. The Chinese, on the other hand, tend to feel uncomfortable with this style and will usually communicate, particularly with strangers, in a less direct stance.

Apparel

Clothing is also a reflection of both cultural values and a culture's approach to communication. In the United States, as we have already mentioned, being informal is highly valued. This value is often reflected in how people dress in the United States. It usually takes a very special occasion for men to wear suits and women to dress in clothes that call for high heels and hose. In other cultures, where formality is valued, such attire is worn on most occasions. In the Arab, Spanish, English, and German cultures, formal attire is appropriate even in very warm weather. If your audience is composed of members from these cultures, it would behoove you to dress in a rather formal and conservative manner.

Facial Expressions

It is good to remember that when and how facial expressions are displayed are subject to the dictates of one's culture. For example, Koreans, Japanese, and Chinese usually do not show outward signs of emotion through their faces. In fact, in these cultures people have learned to mask their emotions. Japanese men will even go so far as to hide expressions of anger, sorrow, or disgust by laughing or smiling.

In many Mediterranean cultures people take a very different view of facial expressions. In these cultures both men and women will be very animated when they speak, and expect others to be expressive in their emotions. Within the United States, there are groups that use facial expressions in ways that differ from the majority of the population. Some Native American groups, for example, use far less facial animation than do other North Americans. Evidence also suggests that men and women use facial displays differently, with women displaying more facial animation and smiling more than men do. Thus, in your role as either speaker or audience member, take into account the cultural norms of your communication partners.

Although people everywhere use eye contact for similar reasons, cultural norms govern the amount of eye contact we can engage in and with whom. In the United States people expect direct eye-to-eye contact with their communication partners. In fact, we tend to hold suspect anyone who does not look directly at us; however, in certain other cultures, such directness of eye contact may be interpreted as a sign of disrespect. The Chinese, Koreans, and Japanese usually avoid sustained eye contact. Some Nigerians and Puerto Ricans also have been raised to think it is impertinent to have prolonged gazes. The same socialization process often has Latino children avoiding eye contact as a sign of respect. At the other end of the spectrum, Arab culture subscribes to direct and prolonged eye contact as a sign of showing interest in the person with whom one is communicating.

> **Eye Contact**

    The way in which the men and women of a culture relate to one another also has implications for eye contact. In some Middle Eastern cultures, women are not expected to look directly into the eyes of men. Accordingly, the men of those cultures respectfully avert their eyes from the women, in contrast to the directness of their gaze at other men. French and Italian men have no such inhibitions about staring openly at women. Studies indicate that American women maintain more eye contact and hold eye contact longer with their communication partners than do American men.

When we talked about movement earlier in the chapter, we were discussing the subject as it applied to the dominant culture in the United States. As we have mentioned throughout this book, the influence of culture is echoed in nearly every aspect of human communication. For example, there are cultures (Arab, Jewish, Italian) in which a great deal of activity and animation is the norm; however, in many other cultures (Japanese, English, German), people are expected to be reserved in both manner and movement. There are even cultural differences in greeting behavior. Someone from Japan might bow as a way of first addressing an audience, while a person from India would find it appropriate to place both hands together just in front of his or her chest. It is important for you to become aware of some of these cultural variations so that you can adapt your delivery as you move from audience to audience.

> **Movement**

    We can also observe significant differences in the use of gestures by looking at co-cultures in the United States. For example, as compared to males, women tend to use fewer and smaller gestures. African Americans, because they value a lively and expressive communication style, display a much greater variety of movements than whites when communicating.

The way we use and respond to space is colored by our cultural orientation. The people of cultures stressing individuality, for example, demand more personal space than do the people of cultures that are more communal. Thus, two friends conversing in the United States might sit or stand farther apart than their counterparts in Israel, Greece, Mexico, Italy, and Brazil. It is not uncommon for students in Asian cultures to place themselves farther away from their teachers than do North American students. This added distance reflects their respect for teachers.

> **Space**

Aural Dimensions of Presentation

The famous classical rhetorician Aristotle wrote that "it is not enough to know what to say—one must know how to say it." He was, of course, referring to the importance of the vocal aspects of communication. We have already seen how part of the message you send to an audience is visual; however, it is ultimately by vocalized sound that the linguistic elements of your message are carried. Your voice does a lot more, though, than simply make your words audible to the audience; it enables you to impart different shades of meaning to those words. Your voice, like your posture, gestures, facial expressions, and movements, tells things about you quite apart from the verbal message you are uttering. Thus, you need to be aware of the voice's potential to help or hinder you in each communication endeavor.

Voice and Word Meaning

How does your vocal behavior affect the sense of the words you are uttering? In the simple expression "John loves Mary," shift the emphasis from one word to another:

John loves Mary. (It isn't Fred who loves her.)
John *loves* Mary. (He doesn't dislike her.)
John loves *Mary*. (Not another woman.)

In another example, note how many inflectional variations you can give to the word *well* in order to modify its meaning:

Well! (That surprises me.)
Well? (Finish what you were saying.)
Well . . . (You are stalling for time.)

These examples illustrate how important your vocal behavior is in adding dimension to the meaning of your spoken words. The rate at which you utter your words, the degree of intensity you impart to each word, the variations in pitch you use, the harshness or mellowness of the sound of each word you speak—all add shades of meaning to your spoken words, just as punctuation marks, certain typefaces, and indentations modify the meaning of the words you write.

Voice and Personality

The sound of your voice also affects the audience's impression of you as a person. Your voice may tell the audience that you are from a certain socioeconomic class, that you hail from a particular part of the country, that you have a certain educational background, that you are in a particular emotional state, or that you are entertaining a certain attitude toward those being addressed. However, the audience's impressions may be inaccurate; your voice may "lie" about the kind of person you really are. A thin, weak voice may hide a person of vigor and courage. A monotonous voice may mask great inner enthusiasm. A speech impairment may create a false impression of the speaker's professional competence. A great Greek orator, Demosthenes, is said to have been so concerned that his speech impediment would create false impressions of his true worth that he practiced giving speeches at the seashore so that he could be heard above the crashing waves and that he put pebbles in his mouth to try to improve his articulation.

Voice and Attention

As you read earlier, body movements and gestures can help hold an audience's attention. In like fashion, vocal movements—vocal variety—can help keep an audience attentive. If you fail to vary the pitch, loudness, rate, or quality of your voice, you may have difficulty sustaining audience attention for any appreciable length of time unless your verbal message is especially compelling. Naturally, your vocal variations should be properly motivated. It would be ludicrous, for example, to alter your rate of speaking just for the sake of gaining attention. That would only call attention to the artifice itself,

The first requisite of vocal sound is that it be loud enough for comfortable hearing.

not to your verbal message. No delivery technique should call attention to itself—it should direct attention to the message.

Whenever a speaker's vocal behavior fails to gain and hold attention, fails to enhance word meaning, or conveys an inaccurate impression of the speaker's personality, there is always the temptation to blame these shortcomings on nature. A popular lament is "I just wasn't born with a good voice." To be sure, nature does impose limitations on us, and our vocal equipment may be inferior to that of someone else, but it is in the use of the vocal apparatus that we are more apt to find the cause of success or failure. Much of our vocal effectiveness depends on the way we control the (1) loudness (volume), (2) pitch, (3) quality, (4) rate, (5) distinctness (articulation), and (6) correctness (pronunciation) of the sounds we produce.

The first requisite of vocal sound is that it be loud enough for comfortable hearing. Listeners may be willing to exert extra effort to hear a person with a weak voice if that person has something compelling to say. Even so, it is likely that the sheer physical exertion of straining to hear the speaker will ultimately cause the listeners to abandon further effort.

Loudness (Volume)

Although attaining a comfortable volume should be our first concern, we must not overlook the need for changes in loudness level. By varying our loudness, we enhance word meaning and sustain attention. A speech delivered without variations in loudness is analogous to a symphony played without crescendo or diminuendo. As we saw earlier, changes in loudness are particularly helpful in giving emphasis to words or phrases. Uttering a word at an intensity level different from that used with the other words in a sentence directs audience attention to its importance. Such emphasis may be attained by making the sound suddenly either louder or softer; recent research suggests that a sudden change to a softer level is apt to be the more effective means of emphasis.

Pitch

The musical scale of a piano ranges from very low notes, called bass notes, to very high notes, called treble notes. A piccolo, however, is much more limited in the spectrum of notes it can produce. Like a piano and a piccolo, your voice has its own pitch range. If someone tells you that you are a tenor, baritone, or soprano, he or she is referring to the pitch range of which your voice is capable.

Whether the pitch of any "note" that you vocalize is high or low is determined by the rate at which your vocal cords (or vocal folds) vibrate. The slower they vibrate, the lower is the key, or pitch, that you will produce and, conversely, the faster they vibrate, the higher the pitch. The extremes of pitch that your voice is capable of producing (i.e., from highest to lowest notes) depend on the length and thickness of your vocal folds. If you have relatively long, thick vocal folds, for example, you probably have a bass or baritone range. Whether your natural pitch range is classified as bass, tenor, or soprano, you have a great flexibility of pitch levels within that range. Whenever you want to produce a high note, for example, a series of muscles causes your vocal folds to stretch, much in the same manner as you might stretch a rubber band, and, when you relax those muscles, your vocal folds slacken and produce a lower note.

Changes in pitch level (called inflectional variations) provide you with a very effective means of giving different shades of meaning to your spoken words. Moreover, such changes tend to help hold audience attention. Under the duress of a formal speaking situation, however, you might become tense and inhibit your natural tendency to vary your pitch level. The resulting effect, monotony, robs your words of much meaning and deadens the listeners' attention. Of course, some persons' voices are always monotonous, even in informal conversation. Although their monotony may be hearing related, more often it is the product of long conditioning. For example, a person raised in a family opposed to any display of emotion probably learned by example to inhibit vocal and/or visual animation in speaking.

Quality

Whenever you hear someone's voice described as mellow, harsh, strident, rasping, whispery, orotund, or aspirate, the reference is to that person's voice quality. Your vocal quality can be one of the most obvious signs of your emotional attitude at the moment you are speaking. Usually, if you are nervous, you tense the throat muscles inadvertently, and the resultant voice quality is apt to be thin and strident. As you relax, the throat cavity enlarges, and your voice quality becomes much more pleasant. When you become angry, your voice quality tends to become harsh and aspirate; when you grow nostalgic and indulge in reverie, your voice takes on an almost whispering quality.

Television advertisements occasionally feature an actor who specializes in delivering his lines at an incredible rate of speed. He seems to be enunciating clearly, but his words go by so fast that it is difficult to keep up with him. His routine is very amusing but not very enlightening.

Rate

Intelligibility, meaning, and attention are all affected by a speaker's rate of utterance. If the rate is too fast, intelligibility suffers. If the rate is slow when it should be fast or fast when it should be slow, meaning may suffer. If the rate is not correctly varied, attention may wane.

Rate is measured in terms of the number of words uttered per minute. It is generally agreed that 125 to 150 words per minute constitute a satisfactory rate for public speaking, but modifications must be made to adapt to room acoustics, audience reactions, the atmosphere of the occasion, and, most important, the speech material.

One of the key factors that influence our rate of speaking is the duration of sound. **Duration** is the time consumed in uttering vowel and consonant sounds. In particular, the duration of vowel sounds affects word meaning. To illustrate, utter the word *long*, holding the vowel sound only briefly; now, utter the word again, prolonging the vowel sound. The emotional coloration of words, thus, is modified by changes in duration.

The number of words uttered per minute, then, depends on how much time is spent in pausing, as well as in actually producing the individual sounds of each word. If you are accused of talking too quickly or too slowly, try to ascertain whether your problem is faulty management of duration or of pause. It is not unusual for a person, when asked to slow down his or her rate of speaking, to maintain the usual duration while pausing more often or pausing for longer periods. Often, the real culprit in such cases is faulty management of duration rather than an excessive number of words per minute. Eighty words per minute may seem excessive if each word is given inadequate duration.

Variety of rate is as important as variety of pitch or loudness. A speaker who seems to be following a metronome in his or her rate of utterance can cloud meaning and diminish attention almost as quickly as a person with a monotone. Emphasis and mood changes can be effectively expressed by variations in rate. For example, when a speaker wishes to emphasize one particular statement of a paragraph, he or she tends to utter it more slowly than the sentences that precede or follow it. A mood of excitement is usually accompanied by an acceleration in rate; a mood of sobriety, with a slowing down in rate.

Your use of a **pause** is yet another way rate can be put to your advantage. The English dramatist W. J. Lucas wrote, "It is the wise head that makes still the tongue." Although he may not have been talking about pausing, his advice is nevertheless sensible. A pause, when used effectively, is an excellent vocal device. However, most novice speakers are reluctant to use silence as a form of communication. This is a mistake, for a pause, like other vocal techniques, can serve a variety of functions. First, *the silence inherent in a pause allows the listeners an opportunity to think about what has been said.* Second, *a pause can dramatize and emphasize key points.* Imagine how startling it would be if someone talking about violence in the United States were to pause in some of the following places: "Think about this (pause)—more than 2 million Americans are beaten (pause), knifed (pause), or shot each year, 23,000 of them fatally (pause)." Third, *a pause can serve as a transition as you move from point to point.* It is a type of "oral punctuation" that can take the place of a comma, a colon, parentheses, or a dash.

Many inexperienced speakers use a pause as an unconscious excuse to use what are called "vocal interferences." These interferences take a variety of forms and should always be avoided. A few of the more common sound hindrances are "uh," "er," and "um." Vocal clutter to fill silence and the uneasiness of the pause can be "well," "OK," "like," and "you know."

Distinctness (Articulation)

Throughout this chapter, you have read that the manner in which you speak is directly related to how you are perceived. When we talk about your use of language in chapter 12, we will point out that if your language is coarse, impudent, crude, and riddled with slang, you will not be viewed as a highly credible source. What is true of the words you use is also true with regard to how you say those words. Simply put, your success as a speaker is directly linked to the clarity, or distinctness, of the sounds you produce. We are, of course, referring to the manner in which you articulate and enunciate your words.

Although some articulation problems are serious enough to warrant work with a speech therapist, most are caused by the way you manage your organs of articulation. Some sounds depend for their clarity on precise lip movements, others on critical placement of the tongue, and still others on full mobility of the jaw. If you use these three organs with care, you can overcome most of the problems associated with poor articulation.

Poor enunciation of consonants such as *p*, *b*, *v*, and *f* is usually the result of lip laziness. For example, the distinction between *have* and *half* depends on your lip movements. Your tongue placement must be correct for the clear production of consonants such as *t*, *d*, *k*, and *g*, as in *cat* and *cad* or *dock* and *dog*. The part that jaw mobility plays in clarity of enunciation is apparent when you try to recite the alphabet through clenched teeth. As you strive for greater precision, however, avoid becoming overly precise, because your audience might interpret that as a sign of affectation.

Your instructor may offer suggestions for improving your enunciation. If so, get into the habit of implementing those improvements into your everyday conversation; then the demands of other speaking situations will be much easier to fulfill.

Because poor articulation can harm both your message and your credibility, let us examine a brief list of words and phrases that tend to call forth deficient enunciation. As you practice the following list, remember that most articulation problems stem from sounds that are left out, added, distorted, or run together.

Incorrect	Correct
wanna	want to
soun	sound
otta	ought to
dint	did not
comin	coming
I et	I eat
nuthin	nothing
swimin	swimming
gimme	give me
hafta	have to
seeya	see you
wilya	will you

didja	did you
gonna	going to
whadayado	what do you do
lemme	let me
mornin	morning
wep	wept
skien	skiing

While enunciation has to do with the distinctness of a spoken word, pronunciation has to do with its correctness. It is possible to enunciate a word with the greatest clarity while grossly mispronouncing it. Listeners are less likely to forgive faults of pronunciation than faults of enunciation, because faulty pronunciation seems to reflect the speaker's intelligence rather than just his or her muscular dexterity in manipulating the organs of speech. This negative connotation associated with poor pronunciation is usually detrimental to a speaker's credibility. To avoid faulty pronunciation, become familiar with the following words, which are often mispronounced.

Incorrect	**Correct**
uh-crost	a-cross
burg-you-lur	bur-glar
pur-fess-ur	pro-fes-sor
rev-uh-lant	rel-e-vant
deef	deaf
Feb-u-ary	Feb-ru-ary
De-troit	Detroit
gun-u-wine	gen-u-win
wit	with
ath-a-lete	ath-lete
thee-a-ter	theater
then	thin
nu-cu-lar	nu-cle-ar
pich-er	pic-ture
hunnert	hundred
ly-ber-y	li-brar-y
git	get
worsh	wash

If you have any doubts regarding the correct pronunciation of any word, look up that word in a standard dictionary, which offers guidelines for pronunciation.

A dialect represents a language variant used by a collection of people from a similar geographic region and/or ethnic background. Dialects can be troublesome in public speaking because many listeners use dialect as a variable in person perception. Although this is unavoidable, it is important to remember that there is no such thing as a correct or incorrect dialect, or accent. This is especially true in the United States, where so many dialects are spoken. First, there are dialects peculiar to a geographic region. Someone from the Midwest, for example, pronounces the word *hard* with the *r* sound uttered prominently. A Southerner drops the r sound and the word becomes "haahd." A New Englander may even pronounce that same word as "had." What is acceptable in New Orleans might not be acceptable in Milwaukee or Seattle.

Then there are dialects peculiar to people who share a common cultural background. Not only is their pronunciation of some words different from that of the majority of the people in a geographic area, but their grammar and syntax may differ as well. The dialects of Hispanic Americans, African Americans, and Asian Americans are cases in point. Each group has its own standards of pronunciation, grammar, and syntax for communication within the group. When group members interact with members of the larger community, which has other standards, they face the problem of deciding which set of standards to follow—the ethnic standard or the majority standard. In such communication encounters, to follow the ethnic standard is to run the risk of being perceived by some members of the majority culture as somehow deficient in language development. But then if you follow the standards set by the majority, you are apt to be perceived by some members of your own culture as somehow disloyal. However, as intercultural understanding grows, respect for the speech patterns of others may grow. Moreover, with the increasing mobility within our society and the pervasiveness of mass communication, regional and cultural differences in pronunciation are becoming less evident.

Perhaps the most practical way of discovering what constitutes acceptable pronunciation in your region or culture is to listen to the way words are pronounced by educated speakers of that area. Also, a good contemporary dictionary is a reliable guide to the pronunciation of little-used words, names of places, and foreign expressions.

Aural Dimensions and Culture

As listeners, we should not be hasty in equating a speaker's voice with his or her character or emotional state. We need to consider the possibility that the speaker's voice may be part of a "mask" hiding his or her real identity or that the speaker may be observing cultural norms that differ from our own. For example, the people of some cultures speak in a loud voice because loudness is equated with strength and conviction, while people of other cultures speak softly because they regard that as a sign of politeness and intelligence. You can imagine the possibilities for misunderstanding that can occur when people of diverse cultures attempt to interact. When a soft-spoken Thai hears a louder North American speak, he or she may think that the North American is angry or disturbed about something. In Japan, laughter is not always a sign of mirth, because the Japanese often use laughter to mask embarrassment, sadness, disapproval, and even anger. Thus, we need to be wary of making snap judgments about others based on their vocal behavior. At the same time, we should remember that, as we speak, our listeners form an impression of our personality and character on the basis of the words we utter and the sound of our voice.

As we have said elsewhere, it is important that you become aware of cultural differences in how people use their voices. Volume, either loud or soft, is a case in point. For example, Jews, Italians, and Arabs tend to speak louder than North Americans and can even give the impression, at least to those that do not understand these cultures, of shouting. This intensity of volume is in stark contrast to the Native American population and to that of East Asia. People in these cultures speak in much softer tones. Women, at least in the United States, also tend to employ less volume when speaking than do males. Discovering the cultural composition of your audience will assist you in adapting your volume to the people in your audience.

Pitch is yet another vocal characteristic that is influenced by culture. For example, Arabic speakers are often perceived to speak in an unusually high pitch, which often carries the unintentional meaning of intense emotion. Be careful not to apply North American standards to other cultures; this can lead to misinterpretations and misunderstandings.

There are cultural differences in the use and perception of long pauses. For many North Americans, an extended pause can cause tension and anxious feelings. Hence, your pauses should not be drawn out. In India and Japan, there is less uneasiness with silence and long pauses. For members of these cultures, a prolonged pause is perceived as a time for reflection and the gathering of one's thoughts—it is a positive message, not a negative one.

Improving Your Speech Delivery

Now that we have discussed the factors that combine to form speech delivery, let us explore some ways in which you can use this information. Many of these ideas have been presented elsewhere; however, they are all important enough to be cited one more time.

Your Body

Although we will arbitrarily begin with the behaviors that the audience sees, it is important to keep in mind that skillful delivery involves the body as a whole. Because we can talk about only one idea at a time, sometimes our discussion of delivery must separate the visual from the oral. However, in reality, the body works as a single unit, and therefore delivery involves the whole person.

1. *Practice good posture, and you will find it easier to move spontaneously from one point to another on the platform.* Moreover, the audience will view good posture as a sign of your being alert and at ease.

2. *Dress in such a way that your apparel does not call attention to itself.* Avoid gaudy colors, T-shirts that have logos, or any kind of distracting jewelry or ornamentation.

3. *Pay close attention to your grooming.* A slovenly appearance may suggest that you have contempt for your audience.

4. *Do not wear a "poker face."* Give your audience a friendly smile from time to time and let your feelings be reflected in your facial expressions.

5. *Establish and maintain good eye contact with your audience.* You might start by picking out a friendly face and talking to that person for a moment, then switch to another friendly face somewhere in the room. Soon you will find it easier to look at more and more people. Remember, not only does eye contact let your listeners know you are aware of them, but it provides you with invaluable feedback on how they are responding to your speech.

6. *Try to make use of meaningful gestures to reinforce your points.* If you avoid gripping the lectern or otherwise immobilizing your hands, you are more likely to gesture spontaneously. It is best not to plan your gestures, because they will probably look planned. Instead, keep your hands free and they will likely work for you.

7. *When you want to emphasize a point or make a transition, consider moving from one location to another on the platform.* A good posture, with weight evenly distributed on both feet, makes such movements easier to execute spontaneously.

8. *Avoid letting physical remoteness come between you and your listeners.* Try to get your listeners seated close to one another near the front of the room, where you are standing. Such physical closeness tends to promote a feeling of mental closeness and helps establish rapport between you and your listeners.

Your Voice

Now we will review some ways in which you can make optimal use of your speaking voice.

1. *Cultivate vocal variety.* Remember, a voice that features meaningful variations in pitch, rate, loudness, and quality tends to hold a higher level of attention than does a monotonous one. Using vocal variety also means not being afraid of silence. Remember the saying that silence can speak volumes.

2. *Remember to enunciate your sounds clearly, avoiding slurring your words or mumbling because of lip laziness.* If you keep your jaw relaxed, you will avoid the clenched teeth tightness that muffles sound; however, remember to avoid being overly precise as you enunciate, because listeners may perceive it as an affectation.

3. *When you are in doubt about the pronunciation of a word, find out how it is pronounced by the educated speakers in your area.* Remember that there are regional standards of pronunciation rather than one universal standard. You can always use the dictionary's recommended pronunciation.

Finally, you should carefully take an inventory of your current delivery practices in various communication situations. Ask friends to offer candid views of your assets and liabilities in informal conversation, discussions, and conferences. Ask your speech instructor for an analysis of your needs in public-speaking situations. Try to find answers to questions such as these:

- To what degree do I use bodily action and effective vocal variety in each of the various communication situations: to an insufficient degree in public speaking, a sufficient degree in conversation? to a distracting degree in some cases?

- What is the quality of the action I use? Does it help or hinder the communication of my ideas? Is it meaningful action? Does it call attention to itself? If so, why?

- Does my posture communicate a positive impression? Does it combine ease with alertness? Are my movements and gestures graceful and decisive, or are they hesitant, tentative, and lacking vigor and enthusiasm?

- Do I have any annoying mannerisms that should be curbed? Does my use of my voice add to or detract from the communication situation?

Securing answers to these and other pertinent questions will enable you to chart your course toward greater effectiveness in the use of the visible and audible aspects of communication.

Perhaps the best way to improve your delivery is to follow the words of the Roman poet Virgil when he wrote, "They can do all because they think they can." Virgil was, of course, talking about your having self-confidence and believing in yourself. Although it may sound somewhat simplistic, it is nevertheless true that if you deem yourself a failure you will be. On the other hand, if you believe that delivery is something that can be controlled, and it can, *you* can control and manipulate your delivery. Gaining this control will improve the manner in which you deliver your speeches and add to your self-confidence. As we noted in chapter 2, your confidence level can be greatly increased if you (1) know your subject and your outline, (2) allow sufficient time to practice, and (3) develop a positive mental attitude toward the speaking situation.

Your Confidence

For effective oral communication, it is essential that the verbal and nonverbal elements of the message work in harmony. The nonverbal elements of the message are visual and vocal. The visual constituents include the speaker's general appearance (posture and apparel), facial expressions, eye contact, movements, and spatial relationship to the audience. The speaker's appearance should provide nonverbal cues that are compatible with the verbal message being uttered. Movements convey meaning and help sustain audience attention. The speaker should adopt a bodily position that does not inhibit spontaneous movement. Movement on the platform is generally motivated by a desire to make an idea emphatic or to suggest a transition from one idea to another. The speaker's action should be sincerely motivated; should be appropriate to the subject, to the audience, and to the occasion; and should not be overused. The amount of space between the speaker and listener can affect the quality of the communication encounter. The speaker should use spatial cues in a manner consistent with the speech purpose.

The voice does more than simply render a word symbol into audible form. It enables a speaker to impart various shades of meaning to the spoken word, it transmits an impression of the speaker as a person, and it acts as a factor of attention. The controllable elements of voice are loudness, pitch, quality, and rate. These elements should be varied in a manner consistent with the sense of the verbal element of the message. Faults in distinctness of vocal sounds (enunciation) are more readily forgiven than are faults in the correctness of the sounds (pronunciation). Acceptability of pronunciation varies from region to region. You are advised to emulate the pronunciation of the best-educated speakers in your geographical area.

A successful speaker needs to be aware of the influence of culture on all aspects of nonverbal communication. Whether it be our bodies or our voices, our culture affects our delivery. A successful speaker also seeks a variety of methods that lead to improved delivery and greater self-confidence.

Summary

The reason why we have two ears and only one mouth is that we may listen the more and talk less.

Zeno

Chapter 5

Listening

Evaluation and Criticism

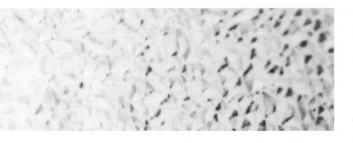

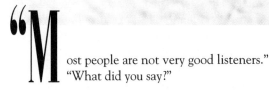

Hear the other side.

St. Augustine

"**M**ost people are not very good listeners."

"What did you say?"

This simple two-line conversation tells us a great deal about the topic of listening. What it says is something most of us probably already know—that it is often difficult to pay attention, comprehend what we hear, and remember that information at a later date. It seems that even though listening is an important human activity, most of us are not very good at it. The irony of being a poor listener is that listening is an extremely important activity. Much of what we know about the past has come to us through listening. Small children learn about their new world through listening, for it is their first means of acquiring information and ideas about their environment. As adults, we use listening more than any other communication skill. The time we spend listening far exceeds the time we spend reading, writing, or speaking. It has been estimated that we spend 40 to 50 percent of our total communication time engaged in listening. In fact, one of the authors of this text conducted a research project that concluded that we spend more than one-third of our waking hours listening. Stop in the middle of what you are doing a few times during the day, and you will discover that the statistics concerning listening are valid. We listen at home, on the job, at school, and at play. The outcome of these listening experiences can influence everything from how much money we earn to the success or failure of our most intimate relationships.

Inherent in our earlier definition and explanation of communication was the idea that speech is a *two-way process*. Speaking and listening are two indispensable ingredients of communication: there can be no effective transaction without someone on the other end. If our discussion of oral communication is to have real meaning, we must give a proper share of attention to listening.

Rewards of Listening

The rewards of effective listening are numerous. First, listening carefully can make a speaker's remarks more informative and interesting. You are apt to discover things you never knew before—things you would have missed had you not been fully focused on the interaction. In this sense, *listening adds to your fund of knowledge*. It also lets you update your collection of facts, attitudes, and beliefs.

Second, becoming a more *effective listener can make you more critical* of the thousands of messages that are sent your way each day. This need for improving listening, as part of the communication process, has gained importance with the onset of the "era of communication." Most of us are confronted with about a million advertising messages each year—messages that ask us to take certain actions. Not only do we have to listen to more advertisements, but we are confronted with a large variety of individuals making specific demands on our actions and thoughts. Some of these individuals rely on the supposition that we are poor listeners. Cult leaders want our minds, politicians want our votes, and hucksters want our money. Listening is extremely important in a time when the mass media attempts to determine our tastes and to run our lives. In short, improved listening is good protection against the devices and techniques of an unethical and sophistic speaker.

Third, an improved listening attitude can also help us *cope with those countless situations when the person we are communicating with is not fluent in English.* Throughout this book, we have stressed the idea that many of our communication encounters are with people from different cultures, and that these individuals may speak English as their second language. It may be difficult to understand certain dialects; however, if you try to be a conscientious listener, you greatly enrich your chances of comprehending messages.

Fourth, we are apt to find that with improved listening skills *we can appreciate and enjoy what we hear with greater intensity.* So very much of our time is spent listening, yet we often miss the little nuances of what we hear. How very different the sound of singing birds can be when we give this simple pleasure our full attention. This chapter seeks to help you direct and control that attention.

Finally, *good listening helps improve your speaking.* By listening to the speeches of others, you will be able to distinguish between the characteristics of content and delivery that ought to be emulated and those that should be avoided. As the English author Lord Chesterfield noted, "We are, in truth, more than half what we are by imitation." Therefore, learn how to listen so you will know what to imitate and what not to emulate.

You will discover that most of your time in speech class is spent listening to student speeches and to the instructor's remarks. In fact, you may listen to over one hundred speeches in your class, although you will deliver only five or six. Take full advantage of this listening time to sharpen your perceptions, and you will be a better speaker, as well as a better listener, for the experience.

Having noted the importance of listening, we are now ready to ask the question, What kind of listeners are we? There is sufficient evidence to support the generalization that, as a whole, people are poor listeners. Countless studies have concluded that a large percentage of those tested could not locate a central idea after listening to an exposition that had been designed for clarity and simplicity. Other research results point to the generalization that listeners comprehend only a small percentage of what they hear. Perhaps you can provide the best proof for these assertions with some serious introspection. Simply ask yourself these two questions: Do I pay attention when other people talk? Do I remember very much of what I hear? If you have been honest in your response, you most likely answered "no" to both questions.

Fear not, for one of the most gratifying aspects about listening is that with motivation and hard work you can substitute good listening habits for poor ones. This improvement is possible for one simple reason; as stressed in chapter 1, human beings have free choice. You can choose what you pay attention to. You can decide to focus on the speaker and the message or to let your mind dart from daydream to daydream. Again, you have free choice. Because of this freedom we have the power to listen or not to listen. The central message of this chapter is to urge you to use that power. As poet Oliver Wendell Holmes, Sr. noted, "It is the province of knowledge to speak and it is the privilege of wisdom to listen."

Process of Listening

One of the major reasons people are poor listeners is that they fail to understand the complex nature of listening. Because the act of hearing sounds is such a simple process they often assume that hearing is listening. This belief is wrong. In actuality, *listening involves six interrelated steps*. Knowing these processes, and the choices a listener makes at each stage, will help you improve the manner in which you listen. Before we briefly identify these six steps, we should note that, although all six steps are listed separately and are described in a linear fashion, in reality the time between steps is often less than a millionth of a second. The six steps can even work in combination:

> (1) **Hearing** (physiological process of listening—the reception of sound waves), (2) **Attending** (focusing on a specific sound or series of sounds and rejecting others), (3) **Understanding** (the brain interpreting the message and assigning meaning), (4) **Remembering** (storing the message for later use), (5) **Evaluating** (making a judgment about the message), and (6) **Responding** (giving an overt response to the message).

As you can see, this description incorporates much more than simply hearing sounds. It includes focusing on certain sounds, excluding others, making sense out of what has been selected, and using what is remembered. What should emerge from these six steps is the impression that listening is a highly active process that demands concentration and attention.

Purposes of Listening

You will recall that there are different reasons for speaking and that, by identifying your reason for speaking, you can better accomplish your goal. The same is true with regard to listening. We all listen for a variety of reasons and for different purposes. By knowing why you are listening, you can adapt to each communication situation. Listeners as well as speakers must alter their behavior as they move from encounter to encounter. Although the purposes for listening often overlap, they generally fall into four basic categories: (1) empathic, (2) informational, (3) evaluative, and (4) appreciative.

Empathic Listening

Empathic listening occurs in countless communication contacts when we share feelings and build and maintain supporting relationships. For example, imagine that a close friend has just had a major accident involving his new car and tells you how frustrated and upset he is. In this circumstance, there might be nothing you can do, yet your friend feels better because you have listened and offered moral support. If you are going to respond, and not only listen in an empathic manner, it also behooves you to listen carefully. Then your response will reflect the fact that you have heard your friend and thought about your response. This kind of emotional sensitivity demands that you listen carefully so that the other person will know you appreciate and understand his or her dilemma.

Informational Listening

The human mind is a marvelous and amazing instrument. It is capable of receiving and remembering an endless amount of facts and information. Think for just a moment about how much of your day is taken up with listening that in some way teaches you something. Listening for learning is listening that has you *gathering information*. If you are like most people, these occasions range from the superficial to the significant. You may ask directions and listen to the words to keep from getting lost, or you may listen to a lecture in class so that you could receive an A on the next examination. Perhaps you listen in order to learn how to saddle a horse, change the oil in your car, repair your computer, or know how to make the intelligent choice in the voting booth. In all these instances, your purpose is to gather information. Knowing that your purpose is informational will enable you to make the necessary decisions regarding *how* you want to listen. Decisions about taking notes, watching for nonverbal cues, asking questions, and answering questions are all related to informational listening.

Evaluative Listening

We also listen to a great deal of material intended to persuade us. In these occasions, our purpose for listening is *to evaluate* what we hear. Whether the mayor is asking for our support, someone is asking us to buy a certain car, or a friend is wanting a loan, we are always confronting people asking us to believe in their message. In these situations, we assume a listening attitude that is critical yet fair. Later in this chapter, we will look at some specific guidelines for critically evaluating what we hear.

Appreciative Listening

The *appreciative* aspects of listening are rather obvious. We listen to music, watch television, go to movies and plays, and engage in a great deal of social conversation. In all these situations, the experience is greatly enhanced, and more appreciated, if we listen carefully. As we noted earlier, even the sounds of nature take on new meaning when we learn to be mindful of what we are taking in.

Misconceptions About Listening

It should be clear from the last few pages that listening is not the simple matter that some people believe it to be. This, of course, can cause problems. Having a number of misconceptions regarding listening can also cause problems. Since these misconceptions can seriously affect the quality of our communication behavior, it might be helpful to look at five of the more common myths that influence what we hear and what we remember.

First, *many people believe that listening is a natural activity and that hearing is the same as listening; it is not.* Hearing is a physical act, while listening is the process of giving meaning to electrochemical impulses. You can, therefore, hear without listening. Do not be misled into believing that, because you are receiving sounds (voices, music), you are listening.

Second, *the belief that once sound is produced everyone receives the same message is also false.* Communication is first and foremost a subjective activity. It is what happens inside of us. Each person responds in a unique and highly personal manner. Think for a moment about the words *Doberman pinscher*. For a person who raises and trains these dogs, the internal response will differ greatly from the response of a person whose only experience with Dobermans is seeing them, teeth exposed, being used by local police to control an unruly crowd. Obviously, both parties hear the same sounds ("Doberman pinscher"), but their internal responses contrast sharply.

Third, *many people make the mistake of believing that listening is a passive activity.* They feel that one merely has to sit back and relax and listening will take care of itself. This is simply not true. Listening requires active participation. To be a good listener,

Even the sounds of nature take on new meaning when we learn to be mindful of what we are taking in.

you must stay focused on the moment; you cannot remain passive and expect to retain much of what is said. The notion of being alert and concentrating on what is transpiring is eloquently stated by Lord Chesterfield: "One should always think of what one is about; when one is learning, one should not think about play; and when one is at play, one should not think of one's learning."

Fourth, *people are often deluded into believing that effective interaction is the exclusive responsibility of the speaker.* Think of how often you have left a college classroom believing that if you did not receive very much from the lecture it had to be the professor's fault. Although in some instances this excuse may be a valid one, too often it is a reflection of the misconception that the burden for success resides with the sender of the message. Again, this is not true. As we have said throughout this book, communication is composed of circular processes involving both the sending and receiving of messages.

Finally, *there is a misconception about listening that perpetuates the myth that people are born either good or bad listeners and that there is very little they can do about it.* This false idea often gives listeners an excuse for not trying to improve their listening ability. Listening skills can be developed like any other skill; however, improvement comes only if one is

Listening requires
active participation.

willing to practice and work hard. You may have heard the saying, "He that would have the fruit must climb the tree." Climb the tree; the rewards are worth it.

Barriers to Listening

We have repeatedly alerted you to the fact that listening is a complex activity and that being a good listener is not a simple matter. Effective listening can be impeded by many factors. Some of these factors are worth examining in detail, for if you can identify what you are doing wrong, you are in a better position to take the next step and start to improve your listening behavior.

Poor Listening Habits

Over two thousand years ago, the Roman poet Ovid indirectly offered us an excellent introduction to our first barrier when he wrote, "Nothing is more powerful than habit." Like so much of human behavior, listening tends to follow consistent patterns. Most of us fall into listening patterns that become so habitual that we fail to realize fully that we are creating a listening barrier. Although all the barriers discussed in this section can become habitualized, Ralph G. Nichols and Leonard A. Stevens have suggested the six most common bad listening habits. Although Nichols and Stevens prepared their list many years ago, it is interesting to note that these problems seem to persist. This, of course, adds credence to the notion that these bad listening traits are indeed habitual.

1. *Faking attention.* Perhaps most of us have learned to fake attention so as not to appear discourteous, or maybe we want a teacher to think we are interested in learning. All cultures teach their young people to have good manners and therefore place a very high premium on politeness. In some instances these two traits might teach us to look as if we are listening when we are actually faking attention. The danger of such action is that it may become habitual.

2. *Listening only for facts.* Because North Americans value time and are impulsive, they view many communication encounters as situations where something has to be done. This attitude often translates into a listening habit that only seeks specific facts. Even the overused expression "Just give me the bottom line" is actually saying all I want is the specific point. This habit, when carried to an extreme, often leads to a listening personality that is narrow. For once the so-called "facts" are obtained, the person stops listening.

3. *Avoiding difficult material.* Most of us feel comfortable with what we know and avoid what is unfamiliar or difficult. We turn off those listening situations requiring too much energy. Such avoidance becomes a habit—whenever the material becomes slightly difficult, we drift away mentally, if not physically. We approach the communication situation without being in the right frame of mind. Not only do we avoid difficult material, but we take a casual attitude toward listening in general. All day long, we move in and out of listening situations that have different purposes. We listen to music or talk to friends in a very relaxed and casual manner, and then quickly go to our history class where we need to pay close attention to each word so that we can receive an A on the next examination. Without even realizing it, we slide from situations that demand very little concentration to informational encounters that call for higher levels of emotional commitment. Although a casual listening attitude is permissible in a pleasurable encounter, it is a serious barrier to listening for information.

As noted earlier in the chapter, in the United States in the 1990s, the problem of avoiding difficult material has become very serious. More and more we find ourselves interacting with people whose primary language is not English. As they attempt to speak their "second language" (English), your listening skills will be challenged, for on many occasions you will have to strain to understand them. If you give in to the habit of avoiding arduous listening situations, you will not receive much from experiences that contain some element of cultural diversity.

4. *Avoiding the uninteresting.* We often make the mistake of equating "interesting" with "valuable" and, hence, stop listening too soon. Our culture puts a premium on being entertained, and because of this we tend to listen only to what is "fun." If the messages we are confronted with do not fall into these categories, we habitually stop listening. Television viewing, of course, contributes to the speed with which we are willing to stop listening. From the MTV channel to the action films that fill our screens, we have come to demand rapid activity and short bits of information. When asked to pay attention to what may not be lively, funny, or interesting, we tend to cease listening.

5. *Criticizing the speaker.* This is perhaps one of the most common problems we face in listening. Too many of us are guilty of becoming overly concerned with *who* someone is and *how* he or she is talking instead of listening to what he or she says. Thus, we reject speakers based on our image of them or how they deliver their messages.

This rejection or acceptance of what a speaker says goes beyond how that person delivers the message; it also includes our perception of his or her role, culture, and status. We know that, when we like and respect someone, we tend to listen more attentively. Unfortunately, we may become overly concerned with the speaker as a person and neglect to think critically about what is being said.

This barrier is perhaps most manifest in the area of gender, cultural, and ethnic stereotypes. Too often, people see the gender, skin color, hairstyle, or traditional attire for a specific culture, or hear a dialect or accent they are not familiar with, and immediately leap to an unfavorable reaction. These responses keep us from listening to the content of the message.

A good listener must recognize that culture, gender, race, status, and the like are factors present in all communication situations and must not let these considerations prevent maximum comprehension.

6. *Yielding to distractions*. The English writer Thomas Fuller once remarked that "If you run after two hares, you will catch neither." He may well have been talking about how easy it is to learn to be distracted. In a sense, all the bad habits we have discussed thus far are a kind of yielding to distractions, chasing that second rabbit, but there are some additional distractions that merit special consideration. These are the distractions that fall into three broad categories—mental, semantic, and physical.

Mental distractions are perhaps the most common of all the distractions and the most difficult to overcome, for they occur when we talk silently to our favorite companion—ourselves. It is a very natural tendency to make ourselves the central character in our daydreams and fantasies. However, when we "visit" with ourselves we often forget about the speaker. Ask yourself how many times a day you are supposed to be listening but, instead, find yourself thinking about your next meal, planning tomorrow's activities, or evaluating what you did yesterday. Throughout this chapter, we will return to the advice that you need to learn how to *stay in the moment* and concentrate on what the other person is saying.

Listeners also yield to *semantic distractions*. Persons often have different meanings for the same word, and if these differences are too great, a semantic distraction can occur. For example, if a speaker and listener are from different generations and cultures, a phrase such as "Man, that is bad" could cause a semantic distraction. What usually happens is that the listener must stop to think about specific meanings while the speaker continues his or her presentation.

As you listen to more and more speakers who have English as their second language, you must work very hard not to allow semantic distractions to keep you from staying focused. If a word fails to make sense to you, try to place it in the context of the moment and see if you can define it in that manner. You may also be given an opportunity to ask the speaker how the word is being used.

As listeners, we can also experience a number of *physical distractions* that make demands on our attention. A cold auditorium, the wind howling outside the window, a man next to you tapping his finger on a desk, someone entering the room when the speaker is talking, odor from someone's strong perfume, and an uncomfortable chair are all distractions to which we often yield. The real danger of physical distractions is that listeners use them as an excuse for tuning out the speaker. We all know from personal experience that we can yield to any distraction quite easily and, thus, make the distraction more important than what is being said.

Having examined the poor listening habits advanced by Nichols and Stevens, we are now ready to discuss a few additional barriers to listening.

Defensive listening is present in situations in which we select only the negative aspects of what is being said and fail to listen to what else the speaker is discussing. None of us delights in being criticized or attacked, so it is quite easy to adopt a defensive attitude when we perceive that what the speaker is saying is challenging some of our beliefs and values. However, this defensive attitude usually keeps us from listening and, in many instances, from learning. A good example of this barrier might be drawn from your speech class. If your instructor were to be critical of your use of evidence and were to say so, you would probably become defensive and stop listening. However, while you were responding defensively, she might go on to offer you some excellent advice about how you could remedy the problem. By being defensive, however, you would allow the negative comments to represent the entire transaction.

Defensive listening makes abundant use of prejudices. These attitudes are usually deep-seated, they have developed over a long period of time, and it is not always easy to create a posture of open-mindedness. For instance, persons with predetermined views toward Arabs would be less likely to give their full attention to a speaker who is talking about Islam. The speaker is not receiving a fair hearing because of the listeners' preconceived attitudes. To break this barrier, we must try to exert some command over our emotions and initial responses. We must try to withhold judgment until we have listened completely and objectively to what has been said. Remember, it is rather easy to be critical of others and their ideas. If we want to be negative, there is always something to focus on. As an old Yiddish proverb states, "If you're out to beat a dog, you're sure to find a stick." If you are determined to be defensive, you will find a stick.

The Roman playwright Terence was correct when he told us over two thousand years ago something very basic about human nature: "My closest relation is myself." What he was referring to is something we talked about earlier in the chapter when we noted that most of us are primarily concerned with self. There are many reasons why we all see ourselves as the center of the universe, but we shall only look at two of them. First, our listening is obstructed when we adopt the "I must defend my position" attitude. In these instances, we stop listening to engage ourselves in mental debate. If someone says to us, "We don't need gun laws in this country," and to ourselves we say, "What is he talking about? Last year there were over six thousand people killed with handguns in the United States," clearly a barrier to listening has arisen, for we have stopped listening and are now debating the speaker in our head.

Second, many of us adopt the "I already know what you have to say" attitude. This barrier begins to form when we say to ourselves, "Oh no, not another speech on drug addiction." When we assume this position, we miss a great deal of life. Think of what a narrow view we have when we are so dogmatic as to believe we know all there is to know on any subject. Much of what we have learned has been acquired by listening, and we would be foolish to stop listening before we hear the speaker's entire position.

Earlier in this chapter, we talked about the importance of listening and how we use listening more than any other communication skill. We thus encounter a large number of words during a normal day. If you think about it, we most likely hear over one billion words each year. It is often this constant bombardment of words that creates yet another barrier

Defensive Listening

Constant Self-Focus

Message Overload

to listening. It is not surprising that when we are faced with so much verbal input, we often just stop listening to *everything*. We simply shut down the brain to all outside noise. When this happens, the important words as well as the frivolous ones are not brought into our consciousness. If you often suffer from message overload, you need to learn to concentrate on entire messages so that you can extract what is important and worthy of your energy. Being faced with message overload is a common occurrence; hence, learning how to be selective is crucial if you seek to improve your listening performance.

Thinking-Speaking Rate

Recall that it is estimated that we speak an average of 125 to 150 words per minute. Our minds, however, are able to cope with approximately 400 words per minute. This means that the mind has a great deal of idle time. This excess time forms one of the major barriers to proficient listening. In most instances, the extra time is spent wandering away from the task of critical and careful listening. Many listeners use this listening-thinking gap for mental excursions ranging from daydreaming to thinking about the speaker's hairstyle. It would be far more beneficial to both sender and receiver if this time were spent analyzing the message.

Short Attention Span

In many ways our final barrier is inherent in all of the others, yet by giving it its own classification we can underscore the significance of this barrier. We begin our discussion by asking you to spend a moment or two the next time you are listening to someone talk (or even reading this chapter), and observe the manner in which your mind leaps from idea to idea. You will begin to notice at once how your attention span is very brief. There is something about the brain, and our need for stimulation, that has us jumping from stimulus to stimulus. Perhaps the first step in overcoming this barrier is simply admitting that it exists. This recognition, if sincere, might well improve our concentration.

Improving Listening

We have pursued two fundamental themes throughout this chapter. First, *by listening carefully, you can reap countless benefits*. As Plutarch noted, "Know how to listen and you will profit even from those who talk badly." Second, *listening is a communication skill that can be improved with serious practice and training*. If you genuinely desire to improve, your speech class offers an excellent arena for that improvement. You will have an opportunity to listen to a variety of speakers discussing a wide range of topics. We would recommend that you begin your efforts at improvement by incorporating some of the following suggestions into your listening behavior.

Identify Personal Listening Characteristics

Introspection, while often difficult, is crucial if you are going to improve the manner in which you listen. Therefore, your first step to enrichment is an analysis of your current listening habits. In a sense, we are advocating that you begin by heeding the maxim "know thyself." This self-analysis should include both your (1) outward and (2) inward listening characteristics. *Your outward characteristics represent how others perceive you as a listener.* Your posture, eye contact, and the like influence the kind of messages speakers send you. The way in which people relate to you correlates with how you listen, or at least appear to listen, to them; hence, try to identify how you present yourself to others. Do you appear interested, enthusiastic, sincere, or bored? The answers to these and other such questions will help you understand your role as a listener.

Your inward listening characteristic relates to what is going on in your head. What are you thinking about while the speaker is talking? We have already discussed the importance of being objective and not jumping to conclusions too soon; now you can take this objectivity one step further and try to recognize the biases you carry around. For example, if you have a negative attitude toward homosexuals, and a member of the Gay Students' Union speaks to you, your prejudice will affect how you listen.

If you find that you have some negative reactions to other people based on their culture, you are apt to be engaging in ethnocentrism. Here your culture becomes the prism through which you judge all other groups and cultures. Starting from this subjective position, it is easy to see how many of your conclusions about other cultures could be negative. How do you regard Japanese, Germans, African Americans, Mexicans, Arabs, or Jews? In most instances, we evaluate them by standards we have learned in our culture. How easy it is for all of us to say, "We do it this way; why don't they?" Feelings of "we are right" and "they are wrong" cover nearly all areas. We can observe examples of this type of listening orientation ranging from superficial conclusions based on dress standards to significant evaluations centering on contrasting attitudes.

To overcome feelings of ethnocentrism, identify your culture's role in how you perceive and listen to the remarks of people from different cultures.

Be Prepared to Listen

There is a saying that the time to repair the roof is when the sun is shining. The same point holds true with regard to listening—the time to think about listening is *before the speaker begins*. There are some specific ways you can prepare your communication profile before a listening experience. Let us look at four of them.

1. *Learn all you can about the subject, speaker, and situation.* This knowledge, much like an audience analysis, will help you understand and appraise what the speaker might be saying. If you know that you will be listening to someone from Mexico talking to a college class in international business, you can make some predictions related to the subject, speaker, and setting.

2. *Minimize physical barriers by placing yourself in a position where you can easily see and hear the speaker.* Being in the back row of a noisy auditorium is hardly conducive to effective listening. Try to find a location where you can use the speaker's nonverbal cues to increase your understanding of the speech.

3. *Eliminate all distractions in your environment that might call attention away from the speaker.* For example, leave the school newspaper outside the classroom; it might become a distraction.

4. *Bring the necessary materials to the communication event.* This advice is intended to remind you that being prepared means that you do not search for paper and a pen five minutes after the speaker has started. If you plan to use paper and a pen, or even laptop computer, they should be in front of you *before* the speaker begins.

Have a Specific Listening Purpose—Be Motivated

We have stressed throughout this book that, as a public speaker, you should know in advance what you hope to accomplish by the conclusion of your talk, the process called "selecting a specific purpose." What is true of speaking is also true of listening. As a listener you must also decide on a specific purpose. Ask yourself what you want to know by the conclusion of the speaker's remarks. Obviously, your purpose will change radically from speaker to speaker and from situation to situation. On one occasion, you may decide that you want to know more about the stock market by the time a stockbroker finishes her talk. While listening to a politician, however, your goal might be to decide whether or not you wish to vote for the proposal being advanced. In either case, stock-broker or politician, *your comprehension and retention will be enhanced if you settle on a specific purpose or goal before the talk begins*.

One of the most important aspects of selecting a listening purpose is to make sure that you are motivated by that purpose. *Efficient listening begins with motivation.* Researchers in the area of listening have concluded that, if you are motivated to listen, you are a more alert and active receiver. Ask yourself this simple yet important question: Do I learn more when I am interested or when I am bored? The answer is obvious. If you believe that the material affects you personally, you listen. What prompts you to listen might be something as pragmatic as making a sale if you listen carefully to what your customer is saying or as abstract as listening because the speaker deserves your attention. In either case, if you are motivated, if you have a purpose for listening, you will discover that you cannot be easily distracted. Benjamin Disraeli said it best when he noted, "The secret to success is purpose."

Make Use of the Thinking-Speaking Time Difference

As noted earlier, we normally think at a pace about three times faster than our speaking pace. As good listeners, we can use this time to think about what the speaker is saying. We can ask ourselves, How does this item relate to the speaker's main purpose? How does this main point support that purpose? As alert listeners, we can make this time gap work for us instead of against us. By concentrating on what is being said, instead of worrying or mentally arguing with the speaker, we can put the time difference to efficient use. Later in the chapter we will talk about those situations that call for note-taking, and how you can use your "free" time to engage in that specific activity.

You can also use the thinking-speaking time difference to observe clues to the meaning of the elements of the speaking situation. The setting, the staging of the event, and the program notes can give insight to what will be said. The speaker's inflection, rate, emphasis, voice quality, and bodily actions can offer clues to the meaning of what is being said and what the speaker feels is most important.

Clues naturally abound in the content and arrangement of the material. A vigilant listener makes note of the speaker's use of partitions, enumerations, transitions, topic sentences, and internal and final summaries. Clues common to writing, such as boldface type, italics, and quotation marks, are replaced with clues of voice, body, material, and arrangement.

Focus on Matter Rather Than Manner

Listening is concerned with a response to what people say. People talk to us so that they can share their internal state. Learn to focus on speech content, and not on the speaker's personality traits and extraneous considerations, so you can better understand what the speaker is trying to say. This is not to imply that nonverbal messages and the speaker's personality are not part of the communication process, but too much emphasis on these issues can de-emphasize the speaker's main mission. By forcing yourself to focus on content, you can avoid the tendency to make superfluous items seem more consequential than they are.

Be an Active Listener

Much of what we have discussed thus far implies that listening is an active process. What this means is that you cannot sit passively and expect to automatically receive the full impact of the speaker's message. As noted elsewhere, active listening requires that you consciously think about what the speaker is saying. There are some very specific mental responses you can choose that will improve your ability to be an active listener.

First, *whenever possible try to recognize patterns*. Ask yourself what organizational pattern the speaker is using. Is he or she speaking in terms of a linear time frame or talking about a problem that needs to be solved? If you cannot discern a pattern, then you must become even more active. This means mentally organize the material for the speaker so that it will be easier for you to comprehend which are the major and which are the minor points.

Second, *you might also find it helpful to regroup material under headings that are easy to remember*. By being an active listener, you can compensate for speakers who offer long lists and expect the audience to remember ten or eleven items. You, not the speaker, become responsible for sensible groupings.

When regrouping what the speaker is saying, you might use the following three-step sequence.

1. Identify the speaker's primary point. Ask yourself this question: What was the speaker's central thesis when he or she decided to give this talk? You should try to word the main thesis in a sentence or two.
2. Identify the supporting ideas the speaker used to clarify and/or prove the central thesis of the talk. Did the speaker use illustrations, analogies, statistics, and the like to explain his or her basic purpose?
3. Consider the adequacy and effectiveness of material used to explain the main ideas. Was the material clear and relevant? Did the material support the main thesis?

Third, *try to paraphrase the speaker's remarks*. This means attempting to put the speaker's ideas into your own words as a "shorthand" summary of what has been said. For example, suppose someone says, "Today 80 percent of deforestation results from population growth; if the numbers keep rising until the year 2050, the U.N. estimates, an additional 2.3 million square miles of land will have to be turned over to farming, roads, and urban uses." You might paraphrase by saying to yourself, "Deforestation is growing at an alarming rate and will cause serious problems in the future if something is not done." The technique of paraphrasing represents yet another way of separating the main ideas from the minor ones, and the insignificant from the significant.

Finally, *when appropriate, an active listener takes notes*. Taking notes allows you the opportunity to have a record of the most important points of the speech. In taking notes, it is essential to remember a few important ideas.

1. As soon as you identify the main thesis, you should immediately write it down.
2. If you are the only person who is going to be using the notes, there is no need to use complete sentences.
3. Organize the notes in the same manner in which you would organize a speech. This means showing major, minor, and subpoints by proper indentation.
4. Good notes are brief and usually contain only the salient points and facts.

Ask Questions

Asking proper and appropriate questions, which is obviously a speaking activity, is nevertheless another skill that can improve listening. You might ask a question to clarify a key point, to gather additional information, or to help direct the flow of the conversation. Regardless of your purpose for asking questions, you need to keep the following points in mind.

First, you need to think about the timing of your question. You should wait until the speaker has finished the speech before you ask your question. In addition, interrupting the speaker is both rude and disrespectful.

Second, know specifically what additional information you are seeking. You can usually obtain that information by using closed-ended questions, open-ended questions, or probes. *Closed-ended questions* ask for a specific answer and narrow the options you offer the speaker. The response to the question is usually brief, and you hope, to the point:

Question: "Exactly how many students did you say would be affected by this change?"

Answer: "I said it should affect about 300 students."

Open-ended questions encourage longer responses as you are asking the speaker to explain some of the points that you did not understand.

Question: "Why did you say we needed to take action on the proposal?"

Answer: "There are a great many reasons why we need to act at this time. First . . . "

Although *probes* can take a variety of forms, they are primarily used after a question and encourage the speaker to develop the last answer he or she gave in more detail.

Question: "Why did you say we needed to raise student fees at this time?"

Answer: "The ruling came from the administration."

Probe: "Did you mention in your talk who you were referring to when you used the word administration?"

Third, remember that, although you are asking a question, you are actually in the role of listener—you are not the principal speaker. Therefore, do not let your question turn into a long speech. You are seeking information, not pursuing a cause.

Use Vocal and Nonverbal Cues

The psychologist Sigmund Freud once noted that "No mortal can keep a secret, for betrayal oozes out of us at every pore." Freud was simply echoing an idea we noted elsewhere in the chapter when we alluded to the fact that an effective listener knows that people "speak" with their bodies and their voices in addition to their words. This idea is of such importance that we will now pause and develop it in more detail.

Vocal Cues

Most discriminating listeners have learned to read meaning into a speaker's use of volume, pitch, and rate. For example, most people show enthusiasm and emphasis by increased volume. Nervousness is often reflected, because of a tightening of the vocal cords, by a high pitch. And increases in rate usually demonstrate excitement.

Nonverbal Cues

Most of the research in the area of nonverbal communication suggests that people are very good at accurately reading nonverbal messages. Therefore, we ask you to read these messages so that you can gain insight into a speaker's meaning and mood. Although you might be familiar with most of the nonverbal behaviors we engage in, let us quickly review some of these actions and relate them to listening.

Facial expressions are one of the most reliable and available indicators of a person's attitude. By reading a person's face, we can often decide if the person is passive, intense, nervous, or enthused. Eye contact, or a lack of it, reveals levels of intimacy, self-confidence, nervous states, and interest. Posture and body movements offer us clues into status, enthusiasm, the importance of the point being made, friendliness, and emotional states.

Proficiency in any skill results from a great deal of conscientious effort. You should, therefore, practice listening. A poor listener avoids difficult listening situations and evades tedious material. A case in point might be a college lecture on a highly abstract concept that defies the application of interest devices by even the most skillful speaker. In such cases, listeners must work along with the speaker at gaining meaning. It is a great temptation to stop listening when it requires effort. Because of this, a weak listener never improves. Force yourself to practice; make yourself listen to music, speeches, and conversations that seem to hold no obvious interest value. If you practice this important skill, you will improve. Remember the words of the Greek playwright Euripides: "Much effort, much prosperity."

Practice

The act of listening, as noted at the start of this chapter, ends with our response to what we are exposed to. After we perceive and comprehend, we need to decide if we want to use or reject what the speaker has said. This final step is a complex one. It asks us to combine the best of our listening skills with some reasoned subjectivity. *We must first understand what we have heard and then decide its merits.* The need for such careful analysis should be obvious.

Evaluating Speeches

We are constantly besieged with requests to vote, give, buy, feel, and think in one way or another. A poor listener is easy prey for sophists, hucksters, shysters, and propagandists. Our major defense against those who attempt to influence or control our behavior is a combination of critical thinking and cautious evaluation. Both of these skills can be learned, and your speech class, by allowing you an opportunity to hear over a hundred speeches, is an excellent place to refine your listening ability. At the end of most classroom speeches, you will have an opportunity to present an informal critique, either oral or written. By evaluating and discussing the speeches in your classroom, you are not only helping your classmates improve their speaking ability, but you are developing a skill that can be transferred to situations outside the educational setting. As you critique the speeches of others, try to implement the broad principles discussed by your instructor. In addition to using the criteria your instructor suggests, you can evaluate speeches by applying the yardsticks offered in the next few pages.

Whenever we speak, we occupy both the life and time of another individual. Therefore, all listeners have a right to ask whether or not the purpose of a speech justified the amount of time and energy they gave it (or were asked to give it). Was the purpose clear or were the speaker and audience part of an ambiguous encounter? Aimless rambling touching on topics from pets to pollution serves no purpose and only contributes to confusion.

Purpose

Following are a few questions listeners can ask of a speaker regarding his or her purpose:

1.   Was the subject worthy of my time?
2.   Was the purpose suited to this audience?
3.   Were the values stressed justified by the speaker?

4.   Was the purpose an ethical one?
5.   Was the purpose clear and easily recognizable?

Substance

Closely related to the issue of purpose is the criterion of substance—whether or not a speech has something worthwhile to say. A number of questions can be asked with regard to the substance of a speech:

1.   Was the speaker prepared? Did the speaker attempt to be objective and fair to himself or herself, to the audience, and to the subject? Did the speaker seem to care about communicating, or was he or she simply going through the motions of fulfilling an assignment? For example, did the speaker appear to have practiced the speech?
2.   Were there indications that the speaker had analyzed the audience? Were factors such as the audience's age, sex, culture, education, and attitudes taken into consideration? Did the speaker indicate that the speech was being directed at the classroom audience or at a hypothetical audience?
3.   Did the speech seem to be original and creative? A unique and imaginative effort should be noted, as should one that is mundane and dull.

Argument

The success of any attempt to influence beliefs or actions depends heavily on the merit of the arguments the speaker offers. What claims did the speaker make and how did he or she support them? Listeners should be especially alert to the following:

1.   Did the speaker separate facts from inferences? Was personal opinion identified and not confused with evidence?
2.   Did the speaker make extravagant and exaggerated claims? Did his or her support and reasoning directly relate to these generalizations? Did the generalizations go beyond the confines of the speaker's purpose?
3.   Did the speaker's illustrations, examples, statistics, testimony, and analogies meet the tests of evidence? Did the speaker use enough evidence to support each point?
4.   Was the material varied?
5.   Was the evidence suited to this audience?

Structure

The ingredients of a message may have great merit, but, if they are not arranged in the proper order, they may not make much sense to the audience. Therefore, clear structure is an essential requirement for the successful communication of ideas. After you have listened to a speaker, apply the following tests of clear speech structure:

1.   Was a central unifying theme made apparent?
2.   Was the main theme of the speech easy to follow?
3.   Was an organizational sequence clearly discernible?
4.   Did the introduction of the speech set a tone that encouraged you to listen to the rest of it? Did the beginning of the speech offer a preview of what the rest of the speech would cover?
5.   Were the major segments of the speech well balanced? The speaker should not spend 80 percent of his or her time on only one point if the speech has six major ideas.
6.   Did the ending of the speech tie all the key points together?

Style

Style is concerned with the ways in which a speaker uses language. Remember, language represents our feelings and ideas. The way a speaker uses language is an important aspect of any communication encounter. The questions asked of a speaker's style might include some of the items in the following list:

1. Did the speaker use words and phrases that were adequately defined? Ambiguity and vagueness confuse the listening process.
2. Were imagery and word pictures used in a manner that made the speech colorful, vivid, and interesting?
3. Did the speaker avoid clichés, slang, and poor grammar? Was the speaker's language appropriate to the audience, the occasion, and the subject?
4. If English was the second language for some of the audience members, did the speaker attempt to paraphrase and/or explain words that might be misunderstood due to cultural and language differences?

Credibility

As a speech critic, you need to evaluate a speaker's credibility as well as his or her speech content. Credibility consists of the characteristics a speaker manifests during a speech that make listeners perceive him or her to be trustworthy and competent. Among the questions relating to speaker credibility are the following:

1. Did the speaker demonstrate a mastery of the subject matter?
2. Did the speaker show genuine concern for the listeners' welfare?
3. Did the speaker's words, actions, and dress contribute to the believability of the speech?
4. Did the speaker behave in ways that detracted from his or her credibility?
5. Did the speaker appear to be trustworthy?

   We will discuss much more about cultural differences in the perception of credibility when we arrive at chapters 14 and 16, but for now it is important to keep culture in mind as you assess a speaker's credibility. That is to say, not all cultures use the same guidelines for deciding who is a credible speaker. For example, in many Asian cultures, where silence and reflection are valued over talk and action, someone who is quiet, calm, and pensive would be perceived as having higher credibility than would a speaker who is enthusiastic and spirited. In most Mediterranean and Latin cultures, being credible means being verbal, displaying rhetorical skills, and being extremely animated. There are even different standards of dress that need to be considered in deciding what is credible attire. In short, make sure you take a speaker's culture into account before you judge his or her credibility.

Delivery

Recall that delivery is the way in which a speaker uses his or her voice and body to communicate a verbal message. It is important to consider the following questions when assessing a speaker's delivery:

1. How effectively did the speaker use the visual aspects of delivery? Did he or she maintain good eye contact? Did he or she have good posture and skillfully execute gestures and movements? Did the speaker use animated facial expressions? Did the physical dimensions of the speech detract from the message?
2. How effectively did the speaker use his or her voice? Was there sufficient variety of rate, pitch, and volume? Were enunciation and articulation clear and was pronunciation correct?
3. Did the speaker appear to be familiar with the speech?
4. Was the overall delivery an aid or a hindrance to the speech?

Effects   One of the major themes of this book is that public speaking is a goal-directed activity that produces a response from listeners—a response that the speaker decided on before beginning the speech. Therefore, an evaluation of any speech must include a discussion of how well the speaker accomplished his or her purpose. To examine the consequences of the speech, you should ask these questions:

1. Was the time you spent listening to the speech worthwhile, or was your time wasted?
2. Did the speaker add to your fund of knowledge, change your views on a topic, or entertain you?
3. Did the speech seem to have a long-range goal as well as an immediate goal?
4. What was the total impression left by the speech? As a listener, you should evaluate the main idea as well as the subpoints. At the end of every speech, you should ask yourself, What is the overall effect of the speech?
5. Was the speaker ethical in his or her overall treatment of the topic and the material?

Listener and Speaker Responsibilities

As you have learned by now, *communication is a two-way process.* This is another way of saying that speaker and listener are interrelated and need each other for a variety of reasons. If the communication encounter is to be successful, each must realize his or her obligation to the other. Let us examine this tandem relationship and some of the responsibilities each party should assume in an attempt to increase the likelihood that a communication event will be a rewarding one.

Listener Responsibility   *To be effective listeners, we must do more than listen: we must assume some of the responsibility for the total communication act.* Not only should we evaluate the messages we have received from the speaker, but we should also be aware of what messages we have given the speaker. What have we "told" the speaker by the manner in which we listened? Did we make the speaker feel we were interested or uninterested? Were we rude or attentive? Did we encourage or discourage clarity? Did we contribute to the speaker's sense of speech anxiety or did we help reduce it? The answers to these, and countless other questions, deal directly with the type of feedback given the speaker. You will recall from chapter 1 that feedback is the response you give to another person about his or her communication. Let us once again return to the topic of feedback and see how it can be used to facilitate communication and then briefly look at some ways that feedback can thwart communication.

Offer Positive Feedback   Speakers not only feel better about themselves and others, but they communicate more effectively when they receive positive feedback from listeners. How much incentive would you have to continue speaking if the persons before you were balancing their checkbooks, frowning, or reading newspapers? In short, our behavior as listeners affects the speaker.

Responding to what you hear is a form of feedback. As indicated earlier, your feedback is the way you "talk back" to the speaker. There are a number of general ideas that you should keep in mind when offering feedback. First, *the speaker must perceive the feedback you are sending.* Your requests for clarification cannot be acted upon if they are not received.

Second, *the feedback should be specific, not ambiguous*. The feedback should be clear and should contain the information that tells the speaker how he or she is doing. As we indicated earlier, even the questions you ask of the speaker, as a form of feedback, should be clear and concise. Third, *the feedback you give the speaker should directly relate to what is going on*. It is of little benefit to either party if your response is delayed to the point that it is no longer germane. Feedback is most effective when it is immediate. Waiting until after a speech to send positive messages to the speaker might help his or her ego, but offering that feedback immediately, through posture or facial expression, would encourage the speaker when he or she needs it most. Finally, *your feedback will help you get more from the encounter if it is descriptive, not evaluative*. Telling someone their report was detailed and clear, but you still have one or two questions, is better feedback than saying the report was very weak and left a great many unanswered questions.

In addition to the general considerations just mentioned, you can take some specific actions to help both you and the speaker. Some of the following suggestions apply to platform speaking, while others are useful in group discussion, interviewing, and everyday conversation.

1. Eye contact establishes rapport between a sender and receiver and encourages communication. Research indicates that we seem to look at people more when we feel comfortable around them.
2. Nodding the head slightly also tells a speaker that the listener is part of the communication process and is tuned-in to what is going on.
3. An act as simple as smiling can offer warmth and support to a speaker. It may be just what he or she needs to get over the nervous feeling that often confronts speakers.
4. Casual remarks such as "I see" and "Is that so?" involve listeners with a speaker. Even vocalizations such as "uh-huh" can be encouraging.
5. Asking relevant questions helps a speaker in two ways. First, your question may enable the speaker to clarify a point of confusion that might be troubling other members of the audience. Second, by asking your question, you are demonstrating your interest both in the speaker and in the topic.
6. There are times when you can help a speaker by remaining silent. Too often, we contaminate a communication encounter by talking when talking is highly inappropriate.
7. Try to lean your torso slightly forward in a natural manner. This nonverbal act makes a speaker feel that you are interested in what is being said.
8. Try to maintain a relaxed involved posture. This tells the speaker that you are not tense. This message should help put the speaker at ease.

These suggestions should not be carried out in an artificial or deceptive manner. Remember, faking attention is a poor listening habit. Actions that offer support should be genuine.

Although the items mentioned thus far tend to help speakers, some listener behaviors can have the opposite effect. Let us suggest a few actions that you should avoid if you want to help a speaker perform at his or her optimum level. Notice as we move through this list how uncomfortable you would feel if your listeners sent you these negative messages:

Avoid Negative Feedback

1. Frequent shifting of your body position can be a signal to a speaker that you are disinterested and/or bored with the talk. Think of the message conveyed by feedback such as bouncing a leg up and down as if the listener has a train to catch and might be late if the speaker doesn't speed up.
2. A slouching posture can give the impression that you would rather be someplace else. If you sit as if you are a candidate for a chiropractor, the speaker will surely feel that he or she is intruding on your time. This mental picture can impede the speaker's efforts.
3. Engaging in other activity while a speaker is talking is not only discourteous but it can keep the speaker from relaxing and doing his or her best work.
4. Try to imagine how disconcerting it would be to have someone respond to your words with a long, loud sigh. We all know the meaning of a sigh in our culture, and it is not a positive one.
5. Facial expressions such as frowning, raising an eyebrow, scowling, and rolling the eyes all send negative messages.
6. Shaking your head in a negative fashion will also bruise a speaker's confidence.
7. In the United States, having your arms folded in front of your chest sends a rather negative message to a speaker.

Speaker Responsibility

Throughout this book, you have read that, as a speaker, if you hope to accomplish your purpose, you need to perform certain tasks, one of which is to hold audience interest and attention. The reason is obvious; if the listeners are not listening, they cannot respond to what you are saying. Let us examine a few of the more common techniques that speakers can use to encourage more effective listening. Many of these techniques will be discussed in more detail later in the book.

Try to Empathize

In chapter 3 we spent some time discussing the place of empathy in human communication. Basically, we noted that empathy is the process of putting yourself in the place of someone else so that you could shape your messages to meet their needs.

What was said then applies to this chapter. For as a speaker, you must understand your listeners and how they will react to you and your message. This is best accomplished by trying to hear your ideas and words as the listeners will. For example, if you have not thought about your listeners, you might talk on a subject that holds little or no interest for them. By using empathy, you can view your speech content as the listeners will, and you will not be asking them to listen to material that is inappropriate and uninteresting.

Adjust Your Delivery

In chapter 4, we talked about how a speaker's voice and body can aid listeners in understanding his or her verbal message. Always make sure you can be heard. It is very frustrating for a listener to strain in order to know what is being said. Moreover, delivery should be animated enough to arouse and maintain interest.

Another dimension of delivery adjustment can be found in the area of culture. You need to accommodate the listeners if they are from a culture different from your own. If English is their second language, you can help them listen by talking more slowly and paraphrasing extensively. If they are from a culture that values calmness, you can tone down your volume and level of animation.

Listeners must use feedback to improve their listening skills.

Listeners must use feedback to improve their listening skills; the same principle applies to speakers. As speakers, we should be sensitive to what our messages are doing to the people who receive them. Are they paying attention? Do they look interested? Do they look confused? Are they seeking more information? These are but a few of the questions feedback may answer. Once we secure this information, via feedback, we are in a better position to make the necessary adjustments. If we sense apathy, and the fact that the audience is not listening, we can try to arouse attention and point the material directly to the needs of the audience.

Use Feedback

You can do a number of things to improve the quality of the feedback you receive. First, although it may not be appropriate in all instances, you can tell the audience that you want feedback. This lets them know that you want them to keep you informed as to how they are reacting to your message. Second, you can learn to be sensitive to nonverbal communication. As you recall, nonverbal messages carry approximately 55 percent of the meaning of an utterance. Learning to read those meanings will tell you if the audience is listening. Be careful how you read this nonverbal feedback, however, when your audience represents a variety of cultures. As noted elsewhere, people from the Mediterranean area are likely to be very animated, while people from Eastern Asia might not outwardly show you what they think of your talk. Third, if the situation allows for it, you can even ask questions of the audience as a way of determining if they are listening. A Danish proverb offers the following advice: "Better ask twice than lose your way." As a speaker, you can modify this maxim to read, "Whenever appropriate, I should ask questions of my listeners." Their responses give you the opportunity to measure how well they understand you. By asking questions, the listeners are able to seek additional information in those areas that are not clear.

Be Clear   You know from your own experience that it is very difficult to listen to a speech that rambles aimlessly. As speakers, we can meet part of our responsibilities by being well organized. We will discuss much more about clarity and organization later in this book, but for now remember that it is unfair to ask a listener to make sense of disjointed wanderings. If the listeners represent dissimilar cultures, you might also want to make extensive use of transitions, previews, and other devices that contribute to clarity.

Be Interesting   If material lacks interest for us, it is difficult to listen; hence, as speakers we must strive to make our content lively, stimulating, and relevant. This means learning how to establish and maintain audience attention with techniques such as suspense, humor, and novelty. These, and many other attention devices, will be developed in detail later in this book, but for now we simply need to underscore the importance of enhancing the listening process by not being colorless and dull.

Culture and Listening

One of the major themes of this book has been that the ways in which we communicate, the circumstances of our communication, the language and language style we use, and nonverbal behaviors are primarily all a response to, and a function of, our culture. We would now add that what is true about verbal and nonverbal communication is also true about listening. That is to say, listening, like most communication variables, is influenced by culture. That influence is seen in a number of different ways. To help you better understand the role of culture in listening, let us look at some of the specific links existing between culture and listening.

First, in many cultures in the Far East, the amount of time spent talking, and the value placed on talking, is very different from those cultures that value conversation and public speaking (Middle East, Mexico, the United States). In Japan, for example, the culture is very homogeneous and most people share similar experiences. The commonality often allows them to know what the other person is thinking without the use of words. In fact, they often believe words get in the way of understanding. Think for a moment of the message contained in the Asian proverb, "By your mouth you will perish." Or what about the view toward silence versus talk in the Buddhist saying, "That there is truth that words cannot ever reach." It is easy to see how these two orientations, one favoring talk and one preferring silence, could influence the listening process.

Second, when judging delivery as a clue to what is being said, remember to allow for cultural variations. That is to say, some cultures are active speakers and some are passive. For example, in Japan, Thailand, and Korea, speakers tend to talk in soft voices, while in the Mediterranean area, the appropriate volume is much more intense. Even the size and number of gestures are controlled by culture. You cannot expect people from a culture that values reserved behavior to engage in the same number of gestures as one that has a very energetic communication style.

Third, a person's culture will even be reflected in the question-and-answer period we discussed earlier in the chapter. If the speaker was from the Chinese or Japanese culture, for example, they would not expect questions from the floor. Questioning a speaker would cause both the speaker and listener to lose "face"—or, by Western standards, be embarrassed and humiliated in front of other people. Questioning the speaker would bring discomfort because it would appear the speaker was not clear in expressing his or her views—hence, the need for a question. The listener would lose "face" because having to ask a question would indicate they did not understand what was being said.

Fourth, as you listen you will experience the sway of culture as it affects accents and vocabulary. Accents by people trying to speak English as a second language, and the confusion they may experience with vocabulary, often makes it more difficult for you to listen and comprehend what is being discussed. In these instances, our advice is rather simple and straightforward—be tolerant and practice being patient. You might also put yourself in place of someone trying to speak a second language that is new and often strange. This attempt at empathy will usually increase your concentration and your compassion.

Finally, developing empathy as a listener is also influenced by culture. As you would suspect, it is very hard to develop empathy toward someone you do not know. If you are talking to your best friend and she has a look on her face that you have seen many times before, you are apt to be able to read that expression with a degree of accuracy. An expression on the face of a stranger might be more difficult to interpret. If you add the variable of culture, the process of reading internal states becomes even more difficult. For example, not all cultures display their emotions in the same manner. In cultures such as the Asian and Native American, outward signs of emotion are very uncommon. Members of these cultures are taught to "keep things inside." As you can imagine, it can be very perplexing to try to empathize without sufficient information about what a person is thinking and feeling.

You will even be confronted with situations in which the verbal information listeners offer cannot be used to develop empathy. For example, in North American culture, you can ask people to respond verbally to what is going on at a particular moment and they will supply you with the data you need to determine if they understand what you are talking about. However, remember that people in some cultures will not answer your request for information about how they feel about what you are discussing. In the Japanese and Chinese cultures, people often say yes even when they mean no, as a way of saving face. In many Latin cultures, where social harmony is important, people supply the response they think you want to hear rather than answering truthfully, which they believe might upset you. You need to approach the subject of empathy carefully if the audience is composed of people from diverse cultures.

Summary

Listening is one of our most important communication skills. Effective listening is an active process that demands conscientious effort. Virtually everyone can improve his or her listening ability simply by becoming aware of some of the problems of listening and their remedies.

A listener who is sincere about improvement should be alert to the major barriers to effective listening: poor listening habits (faking attention, listening only for facts, avoiding difficult material, avoiding the uninteresting, criticizing the speaker, yielding to distractions), defensive listening, constant self-focus, message overload, the thinking-speaking rate, and short attention spans.

You can become a better listener if you identify your personal listening characteristics, prepare to listen, have a specific listening purpose, make use of the thinking-speaking time difference, focus on matter rather than on manner, be active, ask questions, use vocal and nonverbal cues, and practice listening.

Speech criticism and evaluation were also explored in this chapter. Listeners should question much of what they hear and, whenever possible, offer constructive criticism to the speaker. This criticism can be centered around questions of purpose, substance, argument, structure, style, credibility, delivery, and effects.

Both listeners and speakers have certain communication responsibilities that are built into each encounter. Listeners should create a positive psychological environment by adopting a listening attitude and posture that encourages the speaker to reach his or her full potential—the listeners should try to put the speaker at ease. The speaker can meet some of his or her obligations by (1) trying to empathize with the listeners, (2) making adjustments to the delivery, (3) using feedback, (4) being sure that the message is clear and well organized, and (5) seeing that content is interesting, lively, stimulating, and relevant.

Finally, to be an effective listener, you must adapt to the countless communication events that have you interact with people from different cultures. On those occasions, it is important that you practice tolerance, patience, and empathy.

Part II
YOUR IDEAS

Thinking is the endeavor
to capture reality
by means
of ideas.

José Ortega Y Gasset

Chapter 6

Evidence

The Foundation of Your Ideas

127

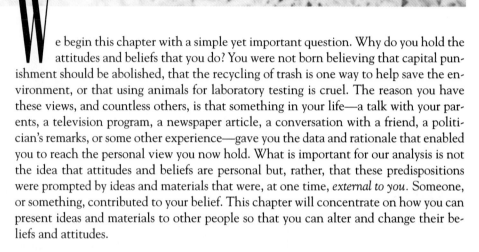

Such is the irresistible nature of truth all that it asks, and all that
it wants is the liberty of appearing.

Thomas Paine

We begin this chapter with a simple yet important question. Why do you hold the attitudes and beliefs that you do? You were not born believing that capital punishment should be abolished, that the recycling of trash is one way to help save the environment, or that using animals for laboratory testing is cruel. The reason you have these views, and countless others, is that something in your life—a talk with your parents, a television program, a newspaper article, a conversation with a friend, a politician's remarks, or some other experience—gave you the data and rationale that enabled you to reach the personal view you now hold. What is important for our analysis is not the idea that attitudes and beliefs are personal but, rather, that these predispositions were prompted by ideas and materials that were, at one time, *external to you*. Someone, or something, contributed to your belief. This chapter will concentrate on how you can present ideas and materials to other people so that you can alter and change their beliefs and attitudes.

The Importance of Evidence

We all know that stating a point does not necessarily render it believable or true. There may be assertions that listeners will accept at face value because the assertions are consistent with their existing beliefs and prejudices. Students who have difficulty finding a parking space each day when they drive to campus do not need much proof when you assert that "parking at this college is a serious problem." The "facts" for them are apparent and compelling, much like the quotation from Henry David Thoreau, "Some evidence is very strong, as when you find a trout in the milk." More frequently, however, our statements by themselves are not "strong"; therefore, listeners require that our assertions be supported and explained with evidence. For example, a speaker on a college campus advocated that the football team be disbanded on the grounds that it was a financial burden to the student body and that it benefited only a small number of students. Because this charge was merely asserted and not supported with proof, the speaker's plea was not heeded. The speaker needed evidence to support his or her assertion. *Evidence is a necessary component of successful communication because it helps prove and clarify the validity of our ideas.* In this chapter we will talk about what those supporting materials are and how you can use them to accomplish your specific purpose.

Verbal Support

Some of the things we say about a particular subject are incidental; we use them to get and hold listeners' attention. On the other hand, some points are fundamental and vital to the accomplishment of our speaking purpose. Therefore, one of our basic tasks as speakers is to study our subject until we recognize the elements in it that are essential to accomplishing our purpose. The essential components that help render our ideas understandable and believable are called *forms of support*. The word *support* accurately describes their function because the materials we select provide sustenance for the central theme of our speech. Just as a builder uses certain materials to construct a house, so you, as a speaker, have to supply the materials for developing and proving your ideas. Using supporting materials enables us to say to listeners, "Driving at fifty-five miles an hour was an excellent law, and we should all work to have Congress and the President reinstate it. And here is why. There is proof that the fifty-five-mile-an-hour speed limit saves lives and fuel. Let me explain." The "whys" enable you to offer reasons that might make your opinions believable and acceptable to another person. They are your forms of support.

Let us consider some of the specific forms of support available to clarify and/or prove an important and fundamental assertion. Although our analysis discusses only one form of support at a time, in reality you will seldom be able to prove your point with a single piece of evidence. As Aristotle reminded us over two thousand years ago, "One swallow does not make a summer," similarly, one form of support does not prove a point. The content of your speech is much like a jigsaw puzzle, for, just as it takes many pieces to complete the picture, your forms of support work in combination.

Regardless of the culture, storytelling has commanded and held attention since the beginning of recorded history. These narratives, be they on television, in books, on computer or movie screens, or transmitted face-to-face, are essential devices for proving and clarifying a point, while at the same time maintaining interest. The fact that a story or an example holds attention renders it an excellent tool in nearly all communication situations. As Mark Twain noted, "Few things are harder to put up with than the annoyance of a good example." Put yet another way, good examples help a speaker accomplish his or her purpose.

Illustrations

An **illustration** is the narration of an incident that amplifies, proves, or clarifies the point under consideration. It is, in a sense, a speaker saying to the audience, "Here is an example of what I mean." It can also be thought of as a story that supports the point the speaker is trying to make. Illustrations generally take one of two forms: (1) detailed, factual illustrations or (2) hypothetical illustrations.

Detailed, Factual Illustrations

Think of a **detailed, factual illustration** as a striking and vivid story that answers the questions *who? what? where? when?* and *how?* Because of the detail in the story, and because the story is true, a factual illustration can be both lifelike and meaningful to the audience. The knowledge that something actually occurred is a source of interest. Notice how interest is stirred when we hear someone say, "Let me tell you about this frightening thing that happened to me last week as I was walking to my car," or "Yesterday I read where a cow . . ." The popularity of biographies and "reality" television programs gives further credence to the idea that most of us like hearing about other people and events, and we like it best when it comes in the form of a detailed, well-told story. The captivating nature of a true story was cleverly explained by Englishman Edward Stillingfleet: "The story should, to please, be true, be apropos, well told, concise, and new; and whensoe'er it deviates from these rules, the wise will sleep, and leave applause to fools."

Trying to convince an audience that the drug called angel dust is dangerous, a student speaker used the following detailed, factual illustration *to help prove his assertion and gain support for his idea:*

A friend of mine had heard so much about a new street drug called angel dust that he decided to try some. Although I urged him not to experiment with this substance, he and a few friends went to a rock concert, and he thought it might be a good place to try out this new drug. He took the angel dust and waited for something to happen. And it did! At first, he became very irritable and anxious. He then started arguing with his friends for no apparent reason. The arguing quickly escalated to hostility and violence. The confrontation became so intense that the police had to be called to the section of the stadium where he was sitting. By then, my friend had become so violent and out of control that it took six police officers to subdue him and take him to jail. During the course of his thrashing around, he cut his head badly enough to need seventeen stitches. When the drug finally left his system, he was still not fully recovered. For months afterwards, he had a paranoid tendency toward the police and believed that they were trying to capture him. It became so bad that he had to leave school and go to a hospital for treatment. For my friend, angel dust was indeed dangerous.

As we indicated, factual illustrations are also *useful for clarifying as well as proving a point*. Notice in the following example how the speaker gives an illustration to explain what she is referring to when she talks about the problem of solid waste. The illustration lets the listeners see an actual case so that the concept will be clear:

There it was—the ship from New York bobbing down the Atlantic Coast and through the Caribbean. It was a 3,100-ton barge loaded with unwanted trash. After 41 days and more than 2,000 smelly miles at sea, the barge was still searching for a home. With an end to its odious odyssey nowhere in sight, the scow raised once again the dilemma of a throwaway society, quickly running out of room for all its solid waste.

Illustrations can also add *a touch of reality* and *personalize* the story by dealing with "real" people:

Let me tell you about Molly, a typical victim of domestic violence. I first met Molly huddled on my front porch at six in the morning, when I was leaving for work. She was wearing only a bathrobe. Her hands were bleeding; she had cigarette burns on her arms and large, dark bruises on her neck. Molly told me that she and her husband had fought, and that he had tried to kill her. When he started to get a knife from the drawer, she decided to run, and that is how she ended up on my front porch. Molly told me that this was not the first time she had needed to flee for her life. It seems that Molly, like so many other women, was a victim of ongoing domestic violence.

A well-told story *can capture and focus attention*. In the following example, notice how the narrative attracts attention:

So you believe that carjacking is only a series of statistics? Not for my best friend Janet. On a warm summer night last month, Janet was walking to her car after working in the library all day, when, without any warning, two teenagers stepped out from behind a pillar and accosted her. They forced her into the trunk of her 1989 Ford Mustang. Five hours later, after being tossed around in the trunk of her car, she was eventually hurled out onto the pavement as her abductors drove away. She was comatose and suffering from dehydration as a result of the 130-degree heat in the trunk when the police found her forty minutes later. After two weeks Janet finally regained some consciousness, but doctors fear she may have suffered irreversible brain damage. For Janet, carjacking was more than a statistic. Carjacking changed her entire life— forever and ever.

An illustration *can serve as the springboard for the presentation of additional and more specific evidence.* For instance, in the following example, a speaker is able to use his factual illustration as an introduction or transition for other pieces of evidence in a speech on the importance of recycling:

> The other day, while I was enjoying a walk along the beach, I noticed a number of shiny objects floating in the water. At first, I thought they were fish, so I decided to walk closer and have a better look. Much to my surprise, my nose and eyes soon told me that what I was smelling and seeing was not fish but tin cans, plastic trash bags, and garbage sacks. I was seeing the negative effects of what is called ocean dumping—a waste disposal system that I have since discovered is bringing harm to those areas that have tried to dispose of their trash in this manner. The problem, however, seems to be that incineration and sanitary landfill methods also present serious problems. Let us look at those problems.

Notice in our next example, on a speech dealing with suicide, how a speaker is able to use a factual illustration to prepare us for statistics.

> I was touched by the sadness that suicide can bring last year when my roommate Scott killed himself during spring vacation. By all outward signs you would never suspect that Scott would be someone who would take his own life. He was a good student, well liked by his peers, had a winning smile, a delightful sense of humor, and appeared to have specific career goals. Yet on April 7th, Scott took his father's handgun, held it up to his head, and pulled the trigger. I was shocked when I heard the news. I, like all of you, knew about suicide, but thought it was one of those things that happened to other people, not to people I knew. But since Scott's death, I have discovered that suicide is *not* uncommon in the United States. In fact, in the United States there are approximately 30,000 suicide deaths annually, which averages to 17 Americans per day.

All of the illustrations in the last few pages had some common characteristics that contributed to their overall effectiveness. First, *notice that they talked about concrete places and events.* Second, *they all made references to familiar topics* (drugs, trash, domestic violence, carjacking, suicide, etc.). Third, *they used colorful and vivid language.* Fourth, *the situation (story) had some interesting aspects.* Fifth, *the illustrations all related directly to the point being made.* Finally, *many were made personal and were presented in a manner that allowed the audience to identify with the story* ("My roommate . . .").

A **hypothetical illustration** is a detailed, fictional illustration that allows the audience to see "what could be" or "what could be supposed." Hypothetical illustrations are most often used to depict future events or to make the future seem graphically clear. In a

Hypothetical Illustrations

speech dealing with a proposal to raise school taxes, you might offer a hypothetical illustration of how the proposal would affect the audience. If you were telling the audience that there are dangers associated with being a "latchkey child," you could ask the listeners to imagine a child coming home to an empty house and playing with matches. You might offer a detailed hypothetical illustration to convince the listeners that high school dropouts have a difficult time securing employment—as in the following:

> Suppose a friend of yours, who is still in high school, decides that he has had enough school. He is doing poorly in math and English and feels there is no real need to finish the semester. On Saturday, he asks the owner of a local market to give him a job. The market owner can pay only $5 an hour, but your friend, having never made that much money, decides to take the job instead of reporting back to school on Monday. After about two weeks on the job, he is dismissed. Business is off at the store and the owner can't afford any extra help. Your friend then goes from store to store and from factory to factory, looking for employment, but he soon discovers that employers are not interested in hiring someone without at least a high school education. Your friend, in essence, is unable to find work because he left school.

Depicting the future with an illustration can place listeners in a situation that affects them personally and emotionally. A question such as, What happens if you reject the idea of added security patrols on campus? affords the speaker an opportunity to place the audience in the center of a hypothetical picture. For example, the speaker, talking about campus security, could have the audience visualize the point he or she is trying to make by saying, "Imagine you are walking to your car late one night after studying in the library. . . ."

In the following example, from a speech on cigarettes and lung cancer, we can see how the speaker let the listeners see themselves as the central figure in the illustration:

> Let us assume for a moment that you are a smoker, and as a smoker you find yourself in the following situation. You wake up one night and discover that your chest is burning. At breakfast, you seem to be coughing more and are having difficulty catching your breath. You decide it is just a cold, so you put off going to the doctor. As the day goes on, the pain and the cough get worse, so you make an appointment to see the doctor. As part of your examination, the doctor takes an X ray of your lungs, which reveals grave damage. The doctor tells you what you already know—that if you had not smoked this problem would have most likely never have happened.

When used effectively, hypothetical examples propel listeners into the future by telling what can happen if this or that proposal is not followed. In our next example, an effective hypothetical illustration shows us what an earthquake would be like if we were not prepared:

> You now begin to feel the room rock back and forth. It is an earthquake, and now you must make some decisions. You can't decide if you should stay in one spot or try to locate a safe place. But, you ask yourself, what is a safe place? As the room shakes with even more force, you find yourself also wondering, Where is the first aid kit if I need it? How do I turn off the gas, water, and electricity? And what will I eat and drink? If you listen to my talk today, you will be able to answer these and other questions concerning what to do before, during, and after an earthquake.

As was the case with factual illustrations, the hypothetical illustration should be a story that is vivid and interesting. In the next example, from a speech dealing with the overcrowding at the Grand Canyon, a speaker uses a hypothetical example to make his point:

> Imagine that you and some friends have just arrived at the top rim of the Grand Canyon and you are ready to start a hike that you have been planning for over a year. After you park your car in a parking lot that reminds you of a large shopping mall, you approach what you believe to be the start of the trail. However, you suddenly stop. You can't believe your eyes. There in front of you is a line that is similar to what you experienced when you visited Disneyland. This line seems to run on for miles. It appears that all of the 5 million visitors to the Grand Canyon have decided to hike on the same day. As you and your friends slowly make your way down a well-worn path to the start of the trail, you notice the ground is covered with trash. At that moment, you begin to realize that the large crowds will keep you from your dream. You have discovered what other people now know, that the Grand Canyon is too crowded to be enjoyed. But there is something we can do about it, and that is what I would like to talk about today.

In using a hypothetical illustration, a few key points need to be kept in mind. First, you should never present an imaginary story as being a true one. Use phrases such as "imagine a situation such as this," "suppose you discover," or "what would happen if" to allow the audience to separate fact from fiction. Second, if a hypothetical illustration is going to be effective, it must seem reasonable and capable of happening. An obvious exaggeration will offend your listeners. Third, always remember that an imaginary story, although very interesting, proves very little. As a student of communication, you should try to locate other forms of evidence if you are trying to prove a point. This will let you rely on hypothetical illustrations to clarify a point or arouse emotions. Fourth, in using a hypothetical example, like a factual example, make certain that it is appropriate and related directly to the point in question. The story must not be in the speech for its own sake, but for the purpose of supporting or clarifying an idea.

A **specific instance,** although somewhat similar to an illustration, is actually a very specific example that omits much of the detail and development of an extended factual illustration. In many cases specific instances are no longer than a sentence or two. As such, several condensed examples are advanced by the speaker as a means of indicating the widespread nature of a situation or to suggest the frequency of an occurrence. Since it is short and takes little time to present, it allows the speaker to offer a great deal of material in a short amount of time. For instance, if you are asserting that college graduates are having very little trouble locating good teaching positions, you might establish your point by stating, "John Timmons, a friend of mine who majored in education, found an excellent teaching position after he graduated from college. Graduates from San Francisco State University and from UCLA are also reporting very little difficulty in locating good teaching jobs." Speaking on the topic of new research on alternative fuels, a student recently told her audience that "Nissan was testing a methanol-fueled vehicle, BMW was working on a hydrogen-powered car, and Italy's Fiat was about to offer an electric car to interested buyers."

Specific Instances

Still another example of a specific instance might appear in a talk about the value of the honor system. The case could be aided by saying, "The University of Indiana has found the honor system to be successful; Purdue University and the University of California at Davis have also reported satisfactory results from the honor system." By using actual people, places, events, and things, the speaker makes the material both meaningful and persuasive.

Some examples may require only a few words: "College tuition at state universities is so high that my friend Roger could not come to school this year, nor could my roommate from last semester." Other examples may call for a sentence or two:

> There are countless endangered species that are found all over the world. In North America, we see the humpback whale has now been added to the list of animals in great peril. It is estimated by the year 2000 that the golden toad of Central America will disappear from the earth, and, in South America, the black lion tamarin also faces extinction.

Regardless of the length of the specific instances, they add strength and understanding to an idea. They provide excellent proof and *are often most effective when they directly follow a detailed, factual illustration*. For example, a student who wanted to prove that a recent strike had adversely affected the workers supported her position by relating a true story (factual illustration) of a worker who had to sell his home and relocate his family because of the strike. The speaker then bolstered the case by offering two undeveloped illustrations that showed how other families were touched by the strike:

> Because of the prolonged strike, Tom Gemhouse had to watch his car being repossessed, and Sally Peters, for the first time in her life, had to accept food stamps.

As is the case with so many of the forms of support, specific instances often work best when they are used in combination with other pieces of evidence. In the next extended example, notice how the earlier speaker, the one talking about endangered species, used specific instances along with statistics and expert testimony:

> Everywhere we look we see animals vanishing from the planet. In Asia, the Asiatic lion, snow leopard, giant panda, and kouprey are nearly extinct. Scientists now tell us that, at the rate we are going, we are eliminating fifty to one hundred species every day. So rapid is this extermination that Thomas Lovejoy of the Smithsonian Institution recently noted that "insects, birds, and mammals are vanishing at a rate much faster than we can calculate."

Guidelines for Using Illustrations

When you use narratives to clarify or prove your point, it is important that they meet certain requirements. Remember, when you use an example or illustration, you may be asking the listener to draw a conclusion and believe your assertion from the illustration. For instance, someone might try to condemn all student athletes because of a football player he or she knows who failed three classes. In drawing a generalization from that one example, the speaker is suggesting that the example supports the assertion. To avoid such errors, ask the following questions when you use or listen to illustrations presented as a justification for a specific hypothesis:

1. *Is the illustration a typical case?* There can be no absolute measure of "typical" in applying this test. The answer depends on many factors, but largely on the phenomenon being discussed. If the conclusion is controversial and primarily a value judgment, a listener should expect more than one or two illustrations. Just as someone cannot indict all football players by a single example, you cannot prove that downtown Burbank is not a safe city because your friend was beaten and robbed there.

2. *Is the example clearly relevant to the idea?* When we talked about critical listening in chapter 5, we observed that a careful listener learns to ask, So what? of certain information. Checking the relevancy of examples is merely an extension of that idea. If we were to talk about the dangers of night driving and cite only an illustration of someone whose brakes had failed, we would be guilty of offering an irrelevant case.

3. *Is there other evidence to support the conclusion being made by the generalization?* This test should be applied to any evidence, whether it is presented in the form of an illustration, a statistic, testimony, or an analogy. Before you are satisfied that the example proves the point, you should ask for other facts and authoritative opinions that might suggest the falsity or validity of the generalization. Suppose, for example, that you are urging reforms in college registration procedures and have offered a single illustration to substantiate the need for reforms. Your position will be enhanced if you offer additional support, such as citing remarks of the dean of admissions, which adds believability to your thesis.

Statistics

While the use of narratives has a long history dating back as far as people have been coming together, statistics is a relatively new science. Ancient activities in the use of statistics can only be traced back to the Old Testament and to population records commingled by the Babylonians and the Romans. Even with this short history, scholars and social critics have had a love/hate relationship with numbers and statistics as a device used to prove a point. English writer Sir Thomas Browne was almost poetic when he wrote, "I have often admired the mystical way of Pythagoras, and the secret magic of numbers." However, Mark Twain, disturbed by the misuse of statistics, had a very different view of numbers when he wrote the famous lines, "There are three kinds of lies, lies, damned lies, and statistics." In many ways, both men are correct. That is to say, statistics are a powerful and useful tool, but they must be used correctly.

It is best to view *statistics as examples*. They are a numerical method for proving or describing something. You will recall that this was the same function we attributed to narratives. However, with statistics you are not talking about one or two cases or instances, you are attempting to measure and define them quantitatively. Because **statistics** are facts or occurrences represented numerically, they compare or show proportions as a means of helping a speaker develop and prove a point. Used in this way, statistics help compress, summarize, and simplify facts that relate to the issue in question. They are generalizations derived from comparisons of individual instances. For example, instead of talking about how alcoholism affects one person, a speaker can use statistics to examine how the disease harms many people. Notice how much more serious and widespread alcoholism appears as a speaker says, "There are an estimated 12 million alcoholics in the United States. They account for 50 percent of all auto fatalities, 80 percent of all home violence, 30 percent of all suicides, and 60 percent of all child abuse."

Although it is not our intent in this section on statistics to ask you to become an expert in statistical analysis, we believe that to use statistics effectively you need to understand a few basic terms that you find in the material you read and that you might want to use in your speech. Many of these ideas have most likely been introduced to you in your mathematics classes. Specifically, let us explain what is meant by range, mean, median, mode, and percentage.

The *range* is the extent and amount of variation of anything. It is the difference between the highest and the lowest numbers that are being examined. It can be the high and low temperature during the month of December or the difference between the number of handgun accidents in 1994 compared with 1995. The *mean* is the average that describes the central tendency of what is being examined. As you might remember from your mathematics classes, the mean is obtained by adding up all of the items and then dividing by the total number of items. Another useful descriptive statistic is the *median*. The median is the middle point in a series of numbers arranged in order from highest to lowest. The median number will then mean that half the numbers lie above that number and half fall below it (2, 5, 8, 10, 13—the median number is 8). The *mode* is the score (number) that occurs the greatest number of times (2, 2, 5, 5, 5, 8, 10 —5 is the mode). Finally, there are statistics discussed and shown in *percentages*. Percentages show the relationship of a portion to a whole, expressed in hundredths. For example, if you said "75 percent of the 852 students polled approved of this plan," you would be automatically saying that out of all the students in the survey (100%), three-quarters approved the plan.

Statistics, like illustrations, may be either brief or detailed. Let us look at just a few examples of how concise statistics can be. Speaking on the subject of heart problems, a speaker might simply say, "*Time* magazine noted that heart attacks claim about 550,000 lives each year." If the subject were the growing population of the elderly, a speaker could quickly say, "In 1980, 11 percent of the population was over sixty-five years of age; that figure is now 14 percent."

Even when they are short, statistics can be tied together in a series. Speaking on the topic of violence in public schools, a speaker noted the following:

> According to the National Education Association, every school day sees at least 100,000 students toting guns to school. Forty students are hurt or killed by firearms, 6,250 teachers are threatened with bodily injury, and 260 teachers are physically assaulted.

Another speaker used a string of statistics to prove that family violence is a serious problem when she said, "At least 1.8 million women are battered every year. Twenty percent of the women seeking emergency surgical procedures are victims of domestic violence. More than twelve hundred children die each year through child abuse."

There are also occasions when statistics take a slightly longer form. Discussing the topic of waste disposal, a speaker used the following statistics to show just what people are trying to discard:

> What to do with waste material in this country is a very serious problem. In one year, we needed to find a place to dump 2 million tons of major appliances; 22 million tons of food; 10 million tons of newspapers; 3 million tons of plates, towels, and napkins; and 52 million tons of bottles and containers.

You should not assume that because statistics are numbers they are automatically uninteresting. A well-trained speaker can make them appealing. In the following example, notice how a speaker used statistics to make the topic of ecology interesting:

> Let us look at what could happen if just one typical office practiced measures to conserve and preserve the world's natural resources. For instance, if just one person were to use his or her own ceramic mug in the office each day, it would eliminate as many as five hundred throwaway cups a year. The same office worker using a half-page cover sheet for a fax instead of a full page, and sending five faxes a day, would save about six rolls of paper each year. And, if the other employees in that fifty-person office used both sides of the paper just 10 percent of the time, the office could save ten trees and $750 a year just in reduced paper cost.

Statistics often enable a speaker to make quite striking comparisons. Note how a speaker, who is *opposing* a petition that would have Congress and the President reconsider the fifty-five-mile-per-hour speed limit, used comparisons to make his point:

> According to the calculations of most economists, the fifty-five-mile-per-hour speed limit causes enough of a traffic slowdown to waste about $6 billion worth of travel time per year. The National Highway Traffic Safety Administration says we save about forty-five hundred lives per year because of the speed limit; hence, it costs about $1.5 million per life saved. Is this a bargain, or are there other social policies that might save more lives for less money? Well, it has been estimated that placing a smoke detector in every home in the United States would save about as many lives in total as the fifty-five-mile-per-hour limit and would cost only $50,000 to $80,000 per life saved; more kidney dialysis machines could save lives for only about $2,000 per life saved; and there are even a number of highway improvements that could be made, through reducing roadside hazards, that cost only about $20,000 to $100,000 per life saved. At a cost of $1.5 million per saved life, the fifty-five-mile-per-hour speed limit is hardly a bargain.

The *comparative* nature of statistics was also evident when a speaker, trying to demonstrate how much we spend on the military compared with what we spend on social problems, offered the following comparisons:

> The United States is first in military spending, first in military technology, first in total global military bases and naval fleets, and first in the number of nuclear bombs and warheads. Yet we rank seventh in life expectancy, tenth in spending for public education per student, fourteenth in proportion of population with access to safe water, and seventeenth in infant mortality rate.

Although we are treating each of the forms of support in separate units, they actually *work in combination*. In the following example, dealing with the government's increased interest in synthetic fuels, notice how a speaker used both statistics and expert testimony to help prove her point:

> The lure of getting in on the ground floor of new energy developments—with government help—is attracting applicants to the synthetic fuels. Sixty-one companies in twenty-four states have applied for loan guarantees and price supports from the U.S. Synthetic Fuels Corporation, which was created by

Congress to stimulate the development of commercial plants to produce liquid and gaseous fuels. The corporation has $17.5 billion in government subsidies to distribute over three years. According to Acting Chairman John J. McAtee, Jr., completion of the projects could enable the country to produce the equivalent of 2 million barrels of oil per day by 1996. That amount would represent one-third of the oil the nation now imports.

In our next example, dealing with one of the causes of high health-care costs, a speaker linked statistics with expert testimony as a way of further proving her point:

For all its sophistication and ingenuity, the health-care industry has a low-tech problem—paper. Sorting, shuffling, and processing billions of pieces of paper cost at least $40 billion a year. Experts agree that paperwork is indeed part of the health-care dilemma. Richard Landen of the Health Insurance Association of America recently noted that "people—the payers, patients, doctors, and hospitals—are drowning in paperwork."

Statistics are a strong form of proof and should be gathered and presented in the most effective manner possible. The following few rules may increase your competency when using statistics:

1. *Whenever possible, present your statistics as round numbers, especially when offering several.* It is much easier to remember the population of a city if we hear "one and a half million," instead of "1,512,653," or that "8 million acres of Alaskan oil lease sales surround Native coastal villages" instead of dealing with numbers such as "7,987,898 acres." There are, of course, instances where exactness is essential.

2. *Give specific and complete source citations for your statistics.* Saying "these statistics prove that" or "quoting from a reliable source" does not tell your audience where you located your information. If the material is controversial, it is useful to cite the magazine or book, specific pages, and the date. In most cases, however, the date and name of the magazine or book are sufficient—for example, "According to the June 14 issue of *Newsweek*, only 10 percent of the teachers in the United States believe that their training did a good job of preparing them for the classroom." You might cite your source by saying, "A few statistics from the Justice Department's recent 'Report to the Nation on Crime and Justice' will illustrate my point." Documentation adds to the credibility and acceptability of your arguments.

3. *Avoid presenting too many statistics at one time.* A speech crammed with numbers can create confusion and boredom. Imagine a speaker who says, "Let us look at what happened in 1995. On January 14, the profits for IMT went up 3 percent, a rise of 1 percent over 1994. This is a dollar increase of $2,474,743.32. When compared to April of 1993, which had a 4 percent increase, we can see a net gain of over $3,499,812.79." Think of how difficult it would be to comprehend the following set of numbers from a speech on the economy: "Consumer confidence is down 0.08 percent, commodity prices down 0.17 percent, unfilled orders for durable goods down 0.12 percent, new plant equipment down 0.02 percent, manufacturing labor hours down 0.15 percent, and the index of leading indicators down 0.3 percent."

4. *Make certain that your statistics relate directly to the point you are making.* The relationship between your statistics and your assertion would be hard to discern if you

were to say, "Last year the sale of riding horses increased by 100 percent, so we can see that most people are tired of paying for gasoline." Consider a speaker who fails to relate his statistics directly to his conclusion by saying, "A Roper survey reports that 57 percent of U.S. military personnel favor a no-combat policy for women. Hence, we should not let gays into the military service."

5. *Make sure that your statistics are accurate.* Remember the quotation by Mark Twain; he underscored many people's feelings regarding the use of numbers to prove a point. There are countless instances, be they intentional or unintentional, where statistics were presented in an inaccurate and misleading manner. A factual example will demonstrate how statistics can be vague and deceptive. A widely quoted book on human sexuality sent out 100,000 questionnaires, but collected only a few thousand responses. From this very limited and unrepresentative sample, which of course produced a highly distorted picture of the phenomena, the researcher advanced what he called a "series of reports." Again, we remind you that you must be extremely careful when using statistics. Any kind of fraudulent activity is highly unethical and will greatly damage your credibility.

6. *Whenever possible, try to personalize your statistics.* Numbers are much more meaningful when the people hearing them can visualize their significance on a personal level. A speaker talking on the subject of illegal marijuana pointed his material directly at the audience when he said, "Last year, Americans used over 30 million pounds of marijuana. This quantity made over 30 billion cigarettes. This works out to about 125 marijuana cigarettes for each man, woman, and child in the nation." Another speaker pointed her statistics even more directly to the audience when she noted, "Each recycled beverage can you return to the store will save you the equivalent of six ounces of gasoline."

7. *At times, repeat and interpret the statistics in your own words.* We have already noted that numbers are difficult to comprehend and remember. Therefore, a verbal elaboration of the statistics is normally very useful. For example, a speaker who was examining teenage drivers first said, "Automobile accidents account for almost half of the deaths of sixteen-to-nineteen-year-olds in the United States." She followed this sentence with her own reading of the statistics: "This means about 50 percent of our teenagers will die needlessly."

8. *Make your statistics interesting.* A speaker, talking about the deadly effects of smoking, offered the following appraisal of smoking:

> Just how harmful is smoking? The World Health Organization and the San Diego Cancer Research Group estimate that the number of people who die from smoking each year is now over 3 million. This number is equal to the entire populations of San Diego and San Francisco.

Testimony

In our complex world, we cannot be an authority on all topics. We have become increasingly dependent on the testimony of experts to help us find the relevant facts of an issue or a concept. A public speaker must also, on many occasions, turn to an expert. An expert is someone who, because of their training, experience, and background, is an authority on the subject being discussed. *Testimony of an authority, as a form of support for a specific point, is often the most important type of evidence a speaker can use.* It can show that the opinions of persons of authority, or experts in the field, corroborate the speaker's own views. For example, if a speaker were trying to convince an audience that periodic chest X rays could save lives, she might quote the testimony of the surgeon general of the United States: "Our office has long held the belief that systematic and regular chest X rays could help save the lives of many cancer and TB victims." A speaker giving a talk to convince an audience that former convicts have a difficult time reentering society used expert testimony in the following manner:

> Lester N. Smith, who served as head warden of Sing Sing Prison for eleven years, indicated the scope of the problem faced by former convicts when he stated that society rejects former convicts right down the line. It is hard for them to locate a job, almost impossible for them to own a home, and difficult for them to lead a normal life. The labor unions often bar them and big companies fear them. In a very real sense, they find most roads back to a normal life filled with social and economic blocks.

In both examples, the persons quoted, because of their positions and expertise, knew a great deal about the topic under discussion. In the next two instances—one about drugs, the other about welfare—notice how the persons cited echo the speaker's view while adding to their own credibility as experts:

Drugs

Dr. David Sanders, who is the head of the San Diego Drug Rehabilitation Center and a leading researcher into the effects of drugs on the brain, offered the following commentary as to the dangers of the street drug called angel dust: "It's the most dangerous drug I've seen. And I've been in contact with every imaginable drug on the street for the past fifteen years."

Welfare

As one of the commissioners of welfare in Erie County, May Edgar is well aware of the problems faced by most welfare workers. In a recent article in *Newsweek* magazine, she noted, "Welfare workers do not have time to know their cases or to acquire the necessary skills in rendering services to people and preventing them from becoming permanently dependent on public aid."

Earlier, we noted that on most occasions speakers use more than one form of support at a time. Notice in the following three examples how testimony is linked with other pieces of evidence:

Declining Worldwide Elephant Population

We desperately need to do something or we will soon see the complete elimination of elephants in the world. Curtis Bohlen, who is senior vice-president of the World Wildlife Federation, recently stated that "poachers are now killing off elephants at a faster rate than they are reproducing." This dwindling population is clearly seen when we begin to realize that the elephant population has gone from 1.3 million in 1979 to around 600,000 in 1995.

AIDS

Dr. David Baltimore, a Nobel prize–winning biochemist at MIT, put it bluntly. "AIDS is a problem for everyone—gay and straight, urban and rural. We are at a critical point in the progress of the epidemic, and we are quite honestly frightened by the future prospects." Frightened is indeed the right word when you think that by 1995, 270,000 Americans will have been diagnosed as having AIDS, the death toll will have risen by 54,000 a year, and the virus, in all probability, will have spread to between 5 million and 10 million persons. How many of those 5 million to 10 million Americans will eventually die of AIDS? Perhaps half—but no one really knows.

In the next example, from a speech dealing with the dangers of drinking and driving, the speaker was able to move from a factual illustration, to some statistics, and then to expert testimony:

Drinking and Driving

There we were: some friends and I having a good time while driving down old Route 78. Then, without any warning, I noticed a driver coming the opposite direction in an extremely erratic manner. Within an instant, I saw the speeding car hit the guard rail, become airborne, and start veering toward our car. And that is the last thing I remember before waking up paralyzed in a hospital bed, paralyzed for life because of the intoxicated driver that happened to be on old Route 78 the same night I was there with my friends. But I am, of course, lucky to be alive. Last year alone, drunk drivers killed twenty-seven hundred young people between the ages of fifteen and nineteen. As Dr. Kenneth Lyons Jones of the University Medical Center noted, "Our young people are being killed by drunk drivers at an alarming rate."

Expert testimony can be used to support and clarify informative as well as persuasive material. In the following example, from a speech about the possible link between alcoholism and genetics, a speaker used testimony to inform the audience of the validity of this assertion:

Dr. David Cendelsom, professor of psychiatry at Harvard University, noted there is now mounting research to bolster the claim that children of alcoholics inherit certain physiological traits that may indicate a tendency toward alcoholism.

On most occasions the audience may not be familiar with the person you are using as expert testimony. This is why in all of the examples we offered in this section we made certain the speaker's credentials were offered as part of the evidence. It is not enough to say that "Dr. Harrington stated that the number one cause of skin cancer is overexposure to the sun." You must say, "Dr. Harrington, Head of the Dermatology Department at State University Medical Center, and the author of the book *Skin Cancer: Causes and Cures*, stated that the number one cause of skin cancer is overexposure to the sun."

When using testimony, you must guard against confusing lay opinion with that of an expert. Over two thousand years ago, the Roman playwright Terence warned that "there are as many opinions as there are people." Testing the authority of your expert is not the only guideline to follow when using testimony. Let us look at some other rules you should try to adhere to when using this form of support.

1. *Cite complete sources when using testimony.* Let the listeners know where you found your evidence, whether in a magazine, book, newspaper, television program, or personal interview. You will increase your personal credibility, as well as the credibility of your sources, if you say, "According to the Sunday, January 15, 1995, issue of the *New York Times*, the Supreme Court, after reviewing obscene material from the Internet case in Florida, concluded that. . . ."

2. *Select experts who will carry considerable weight with your audience.* In all circumstances, you should establish the person's credibility and explain to your audience why he or she is an expert. That is, make it clear to your listeners that this particular person should be respected. The audience's acceptance of the expert will go a long way toward proving your point. A college professor may teach eighteenth-century English literature, but this does not qualify him or her as an expert in economic affairs. There is also a common tendency for many speakers to equate expert testimony with testimonial. For instance, Bill Cosby may be a good comedian, but that does not qualify him as an expert on tooth decay.

3. *Do not try to memorize your quotations.* By reading your quotations directly, you can assure accuracy and avoid forgetting parts of them. Reading small portions of your speech, such as some of your evidence, will offer your audience a change of pace. Furthermore, the act of reading a particular quotation will enhance its credibility. A small card, if handled correctly, will not detract from your speech.

4. *Testimony should be relevant to the point being discussed.* Speakers often cite an authority to prove a position but, on closer examination, listeners discover that the expert is talking about another problem. Imagine how ineffective it would be if you were talking about mental health and quoted this testimony, "There are a great many people in hospitals today who would not be there if they were not rushing to keep an appointment." On some occasions, you might find it helpful to explain the relevance of a piece of testimony in your own words. You could say, "Police Chief Jones is telling us that. . . ."

5. *Whenever possible, use brief quotations.* Long quotations are often quite difficult to follow and may hinder the audience's concentration. Even when paraphrasing, you should aim at brevity.

6. *Carefully attend to the means of introducing quotations.* Lead-ins, such as "In a speech last week the Secretary of State noted" and "So we see, as Professor Jones pointed out, that overpopulation and food shortages present serious problems" can help hold the audience's attention and, at the same time, reveal the source of the quotation and when it originated.

7. *Indicate the beginning and end of any quotation so that the audience will be able to distinguish your opinions from those of the expert you are quoting.* However, avoid the all-too-common practice of saying "quote" and "unquote." A change of voice, a pause, a move, or a certain phrase can better indicate the beginning and end of a quotation.

8. *When reading lengthy testimony, maintain eye contact.* On occasions when you must read to your audience, do not let your notes become more important than your listeners. This advice applies not only to reading testimony but to reading any material, whether it is a quotation, a set of statistics, or an example.

On occasions when you must read to your audience, do not let your notes become more important than your audience.

Analogy

All of us, whether in everyday conversation or on the public platform, use analogies to help explain and/or prove our points. Analogies are not only popular, but they can also be powerful. The English writer James Colton alluded to this power when he wrote, "The analogy, although it is not infallible, is yet that telescope of the mind by which it is marvelously assisted in the discovery of both physical and moral truth." We are using analogy when we ask someone to compare one idea or item to another. In trying to make our ideas clear, interesting, and compelling, we suggest that A "resembles," "is similar to," or "is not as good as" item B. By using comparisons we try to support our main thesis and explain our principal ideas. For example, when a contemporary tennis champion says, "Trying to run my business affairs without a Silver-Reed computer would be like trying to win Wimbledon without my tennis racket," she is making a point by using analogy—comparing the known (the importance of a tennis racket) to the unknown (the importance of Silver-Reed computers).

Comparison frequently takes the form of analogy. In an **analogy,** *similarities are pointed out in regard to persons, ideas, experiences, projects, institutions, or data, and conclusions are drawn on the basis of those similarities.* Because analogies compare the unknown to the known, people find them easy to relate to. As Freud once remarked, "Analogies, it is true, often decide nothing, but they can make one feel more at home." Think of how much more "at home" we feel if someone is trying to explain the European game of rugby by comparing it to the American game of football.

As just indicated, the main function of an analogy is to point out the similarities between what is already known, understood, or believed and something that is not. For example, trying to make the point that the requirements for securing a marriage license are deficient, a speaker offered the following analogy comparing the known to the point she was trying to make: "Why is it we place more demands on securing a license to drive than we do on obtaining a license to get married?" Using this technique as support or clarification, you show the listener that what he or she already believes or knows (that it is easy to get a driver's license) is similar to what you are trying to prove or explain. For example, if you suggest that it is dangerous to drive while intoxicated, you might offer the following analogy:

> We all know that driving a car at high speed during a foggy night is dangerous because of our impaired vision [known]. The same can be said of those who try to drive after consuming alcoholic beverages, for their vision is also obscured and their life is in peril [unknown].

In arguing that a baseball players' strike against the owners of the teams is detrimental to both parties, a speaker could use an analogy in the following manner: "Let us not have another baseball players' strike. What we learned from the last strike was that it resembled a war that neither side could win. Both factions suffered heavy losses in dollars, fan support, and credibility."

A speaker recently used an analogy to gain acceptance for a proposal that would forbid children under the age of twelve from riding three-wheel off-road vehicles: "We don't let children play with real guns because they are dangerous, yet we have allowed 559 children to die since 1985 because we have let them play with three-wheel off-road vehicles."

Another speaker, trying to make the point that nurses are underpaid, made effective use of analogy by suggesting that a nurse makes in one year what some rock stars earn in the time it takes to sing two songs at a rock concert.

Analogies are divided into two types, **figurative** and **literal.** *Figurative analogies compare things of different classes,* such as the workings of a college library with the workings of the human circulatory system, smoking cigarettes to drinking poison, not wearing a helmet when driving a motorcycle to deep sea diving without oxygen tanks, growing teenage violence to cancer, or the theory of airplanes with the flight of birds. To say that writing a term paper is like learning to swim, because both have certain basic rules that are difficult at first and get easier with time, would be an example of a figurative analogy. A speaker comparing the growth of the number of millionaires in the United States with the growth of McDonald's fast-food outlets, would also be using a figurative analogy. Figurative analogies are generally creative, vivid, and often interesting, but, because they do not contain statistics or other facts, they often have limited value as proof when they are not used with other forms of support.

Much more useful and valid is a *literal analogy, whereby you compare items, ideas, institutions, persons, projects, data, or experiences of the same class.* You might compare one instructor and another, one political creed and another, one city and another, similar historical events, or similar athletic teams. On the basis of the similarities, you build a theorem. You reason that, if two or more things of the same class contain identical or nearly identical characteristics, certain conclusions that are true in one case may also be true in the other(s). For example, Winston Churchill used a literal analogy when he compared the turning point of the Civil War to what he believed to be the turning point in World War II.

Again, we remind you that, when using literal analogies, it is the similarities of the ideas being discussed that gives the literal analogy its persuasive influence. A speaker recently made effective use of a literal analogy when she spoke to the Board of Supervisors about flooding in her community. Notice her strong use of comparison.

> Our city, just like El Cajon, suffers from dangerous flooding each time there are heavy rains. El Cajon recently solved this problem by rechanneling the water that flows from Sutherland Dam. We should do the same thing.

In a speech dealing with the unfair treatment of people suffering from AIDS, a speaker made effective use of a literal analogy with the following comparison:

> A hundred years ago, people with leprosy were sent off to remote islands and treated in the most inhuman manner. There was a prevailing belief, later proved wrong, that the general population would all contract leprosy if it had contact with lepers. We are now acting as if people who have AIDS were lepers. More and more, we are hearing suggestions that we isolate them from the population, just as we did with lepers.

Another example can be found in a speaker trying to persuade an audience that the United Nations Charter should be obeyed by all member nations:

> We Americans take a great deal of pride in the Constitution and the Bill of Rights. We know that our country would not be as great and as strong as it is if we were to discontinue our obedience and allegiance to the laws and regulations contained in these documents. The same can be said of the United Nations Charter, for just as each of us, as individuals, must comply with the Constitution and its provisions, so must the members of the United Nations comply with its laws and rules. If the individual nations do not observe and obey the laws of the Charter of the United Nations, it will not be an effective instrument for world peace.

The comparison and similarities are obvious: we are aware of the concepts behind the Constitution (known); the speaker suggests that the same concepts are inherent in the United Nations Charter (unknown). In summary, you believe and understand one; therefore, you should believe and understand the other, for they are basically the same.

When selecting and using analogies, either figurative or literal, you need to apply the following guidelines.

1. *Do the points of likeness outweigh the points of difference?* If the differences between the essential features being compared outweigh the similarities, one can hardly establish a logical connection. If we compare a supermarket to a high school in order to make the point that each must keep its customers, we have overlooked some fundamental differences existing in the two cases.

2. Is the premise (generalization) on which the analogy is based accurate? Saying "just as a ship sinks without a captain, so will our club be destroyed without a president" is an example of a false circumstance being used as a basis for a generalization, because a ship does not necessarily sink without a captain. The premise for the entire analogy and conclusion is therefore inaccurate and invalid.

3. Is the analogy appropriate to the audience? It is important for the audience to observe clearly the likenesses and the essential characteristics of the analogy. If one-half of the comparison confuses your listeners, you may find that your analogy has hindered rather than aided your speech. It would probably be confusing to a group of high school freshmen if you were to say, "The workings of the rotary engine are much like the working of the epiglottis."

The need to concentrate on appropriateness is especially important when using analogies with people from different cultures. It may well be that the part of the analogy that you believe to be known by the audience is actually not part of their cultural experiences. A culture that does not have a concept for "window shopping" would not understand an analogy that said, "Just as we all window shop before we buy, we need to slow down before we rush into this decision." Think of how someone from a culture in which basketball is not played might have difficulty relating to the following analogy: "We all know that the more agile the player, the easier the slam dunk. The same is true of a person trying to master figure skating."

Other Forms of Verbal Support

At the beginning of this chapter, we noted that the forms of support occasionally overlap—that a factual illustration might well contain statistics. Certain other forms of support are closely related to the six already discussed. Many of these are further extensions and refinements of those just mentioned. A case in point is all the variations found in illustrations: an anecdote is an amusing story in which real-life characters are usually featured; in fables, animal characters speak and act as if they were human; and parables are fictitious stories from which a moral or religious lesson may be drawn. As you can see, all three of these are forms of illustration.

There are also forms of support, such as explanations and descriptions (which we will explain in detail in chapter 13), that serve more to clarify than to prove a point. For example, a speaker might explain in great detail the complicated role of the federal government in public welfare payments. Though this explanation might help support a premise dealing with the need for reorganizing our nation's welfare system, it does not, in and of itself, prove that there are major evils in the status quo. We shall return to some of these ancillary forms of support when we talk about informative speeches in chapter 13.

Other devices for developing and clarifying, such as restatement, repetition, and description, will also be discussed in detail in chapter 13. The important point to keep in mind is that, in most situations, it is best to use a combination of devices. For example, you may have occasion to begin by defining what you are talking about even before you offer an illustration of the point. You could follow this bit of evidence by quoting an expert who, in turn, cites statistics or uses an analogy. You then might move to a detailed description of the central point. What is important to remember is that any of the techniques discussed in this book should be used if they will aid in securing the desired response. The various classifications are a guide for specific occasions; the real communication situation must determine your final selection.

The Ethical Use of Evidence

In every chapter to this point in the book we have attempted to alert you to the ethical responsibilities associated with communication. As you move through the remaining chapters, you will see how this important topic reemerges. Our rationale, whether we are talking about the use of language (chapter 12) or appearing on television (chapter 15), is the same—when you send a message to another human being, you are gaining access to their life space and therefore influencing how they might think and act in the future. This influence demands that you consider your actions. Let us examine those actions as they apply to the ethical use of statistics and testimony.

The Ethical Use of Statistics

Statistics can have a telling effect on an audience. Unfortunately, as we noted earlier, statistics are highly susceptible to error and abuse. An ethical and conscientious speaker, as well as a critical and careful listener, must be willing to apply certain criteria to the statistics they confront.

1. *Are the units being compared actually comparable?* It may be said that Los Angeles has twenty-five hundred more crimes than does Dallas, but, if Los Angeles counts *all* crime and Dallas counts *only crimes against people and not those against property*, the statistics are unreliable. In addition, the city of Los Angeles may have a population of four million, while Dallas has only one million residents. In both of these cases, the units are not comparable. To present them as being equivalent would be an unethical act.

2. *Do the statistics cover a sufficient number of cases?* A statement that 50 percent of the voters polled favored Proposition II would be quite misleading if only ten people out of forty thousand were asked their opinion.

3. *Do the statistics cover a sufficient period of time?* There are two considerations in applying this test. First, if one is going to talk about the high cost of foreign aid, one must give current statistics. The foreign aid bill changes each year, and what was valid five years ago is likely to be outdated today. Second, if you wish to draw conclusions from your data, you must be sure that the period covered is not exceptional. The flow of mail in December, unemployment figures related to seasonal companies, and traffic after a football game are obviously exceptional cases.

4. *Were the gatherers of the statistics strongly interested in the outcome?* Whenever you gather and analyze evidence, it is crucial that you examine the biases and attitudes found within the special groups that originally compiled the data. For example, if you were considering the problems associated with the cutting down of the California redwoods, you might find different results whether you approached the lumber industry or the Sierra Club. In these instances, the speaker should consider as many different sources as possible and try to locate a neutral source. Napoleon once remarked, "Neutrality consists of having the same weights and measures for each."

The Ethical Use of Testimony

In using and listening to testimony, remember that an expert's opinion may not be based on concrete and comprehensive data. There are some safeguards and ethical considerations you should observe whenever you use expert testimony:

1. *Is the person an unbiased observer?* Objectivity is essential if we are to respect and believe the testimony of an expert. The chairperson of the Republican National

Committee would hardly be qualified to give an objective account of a Democratic president's term in office. Nor could a chemist for a chemical company offer unbiased testimony on the need to destroy the sawtoothed grain beetle to preserve U.S. food crops.

2. *Is the reference to authority specific?* Quotations such as "according to an eminent authority" or "an expert in the field concluded" are vague and misleading. The audience should know exactly who is being quoted and why he or she was selected.

3. *When and where was the opinion expressed?* Statistics, theories, and findings are soon outdated. What an expert said in 1986 may not accurately express his or her views today. In addition, the place where a statement is made may well influence what is said. The Secretary of Labor might state one view at the Teamsters' convention and expound another position, on the same theme, before the Chamber of Commerce.

4. *Have you accurately recorded and presented the statements of the expert?* This current ethical objective is actually rather self-evident. That is to say, it is obvious that to misquote someone, on purpose, is unprincipled and unethical. How would you like to be told that Dr. Jones said that "smoking during pregnancy is not dangerous," when, in reality, Dr. Jones never uttered those words?

5. *Are you confusing expert testimony with lay testimonials?* In this era of mass communication, we are often confronted with famous celebrities being presented as experts. Someone who has a successful situation comedy on television may not be qualified to evaluate and comment on the health benefits of ice cream.

When to Use Verbal Support

Determining when the various forms of support are needed is no easy task. Every audience, occasion, and topic has special demands that make each communication encounter a unique and dynamic experience. There are, however, basic questions to ask when you are trying to decide where and when you should use support.

1. *Are you making a statement that will be accepted as true simply because you assert it?* For example, if you want to convince an audience that educational benefits for veterans should be increased, you must do more than say, "The meager grants now awarded under the GI Bill are so small that many veterans cannot attend college." Any intelligent listener would respond by saying, "What do you mean?" or "How do you know this is true?" You should use forms of support when you are making a statement that needs substantiation as a means of establishing its authenticity, believability, and plausibility.

2. *How much substantiation is needed?* There is no simple formula for deciding how much support any assertion will require. In most instances, you will have to depend on your own good judgment and common sense. View the assertion or statement from the perspective of your audience. Your audience analysis will let you see things from the listeners' point of view. Ask yourself this question: "Would I need and demand proof for the opinions being expressed?" Most audiences would accept the contention that a college education is useful, but they would be skeptical, and demand support, if you were to say, "The President's health plan is not costly."

3. *Are you making a statement that requires no further clarification?* We have already mentioned the need to ask if an idea needs proof; now the issue is one of clarity. As pointed out earlier, the forms of support are often used for clarification as well as for proof. Ask yourself, Is my idea clear? If the answer is no, support is needed. If you were to say, "There is often a stigma attached to persons who have been mentally ill," you would run the risk of the audience not knowing what you mean. However, you could clarify your point with an illustration about someone who has been stigmatized because of confinement in an institution.

4. *Are you making statements that might be attacked or refuted by other speakers?* Evidence tends to operate as a neutralizing agent. If someone offers evidence, and you do not, the other person is more apt to be believed. However, if during your speech you buttress your arguments with proof, it will minimize the impact of the evidence your rival offers.

How to Use Verbal Support

Nearly every speaker faces the problem of trying to decide what to do with the material he or she has gathered as part of the preparation process; learning how to use your supporting material takes practice and experience. Each time you give a speech, you will find that integrating your supports into your speech becomes smoother and easier. There are, however, some specific techniques that you can use. Many of these were mentioned earlier with some advice following each of the forms of support. However, a few of these suggestions warrant reexamination.

Direct Quotations and Paraphrases

First, *there will be times when, because of the nature of the evidence, you will want to present it as a direct quotation.* This is usually the case with statistics and expert testimony. In fact, your credibility is enhanced and the impact of the statistics or testimony is often greater when you present it in its original form. In offering testimony about the dangers of freebasing cocaine, a speaker might use a direct quotation in the following manner: "Dr. George R. Gray, director of emergency medicine at San Francisco's Haight-Ashbury Free Medical Clinic, said, 'Freebasing is like putting your finger in an electric socket. It can only lead to your eventual collapse.'"

Second, *there will be times when the technique of paraphrasing may be appropriate.* When you paraphrase, you restate a passage in your own words. This restatement often helps clarify as well as support an assertion. It is not so much a summary of what has been said as it is a recasting of the original passage into a style that is more suited to the speaker and the audience. For example, notice the difference in style between the original source and the speaker's paraphrase:

Original: Although cocaine is not a leading cause of drug-related deaths, in a number of cities, including San Diego, San Francisco, and New York, it is now the fastest-growing source of serious drug-related medical problems, according to epidemiologists for the National Institute on Drug Abuse, who met last week in Washington.

Paraphrase: The increase in the number of deaths by cocaine is a serious matter. Although it is not yet the leading cause of drug-related deaths, epidemiologists for the National Institute of Drug Abuse say it is now the fastest-growing source of serious drug-related problems.

Original: The number of women inmates has almost tripled in the past 10 years. In 1985, there were 12,000 women behind bars, 20,000 in 1990, 28,000 in 1992, and 40,000 in 1995.

Paraphrase: From 1985 to 1995, the number of women inmates more than
                     tripled from 12,000 to 40,000.

You will recall from the previous chapter the importance of paraphrasing as it relates to listening and culture. We once again examine this idea, but this time in the context of asking your audience to understand the evidence you are offering. If your listeners, because of language problems, fail to interpret your evidence correctly, you will not
accomplish your purpose. Hence, the need to paraphrase takes on added significance
when the listeners have English as their second language.

Transitions

*The correct use of transitions, which can be words, phrases, or sentences, is an essential in-
gredient in the correct use of evidence.* Transitions serve several functions. Primarily, they
provide your speech with a smooth flow as you move from idea to idea. As we shall see
when we discuss the speech to inform (chapter 13), transitions make it easier for your
audience to remember key ideas. When used with evidence, they show relationships between your ideas and your evidence. Transitions tell listeners you have completed one
thought or piece of evidence and are about to move on to something else. ("Having
spent the past few minutes talking about why college tuitions have been rising, we are
now ready to discuss what we can do about this problem.")

Transitions can also link together several items of support. ("There are other statistics that support the danger of passive smoke to one's health. Let us look at some of
them.") They can lead the audience from one point to another. ("We have seen what
the experts say about the dangers of passive smoke. Let us look at other evidence to substantiate their claims.") Notice in the examples thus far that the transition stated both
the idea the speaker was finishing and the one that he or she was about to treat next.

A good transition can also highlight the importance of a specific piece of evidence while moving the audience on to other evidence. For example, after presenting
a factual illustration, statistics, and testimony, a speaker used the following transition
for both emphasis and clarity:

Mr. Miller's sad experience with escalating nursing home care costs is not an
isolated case. The number of uninsured elderly suffering the same fate as Mr. Miller
grew from 25 million ten years ago to about 37 million in 1990. And, according to
Mr. Fazlur Rahman, chief of hematology and oncology at Angelo Community
Hospital in San Angelo, Texas, the problem is only going to get worse.

There are some occasions when the transition takes the form of a single word or
phrase. Some of the more common words and phrases appear in the following list:

in other words	moreover
in addition	for example
therefore	thus
finally	consequently
on the other hand	to be more specific
for instance	to illustrate this point

As you have observed, transitions can take a variety of forms. Let us look at a few
additional types of transitions so that you can introduce your point and move from one
piece of evidence to another.

Bridging, perhaps one of the most common transitions used in public speaking, directs your audience from what you are talking about at the moment to what you want to treat next. For example, if you have been talking about the widespread nature of crime in the United States and were now ready to offer some specific statistics to substantiate your assertion, you might introduce your statistics in the following manner:

> There are simply too many criminals in the United States. Let me show you what I mean. The best estimates suggest that 36 million to 40 million people, or 16 to 18 percent of the population, have arrest records for nontraffic offenses.

If you wanted to add to this idea, another bridge could be used:

> The statistics I just shared with you tell only part of the story. They don't tell us just how many criminals we have already identified. For example, we currently have 2.4 million people under correctional supervision, 412,000 of them locked away in cells.

Signposting is also an effective transitional tool. Not only does signposting enable you to direct the audience's attention to the point immediately ahead, but it also allows you to preview what lies beyond. In the next example, notice the twin functions of signposting:

> Let me offer you some evidence showing just how much crime costs us in the United States. Then we can discuss what to do about this problem.

Good speakers can use signposting as a way of reminding their audience of a number of points at the same time. In the following example, the transition reviews what has been accomplished and highlights what is to come:

> So far, we have seen how easy access to handguns causes needless accidents among children and increases the rate of murder, and handguns are used in most suicides. Now let us spend some time talking about why these handguns are so easy to secure. Once we have done that, we can examine some solutions to this serious problem.

There are many occasions when signposts simply take the form of numerical indicators. For example, if you are talking about the fact that Iran might be a major trouble spot in the near future, you could use signposting in the following manner as you move from point to point:

> Today I want to talk about four reasons why I believe Iran might represent a major conflict area for the United States. First, Iran continues to support terrorism throughout the Middle East. Recently, Iran . . . Second, Iran is actively supporting Islamic revolutions that are highly anti-American. For example, the leaders of Jordan and Egypt are both saying . . . Third, Iran is working to undermine the Arab-Israeli peace process. Last week, for instance, . . .
>
> Finally, Iran continues to arm itself at an ever increasing rate. In the past two years, Iran has spent an estimated . . .

Before we move on to other transitional devices, let us briefly summarize some words and phrases that can be used as signposts:

first	finally
second	in conclusion
one	next
let's now look at	in overview
lastly	in closing
to reiterate	in review

Spotlighting is a transitional device that actually serves two purposes. First, like all transitions, it tells the audience that you are moving on to another idea or piece of evidence. In addition, it signals the audience that what is coming next is important. Notice in the examples that follow how the speaker alerted his or her listeners that something significant is about to be talked about.

- I would urge you to think about this if you were to remember only one idea of this talk.
- We now arrive at the most meaningful part of this speech.
- I am now going to explain the single most important element in this entire debate.
- The most significant thing I can tell you about this new proposal is that . . .

Transitions can be nonverbal as well as verbal. Leaning forward, smiling, pausing, and moving in one direction or another all signal to the audience that a new idea or form of support is about to be introduced.

Finally, *there may be times when you simply want to summarize your supporting materials.* We talked earlier about how statistics serve as a kind of summary of facts. In a sense, specific instances also constitute a type of abridgment. In both cases, you are eliminating some of the detail for the sake of time and clarity. The value of a good, concise summary may be seen in the following comparison:

Original source:	There are a great number of inmates on death row, waiting for the courts to decide their fate. For example, Florida has 294 prisoners on death row, Texas has 283, California 247, Illinois 120, Pennsylvania 115, and Georgia 102.
Summary:	There are 1,161 prisoners on death row in the five states that have the largest number of inmates awaiting the results of various court decisions.

When we talk about summaries, we are referring to two different types of summaries—initial summaries (previews), and internal summaries (running). Although all of these devices will be discussed in detail during the chapter on informing (chapter 13), we introduce them now so that you might be able to use them as you present your evidence to the audience.

Initial summaries are useful when you are about to introduce a series of forms of support.

So that you will fully understand just how serious the problem of air safety actually is, I will begin by offering you the views of experts in this area and, second, share with you some startling statistics that will substantiate their concerns.

Internal summaries, when used as transitions, move the audience from a set idea or piece of evidence to a new point.

Visual aids are a useful means of supporting, explaining, and proving an idea.

Having seen what the experts believe about air safety, and how their views are supported by the facts, we are now ready to talk about what can done about this problem.

Because transitions are such an important tool, we will also discuss them elsewhere in the book. For now, however, make abundant use of them as you move your audience from one piece of evidence to another and from one point to another.

Visual Support

The importance and use of visual aids will be the subject of the next chapter. However, because visual aids are a useful means of supporting and proving an idea, a principle, or a concept, we need to discuss them briefly at this time. By seeing what is talked about, the listener brings still another of his or her senses into play. In trying to convince a judge that a stop sign was blocked from view by a large tree, a lawyer brought forth a photograph. On seeing the picture, the judge ruled the defendant could not have seen the sign from his car. The old adage "seeing is believing" made the point both real and believable. By using a chart, a model, a graphic, a demonstration, or an exhibit, you prove the assertion you are advancing. In addition, statistics that are detailed and confusing can be clarified and reinforced by a graph, table, or poster that highlights the main features. Notice how "seeing" the following statistics reinforces the assertion that sex education is needed in public schools:

IN ONE DAY

2,753 TEENAGERS GET PREGNANT

1,099 TEENAGERS HAVE ABORTIONS

367 TEENAGERS MISCARRY

1,287 TEENAGERS WHO ARE NOT MARRIED GIVE BIRTH

As you can see in this example, visualizing the statistics adds to the persuasiveness of the idea. Visual support is also useful when you are speaking to an audience of mixed cultural backgrounds that might have English as a second language. Comprehension and persuasion are enhanced when the audience can see as well as hear your important points. Therefore, do not hesitate to use visual support to aid your cause.

The Role of Culture in the Use of Evidence

You must also take your audience into consideration when deciding how and when to use your evidence. It should not surprise you that there are cultural variations regarding the selection of forms of support. For example, cultures such as the Latin, Arab, and African favor illustrations and stories over "facts," while most Germans, North Americans, and English demand statistics and the advice of experts if they are to be persuaded. There are even cultural differences as to who can be called an "expert." In one culture, it might be an elderly person; in another culture, it could be someone with impressive professional credentials. In short, a full audience analysis is needed before you decide on what evidence you will cite and how you will use it.

Summary

In this chapter, we were concerned with the topic of evidence, more specifically, the devices we use to support and clarify assertions and observations. The forms of support we examined were factual illustrations, hypothetical illustrations, specific instances, statistics, testimony, analogy, and visual support. We indicated that you need to be concerned with the ethical issues involved in evaluating, presenting, and listening to the various forms of support.

This chapter also offered advice as to when and how to use evidence. Techniques such as using direct quotations, paraphrasing, and transitions were discussed. It was noted that the most effective transitions take the form of bridging, signposting, spotlighting, nonverbal actions, and summarizing.

We concluded the chapter by alerting you to the role of culture in the use of evidence.

Chapter 7

Visual Aids
Displaying Your Ideas

Our sight is the
most perfect and most
delightful of
all our senses.

Joseph Addison

Our ears are less accurate than our eyes.

Greek proverb

Ask yourself this simple question: Why do most of us enjoy going to the movies, watching television, going to sporting events, and playing computer games? The answer is obvious—we are all captivated by what our eyes behold. We are drawn to movement. This chapter is about how you can use the audience's desire to see as well as hear to help you accomplish your purpose.

The value of visual aids to speech making cannot be overstated. Although they might be trite phrases, there is some truth to the expressions "seeing is believing" and "one picture is worth a thousand words." Like all cultures, ours encourages both visual and oral expression. As we indicated in the first paragraph, we all grow up seeing films, attending to our television sets, enjoying video games, watching music videos, and moving a little mouse from one icon to another. All of these action-oriented messages are successful because they have something happening besides words. Today, more than ever before, audiences expect speakers to use more than just verbal messages. Because of this requirement, public speakers should include visual aids in their presentations whenever they are appropriate.

Importance of Visual Aids

Utilizing visual aids during your talk can help you in a variety of ways. First, they can assist the audience with both *memory and recall*. When people *see* as well as hear the message, there is a much better chance that they will remember the point being made. By some estimates we retain only 20 percent of what we hear, yet when hearing is combined with seeing, the percentage jumps to nearly 50 percent. If you were talking about the early Plains Indians of North America, and put the names ARAPAHO, ARIKARA, CHEYENNE, HIDATSA, MANDAN, and PAWNEE on a large poster, it would assist the audience in retaining the information.

In chapter 6, you saw the value of visual aids as a *means of support*. We noted how visual aids can make an idea concrete and persuasive. A picture of a child as a victim of a drunk driver has a greater impact than the citing of statistics on the same subject. Think of how you could support your assertion about the increased number of deaths due to handguns if you had a bar graph depicting the steep rise in deaths over the past five years.

Visual aids can also *simplify complex material*. The word *larynx* might be unfamiliar to the listeners, but a model or diagram can offer a definition of the term. A common principle of learning maintains that it is worthwhile to use as many physical senses as possible: the more sensory associations one has with an idea, the better are one's chances of remembering the idea. Seeing a video, even one you have made yourself, of the pollution of a local lake would make the image much clearer than simply hearing about the filth in the water. Consider how the complex boundaries and borders of the Middle East could be made less confusing by looking at a large map, instead of trying to describe the territorial lines only with words.

A speaker's *organization can also be enhanced* by visual aids. Having a poster that lists the proper sequence in changing the oil in a car will allow your audience to see as well as hear the steps involved.

The English author Samuel Johnson once wrote that "The true art of memory is the art of attention." This advice certainly applies to the use of visual aids, because they help memory by arousing and maintaining *attention and interest.* Although we will discuss interest and attention in many other chapters, let us now mention how the use of visual aids can gain and maintain that attention. A pretty picture, a shiny object, or a drawing provides listeners with an object on which to focus their attention, and they are usually anxious to hear what the speaker has to say about it. In a speech on water pollution, you might display a graphic example by showing a large photo of trash and other foreign matter found in a local stream. This vivid illustration of the problem would certainly get attention, focus interest, and make your speech more dynamic.

There are a number of *psychophysical* reasons that make visual aids so compelling. These factors deal with the interplay between psychological processes and physical stimuli. A brief examination of these optical attention factors might help you decide which aids to select.

As you know from experience, colorful lights and brilliant colors almost demand that you look at them. When you consider the concept of *intensity* when you choose your visual aids, you enhance the chances that your listeners will pay attention. A chart showing the projected rise in the number of Alzheimer's disease cases will take on added meaning if you can demonstrate that increase with a bright red graph that is moving in an upward flow. Think of the impact if you say, "We need to do something about this disease. Roughly 4 million Americans have it today, but that number is projected to grow to 14 million by 2050," while you are pointing to the bold red line that is making the same point.

Contrast is yet another visual device that arouses attention. Try to use aids with a variety of patterns, shapes, colors, and the like. Imagine how clear and compelling your comments about the debris found on the beach would be if, while making this point, you were to place an assortment of this trash on a clean table.

The use of visual aids not only helps with retention persuasion, clarity, and interest but it can add to your *personal credibility.* Listeners will think well of you if you have taken the time to present a professionally prepared learning aid. Clearly, visual aids have a positive effect on the entire communication process.

Finally, visual aids are *useful when speaking to people from cultures different from your own.* The most obvious advantage would be for those who have English as a second language. Seeing what you are talking about would help them understand a concept that is not verbally clear. For example, it might be easier for listeners from China to comprehend a speech on changes in American fashions if they could see pictures of the clothes being discussed instead of only hearing words such as apparel, garments, and accoutrements. There are also cultures whose members are very cautious and deliberate in making decisions. They demand more proof than do North Americans. There is even an Ashanti proverb that notes, "No one should test the depth of a river with both feet." For the prudent members of the audience, regardless of their culture, a visual aid offers additional proof and clarification.

Choosing the Appropriate Aid

In the next section of this chapter, we will discuss the many visual aids that you can use to assist you in your efforts. However, before we examine a register of visual aids, it might be useful to look at some general guidelines to apply when deciding what aid would be most appropriate for your presentation.

First, ask yourself, *What is the purpose of my speech?* The supporting materials you would select for a persuasive speech differ from those you would choose for an informative talk. The same rule applies when considering which visual aids to use. If your aim is to entertain, you might use posters that show whimsical cartoon characters depicting key points. This design, however, would be inappropriate for a speech on the plight of the homeless living in your city. As our examples should demonstrate, in most instances, choosing the most appropriate medium is usually a matter of common sense.

Second, *audience size influences the visual aid you eventually select.* If you were to speak to one hundred people in a large auditorium, they would have a difficult time seeing photographs or flip charts. You would need to adapt to the size of the audience and thus would most likely use overhead transparencies, slides, or other devices that can be enlarged and projected over a long distance. Here again, common sense is your best advisor in matters of audience appropriateness.

Third, *issues such as time, money, and the availability of certain equipment also affect your decision as to which aid to use.* For example, slides take a few days to develop and can be expensive, and certain types of transparencies require special equipment. In short, try to select the medium through which you can produce the best visual aid with the resources at your disposal.

Finally, remember to *think about your audience* when selecting your visual aid. A group of young children you are trying to persuade not to start smoking would not be influenced by a graph showing the rise in teenage smoking. Yet a comical poster containing an easy to remember slogan would facilitate your cause. As we have emphasized throughout this book, try to put yourself in the place of your listeners—even if they are from another generation or culture. Ask yourself: Who are they? What are they interested in? How much do they know about this topic? All of these questions will help you select the appropriate aid.

Nonelectronic Visual Aids

The American philosopher George Santayana once noted that "Imagination is infinite." Although he was obviously not talking about visual aids, he was reminding us that our use and selection of aids is limited only by our imagination. Hence, we urge you to be creative as you adapt the aids we discuss to your particular speech. As you read through our list, keep in mind that, although we will examine each type of aid one at a time, you will usually find them most effective when used in combination. That is to say, if you are trying to explain how to tune up a car, you are well advised to show the tools and replacement parts needed. In addition, a poster showing the engine would be helpful, so the audience can see where the various parts are located. If your purpose is persuasive—you want to convince your audience to vote for placing a new traffic signal at a dangerous intersection—you could present a chart that shows statistically how the number of accidents has increased on this corner. You could also present your own videotape showing how hectic traffic is at peak hours. Let us now examine some of the visual aids that you should learn to use as you try to let others know what you think and how you feel.

Although it might appear somewhat obvious, we will begin with an often overlooked visual aid—**people.** As the main focus of your talk, you are automatically adding a visual dimension to the presentation. You can turn that visual capacity to your advantage by demonstrating various points by using your own body. For example, if you are talking about the correct tennis stroke to hit a "slice," you could demonstrate the correct movements by swinging the racket yourself. If you are discussing the proper attire for backpacking, you can even wear that apparel.

> **People**

You can also ask someone else to serve as a visual aid. To demonstrate the correct way to carry out artificial respiration, you might ask a friend to role-play a person having breathing problems. If you are trying to inform people about water safety, you might have someone lie on a table so you can demonstrate the correct form for holding a victim while swimming to shore. Usually it is not a good idea to call on a volunteer from the audience unless you have contacted the person in advance. You might find that a spontaneous volunteer is unpredictable. The volunteer might be nervous or even try to become "the star of the show."

Reality is usually more compelling than a mere representation of that reality. An **object** being talked about can be displayed to help explain an idea or a principle, while the object captures and maintains attention. For example, on a speech dealing with how to develop film, you can demonstrate with the objects that are actually involved in the developing process. An audience can better understand the process if it could see all of the essential articles such as trays and solutions. Similarly, an audience can better understand a speech on football protective gear if it can view a football player's shoulder pads, hip pads, and helmet. Effective communicators are not satisfied to talk about an idea; they want the listeners to see the object in question. A dog by your side when talking about obedience training, flowers when explaining flower arrangements, rocks when demonstrating gem polishing, and a knife and block of wood when instructing how to carve are all useful in helping you accomplish your purpose.

> **Objects, Specimens, and Models**

On some occasions, you will not be able to bring the entire object to the speech. In these instances, you will have to settle for a **specimen**—a sample of the object. A speaker who cannot show the audience an entire rock collection has to be satisfied with displaying a few chips from larger rocks. Specimens give the audience an approximation of what you want them to visualize.

Because they are facsimiles and replicas of the real thing, **models** can serve three useful purposes. First, they help explain a complex idea. For example, a three-dimensional model of the human heart could greatly simplify an explanation of this intricate organ without distorting any of the heart's main functions. Second, models can be made into any size or shape; therefore, they can be moved from place to place. You could not bring the *USS Nautilus* to class, yet seeing a disassembled model of that nuclear submarine would be helpful to any audience. Third, because models have to be constructed, the model maker can emphasize whatever aspect of the process he or she wishes. Notice in the communication model in figure 7.1 how messages and feedback are emphasized, while concepts such as encoding, decoding, and channels are not even shown. In this visual aid, the speaker was concerned with defining feedback. As you can see, the model helped demonstrate that feedback is the response the receiver makes to the sender's messages.

When selecting and using objects, specimens, and models try to keep three points in mind. First, some items should be avoided because of their potential to create a negative

Figure 7.1
Feedback Model

response. For example, live snakes or guns might make members of your audience nervous. Second, make sure you choose an aid that can be seen by everyone. We recall a student trying to demonstrate how to program a VCR by pushing actual buttons on a machine that could not be seen by all members of the class. Finally, in most instances it is not a good idea to circulate your aid throughout the audience. People are likely to find the object or specimen more entertaining than you. When we talked about listening in chapter 5, we stressed how easily people are distracted. Your aid could thus be a distraction.

Posters, Diagrams, Maps, Paintings, and Photographs

Posters are among the simplest of all visual aids to locate or construct. They can clarify and reinforce any idea or process you select. What is attractive about a poster is that it can be prepared ahead of time and tailored to your needs with very little effort, using some colored pens and poster board. Note that figures 7.2 and 7.3 show how to create posters that help the audience remember the key elements of two speeches—statistical data and a set of directions. In both instances, the speakers, one on horse racing and the other on fire prevention, are engaging the sense of sight as well as hearing.

Diagrams are like models; both attempt to explain and clarify that which is complex. However, models are three-dimensional, while diagrams are two-dimensional line forms. The blueprints for an underground watering system would be an example of a dia-

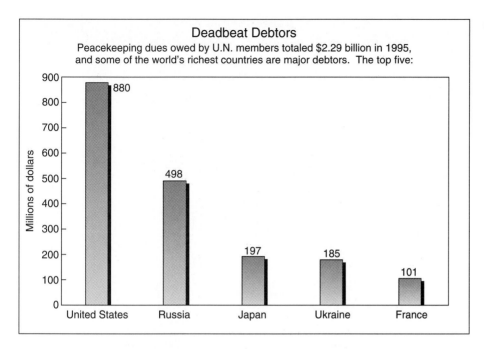

Figure 7.2
Poster

Home Fire-Prevention Plan

1. Remove rubbish from halls and closets.
2. Use appropriate containers for storing flammable materials.
3. Check electrical wiring and appliances and make needed repairs.

Figure 7.3
Poster

gram. A student used a diagram when she was talking about how to plant a vegetable garden (see figure 7.4). She used her visual aid to help demonstrate the importance of what to plant in each row and the distance needed between these rows. Her points were that some vegetables need more room than others and that some plants grow so large they would rob the sunlight from the smaller plants. Her diagram helped clarify these points.

Maps are very helpful in assisting the audience to locate various geographic points of reference. If, for example, you were giving a speech pointing out some of the reasons Israel is concerned about its security, you could display a map showing how Israel is surrounded by Egypt, Jordan, Syria, and Lebanon. The map would clearly indicate the location of these Arab countries to the borders of Israel. Availability is yet another advantage to the use of maps. In most instances, you should be able to secure a map from your local or campus library. Like books, maps can be checked out for short periods of time. The main problem in using maps is that most commercially prepared maps contain too much detail. Hence, the best maps are those you prepare specifically for your speech.

Figure 7.4
Diagram

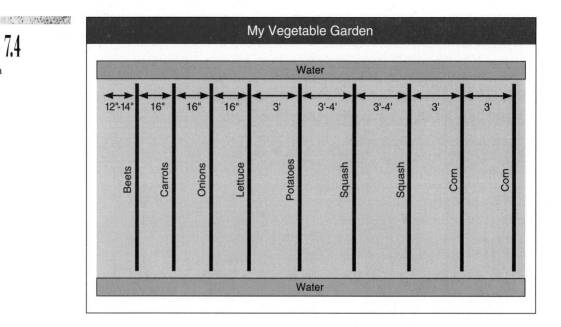

Let us offer a few guidelines to keep in mind when you are preparing a map, poster, or diagram. First, *remember to use light on dark, black and white, or bright colors*. This will not only make your aid easier to see, but it will also hold attention. Second, while it is somewhat obvious, *make sure everyone can see the map, poster, or diagram*. This means you must imagine the size of the room and the distance between the visual aid and the person in the last row. When considering the problems associated with size, you need to make sure that your important points, whether they are lettering on a map or an object on a diagram, are not too small. Third, *use a ruler or a yardstick to draw straight and neat lines*. As we have indicated, an aid that is poorly conceived and constructed will not only impede audience comprehension, but it will also lower your credibility. Finally, *if there is writing on your visual aid, you should use phrases rather than complete sentences*.

Paintings (also sketches and cartoons) are extremely helpful and are readily available to all speakers. Imagine how you could use such visual aids if you were speaking on the history of the American automobile, modern architecture, or cultural differences in the portrayal of animals in art. Paintings would make your material more compelling, interesting, and memorable.

Photographs taken by the speaker can be tailored to any speech. If you were speaking on the topic of tree identification in your community, you could take pictures of various trees, enlarge them, label them, and use them to help the audience see the distinguishing characteristics of each tree. These photographs may not have been available elsewhere, but, with a camera, you can create your own visual aids.

Photographs can also be used to support a persuasive assertion. If, for example, your purpose is to persuade an audience to give money to a relief fund to help flood victims in your community, you can show pictures of the flooding and of people left homeless by the disaster. Remember that the photographs you use must be large enough to be seen by all members of the audience. Most photographs are developed

Photographs taken by the speaker can be tailored to any speech.

in sizes that are too small to meet this criterion. Therefore, long before the speech, make the necessary arrangements to have your photographs enlarged. In addition to your photographs being large enough to be seen, they should be of high technical quality. Although it might be humorous to share your efforts as an amateur photographer, pictures that are out of focus or are cluttered with unnecessary detail detract from your speech.

Recent technology has made the use of photographs, pictures, and paintings an even more attractive proposition. Through the use of color laser enlargement techniques, a small picture or photograph can be greatly amplified. For a very small fee, any copy center can amplify your photograph or picture so that the members of the audience will be able to see it.

Most of us have a difficult time comprehending numbers or abstract and complicated ideas. **Charts** and **graphs** can often help with this problem by making issues more understandable. They also have the advantage of offering a visual summary that can show both processes and relationships. Reflect for a moment on how easy it would be for an audience to see an increase in personal income taxes over the past twenty years on a graph that shows, on the horizontal axis, the years involved and, on the vertical axis, the average amount of taxes paid by each individual.

Charts and Graphs

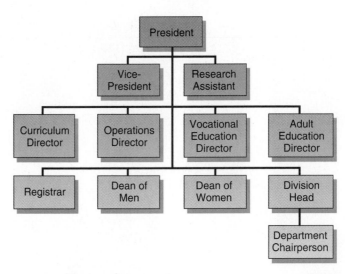

Figure 7.5
Organizational Chart

Figure 7.6
Comparison Chart

Major U.S. Weapons Systems		
Item	Estimated Cost (millions)	Number to Be Produced
F-14 Tomcat	$10,564.0	580
F-15 Eagle	12,603.4	729
F-16 Condor	13,833.3	1,730
F-18 Hornet	12,815.8	811

The four most common charts and graphs are the **organizational chart, which dis**play, by means of blocks and interconnecting lines, an organization's hierarchy of control and responsibility, as well as parts of a process (see figure 7.5); the **comparison chart,** which compares or contrasts two or more quantities, usually of a statistical nature, in terms of each other or in terms of other predetermined quantities (see figure 7.6); the **pie graph,** which is a circle divided into several "slices," each representing a classified item and its relationship to the other items (see figure 7.7); and the **bar graph** and **line graph,** which are used to represent trends and/or compare variables at fixed times (see figures 7.8 and 7.9).

Let us offer a few words of warning about using charts and graphs in speech making.

1. Many "homemade" visual aids suffer from too much clutter. Keep in mind that you will defeat the entire purpose of your chart or graph if it is not clear, simple, legible, and accurate. In short, to prevent chart and graph "overload," limit the data on the visual aid to what is absolutely necessary.

Average Day for Working College Student

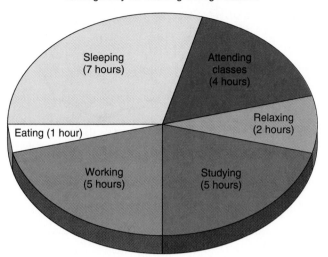

Figure 7.7
Pie Graph

Children Orphaned by AIDS

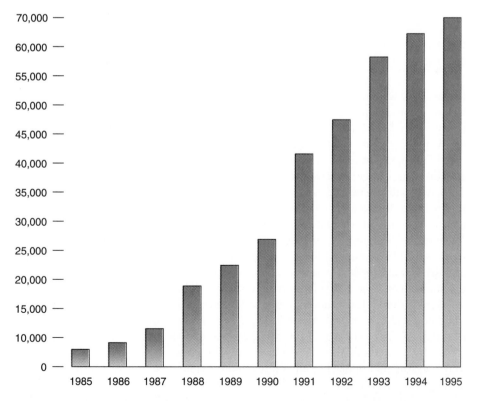

Figure 7.8
Bar Graph

Figure 7.9

Line Graph

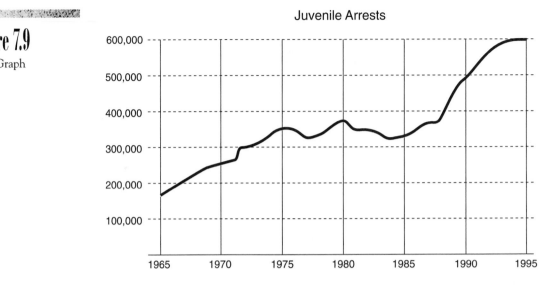

Juvenile Arrests

2. Do not put the graph or chart up without reading and/or interpreting it for the audience. We have seen speakers display elaborate charts in front of an audience and forget to talk about the material depicted on the chart.

3. Charts and graphs can often be rather dull. Whenever possible, try to use bright colors or other creative ways of showing the points you are trying to stress on the chart or graph. For example, you could show the blight of the world's rain forests by using green trees on your graph instead of numbers.

Chalk and Dry-Erase Boards

In this age of action and sophisticated technology, using **boards** might seem a rather dull type of visual aid, yet for many reasons, it can help you accomplish your communication purpose. Let us look at some of the advantages of this aid so that you can decide when and how to use chalk and dry-erase boards.

The main advantage of boards as visual aids should be obvious to anyone who has attended school: they are convenient—items can easily be added or removed at any time. They are usually found in conference rooms and auditoriums, as well as in classrooms. A conscientious speaker should check the speaking environment beforehand to be sure that a chalk or white dry-erase board will be available. One speaker very casually said, "Now let me diagram how this system will work," only to turn around to find there was no chalkboard in the room. Both the speaker and the audience were greatly embarrassed.

A second benefit of boards is that, on some occasions, a board offers an opportunity to present a step-by-step development of the process being explained. Using chalk or special pens for the white dry surface, you can add material as you go along to visually demonstrate how a ship is built from the inside to the outside. Moreover, because chalk and marking pen can be erased, you can delete certain items as a means to clarify your point.

Third, boards also let you adapt to specific and often unexpected situations. If you were speaking on the need to immunize children against life-threatening diseases, you might decide, on the spur of the moment, to turn to the board and write, "Five dollars can immunize a child against six life-threatening diseases." These words would add impact to your message and focus the listeners' attention on your main point.

Finally, boards can help facilitate movement. The act of walking to the board frees you from the constraints of the lectern.

As we have just discussed, boards are handy and helpful, but some words of advice are in order concerning their use and abuse.

1. Because it takes time to write, you need to make sure that you do not lose the audience's attention while lettering and diagramming. Therefore, *you should continue talking and maintaining eye contact while you are at the board.* If you try to overcome this problem and put your material on the board before you speak, your audience may spend more time looking at your artwork than at you.

2. Although you can use a board in a spontaneous manner, *in most instances you should plan the content and mechanics of your drawings well in advance of the presentation.* This means rehearsing with your drawings as you practice your speech. Too often, speakers have turned to the board and written something on it without thinking of its impact.

3. *Print; do not write.* Handwriting is much harder to read than standard bold print. There is nothing more frustrating to an audience than trying to decipher unreadable material. This caution also applies to your artistic abilities. Because it is so easy to pick up a piece of chalk or a marking pen, many speakers start to draw without thinking about the audience. They end up cluttering the board with marks that make very little sense to anyone but themselves.

4. If at all possible, try to secure a variety of colors when selecting chalk and marking pens. The added color will add to both clarity and interest.

Flip charts (sometimes referred to as "butcher paper"), which are large, unlined tablets, combine some of the characteristics of posters and chalkboards. Most of them are two feet wide and three feet high. They rest on an easel and are written on with broad-tipped felt pens. Because the pages can be turned, you can mark on some pages as you move through your talk. Flip charts are useful for speeches that attempt to explain a progression or process. For example, a speech describing the ten steps in learning how to draw mountains could use each page of a flip chart to demonstrate a stage of the process. You can also mark pages in advance of your talk. Regardless of how you use a flip chart, remember to leave the first page blank unless you plan on using what is showing as part of your introduction. If your listeners see a figure on a chart before you start talking, they will try to anticipate what you plan to say.

Flip Charts

Although they appear to be somewhat elementary, we need to examine a few additional guidelines for using flip charts: (1) securely attach the flip chart to the easel, (2) adjust the easel height before you start your presentation, (3) grasp the chart in the middle to flip pages so that the paper moves with ease, and (4) remember to face your audience while you are using the flip chart.

Duplicated material is another highly recommended type of visual aid for a number of reasons. They can be easily and quickly prepared, readily updated, and provide a permanent record once the speech is over. In addition, with the popularity and availability of

Duplicated Material

copy machines and computer printers, it is a rather simple matter to produce duplicated material. Handouts allow each member of the audience to have a copy of a long quotation, a diagram, a chart, or an illustration. Many business meetings and educational settings call for materials to be in the audience's hands as part of the presentation. When you want to use duplicated material (or even distribute blank sheets of paper), you may find the following suggestions profitable.

First, unless you plan to use your handout at the very start of your talk, *you should not distribute the material until you are ready to use it.* Circulated material offers listeners an easy excuse to stop listening. Second, *make sure to give each person a copy of the material.* Trying to read over someone's shoulder can confuse listeners. Third, *your material should be neat and readable.* It is of little value if your words contribute to audience comprehension but, at the same time, the printed material is distracting and perplexing. One will counteract the other, and the result may be a lack of understanding. Fourth, when using handouts, *keep talking while the listeners are looking at the material on the handout.* This will enable you to remain the focus of their attention. Fifth, *references to the handout should be very specific.* Offer comments such as "notice the shape of the bird's wing on page two; this is one reason it can fly faster than birds even twice its size."

Electronic Visual Aids

Thus far, our discussion has focused on aids that could be classified as nonelectronic media; however, there are also a number of very effective electronic devices you can use. If an electrical outlet and a screen are available, you might want to consider some of the following aids.

Slides

Although they often require elaborate preparation, many speeches can benefit from the use of slides. In recent years, because slide projectors are so easy to operate, this aid has become extremely popular within the business and professional context. Like photographs, slides can be selected for a specific purpose or product. They are also useful in that many slide projectors are equipped with remote control units that can advance the slides while the speaker stands in front of the audience or moves around the room. With this device the speaker can control the rate of speed at which the slides appear. Because slides are often colorful and change quickly, they can hold attention while informing, persuading, and entertaining. Imagine how interesting it would be to listen to a speech on how different cultures use masks while you were looking at a variety of masks being projected on the screen. Think of the persuasive impact of showing slides that allow your audience to see the plight of "homeless" dogs and cats being kept at the local animal shelter.

One of the appealing attributes of slides is that you can get them from a variety of sources: media centers, libraries, and friends. You can also take them from your personal collection. If you took pictures during a trip to China, and now want to talk about the Great Wall of China, you can use your slides to help illustrate your points and also create interest.

You should keep a few ideas in mind if you plan to use slides: (1) number and title all slides so that you can use them easily and keep them in correct order, (2) rehearse your talk while using your slides—ideally, with the same slide projector you will use during the actual presentation, (3) time your talk carefully so that you allow sufficient time for the audience to look at each slide, (4) avoid movements in front of the projector's light beam so that you will not block out the picture temporarily or cast distracting shadows on the screen, (5) design visuals for continuous viewing, and (6) if you are converting a photograph to a slide, allow sufficient time before the speech for the slide to be produced.

As is the case with all visual aids, there are a few weaknesses associated with the use of slides. First, since the room must be darkened in order to use a projector, you will obviously have a problem with eye contact. The subdued lighting might also be an invitation for some people to take a short nap. Therefore, your voice and material must remain active unless you want to turn on the lights at the end of your talk and find most of your audience fast asleep. Second, like all films and recorded material, slides are subject to a number of major and minor mechanical problems that can detract from your talk. Loss of electrical power, burned-out fuses, damaged pictures, and an extension cord that is too short are just a few potential hazards that await an unlucky communicator.

Videotape systems represent yet another audiovisual tool that has grown in popularity in recent years. There are two types of videotapes that you can use—those that are prerecorded and those you make yourself. Most college campuses and major business firms have audiovisual centers that catalog, store, and circulate thousands of prerecorded tapes. Nearly every topic has been explored on videotape. You can use these tapes to help clarify and explain various points in your speech. You will also find that many of these centers will let you borrow their equipment so that you can make your own tapes.

Videotape

Making your own videotapes represents one of the newest and most exciting phenomenons in the communication field. The equipment for producing "programs" is relatively inexpensive, lightweight, and simple to use. Because of their portability, these systems enable creative speakers to make tapes that are highly individualistic. You could, for example, take a small video camera to your community's inner city and interview alcoholics for a speech dealing with skid row. You could also make a video on cultural differences in gestures by filming people from various backgrounds engaged in communication encounters.

Most video units are easy to stop and start, so you can speak for a few minutes and then let your tape do some of the "talking" for you. You can, with the aid of a friend, even be the "star" of your own production. There is nothing that prohibits you from being on the screen and "live" in front of an audience at the same time. Think of how effective it would be if, while talking about the newest methods of water safety, you were to show a video of yourself demonstrating the correct methods of rescuing a drowning person from the ocean, a lake, and a swimming pool.

Videocassette players also contain a number of features that can contribute to both interest and learning. For example, most machines will let you replay, "freeze-frame," and use slow motion. These techniques afford you an opportunity to stress particular parts of the videotape. Just remember to rehearse a number of times if you are planning to be creative.

In the past few years, **computer graphics** have become an increasingly useful vehicle for producing visuals before a presentation. Computer graphics now supply a speaker with novel and effective means for visualizing material. These graphics are clear, readable,

Computer Graphics

Making your own videotapes represents one of the newest and most exciting phenomenons in the communication field.

and interesting. Many home computers (and virtually all business computers) have the capability of producing line graphs, bar graphs, charts, and drawings in black and white or color. What is nice about most of these graphics programs is that you do not have to be a computer genius to "run" these programs. Most models let you create and alter your graphics right on the computer screen. When you are satisfied with the results displayed on the monitor, you can print out those same lines, graphs, shapes, or very elaborate and colorful pictures. Once they are on paper, computer graphics can be displayed as easily as any traditional poster, painting, photograph, or object. In addition to constructing creative designs with computers, you can use them to enlarge both the lettering and the design material.

If you own a computer or have access to one, look into the possibilities of producing a unique kind of visual communication that will give your verbal message added clarity and attractiveness. In addition, as we have seen, using creative visual aids also contributes to your personal credibility.

When using computer graphics, you should remember the following advice:

1. Try to strike a balance between creativity and trying to be Pablo Picasso. Because some graphics programs and laser printers allow for detailed and dazzling artwork, there is a tendency on the part of some novices to get carried away. Hence, try not to add extra material simply because it looks nice yet serves no useful purpose.

2. Allow ample time to produce your graphics so that you will be able to practice with them long before you give the speech.

3. Remember, in most instances the material reproduced by the computer will not be large enough for all members of the audience to see. So again we urge you to set time aside to have your graphics enlarged at the copy center.

Transparencies and **opaque projections** are two of the most common visual aids used by speakers. The machines themselves are found in nearly every classroom or business meeting room. They are useful because what is projected onto the screen is inexpensive, easy to store, simple to make, and highly transportable. Transparencies come in a variety of colors and can even be marked on with a special pen. The basic principle behind both of these devices is simple—by enlarging an image and projecting it onto a screen, a group of people can view material that is ordinarily visible to only one person at a time.

Most campus audiovisual centers or copy centers can make transparencies for you. As we indicated, transparencies are very inexpensive and not the least bit complicated to create. The transparency itself is a thin, clear sheet of plastic, on which is an image from any book, magazine, or journal that contains material you would like your audience to see. Perhaps even more important, you can personalize your transparencies by placing your own image on the sheet of plastic. By using a felt-tip pen to write or draw on the plastic sheet, you can stress any process, idea, or concept you deem significant. Transparencies can be made in advance of your talk, or they can be constructed while you are speaking. For example, you could trace the route of an oil spill while discussing each city that was touched by the spill.

Transparencies have the added advantage of letting you face your audience as you display the visual aid. Chalkboards force you to watch what you are writing; however, you can "load" the transparency projector while you look at the audience.

Many speakers find it useful to prepare a series of transparencies. By laying one piece of plastic over another, you can give your aid an overlay image. Each overlay after the first transparency shows a different and more detailed explanation of the point being made. As each overlay is added, a concept can be made more complete, a complex process simplified, sequential stages developed, or additional information presented. Remember, whatever use you make of transparencies, they allow you to control the amount of information your audience receives at any one time. For example, in a speech dealing with acid rain, you could begin by projecting an unadorned map of the United States and then, with each additional overlay, demonstrate the severity of the problem as the map grows darker and the rain spreads.

While a transparency needs a sheet of plastic to allow light to shine through, an opaque projector displays an image printed or drawn on one side of an opaque sheet of paper. Thus, you can show clips from newspapers and magazines as well as diagrams and charts you have drawn on white paper. Most audiovisual centers have opaque projectors and will loan you one.

As is the case with all the aids we have discussed in this chapter, transparencies and opaque projections must be used with great care. If handled incorrectly, they can call attention to themselves and, therefore, reduce audience comprehension. Let us examine a few guidelines you should follow when using either one of these devices.

First, both overhead transparency and opaque projectors have the potential to make you look clumsy. It takes a few seconds to change visuals as you lift a gate and drop each new one into place. If the new insert is not positioned correctly, or the gate is not opened smoothly, the image on the screen will leap around or appear off center. Therefore, be sure that your image on the screen is level and upright. Although it may give everyone a good laugh, you will be embarrassed, for example, if your picture of the Mississippi River shows the water running east to west instead of north to south.

Transparencies and Opaque Projections

Second, too much clutter and detail on a single transparency or opaque projection will only confuse your audience. Because language is linear (you can say only one word at a time), the audience must wait for you to complete one idea before you can start another. However, your aid has the potential to include a great many items all arriving at the same time. Your visual on the Mississippi River would be very confusing if, when it was first projected on the screen, it showed major and minor ports, wildlife areas, all the streams that empty into the river, each city and town, and the main sections of pollution. In short, if there is too much for the audience to see, they will have difficulty finding the focal point.

Third, number your materials so that you will have them in order when you reach for them during your talk. It could be a very embarrassing moment if you were to say, "Perception begins with one of our senses," while your projection showed the differences between right- and left-brain responses.

Fourth, make sure your images—numbers, letters, or drawings—are large enough for everyone to see. You are showing only a projected image. If the original image is small, the projection will be small.

Fifth, as we have said elsewhere, practice your speech while using your transparencies. In this way you will be comfortable during the actual speech.

Sixth, turn the projector to "off" when you are not displaying an image. The bright light of the machine, or a picture you are no longer talking about, might well become a major distraction.

Finally, you need to keep in mind that all electronic aids have the potential to present mechanical problems. Hence, it behooves you to see that the machine is in good working order before your talk and that you know how to operate it. If it does break down during your speech, you should try to handle the "disaster" with wit and humor. Your audience will surely empathize with your situation.

Audio Aids

Although we have called this chapter "Visual Aids," we would be remiss if we did not briefly mention the role of audio in speech making. Compact disks, tapes, and records can make your material more interesting and unforgettable. If you were presenting a speech on the history of jazz, it would be extremely beneficial for the audience to hear actual examples representing each musical period. You could also use audio aids if you were giving a speech about famous American orators and wanted your listeners to hear the Martin Luther King, Jr., speech "I Have a Dream."

Preparing Visual Aids

The philosopher Thomas Fuller once wrote that "A danger foreseen is half avoided." We would add that preparing your visual aids in advance of your presentation cannot only avoid "danger," but can also add to the overall effectiveness of your speech. Hence, when you compose your aids, we would urge you to consider the following points:

1. Conduct an audience analysis for your visual aids in much the same way you would for the verbal content of your speech. Ask yourself this important question: Is this visual aid suited, in both content and form, for this audience? A visual aid that insults your audience's intelligence or one that is much too complex for their backgrounds will hinder, instead of help, your speech. It would be an affront to ask a

group of third-year computer science students to look at a diagram showing a keyboard, monitor, and printer.

2. A visual aid should help you accomplish your purpose; it should not be "window dressing" used to make your speech more attractive. It must be pertinent and serve a purpose. Many speakers, especially those preparing speeches to inform, use the occasion as an excuse to show their favorite pictures or slides. Try to avoid this fault. Remember, your aids should instruct, convince, and motivate or stimulate interest.

3. As we have discussed, be sure that the lettering, artwork, or other main features are large, clear, and of sufficient contrast for everyone in the audience to see. Too many visual aids force the audience to squint and strain as if they were reading the last line on an eye chart. The lettering should allow for sufficient spacing so each word can be easily read. The use of bold type and italics should also be employed to help with clarity and interest. The artwork should also be attractive and free of distracting elements. Most aids suffer from too much clutter, so be sure that all the important items are easy to see. Try to use color, contrasting shapes, and other techniques to keep your aids from being dull and ordinary.

4. If you are using pictures, paintings, posters, graphs, or any other aids involving paper, make sure you use heavy stock or a firm backing. It is much easier to handle stiff paper than material that is thin and flimsy.

5. As noted earlier, check the physical surroundings and furnishings so that you will not discover, when it is too late, that there is no place to put your chart or no electrical outlet for your tape recorder or VCR. Many speakers have had to hold their aids throughout their speech because they failed to investigate the accommodations. How awkward you would feel if you started to show a film in a room that could not be darkened.

6. As mentioned previously, allow for time to prepare your audiovisual aid. It is important to remember that some aids take longer to produce than others. You might be able to design and draw a poster in a single night, but taking pictures and having them enlarged and mounted would take at least two days.

7. Practice your speech with your audiovisual aid. Rehearsing how to use your aid, so that you will be comfortable with it, is as important as practicing the language and delivery of your talk. This practice will help you become familiar with your aid so that its use is not marked by an awkward break in the speech. Too many speakers fail to recognize the importance of this rehearsal and end up having to look at their aid to remember what it contains.

Using Visual Aids

Once you have prepared your visual aids, you must then decide how to use them most effectively. Following are some do's and don'ts that should help you plan the use of your visual aids:

1. Unless the audience will be using your visual aid during the speech, you should avoid passing it through the audience either just before your talk or while you are speaking. Should you want them to carry something away from the speech, pass it out at the end of your talk.

2. Remember the necessity of maintaining eye contact with your audience. Too many speakers enjoy their visual aid so much that they forget their audience and talk to the aid. They also neglect other aspects of delivery; some speakers move in front of their visual aid, blocking it from the view of the audience.

3. Unless circumstances demand otherwise, you should keep your visual aid out of sight until you are ready to use it. There are enough other distractions pulling on your listeners; your aid should not provide another. When you are finished with your visual aid, remove it from the audience's line of vision.

4. Be sure to coordinate your visual aid with your words. Do not point to the location of an air bag on a car when you are talking about antilock brakes.

5. In most instances, it is best to display only one visual aid at a time. To have more than one aid in front of the audience at one time encourages the listeners to divide their attention between the aids and, perhaps, miss certain important points about the one you happen to be discussing.

6. Learn to expect and deal with the unexpected. Although this might seem like a contradiction in terms, it is nevertheless a point worth remembering. The horror stories concerning the use of visual aids are legendary. Slides being placed into the projectors upside down, photographs sticking together, easels and tripods falling apart, colors that have run because they got wet while being transported, videotapes breaking during talks, and "live" subjects that upstage you are just a few of the problems that might beset your presentation. Learn to think about a contingency plan should you be faced with the unexpected. Perhaps the best advice is to stay calm, keep right on going, laugh at adversity, and let your audience know that you are aware that your visual aids conspired against you.

7. Although it seems somewhat obvious, make sure everyone can see, and when appropriate, hear, your aid. As we said elsewhere, posters, pictures, transparencies, and the like need to be large enough for everyone to see. The rule regarding size even applies to models and specimens. We once saw a speaker in a large auditorium talking about and showing gems and rocks that were no bigger than a golf ball. The thing to do is put yourself in the place of the person sitting in the last row. Ask yourself, will they be able to clearly see my aid?

8. Visit and prepare the room in advance. Notice if there will be barriers obstructing the audience's view (desks, podiums, etc.). If you are going to project images on a screen, make sure you know the location of the lights and how to draw the curtains. Thinking about these sorts of issues will help you avoid problems before they occur. Or as Shakespeare once told us, "To fear the worst oft cures the worse."

Summary

You should use visual aids whenever you believe they might assist you in accomplishing your purpose. Although it might be a slight exaggeration, Alfred Lord Tennyson was correct when he noted that "things seen are mightier than things heard." Visual aids let people "see."

Visual aids can help make your verbal message more interesting, more under-standable, more persuasive, and more memorable. In choosing the most appropriate aid, you need to analyze the purpose of your talk, the size of your audience, and the availability of certain aids. You should investigate a wide variety of visual aids such as people, objects, specimens, models, posters, diagrams, maps, paintings, photographs, charts, graphs, chalkboards, flip charts, duplicated material, slides, videotape, computer graphics, transparencies, and opaque projections.

Whatever form of visual aid you choose, you should select it for its appropriateness to the audience, the subject, and the purpose of the speech. It should be easily seen by the audience, it should be easy for the speaker to manipulate, it should accurately represent the concept being discussed, and it should be free of distracting elements. In short, a visual aid should aid. You are advised to practice using your visual aid before making your speech and then to observe certain cautions during the presentation. Remember to look at your audience, coordinate your visual aid with your words, avoid passing your aids through the audience, and display only one aid at a time.

Chapter 8

Research

The Content of Your Ideas

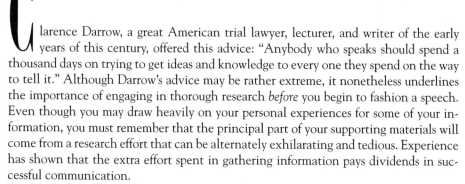

Nothing will come of nothing.

Shakespeare

Clarence Darrow, a great American trial lawyer, lecturer, and writer of the early years of this century, offered this advice: "Anybody who speaks should spend a thousand days on trying to get ideas and knowledge to every one they spend on the way to tell it." Although Darrow's advice may be rather extreme, it nonetheless underlines the importance of engaging in thorough research *before* you begin to fashion a speech. Even though you may draw heavily on your personal experiences for some of your information, you must remember that the principal part of your supporting materials will come from a research effort that can be alternately exhilarating and tedious. Experience has shown that the extra effort spent in gathering information pays dividends in successful communication.

Many students are dismayed when they discover that doing research is part of the public-speaking experience; however, when they begin the process of probing and searching, they discover that the rewards of learning how to do research far outweigh the disadvantages. The elation that comes from discovering new information about a subject you are interested in will often prompt you to search still further. Charles Dickens remarked, "There is a passion for hunting something deeply implanted in the human breast." The goal of this chapter is to urge you to tap into that passion.

Learning how to do research provides you with skills that you will need for life-long learning. Once you master the techniques of digging out and using diverse sources of information, you can apply these talents to different situations as they arise. The payoff that comes from knowing how to perform research for a speech extends well beyond the limits of the classroom.

In chapters 1 and 2, we noted that effective speech making involves following a systematic series of steps. When you have selected your topic, determined your speech purpose, and conducted an analysis of the audience and occasion, your next step is to begin your research. You need to find the materials that will help you accomplish your main objective. As a starting point, we need to realize that doing research is not a random or haphazard activity; it is systematic and tedious. That is to say, although plunging into your research because you are enthused is a noble endeavor, you must also have a plan of action.

Research Agenda

Ralph Waldo Emerson wrote that "there is always a right way of doing everything, even it be to boil an egg." This same wisdom applies to doing research; there is a correct way to approach researching any topic. Most experts agree that, regardless of the subject matter being sought or the questions being posed, successful research involves six interrelated steps. Although many of these steps were mentioned when we discussed speech preparation in chapter 2, it is nevertheless useful for you to see all of them spelled out here again.

1. *Start early.* The advice is simple and clear—good research takes time. The American poet Countee Cullen said the same thing far more lyrically: "And dill-dalliers never yet/Have at the proper moment sallied/To where they were supposed to get." Starting early keeps you from rushing and allows time for a degree of trial and error.

2. *Select a topic.* This will help you determine where you should look for material. Often, the most frustrating part of doing research is getting started. Part of the frustration comes from not deciding on a topic in advance of going to the library or telephoning someone for an interview. Whether your topic is carjacking or test tube babies, you need to know what you are interested in if you expect your time to be productive.

3. *Narrow your topic.* You need to move from a general subject to a specific area within that subject. You cannot easily research a topic as immense as world religion, but you can locate information for a speech that compares the Ten Commandments with the Eightfold Path of Buddhism.

4. *Select a research strategy.* Deciding on a research strategy simply means thinking about the various places you can find material on the subject you are researching. For example, should you interview professors in the Religion Department? Should you locate books on comparative religion? Should you visit a local Buddhist Temple?

5. *Keep records of your research activity.* It is essential that you keep track of the sources you have contacted. In the next few pages, we will talk about what to put on your bibliography and reference cards (or computer), but for now remember that these cards tell you what you have found thus far and usually eliminate your having to redo your work.

6. *Organize your material into specific headings.* For example, if you are researching the Ten Commandments and the Eightfold Path, you could develop headings around the origins of these precepts, the writings that carried the messages, the people who introduced the religious precepts, early translations of the writings, and the like.

7. *Carefully read and evaluate your material.* Is your material up-to-date, free of prejudice, complete, and accurate? Is it from primary or secondary sources?

8. *Take careful notes.* Later in the chapter we develop this idea in more detail. But for now we simply want to include as part of your research agenda the notion that, whether on cards, sheets of paper, or on computer files, you need to abstract the key ideas of what your research reveals.

Finding Material

Resource material is to be found in a number of places. You must learn to familiarize yourself with those places so that you can support your ideas with clear, believable evidence. What follows is a discussion of these sources that successful speakers use as part of their speech preparation.

Lawyer Owen Young remarked that, "Experience is wisdom's best friend." The natural start-ing point for the gathering of speech materials is your own storehouse of knowledge—the place that jurist Benjamin Cardozo referred to as "the archives of my memory." In all like-lihood, you will choose to speak on a particular topic because it holds an attraction for you. Learn to draw on that attraction as a first step. In the course of your life, you have under-gone countless experiences. Whether an experience was firsthand (going through exten-sive treatment for skin cancer) or vicarious (seeing a news clip on *NBC Nightly News*), it is still a part of your private "library." Some of the best speeches use personal experience as a major source of information. For example, a student who left Vietnam at the end of the war as a boatperson vividly explained the horrifying trip in a manner that went well be-yond any account that could be found in a book. Another speaker, who worked as a ski in-structor, talked about survival techniques in the wilderness. A student who was born and raised in a town of only five hundred people talked about how her school experiences pre-pared her for life at a major university. Thus, begin by writing down what you know about the topic. Not only will you start to build a supply of information for the speech, but you will place yourself in a position to identify the areas in which additional research is needed.

It is unwise, however, to rely solely on your personal background as a source of supportive material. All of us have perceptual limitations that can distort our view of reality. What we have learned and what we can recall are subject to our individual prej-udices. A paratrooper who has participated in an invasion would most likely perceive the action very differently than a person who has only read about it or viewed clips of it on television. Personal experiences are useful and necessary, but, when used to the ex-clusion of other sources, they have limited value. As is the case with so many aspects of life, moderation and balance are the watchwords.

Experience and Observation

Not many years ago, research for speeches was confined largely to poring through printed material and conducting interviews with knowledgeable sources; however, in the present era of electronic and mass media explosion, new resources have become available to speakers. Most colleges and universities have media centers, where they catalog and store films, commercial and noncommercial videotapes, audiocassettes, and even student me-dia projects. Learning to use such sources, whether a videotape of a *National Geographic* special on rain forests, or a student project on earthquake preparedness, will add another valuable research tool to your collection. Approaching a television screen as a learning device, as well as a source of entertainment, can help you as a researcher.

Using electronic media as a research tool has become even more attractive in the past decade, as more and more material has been cataloged and indexed. For instance, you can now find media listings in some of the following collections: *CBS News Index, Television News Resources: A Guide to Collections, Film Review Index, International Index of Multimedia Information, Public Television Transcripts, Television Index,* and *Transcript Video Index: A Comprehensive Guide to Television News and Public Affairs Programming.*

Electronic Media

Often ignored are several simple and quick ways of gathering information on a particu-lar topic—sending letters, using the telephone, requesting information via fax ma-chines, and making contact through Internet. Although writing letters has been used for centuries to make contact with other people, the widespread use of the other three devices clearly reflects major changes in our culture that justify the label "Information

Writing, Phoning, Faxing, and Internet

Age." Internet, which is the newest of the "contact devices," is simply a network that links computer networks all around the world. It enables groups and people on the system to communicate with each other. It can also be used to retrieve information from computers in remote locations.

The use of these tools is based on two interrelated premises. First, people besides you are interested in your speech topic, and, second, these groups and individuals are eager to furnish you information on that topic. Locating and contacting these organizations and agencies in the 1990s has become a rather easy task. In the next few pages, we will discuss how to locate and make contact with these groups and individuals.

Countless organizations and agencies are especially designed to gather and disseminate information about certain topics—whether it is the budget deficit, drunk driving, drug abuse, Alzheimer's disease, backpacking, or organ transplants. These organizations can represent commercial interests (National Dairy Council, American Paper Institute, National Automobile Dealers Association, Aerospace Industries Association of America, Chemical Manufacturers Association, American Iron and Steel Institute, Association of American Railroads), health issues (American Lung Association, American Physical Therapy Association, National Rehabilitation Association, American Institute of Nutrition, United Cerebral Palsy Association, American Academy of Allergy and Immunology, National Society to Prevent Blindness, National Association of the Deaf, Leukemia Society of America, American Institute of Nutrition), environmental concerns (National Audubon Society, Nature Conservancy, Water Pollution Control Federation, Air and Waste Management Association, Friends of the Earth, Greenpeace, National Parks and Conservation Association, Save-the-Redwoods League, Sierra Club, Soil and Water Conservation Society, National Wildlife Federation), and specialized interest groups (Aircraft Owners and Pilots Association, Women in Communications, American Civil Liberties Union, Abortion Rights Action League, African-American Institute, Animal Protection Institute, American Council of Education, Handgun Control Inc., Planned Parenthood, National Space Society, National Investigators Committee on UFOs).

It was not our intent in the previous paragraph to list all the places and organizations you could contact, but rather to demonstrate the idea that there are literally thousands of groups that will forward you information upon request. You simply need to contact them via fax machines, letters, phone calls, or Internet. Most of these organizations are listed in the *Encyclopedia of Associations,* a reference book found in most libraries. *The World Almanac,* a popular newsstand reference book, provides the names and addresses of over a thousand groups under the listing of "Associations and Societies."

Government agencies, at all levels, are another source of information that can often be gathered by writing letters, making phone calls, faxing, or using Internet. Topics ranging from organic farming to state lottery revenues are treated in government publications. At the national level, these topics are listed in a resource guide provided free of charge by the U.S. Government Printing Office (Washington, DC, 20402). Libraries have this index in their reference section.

Many foreign governments will answer requests for various kinds of information. For example, if you wanted to know more about how mainland China provides for part-time work permits, you could contact the nearest Chinese embassy or consulate. In most instances, information requests are answered promptly by the appropriate party. If you live near the embassy or consular office, you may be able to pick up the information in person. It is good to remember that, when you request information about any organization representing a specific cause or orientation, you may receive material that does not "tell the whole story." It is advisable to check other sources when using some of the facts and figures from these groups.

Thousands of the groups and organizations you may want to contact can be reached easily by telephone. Not only can you locate most of the phone numbers through "information," but, with the advent of the "800" number, reaching these organizations is rather simple and inexpensive. Most libraries have a special "800" phone directory.

If you are willing to pay a small fee for some of the materials, organizations will gladly fax them to you. All you need to do is locate a fax machine and know its "number" (most colleges and stationery stores have these machines and numbers) and request that the material be sent to that number.

Interviews

Over four hundred years ago, French scholar and writer François Rabelais wrote, "What harm in getting knowledge even from a sot, a pot, a fool, a mitten, or an old slipper." We can add "other people" to that list. The experiences and observations of other persons, who might be in a better position to know more about the subject than you, are often excellent sources of information. To secure that information, you will most likely have to conduct an interview. As a research tool, interviews have several strong points. First, if you want the most current information, an interview can give you access to the person who is currently involved with your topic. Books, magazines, and even CD and computer programs take time to write, print, and distribute; hence, they can be outdated. Interviews are timely; you can talk to someone about what is happening now. Second, an interview allows you a certain degree of selectivity. Instead of simply talking to someone who knows a little about the topic, you can gather data by going directly to an expert—someone with firsthand information. For example, if you were preparing a speech on the training program for Olympic skiers and a member of the Olympic team lived in your community, you could interview this person as a way of gathering firsthand information.

As a college student, you are in a position to make extensive use of interviews. Most professors, because of their teaching assignments and research programs, are experts in specific fields and can offer you valuable assistance. To illustrate, if you were going to give a speech dealing with the problems of interracial marriages, you might gain useful information and new ideas from interviews with professors of sociology, psychology, religion, and marriage and family relations. In addition, you might seek an appointment with some of the campus clergy. In all these instances, you are increasing your knowledge of the topic.

Interviewing as a research tool is also useful in that it lets you gather information on fairly narrow topics. For example, if your subject is the problem of rape on your campus, you can go directly to the campus chief of police and get his or her view of the topic, as well as some valuable facts and figures. Interviews also stimulate interest when they are reported in the speech. The audience wants to hear what you have to say because you have gone to an expert.

Information-gathering interviews, because they are a formal communication activity like a speech or group discussion, require a great deal of forethought and planning if they are to yield useful and relevant material. Let us look at some of the stages of that

Interviews represent a
strong research tool.

planning as a means of improving your interviews. After discussing the preparation
phase of interviewing, we will examine some guidelines for conducting an interview.
We will also offer some counsel on how to convert the interview material into something useful for a speech. The section ends with some advice regarding special considerations when interviewing someone from a culture different from your own.

Preparing for an Interview

First, *set up an interview well in advance, taking pains to arrange it at the convenience of the
interviewee.* He or she is granting you valuable time, so it is only a matter of simple courtesy to take his or her schedule into consideration. You should make your purpose very
clear during this first contact. This means specifying the general nature of the content
of the proposed interview and the amount of time that will be needed to conduct the
interview. Identifying your purpose is not only important for the interviewee, but it will
also enable you to focus on a specific goal. Knowing what you want from the outset
keeps you from wasting time on irrelevant issues. If you want to find out how a person
from Mexico views the United States' role in the Organization of American States, you
would hardly prepare questions on how Mexican citizens perceive our electoral process.

Second, *learn all you can about the person you will be interviewing.* Specifically, what
information do they have because of their position and experiences that drew you to
them? Being knowledgeable about his or her expertise will enable you not only to ask
good questions but to let the interviewee know you are serious about your task.

If the person you are interviewing is from a culture different from your own, it is important that you investigate any cultural "rules" that might have an impact on the interview. For example, many Muslims do not touch other people with their left hand. Hence,
in greeting a Muslim, you need to be careful that you do not violate this cultural rule.

Third, *before the meeting, prepare a detailed, well-organized agenda of questions you want to ask.* An information-gathering interview is a systematic and well-thought-out conversation. Although interviewers may give the impression of being spontaneous and do react to what the interviewee says and does, most successful interviewers know in advance the type of information they need from the other person.

In preparing your questions, you should decide not only the content of your inquiries but also their sequence. In most instances, you will find it useful to move from the general to the specific or from difficult to easy questions.

Fourth, *when preparing and asking questions, try to use open, closed, mirror, and probing questions.* An **open question** invites a relatively unrestricted area of response. When interviewing a Cambodian student about the dietary habits of her homeland, you might ask, "What kinds of foods are popular in your country?" This broad question allows the respondent to choose the approach she wishes to take in dealing with the question.

A **closed question,** which is often the most effective in information-gathering interviews, severely restricts the choices of responses available to the interviewee. "Do you think there is the likelihood of a presidential veto?" invites a yes or no answer. "How much money is available for school lunch programs in this district?" gives the respondent little room for anything except an answer involving some figures. As these examples indicate, closed questions are practical in that they are normally used to elicit brief and specific answers in a rapid-fire series. In this way, they can draw out a great deal of factual information, often in a short period of time.

A **mirror question,** as its name suggests, reflects the answer just given by the respondent. "You said that gang membership is likely to increase?" prompts the interviewee to elaborate on his or her previous answer. Interviewers ask mirror questions, then, to secure clarification of a point raised by the interviewee.

A **probing question** serves somewhat the same function as a mirror question in that it seeks elaboration of a point already raised. "What do you mean by that?" or "Can you explain in a little more detail?" directs the respondent to continue with the present theme. Even a simple "Oh?" or "I see" suggests that you want to know more. Your nonverbal behavior can also serve as a kind of probing question. A fixed gaze and a nodding head can tell the interviewee, "Go on."

Fifth, *in preparing your questions, remember that there are certain types of questions that you should avoid.* For example, there is no need to ask questions you can answer without the interview. To ask someone, "How long have you been in charge of the international studies office?" when the college catalog would supply the answer is a waste of everyone's time. Questions that are too vague should also be avoided.

Finally, *you should consider whether or not to use a tape and/or video recorder* (granting, of course, that the interviewee will allow it). There are advantages and disadvantages to the use of a tape recorder. One of the obvious advantages is that you can obtain an accurate record of the meeting. Also, you are freed from the task of taking notes. The major disadvantage is that a recording device can have an inhibiting effect on some interviewees; hence, you may not get the honesty and spontaneity you desire. In summary, you should consider the comfort of your interviewee, the setting for the interview, the topic to be discussed, and the pros and cons of taping.

Conducting the Interview

In conducting an interview, you would be wise to divide the meeting into three closely related parts—opening, body, and closing.

In the **opening** of the interview, you have two main chores to perform. First, try to establish rapport with the interviewee by setting a relaxed and friendly mood. Putting the interviewee at ease will increase the chances of securing accurate and complete answers to your questions. Second, during the opening, you should preview the purpose and scope of your interview. During this period, you should also ask permission to use a tape recorder if you plan to take one to the interview. Although a recorder assures the accurate quotation of the interviewee's remarks, many people feel uncomfortable having one in the room. If the interviewee does not want to be recorded, make sure you have paper and pen so that you can write down his or her answers.

It is in the **body** of the interview that you cover the essential material of the meeting. That is to say, once you have established rapport and previewed the interview, you are ready to gather the information you need to prepare your speech. To aid you in that effort, you should attend to the following guidelines.

1. *Keep the interview moving and organized.* By asking salient questions, you can control the flow and tone of the meeting. This helps assure you that the key issues get covered.

2. *Remember that the interviewee has the information you need.* Therefore, let him or her do most of the talking. Although most of us like to be the center of attention, in an interview the respondent should be the focal point.

3. *Offer verbal reviews as you go.* By letting the interviewee see what has been accomplished, you can avoid repeating the same ideas throughout the meeting. These reviews also let you verify your findings as you go. By saying, as a review, "So you believe that these four exercises are crucial to all young skiers," you can check your conclusions.

4. *By your words and actions, try to make the interviewee feel comfortable.* Not only is this the polite thing to do, but it helps you maintain rapport and encourages the interviewee to talk freely.

5. *Listen carefully.* Remember, you will be quoting and paraphrasing what you heard the interviewee say. You must not misquote. When you detect a contradiction or fail to understand something the interviewee says, you should ask for clarification; however, you can do this only if you are listening.

6. *Be time conscious.* You are using the interviewee's time, so do not overstay your welcome.

In **closing** an interview, summarize what has taken place ("So today we have. . . ."), discuss a follow-up meeting if one is necessary ("Perhaps we can meet again on Tuesday to finish our talk?"), and show your appreciation ("Thank you very much for your time. You have given me some valuable information.").

After the Interview

Immediately after the interview, you should review your notes and decide what material is best suited for your speech. When selecting what to use, it is best to concentrate on two types of information. First, try to locate the main theme of the interview. If the topic was campus crime and you interviewed the chief of police, the main theme might be how crime is increasing on campus. Second, you will want to isolate specific points you can use as evidence. This support can take a variety of forms: statistics ("Last year we had a 92 percent increase in campus crime"), examples ("Just last night someone attacked a student as she was walking to her car"), and testimony ("I really believe we are seeing an increase in crime on this campus").

After reviewing your notes, if something is unclear you should call the interviewee and ask for clarification. In fact, this entire section of the chapter has been concerned with asking for clarification and information. Asking others for information is an important part of doing research. As philosopher John Locke wrote, "I attribute the little I know to my not having been ashamed to ask for information, and to my rule of conversing with all descriptions of men on those topics that form their own peculiar professions and pursuits."

Throughout this book, we have stressed the impact of culture in all aspects of human communication. We now alert you to the fact that the interview process is not immune from this influence. Therefore, should you decide to interview someone from a culture different from your own, we urge you to keep the following points in mind.

The Role of Culture in Interviewing

First, *you will find that even the method you use to contact someone for an interview is affected by culture*. For example, while most of us might feel it is highly appropriate to contact people by phone and ask for an interview on the next day, this process is not used in many Asian cultures. For these cultures a formal letter, allowing the other person to set the time of the interview, is what is expected.

Second, *the initial greeting you offer the interviewee is yet another area of concern*. When you greet Western Europeans they, along with the Japanese, would expect you to be somewhat formal. First names are never used with cultures that value formality. You should also avoid any attempts at "small talk" when meeting someone from a formal culture.

Third, *be aware of problems associated with language when interviewing someone from another culture*. Although we will discuss cultural differences in the use of language in chapter 12, there is one area of concern that needs to be identified at this time. We are referring to the manner in which questions are asked and answered during the interview. Simply put, the dominant culture of North America uses language in a *direct* manner while many Asian cultures are *indirect*. Most Americans, for example, learn to say "yes" and "no" with great ease. Yet the Japanese and Chinese seldom use the word "no." They find it too harsh and direct. They would prefer to be vague and equivocal rather than offer a direct answer that might offend their communication partner. You can see how this attitude toward directness could affect the entire interview. We would therefore urge you to use open questions instead of direct questions when interviewing someone from a culture that manifests a value towards prescribed language.

Fourth, *the time it takes to conduct the interview will also be swayed by the culture of the participants*. This variable of time shows itself in a variety of ways. For example, the time it takes for the interviewee to answer the questions you ask will indicate the influence of culture. In both the Mexican and Arab culture, talk is highly valued. These cultures take great pleasure in conversation and in demonstrating their rhetorical skills. Hence, the response to your question might consume more time than you had allotted for the answer. The pace at which the interview is conducted is also influenced by culture. In the United States, we are raised to believe that "time is money" and we should not waste it. We even have a tendency to rush through our communication encounters.

However, in many cultures a slower pace is valued. The Asian and Latin cultures are two examples of people who do not like to hurry their conversations. Therefore, be prepared for many different time schedules as you move from culture to culture.

Printed Material

Donald C. Bryant and Karl R. Wallace, in their text on oral communication, noted, "The library is to the speech maker what the laboratory is to the scientist. It is a place of search and research." Although today with many computers a great deal of the searching and research can be done at home, it is nevertheless still true that reading in books, magazines, periodicals, newspapers, and documents places a great deal of information at the disposal of any speaker.

Before discussing the places in which to look for printed material, let us review some of the research strategies proposed at the beginning of the chapter and examine some additional advice:

1. *Read more than you think you will use.* Most beginning students feel compelled to read only enough to get by. You will discover, however, that the most effective speakers have a grasp on the topic that goes beyond the material given in the speech.

2. *Use independent sources.* A good researcher quickly learns the difference between material that stresses a single point of view and that which is free from self-serving interests. Articles on cigarette smoking put forth by the tobacco industry must be questioned in regard to the independence of their conclusions.

3. *Take complete and accurate notes on what you read.* It is important, for ethical as well as practical reasons, that you keep a record of exactly where your material comes from. For example, if your material is from a magazine, you should write down the name of the author, title of the article, name of the magazine, volume, date, and page, and you should cite this material in your speech, outline, and bibliography. Use quotation marks when quoting directly, and avoid plagiarism at all times.

There will be some occasions when your note-taking is in the form of a paraphrase. In these instances, you will be putting the author's main idea into your own words, enabling you to summarize and clarify someone else's findings and conclusions. You might develop the practice of putting paraphrases in brackets ([ ]) as a way of differentiating them from direct quotations (shown in your notes with quotation marks).

When copying notes from your resource material (books, journals), you should use a separate card or notation on your computer for each entry. Your material will be much easier to review and organize if each fact is by itself. This will let you sort your material under the appropriate heading until you are ready to use it.

4. *Know your library and librarians.* Although similarities exist, no two libraries are alike. However, you should try to discover the following aspects of the library that you will primarily be using:

a. The library catalog system, whether in card form or computer format, is the heart of any library

b. The interlibrary loan system

c. Basic procedures for using library material

d. The location of indexes, abstracts, reference books, government documents, special collections, nonprint media archives, and the like.

When using the library, you should feel free to ask questions of those who work there. Timidity may cost you access to valuable information. Remember the Malay proverb "If you are reluctant to ask the way, you will be lost."

Most libraries offer detailed tours of both the facilities and the procedures of the library. Sign up for one of these "expeditions" as part of your speech training.

Having talked about the library in rather general terms, let us now focus on specific sources of information found in most libraries and/or through computer searches.

Reference Books

When we think of reference books, most of us draw a mental picture of long rows of *Encyclopaedia Britannica* and *Encyclopedia Americana*. In many cases, we start the library portion of our research by turning to encyclopedias. They are easy to use in that they are arranged alphabetically, and they are usually kept updated by means of annual supplements. In addition to general encyclopedias, there are a number of specialized encyclopedias. Depending on your subject, you might find some of the following works especially helpful: *Encyclopedia of Education, International Encyclopedia of the Social Sciences, Encyclopedia of Philosophy, Encyclopedia of Psychology, Encyclopedia of Religion and Ethics, Encyclopedia of American and Foreign Policy, Encyclopedia of World Art, Encyclopedia of Educational Media Communications and Technology, Encyclopedia of Information Systems and Services, Encyclopedia of Associations,* and *The McGraw-Hill Encyclopedia of Science and Technology.*

As you would suspect, there are now entire encyclopedias available on CD-ROM. One of the best is *Grolier Multimedia Encyclopedia.* This disk can display thousands of photos (many of which move), maps, and illustrations along with sound and text. A request for material on Mozart offers the user pictures of the composer, the music from numerous selections, and written information about the person. These new disks even come with a "print feature," so you can have a copy of any information you might find useful.

Beyond encyclopedias, there are many other useful references. *The World Almanac, The Statesman's Year Book, The New York Public Library Desk Reference, Information Please Almanac, Guinness Book of Records, Statistical Abstract of the United States, Facts on File,* and *Commerce Reports* all furnish facts and figures that speakers may find useful.

For information about people, it is always advisable to consult biographical guides. A few of the more useful guides are *Current Biography, Who's Who in America, International Who's Who, Webster's Biographical Dictionary, Who's Who,* and *Who's Who of American Women.* Some guides are more oriented toward prominent persons of the past, such as *Dictionary of American Biography,* which profiles persons from American history, and its British counterpart, *Dictionary of National Biography.* Still another work, *Chambers's Biographical Dictionary,* contains more than fifteen thousand biographies, dating from ancient history to the present.

Literary references, anecdotes, humor, and famous quotations can be found in books such as *International Thesaurus of Quotations; Macmillan Book of Proverbs, Maxims and Famous Sayings; Sourcebook for Speakers; Bartlett's Familiar Quotations; Oxford Dictionary of Quotations; The Home Book of Quotations;* and *The Little, Brown Book of Anecdotes.* For information about poets, playwrights, novelists, and major characters in literature, you can consult *Benet's Reader's Encyclopedia.*

In recent years, many reference books have found their way into our computers. That is to say, with the advent of CD-ROM disks, countless companies have produced reference "books" on small laser disks that store electronic data. If you do not own an encyclopedia on a disk, you might ask your librarian or media center representative what reference disks are available.

The list of reference works in this section is but a glimpse of the sources that are available. There are guides to reference books that can put you in touch with a myriad of other possibilities. For example, *Guide to Reference Books*, edited by Eugene P. Sheehy, lists works in medicine, technology, and science; history and area studies; social and behavioral sciences; humanities; and general reference works. *American Reference Books Annual* has an updated list of works in many disciplines.

Finally, *Books in Print* contains a list of books currently in print or scheduled for publication by January 31 of the following year. As you would suspect, *Books in Print* can also be accessed through a computer.

Magazines and Pamphlets

Hundreds of magazines are available in the United States; it would be impossible to list all of them. However, several publications contain articles on a wide range of subjects: *Time, Newsweek, United States News & World Report, Business Week, Fortune, New Republic, Forbes, Reporter, Nation, Atlantic Monthly, Commonwealth, Harper's Magazine, Current History, National Geographic, Foreign Affairs, Yale Review, Vital Speeches of the Day, Aviation Week and Space Technology, Kiplinger's Personal Finance Magazine, Congressional Digest, Consumer Reports, Ebony, Harvard Business Review, New Yorker,* and *Smithsonian.*

Nearly all libraries have *The Magazine Index,* and its monthly supplements, which lists over four hundred magazines you can use to locate material to augment the information you gather from your other sources.

Most libraries also have a large collection of pamphlets that are hard to catalog and index because of their size and subject. These pamphlets, which are printed and circulated by various groups and organizations such as the American Medical Association and automobile clubs, cover a wide range of topics. Normally, this material can be secured from the library's vertical file or by asking the librarian for the location of the college's pamphlet collection. The Vertical File Service Catalog also lists pamphlets published and distributed by various organizations and agencies.

Atlases and Gazetteers

Intercultural interaction is a fact of life. With so many political and social changes taking place throughout the world, we are seeing alterations in geographic boundaries and the renaming of many countries and regions. Part of a good research program is to be aware of these changes, for what happens in one part of the world affects the entire planet. This intercultural interdependence demands that we not only know about other cultures, but that we are knowledgeable about the location of those cultures. Atlases and gazetteers help us obtain that knowledge.

Atlases, of course, are books that contain maps; however, they also contain much more. Most have charts, tables, plates, and even statistical information about the regions, countries, and states. The most widely used atlases of the world are *Rand McNally Cosmopolitan World Atlas, Times Atlas of the World,* and *National Geographic Atlas of the World.* Useful atlases of North America are the *Rand McNally Atlas of the United States* and the *National Geographic Atlas of North America.*

Gazetteers are a type of geographical dictionary. They are arranged by alphabetical headings and can help you with spelling and pronunciation. They also contain a great deal of information related to population, natural resources, elevations, manufacturing, weather, and the like. The most widely used gazetteers are *Webster's New Geographical Dictionary* and the *Longman Dictionary of Geography*.

In addition to the countless magazines written for the general public, there are thousands of very specialized journals and trade magazines written for specific audiences. Whether the topic is advertising, broadcasting, public relations, world affairs, religion, law, psychology, education, political science, sociology, communication, home economics, or engineering, there are academic and trade publications available. Most of these materials are indexed. However, if you cannot locate a specific journal or trade publication, ask any library assistant to help you locate it.

Academic Journals

Information on almost any topic can be secured from newspapers. While books normally take years to be written and published, newspapers are an excellent source of current happenings and information. Several major U.S. newspapers are now indexed, making it much easier to locate specific information. Some of the leading newspapers that are indexed are the *New York Times, Wall Street Journal, Christian Science Monitor, Los Angeles Times, Chicago Tribune, Washington Post (DC), New Orleans Times-Picayune*, and *Atlanta Journal/Atlanta Constitution*. Two highly regarded foreign newspapers are the *London Times* and the *Manchester Guardian*. When you are investigating a regional issue, you will find it helpful to consult your local newspapers.

Newspapers

Because of the large ethnic population in the United States, most libraries carry a number of newspapers from other countries and cultures. Many of these newspapers are printed in English. We would urge you to contact international and ethnic newspapers if you are planning a speech involving topics or people from other cultures.

Students are often surprised to learn that various local, state, and federal agencies produce thousands of reports, books, and pamphlets each year and that these materials are housed in libraries. Any librarian can show you where these sources are kept and how they are indexed. The most workable indexes for federal publications are the *Congressional Record* (the daily accounts of the workings of Congress), *Monthly Catalog of U.S. Government Publications* (the main listing of government reports), and *American Statistical Index* (government statistical reports). Various government agencies such as the Departments of Commerce, Health and Human Services, Transportation, Housing, and Labor also produce countless reports.

Government Publications

As you would suspect, the topics treated by all these organizations range from acid rain to zoos. Hence, regardless of the topic you have selected, you should examine the documents and reports generated by government agencies.

As you explore the sources available to a researcher, you will undoubtedly come in contact with subject abstracts. These abstracts offer concise summaries of articles, books, and other publications. If you read the abstract, you can then decide whether or not the entire work justifies further investigation.

Subject Abstracts

While there are many subject abstracts, the following are a few you might find the most helpful: *Communication Abstracts* (advertising, broadcasting, interpersonal communication, journalism, public relations); *Criminology and Penology Abstracts* (criminal behavior, delinquency, treatment of offenders, criminal procedures);

Environmental Abstracts (air pollution, ecology, wildlife); *Psychological Abstracts* (all areas of psychology); and *Sociological Abstracts* (social control, group behavior, mass phenomena). Again we urge you to consult a librarian as to the location and availability of these and other subject abstracts in your library.

Indexes

Any person who has ever conducted library research knows how fortunate we are to have indexes. They save us countless hours of tedious drudgery by cataloging and listing materials on nearly every subject imaginable. The most common index is the library card catalog, with its subject, title, and author indexes. This is, of course, a superb starting point for your research. In this file, you will find a complete listing of books found in your library. *The Reader's Guide to Periodical Literature*, published each month, is a cumulative index of articles published in more than a hundred selected periodicals. Articles are listed alphabetically according to author, title, and subject.

In addition to the indexes just cited, you might have occasion to consult the *Bulletin of Public Affairs Information Service* and the *International Index*. Also, as indicated previously, the activity of the United States Senate and the House of Representatives is completely indexed in the *Congressional Record*.

There is also a vast array of indexes focusing on specific subject areas. Some examples are the *Biological and Agricultural Index, Applied Science and Technology Index, Art Index, Biography Index, Education Index, Criminal Justice Periodical Index, General Science Index, Psychological Index, Psychological Abstracts, Business Periodicals Index, Index of Legal Periodicals, American Statistical Index, Statistical Reference Index, Business Periodicals Index, Humanities Index, Public Affairs Information Index,* and *Social Sciences Index.*

Microfilms, Microfiche, and Ultramicrofiche

In the interest of saving space and facilitating speedy access to printed materials, libraries have turned to the use of film in several forms, collectively known as microforms. Virtually all the kinds of printed material we have been discussing for the past few pages can be found on microfilm, microfiche, or ultramicrofiche. **Microfilms** are reels of film on which printed matter is photographed in greatly reduced size. Newspapers are often put onto microfilm. A **microfiche** is a microfilm sheet about the size of an index card that contains rows of printed or written pages. **Ultramicrofiche,** although less than half as large as a microfiche, contains many more pages of materials. All these microforms use projection devices for the readout. Assistance in the operation of any of these devices is available from members of the library staff.

Computer Searches

You could not have read the last few pages without realizing the importance of computers as a research tool. As we have seen, it is easy to use computers to conduct searches and retrieve customized bibliographies and abstracts on almost any topic—and in an amazingly short period of time. Most public libraries, and virtually all college and university libraries, currently have the electronic equipment necessary to search through indexed files from journals, magazines, and research reports. In fact, many personal computers are now "programmed" to conduct these searches so that the researcher can access material from home. When you use computers in this fashion, you are conducting *on-line searches*, and the indexed files that are being scanned are referred to as *databases*.

You are most likely already familiar with, or at least have seen, the computer search system being used by your public, college, or university library. A very popular system to locate material within a library is LUIS (Library User Information Service).

Because most systems are alike, we need only to discuss LUIS for you to get a feel of how computer searches function.

As you approach the system, you will see a keyboard and a terminal screen containing the following information:

Search	**Options Commands**
To search by	TITLE: = T
	AUTHOR: = A
	SUBJECT: = S

If you are looking for a specific book, and you know the title, you would type on the screen, following the prompt T = *Oral Communication: Speaking Across Cultures*. If the book is in the library, you will immediately see the author's name, the title of the book, the date of publication, and the call number. If you know only the name of the author, but not the title of the book, you would type on the screen A = Samovar. All of the books in your library written by that author would appear on the screen. If you were interested in a specific topic, such as public speaking, you would type S = Public Speaking. All of the books in your library on this subject would appear on the terminal screen.

Many computer search systems have printers. Hence, once you have selected the books you are interested in, you simply tap the "print" button on the keyboard, and you will get a printed listing of these books. You need only stroll to the stacks, list in hand, and locate your materials.

In addition to locating books, magazines, and journals within the individual library, computerized databases have now become popular tools for anyone doing research. These databases are, of course, faster and easier to use than the indexes we discussed earlier in the chapter. The most widely used databases for general references seem to be *InfoTrac, ProQuest,* and *Academic Abstracts*. Depending on the library and computer, these databases can be accessed through CD-ROM players, on-line searches, or mainframe computers.

The number of companies that now retrieve information for researchers is growing so rapidly that any attempt to provide a complete listing is bound to become obsolete in a short time. Nonetheless, we will examine a sampling of the available services.

One of the earliest and most popular systems used by college students is the Educational Resources Information Center, or ERIC. ERIC is composed of a series of clearinghouses that gather, organize, and catalog unpublished materials, such as project reports, conference reports, and other research findings. The ERIC service is especially helpful if your topic falls into one of the following subject areas: career education; counseling and personnel services; early childhood education; educational management; handicapped and gifted children; higher education; information resources; junior colleges; languages and linguistics; reading and communication skills; rural education and small schools; science, mathematics, and environmental education; social studies and social science education; teacher education; tests, measurement, and evaluation; and urban education.

ABI/FORM is an index of over 1,400 periodicals in business and related fields. The databases also include detailed abstracts of the articles. The AMERICAN STATISTICS INDEX (ASI) indexes and abstracts U.S. Government statistics and statistical publications. NEXIS provides indexing and full-text access to newspapers, wire services, and some government publications.

Bibliographic Retrieval Services (BRS) enables you to gain access to bibliographic and full-text databases on subjects as diverse as dentistry, agriculture, social sciences, chemistry, mental health, medicine, and books in print.

The DIALOG (Dialog Information Services) retrieval service can search over hundreds of databases containing more than a million references. DIALOG organizes its many databases by headings such as business, science and medicine, law, news, energy and environment, humanities, and people. You simply identify your specific subject area and ask the computer to show you what it has. It will search thousands of newspapers, magazines, and other publications in a few seconds. Among its databases are those compiled by Dun and Bradstreet, Harvard Business Review, UPI News, Historical Abstracts, Standard and Poor's, Moody's Investor's Service, and many others.

WILSONLINE has on-line access to *The Reader's Guide to Periodical Literature* (an important index we mentioned earlier), the *Business Periodicals Index*, the *Education Index,* and many other periodical resources. More than three thousand periodicals and half a million books are covered by its databases.

Dow Jones News/Retrieval is an on-line computer service offering the latest financial information on request. Articles appearing in the *Wall Street Journal, Barron's,* and *Dow Jones News Service* go back as far as three months.

ORBIT search service is a bibliographic database focusing on scientific and technological data. You can obtain copies of full-text documents from any of the available services.

CD-ROM (Compact Disc Read-Only Memory), which we discussed earlier, is yet another important new data storage medium. Simplistically described as a PC hooked onto a compact disc player, one CD-ROM can hold an entire year of ERIC information. CD-ROM searches access more current information than either periodical indexes or on-line searches such as ERIC.

One computer search available at no cost at many college libraries is one we mentioned earlier—InfoTrac. Information is stored on microfilm or laser disc in InfoTrac and can be accessed by using methods similar to those in using the *Reader's Guide*. The main differences between InfoTrac and indexes are (1) the use of a monitor instead of a book, (2) the availability of a printed copy of the appropriate sources, and (3) the speediness of a computer search over the manual use of indexes.

Although the computer search systems themselves are simple to operate, the large number of options available can often cause confusion. In addition, there will be many new computer research tools in the near future because the number of systems is rapidly increasing. Therefore, it is important to remember to ask your librarian which service your school subscribes to so that you will know what types of information you can look for.

Regardless of what system you use, you should keep three points in mind. First, as we have mentioned throughout this chapter, seek the aid of the people in your library who operate the various computer services. They will be glad to offer you some tips on how to use the system. It does not take a computer science major to use these systems, but you might need some instruction.

Second, remember that computers do not think for you—they are only an aid. In some instances, they are an aid that costs money to use. Therefore, you must do some creative work before you ask the machine to offer you what it has stored in its memory bank. While a printed index is created with one heading at a time, computer searches can examine many requests simultaneously. This is why you should request information carefully. If you are lackadaisical in your requests, the bibliography produced by the computer may not access the information you need. Many students have wasted time, energy, and money because they were vague in what they asked of the computer. In short, be specific and know what you are looking for before you use the computer.

Third, most computer databases have stored information only for the past fifteen or twenty years. Therefore, if you are looking for information published before the 1970s, you may have to bypass using the computer search.

Learn these computer systems as part of your speech training. Computer searches, and the services they offer, are going to grow in both numbers and sophistication in the next decade. As we indicated, many of these services can even be used in our own offices and homes. Therefore, you need to understand the workings of these systems if you are going to take advantage of this research tool of the 1990s.

Recording Material

You will find that it is difficult to keep track of all that you read and hear as you do your research. In the interest of accuracy, you should not attempt to keep facts, figures, and quotations in your head. Unless you have a phenomenal memory, you will need to record your information for further use.

Ensuring that the information is usable should be one of your primary concerns when recording your data. Hence, you should try to develop a research and recording style with which you feel comfortable. Since most libraries have photocopy equipment, the recording process often begins with you making copies of the material you deem most useful. Or, as we have said elsewhere, if you are using a computer that is attached to a printer, you simply have to press the "PRINT" button or move the "mouse" to the appropriate spot. However, whether you copy, print, record your material on index cards, or create "files" in your computer, there are some guidelines that will aid you in making the most efficient use of your research:

1. It is essential that your material be recorded in an accurate manner and a usable form. This means that the complete reference should be shown on the card or computer so that you can cite the source in your outline and, when appropriate, mention it in your speech.

Although there are numerous methods for citing research data, three of the most popular bibliographic formats are Modern Language Association (MLA), the University of Chicago (often referred to as Turabian), and American Psychological Association (APA). While all three formats have merit, we have found that our students find MLA style most useful. Hence, we will offer some examples of how to use this classification system for recording bibliographical citations. You, of course, may choose to purchase a reference book that includes all three styles.

a. Book with one author: Brownell, Judi. *Listening: Attitudes, Principles, and Skills.* Boston, Mass.: Allyn and Bacon, 1996.

b. Book with two authors: Andereck, Paul A., and Pence, Richard A. *Computer Geneology: A Guide to Research Through High Technology.* New York: Ancestry, 1985.

It is essential that your material be recorded in an accurate manner and a usable form.

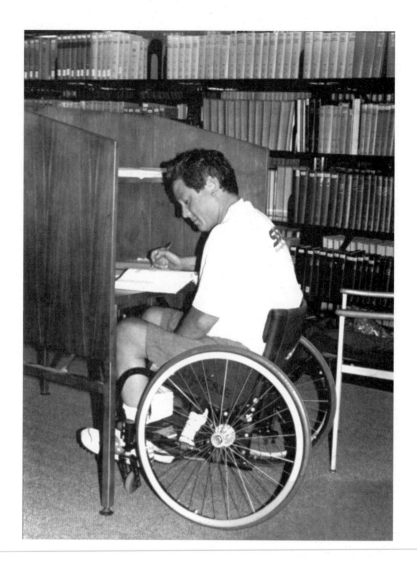

c. Pamphlet: Chicago Women in Publishing. *Equality in Print: A Guide for Editors and Publishers*. Chicago: Chicago Women in Publishing, 1994.

d. Article from a journal: Zimmerman, Stephanie. "Perceptions of Intercultural Communication Competence and International Student Adaptation to an American Campus." *Communication Education* 44 (1959):321–335.

e. Article from a monthly magazine: Rodriguez, Richard. "Late Victorians: San Francisco, AIDS, and the Homosexual Stereotype." *Harper's* 281 (October 1995): 57.

f. Article from a weekly magazine: Adler, Constance. "Foul Ball." *TV Time* I (13 October 1990): 20.

g. Article from a daily newspaper: Stein, Mark. "Quake Solemnly Remembered in Bay Area." *Los Angeles Times*. 18 October 1990. Sec. 1, P. 1, Col. 4.

h. Television program: *The Civil War*. Writers, Geoffrey C. Ward, Ric Burns, and Ken Burns. Producers, Ken Burns and Ric Burns. PBS Miniseries Event, September 23, 24, 25, 26, 27, 1990.

i. Personal and telephone interviews: Day, Thomas. Telephone interview. 3:30 p.m., 7 May 1995. Sagan, Carl. Personal interview. 5:00 p.m., 10 October 1992.

j. Compact disc: Trzetrzelewska, Basia. *Time and Tide*. Epic, EK40767, 1994.

k. Motion picture film: Levinson, Barry, dir. *Avalon*. With Armin Mueller-Stahl and Joan Plowright. Tri-Star Pictures. 1990.

l. Anonymous article: "The Dawn of the Laptop Computer." *Consumer Reports*. 55, No. 6 (June 1990): 377.

m. Work in a collection of pieces: O'Connor, Flannery. "Everything That Rises Must Converge." In *Mirrors: An Introduction to Literature*. 2d ed. Ed. John R. Knott, Jr. and Christopher R. Reaske. San Francisco: Canfield, 1995, pp. 58–67.

n. Encyclopedia: "Reconstruction." *The New Columbia Encyclopedia*. 4th ed. 1975, pp. 2286–7.

2. Your research cards or computer should not only include the correct citations and quoted material but they should also contain your personal evaluations of the material. Notes to yourself will come in handy as you begin to piece the speech into the organizational scheme you eventually select. In short, each card should include (a) the complete citation, (b) the quoted material, and (c) your personal comments. Following is a typical card or computer evaluation.

Crewdson, John. "AIDS : A Million Cases Feared by End of Century." *San Diego Union*, 14 June 1993, sec. C, p. 5, col. 2–5.

"Earlier this year, when more than 50 prominent American scientists were asked by a pharmaceutical company to chart the future of the AIDS epidemic, they predicted that by the turn of the century more than one million Americans will have fallen ill from the disease."

GOOD GENERAL QUOTATION SHOWING THE FUTURE OF THE PROBLEM.

Ethical Considerations in Conducting Research

Now that we have considered some of the skills necessary for productive research, we need to pause and return to one of the major themes of this book—the ethical responsibilities associated with human communication. No where is this topic more relevant than when you are conducting research. For as you have seen, doing research demands a delicate balance between combining your own creativity with the work of others. In this final section, we offer some advice as to how you can achieve that balance.

First, ask yourself if you have conducted a meticulous and careful search of all the available materials. Too often speakers only consult materials that are easy to locate or buttress their own thesis. The weakness of this position is that they may not be obtaining an accurate representation of the question they are investigating. For example, to research and utilize material on the topic of abortion only from the National Organization for Women would greatly limit your findings on this topic. To be ethical, you should try to control bias and be eclectic in your search for material.

Second, in both written and oral form, you must always avoid plagiarism. As you know, plagiarism occurs when a writer or speaker offers the words of someone else as if they were their own. This practice is a form of intellectual thievery, for you are stealing from someone else. To be ethical and to avoid ever giving the slightest appearance of plagiarism, we suggest you follow the following guidelines when finding and using research material.

1. Never use another person's exact words without giving proper acknowledgment. In written form, this means showing the entire source. When delivering the talk, you cite the complete reference.

2. When conducting your research, take careful notes so that you can always identify what comments and findings are yours and which belong to someone else.

3. If you are going to paraphrase, either in your outline or your talk, you should still follow the rules of honesty and tell your audience the remarks are not yours.

4. If you have any doubts whether or not you should assign credit to someone else, do so! The key is always to be truthful. The Swiss philosopher Henri Frédéric Amiel said it with shining prose when he wrote, "Let us be true: this is the highest maxim of art and of life, the secret of eloquence and of virtue."

Summary

In this chapter, our main concern was with ways of locating the material you will need in order to accomplish your purpose. You should begin by developing a research agenda. Once you decide what you know and do not know about the subject in question, you can use electronic media; write and telephone for information; conduct interviews; use reference books, magazines and pamphlets, academic journals, newspapers, subject abstracts, indexes, and computer searches.

We also discussed how to record your material so that you can use it when your research is completed. We examined the importance of using notes, of being accurate when reproducing material, of being complete with regard to content and source citation, and of jotting down some personal evaluations on your card. We concluded by asking you to always be ethical in carrying out all of your research projects.

*C*ommon sense is
not so common.

François de Voltaire

Chapter 9

Critical Thinking
The Appraisal of Your Ideas

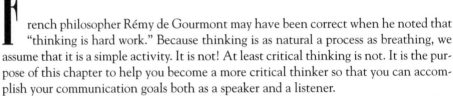

It is the hardest thing in the world to be a good thinker without
being a good self-examiner.

Anthony Shaftesbury

rench philosopher Rémy de Gourmont may have been correct when he noted that
"thinking is hard work." Because thinking is as natural a process as breathing, we
assume that it is a simple activity. It is not! At least critical thinking is not. It is the purpose of this chapter to help you become a more critical thinker so that you can accomplish your communication goals both as a speaker and a listener.

It is only fitting that we pause at this juncture in the book to examine the topic
of critical thinking, for the manner by which you approach data from the outside world
touches every aspect of speech making. The material you select for your speech will be
influenced by your ability to make sound judgments. In addition, the way you use that
material is also affected by critical thinking. Even how you listen to the words of others
is partially controlled by the important skill of analytical and judicious thinking.

In chapter 6 we talked about the need to use evidence to augment your ideas, and
in chapter 8 the places to locate that evidence. Thus far, however, we have not discussed
in detail the various ways you can think about your ideas and evidence. That is to say,
although systematic research can help you locate speech materials, you need to analyze
those materials before placing them into your speech. As you appraise the materials you
have gathered through reading, listening, and observing, you need to make a conscious
effort to think critically—to distinguish fact from judgment, belief from knowledge,
sound reasoning from fallacious reasoning. Critical thinking enables you to avoid the
errors in reasoning as you collect the material for your talk. It also contributes to the accuracy with which that material is presented. Critical thinking, as we noted in the chapter on listening (chapter 5), even affects the manner in which you receive messages.
The very word *critical* implies learning how to discriminate between reasoning that is
reliable and reasoning that is marked by omission and inaccuracies.

Before we talk about ways to evaluate a piece of material, we should ask ourselves
if we have any tendencies of thought that might impair our ability to judge that material fairly. All of us are subject to lapses of good judgment from time to time. We fall into
habits of thinking that make objectivity hard to attain. Therefore, in the early part of
this chapter, we will deal with some of the habits we often develop over our lifetime that
can become barriers to critical thinking.

The second part of the chapter will deal with flaws that may appear in the materials gathered through research. Patent attempts to mislead as well as innocent blunders
will be examined as we investigate a variety of fallacies. In particular, we will look at fallacies that stem from (1) the misleading use of words, (2) the use of materials that are
not truly relevant, and (3) violations of logical consistency.

Personal Barriers to Critical Thinking

Chapter 5 included a discussion of some of the personal factors that reduce our efficiency as listeners. Such barriers as constant self-focus, defensiveness, and avoidance of difficult and uninteresting material were mentioned in that chapter. There are, however, other personal barriers that often impede critical thinking. Let us examine some of these barriers so that we can hold them in check as we gather material, present that material, or listen to the remarks of other speakers.

Frozen Evaluations

Over two thousand years ago, Greek philosopher Heraclitus wrote that "nothing is permanent but change"; however, when it comes to our personal beliefs, we seldom seem to agree. Once we have made up our minds about something, it is annoying to have to reconsider our decision. It is more comfortable to hold fast to our original conclusion. Because of this universal tendency, we are apt to harbor frozen evaluations about everything from events, to people, to ideas. For example, once we have labeled a person a "liberal" or a "conservative," with all of the associations those labels bring to our mind, we tend to be blind to changes in that person that would invalidate that label. Maybe you can recall some of the foods you disliked as a child and that you refused to eat until sometime in adulthood, when you finally gave in and tried them, and much to your surprise, often liked them. Our simple example about foods can be applied to other things, including ideas and people. You need to learn to suspend such frozen evaluations and look for evidence of change. If, after you have reconsidered the material in question, and you still adhere to your original belief, at least you know that you have been open-minded and fair. You might also find that you have learned something new, even if you do not agree with it. There is a famous saying that creates the same idea in slightly different words: Minds are like parachutes. They only function when they are open.

Self-Interest

The degree to which we are personally involved in something affects our perception of it. Self-interest often leads us to refuse to look for evidence that we do not want to face. Ostrichlike, we ignore the facts. We build false expectations on wishful thinking, not critical thinking. On other occasions, we are even unwilling to identify our self-interests. For example, coastal residents, who have homes along the beach, are apt to be more concerned with proposals for offshore oil drilling than are inland residents, yet because of self-interest do not listen to all sides of the issue. If a piece of legislation means money in our pockets, we tend to view it with favor; if it means money out of our pockets, we tend to dislike it. Self-interest, then, is a powerful determinant on the way we look, or fail to look, at things. How fair are judgments clouded by self-interest? To achieve a greater degree of objectivity when we are making judgments, we need to be aware of the role that our self-interest is playing and then make allowances. When we encounter a magazine article that tells us that we will suffer financially if a certain measure is passed by the legislature, we need to ask ourselves, Am I opposed to this measure because it lacks all merit, or am I just concerned about holding onto my money?

Ego-Defense

We begin our section on ego-defense, and its impact on thinking, with a quotation:

> It is a curious fact that of all the illusions that beset us, none is quite so curious as that tendency to suppose that we are mentally and morally superior to those who differ from us in opinion.

Although the source of this commentary is anonymous, the observation is one worth considering. It is only human nature to want to protect both our physical and emotional well-being, and one way we do this is by rejecting the ideas of other people. If another person, or even a piece of evidence, tells us our beliefs are wrong, we might react in an irrational manner. We usually engage in a series of mental activities that keeps us from systematically evaluating the concept under investigation. We often resort to excuses and self-delusion in order to preserve our self-esteem. This face-saving behavior can lead us to ignore evidence that runs counter to our beliefs, no matter how valid that evidence might be. It can cause us to shift the blame for our conduct onto others. It can cause us to invent rational explanations for irrational actions. Of all of our bad habits of thinking, the practice of ego-defense poses one of the greatest barriers to objectivity. It is not by chance that almost one hundred years ago philosopher Gilbert Chesterton wrote, "One may understand the cosmos, but never the ego; the self is more distant than any star."

Ethnocentrism

As we have just indicated, it is difficult to avoid judging others and their ideas without thrusting ourselves into the equation. It is additionally hard to be open and tolerant of the customs, beliefs, and values of other groups and cultures when they run counter to our own. All of us are molded and shaped by the experiences of our culture, and automatically develop the habit of evaluating all other cultures by these experiences. You will recall that this barrier to critical thinking is so common that anthropologists have given it a name: **ethnocentrism.** In effect, when engaging in ethnocentrism, what we are doing is placing our own culture in the central position of priority and worth. Ethnocentrism can induce an attitude that says, either consciously or unconsciously, "our way is not only the right way, it is the only way." If in our culture dating rituals call for flowers or tickets to a rock concert, and somewhere else in the world the suitor offers a handful of raw fish, is one right and one wrong? Christians and Muslims speak to a single God, the Hindu to many gods, and the Buddhist has no god; is one right and one wrong? Of course not, they are only different views of the world that have developed over a long period of time and for specific cultural reasons.

The danger of ethnocentrism is that it produces a type of perceptual blindness leading to a subjective evaluation that greatly limits what we take in and what we use. We are not advocating that you arrive for your next date with a handful of fish, but rather that you develop the view that although many great ideas are founded on Euroamerican principles, they are not the only principles. This new receptiveness will let you seek out the writings, philosophies, and worldviews stressed in other cultures. It is a provincial and naive belief that the Western world is the exclusive creator of wisdom and information. We need to broaden our perceptions and not limit our thinking to one point of view. Knowledge does not know color, gender, nationality, or boundaries. Hence, we again urge you to be alert to the dangers of narrowness and dogmatism in your thinking. St. Thomas Aquinas said much the same thing two thousand years ago: "Beware of the man of one book."

Stereotyping

Stereotyping, our final personal barrier to critical thinking, is closely related to the concept of ethnocentrism in that both involve classifications. The word *stereotype* was originally a printer's term, referring to a metal printing plate made by casting metal in a

Knowledge does not know color, gender, nationality, or boundaries.

mold. The word has now taken on a figurative meaning, referring to a long-standing, oversimplified, exaggerated, inflexible judgment (one cast in a mold). In reality, a stereotype is actually two things. First, it is a special kind of frozen evaluation—a pre-judgment of another's religion, race, profession, sexual preference, affiliations, and so on. Second, stereotypes are an outgrowth of selective perception in that we let ourselves see only a small slice of the world. More often than not, we acquire these prejudgments from our friends and relatives. We accept them uncritically and make them our own. Thus, we harbor stereotypes of college professors, Asians, hairdressers, environmentalists, used-car salespeople, the elderly, Southerners, Democrats, preachers, and rock musicians. Even if we have never met a person from Iraq, we have our ready-made judgment on hand in case we do, and that stereotype will bias the way we perceive that person. If, in our research, we find an article written by a person whom we have prejudged, our reading of that article is not likely to be objective.

Not all stereotypes are acquired from friends and relatives, however. Sometimes we manufacture our own. For example, a single bad encounter with a person from another country might lead us to an unfavorable prejudgment of the next person we encounter from that country. This act of attributing to all members of a group the qualities of a single member is an example of hasty generalization, one of the fallacies we shall discuss later in this chapter.

What we have been saying is that stereotypes contaminate our thinking in a number of ways. First, when applied to people, ideas, or cultures, they cause us to conclude that a belief is true when in reality it is not. To conclude that *all* Germans *only care* about hard work is to engage in a damaging and misleading stereotype. Germans have a long history of loving the arts, being outdoors, enjoying fine foods, and the like. To stereotype them as being obsessed with only work limits one's ability to accurately think about Germans and the ideas they produce. Second, stereotypes hamper critical thinking because when they get reinforced often enough they are difficult to overcome. Think for a moment about the myths we presented with regard to women, Arabs, and the elderly. From a host of sources, the images and stereotypes are repeated with such regularity that it takes constant vigilance if we are to avoid lumping these groups into three rigid categories. It is this type of classification that limits our thinking process.

We have discussed only five of the major barriers to critical thinking. As you would suspect, there are many more. However, we have singled out some of the most destructive ones. Master these and your ability to think critically will be greatly increased.

Detecting Fallacies

Now that you have attempted to identify some personal and potential flaws in your thinking process, you are ready to take the next step and examine your evidence, reasoning, and ideas. Richard Whately, a nineteenth-century logician, classified as a **fallacy** "any unsound mode of arguing which appears to demand our conviction, and to be decisive of the question in hand, when in fairness it is not."

Logicians, social psychologists, and rhetoricians make repeated attempts to classify types of fallacies, but no one has been successful in devising a system that has won universal support. Not only is there a problem of classification and division, but there is also a question as to what to include and what to exclude. Discussions of fallacies often contain lists with as many as fifty or sixty kinds of fallacies. We shall not attempt to investigate all the possible fallacies, but will examine those that you are most likely to encounter as you assess and present your materials and ideas. For the sake of convenience, we shall group fallacies under three principal headings: (1) language deceptions, (2) extraneous appeals, and (3) faulty logic.

As we move through our list of fallacies, our focus will be twofold. First, an awareness of fallacies should assist you in detecting errors in thinking as you confront the ideas of others. Second, you should also find yourself scrutinizing your own thinking and speaking more carefully as you become familiar with these intentional and unintentional deceptions.

Language Deceptions

What the author T. S. Eliot called "the intolerable wrestle with words and meanings" is a problem that constantly confronts a speaker, reader, or listener. We need to be on guard against words, phrases, and sentences used in a way that obscures or distorts meaning, produces confusion, or misleads us in our use or appraisal of a message. For the next few pages, we will explore some of the more common fallacies of word management: semantical ambiguity, syntactical ambiguity, equivocation, innuendo, separation from context, and infusion of emphasis.

Semantic Ambiguity

Richard Sheridan, the famous Irish playwright and witty parliamentary orator, was once asked to apologize for insulting a fellow member of Parliament. "Mr. Speaker," replied Sheridan, "I said the honorable member was a liar it is true and I am sorry for it. The honorable member may place the punctuation where he pleases." Language can be ambiguous. In everyday speech, it is not unusual for a word or phrase to suggest a variety of different meanings. The fallacy of *semantic ambiguity* occurs when the context of the statement (word or phrase) does not make clear which of several meanings of a word is intended. If the context does not help clarify the intended meaning of the term in question, it is quite possible that the listener might interpret the word in another way and thus arrive at a false conclusion. Think for a moment of the built-in ambiguity if someone says "The shooting was terrible" and you failed to know the context. Did a friend have a poor hunting trip? Did the makers of the movie have a bad production day? Were two police officers discussing a murder? Even the simple sentence, "Honey please get my coffee" changes meaning if the words are uttered to wife, stranger, or secretary.

Examples of the fallacy of semantic ambiguity abound. If someone were to say, "He is a liberal talker," we might interpret *liberal* as a label for that person's political stance, or we might take it to mean that he or she is very talkative. Unless the user of the word offered a clue as to the intended interpretation, we would have to rely on mere guesswork. If we were to hear a movie critic say, "Spike Lee's role was better than most," we would be left to speculate about whether the allusion to Spike Lee's role referred to the character part he was asked to play or whether it referred to his acting. Moreover, the claim that the role was better than most might be construed to mean that it was better than the majority of the parts he has been given in films or that his performance excelled that of most of the other performers in the film.

Although it is probable that many semantic ambiguities are merely the result of sloppy wording, it is not unusual for advertisers, salespeople, and politicians to use them deliberately. A TV commercial that trumpets a product as "new and improved" is depending on the vagueness of the terms for its effectiveness. The advertiser has a belief that we will attach favorable associations to the terms. *New* becomes *fresh, pristine, radically different,* and *youthful,* while *improved* becomes *decidedly better, without rival,* and *flawless.*

As a speaker, it is important for you to give the listener a clear indication of which meaning is intended. As a listener, you might be able to ask the speaker for the meaning they had in mind. If it is not possible to make such a request, use your own knowledge of the subject and what you might know about the speaker to decide on the meaning. It is important for your conclusion to be tentative because you were confronted with semantic ambiguity.

Syntactical ambiguity involves the use of a word or phrase that is liable to more than one interpretation because of its unique placement within the structure of a sentence. The problem, then, is not one of word selection, as is the case with semantical ambiguity; it is the position that the word or phrase occupies within the grammatical structure of the sentence that is the source of confusion.

Syntactical Ambiguity

Consider, for a moment, the following statement: "The principal scolded the custodian because she was angry." Does it mean that the principal, in a fit of anger, scolded the custodian, or does it mean that the principal scolded the custodian because the custodian had exhibited anger? Just who is "she"? How would you rewrite the sentence to make it clear? What about a sentence that says "During my four years of college I had about thirty odd professors"? Is odd being used to indicate an imprecise number of professors or is it a description of personality traits?

Suppose you are a prospective home buyer and you encounter an advertisement in the realty section of the newspaper: "Large home and ten acres needing attention."

What needs attention? The large home? The ten acres? Both? For the advertisement to be clear, some restructuring of the wording is necessary.

Unlike semantic ambiguity, syntactical ambiguity is seldom intended. Writers and speakers simply become careless in the way they put sentences together. After all, the meaning is clear to them. Why should it not be clear to others?

It should be noted that the fallacy of syntactical ambiguity most frequently occurs when a writer or speaker fails to indicate the referent of words such as "his," "hers," and "its" or does not make clear what a word or phrase modifies.

Syntactical ambiguity also occurs when we attempt to translate material from one culture to another. Difficulties can arise for a variety of reasons. There might not be an equivalent part of speech in the language into which a message is being translated. For example, in the Urdu language (the official language of Pakistan), there are no gerunds (a verbal noun ending in "ing"), and it is difficult to find an equivalent form for an English gerund. Even the placement of nouns and verbs vary from culture to culture. In the Japanese language, for instance, the verb usually comes at the end of a sentence. It is easy to see how these variations, and there are many others, could cause ambiguity.

Equivocation

The fallacy of *equivocation* is committed when a speaker makes a word or phrase appear to have only one meaning, when, in fact, he or she is using it in two different senses.

Let us suppose that a high-ranking public official made the following statement:

> This great nation of ours has a record of lending assistance whenever and wherever it is needed. If we are lending funds to any nation, however, we should have a reasonable expectation of being repaid.

Note the shift in meaning of the word *lending*. The context in which it first appears is typical of those where lending means "giving." Thus, we "give assistance" to those in need. In the second sentence, however, the context would suggest that lending means "loaning." When we loan funds, we expect to be repaid (with interest). Perhaps the speaker wants the connotation of unselfishness that surrounds the first use of lending to preclude the connotation of usury that might be evoked by the second use of the word.

Those who commit the fallacy of equivocation may not be aware of their error. For example, it is conceivable that a person might be unaware that the word *rational* can mean "logical" or "sane." That person might observe

> The psychiatrist says that rational people don't act the way Bill's been acting, but I was in a discussion with Bill just yesterday and found his arguments to be very rational. He backed up every one of his arguments with lots of good evidence.

It might well be that the person does not understand that the psychiatrist is making a judgment about Bill's sanity, not his ability to construct a logical argument. Whether the equivocation is intentional or unintentional is not particularly important. What is important is that the equivocation is detected and taken into account as part of the appraisal of the message. The fallacy is not always easy to detect, especially when the two different usages of the word or phrase are separated by several sentences, as they might be in a complex argument.

If you believe, as part of your research efforts, that the material you are reading is an equivocal message, or if you are listening to a speaker who is engaging in the fallacy of equivocation, you should try to identify the problematic word or phrase. Although precise definitions are never possible, focusing on the culprit is the first step to avoid becoming a victim of this common fallacy.

Equivocation and ambiguity are fallacies that stem from what is actually stated. *Innuendo,* on the other hand, is a matter of what is hinted at rather than explicitly stated. We see this fallacy when a writer or speaker, often through a skillful choice of words, brings us to the brink of a conclusion that would put someone or something in a bad light. Yet, as we indicated, the person committing this fallacy usually stops just short of asserting that conclusion. Because the fallacy of innuendo relies on suggestion instead of proof, innuendo is particularly insidious.

Innuendo

If someone were to state, "These street people may eventually get around to looking for a job," he or she would seem to be implying that the street people have not yet started a job search. Since no overt claim to that effect has been made, the speaker escapes the responsibility of providing any proof. In a like fashion, if someone were to state, "These college kids may get around to doing something worthwhile someday," he or she would be implying that college students presently are doing nothing worthwhile. By hinting at something rather than making an outright claim, the speaker avoids having to offer proof.

As you can see, innuendo enables an unscrupulous writer or speaker to attack someone or something while maintaining an avenue of escape. If a salesperson wanted to undermine a prospective customer's favorable opinion of a competitor's product, he or she might say, "Of course, if you're satisfied with that level of quality, I can see why you might want their product." The implication is that the competitor's product is of inferior quality, even though no such claim is made. Should the customer challenge the implied attack on the competitor's product, the salesperson could always say, "I didn't say their product was of inferior quality. I was simply noting that you are the ultimate judge of what you want." Thus, the salesperson can attack and then deny that he or she is attacking.

To the user of innuendo, its great utility resides in the freedom from responsibility it affords. There is no need to furnish evidence to back a claim that is only implied. This is particularly useful when there is no evidence to be found in the first place.

Although argument by innuendo can be encountered in many communication contexts, it is particularly noticeable in situations in which character attacks are a popular method of combat. In political campaigns, candidates try to undermine public trust of opponents; in courtrooms, lawyers try to shake jury confidence in the reliability of witnesses; in editorials and commentaries dealing with emotionally charged issues, exponents of competing ideologies try to impugn the motives of one another. In gathering supporting material for a speech, if you collect evidence from campaign speeches, trial transcripts, editorials, or commentaries, be especially alert to the possible presence of innuendo. If you hear innuendo in a speech, ask the speaker to spell out the evidence that led them to the conclusion they advanced. In no case should you blindly accept an implicit claim without being satisfied that the logic and support justifies the claim.

Separation from Context

When we take anything out of its usual surroundings and view it in isolation, it tends to take on a new dimension of meaning. We may see things in it we had not seen before; we may discover that it loses some or all of its former meaning.

When we take words, phrases, sentences, or even paragraphs out of the larger work of which they are a part, they can suggest meanings they did not suggest before. Thus, a person encountering something quoted out of context may make a judgment about the material that he or she would not make if seeing it in its original context. A few examples may illustrate this point.

Let us assume that you turn to the entertainment section of the newspaper in search of information about movies playing in your area. You see one advertised with testimonials worded as follows:

> ". . . something great." *Evening Sun*
> ". . . overwhelmingly beautiful." *Morning Post*
> "This film takes the prize. . . ." *Freeway Weekly*

You might conclude that the critics recommend the movie; however, the ellipses, which tell you that something has been omitted, are danger signals. Perhaps you ultimately discover that the *Evening Sun* said: "This modest little film pretends to be something great." The *Morning Post* may have stated: "Although the plot is absurd and the acting is abysmal, the scenery is overwhelmingly beautiful." *The Freeway Weekly* could have observed: "This film takes the prize for movies that will never make it to the video rental shelves."

A more serious example might be encountered on the editorial page, where a writer is giving reasons for opposing the confirmation of a presidential appointee:

> The candidate's own words convict him of partiality to the interests of the tobacco industry. How can we expect a fair ruling on legislation curtailing the sale of cigarettes in hospitals receiving federal subsidies from a man who has stated publicly, "My right to smoke cannot be abridged at the mere whim of those who happen to prefer a smoke-free environment"?

It is possible that the candidate may have made that remark in the context of an abstract discussion of the rule of law. He might well have said,

> Our legal system ensures that our rights cannot arbitrarily be abridged, however repugnant to others the exercise of our rights might be. Until their repugnance is translated into laws that meet the tests of constitutionality, our rights remain unfettered. My right to drink myself into a drunken stupor in the privacy of my home cannot be abridged at the mere whim of a neighbor who hates to see me self-destruct. My right to smoke cannot be abridged at the mere whim of those who happen to prefer a smoke-free environment. My right to do any number of equally irrational things cannot be abridged arbitrarily. There must be a law in place that, in principle, restricts the exercise of those rights.

Viewed in context, the quoted sentence suggests quite another meaning than the one assigned by the writer who quoted it out of context. Quoting out of context is not necessarily motivated by a desire to twist the meaning to suit the speaker's argument. Our perceptions are highly selective, so it is possible that the speaker sees only what he or she wants or expects to see and may not even have read the entire paragraph. Noticing that one sentence, the speaker may have assumed that the rest of the material was in harmony with his or her preconceived notions.

It was once said of a famous actor that he could read the telephone book aloud and make it sound like Shakespeare. By reading names, addresses, and numbers in a certain cadence and in a particular tone of voice, he could create the illusion of someone reading a sonnet or soliloquy. Although the illusion the actor created could hardly be classified as a fallacy, the practice of placing emphasis on another's words, phrases, or ideas that were never intended to be emphasized can constitute a fallacy if it misleads the reader or hearer. An example might be observed in a jury trial. Suppose the defendant, in replying to a question about his reason for striking the victim with a blunt instrument, replied, "I didn't *mean* to hurt him." The prosecutor, in his summation speech, might say to the jury,

> Let me remind you of the defendant's own words: "I didn't mean to *hurt* him." No, he had something much more lethal in mind. He wanted to *kill* him.

Infusion of Emphasis

The defendant's emphasis on the word *mean* suggests that he had no intention of inflicting harm. The prosecutor's emphasis on the word *hurt* suggests that the defendant had a sinister motive.

Another example might be afforded by news reports of a political candidate announcing her decision to quit the race for office. In a letter to the press, the candidate states,

> Nothing is more important to me than the welfare of my family. The prospect of a long and bitter campaign and the toll it would exact upon my family has made me reconsider my priorities. Accordingly, I am removing myself from consideration for the nomination.

Let us suppose that three different newspapers print the candidate's letter, but each provides a different headline for the story. One newspaper emphasizes the coming campaign in its headline: "Candidate sees bitter campaign and quits." Another headlines the matter of priorities: "Candidate shuffles priorities and deals herself out." The third newspaper has a headline that calls attention to the candidate's devotion to her family: "Candidate chooses family over nomination." All three newspapers have, in some measure, distorted the candidate's message by emphasizing only a small portion of the ideas contained in the letter.

Constant vigilance is necessary on the part of anyone who is listening to a speech or sorting through the evidence to be used in a speech. If you have encountered evidence through the spoken word, remember that vocal shadings can change the points of emphasis within a message. If you are looking at headlines for clues to the content of a printed message, remember that headlines are selective in their content and may not fairly represent the information to follow.

In addition to being sensitive to the various word deceptions just examined, a critical thinker should be on the lookout for extraneous and irrelevant appeals that may be used to cloud issues and hide inadequacies of evidence and reasoning. Such appeals can have a telling effect on an unwary researcher or listener, diverting attention from the real issues by the strong allure of emotionally charged material.

Extraneous Appeals

Of the fallacies involving the introduction of extraneous matter, perhaps the most common are (1) character attacks, (2) emotional appeals, (3) appeals to authority, and (4) biasing the case. Let us look at each of these fallacies so that you can be aware of their impact on the communication process.

Character Attacks

Called the *argumentum ad hominem* fallacy, this tactic involves discrediting an opponent's character instead of dealing with the relevant issues at hand. Thus, the arguments are transferred from principles to personalities. Such arguments seem to suggest that truth can be forthcoming only from persons of good character; hence, one should reject anything said by a person whose character is suspect.

You would encounter this fallacy in listening to a speaker say, "Professor Jones says cleaning up the environment should be this nation's top priority, but what does he know about cleanliness? He has worn the same dirty jacket to class the last two weeks." An *ad hominem* fallacy is also taking place when a speaker recently noted, "The city's new highway program should be vetoed. The highway commissioner is a notorious troublemaker and philanderer." In another example, a columnist, in expressing opposition to a proposed trade agreement with a foreign nation, might impugn the character of that nation's representative rather than addressing the trade agreement itself:

> So we have a proposal brought to us by a man who lied to his fellow citizens about his personal wealth, who spent his official salary on caviar and cars while others starved from want of bread, who made pious declarations of his devotion to the ending of world hunger while feeding his kennel of dogs the most expensive meat to be found anywhere.

Ask yourself if the person's alleged character flaw is germane to the issue being discussed.

Reference to another's personal circumstances or lifestyle is often made in an effort to detract from the merit of what that person is saying. For example, suppose that a millionaire member of Congress sponsors a bill to aid the homeless. An opponent of the bill might make this observation: "How can a wealthy person like my distinguished colleague here possibly understand the plight of the street people? She has never been cold or hungry." In another instance, a priest's argument for salary increases for schoolteachers may be met with the reply, "It's easy for Father Dawson to ask us to raise our own taxes. He doesn't have a houseful of kids to raise." The person's lifestyle is hardly relevant in either instance, yet every day views are questioned simply because they emanate from someone whose circumstances are unlike those of the majority of people.

When you are confronted with *ad hominem* thinking, it is often a good technique to ask the creator of the fallacy to offer you other good reasons, apart from those related to the personal attacks, for believing as they do. In most instances, you are apt to be confronted with even more fallacies, for people who use *ad hominem* are usually unaware that they are using such appeals.

Emotional Appeals

Playing upon the emotions of people to color a cause and/or distract from the merits of that cause is one of the most common of all fallacies. We are not trying to suggest that there is something inherently wrong with asking people to become emotionally involved with an issue; what we are saying is that the use of emotion should not be a substitute for sound logic and appropriate evidence. When emotion is used as a substitute, it becomes an error in reasoning and thinking. Appealing to the emotions and prejudices of readers or listeners is called *argumentum ad populum*. As we just noted, instead of presenting empirical evidence and logical argument, an *ad populum* speaker or writer attempts to win support for his or her point of view by enlisting our nonrational impulses. There is no denying the fact that emotional appeals can be very persuasive. It is up to us as consumers of persuasion to be on our guard against any attempt by others to bypass the rational grounds for belief or action. Fortunately, appeals to passions and prejudices become less successful as individuals learn to recognize such appeals.

In this section, we will sample a variety of fallacies resulting from unwarranted appeals to emotions and prejudices. Bear in mind, however, that the possibilities for fallacious use of such appeals extend far beyond the range that our samples may suggest.

Fear Francis Bacon, Henry David Thoreau, Franklin Roosevelt, and Bertrand Russell entertained similar views of fear. In 1623, Bacon observed, "Nothing is terrible except fear itself." Thoreau wrote in 1831, "Nothing is so much to be feared as fear." Roosevelt declared in 1933, "Let me assert my firm belief that the only thing we have to fear is fear itself." In 1950, Bertrand Russell concluded, "To conquer fear is the beginning of wisdom." All were alluding to the kind of fear that lacks a rational basis—nameless, unreasoning fear. It is an appeal to this kind of fear that we brand as fallacious.

You have probably seen advertisements for home security systems that depict a shadowy, menacing figure slipping through a window that has been forced open or standing silhouetted in the doorway of a dark bedroom. These manufactured threats may have their counterparts in the real world, but the point is that the advertiser wants you to use your imagination as a substitute for tangible evidence of a threat. Unless the advertiser can couple the imagined threat with hard evidence of a real threat, the advertisement is nonrational.

Fear arising out of presumed threats to personal safety and well-being can exert a coercive force on our judgment. However, equally coercive in its effect is fear of scorn or rejection. A publisher who touts a beauty book with the slogan "Learn how to hang onto your mate" is hinting that the permanency of a relationship is threatened by ignorance of the information contained in the book, yet no evidence is produced to show the likelihood of such a consequence. To take another example, note that some fitness salons seldom sell fitness in their advertising. They sell freedom from the fear of being ostracized; nowhere do they offer any evidence that one is in danger of being ostracized.

Naturally, there are times when it is perfectly logical to experience fear. If someone offers you evidence of an imminent threat to your personal safety, you ought to feel fearful; however, you should be skeptical of appeals to fear that fail to provide evidence of the reality of a threat.

Pity The acceptability of a product, a proposal, or an idea ought to depend on its demonstrated worth, yet there are those persons who try to persuade us to buy, to support, or to believe something not because it has merit but because we are made to feel sorry for the persons themselves or those they represent. Appeals to pity and compassion are aimed at us from many quarters.

Perhaps you have had experiences similar to the following. Someone asks you to purchase a magazine subscription, not because of the merits of the magazine but because "it will help us earn enough money to bring our grandfather here from overseas." A friend begs you to date his cousin, not because you might find the date a pleasant experience but because "that poor kid hasn't had a date in ages." Someone asks you to overlook a violation of confidence, not because the violation was without harmful consequences but because "I had just flunked a midterm exam and didn't realize what I was saying."

It is entirely possible that you may encounter an appeal to pity or compassion in the speeches or writings of those who have broken the law, exceeded their authority, or violated the public trust. Unable to defend their actions, they attempt to portray themselves as martyrs, as victims of circumstance, as well-intentioned patriots trying to do what is best for their country, thereby hoping to escape deserved punishment. The records of criminal trials and congressional hearings offer ample evidence of the popularity of this type of appeal.

Because we all have feelings and are not made of stone, overcoming calls for pity is often difficult to conquer. We are all compassionate people who care about the welfare of others. However, if we allow ourselves to be swayed by pity, without either recognizing it or asking for other evidence, we might be guilty of thinking in a noncritical manner. It is best to grant that our emotions are involved, but at the same time we should ask the maker of the message if a call to pity is the only reason we should adopt the proposal.

Sentimental Attachment   Closely allied to pity is our need for sentimental attachments. Many of our actions are guided by a strong desire to preserve the things we cherish. Love of our family, friends, nation, and traditions are sentiments that are deeply ingrained and exercise a strong influence on the way we see the world.

Appeals to these sentiments are, in many cases, fully justified. The abuse occurs when they are used as a shortcut to persuasion. A politician urges us to support a particular policy because "I know you love this country as much as I do," yet she fails to explain why support of the policy is necessarily the best way to demonstrate that love. "Loyal opposition" might be an even better way. Witness the plea of a ruler who calls on his neighbors to join him in a "holy war" even though his private agenda is anything but holy. History affords numerous examples of the misuse of appeals to sentiment.

Prominently displayed symbols of things we cherish are often used in connection with a variety of messages. The "halo effect" of the flag displayed behind a political candidate supposedly lends credibility to his or her message. The picture of a happy family seated at the Thanksgiving table in a grocery advertisement suggests that the purchase of turkey, at this particular market, is a demonstration of love for your family.

A critical thinker must be on guard against subtle applications of the tactic. Whenever you feel yourself warming to an argument, pause for a moment and consider whether sentiment is an influential factor. If it is, then you would do well to reexamine the argument to see if there are logical elements that support the sentiment.

Vanity   Sir Richard Steele, writing in *The Spectator* in 1711, stated, "Among all the diseases of the mind there is not one more epidemical or more pernicious than the love of flattery." We all enjoy a compliment, especially when it is well deserved, but we have learned, often through bitter experience, that compliments can blind us to factors that may be detrimental to our welfare.

Persuaders have long recognized the power that flattery can exert. When used with subtlety and seeming sincerity, it disarms the flattered person and predisposes him or her to be more receptive to the flatterer. Therein lies the danger. Once the critical faculty is put on hold, the person becomes more susceptible to suggestion without any proof.

A common ploy used by speakers is to pay a compliment, perhaps praising the community, the auditorium, a local hero, or something that evokes civic pride. Then the speaker may compliment the audience itself for its generosity, openmindedness, or maturity. Having done so, the speaker moves into his or her message with the presumed goodwill of the audience. Then comes the mischief. An assertion is made, but, instead of offering proof for the assertion, the speaker says:

> I know you folks are well read enough to be familiar with the facts, so I won't bore you with reciting them here tonight. Needless to say, they demonstrate the magnitude of the problem.

You do not need to become cynical of every compliment you receive, but remind yourself of its irrelevance to the matter you are supposed to be judging.

Appeals to Authority

If one attempts to prove the soundness of a position by citing the testimony of a person well qualified to express an informed opinion on the matter, then one is making valid use of expert opinion. However, if one attempts to support an argument by quoting the judgment of a person who is not an authority in the field, the views of an unidentified authority, or the testimony of a person who is likely to be significantly biased in some way, then one is engaging in the fallacy of appealing to authority. Although we alerted you to the danger of this fallacy in chapter 6, when we discussed evidence, it is important enough to justify a second presentation.

The fallacy of appeals to authority is known as *argumentum ad vercundiam*. As we indicated, this fallacy often shows itself when a speaker offers proof for a position by improperly making an appeal to a "name," to an institution, or to an authority; for example, "George Washington, the father of our country, warned us against the danger of foreign alliances; therefore, I maintain that we should withdraw from the United Nations." Granted, George Washington was well qualified to offer sound advice on American policy in the context of his time, but the needs of modern foreign affairs are quite different from the needs expressed in Washington's time. Recently we heard a speaker committing the fallacy of irrelevant authority when they stated, "I do not see how we can cut the budget one more penny. Reverend Smith, my minister, said we did not even have enough money at the present time to finance the football team."

In preempting this fallacy, we urge you to do three things. First, if the speaker or writer is invoking an unidentified source, you should immediately ask for the authority to be identified. Second, try to determine if the authority is biased. Someone from PETA (People for the Ethical Treatment of Animals), while well meaning, may not be the best person to comment on the use of horses for rodeos. Third, and most importantly, don't be intimidated when someone with a famous name is improperly used to support an argument. An expert in one area is not automatically an expert in all other areas. William Shakespeare, Mark Twain, and Carl Sandburg are great writers, but they should not be used to support an argument for a balanced budget.

Biasing the Case

This fallacy consists of an attempt to inoculate a reader or listener against an argument about to be advanced by an opponent. In effect, it asks the reader or listener to pay little heed to what will be said by the opposition. The reasons given are more emotional than logical. In fact, they are frequently *ad hominem* attacks or appeals to prejudices. For example, a president might say, "You can be sure that the wolves on Capitol Hill are going to try to tell you that this policy will lead to fiscal disaster, but, when you hear them, you will be hearing nothing new—just a rerun of the same old line."

Faulty Logic

What the French writer Jean de la Bruyère said over two hundred years ago is still true today: "Logic is the art of making truth prevail." In the next few pages, let us look at some ways that search for truth might be hindered.

Violations of logical consistency, whether intentional or unintentional, are to be found in the messages of saints and sinners alike. Their capacity for misleading should be a matter of great concern to anyone who wishes to make sound judgments.

Hasty Generalizations

Snap judgments, jumping to conclusions, and generalizations based on insufficient evidence are all examples of the hasty generalization fallacy. In this fallacy, a speaker draws a universal conclusion from evidence warranting only a restricted conclusion. An example of a hasty generalization is saying that marijuana has great health benefits because you read *one* article about *one* sick person who felt better after smoking marijuana.

This fallacy is common in daily life. Most of us can recall instances in which travelers have experienced one or two unpleasant situations and then reached conclusions concerning the honesty and character of all the people in that particular city. Another example is a speaker who concluded that all supporters of the Libertarian Party are rich. The speaker stated, "Eric Foresman supported the Libertarian party and he is a millionaire; Scott Allen supported them and he is very rich; so, you see that all supporters of the Libertarian party are rich."

One of the reasons it is so very difficult to deal with hasty generalizations is that the people who present them are usually sincere in their belief regarding the conclusion reached by the generalization. In addition, most generalizations do not stem from the facts, but rather from personal experience. Because these experiences are meaningful and real to the people offering the generalizations, they usually do not realize that their conclusions are mistaken. In some instances, you might simply say to the person, "That is an interesting illustration, do you know of any other cases?"

Begging the Question

The fallacy of begging the question can take many different forms. But what they all have in common is that the person committing this fallacy is assuming at the outset of an argument the very point that is to be established in the conclusion. Put in slightly different terms, the conclusion appears as a premise in this fallacy. In addition, begging the question is a serious fallacy because a speaker often assumes the truth or falsity of a statement without proof. If someone making a speech were to state that "the widespread cheating among our students is bad and, therefore, should be abolished," he or she would be begging the question. In this example, the speaker is taking for granted that cheating exists, when the statement cannot justify such a conclusion.

Begging the question normally appears in the form of "arguing in a circle." If you use one proposition to prove another proposition, you are engaging in this fallacy. Arguing in a circle usually appears in the following form: "Medical Plan X is best because the experts say so. How do we know who the experts are? They are the persons who prefer Medical Plan X." In this case, begging the question is illustrated by taking as a premise what is true only if the conclusion has been granted to be correct. In another example, a speaker also assumed the conclusion at the outset when he said, "The deterioration and corruption in government, which we all see every day, is the direct result of the fact that we have too many Democrats in the Senate."

We suggest two defenses against begging the question. First, keep track of the logical structure of the argument. This will help you discover if the main premise and the conclusion are exactly the same. Second, you can directly confront the person engaging in this fallacy. Ask them why the conclusion should be assumed without evidence.

Card stacking is one of the most reprehensible of all the fallacies we have discussed. It depends upon exaggerations, false evidence, misstatements of facts, and often outright lies. Card stacking involves the use of distractions and/or illogical statements in order to give the best or the worst possible case for an idea, a program, a person, or a product. The speaker selects only the items that support his or her position, regardless of the distortion they produce. Listing a few of the accomplishments of one's administration while leaving out all the failures is an example of this technique. This one-sided presentation often passes as the truth if the recipients of this fallacy fail to ask themselves, and eventually the speaker, if there is another side to the issue. Aesop, the Greek fabulist, reminds us that "Every truth has two sides; it is well to look at both before we commit ourselves to either."

Card Stacking

A half-truth, as a fallacy, is much like card stacking. In this case, a speaker tells only part of the story or offers a small portion of the facts. Notice the half-truth in the following example:

Half-Truths

> In selecting an area hospital for our trauma center, we ought to rule out Rosewood Hospital, because it has a higher death rate among patients than any other hospital in the county.

What the speaker is neglecting to mention is that Rosewood Hospital accommodates three times as many geriatric patients as any other hospital and would naturally have a higher death rate. Hence, what is happening is that the speaker is leaving out evidence and offering half-truths by only presenting us with half the facts.

Applying to the part what may be true of the whole is known as the fallacy of division—for example, "His home state is called the 'Land of Lakes,' so he probably has a lake, or at least a pond, on his property." The speaker would be committing the fallacy of division if he said, "John belongs to the fraternity that was just suspended from campus. Therefore, I would conclude that John cannot be trusted." Here is a clear example of taking a part of a larger premise and misapplying it to an individual case. Earlier, when we talked about stereotyping, we were dealing with notions that probably had their origin in fallacies of division.

Fallacy of Division

The opposite of the fallacy of division is the fallacy of composition, in which properties of the part are assumed to be properties of the whole. Thus, if one house in a subdivision is contaminated by radon, a person might say, "I sure wouldn't live in that contaminated subdivision." We would also be seeing this fallacy if someone said, "Since Tom

Fallacy of Composition

is a great football player, the team he plays for must be a great team." Again, the major problem in the mental error is that someone is asking us to assume that a characteristic *automatically* passes from the parts to the whole.

Non Sequitur

In a broad sense, any argument that fails to establish its conclusion may be said to be *non sequitur*, because the meaning of the phrase is simply "it does not follow." More specifically, the fallacy of *non sequitur* means that a conclusion is drawn from premises that provide no adequate logical ground for it, or that have no relevant connection with it. Notice in the following two examples that the points being linked together do not make much sense, yet the speaker, employing weak or counterfeit reasoning, asks us to connect them. "Because Jones is a good husband and a fine father, he ought to be elected mayor." "Since only a few people are smart enough to handle complex problems, the wealth of this country should be in the hands of the very rich." It is quite obvious in both examples that a logical cause-effect relationship cannot be made. Still other statements point out how speakers reach false conclusions as they try to establish cause-effect connections. "Since only men can run a mile in under four minutes, they should be the only ones flying jet airplanes." "The child is unhappy, beautiful, and a college freshman; she must therefore come from an average American family."

One of the most common and insidious forms of this fallacy is *post hoc, ergo propter hoc*—"after this, therefore because of this." This fallacy assumes that because one occurrence precedes another in time, the one is the cause of the other. Superstitions belong here. If you walk under a ladder on your way to class, receive an A that same day, and then conclude that walking under a ladder gives a person high grades, you are guilty of *post hoc, ergo propter hoc*. A speaker noted, "Since minority groups have been given more educational opportunity, we have had an increase in the crime rate throughout the United States. I would conclude, therefore, that the growth in crime is directly related to education." Here again, it is not sufficient to say there is a connection simply because one thing followed the other. In short, because two things happen in sequence does not mean that they are logically or causally connected.

Either/or Thinking

Either/or thinking, often called *polarization*, is when we see issues only in terms of two extreme positions and therefore polarize the arguments. Polarization is a problem because the English language has many words that are extremes and therefore speakers are tempted to use these words to make their speeches startling and dramatic. Think for a moment of the countless words that represent two ends of a continuum: hot/cold, tall/short, relaxed/nervous, friendly/unfriendly, legal/illegal, good/bad, and so forth. The problem is that in reality very few issues and questions actually involve extremes. Most problems and solutions are located in the gray areas. That is to say, most of the challenges we face are not as simple as good or bad, right or wrong, yes or no. When a speaker says to you, "One has to believe that capital punishment is the only way to stop the crime on our streets," he or she is using the simplistic logic found in either/or thinking. You should learn to avoid polarization, both in perception and language. In viewing the world, speakers should realize that people are seldom one thing or another. You can also learn to describe the world with words that are less extreme if you increase your vocabulary.

The logical fallacy of allness occurs when we posit that we have either observed all there is to observe or that we have said all there is to say on a subject. It is a narrow and naive view to believe that any of us can perceive all that is outside of us or describe every nuance of an event or idea. Both perception and language leave things out, and to assume otherwise is an error in our thinking. Hence, be attentive to a speaker who says, "I have researched and examined every single aspect of this issue, and it is my contention that it is a bad idea."

Allness

Summary

In making a fair assessment of the materials discovered through research, one has to use critical thinking. In order to improve our ability to think critically, we must first take an inventory of our present way of thinking. Some of the bad habits people can acquire include relying on frozen evaluations, seeing matters in terms of their own self-interest, practicing ego-defense, getting involved in ethnocentrism, and harboring stereotypes. Once we are aware of our own thinking habits, we can make corrections where needed.

As we turn to an examination of the thinking of others, we need to be sensitive to the presence of unsound modes of arguing, called fallacies. Fallacies involving verbal flaws include semantical ambiguity, syntactical ambiguity, equivocation, innuendo, isolating words from their context, and adding undue emphasis to certain words or phrases.

Fallacies involving the use of irrelevant matters include character attacks, emotional appeals, appeals to authorities, and biasing the case.

Fallacies of reasoning include hasty generalization, begging the question, card stacking, half-truths, fallacy of division, fallacy of composition, *non sequitur*, either/or thinking, and allness.

One never goes
so far as when
one doesn't know
where one is going.

Johann Wolfgang von Goethe

Chapter 10

Organization
Assembling Your Ideas

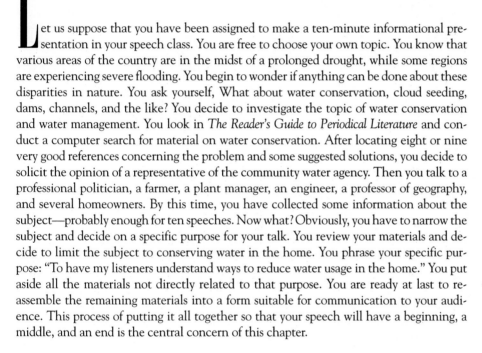

Order is half of life.

German proverb

Let us suppose that you have been assigned to make a ten-minute informational presentation in your speech class. You are free to choose your own topic. You know that various areas of the country are in the midst of a prolonged drought, while some regions are experiencing severe flooding. You begin to wonder if anything can be done about these disparities in nature. You ask yourself, What about water conservation, cloud seeding, dams, channels, and the like? You decide to investigate the topic of water conservation and water management. You look in *The Reader's Guide to Periodical Literature* and conduct a computer search for material on water conservation. After locating eight or nine very good references concerning the problem and some suggested solutions, you decide to solicit the opinion of a representative of the community water agency. Then you talk to a professional politician, a farmer, a plant manager, an engineer, a professor of geography, and several homeowners. By this time, you have collected some information about the subject—probably enough for ten speeches. Now what? Obviously, you have to narrow the subject and decide on a specific purpose for your talk. You review your materials and decide to limit the subject to conserving water in the home. You phrase your specific purpose: "To have my listeners understand ways to reduce water usage in the home." You put aside all the materials not directly related to that purpose. You are ready at last to reassemble the remaining materials into a form suitable for communication to your audience. This process of putting it all together so that your speech will have a beginning, a middle, and an end is the central concern of this chapter.

Importance of Organization

Putting your ideas and information into a logical sequence is an essential step in successful communication. The famous Russian mystic Madam Swetchine said it far more eloquently when she wrote, "To have ideas is to gather flowers, to put them in order is to weave them into garlands." Knowing how to organize your ideas and materials can benefit you in any kind of communication encounter, whether it is a casual conversation, an interview, a group discussion, or a formal public speech. The specific advantages of being well organized are numerous. First, *the organizational process enables you to put your material together in a variety of ways to help you determine the sequence of ideas best suited to your listeners and to your purpose*. In this way, it enables you to detect the places where more evidence is needed to support a point or where logical flaws might be present.

Second, *clear organization helps both you and your audience retain ideas with greater ease during the presentation*. You benefit because, during the pressure of delivering the speech, you do not have to search for a sequence or an order; these decisions have already been made deliberately and systematically. The audience is rewarded in that the

Clear organization
promotes greater
understanding and
encourages listeners to
remain attentive.

material "makes sense." You know from your own experiences that it is easier to comprehend and retain information if its flow and arrangement is self-evident and vivid rather than murky and disjointed. Clarity of organization adds to that flow. Remember, your listeners must understand your message at first utterance, for, unlike reading, they cannot go back and reread what you have said.

Third, *by organizing your material into a meaningful sequence you can see the relationship between the main ideas and subordinate ones.* This process of sorting everything out before the talk also enables you to very early on observe both gaps and redundancies in your material.

Fourth, *if what you say is well ordered, your listeners will assign it greater credibility.* They will, of course, also perceive you in a more credible light if your material is well sequenced and free from distracting verbal excursions. On many occasions, we deem a speaker to be poorly prepared if we have a difficult time following what he or she has to say; yet, if that speaker is clear, we see him or her as credible. In short, clear organization promotes greater understanding and encourages listeners to remain attentive.

Although there are a variety of approaches to speech organization, we shall concentrate on the method that involves (1) formulating a core statement that expresses the central idea of the speech, (2) phrasing main points and subpoints that support the core statement, and (3) choosing appropriate patterns to show how the main points relate to one another. We will talk about how to devise an overall speech plan and discuss the mechanics of outlining. Our approach to speech organization is based on the assumption that the message will be divided into three major parts—the introduction, the body, and the conclusion. Although not all messages need to use this format, it is workable in the majority of cases.

As you begin to put together the materials that will go into the body of your speech, you will find it useful to have your general purpose (to persuade, inform, or entertain) and a specific focal point always in mind. We have already discussed general and specific purposes elsewhere in the book, so now let us examine some methods of narrowing your concentration even more precisely. One way to further compress your general and specific purposes is to compose a sentence that, in effect, crystallizes your speech into one sentence, called the **core statement.** A core statement serves as the unifying element around which you can assemble the materials that will help you accomplish your general and specific purposes. It is, in short, a specific declaration of what you expect to accomplish with your speech. For example, if your general purpose is to inform and your specific purpose is "to have the audience understand ways to reduce water usage in the home," your core statement might be "There are seven things you can do to reduce water usage in the bathroom, kitchen, and laundry." With that core statement as a focal point, you can arrange your materials into those that concern water usage in each of the separate areas indicated. If your general goal is to inform and your specific purpose is "to have the audience understand the features to look for when buying a laptop computer," your core statement might be "The principal features to look for when buying a laptop computer are display clarity, keyboard adequacy, speed, and portability." Again, you can see how the core statement suggests the ways in which the materials can be put into orderly groups.

If your speech is designed to persuade, your core statement might be phrased as a declaration of policy, such as "Off-shore oil drilling should be prohibited along the southern California coastline," or it might be worded as a value judgment, such as "Air travel is safer than rail travel." Perhaps it takes the form of a statement alleging something to be true, such as "Loud music has caused hearing loss in many teenagers."

The core statement of an informative speech might suggest the steps in a process, such as "Cheese making involves coagulation, compression, and curing." It may suggest the parts of a whole, such as "The principal parts of a sailboat rudder are the tiller, the head, and the blade." It may suggest the characteristics that distinguish the subject from other closely related subjects, such as this definition of stage fright: "Stage fright is a form of communication apprehension specific to a given communication encounter." As you can see from the examples cited in this paragraph and the preceding paragraph, the core statement calls for development by supporting material in order to carry its intended meaning to the audience.

When do you formulate your core statement? Ideally, just as soon as you have completed your investigation and analysis of the subject. With the results of your research before you, you will be in a position to ask yourself, What does all this add up to? Your answer should provide you with the elements necessary to compose your core statement.

In wording your core statement, be careful to phrase it in terms broad enough to cover all the major areas to be included in your speech, yet specific enough to suggest what will not be included. Compare the phrasing of the following statements:

Core Statement A: Successful weight loss involves several considerations.

Core Statement B: Successful weight loss involves a proper diet, proper exercise, and a proper mental attitude.

Statement A suffers from the ambiguity of "several considerations." Statement B indicates precisely what will be discussed.

Core Statement

One of the benefits of composing a core statement at the outset of the organizational process is that it provides you with a way to test the relevance of any material you expect to introduce into the speech. If any proposed main point, subpoint, or piece of supporting material doesn't relate to the core statement, then you can discard it as irrelevant. In this way, the unity of the speech is maintained.

Up to this point, we have discussed the core statement as a device that helps a speaker organize materials efficiently. You may be wondering whether the speaker actually utters the core statement while presenting the speech and, if so, at what point. It is entirely possible that the core statement need not be uttered if it is clearly implied in the way the speech unfolds. However, it is usually a good idea to state it, especially in a speech to inform. You can state it just prior to the first main point of the speech so that the audience knows what to expect and what not to expect in the way of information. Hearing the core statement enables the listeners to adjust their expectations and, thus, listen with greater efficiency. Sometimes the core statement is repeated at the end of the speech to help reinforce the learning process. In speeches to persuade, the core statement (sometimes called the thesis or proposition) may precede or follow the arguments designed to support it. There is no set rule that prescribes when it should be uttered or if it should be uttered. Your careful analysis of the audience and the situation should afford clues as to your best strategy.

Let us conclude our discussion of the core statement by reminding you that a core statement should (1) have but one central idea, (2) be worded in very specific language, (3) be a complete sentence, and (4) be audience centered.

Formulating Main Points and Subpoints

Once you have formulated your core statement, you can lay out the main points that will clarify, reinforce, or prove the core statement. These main points serve as the principal units of the body of the speech. Even though it is your introduction that will begin the speech, in the preparation stages it is far more beneficial to plan your body before you worry about the introduction and conclusion. Usually, the device you use to start your speech takes its impetus from the body. Hence, you begin the organizational process by translating your core statement into main points and subpoints.

Most speeches have two to five main points. Like the core statement, the main points are also worded as statements, but each point deals with only one aspect of the core statement—for example:

Core Statement:	The key factors in selecting a room air conditioner are ease of installation, cooling efficiency, and energy consumption.
Main Point:	I. Ease of installation depends on the size of the window opening, the weight of the cabinet, and the type of mounting hardware.
Main Point:	II. Cooling efficiency is dependent on the unit's BTU rating, the thermostat, and the size and condition of the room to be cooled.
Main Point:	III. Energy consumption is directly related to the size of the motor.

The following guidelines may assist you as you select and phrase the main points of your speech. First, *make certain that each main point is a direct outgrowth of the core statement.* Second, see that *each main point is clearly distinguishable from the other main points of the speech.* Third, be sure that *the main points, taken collectively, develop the core statement completely.* Let us now examine each of these guidelines in detail.

To be considered a main point, a statement must contribute directly to the proof, explanation, or illustration of the core statement. One way to determine whether or not a statement is a main point of a persuasive or argumentative speech is to place such connectives as *because* and *for* between the core statement and the main point in question. Following is an example:

Core Statement: You should buy term insurance, *because*
  I. It provides sufficient coverage at less cost than whole-life.
  II. It is convertible to whole-life.
  III. It is usually renewable.

The relationship between the core statement and the main points of an expository speech may be checked by using expressions such as *namely, for example,* and *in that.*

Core Statement: Synthetic cooking oil has attractive features, namely,
  I. It has no cholesterol.
  II. It has no calories.
  III. It tastes the same as vegetable oil.

Can you tell which of the following main points is not clearly related to the core statement?

Core Statement: There are myths regarding the effectiveness of some vitamins.
  I. Vitamin C does not prevent colds.
  II. Vitamin B_6 is not useful in treating premenstrual syndrome.
  III. Vitamin C is not found in all four food groups.
  IV. Vitamin E does not help women with mammary dysplasia.

Although the main points have a common kinship to the core statement, they should nonetheless be separate from one another. Which of the following points seem to overlap one another?

Core Statement: You should buy generic drugs.
  I. They are just as effective as brand-name drugs.
  II. They are cheaper than brand-name drugs.
  III. They are often more available than brand-name drugs.
  IV. They are a godsend to people on a tight budget.

Points I and III are apparently dealing with separate issues, but point II sounds more like a subhead of point IV. Unless the main points are clearly distinguishable from one another, listeners are apt to become confused by the developmental pattern.

Relationship to the Core Statement

Separation from Other Main Points

Collective Completeness of the Main Points

How can we tell when we have formulated all the potential main points of a speech? Only when every facet of the core statement has been indicated for development somewhere. We do not consider an airplane complete if one of its wings is missing. Similarly, if one aspect of the core statement does not find a place in the main points already formulated, then another main point is called for.

Determining all the essential parts is seldom easy. If you are selling automobiles and want to convince a customer that a particular model is the best one to buy, you should determine what constitutes a "best" car, not from your own personal view, but from the probable vantage point of the customer. To your customer, the "best" car might be the most stylish or the most powerful or the most economical to operate, so try to look at your core statement through the eyes of your listeners and ask, What points will the speech have to cover before winning audience agreement? or What points will the speech have to clarify before listeners fully understand?

Although our discussion in this section has centered on the selection and phrasing of main points, all the principles discussed are equally applicable to the selection and phrasing of subpoints. A subpoint bears the same relationship to a main point that a main point bears to the core statement.

When deciding on and arranging your main points, we remind you to ask yourself: (1) can some main points be combined? (2) are the main points clear? (3) do they directly relate to the main assertion you are advancing? and (4) are they of equal weight? The answers to these four questions will enable you to organize the remainder of your speech into a clear and logical form.

Organizational Patterns

We have all had the experience of recognizing a familiar face but then finding it almost impossible to remember just where we have seen that face before. We struggle to remember the occasion or the surroundings in which we have seen the person. Sometimes we give up in exasperation; at other times, we remember that the face belongs to the person who sat next to us on a flight from New York to Atlanta, to the supermarket checker, or to the mail carrier. Psychologists tell us that things perceived in isolation do not have as much meaning as when they are seen in relationship to other things, which give them meaning. We develop habits of organizing our perceptions into meaningful contexts. Some things we perceive within a time frame, others in terms of their spatial placement, and still others in terms of logical parts, components, or divisions. We organize our perceptions of argumentative and nonargumentative relationships in special ways.

A list of organizational patterns that we use could go on and on, but we will concentrate on those that have proved to be particularly serviceable to speakers over the years. Keep in mind that no one pattern is suitable for all topics and purposes. Therefore, an organization scheme must be selected with great care. Your ultimate plan should take into account certain predictions you have made about your potential listeners. Your audience analysis should have told you about their probable level of acquaintance with the topic, their probable attitude toward your specific purpose, and their probable attitude toward you as a spokesperson on the topic.

One more introductory observation is called for before we explore some of the more widely used organizational patterns. Please keep in mind that we will reexamine most of these patterns later in the book, when we discuss the speeches to inform, persuade, and entertain. Our purpose at this point is simply to look at the various patterns so that you can use them to prepare your outlines and your speeches.

Many subjects can be developed in terms of a chronological (time) sequence. Most obvious are speeches that deal with the steps in how to do something or make something or speeches that treat historical matters. For example, in the fall season of the year, speeches about the origin of holidays, such as Halloween and Thanksgiving, are popular. If you were asked about the origin of one of the later holidays, such as St. Valentine's Day, you would probably devise a speech pattern that would start with the first known traces of the celebration and then work forward to the present time. The design of your main points might resemble the following:

Chronological Pattern

Core Statement: St. Valentine's Day has a long history.
  I.   The annual Roman feast of Lupercalia, held on February 15, was its most likely predecessor.
  II. The feast was Christianized in A.D. 270 to commemorate the martyrdom of Saint Valentine.
  III. The holiday was celebrated thereafter by west European Christians on February 14.
  IV. In the 1840s, the first commercial Valentine greeting cards were sold in the United States.

The chronological pattern is also effective when examining a person's life. Notice the time sequence in the example shown below:
  I.   The life of Martin Luther King, Jr., clearly reflects the many influences on his nonviolent philosophy.
      A.   The influence of his family.
      B.   The influence of his education.
      C.   The influence of his meeting with Mahatma Gandhi.

Historical events do not necessarily have to be "old" to use the chronological pattern. For instance, a student talking about federal income tax regulations looked at those regulations under the Reagan, Bush, and Clinton administrations.

As indicated earlier, historical time sequencing is just one of many topics that can fit into the chronological pattern. When someone offers instructions or describes a process, he or she is using a step-by-step method, which is a kind of time pattern. The following example illustrates how the time pattern applies to a speech describing the manufacture of soap.

Core Statement: The manufacture of soap involves four basic procedures.
  I.   Fats, oils, alkali, and salt are boiled.
  II. The resulting curd is washed and allowed to settle.
  III. The upper layer of the curd is churned.
  IV. The resulting product is cut, shaped, and stamped.

Instructions for changing a tire might include these steps: (1) laying out proper tools, (2) jacking up the car, (3) removing the lug nuts, (4) taking off the flat tire, (5) putting on the spare tire, and (6) letting down the jack.

It is a good idea to keep the number of main points in a time pattern to no more than five—three to five is the ideal range—for ease of understanding and retention. Consequently, you will find it convenient to group a number of chronological details under general headings, such as "The first era was . . . ," "The first decade was characterized by . . . ," or "The ancient Greeks were the first to systematize the study of public speaking."

The chronological pattern is a popular organizational scheme in that nearly everyone perceives events and processes in this linear fashion. The weakness of this pattern is that it does not easily lend itself to complex discussions or issues related to causes and effects.

Spatial Pattern

As the name implies, spatial patterns organize main points around the relationships based on how various parts connect to each other. Geographical topics fit neatly into this pattern. If, for example, you were talking about population growth around the world, you could discuss various regions of the world:

Core Statement: The increase in the world's population is a serious problem.
  I.   Population growth in Africa.
  II. Population growth in Asia.
  III. Population growth in Latin America.

Speeches involving locations or tours usually lend themselves to the spatial pattern.

Core Statement: There are many special sites to see when visiting Yosemite Valley.
  I.   As you enter the park, you see a magnificent view as you descend into the valley.
  II. Once you reach the bottom of the valley you experience the beauty of Yosemite Falls.
  III. From the middle of the valley you will be able to see Half Dome.

Speeches about the spread of an empire, the encroachment of a disease, or the location of natural resources are all examples of how one might use a spatial pattern with a geographical topic. If you want to visualize the layout of a proposed passenger station on a new suburban trolley line, for example, you might arrange your materials in terms of a familiar configuration:

Core Statement: The trolley stop will be laid out in an L-shaped configuration.
  I.   The vertical axis of the L will be a 50-foot-long waiting platform at trackside.
  II. The short horizontal axis of the L will contain ticket-vending machines.
  III. The open space to the right will be a one-acre parking lot.

If you are describing a building, you might arrange the details from basement to attic, from east wing to west wing, from entrance to exit, or from front to rear.

Core Statement: The Campus Center Building will have four levels.
  I.   The basement level will house a snack bar, bowling alley, and game room.
  II. The ground level will have shops, a restaurant, and reception lounges.
  III. The next level will have a small library, facilities for using audiovisual materials, and office space.
  IV. The top level will house guest rooms for visiting dignitaries.

Sometimes you can combine a spatial pattern with a time pattern if the subject is suitable—for example:

Core Statement: Museums devoted to children have been opened throughout the United States.
   I. The Brooklyn Children's Museum was founded in 1899.
   II. The Children's Museum of Boston was founded in 1913.
   III. The Eugene Field House and Toy Museum in St. Louis was founded in 1913.
   IV. The Exploratorium in the Palace of Fine Arts in San Francisco was founded in 1969.
   V. The Please Touch Museum in Philadelphia was founded in 1976.

When you use a spatial pattern, you are "telling" the audience that there is a specific reason you are arranging your material in this order. For example, if you are explaining a proposed Community Plan to the Board of Supervisors, your main points might look like the following:

Core Statement: Ramona's New Community Plan touches all portions of the area.
   I. The results of the plan on the valley
   II. The results of the plan on the lower foothills
   III. The results of the plan on the upper mountains

Notice that, in the last example, even within the pattern the sequencing made sense in that we moved from low to high. Space patterns often go from left to right, top to bottom, bottom to top, or front to back. They can also move in a descending order of importance. For example, if your topic is preparing your home for an earthquake, you could divide the house into the sections that are most dangerous (the garage area because of oil and gasoline) and those that are least dangerous (making sure there will be enough food in the pantry).

Topical patterns are one of the most widely used sequences in speech making. If you want to call attention to natural divisions and categories of a topic, you will find that the topical pattern is very effective. Here you are suggesting that there is a classification and/or relationship among the parts of a subject. That classification can relate to such things as roles, functions, component parts, qualities, features, and levels of hierarchy. Some examples may illustrate the wide array of speech subjects that can be treated topically.

Topical Pattern

Core Statement: A good athlete combines three qualities.
   I. The athlete has intelligence.
   II. The athlete has agility.
   `III. The athlete has stamina.

Core Statement: We communicate with many parts of our body.
   I. Our eyes send messages.
   II. The way we move sends messages.
   III. Our facial expressions send messages.

Core Statement: Automotive trouble is most likely to occur in one of the three systems.

    I. It may occur in the electrical system.

    II. It may occur in the fuel system.

    III. It may occur somewhere within the transmission.

Core Statement: The Ramona Community Plan is environmentally sound.

    I. The plan protects the lakes from pollution.

    II. The plan protects the wildlife.

    III. The plan protects endangered plants.

Patterns of topical relationships, time, and space are especially useful in presenting nonargumentative thought relationships, such as in speeches of exposition, description, and narration. Moreover, it is possible to combine a variety of these patterns within the same speech. The main points, for example, might follow a spatial pattern, the subheads developing a main point might follow a topical pattern, and the subheads developing still another main point might use the time pattern.

We will make one final observation before we conclude our discussion of the topical pattern. Be careful that the topical pattern does not become a formless sequence where you can deposit any topics that fail to make sense anywhere else. Students often make the mistake of calling anything a "topic" and therefore end up tossing in items that fail to relate. An example of calling anything a topic is to discuss solutions to sleep disorders by examining prescription drugs, herbs, and the history of sleep disorders. So again we remind you that, regardless of the pattern you select, the link between major and minor topics must be obvious to the audience.

Causal-Effect Pattern

The causal-effect pattern organizes the content of the speech around a set of conditions such as the cause of an event or a phenomenon. What you are suggesting in this organizational sequence is why a particular "thing" occurred (causes) and that it is instrumental in bringing about certain results (effects). Notice in the following arrangements how each main point (the cause) resulted in certain consequences (effects).

Core Statement: The reduction of funds for after-school programs has caused serious problems.

    I. The remedial reading program has been eliminated.

    II. Free hot lunches have been eliminated.

    III. Street crossing guards have been eliminated.

Core Statement: Not getting enough vitamins in your diet has serious consequences for your health.

    I. A lack of vitamin K can produce increased blood hemorrhaging.

    II. A lack of vitamin C can produce scurvy.

    III. A lack of vitamin B_6 can produce anemia.

Core Statement: There are many reasons why trial by jury is ineffective.

    I. Trial by jury is costly.

    II. Trial by jury is a lengthy process.

    III. Trial by jury is unfair to minorities.

As you can see, this pattern looks at specific results, or at least the predicted results, that stem from an event or a factor (budget cuts, a lack of vitamins, trial by juries).

The problem-solution pattern is often conceived as a longer and more elaborate version of the causal pattern. Many persuasive speeches lend themselves to the problem-solution pattern. In these situations, you are urging the adoption of a new policy or plan. It involves (1) presenting a problem area, (2) proposing a solution to the problem, and (3) defending the proposed solution. Suppose, for example, that the houses in your neighborhood have been defaced by graffiti that you suspect has been applied by youngsters with cans of spray paint. You think the best solution to the problem is to ban the sale of spray paint to minors. You might arrange the main points of your speech as follows:

Problem-Solution Pattern

Core Statement: The sale of spray paint to minors should be prohibited by law.

Problem:
I. Some minors use spray paint destructively.
   A. They deface public buildings.
   B. They deface private residences.
   C. They deface pavement and sidewalks.

Solution:
II. A ban on sales of spray paint to minors represents a solution to this problem.
   A. It would make access to spray paint much more difficult for minors.
   B. It would make minors more fully aware of community feeling about defacement of property.

Defense:
III. Such a ban is feasible.
   A. It is legally feasible.
   B. It is administratively feasible.

Defense:
IV. Disadvantages of a ban are minor.
   A. Stores selling spray paint would experience little decline in sales.
   B. Minors needing spray paint for legitimate use could obtain it through parents.

Defense:
V. Banning sales is the best solution.
   A. It is less costly than surveillance systems.
   B. It is a better deterrent than the threat of harsh punishment.

You will notice that both main heads and subheads are topical groupings. The main heads involve the topics of problem, solution, and defense of solution. The subheads are groupings of such topics as defacement, accessibility, awareness, and legal and administrative feasibility.

The problem-solution pattern can take a number of forms. Obviously, the number of problems you isolate and the solutions you propose will depend on the complexity of the problem and the amount of time you have been allocated. For example, your pattern might be as simple as the following:

Core Statement: We need an evening security escort service on campus.

Problem:
I. The incidence of rape has grown significantly on our campus.
   A. Statistics show the increase.

B. Experts confirm the increase.

Solution:

    II. An escort service would provide students protection as they walk on campus at night.

      A. The escort could walk students to their dormitories.

      B. The escort could walk students to their automobiles.

One of the major advantages of the problem-solution sequence is simplicity. By convincing the audience that there is something wrong with the status quo (too many car alarms going off during school hours), they will be receptive to your solution (having car alarms turned off during school hours).

Level-of-Acceptance Pattern

The level-of-acceptance pattern, sometimes referred to as the withheld proposal or indirect sequence, moves the audience through a succession of points that gradually leads to a conclusion. This pattern is usually used when the audience analysis reveals that the speaker is likely to encounter strong listener resistance to the point of view he or she is upholding. In these cases, it is wise to start with ideas that are acceptable to the listeners and then work progressively toward less acceptable ideas until the least acceptable idea (perhaps your solution) is reached. In the early stages of this sequence, then, you would be using the "common ground" technique. An example of this strategy is seen in the following outline:

Most Acceptable Idea:

    I. Every person values his or her job security.

    II. All of us are concerned about how our jobs are threatened by foreign competition.

    III. All of us want steps taken to preserve our jobs.

    IV. Any equitable solution requires the participation of every person in the firm.

Least Acceptable Idea:

    V. The most equitable solution is an across-the-board 10 percent salary reduction.

Core Statement: All employees of the firm should take a 10 percent salary reduction.

The first point is a statement of common ground. The presumption is that most listeners will not challenge this idea. The second and third points may require some demonstration, although they, too, are likely to be areas of common ground. The fourth point may be more difficult to establish, particularly if the prevailing attitude is to "let Joe do it." The fifth point would most likely receive the greatest resistance. However, if the speaker succeeds in establishing these points in order, the core statement is more likely to be heard with favor than if it were announced at the outset.

As indicated in the introduction to this particular pattern, your appeal to a specific common ground is directly related to your audience analysis. When talking to people from cultures different from your own, the area of "what is common" takes on added significance. That is to say, what is believed in one culture may not be "common" to another culture. In our last example, the common ground approach was very North American. However, the Japanese have a very different view of the workplace and employment. They believe in great loyalty to their companies and would not necessarily agree with the premises being advanced by the speaker in the example. Speeches dealing with women's issues need to be given special attention if you are using the indirect approach to diverse cultural groups. In much of Latin America and the Arab world, women are perceived quite differently than in the United States. If your starting point is faulty, at least from the Latin or Arab point of view, your entire organizational sequence will suffer.

A design applicable to both informative and persuasive speeches is the extended illustration. If you want to explain the duties of a television anchorperson, for example, you might build your speech around a typical day in the life of a real or hypothetical anchorperson. By translating the facts into narrative form, you would be using an effective technique for keeping audience interest at a high level.

Extended Illustration Pattern

    A persuasive speech urging donations to CARE might be translated into a narrative involving a family struggling to stave off hunger in a drought-stricken, underdeveloped country.

    One student spoke about three common treatments for patients suffering from acute myelogenous leukemia. As a way of explaining these treatments, she introduced her friend Brian. By means of a vivid and compelling factual illustration, she walked the audience through Brian's experiences with chemotherapy, radiation, and a bone marrow transplant. Her narrative, using who, what, where, and how, helped listeners learn about the three treatments; at the same time, she made the material interesting by personalizing it.

For over fifty years, Professor Alan H. Monroe's motivated sequence has been a very popular method of organizing speeches. In his book, *Principles and Types of Speech Communication,* he divided the motivated sequence into five steps. When applied to persuasive speeches, this format involves: (1) the attention step, wherein the speaker secures initial audience attention; (2) the need step, wherein the audience is made aware of the existence of a problem; (3) the satisfaction step, wherein a solution to that problem is explained and defended; (4) the visualization step, wherein the speaker envisions what the future will be like if the recommended solution is (or is not) put into practice; and (5) the action step, wherein the audience is given directions for implementing the solution. Note the similarity between the problem-solution sequence described earlier and the need and satisfaction steps of the motivated sequence.

Motivated Sequence

    Professor Monroe indicated that, when this sequence is applied to informational speeches, the visualization and action steps could be omitted. The attention step would serve the same function as in a persuasive speech, while the need step would be aimed at making the audience feel a need for the information to be presented. The satisfaction step would, of course, provide the needed information.

    Because the motivated sequence is such an effective organizational scheme, we will discuss it in much greater detail in chapter 13, when we look at the informative speech, and in chapter 14, when we examine speeches to persuade.

Other Patterns

As noted at the outset of this section, there are countless ways to organize your materials. As we close this section on organizational patterns, let us look briefly at a couple of additional sequences you might use.

The placement of ideas in order of increasing difficulty is as old as the history of teaching. Instruction frequently follows the sequence from the simplest idea to the most complex. For example, multicellular speech structure can be better comprehended if one begins by understanding the simplest form of speech—the single cell—and then moves in increasing complexity toward the most sophisticated forms.

Another application of placement in order of increasing difficulty is movement from familiar ideas to unfamiliar ideas. It has become virtually axiomatic that explanation is the process of relating the unknown to the known. Extended comparisons or analogies likewise epitomize this expository design.

The Role of Culture in Organizational Patterns

Throughout this chapter, we have talked about the organizational patterns that are most effective if your audience is composed primarily of members from the dominant North American culture. Our cultural experiences have taught us to string ideas together in a manner that, while common for us, is not universal. Four examples will help us clarify this idea. First, in North America the deductive organizational pattern is very common because it is highly structured and rigid—characteristics admired in our culture. Hence, we often introduce broad categories and then move to specifics to explain the assertions. As we shall see in a moment, not all cultures employ this pattern. Second, because people in this culture normally look for causes behind events, the cause-effect pattern is a popular method of organization. This pattern assumes there are reasons (causes) for all actions. Again, this is not the approach taken by many cultures. Third, as we have previously discussed, much of the thinking in the Western world is linear—direct and straightforward. The connection between each point when we organize our thoughts, prose, or speaking is clear and easy to see. We often hear people praise someone because their "ideas flowed together." Like so many mental processes, this form of organization is not used by all cultures. Finally, and this may simply be a corollary of the first three, we often introduce broad categories and then move to specifics to explain the assertions. Throughout school, we are taught to "make a point and then subordinate it."

Unless we have had experiences with people from other cultures, it would be easy to assume that everyone in the world organizes their thoughts in the same manner. This is simply not the case. The mental processes of reasoning (discussed in the previous chapter) and ways of organizing ideas are influenced by culture. In many Eastern cultures, such as the Korean, the pattern is to start with specific observations and then extract generalizations. In addition, many cultures employ configural logic instead of linear methods. In configural schemes, often used by Asians and Native Americans, the association between each point is not direct and spelled out. This type of pattern assumes the listener will make the connection on his or her own. Gaining this type of information from audience analysis will help you select the most appropriate organizational pattern. This is not to suggest that you completely abandon the Western organizational patterns that you are comfortable with, but rather that you make some attempt at understanding and, when appropriate, incorporating other organizational patterns.

Benjamin Franklin wrote, "A place for everything, and everything in its place." The truth of his adage is perhaps most evident in the preparation of a speech outline. It is here that all the pieces begin to fit together. However, outlining is usually misunderstood and personally dreaded by students. One common misconception is that outlining is something you do after you have composed a speech—a frivolous requirement instructors impose on students. Those who entertain such a view of outlining are depriving themselves of one of the most valuable tools for ensuring that their speeches are organized in a clear and unified manner. An outline is essentially a visual representation of the cognitive process you go through as you put a speech together. However, because the process is visualized, you are better able to tell where gaps exist, where reasoning is faulty, where illustrations are needed—in short, where revisions will make your ideas easier for the listener to absorb (and for you to remember). A good outline enables you to see the interrelationships of the parts of your message, their proportions, the adequacy of their development, and how well they function as a whole.

Outlining the Message

A speaker making optimum use of the outlining process first assembles a master outline (sometimes called a brief) designed to promote understanding of a subject in all its dimensions. Such an outline contains far more material than ever reaches the presentation stage. It serves as the warehouse from which to draw materials for a presentation outline. The presentation outline—the one with which we will be primarily concerned—is designed with the audience in mind; thus, it is much more selective than the master outline, or brief.

Although experienced speakers may use an abbreviated outline featuring the use of key words or phrases, beginning speakers profit more from using a complete-sentence outline. It is especially important to use the complete-sentence form when outlining argumentative speeches, because logical relationships cannot be clearly expressed through the use of key words or phrases. Moreover, the extra effort required to construct a complete-sentence outline helps you remember your ideas more readily during your speech.

It is difficult to say just how much of your actual speech should appear on your outline. Many variables affect this decision. They range from how familiar you are with the topic to the amount of time you have been allotted. However, as a general rule of thumb, the total number of words in your outline should equal no more than one-third to one-half of the words you think you will say during your talk. Regardless of the formula that meets your needs, observe the following principles as you prepare your outline:

1. *Assign only one idea or statement to each unit of the outline.* In this way, you will be able to ensure that your material is clear and free from auxiliary points. Notice in the following two illustrations of this point how Example B is much more explicit than Example A.

   Example A
   I. Because it is cleaner and cheaper, solar power is preferable to fossil-fuel power; moreover, it has unlimited availability.

   Example B
   I. Solar power is preferable to fossil-fuel power, for
      A. It is cleaner.
      B. It is cheaper.

A good outline enables you to see the interrelationships of the parts of the message.

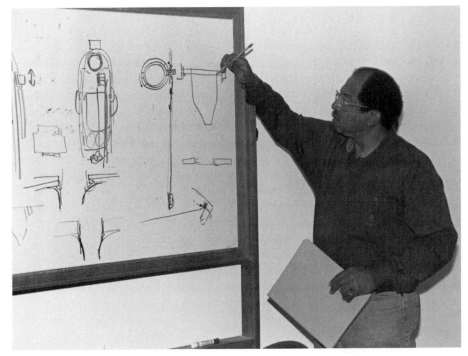

    C. It has unlimited availability.

Example A

  I. The proposed development is bad for everyone in that it takes away greenbelt areas and opens up the park regions to commercial development.

Example B

  I. The proposed development would harm our community.

    A. It takes away greenbelt areas.

    B. It opens up park regions to commercial development.

2. *Do not allow points to overlap.* The following example represents an infraction of this rule.

  I. Skateboarding is popular in the United States.

    A. It is popular in the East.

    B. It is popular in the West.

    C. It is popular in the North.

    D. It is popular in the South.

    E. It is particularly popular in urban areas.

The inclusion of E throws the pattern into confusion, since urban areas are found in each of the regions named.

3. *Maintain consistent levels of importance among coordinate points.* Units that are labeled as main points, for example, should share common elements. The inclusion of a unit of greater or lesser magnitude will destroy the consistency of the pattern—for example:

  I. Consumption of meat is declining in the U.S.A.

    A. Sales of beef are down.
    B. Sales of pork are down.
    C. Sales of lamb are down.
    D. Sales of fish have increased.
The inclusion of D breaks the consistency of the pattern and introduces an
annoying element of disproportion.

4. *Maintain clear levels of subordination.* Through the proper use of symbols and indentation,
   the hierarchy of points is indicated. Compare Examples A and B that follow.
   Example A
   I. Advantages of paper packaging are
       A. Light weight
       B. Strength
       C. Biodegradable nature
       D. An important export item for many years
           1. In the early twentieth century
           2. At mid-twentieth century
           3. In the past decade
   Example B
   I. Advantages of paper packaging are
       A. Light weight
       B. Strength
       C. Biodegradable nature
   II. It has been an important export item
       A. In the early twentieth century
       B. At mid-twentieth century
       C. In the past decade

5. *Use a consistent set of symbols and indentations to indicate relationships among main
   headings and subheadings.* The usual system is
   I. Main heading _____
       A. Subheading _____
           1. _____
              a. _____
                 (1) _____
                 (2) _____
              b. _____
           2. _____
       B. _____
   II. _____
   Note that main headings are consistently designated by Roman numerals; that
   subheadings that explain, illustrate, or prove the main headings to which they are immediately subordinated are designated by capital letters; that the level subordinate to the
   subheadings is designated by Arabic numerals; and so on down the scale of importance.

6. *Supporting points, whenever possible, should be worded in parallel sentence form.* By
   using corresponding structure and language, you test the logic of your material and
   make it clear for your audience. Notice how Example B is much clearer than

Example A in that each point in B begins with a common and consistent vocabulary.

Example A

I.   Vitamins in your diet might be essential to good health.
  A.   Some people say that niacin might be a possible cancer initiator.
  B.   It has been suggested that folic acid may help protect against heart disease.
  C.   It could be that vitamin D is related to some kidney diseases.

Example B

I.   Vitamins in your diet might be essential to good health.
  A.   Niacin may inhibit certain kinds of cancer.
  B.   Folic acid may help protect against heart attack.
  C.   Vitamin D may help prevent certain kidney diseases.

7. *Your outline should have an introduction, body, and conclusion.* Including these three elements in your outline can help you visualize how all of the parts of the speech fit together.

Introduction

I.   Be careful the next time you approach that cute little boy playing with a toy gun—it may not be a toy.

Body

II.   Juvenile crime is on the increase.
  A.   Murder is on the increase among juveniles.
    1. Evidence
    2. Evidence
  B.   Armed robbery is on the increase among juveniles.
    1. Evidence
    2. Evidence
  C.   Aggravated assault is on the increase among juveniles.
    1. Evidence
    2. Evidence

Conclusion

III.   Juvenile crime is on the increase.

We should point out that while introduction, body, and conclusion is the appropriate sequence in North America, much of the world does not use this succession. In India and parts of Asia, for example, people will often begin talking without giving any consideration to an introduction or a conclusion.

A Sample Outline

As we have indicated elsewhere, an outline for an entire speech would probably be divided into four parts: introduction, core statement, body, and conclusion. In some speech classes, the instructor may require a statement of general and specific purposes, and a bibliography of sources consulted. In some instances even a title will be assigned. The following is an outline of an informational speech:

VACATION AFLOAT

Introduction

I. My idea of relaxation is to sit in a rowboat in the middle of a lake, with a fish on the line and some lemonade in the ice chest.

II. My boyfriend's idea of relaxation is to be somewhere next to nature but with most of the creature comforts still available.

III. Today, I want to tell you how both kinds of relaxation can be achieved simultaneously in the same location.

Core Statement: Houseboating on Lake Powell is a vacation that is both comfortable and affordable.

Body

I. Houseboating offers something for the camper.
  A. There is the change from everyday urban life.
    1. There is no freeway traffic to fight.
    2. There is no time clock to punch.
  B. There is solitude in a beautiful setting.
    1. There are many secluded coves where you can anchor your boat.
    2. The water is blue and clear.

II. It offers something for the person who wants to fish.
  A. You can fish in comfort.
    1. Because there is water all around, you don't have to get up at 4 A.M. to drive somewhere to start fishing.
    2. You can fish right from your own front porch.
  B. Lake Powell is well stocked.
    1. There is a large variety of fish in the lake.
    2. Here is a picture of a fish we caught during my last trip on a houseboat.

III. Houseboating offers something for those on a budget.
  A. The cost can be shared.
    1. A group of four can share the cost of a thirty-five-foot houseboat.
    2. A group of ten can share the cost of a fifty-foot boat.
  B. Special rates are available.
    1. Three-day rentals during weekdays are 40 percent less than on weekends.
    2. Weekly rentals during off-season are less than half the rate of peak-season rentals.

Conclusion

I. For fun in the sun, I recommend a vacation on a houseboat.
  A. It offers seclusion.
  B. It offers good fishing.
  C. It is not very expensive.
      An abbreviated outline of the same speech might appear as follows:

Introduction

I. My idea of a vacation.

   II.   My boyfriend's idea of a vacation.

   III.   How to achieve both simultaneously.

Core Statement: Houseboating on Lake Powell combines the best of outdoor
vacationing with affordable rates.

Body

  I.   For camper
-    A.   Change from city
  - 1. No traffic
  - 2. No time clock
-    B.   Nice setting
  - 1. Cove anchorage
  - 2. Clear blue water

  II.   For the person who likes to fish
-    A.   Comfort
  - 1. No need to rise early
  - 2. Fish from porch
-    B.   Good fishing
  - 1. Well stocked
  - 2. Large fish

  III.   For budget
-    A.   Share cost
  - 1. Group of four
  - 2. Group of ten
-    B.   Special rates
  - 1. Weekdays
  - 2. Off-season

Conclusion

  I.   Great vacation
-    A.   Location
-    B.   Fishing
-    C.   Cost

Using Transitions

In chapter 6, we looked at a number of different kinds of transitions and talked about how they link your forms of support into a cohesive unit. Let us briefly return to the topic of transitions so that you can learn how to include them as part of your outline.

You will recall that transitions are words, phrases, and sentences that connect your ideas to one another. Their major function is to tell your listeners what you have done ("The statistics we have just looked at clearly demonstrate the widespread nature of this problem") and where you are going next ("Let us see if the experts agree with the numbers I have just presented").

As noted in chapter 6, a transition can take a number of specific forms. Four of the more common ones are the (1) *preview* ("Now would be a good time for me to talk about the reasons our college does not have a suitable student health plan"),

(2) *summary* ("Having looked at the major funding programs on campus, you can see why we do not have a suitable student health plan"), (3) *summary-preview* ("We now know what is wrong with the student health plan, but what can we do about it?"), and (4) *enumeration* ("There are three reasons our health plan is not working. First, . . .").

As a general rule, transitions are not absorbed into the same system of symbolization and indentation that are part of a normal outline. They are usually shown in the following manner:

I. _____.
   A. _____.
      _____.
   B. _____.
      _____.
      1. _____.
      2. _____.
(*Transition*) _____.
II. _____.
   A. _____.
      _____.
   B. _____.
(*Transition*) _____.
III. _____.

You may want to review chapter 6, where you will be able to find a much more detailed discussion of this important communication tool.

Summary

The process of assembling a speech usually begins with the formulation of a core statement embodying the central idea of the speech. Growing out of the core statement are the main points, subpoints, and supporting materials. Coordinate points should (1) relate to the core statement, (2) relate to one another yet be separable from one another, and (3) collectively develop the statement under which they stand. Material should be meaningfully organized around a logical sequence. Among the most common patterns of grouping are chronological, spatial, topical, causal-effect, problem-solution, level-of-acceptance, extended illustration, and the motivated sequence.

An outline is a tool for arranging constituent parts of a message into an orderly sequence. Good outline form features the use of a consistent set of symbols to show proper subordination of ideas. Each unit of the outline should contain only one idea; points should not be allowed to overlap; and coordinate points should be consistent.

A journey of
a thousand miles must
begin with
a single step.

Lao-Tzu

Chapter 11

Introductions and Conclusions

Connecting Your Ideas

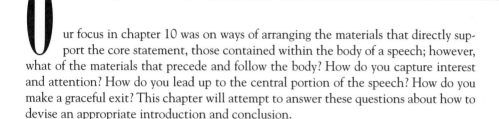

All's well that ends well; still the finis is the crown.

Shakespeare

O ur focus in chapter 10 was on ways of arranging the materials that directly support the core statement, those contained within the body of a speech; however, what of the materials that precede and follow the body? How do you capture interest and attention? How do you lead up to the central portion of the speech? How do you make a graceful exit? This chapter will attempt to answer these questions about how to devise an appropriate introduction and conclusion.

Preparing the Introduction

An old English proverb states, "A good beginning makes a good ending." A good beginning helps makes a good speech, for, whether your intent is to inform, persuade, or entertain, your introduction is crucial. It is your first exposure to your listeners. You know from your own experience how quickly we form first impressions and just how important these images can be. Research in interpersonal relationships suggests that, when we meet someone, within the first fourteen seconds we decide if they are friendly, likeable, attractive, and trustworthy. We would suggest that what is true in informal interaction also applies to public speaking. Therefore, a vital beginning is crucial if you are going to accomplish your purpose.

Some experts believe that, in addition to being important, the introduction is also difficult to prepare. The reason is that the introduction must be relatively short but, at the same time, must accomplish a number of purposes. For instance, an efficient introduction should (1) *secure the listeners' attention,* (2) *motivate them to want to listen to the entire speech,* (3) *establish the speaker's goodwill and credibility,* and (4) *prepare the listeners for what is to follow.* Although these four purposes are often combined, they all set the tone for the remainder of the talk. In the first part of this chapter, we will examine how you can achieve all of these purposes at the beginning of your speech. We will return to the topic of introductions in chapters 13 (speeches to inform), 14 (persuasive speeches), and 15 (special occasion speeches), when we examine specific types of speeches. However, for now we will explore some of the more popular approaches of beginning a speech that apply to all situations.

Gaining Attention

The kind of attention a speaker should seek is not the momentary, fleeting attention that inevitably occurs when the speaker appears on the platform. Rather, it is the kind of attention that attracts and holds the audience. In order to do so, the speech has to provide a stimulus that overrides all the other stimuli that are competing for the audience's attention. Perhaps the audience is more concerned with the discomfort of sitting in a hot, stuffy classroom. Maybe a number of the listeners are engaged in animated conversations, while others are enjoying private daydreams. Whether you confront one of these situations, or you face the kind of captive audience found in required speech classes, you may have to use ingenious ways to gain favorable attention. Let us look at some of the best methods to gain and maintain attention at the outset of your talk.

Quotation   A favorite device for opening many speeches is a thought-provoking or curiosity-arousing quotation. The interest value of this technique is that someone else has made a striking observation about the issue you plan to discuss. For example, if you wanted to explain ways of building self-esteem, you could start out with this quotation:

> "No one can make you feel inferior without your consent." This observation made by Eleanor Roosevelt strikes directly at one of the reasons so many of us hold low opinions of ourselves.

A speaker discussing the popularity of magazines that feature sensationalism and gossip opened with this quotation from Alice Longworth:

> "If you can't say anything good about someone, sit right here next to me." Alice Longworth, who had these words embroidered on a pillow in her sitting room, could have been describing the allure of those gaudy magazines that you find next to the checkout stand in the local supermarket.

Yet another speaker, examining the topic of animal rights, started her talk with the following quotation: "Henry Beston was right when he wrote that animals are not underlings; they are instead like us, caught in the net of life and time." Recently a speaker, talking on the topic of cultural differences in doing business, started with the following introduction:

> There is an Arab proverb that states, "Live together like brothers, and do business like strangers." This seemingly simple proverb offers great insight into how each culture perceives the business arena.

Quotations can be brief or long. Notice in the next two examples, both dealing with the topic of the freedom of the press, how attention is aroused in just a few words or in an entire paragraph.

> (Short)
> The free press is the foe of rhetoric but the friend of reason.

> (Long)
> The invention of the printing press added a new element of power to our race. From that hour, the brain and not the gun, the thinker and not the soldier, words and not kings, were to rule the world; and weapons, forged in the mind, keen-edged and brighter than the sunbeam, were to supplant the sword and the battle-ax.

In selecting an opening quotation, you should be guided by three criteria: *relevance*, *provocativeness*, and *good taste*. If you cannot build on a quotation, then the listeners may feel resentment when they realize you have cited it simply to gain attention. It must bear a connection to your subject. A quotation that is not provocative simply fails to attract the audience's attention in the first place. A quotation that is in poor taste will get the wrong kind of attention and will work to your disadvantage. Recently a speaker, talking about American buying habits, alienated most of the women in the audience by using a quotation that reinforced a common and insulting stereotype when he said,

> "Edgar Howe was right when he noted, a woman does not spend all her time in buying things; she spends part of it in taking them back."

Chapter 8 mentioned a number of excellent books of sayings and quotations you could consult as part of a research program for a particular speech. You might also start the practice of collecting interesting quotations on your own so that you might create your own personal library.

As noted in chapter 6, everyone enjoys a good story. Hence, if properly handled, stories, anecdotes, and illustrations can be among the most effective openings you can use. These narratives cause the audience to listen effortlessly. They are also useful in that they can take a variety of forms. Illustrations give you an opportunity to be creative. Before you decide to open a speech with a story or an illustration, take pains to see that (1) it is fresh (old stories told from a new slant are as fresh as brand-new stories), (2) it is pertinent to the main theme of the speech, (3) it can be effectively related (your limitations as a storyteller should be considered), and (4) it is in good taste. The importance of this last quality cannot be overemphasized, especially if the story is a humorous one. In your audience analysis, look for any information that would alert you to matters of taste. Generally speaking, it is wise to avoid stories that derive their humor from the ridicule of religion, racial origin, culture, or gender. Self-directed ridicule is, perhaps, the safest form of humor in a story or an illustration. (See the treatment of illustrations in chapter 6 for additional guidelines.)

Illustrations and Anecdotes

Illustrations can call attention to an event that both captures attention and points to your topic. A student gave a speech to inform on some of the overlooked personality traits of Abraham Lincoln. To stress Lincoln's sense of humor, she started with the following story:

> When the Confederate forces were attacking Fort Stevens, Lincoln made a tour of inspection of the Union troops. He was shown around by the general's aide, Oliver Wendell Holmes, Jr. As Holmes pointed out the enemy lines, Lincoln, wearing his customary tall hat, stood up to get a better view. At once, there was a crackle of musketry fire from the opposing trenches. "Get down, you fool!" shouted Holmes. An instant later, he realized what he had said and wondered what kind of disciplinary action would be taken against him. As Lincoln was leaving, he said good-bye to the young officer and added, "I am glad you know how to talk to a foolish civilian."

Illustrations are also useful if you can personalize them by making yourself the main character. Notice the impact in the following incident because the person in the story is the speaker:

> My name is Kevin Kirk. On April 17, 1995, a beautiful spring night in Ramona, California, I was a passenger with six of my best friends in a van that was

headed for a camping trip in the mountains. We were laughing, joking, sharing stories, and getting more and more excited as we approached our destination. But we never reached our destination. We were struck by a drunk driver. I remember being thrown from the van. It seemed like hours before I was moved into an ambulance. Once they started loading us, I began to realize that some people were missing. The reason for their absence became obvious within the next few minutes. Four of my friends were killed in the crash. I am here to tell you my life has never been the same because of that drunk driver.

A good factual illustration not only awakens attention, but it also points the audience toward the main point of the speech. A speaker recently combined attention with motivation by starting a talk on how gang violence is a problem of small as well as large communities in the following manner:

The car screeched to a halt at the corner of 34th Street and 17th Avenue and someone inside the car fired two shots at point-blank range. Hit in the arm and back, 13-year-old Kevin Franks, an innocent bystander, ran half a block before he collapsed and died. The murder was a classic drive-by large city shooting. However, the shooting took place in a small midwestern town like ours, not in Los Angeles, Chicago, Detroit, or New York.

In chapter 6, we also noted that illustrations can be hypothetical. These represent the accounts you offer to listeners that place them in the key positions of the story. One student started her speech on the need to spay or neuter pets with the following hypothetical illustration:

Please come with me as we take a tour of the county Humane Society. As we approach the first outdoor enclosure, we see four cute little puppies wagging their tails. They are, of course, anticipating the attention they know we will give them. Next to the puppies, we see a full-grown German Shepherd. He is as beautiful as any dog we have ever seen in a movie. From the inside cages, we hear the cats demanding that we pay them a visit. As we enter the cat area, we quickly notice two things. First, how sweet and engaging they all look. And, second, how many of them there are in the kennel. You are even more surprised when I tell you that there are more dogs and cats in areas we have not even visited. But the real shock and astonishment arrives when I tell you that these cats and dogs will soon be killed. It seems our county has a serious animal overpopulation problem.

Reference to a Recent Event

Associating the theme of your speech with something currently in the news is another good way to make the audience attentive. For example, if you wanted to discuss the plight of migrant workers, you might refer to a newspaper article dealing with a local ordinance affecting hiring: "Yesterday, the *Times* reported that the City Council is on the verge of passing an ordinance that would make it illegal to try to hire migrant workers off the streets. This kind of action will deprive a large number of migrant workers of their principal means of support."

By associating your theme with a recent happening, you impart an air of freshness and immediacy to your ideas that is likely to make the audience want to listen further. Notice in the next example that the student captured attention by directly linking her introduction to a common and current event:

I would suspect all of you were appalled last week when you saw your
television screens filled with pictures of the riot that took place at the local
amusement park.

At this moment, try not to think of your first roller coaster ride. Whatever you do, make
sure you do not picture that ride. You are probably unable to keep that experience from
your mind. The reason is simple; the brain has a mind of its own, and it does not take
much to activate it. This concept is the idea behind rhetorical questions.

Rhetorical Question

A rhetorical question "forces" the listener to want the answer to the question
the speaker poses. A skillfully phrased question creates a feeling of suspense that
makes the audience want to "stay tuned." However, not just any question will do.
Remember that very important qualification—one that makes the audience anxious for an answer. Lacking that element, a rhetorical question is ineffectual as an
attention device. Naturally, what makes an audience curious for an answer depends
on the nature of that particular group of listeners. A group of entering freshmen
would probably be attentive to a dean of admissions who asked this rhetorical question at an orientation meeting: "How many of you will still be in college next year
to start your sophomore year?" However, a group of chemistry majors would hardly
come to attention on hearing a speaker ask them, "Where can you buy a first edition of Hugh Blair's *Lectures on Rhetoric and Belles Lettres* for only forty-eight cents?"
Their unspoken answer probably would be, "I don't know and I don't care."
However, if that question were addressed to an audience of graduate students of
rhetoric or to a group of dedicated bibliophiles, it might have an electrifying effect.
It is evident, then, that you need to know something of your listeners' interests before you plan your strategy.

In using rhetorical questions, you can state a single sentence ("Ever wondered
what it would be like to work alongside a robot?") or you can ask a series of questions:

What would you do if, at this very second, you felt an earthquake? Would you
run for cover? Would you hide under your seat? Would you head for the casing
around the door? Would you just sit still and review your life?

Perhaps your audience analysis will reveal that your listeners are likely to feel apathetic
about your topic. In that case, you can usually make them attentive by saying something
about your subject that is startling. A speaker wanting to talk about the ease with which
someone can secure a handgun started with the following startling statement: "I could,
at this moment, take a gun out of my pocket and point it directly at any of you. This is
how easy it is to secure a weapon in our city."

Startling Statement or Fact

A startling statement can be very useful when you have to introduce a speech on
a familiar theme, such as asking for contributions to the March of Dimes or urging people to wear seat belts or stop smoking. In such cases, you can refer to audience members
in a startling statement—for instance:

Isn't it too bad about these three people sitting in the front row? They are
going to be hospitalized for quite a while—probably long enough to exhaust all
their savings. They may have to sell everything they own—car, furniture, even
their homes.

Undoubtedly, the "three people" would be startled by this introduction, and it is likely that the remainder of the audience would find their curiosity aroused. To be effective, the startling statement or fact, like all attention-seeking devices, should be relevant to the topic and should be based on an understanding of the audience. It is easy to see that indiscriminate use of this device could be self-defeating.

As you recall, many introductions work in combination. Therefore, you might find many occasions when your startling statement takes the form of a rhetorical question: "How many of you realize that the United States, with only 5 percent of the world's population, has more greenhouse emissions than any other country on earth?"

Promise of Reward

Promising a reward for careful listening can generate suspense in much the same way as a rhetorical question. Therefore, it is applicable to a wide variety of topics.

Here are some examples from speeches that have generated suspense by promising a reward: "You are going to be at least three hundred dollars richer by the end of this semester just by following the suggestions I'm about to make" was the preface to a speech on deceptive food packaging. "The next five minutes may be the most important five minutes you'll spend this semester," said another speaker prior to giving instructions on how to aid a person choking on a food particle. Still another speaker caught attention by saying, "You are about to find out why some of your driving habits are making you a major contributor to air pollution in this country."

Reference to the Subject

The use of this device should be reserved for subjects in which your audience is already involved, so that the mere mention of the topic will provoke a high level of interest. If your topic does not possess an inherent interest value for your audience, avoid this type of opening. To illustrate, we can guess that an audience will be inherently interested in gossipy information about famous public figures. Therefore, we can, with impunity, open with, "Today, I'd like to share with you some little-known facts about the after-hours behavior of one of our highest-ranking government officials." We can also guess that an audience will not be inherently interested in an explanation of an esoteric subject. Thus, "Today I'd like to talk about residual disjunctive enthymemes" will probably produce a yawn from the listeners.

Reference to the Occasion

If you have to make a speech on a relatively formal occasion, such as a banquet, a graduation ceremony, a dedication, an induction of club officers, a special lecture, or any situation in which the occasion is the dominant factor, a reference to that occasion and its significance is an appropriate opening device. In the usual speech class, however, such a formal opening would seem stuffy and affected, unless it happened to be the first or last day of the class. But if your sailing club had just won a major sailing event, you might begin by saying "We are here today because we are the best. We worked hard each and every afternoon for two years, and tonight we get to enjoy the rewards of that labor."

Humor

In chapter 15, when we examine special occasion speeches, we will deal with the topic of humor in great detail. However, because it is an effective attention-getting device, we need to touch briefly on humor at this time.

Humor, if relevant to the topic and done in good taste, can get a speech off to an excellent start. The following humorous anecdote was used to open a speech dealing with the importance of being able to adapt to any situation:

Humor, if relevant to the topic and done in good taste, can get a speech off to an excellent start.

A doctor at the health service office for our university had an urgent call from a student. The student told the doctor his roommate had accidentally swallowed his fountain pen. The doctor told the student to bring his roommate to the office. The doctor then asked the student what he had been doing since the accident. The student replied, "Using a pencil."

As is the case with all introductions, it is important that the humor point the audience in the direction of the topic. In the next example, the speaker planned to talk about cultural differences in the use of language. To arouse attention while introducing the topic, she used the following humorous opening:

A Frenchman learning English said his teacher noted that English is a strange language. He asked, "What does this mean—'Should Ms. Noble, who sits for this constituency, consent to stand again, she will in all probability have a walkover'?"

Visual and Audio Aids

In chapter 7, we discussed how visual aids can both clarify an idea and arouse interest. This twofold advantage makes visual aids excellent devices for starting a speech. A few examples from recent student speeches using visual aids will demonstrate the utility of these tools.

To create interest in a speech on animal abuse, a speaker simply started by turning on a VCR that showed a tape of lions and bears being kept in extremely small quarters. For a speech dealing with the earliest stages of organized culture, another student had a transparency projected on a screen of a mural from a subterranean cave in France that dated back 40,000 years. To persuade an audience that schools need to teach more

geography, a student had a map on the board and asked the audience if they could identify the ten major countries outlined on the map. Finally, on a speech dealing with the
history of jazz, another student began her talk simply by having the audience listen to
some music. As you would suspect, this approach captured everyone's attention.

We conclude this section on gaining attention by once again asking you to be creative. What this means is not to leap to the first introduction that crosses your mind, but
instead put yourself in the position of the listeners. Ask yourself if the introduction you
have selected will make them stop whatever they are doing and focus on you and your
message. If your truthful answer is "yes," you have a good and innovative introduction.

Preparing Your Audience for the Speech

Once you have obtained the favorable attention of your audience, then you need to get
them ready for what is to come. On many occasions they will, of course, have an idea
of your topic by the material you included in your opening remarks. If you tell a story of
drunk driving or show a video of abused animals, the audience will know the general
nature of what you plan to discuss. However, under normal circumstances, one or more
of the following things will need to be done in order to prepare your audience adequately: (1) justify the topic, (2) delimit the topic, (3) present your speaking credentials, (4) define your terms, (5) provide background information, and (6) establish a
common ground with the audience. Again, depending on the time you are allotted and
the topic, you might combine some of these tasks.

Justify the Topic

When your listeners have not gathered for the express purpose of hearing you talk about
a given topic, you need to offer them a reason for listening. "So you're going to talk
about paper manufacture. What's in it for us? Why should we listen?" may be the audience's reaction to the announcement of your topic. Well, what is in it for them? Will
your treatment of the subject benefit them in a tangible way? Will it help them be
healthier and more productive? Will it satisfy their sense of curiosity or their need for
emotional expression?

In speeches to inform, the justification of the topic answers the question, Why do
I need this information? In a speech to persuade, it answers questions such as How does
this issue affect me? and Why should I be concerned about this problem and its solution? If traffic around the campus was causing hourly delays, you could easily justify the
topic if you plan to offer remedies for the specific predicament.

Sometimes the device used for gaining attention can also justify the topic. For example, a rhetorical question may provoke attention and instill a need for information—
"How many of you realize that a lack of exercise can adversely affect nearly every part
of your body?"

Delimit the Topic

You may find it necessary to draw the boundaries of your discussion when approaching
certain topics. If you were to say, "Today I'm going to talk about AIDS," you might
cause the audience to anticipate any number of possibilities. Will you be discussing
treatment methods? Future research directions? Legislative efforts to require universal
testing for AIDS? Where AIDS is most frequently encountered? In such cases, it may
be good for you to point out what you are going to exclude as well as what you are going to include in your discussion. By doing so, you enable your listeners to adjust their
expectations accordingly. If listeners know the boundaries of your discussion, they can
listen more efficiently.

If your authority to speak on a subject is not known to your listeners, you may need to establish it during the speech.

There are occasions when it is unwise to indicate the boundaries of your discussion, especially if the creation of suspense is essential to the accomplishment of your purpose. (Be sure this is not a rationalization resulting from confusion in your own mind about the boundaries of your discussion.)

Once again, as we have throughout this book, we are emphasizing the important topic of credibility. In chapters 13 and 14 we will have a detailed discussion of credibility, but for now we need to tie this topic to the introduction of your speech.

Present Your Speaking Credentials

If your authority (credibility) to speak on a subject is not known to your listeners, you may need to establish it during the speech. On some occasions this would be done for you by the person introducing you to the audience, but, if the introducer fails to do so (or if there is no introducer), the task falls on you. How shall you make your credentials known? This can usually be accomplished without creating the impression of immodesty. Following are a few examples:

"I want to share with you some information about human nutritional needs that I learned in my health science class last semester."

"I know you are all familiar with the jokes about the preacher's son. As a preacher's son, I'd like to set the record straight about what it is really like to be a member of a minister's family."

"I've long been intrigued by the story of the duel between Alexander Hamilton and Aaron Burr. What series of events led to the duel? Could it have been avoided? What might have been the consequences of a peaceful solution to their differences? Speculation about these matters has been one of the subjects of a history seminar I'm taking. Today, I want to give you the results of my inquiry into this famous incident in our nation's early history."

"You have read and heard about the dangerous aspects of street gangs. From second- and third-hand sources, you have been exposed to the violence associated with gangs. Well, I was a gang member in junior and senior high school, so I can tell you first-hand about this lifestyle. I know from my own experiences why people join gangs and how they can get out of them. Let me share some of these observations with you during the next ten minutes."

"For forty days last summer, I was with a group of other students who hiked through the mountains of Tibet. I visited many places so far removed from civilization where there were some villagers who had never seen outsiders. The villages had no electricity, no running water, and no roads for vehicles. Today, I would like to share some of my experiences with you."

Define Your Terms

On some occasions, your subject might involve special terminology, jargon, or technical vocabulary that should be defined early in the speech. If your subject is dealing with computers, you may want to define words such as *interface, integrated circuit, megabyte,* and *microprocessor* early in your talk. One student, speaking on the importance of proper eye care, defined *myopia, hyperopia, astigmatism, cataracts,* and *glaucoma* during the introductory portion of her talk. You can set aside part of the introduction to define all the terms to be used, or you can define each term when it first appears in the speech.

Remember that defining terms and concepts takes on added significance when you are talking to a culturally diverse audience. For example, if your subject is drugs in the workplace, and your audience is composed of people new to the United States, you need to explain such things as the differences between depressants and stimulants. For people from countries other than the United States, even differences between "over-the-counter" and "prescription" drugs might need clarification.

Provide Background Information

Sometimes your listeners cannot gain a full appreciation or understanding of your subject unless they are familiar with certain background information, often in the form of historical details. To discuss a great event without indicating the historical context in which it occurred is to deny listeners an important dimension for understanding this event.

As is the case with defining terms, supplying background information is an important consideration if the audience members are not familiar with the major premises of your speech. For example, a student talked about the historical aspects of African-American culture before she moved to the main sections of her speech, which dealt with the differences between forced and selected immigration. She contended that this information had to be given early in the speech so that the audience could clearly understand the points she wanted to make later in her talk.

Other background materials may be physical in nature. For example, if you want the audience to sense the magnitude of the Grand Canyon, you have to put it in a physical context. How does it compare to the size of other topographical features with which the audience might be familiar? To give an audience a notion of the grandeur of the Lincoln Memorial, you have to put it in a physical context. An architect's genius cannot be fully appreciated by simply examining the building he or she designed. One has to see how the building integrates with its physical environment.

Occasionally, you are forced to take an unpopular stand on a controversial issue. If you wish to win audience support for your position, you must pave the way carefully. One method is the establishment of a common ground of belief between you and the audience. Essentially, it means that you will take pains to stress the areas in which you and the audience agree before you turn to the issues on which you and your audience hold divergent viewpoints. For instance, if you are eventually going to advocate that certain areas of a park should no longer be used by people on motorcycles, you might want to begin by talking about what is happening to the plants and animals in the park. By establishing an interest in plants and animals, you might be building common ground.

Establish a Common Ground with the Audience

Conceivably, if the audience is from a culture vastly different from your own, this act of establishing a common ground could occupy a major share of your speech. For example, if a speaker from Japan wanted to talk on how quality circles are useful in problem solving, he might have to demonstrate how the organization of these groups is much like groups the audience is already familiar with.

Introductions and Culture

A major theme of this book is that not all cultures approach communication in the same manner, nor do they necessarily have the same communication patterns. The topic of introductions is a clear example of how culture and communication are interrelated. As we noted earlier, the whole idea of a speech having an introduction, a body, and a conclusion is a Western concept. In many cultures, people simply start talking without any concern for having to gain attention and interest. Let us look at three cultural variations in starting a speech so that you will be able to appreciate the role of culture in forming introductions.

First, it is not uncommon for people from Japan to start their talk with an apology. Being modest and humble is highly valued in that culture. Therefore, to reflect that deferential attitude, a speaker may start by implying that she wishes she could have had more time to prepare or that she hopes the speech will benefit the listeners. If your audience is composed of many people from Japan, you might attempt to offer a mild apology as part of your introduction:

> I know all of you are familiar with my topic, so I don't want to tell you what you already know, but, if you are patient with me, I might be able to add to what you have already learned about this important subject.

Second, in Latin American cultures, establishing rapport and feeling comfortable with the people you are around is very important. Hence, if you were talking to people from Mexico or any other Latin culture, it would be wise to spend some time putting everyone in a relaxed and amiable mood before you go to the body of your talk.

Third, in Western cultures, people often admire the speaker who is witty, clever, has a keen sense of humor, and can begin a speech with a joke. This book has even recommended that you use humor as a method of gaining attention. However, we must alert you to the fact that, while laughing is universal, many cultures believe that the telling of jokes is the domain of the professional comedian, *not* the public speaker. They believe that people get paid for telling jokes and that the occasion of speech making is a serious matter.

As we leave the topic of introductions, let us summarize a few key points that you should keep in mind when thinking about this important part of your speech.

1. Although it should not be memorized word for word, the introduction should be thoroughly learned and delivered in a clear manner. The first few minutes are so crucial that you should not leave the success of the introduction to chance.
2. Let the body of your speech help you decide on your introduction. This means you should not begin your speech preparation by writing your introduction. Your introduction must relate to the body of your talk, and thus deferring its preparation will help you establish that link.
3. Your introduction should be neither too long nor too brief; that is, try to strike a balance. Some speakers utter a word or two and believe that is a sufficient introduction, while others allow the introduction to become the entire talk. Again, balance is the key.
4. Avoid tacky irrelevant gimmicks to get attention. A tie that glows in the dark or pulling a rattlesnake out of a burlap sack are two examples of introductions that are neither original nor clever.

Preparing the Conclusion

All too often, speeches end with these words: "Well, I guess that's about all." Judge for yourself whether this ending accomplishes the desired functions of a speech conclusion: (1) Does it redirect the audience's attention to the central point of the speech and tie together the main content of the speech? (2) Does it conduct the listener into the frame of mind that should be dominant at the end? (3) Does it leave the listener with a sense of completeness?

Preparing Your Audience for the Conclusion

There is a tendency for beginning speakers to give less thought to the preparation of the conclusion than to any other portion of the speech, yet the conclusion can be the most critical part. A poor conclusion can undermine all the speaker has accomplished to that point. It is in order, then, to examine some of the possible means of ending a speech effectively.

Summary

A brief recapitulation, or summary, of the main points of the speech is a common device used in concluding. It is particularly valuable in instructional speeches because it reinforces the instructions that the speaker wishes the audience to recall. For example, in concluding a speech on the fundamentals of tennis, a speaker would use a summary in the following manner: "Today, having learned some of the elementary techniques of tennis, try to remember that (1) you should always keep your eye on the ball, (2) you should keep your arm firm, and (3) your swing should follow through." In another informative speech, offering smokers some tips on how to discontinue the habit, a speaker used a summary in the following manner:

> During the last fifteen minutes, five important points were made concerning how you could quit smoking. First, I suggested that you set a specific date to quit; second, consider some of the healthy alternatives I recommended; third, remove reminders of smoking; fourth, avoid settings that you associate with smoking; and finally, drink plenty of water. Good luck. I am sure you will be successful.

In persuasive speeches, a summary can remind listeners that sound reasons have been advanced for the belief the speaker wishes them to hold or for the action he or she wishes them to take. In the following example, dealing with a speech on trial by jury, the speaker reminded the listeners of points she had stressed throughout her speech:

> Today, we have seen that trial by jury is costly and time consuming, and it often produces unfair decisions. This is why I urged you to support the plan that would replace all jury trials with a panel of three experts.

Usually, a summary is used in conjunction with other concluding devices, because by itself it may not accomplish all the purposes of a conclusion that we have discussed. For instance, the student in the previous example added the following lines to her speech as a means of intensifying her main thesis:

> If we don't change this antiquated system of justice, we will all be guilty of sending innocent people to jail because we let their fate be decided by twelve people who had absolutely no expertise in dealing with legal matters. If you thought you needed surgery, you would want a doctor to decide the seriousness of your problem. Why, then, do we allow untrained "strangers" to decide legal problems?

Quotation

Journalist Hendrik Van Loon once wrote that "somewhere in the world there is a quotation for everything." We have already seen that a quotation can serve as an effective opening of a speech and, with equal effectiveness, as part of the conclusion. Sometimes you can have two quotations from the same person, citing one quotation at the outset of the speech and the other at the end. In a speech on the topic of ecology, a student was able to use two excellent quotations by Walt Whitman, the first to open the talk and the second to end the speech:

Introduction

I believe a leaf of grass is no less than the journey-work of the stars,
And the pismire is equally perfect, and a grain of sand, and the egg of the wren,
And the tree toad is chef-d'oeuvre for the highest,
And the running blackberry would adorn the parlors of heaven.

Conclusion

The earth does not argue,
Is not pathetic, has no arrangements,
Does not scream, haste, persuade, threaten, promise,
Makes no discriminations, has no conceivable failures,
Closes nothing, refuses nothing, shuts none out.

In a speech stressing the need for cultural understanding, a speaker used a quotation by John F. Kennedy to reaffirm her specific purpose: "Our most basic common link is that we all inhabit this planet."

You might find that an opening quotation could be repeated at the end of the speech. This is often a very effective rhetorical technique. Whatever quotation you choose, it should meet the tests of relevance, good taste, and impact.

Illustration or Story

An illustration, like a quotation, can be used as effectively in the conclusion as it can be in the introduction. You will find it particularly useful as a means of visualizing for your listeners the importance of the ideas you have discussed in the body of your speech. A hypothetical illustration works well in that the characters in the story are the members of the audience. In a speech on the topic of government-sponsored immunization for young children, a speaker ended her talk with the following hypothetical illustration:

> As I said during my speech, it would cost the government only five dollars per child to immunize the children of this country against six diseases that threaten all of them. Should the government refuse to be part of such a program, you might see the day when your child comes down with a crippling disease that could have been avoided by a simple vaccination. Imagine how you would feel if your little boy or girl was the one lying in a hospital bed because our government did not grant the funds necessary for this program.

Illustrations distill the essence of your message and present it in a form that makes it memorable to listeners. If the prevailing mood of your speech has been very sober, then you might find that an illustration or a story in a light vein can provide the touch needed to leave the audience in the right frame of mind. A student concluded a speech dealing with cultural differences in the perception of death with the following humorous anecdote:

> One of the main points of my speech is that cultures do not agree as to what happens at the end of life. Well, cultures are not alone; most individuals don't know for sure about an afterlife. Comedian George Burns worked for over thirty years with his wife, Gracie Allen. After her death, he has visited her grave regularly. Someone once asked him if he told Gracie what was going on in his life. "Sure, why not?" was his reply. "I don't know whether she hears me, I have never been dead, but I've nothing to lose and it gives me a chance to break in new material."

Challenge   Speeches designed to stimulate the audience to greater efforts or stronger devotion to a cause or an ideal often end with a challenge: "If we all work together, we can stop the land developers from making our city one large parking lot and shopping mall. I implore you to help me preserve the little bit of open space we have left in our town." Occasionally, an informative speech can also use this kind of ending if the speaker wishes the audience to seek more information about the subject that has been discussed in the body of the speech. In any case, the challenge should be worded so as to encourage a spirit of confidence in the audience's capacity to meet the challenge. Our earlier example concerning smoking could have ended in a challenge and with encouragement if the speaker elected to say, "I have no doubts that, with willpower, determination, and a strong resolve, you will stop this unhealthy habit and join the millions of others who have said *no* to smoking."

One of the most famous uses of the challenge was that issued by John F. Kennedy in his inaugural address, the much quoted "Ask not what your country can do for you—ask what you can do for your country."

Declaration of Intent   Speeches intended to induce action can be concluded effectively when the speaker sets an example for the audience by declaring what he or she personally plans to do. "I will be the first one. I have now fastened a donor tack to my driver's license. Please join me in this action so that other people can enjoy life after you are gone." Patrick Henry's famous closing remarks in his "Liberty or Death" speech is a well-known example of this concluding device.

Recently a student used declaration of intent when she said the following:

> I will not stop working for the homeless in our community until every single person on the street has a warm place to sleep and hot food to eat. To do less would be closing my eyes to the suffering of those who live but a few miles from where we are sitting at this very instant.

Alluding to the Introduction

Returning to the introduction of your speech is often an effective method of concluding your talk. You can reestablish your introduction in a variety of ways. For example, if you start with a rhetorical question, you might end by restating the same question, but now you can offer the answer:

> I asked you ten minutes ago if you knew what to do if an earthquake were to take place at this instant. Now, when I ask that question, the answer should be yes.

You can also return to the introduction by finishing an illustration you started at the beginning of the talk:

> We now know we have to do something about domestic violence. We may not have faced situations like the one that confronted Susan. Remember, she had no place to go and no one to turn to. The new downtown center for battered women will now give people like Susan somewhere to go and people to comfort and protect her.

In planning your conclusion, we would ask you to keep some of the following ideas in mind. First, practice the conclusion so that it does not wander aimlessly. Too many speakers fail to develop an incisive conclusion and thus end up dragging it out for a long period of time as they drone on about insignificant issues. Still others, because they have failed to prepare an effective conclusion, end too abruptly. Again, balance and moderation are the keys. Second, try not to add any new points to the conclusion of your talk. If something is simply tossed out at the end, it will only confuse the audience and detract from your specific purpose. Third, regardless of the form your conclusion takes, it should stress your strongest ideas. Remember that it will be the last thing your audience hears before you sit down.

Summary

After designing the body of the speech, the speaker must give considerable thought to the introduction and conclusion. An introduction gains attention and prepares the audience for the remainder of the speech. Among the methods of gaining attention are quotations, illustrations or stories, references to recent events, rhetorical questions, startling statements, promises of reward, references to the subject, references to the occasion, humor, and visual aids. An introduction also justifies and delimits the topic, offers an opportunity to present your speaking credentials, defines key terms, provides background information, and establishes common ground.

The conclusion redirects the audience's attention to the core statement and tries to give the audience a sense of completeness. Some methods of concluding are summary, quotation, illustration or story, challenge, declaration of intent, and allusion to the introduction.

Chapter 12

Language
The Medium of Your Ideas

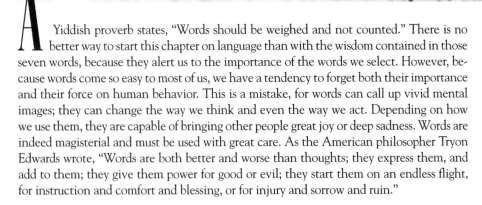

Why does language provide such a fascinating object of study? Perhaps because of its unique role in capturing the breadth of human thought and endeavor.

David Crystal

A Yiddish proverb states, "Words should be weighed and not counted." There is no better way to start this chapter on language than with the wisdom contained in those seven words, because they alert us to the importance of the words we select. However, because words come so easy to most of us, we have a tendency to forget both their importance and their force on human behavior. This is a mistake, for words can call up vivid mental images; they can change the way we think and even the way we act. Depending on how we use them, they are capable of bringing other people great joy or deep sadness. Words are indeed magisterial and must be used with great care. As the American philosopher Tryon Edwards wrote, "Words are both better and worse than thoughts; they express them, and add to them; they give them power for good or evil; they start them on an endless flight, for instruction and comfort and blessing, or for injury and sorrow and ruin."

Importance of Language

For students of communication, there can be no topic of greater importance than language, for, with your words, you express your ideas and share your internal states. You would be living a solitary life if you could not tell others what you know and what you want to know. One of the charming aspects of language is that you can make choices as to what words to use and which not to use. With practice, you can learn to choose words consciously and purposefully—words that help you accomplish your purpose and let you exercise some control over your environment. This chapter is about making the proper choices. However, at the outset we must once again remind you to be ever vigilant and meticulous when you make those choices. As we have said repeatedly, words are powerful and once they are received they have a commanding effect on people. The words of the English writer Robert Burton said it even more eloquently, "A blow with a word strikes deeper than a blow with a sword."

As noted at the start of this chapter, language serves you in many ways. It enables you to share your feelings and ideas with others; it lets you affect the behavior of others; it helps you gather information from others; it provides a way for you to give and receive comfort; and it enables you to know yourself, for you form your self-image in great part from the way others relate to you through language.

Have you ever stopped to consider just what language is and what its possibilities and limitations might be? Have you seriously examined the way in which you use this valuable gift? Are you making the most of your ability to use words or are you, like most people, content to use only three to four thousand words from a potential "list" of nearly a million? These are some of the matters we will address in this chapter. First, we will talk about the need to be aware of some general characteristics of language in order to use language to your advantage, and, second, we will discuss some techniques of language use that you need to develop in order to become an effective speaker. And finally, we will offer some advice as to how you might be able to improve your use of language.

Nature and Limitations of Language

If you understand something about how language operates, you are able to make intelligent decisions concerning which words to select and which to reject as you seek to accomplish your speaking purpose. For example, if you know that your listeners' background and culture influences the meaning they attach to words, you will choose words that are commensurate with their experiences.

Let us start with a definition of language. **Language** may be thought of as an organized system of symbols, both verbal and nonverbal, used in a common and uniform way by persons who are able to manipulate these symbols to express and communicate their thoughts and feelings. Words are the symbols used in verbal language, just as certain gestures, movements, and facial expressions are the symbols of nonverbal language. We examined nonverbal symbols in chapter 4, when we discussed the topic of delivery. Therefore, let us now turn our attention to the verbal symbols you use as a means of sharing what is going on inside you.

Words Are Only Symbols

We begin by examining the concept of symbols. In rather unadorned terms, we can say that a **symbol** stands for something else. Words, the symbols used in verbal communication, are substitutes for "the real things." Try as you will, you cannot eat the word *apple* or drive the word *car*. Words only represent the things—in this case, apple and car. It is important to remember that there is no necessary relationship between a word and the thing it symbolizes. In reality, words are only sounds or scratches on paper that we use to talk about the world that is in our heads. In this sense, you need to appreciate that we actually live in two different worlds: the one made up of words and the world composed of what the words stand for. In short, *words are arbitrary symbols*. People who share the same culture and language have simply agreed that a certain sound or combination of sounds stands for a given thing, concept, or experience. The word *elephant* could just as easily represent a winged creature if people were to agree to that meaning.

As a speaker, it is important to always remember this simple yet profound notion that language is symbolic, and that words have no meaning in themselves. This realization should guide you in your selection of the words you finally decide upon. Words are the tools you use as you attempt to share your reality, but because they are only symbols they can, as the English novelist Joseph Conrad reminds us, "be the great foe of reality."

Words Have Many Uses

A common problem encountered in our use of language involves the belief that every word has but one meaning. This, of course, is simply not true. In fact, the two thousand words most frequently used have approximately fourteen thousand different meanings. In your vocabulary, you probably have countless words with multiple meanings and uses. The word *cat*, for example, can refer to a jazz musician, a form of tractor, a type of fish, a type of boat, or a whip. In similar fashion, the word *lap* can represent the distance around a track, a portion of one's anatomy, the drinking method of a cat or dog, or the sound of water washing gently against the side of a boat. And the simple word *flush* can mean someone is red in the face, water rushing and flowing, chasing an animal out from a hiding place, being level with another surface, or a hand of cards in poker. A quick glance at any page of the dictionary will yield thousands of words with multiple meanings.

Thus far, our examples of multiple meanings have been rather unostentatious and plain (*cat*, *lap*, and *flush*). What happens when the words you select are complex and controversial? Do the meanings for the following words and phrases have a single, one-to-one relationship: *freedom, human rights, obscene, sexuality, gay, democratic, liberal, conservative,* and *birth control?* The answer to our question is no. There is indeed more than one meaning and interpretation for each of these words, and, when you add the variable of culture, the meanings become even more confounded and ambiguous. How would you explain a single meaning for the phrases *laptop computer, affirmative action, free choice,* and *teenage gang violence* to someone from a culture that does not have these experiences or expressions as part of its working vocabulary?

Awareness of the multiple-meaning characteristic of language is the first step toward minimizing some of the communication problems that are bound to arise when we use symbols. Another step is to realize that what is being said may not represent what the user intended or assumed. Whenever appropriate, we can develop the habit of asking directly how a person is using a particular word or phrase. Moreover, when we speak, we should try to select words that lend themselves to direct translation and define those words and phrases that have a variety of meanings.

As we have discussed throughout this book, selecting your words to avoid ambiguity and confusion is especially important when speaking to an audience composed of people from diverse cultures. Knowing that words can have more than one meaning, try to imagine how people who have English as a second language would interpret the following expressions:

"There are people all over this world who are born with two strikes against them."

"I will put this plan to the acid test by seeing how it deals with the nuts and bolts of the problem."

"If we stop being wimps and adopt this plan, we will be able to stop beating our heads against a brick wall."

"We need to be careful that the tail does not wag the dog."

"Do not listen to John; he has an ax to grind."

"The use of humor was so bad, Janet laid an egg."

"Jane dropped the ball this time and is she ticked off."

"What we need to do with this proposal is go tell David to take a hike."

"He split a gut laughing to the point I thought he would have a cow."

"If you don't think we are on the same wavelength, just give me a buzz."

"We can no longer dilly dally; it is time to get off the dime."

After reading these examples, you should be able to see the need to be aware of the language principle that *words have many uses, some of which are tied directly to culture*.

Words Evoke Denotative and Connotative Meanings

We have already explored the idea that, when someone selects a particular word, he or she is not using it in precisely the same way someone else might use it. Because meanings exist only in the mind, not in the object, thing, or concept being described, people possess different meanings for the same word. *Meanings are also affected by the denotative and connotative aspects of words*. Let us look at each of these dimensions of meaning and see how they affect communication.

Denotative Meaning

When someone asks the meaning of a word you have just used, he or she is usually seeking its denotative meaning. The **denotative meaning** is the one that society has sanctioned as the "official" or literal meaning of a word, the meaning furnished by the dictionary. It is often referred to as the "core" meaning of a word. Denotative meanings are somewhat impartial and neutral. There can be general agreement as to what is a car, tree, chair, table, and the like. As we discussed earlier, however, the dictionary may furnish several "official" meanings for a given word. The word *land*, for example, is variously defined as the solid portion of the earth's surface, as a country or nation, as a piece of real estate, as the act of arriving at a destination, and as the act of catching a quarry such as a fish or gaining a prize such as a job.

The context in which a person uses a word usually suggests its intended denotative meaning. Dictionary definitions ordinarily are phrased in nonjudgmental language. They tend to be factual and concrete. These denotative meanings normally cause public speakers very little trouble. It is the second category of meaning, connotative, where problems arise.

Connotative Meaning

As we have already noted, **connotative meaning** is anything but neutral or nonjudgmental. It is the private, emotional meaning that the word evokes. It is the meaning that reflects your personal experiences and feelings with the thing or event the word represents. The connotations you have for a word are more likely to determine your response than the denotations, because you learned most of your connotative meanings through subjective experiences. For example, when you hear the word *plumber*, you may think of the quiet little man who solved your drain problem in five minutes and charged you less than half the usual amount for a service call, or you may be reminded of the fast-talking con artist who discovered that you had twenty other problems with your plumbing that needed immediate attention. Even the word *dog* can elicit powerful connotative meanings. Imagine your response to the word *dog* if you were badly bitten by a dog when you were a child. However, if you were raised around dogs, and had fond memories of dogs, your connotative meaning for the word would be positive. Obviously, each of us has our own connotative meanings for words, and, therefore, no two people have identical meanings for a single word. After all, *meanings are not in words; meanings are in persons*.

Words Convey a Partial Picture of Reality

Each of us sees the world in a restricted way because we perceive things selectively. Looking at the same city, many people might well observe different characteristics. One person might look at the city's mountains and streams, while another notices its traffic and pollution. What is common with our example of a city applies to all the things in our surroundings—we notice some features of the outside world and others we ignore.

What is true about perception is also true about language. That is to say, at any one instant, *we can talk about only a portion of reality*. This notion, often referred to as *allness*, is based on the assumption that, when we say something about a "thing" or an idea, we are *not* saying all there is to say on the subject. In most instances, a great deal is being left out. The problem, of course, is that on many occasions what is omitted may well be more important than what is included. If a friend tells you about her history class, she can tell you about only a small portion of that class. Most of what happened and what she saw and experienced must be left out. You may hear about the lectures, but what about the textbook? You may hear about the examinations, but what about the class activities? We could go on and on with examples of what your friend shared with you and never accurately describe the class. What you are always going to get will be but a small slice of her total reality, and that portion will be difficult to describe because she has to decide what to include and exclude. If someone asks you about your new car, you must select what to say. From your total impression of your car, you might say, "It is a black Ford." You have abstracted only part of your impression. Think for a moment of all the things you could have said. You could have said it was a 1997 truck with four-wheel drive and a cab on the back. Even with the added words, you could not say all there was to say about the truck. What is true of the simple examples of the truck and the history class is characteristic of all words. The concept is simple—no single word captures the total essence of what the word is trying to describe. *Language forces us to discriminate.*

As we have already noted, what we leave out may be just as important as what we include. If a speaker says, "Our city has the best beach on the entire coast; there's never any litter or seaweed to spoil its visual beauty," he or she has decided to focus on the visual character of the beach. However, because language forces selection and makes it impossible to tell all there is to tell, the speaker does not tell you about the underground sewage spills that make the beach off-limits for bathers. This omitted fact could be more important than what was actually related.

The details we can include in our verbal accounts of reality are limited by our vocabularies and our experiences. If we do not have a label (word) for something we perceive, it is very difficult to talk about it with any degree of clarity. A speaker would have a difficult time explaining a hospital's computerized axial tomography (CAT) scanner if his or her vocabulary did not contain the words necessary to talk about its essential processes and components. What we choose to say about a topic is also influenced by our personal experiences. If someone holds biased and prejudiced views toward African Americans, and you ask them about the famous "I Have a Dream" speech by Martin Luther King, Jr., what they decide to tell you will be impacted by their bigotry. As the German philosopher Friedrich Nietzsche observed, "Every word is a preconceived judgment." It is important, then, for us to remember that what we say is a reflection of our vocabulary and background, and we can never say everything about anything. What is equally important is that we realize that the limiting nature of language demands that we be exact when we select our symbols. Knowing that we will be leaving things out obliges us to choose the best possible words and phrases.

Words Do Not Change As Quickly As Reality

Everything in the world is continuously changing and constantly in process, but our language tends to remain static. Hence, some of our trouble with word usage comes from our forgetting that *the world changes more quickly than words*. For example, we might label a politician as "conservative" today and continue to refer to her as a "conservative" in the future, even though she increasingly becomes more liberal in her rhetoric and voting record. A successful communicator is aware that reality changes but often words do not. Think for a moment of how our image for the words *Arab, Women's Rights, Yuppie, smoking, pit bulls, emigration,* and *Russia* have changed as new data about each of these concepts have been added to our fund of knowledge. Hence, be aware that everything that is said applies to a particular time. When you communicate, try to let others know the time frame for what you are saying, and ask others to do the same.

Words Reflect Our Experiences

The last characteristic of language we will discuss is one we have alluded to earlier. We will now develop it in detail, because it can present potential problems if we fail to consider it. Simply stated, *our meaning for any word is determined by our experiences with that word*. Put in slightly different terms, the meaning for any word grows out of the meaning we have learned for the word. As you recall, meanings are in people, and as people have different experiences they will have different meanings. In this sense, *language is a collection of symbols that represents the experiences of a group of people within a geographic or cultural community*. We hear the word *dog* and see a domesticated pet that is often a member of the family and might even sleep on the new furniture. In other parts of the world, however, *dog* elicits a different image and definition. In Hong Kong, China, and Korea, dogs are often considered to be food. Different personal and cultural experiences equal different definitions.

It is important to remember that what is true with our elementary example of *dog* applies to ideas and concepts that are much more involved. Think for a moment of how people from different cultures, with their unique backgrounds and experiences, might define words such as *abortion, AIDS, affirmative action, sexual harassment, free choice,* and *manifest destiny*. With over three thousand languages in the world, you can see why our list of cultural definitions is endless.

What the previous examples are telling us is that all people, regardless of their culture, develop both shared and private codes. *Shared codes* designate those aspects of language whose meanings are generally agreed upon by most members of the language community. These words are somewhat like those we discussed when we examined denotative meanings. In public speaking, it is often the private codes that cause problems. *Private codes* refer to the aspects of language whose meanings are agreed upon by a specialized segment of the language community. Private codes can take a variety of forms. For example, private language may consist of common words that take on a different meaning because of the affiliation of the user. See if you can determine the meaning of the following private code:

> There we were, we thought we were tanked. Sure to be a pickle boat when along come the black gasser. What a smooch. Three turkeys in front of us bottled immediately.

The above example, taken from the community of sailboat racing, is simply a description about how a poorly skippered boat almost sunk the boat in question before a strong gust of wind came along and saved the day.

Private codes refer to the language whose meanings are agreed upon by a specialized segment of the community.

Private codes are very common in professions and cocultures. Horse trainers might know about a bug boy (apprentice jockey), chalk (the horse expected to win the race), and being rank (running down the racetrack in an erratic manner). In the same way, prostitutes would know the private meanings for terms such as date (a client), outlaw (a prostitute working with a pimp), COYOTE (a union of prostitutes), and the life (the world of prostitutes).

We have emphasized in the last few paragraphs that you must think about the other person during all stages of the preparation and communication process. Ask yourself these simple questions: *What are the experiences of my audience, and how will these experiences influence the meaning they give to the words I use?*

Now that we have an idea of what words can and cannot do, let us turn our attention to what constitutes effective language use.

Characteristics of Effective Style

Over 250 years ago, English author Jonathan Swift wrote, "Style may be defined as proper words in proper places." What was true then is true now. Style still means the manner in which someone chooses his or her words and strings them together. This selection process also takes into consideration the manner in which the words fit the audience and occasion. Saying the right thing, in the right way, at the right occasion is not a simple task. Therefore, we will spend much of this chapter discussing how you can improve your style.

A person's style is highly individualistic and is developed over a long period of time. If one is lucky enough from early childhood to be surrounded by those who have good language habits, then one is likely to develop similar language habits simply by imitating those in one's own circle. Parents, siblings, and close friends are particularly influential in the development of our language habits. There are people who have had the good fortune to be exposed to teachers who saw the value of developing an effective style and stressed this subject in their classes. Regardless of whether or not you have been surrounded by good models to emulate, you can always improve your language style through sincere and careful practice, for, although we come to this earth knowing how to talk, we are not born knowing how to use words effectively. It is a skill that is learned and, therefore, can be improved.

Effective Style Is Clear

Clarity is perhaps the most indispensable of all the qualities of good style. It is especially important for a speaker's words to be understood by the listeners at the moment of encounter, because listeners, unlike readers, cannot stop to consult a dictionary and, in many instances, cannot even ask the speaker for clarification. Let us examine some of the ways you can make your message clear.

Oral Style Promotes Clarity

In chapter 1, we talked about how public speaking differs from the essay and from casual conversation. We will now return to that earlier discussion and explore some specific ways an oral style can contribute to clarity.

First, *oral style makes abundant use of rhetorical questions.* You will recall that rhetorical questions are an excellent device to arouse attention because they force your listeners to become mentally involved in the speech. If you were speaking on the subject of recycling, you would be using good oral style if you asked, "How much would you estimate our city spends each year to dispose of our trash?" If your topic is violent behavior in our society, you could even ask a series of rhetorical questions to bring about a clear, interesting, and lively style: "Just how violent are we? How do we rank against the rest of the world in violent behavior? Why are we so violent?" As you can see from the example, rhetorical questions bring listeners into the communication process by offering language that is concise, compact, and clear.

Second, *oral style adds to clarity because it is less formal.* Language that is prim, stiff, or stodgy usually distorts a speaker's message. Later in this chapter, we will discuss some ways to keep your language from being too formal. At this point, however, simply be alert to the idea that words such as *synergistic, digital, dyad, co-orientation,* and *matrix* might be too formal for most audiences.

Third, *oral style uses more repetitions than does written style.* In chapter 6, we talked about making your evidence clear by the generous use of transitions. You will recall the techniques of bridging and signposting as two methods of repeating your main ideas. In chapter 13, we will examine even more formulas for effective repetition. In both chapters, the message is the same—in written communication, the audience can reread a paragraph or page and then move on; in public speaking, the speaker "turns the pages." Therefore, it is important that the audience understands what is going on at all times. Repetition is yet another way to ensure that understanding. If you had just made an important point regarding the overcrowding of prisons, you would further your cause by uttering the following words as a way of clarifying that point: "Having just seen that the prison population in the United States is now approaching the 900,000 mark, we can better appreciate just how serious the problem really is." The stylistic technique of repetition adds to clarity while reminding your listeners of what you deem to be important.

Parallel wording is a type of repetition that can add to clarity at the same time it makes an idea compelling. For example, there can be little doubt as to a speaker's position on the death penalty if they say:

> The death penalty was inhuman when it was conceived hundreds of years ago.
> The death penalty is inhuman as it is applied today.
> And the death penalty will continue to be inhuman if we use it in the future.

Finally, *oral style is usually more personal than written style.* Talking directly to someone and looking into his or her eyes enhance intimacy. So do the words you use. You "connect" with your audience when you use pronouns such as *you, we, us, our,* and *I*. Think about the impact of the following two sentences: (1) "One has to be very careful when deciding if one should take that final drink before getting into one's car." (2) "You need to be very careful when deciding to take that final drink before getting into your car." To further personalize your material, you can use specific names from your audience: "John was telling me just the other day about his friend Robert, who got arrested for drunk driving during spring vacation."

We begin this section with advice from someone who knew how to use language effectively—William Shakespeare. Over three hundred years ago, Shakespeare wrote, "When words are scarce they're seldom spent in vain." What he was telling us is that, whenever possible, use one word instead of two, a word with a clear meaning, and one sentence instead of two. Which is the clearer word in each of the following pairs? *Prevarication* or *lie? Risible* or *laughable? Ennui* or *boredom? Sanguine* or *optimistic? Betrothal* or *engagement? Edifice* or *building? Recapitulate* or *summarize? Denouement* or *end? Eschew* or *avoid?* Is the user of the first word in each pair really aiming for clarity, or is he or she trying to exhibit an impressive vocabulary? Simpler words generally increase understanding and reduce ambiguity.

Simple Language Promotes Clarity

There might be times when even what appears to be a simple word can cause confusion. Think for a moment of the ambiguity in the next two sentences: "These minks were harvested in California." "Our chickens are grown in Iowa." The words *harvested* and *grown,* because they are used in a context that actually doesn't apply, are not very clear.

The purpose of communication is to share ideas, information, and feelings. If the language you use does not promote meaning similarity, then your communication purpose cannot be achieved. We have not intended to give the impression that using simple language means you are being infantile or dull. For there are many occasions when the appropriate word should be ceremonial and formal. You should use the literary word for those occasions. However, in most instances, you need to realize that vague, complicated, showy words and too many words can cause serious communication breakdowns. As the English writer John Ray advised, "Those that use too many words for explaining any subject, doth, like the cuttlefish, hide themself from others."

If you were to read some of the speeches of American orators of the late nineteenth and early twentieth centuries, you probably would encounter phrases that have an antique ring to them, because trends occur in language style just as they do in clothing style.

Current Language Promotes Clarity

The purpose of communication is to share ideas, information, and feelings.

Expressions that may have been fully understood by everyone a century ago might be incomprehensible to us today, because they allude to a mode of life that no longer exists. Expressions using the terminology of a horse-and-buggy, steam-engine, preelectric, black-and-white-TV age may not only sound quaint, but they often lack the essential property of clarity.

Colloquial expressions are especially subject to changes in meaning as time passes. During the period of the Watergate scandal in the 1970s, a popular expression for an informer was *deep throat*. Use of that expression today generally draws puzzled looks from young audiences. Even the simple word *stooge* would be out of date if you were talking about an informer. Also, how many members of your audience would understand an analogy that referred to "the long gas lines brought about by the revolution in Iran"? How many people from a culture other than the United States would understand a joke that refers to a "space cadet" as part of its punch line? And many young people in your audience would have a difficult time deciding the meaning of "corporate uniforms." In all of these instances, the meaning of the word is directly related to a specific period of time. Even the words *Desert Storm* may not be clear to people who hear them or read them five or ten years from now.

As you recall, it is always important to consider the age and culture of your audience when you select the words and expressions for your message. Try to visualize how an audience twenty years from now might react to some of the expressions that are currently in vogue.

As we have noted elsewhere in this book, in public speaking an audience cannot, as they can with a book or videotape, go back and reread or replay the words they were exposed to. Therefore, as a speaker you need to be clear. Yet most of us are guilty of expressing ourselves rather vaguely at times. We may say, "I saw this man crossing the street," without any further identification of the "man" or the street or the method of crossing the street. A friend might tell us, "I watched this program the other night," with no indication of the program's name, the night of the week it was seen, or whether it was a televised or in-person program. Someone may allude to "that neat little thing" without indicating precisely which "thing" he or she is talking about or whether "neat" is descriptive of its appearance or function. Or think about how often people talk about "that stuff" with no indication of what the word "stuff" is referring to. In all of these cases, word choice falls short of precision because it is not concrete and/or it lacks specificity. As a speaker, if you learn to index by using names, dates, places, and other details, your listeners are apt to get a much clearer mental picture of what is being discussed. For example, "Anais and Asher went to the comic book convention at Golden Hall last Saturday afternoon" is certainly more specific than "They went to something not long ago." We hear general statements such as, "A lot of the people got sick from eating at the fair." A person concerned with communicating a clear picture would say, "Twenty-five first-graders from Polk Elementary School suffered severe stomach cramps after eating candy apples purchased from the concession stand located at the west entrance to the fairgrounds." Here we can see the value of being specific so that the listeners have a reasonably clear indication of what transpired.

In many instances, only a word or two can make the difference between being vague and being clear. Think about how much more apparent your meaning is if you say, "On October 6th" instead of "sometime next month," or if you say, "Gail gets all As" instead of "Gail does well in school."

In the following general and specific comparisons, notice how a more specific word helps a speaker elicit a clearer meaning:

Concrete and Specific Language Promotes Clarity

General	Specific
animal	dog, horse, elephant, camel, cat
vehicle	car, bike, coach, motorcycle
worker	plumber, painter, carpenter, mason
color	blue, red, green, violet, yellow
move	crawl, creep, glide, run, waddle
sports	baseball, basketball, football
vegetables	carrots, broccoli, green beans
exercise	walking, swimming, running
residence	house, apartment, condominium
doctor	surgeon, pediatrician, urologist
educator	principal, teacher, professor
reading material	magazine, book, journal
automobile	Ford, Dodge, Jeep, Porsche

Using the specific and concrete examples in the right-hand column will clarify the discussion for the audience. In short, it is easier to visualize a dog being abused than an animal being mistreated.

Effective Style Observes the Rules of Grammar

Effective style keeps a listener's attention on the subject matter of the speech, not on the manner of expression. Thus, a speaker should try to avoid the distractions that can accompany errors in syntax and grammar. Grammatical errors damage a speaker's credibility and also confuse the listener. For example, "His voice fits him perfect" may appear to be an understandable statement at first glance, but the listener might pay more attention to the grammatical inaccuracy than to the sense of the statement. Note the degree of distraction inherent in these common grammatically incorrect statements:

"I need your help, give me them votes."

"I had wrote this petition after think about this issue for a long time."

"There wasn't no easy way out for any prisoner which hoped to escape."

"She has went there many times in the past."

"He hadn't ought to give to this here charity."

"I had went to this college once before."

"Our college's graduate school has a difficult job before them."

"Having studied them before, the rocks was of a limestone variety."

"Me and my friend are going to the show."

"John can't hardly follow the instructions."

"That there plan ain't going to work."

"I think he done it."

"They was going to do the same thing we did."

"She don't know right from wrong."

Often what is considered improper speech becomes so commonplace that it creeps into our vocabulary without our even being aware of it. The phrases "Tell it like it is," "None of them are going," "It was a real difficult decision," "Solutionwise, this is a good plan," and "She gave 120 percent to this project," are all examples of words and phrases being used incorrectly.

At times, a speaker can break the rules of grammar to good effect if it is obvious to the audience that the speaker is doing so intentionally. What constitutes correct usage may vary from audience to audience. Some audiences will accept, or even expect, certain departures from what is popularly regarded as good grammar, because such departures are part and parcel of the everyday language of that group. In other words, what is correct expression is determined in part by the audience's standards of correctness. Part of your audience analysis, then, should be to find out about the speech patterns of the group you will be addressing.

We have been discussing the idea that the way words are put together to form sentences, clauses, and phrases affects your style. "The man eating turkey was fat" may be clear to a person reading the statement, but a person hearing it might mentally hyphenate "man-eating," conjuring up an image of a turkey devouring a man. Greater clarity might be obtained by saying, "The fat man was eating turkey." If someone said, "The lady in the car breaking records was Evelyn," we would have the option of interpreting the statement in several different ways. Who is breaking the records, the car or the lady? What kind of records are being broken, speed records or old phonograph records? Had the person said, "Evelyn was in the car that broke the speed records," there would have been less chance of our misinterpreting the meaning.

Throughout this chapter, both in latent and in manifest ways, we have accented the power of language. Nowhere is that power more evident than in the area of picturesque language. As important as *clarity* and *correctness* are, these qualities alone may not be sufficient to hold attention, maintain interest, and create a favorable impression. They need the assistance of a third quality—vividness.

Effective Style Is Vivid

To achieve vividness, successful speakers have relied on two fundamental methods: (1) *imagery* and (2) *figures of speech*. What follows is a discussion of how each method makes your ideas come alive in a memorable fashion.

A philosopher noted that we speak so that others can *see* what we mean. The wisdom of that simple observation can be underscored by our asking you to take part in the following experiment. Stop for a moment and ask yourself what happens inside of you when you tell yourself to picture a small, white polar bear sleeping peacefully on a drifting block of ice. You know exactly what happens. You picture that bear. This unadorned example demonstrates that, when using imagery, we are asking our listeners to see a prior event or to experience a new situation that we paint for them. In either case, the objective is to have the audience vicariously experience the sensation we describe. The forms that imagery takes, then, correspond to the human senses. Through language, we can evoke sensations of sight, smell, taste, touch, organic sensation, and kinesthetic sensation. Consider, for example, the various senses aroused by the following descriptions:

Imagery Promotes Vividness

1. As I lay awake in the darkness, I could hear the muffled sound of footsteps on the gravel pathway that led past my bedroom window.
2. When I stepped inside the abandoned miner's cabin, I saw a shaft of sunlight coming through a hole in the roof and falling on a rusty metal basin that lay on the bare wooden floor.
3. The plastic quart bottle slipped from my grasp and the ammonia poured out onto the kitchen floor, filling the room with fumes that made me gasp for breath.
4. Running my fingertips across the smooth lacquered finish of the tabletop, I suddenly encountered a small indentation made by an object apparently dropped by accident.
5. Grasping the dangling vine firmly, I swung out over the water, then released my grasp to plunge feetfirst into the refreshing depths of the river.

6. In great anticipation, I raised a spoonful of the gumbo to my lips, only to discover that someone had emptied what seemed like half a bottle of red pepper sauce into the mixture.
7. Sandpipers darted out into the receding surf to find tiny minnows.
8. After spending all morning tossing bales of hay from the truck to the cattle standing huddled on the frozen ground, I was one mass of aching bones and muscles.
9. As my eyes were fixed on the Yellowstone fire, I had the feeling I was looking directly into the midday sun.
10. If you were there with me, you, too, would remember the outlandish red color of the clamoring birds as they moved from the murky marsh into the enormous trees that gave them asylum from the wandering tourists.
11. I could not force my gaze directly into the eyes of the small, brown puppy, paws against the cage, appealing to me to take it home.

On many occasions, the impression to be communicated takes more detail and development than one can put into a single sentence. In these instances, the singleness of impression might be expressed by an extended illustration. In the following example, the speaker wanted her audience to understand how cruel it is to keep elephants in small cages or in the back of trucks, moving from town to town as part of a traveling circus:

> Elephants, like humans, grieve, cry from frustration and sadness, and help one another. They have a long childhood and remain with their mothers for fifteen years. They are sensitive, intelligent, and affectionate, and they long for social relationships. Now try to imagine one of these magnificent creatures in complete isolation, spending its entire life in either a small cage or the back of a truck, being moved from city to city. Confined, chained, and caged, the elephant quickly learns the futility and brutal repercussion of protesting. Picture this dignified and social animal responding to this isolation and lack of space. Pacing, weaving, rocking, sucking, or chewing on the steel bars of the cage are the animal's response to monotony and loneliness. Many, of course, simply go mad.

Another speaker, trying to encourage a group of smokers to stop smoking, used imagery in the following manner:

> Let us imagine for a moment that you are feeling good as you take a long, deep puff on your cigarette. But let us also add a touch of realism to this scene by asking you to also picture what your body is doing with this invisible and sinister chemical as it invades your body. Your gums and teeth are the first recipients of the poisonous chemical. While the smoke pays but a short visit to your mouth it is leaving enough pollution to increase the risk of painful gum diseases and the agony of mouth and throat cancer. But this is just the beginning. As the smoke continues its journey into your unsuspecting lungs, you will soon find that your breathing is shallow and impaired, for now the smoke deposits insidious toxins that, after a period of time, will increase your chances of crippling and deadly cancer. Your stomach too will experience the corrupt and silent killer of cigarettes. While you cannot see them, small bits of acid are coating your stomach, adding to the chances that you will develop lacerated ulcers. Think about all this the next time you decide that it is okay to take one little puff of this cleverly concealed stick of dynamite.

In some instances, even a single word can make your material more vivid, colorful, and lively:

horse	mount, nag, equine, bronco
hot	scorching, torrid, blazing
walk	stroll, plod, shuffle, slink
violent	turbulent, raging, explosive
cheap	frugal, prudent, scrimping
fast	rapid, nimble, brisk
poor	destitute, impoverished, insolvent
small	diminutive, paltry, scanty
loud	boisterous, deafening, resounding
silent	hushed, muted, quiescent
soft	malleable, delicate, mushy
hungry	famished, ravenous, voracious
painful	agonizing, throbbing, excruciating

Obviously, the context, as well as your analysis of the audience and occasion, will determine which words and phrases you utter. However, regardless of what factors you take into consideration, your language must not be inanimate, dull, or mundane.

On many occasions, you might find it useful to enhance and elevate your speaking style so that it rises above ordinary and everyday speech. When seeking to use variations from literal or common forms of expression, figures of speech are highly effective. They impart vividness to your language usage. Moreover, figures of speech can greatly increase a speech's vigor, clarity, and beauty. In addition, they add to your credibility. Among the most popular figures of speech used by experienced communicators are simile, metaphor, antithesis, personification, hyperbole, climax, onomatopoeia, rhetorical questions, parallelism, and alliteration.

Figures of Speech Promote Vividness

Simile is an expression of the figurative resemblance of one person or thing to another, put in the form of an explicit comparison. A simile normally uses "like" or "as" to compare and link similar ideas. One would be using a simile when saying, "At times, finding a gasoline station that services cars is like hunting for a place to camp on the Hollywood Freeway." A simile involving the importance of child rearing might well state, "A strong tree is like a strong family—both need deep roots." A speaker, talking about the poor attendance at a town meeting, also used a simile when he said, "The auditorium was as desolate as a cemetery at midnight." Another speaker noted, "He was so thorough that he examined the book as if he were a customs inspector." Perhaps one of the most famous of all similes is the one that noted, "Requesting the television industry to police itself is like asking the fox to guard the henhouse."

Closely related to simile is **metaphor,** the comparison of unlike things that allows us to say a great deal with very few words. The comparison is implied and built into a metaphor. Hence, the speaker can omit the words "like" or "as." A simile says that one thing *is like* another; a metaphor says that one thing *is* another. Thus, the simile "He is like the Rock of Gibraltar" becomes a metaphor when expressed as "He is the Rock of Gibraltar." Abraham Lincoln, discussing the danger of two Americas, used the metaphor "A house divided against itself cannot stand." In both of these instances, the speakers created a figurative comparison that suggests that two dissimilar things are alike. To say, for example, that "his eyes reminded me of two flickering candles just before they burn out" is to imply that the person's eyes were actually similar to a candle. A speaker talking about campus violence would be using a metaphor if she were to say, "The hallways in our high schools now resemble war zones."

Style can also be made more vivid by using **antithesis.** In this figure of speech, contrast is emphasized by the position of words. That is to say, strongly opposed notions are put side by side in parallel construction—for example, "The homeless want employment not welfare checks, dignity not pity." When John F. Kennedy uttered the words "Ask not what your country can do for you; ask what you can do for your country," he gave an antithesis that has now become a classic figure of speech. It is often the cadence of the antithesis that gives it added power. In this sense, many speakers use an antithesis to end their talk. Imagine the impact of the speech that ends with these words: "We will not simply get by, we will excel. We will not simply accept, we will demand. We will not simply wait, but we will act."

Personification is a figure of speech in which life and personality traits are attributed to inanimate objects or abstract ideas. The following are some examples of this excellent figure of speech:

"The old house just shuts its eyes to the ugliness springing up around it."

"That piece of cake was begging me to come and taste it."

"The problem has been with us so long that it is a member of the family."

"The trees, knowing they would be spared the power of the chain saw, seemed to be dancing in the wind."

"The cat was so humorous that it, too, seemed to laugh out loud."

"For the first time in history, the wall around Wall Street seemed to resemble a bridge that was bringing even the small investor inside the sacred bastion."

"My car had taken such good care of me for ten years that last week I decided to give it a birthday party."

"Even the stately faces on Mt. Rushmore looked a little sadder the day our astronauts perished in that tragic explosion."

Hyperbole is a figure of speech that magnifies objects beyond their natural boundaries in order to make them more impressive and more vivid. It is based on exaggeration.

"He stood there, tall and proud—taller than Mount Everest and prouder than San Francisco on the day the 49ers won the Super Bowl."

"It took Lisa so long to enroll in the required classes that she was now able to be in the same graduation class as her daughter."

"There was so much hot air coming from those politicians that I thought the convention hall would become airborne."

"He had been living in the back of his truck so long he had to give it an address."

"This dog training method is so effective that one dog became so smart that he trained his master to bring him his dinner at exactly five o'clock each night."

Climax is a figure of speech that presents a series of thoughts or statements arranged in order of increasing importance. It is the building effect of climax that gives the impact of this figure of speech. "First the government takes your apple, then it takes your tree, and before long it takes your whole orchard." "The first fee increase saw me taking a part-time job. The second addition forced me to take full-time employment so I could stay in school. Now, with the additional charge, I must leave school and abandon my education."

Another figure of speech is **onomatopoeia.** While this is often thought of as a vocal device, we shall treat it as a language tool. It is a figure of speech in which the sound of a word or group of words imitates the sound it names or describes. The following words fall into this category: *rumble, crash, splash, boom, buzz, cackle, hiss, smack, chatter, thud, slither, bang,* and *fizzle.*

Even though we have treated it elsewhere, we should point out that **rhetorical questions** are an effective linguistic device. You will recall that a rhetorical question is a query intended to produce a mental response on the part of your listeners. When rhetorical questions are used as a figure of speech, it is often effective to ask a series of questions. Notice the verbal impact in the following example:

Do you believe you are receiving the best education possible? Ask yourself these questions: How crowded are my classes? Do my professors know my name? Am I being challenged to do my best work?

As the last example demonstrated, rhetorical questions are effective when presented as a series of questions:

Why is suicide one of the fastest-growing causes of death among young people in the United States? And do you know someone who is manifesting suicidal tendencies? Is it your brother, sister, best friend?

Parallelism, which we mentioned earlier in this chapter, is the figure of speech in which two or more clauses or sentences are stated in the same manner. The result is a rhythmic pattern that can be captivating and interesting. Notice the parallel structure in the following example:

We will not give up this fight until every homeless child has a safe place to sleep. We will not give up this fight until every homeless child receives three meals a day. We will not give up this fight until every homeless child moves from the streets to the classroom. And we will not give up this fight until every homeless child has adequate medical care. The battle may be arduous, but we will not give up the fight.

Another speaker, challenging the audience to be motivated about animal rights, noted:

Be committed to animal rights for all animals. Care about the cats that suffer. Care about the dogs that languish in small pens. Care about the rabbits that get chemicals put into their eyes in the name of vanity. Care about the tigers that pace all day in small cages. Care about the elephants that travel in trucks that are so inadequate they can hardly move around. Care for all the animals. Care. Care. Care.

The final figure of speech, **alliteration,** is much like parallelism, except that it is the repetition of a sound that adds interest to the point being made. Notice the vividness in the following examples:

"When we entered the cave for the first time, we could sense the approaching perils, pitfalls, and problems we would face."

"I can assure you she will make an excellent candidate. She has both character and charisma."

"This program was doomed to fail. It was too costly, too chaotic, and too complex."

"This law is important for our community. We must persuade, prod, and push our legislature to adopt the proposal."

A word of caution is warranted about using figures of speech when speaking to an audience composed of people who are not familiar with the North American culture. Notice that, in many of the previous examples, the figure of speech has a frame of reference with its roots in North American culture. When you talk about the Hollywood Freeway, the Rock of Gibraltar, or the Super Bowl, you are asking the listeners to know these expressions so that they can comprehend and appreciate the entire figure of speech. If the references are not universal, the simile or metaphor will be confusing.

Effective Style Is Appropriate

There is an Italian proverb that says, "Since the house is on fire, let us warm our hands." This advice, although sublime in its words, underscores the importance of fashioning one's remarks to the situation and circumstance. Adaptability is indeed one of the hallmarks of a successful communicator. When you move from one communication situation to another, you will find it necessary to adjust your language style to meet the unique demands of each encounter. Thus, your style will be appropriate because you have geared it to (1) *the specific audience* and (2) *the occasion*.

Appropriate to the Audience

As one aspect of adaptation, your language may be the most crucial. You know from experience that you often change words and phrases as you move from person to person and place to place. If a professor calls on you in class, you respond with one type of language, yet, if a friend asks you a question, your remarks are far less formal. You are making your language appropriate to the receiver.

You run the risk of not accomplishing your purpose when you use language that is not suited to your listeners. Imagine how you would feel if you had gone to hear a lecture entitled "An Introduction to Perception" and heard a speaker say, "Once we know that we can see electromagnetic radiation with wavelengths of 380 to 760 millimicrons, we should find out what the subjective experience is at each point between the upper and lower thresholds." If the entire audience were composed of persons with very little background in perception, this would be a blatant example of inappropriate language. Suppose you tuned in a television "household hints" program and heard the host say, "So whatever you do, don't put a neutral sulphated monoglyceride detergent on your woolens."

Appropriate to the Culture and/or Coculture Once again we ask you to recall the role of culture in deciding what is appropriate and inappropriate language. For example, as indicated, there are many cultures, such as the German and English, in which formality is a primary value. When speaking to audiences composed of people from these cultures, you need to avoid slang and other types of casual language patterns. If the culture values simplicity in the use of language (for example, Japanese, Chinese, Korean), you should not overstate your points. Finally, if the culture you are talking to values rhetorical artistry (for example, Arab and Mexican), you should aim for a grander and more commanding style. In all these instances, what is called for is a careful assessment of your audience, coupled with a sense of good taste.

There are also times when cultural attempts at adapting can backfire. This is especially true when speakers attempt to "speak the language" of certain cocultures. An excellent example can be found in the engaging language used by African Americans.

Many African Americans use a specialized vocabulary called *argot* to produce group solidarity. This unique language, composed of hundreds of words, grows out of the experiences found in the African-American community. It would be folly and embarrassing if a European-American speaker would try to adapt to an African-American audience by using words such as *shucking, jiving, hussling, woofing, Charlie, bad,* and *oreo.* Such a speaker would not demonstrate an ability to "speak the language" but, instead, would display a lack of tact. The same is true of a middle-aged person who thinks he or she is being inspirational by telling a teenage audience to "take it to the max!" or "let's jam." Trying to make someone else's unique expressions one's own generally results in transparent artificiality. This sham is usually obvious and puts both the speaker and the audience in an awkward situation. Be yourself; to do otherwise is inappropriate and artificial.

Appropriate to Women In recent years, there has been an increasing awareness of the sexist character of some of our everyday language. Much of this language is perceived as belittling others because of their gender. A speaker who is sensitive to the feelings of the listeners avoids words and phrases that might be viewed as demeaning or offensive. Let us examine three aspects of sexist language that are inappropriate.

Our first area of concern deals with the use of "he." Traditional grammar has conditioned most of us to use the pronoun *he* to represent the entire class of humans, whether they are male or female. Saying "each voting member of this community should exercise his right to vote" completely excludes over half the population and even suggests a subtle bias. Let us suggest a few ways that you can avoid masculine pronouns and use language that is more generic.

(1) In the example we used above, it would be better to say, "All persons should exercise their right to vote." (2) The misuse of *he* can also be avoided if you learn to pair the pronouns and use constructions such as "he or she," "women and men," and "her or his." (3) The use of "they" is yet another effective nonsexist device: "As voters learn about the issues, they will make the correct choices." (4) Using the second person ("you") can help overcome the use of masculine pronouns: "As you mark your ballot, think about the importance of today's topic."

Second, *sexist language often omits women from the culture by making maleness the norm.* For example, words such as *fireman, mailman, chairman, salesman, workman, cameraman, paperboy, congressman,* and *foreman* all give the impression that women are excluded from these roles. You should learn to use alternative words such as *firefighter, mail carrier, chairperson, sales representative, worker, camera operator, paper carrier, member of congress,* and *supervisor.*

Finally, *a great many words and phrases are inappropriate because they possess strong sexist overtones.* For example, it would be insulting to most women in your audience to use the word *girl* if you were talking about an adult. Think of the image associated with words and phrases such as *spinster, little old lady, the weaker sex, libber, his better half, chick, hunk, sexy, buns, broad,* and *little woman.*

Appropriate to the Occasion

As noted in chapter 3, the speaking occasion is a very important determinant of what constitutes appropriate style. Religious ceremonies, eulogies, appeals for charity, and the like usually preclude the use of facetious expressions, slang, or obscenity. A small, informal meeting of friends might call for casual language, while a college commencement address demands a more serious tone. For example, a commencement speaker might say, "May the doors of learning, now open to you and your fellow students, remain wide for the future generations of this great state," but, in a small group, that same statement might be perceived as pompous and out of place.

Effective Style Is Free from Distractions

Throughout this chapter, we have explored the notion that effective style benefits you on two counts. It enables you to explain your internal states (what you are thinking about) in a way that other people might better understand them, and it adds to your perceived credibility. However, if your language habits are deficient, clarity is lost and your prestige is lowered. As you would suspect, there are patterns of expression that can interfere with your overall communication effectiveness. We inadvertently choose words and phrases that divert attention from our main ideas. Let us examine some of the types of words and phrases that can lower your credibility and cause your audience to become distracted from your main idea.

Slang

It may be acceptable under certain circumstances to use slang words and expressions, but, more often than not, they lessen a speaker's status and distract from the purpose of the speech. Speakers who use slang usually do so because of laziness. Words and phrases such as *nerd, macho man, bummer, freaked out, ticked off, jazzed, turn off, pad, stoked, kick it, awesome, turkey, rip-off, wiped out, humongous, the pits, outta sight, real awesome, blow your cool, bread, cop out, go for it, uptight, dude, gross, radical,* and *booze* are all examples of slang. Because slang changes with each generation, many of these words may not be used today. Yet when they were used, they did little to clarify an idea, make an image more vivid, or raise a speaker's credibility.

Triteness (Clichés)

Some words and phrases, which are refreshingly novel for a time, lose their novelty through overuse and, thus, become trite. They lack originality and impact because of their commonness. The Unicorn Hunters of Lake Superior State College annually publish a list of words and expressions that they propose for extinction because of their overuse—words and expressions such as the *bottom line, state of the art, networking, play it by ear, time frame, world-class, cutting edge, input, interfacing, empowerment,* and *meaningful dialogue.*

If the previous expressions of relatively recent vintage are already regarded as trite, think how much more so are the following expressions: *high on the hog, madder than a hornet, to each his own, busy as a bee, behind the eight ball, it takes one to know one, it takes two to tango, green with envy, leave no stone unturned, the straight and narrow path, cold as ice, keep a stiff upper lip, happy as a lark, a legend in her time, light at the end of the tunnel, can of worms, unaccustomed as I am to public speaking, dime a dozen, talk is cheap, ax to grind, play it by ear, few and far between, dead as a door nail, it goes without saying, last but not least,* and *beyond a shadow of a doubt.*

It is easy to let many of the clichés in the previous paragraph creep into your vocabulary. The very nature of a trite expression implies that it is commonplace. However, you can be more creative than simply returning to the overused expressions of other people.

Not only does triteness lower your credibility, but it has the added problem of being confusing to people who are not familiar with North American idioms. Go through the previous examples once again and try to imagine what it would be like to discover the meanings of *can of worms, behind the eight ball, networking,* or *cutting edge,* if you were not born and raised in the United States.

Jargon

During a recent congressional hearing, the expression *plausible deniability* was used repeatedly, yet there was always some doubt as to what meaning was intended by that expression. Each profession has its own language, and a speaker must remember that what is clear to a bureaucrat may not be clear to a voter, just as what is clear to a nuclear physicist may be very confusing to an orthopedic surgeon. *French fold* may be meaningful to producers of greeting cards but mystifying to a layperson. Someone without a medical background might have trouble with words such as *xerophthalmia, retrolental fibroplasia, cervical dysplasia,* and *pellagra.* It would also be hard for a heterogeneous audience to decide the meaning of the sentence "The new technology uses synchronized digital time phase projections."

When addressing a general audience, a speaker must avoid jargon and highly technical language. It would be very difficult for someone without a computer background to understand the jargon words and phrases *hard drive, DOS, mainframe, menu, file, scroll lock, data base management,* and *downloading.* And think about how confusing it would be if you were not an organizational manager for a major corporation and hear someone using words and phrases such as *benchmaking, replexity, broadbanding, reengineering,* and *rightsizing.*

Knowing the listeners' background and defining unfamiliar words will help a speaker overcome many of the problems of jargon and technical language.

Loaded Words

There are those who suggest that loaded and emotional words should be used whenever possible. They argue that such words assist a speaker in the goal of "manipulating others." Although loaded words are often colorful, in most instances they are ambiguous and vague. Think of how very different the image created by language is if one person, speaking on the abortion controversy, talks of the *unborn child,* while another person uses the words *undeveloped fetus* to describe the same circumstance. By playing on emotionalism, both sets of words, implicitly and explicitly, ask listeners to respond on a purely emotional basis.

Notice the images called forth by phrases such as *fat cats, stingy, selfish tightwads, health nuts, welfare chiselers, do-gooders, big conglomerates, bureaucrats, male chauvinist, extremists, nonfeeling spinster, demagogue, queer, religious fanatic,* and *barbaric approach.* Are these words really consistent with facts? If a colorful expression can be selected that does not distort reality, it should be used; if the appeal is strictly irrational, the speaker is guilty of a violation of ethical responsibility.

Empty Words

A philosopher once noted that "some so speak in exaggeration and superlatives that we need to make a large discount from their statements before we can come at their real meaning." He might well have been talking about "empty words." In this day of mass appeal, we are barraged by superlatives and exaggerations. This overexposure may condition an unsuspecting communicator to lean heavily on overworked and meaningless terms. Notice the empty quality of the following words and phrases: *super, colossal, deluxe, monumental, monstrous, new and improved, really great, magnificent, terrific, very good, fantastic, extra special,* and *a whole lot.* Many persons have been so bombarded with empty words that they are tempted to discount them and pay little attention to the person using them.

Contractions

It has become popular to use shortened forms of certain words. Although such contractions are derived from words in good use, they often lower the prestige of the speaker and indicate a lack of concern for language. Some common contractions are *exam* for *examination, y'know* for *you know, didn't* for *did not, condo* for *condominium, prop* for *proposition, prof* for *professor, caf* for *cafeteria, auto* for *automobile, letter of rec* for *letter of recommendation, ad building* for *administration building, grad school* for *graduate school, sub* for *substitute,* and *lab* for *laboratory. Frisco, Vegas,* and *DC* are poor substitutes for *San Francisco, Las Vegas,* and *Washington, DC,* and their use by visitors to those cities is particularly irritating to local residents. Perhaps the public-speaking situation also calls for *should not* instead of *shouldn't, we will* instead of *we'll,* and *will not* instead of *won't.*

Taboo Words

The topic of taboo words as a verbal distraction is a difficult one, for every audience and every occasion is different. While one person might consider a certain word a profanity, such as *damn* or *hell,* another person might not be offended by these words. The same, of course, is true of most curse words. Some people view swearing as offensive, while others see it as part of everyday life. Most people, though, find profanity inappropriate in the public-speaking environment.

Derogatory Language

There is yet another category of taboo words that should not be part of the vocabulary of a competent speaker. These are words that are degrading and repugnant to an entire class of people. It would be callous, tasteless, and a sign of ignorance to use words such as *Hymie, Dago, Jap, Spic, Chink, Chinaman, Nigger, Hebe, Frog, Wop, Kraut, Kike,* and *Polack* when referring to people from different ethnic backgrounds. These kinds of taboo words are the mark of verbal bigotry and an insensitive speaker. It is also insensitive not to respect the wishes of your culturally diverse audience if, as a group, they would prefer words such as *Asian* for *Oriental, gay* for *homosexual, Native American* for *Indian, African American* for *black,* and *person with a disability* for *handicapped.*

Ethics and Language

It is perhaps fitting that we move from a section on derogatory and hypercritical language to one dealing with the ethical issues surrounding your use of language. To begin our discussion of the ethical responsibilities of language, we need to return to a theme we have weaved in and out of every chapter. Simply stated, the words we use and the actions we take have an influence on other people. Our messages create change. Therefore, in selecting your words, we would urge you to follow some ethical guidelines.

First, see that words are *accurate*. When you are presenting facts or describing a scene, you should use language that correctly and carefully represents reality. In the following example, a speaker distorted the facts when, in giving a speech opposing the United Nations, she said, "The United Nations does not even respect the United States, because its official languages are Russian and French." The inaccuracy is that the United Nations has six official languages (English, French, Spanish, Russian, Arabic, and Chinese), not only the two selected by the speaker. It would be unethical to use language in this imprecise manner simply to make your case. Language should properly represent the facts. The English author Walter Savage Landor said much the same thing when he wrote, "I hate false words, and seek with care, difficulty, and moroseness, those that fit the thing."

Second, knowing the *emotional impact* of some words could help you avoid language that touches the passions of your audience in an unethical manner. We are not suggesting that you avoid animated and passionate language, but rather when you employ a style to arouse the emotions, you do so in a way that does not exaggerate or falsely embellish the point you are trying to make. Overstated appeals to fear represent a vivid example of language use that is unethical.

Finally, it is unethical to use language that is *hateful*. Words that are racist, anti-Semitic, or speak maliciously of a person or group of people are examples of hateful language. There is nothing wrong in speaking out when you see evil in the world; in fact, as a citizen in a democracy, it is your duty to speak out against injustice. However, your language should not lower you to the same level as your bigoted adversaries. Rise above character attacks and the language of demagogues. History is full of too many examples of how hateful words only produced more hateful words. Therefore, let your language be forceful, honest, and free of hatred.

Perhaps the best advice we can offer concerning the ethical use of language is what we said at the beginning of this chapter. At that time we noted that words have power. We again urge you to respect them and use them with great care, for, as the Greek poet Homer said, "Once a word has been allowed to escape, it can never be recalled." Reflect on their force *before* you let them escape.

Improving Your Language Habits

Some people believe that effective speakers are born, that the ability to speak well is given to some but not others. This is simply not true. Even though language habits and vocabulary develop early in life, they are constantly open to change, and this change can be in the direction of improvement. However, this involves more than memorizing a few rules or formulas. It demands practice and hard work over a long period of time. The English philosopher Charles Spurgeon would even suggest that this practice should last a lifetime: "To acquire a few tongues is the task of a few years; to be eloquent in one is the labor of a life." If you are willing to labor, much of your effort should be channeled into the following activities:

1. *Learn to use a dictionary and a book of synonyms.* These two sources provide clues to new words that are often more accurate and vivid than the ones you have been using. For example, *Roget's Thesaurus* and *The Synonym Finder* can help you widen your vocabulary while increasing your choices when searching for the right words with which to share an experience. In addition to books, most computer writing programs now contain a "built-in" thesaurus. You should learn to use these sources so instead of having to say, "It was good," you could be more specific by using one of the choices afforded by a thesaurus, such as *beneficial, valuable, edifying, salutary, capital,* or even the exotic *rara avis.*

2. *Be alert to new words as you listen and read.* Listening is an excellent method of improvement, for it allows you to perceive the overall impact of a word. Hearing someone say *glistening* instead of *bright* may persuade you that one strikes the ear more pleasingly than the other. Novels, plays, speeches, poetry, and essays illustrate how knowledgeable persons use language. In the correct context, a writer might avoid "the road was dangerous," preferring, instead, something like "the road was hazardous, treacherous, menacing, or perilous."

3. *Develop a habit of careful writing.* Careful writing and revision develop better expression. A diligent writer does not settle for the first word that comes to mind but searches for the word or phrase that promotes clarity and conveys the desired impression.

4. *Be aware of words, respect them, and make a study of language itself.* The field of general semantics, for example, examines the relationship between language and objects. There is a whole new world to explore when one investigates how people use symbols to influence one another and the world they live in.

5. *Be sensitive to the difference between oral style and written style.* Language generated to be heard is somewhat different from language written to be read. Speech making tends to contain more personal pronouns; more repetition of words, phrases, and sentences; shorter sentences; words and phrases that are easy to understand at first encounter; and more colloquial expressions. As you create your speech, then, remember to compose for the ear rather than the eye.

It is probably obvious by now that a large segment of the study of oral communication is necessarily a study of language. Later chapters, dealing with informative, persuasive, and other types of speeches, will also touch on the kinds of language appropriate to each.

Summary

Keep these general language principles in mind as you engage in both public and private communication: (1) words are symbols used to represent objects, ideas, concepts, experiences, and feelings; (2) one word can have many meanings and many uses; (3) words can have denotative and connotative meanings; (4) words convey only a partial view of reality; (5) words do not always keep pace with reality; and (6) words reflect our experiences.

Clarity, correctness, vividness, and appropriateness characterize effective language usage. Clarity is the product of using oral style, simple words, current words, and concrete and specific words. Correctness results from observing the grammatical standards expected of you by your audience. Vividness is obtained through imagery and figures of speech. Appropriate language is that which is suited to the audience's background, culture, and gender. Appropriate language also is adapted to the occasion. Effective style avoids distractions such as slang, triteness, jargon, loaded words, empty words, contractions, taboo words, and derogatory language. Remember the power of language and strive to be ethical in your selection of words and phrases. And finally, language can be improved by sincere study and conscientious practice.

Part III
HAVING AN INFLUENCE

Chapter 13

If you would thoroughly know anything teach it to others.

Tryon Edwards

Informative Speaking

Being Understood

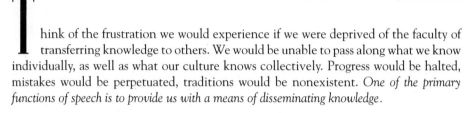

Seldom ever was any knowledge given to keep, but to impart; the grace of the rich jewel is lost in concealment.

Joseph Hall

Think of the frustration we would experience if we were deprived of the faculty of transferring knowledge to others. We would be unable to pass along what we know individually, as well as what our culture knows collectively. Progress would be halted, mistakes would be perpetuated, traditions would be nonexistent. *One of the primary functions of speech is to provide us with a means of disseminating knowledge.*

The Importance of Informative Speaking

The ability to render an idea clear and comprehensible is one of the most highly prized skills a person can possess in our complex and ever-changing society. Being able to tell others, in a clear and interesting manner, how this or that functions or operates is often a measure of someone who is educated. Regardless of the culture, individuals who have knowledge, and can share it, are perceived as being productive and credible. There is even a belief among many cultures that it is wrong to have knowledge and not share it. The Persian poet Saadi once wrote, "Whoever acquires knowledge and does not share it resembles him who ploughs his land and leaves it unsown."

Situations calling for the use of informative discourse are numerous. Virtually all teaching can be labeled informative speaking. Instructing and training workforces and office and sales staffs likewise involve informative speaking. Even directing a stranger toward a particular destination in your city calls for informative discourse. At all levels of communication, both formal and informal, people engage in informative speaking, and, in this "Information Age," it is used with accelerating frequency. We are now experiencing an unprecedented explosion of ideas and information; new concepts are emerging from every direction and from every discipline. As noted earlier, knowing how to organize, clarify, and transmit those concepts is one of the hallmarks of an educated person.

An informative speech imparts materials that increase a listener's knowledge of a given subject. If you know a great deal about fraudulent practices in mail order businesses and give a speech on that topic, you expect your listeners to know more about that subject when you complete your talk. Therefore, *the primary objective of informative speaking is to present information so that it will be easily understood, remembered, and perhaps even applied by your audience.* It is difficult to draw a rigid distinction between speeches to inform and speeches to persuade and entertain. As we observed in chapter 2, what a speaker intends to be a speech to inform may have a persuasive effect on the listeners and may be very entertaining. It is difficult to say that a speech has but a single clear-cut end or purpose. It is more realistic to view discourse on a continuum, with many gradations and variations running from informing to persuading. Charles Colton must have been writing about the difficulty of a single purpose when he wrote, "A windmill is eternally at work to accomplish one end, although it shifts with every variation of the weathercock, and assumes ten different positions in a day." In the final analysis, it is the receiver's response that determines whether a message is informative, persuasive, or entertaining; in most instances, it is a bit of each.

Basic Assumptions About Learning

If our aim is to increase audience understanding of a subject, we should be aware of the important principles that contribute to both short-range and long-range learning. Educators and psychologists have suggested some basic assumptions about how persons learn and retain information. These assumptions should help you select a topic, as well as prepare and present your material. Therefore, once we have identified these postulates concerning learning, we shall then weave them into the entire chapter. This will enable us to show you how theory can be turned into practice.

Learning is facilitated when we are motivated. The results of many experiments to determine how people learn have validated Aristotle's claim that "all that we do is done with an eye to something else." We learn more and retain it longer when we see a reason for listening. If, for example, you have been experiencing difficulty in setting your VCR to record programs during your absence and a speaker says that he is going to remove some of the mystery from VCR operation, you are apt to pay close attention to his talk. Think about your motivational level if you live near a nuclear power plant and hear that a speaker's topic is "reevaluating the risk of living near a nuclear reactor." You can see from these examples that one of the principles of effective motivation is that it points the topic directly at the audience; it makes the subject personal.

Curiosity and interest, as well as anxiety, can motivate people. A speaker once encouraged her audience to listen to a speech on the Japanese yen by declaring that the yen and the U.S. dollar are interrelated. She did what every effective informative speaker is able to do—she made the material interesting.

It is important to remember the role of culture in motivation as you think about your speech to inform. Not all cultures are motivated by the same propositions. While many North Americans are motivated to listen to a speech on the stock market so that they can add to their material wealth, members of other cultures might not find this appeal as challenging. For them, happiness may well derive from sources other than money. Later in this chapter we will talk about some techniques you can employ that will make your material compelling and interesting so that your audience will acquire knowledge from your presentation.

Learning is facilitated when the unknown is coupled with the known. If you have never ridden horseback but can visualize the relationship between steering a car and reining a horse, you might couple these experiences and be able to understand something of elementary horsemanship. Having people visualize how a computer disk is much like an enormous filing cabinet, can help them see the basic function of computer disks. As noted in chapter 6, analogies point out similarities between what is already known and what is not, making these forms of support particularly useful in informative discourse.

Listeners remember a fact or an idea much longer if it is repeated and reinforced.

Learning is facilitated when information is encountered in a logical sequence. Most of us have suffered through speeches that lacked clear direction and seemed to leap from point to point at random. Perhaps we tried to reorganize the speaker's rambling ideas, but more often we simply stopped listening out of frustration. Part of this chapter capitalizes on what researchers now know about the constituents of successful organization. We will examine various organizational schemes, as well as some transitional devices, that can make your speech easier to follow.

Learning is facilitated when key ideas are repeated. A typical television commercial makes certain you don't miss the main point; it is repeated or restated over and over. You most likely can sing the McDonald's commercial because it has been repeated so many times, but can you name the state capitals for all fifty states? A person who places a hand on your shoulder while saying, "I'm very fond of you," is nonverbally repeating a verbal point. This same principle of frequency applies to learning theory and, hence, to informative speaking. Listeners remember a fact or an idea much longer if it is repeated and reinforced. These two principles often take on added significance when you are speaking to people who do not share your cultural background. For example, if you are explaining how to prepare a résumé to people who have no such item in their country, repeating and reinforcing would help them learn about this new procedure. Later in the chapter, when we discuss previews, transitions, and summaries, we will offer some very specific advice on how to use the learning tools of repetition and reinforcement.

Learning is facilitated when multisensory stimulation is used. As pointed out in chapter 7, educators have known for a long time that learning is fostered when a stimulus is presented in a way that involves as many of the senses as possible. This fact is even more accurate since we entered the television and computer age. These are both very visual pieces of equipment. Hence, *we urge you to think about including aids if your goal is having people learn.* For example, if you use a visual aid depicting the topography of the Los Angeles basin while you discuss conditions that foster the formation of smog, you are apt to produce a clearer understanding of why the Los Angeles metropolitan area is so prone to experience this form of air pollution. A speech on how to distinguish an edible mushroom from a deadly one obviously needs visual aids if the audience is going to be able to make such a distinction long after the speech is over.

Being able to call on a variety of senses is extremely important if you are speaking to people from another culture who are not familiar with all aspects of the North American culture. Imagine how much easier it would be to learn about traffic signs and signals if you had posters and pictures so people could actually see what you were talking about.

Throughout this chapter, as you study techniques that contribute to learning, you will see the value of returning to chapter 7 in order to reexamine the visual aids discussed in that chapter. We emphasize that you will find visual aids to be helpful when giving a speech to inform.

Learning is facilitated when the learner is not subjected to communication overload. The human brain, amazing as it is, can process only a certain amount of new material at any given time. Speakers who offer too many pieces of information run the risk of confusing rather than enlightening their listeners. All of us have encountered speeches so filled with information that we were unable to recall even a fraction of it. Trying to explain all the causes of world hunger or how to outfit an army for desert conditions in an eight-minute speech are two examples of topics that could produce overload. Thinking about your audience and narrowing your topic are perhaps the most meaningful steps you can take to avoid problems of excess and overload before they arise. Techniques for reducing overload during a speech presentation will be examined later in the chapter.

Learning is facilitated when the content is perceived as having some depth. At first glance, the principle of depth might seem to contradict what you have just learned about overload, but they are really two different ideas. The principle of overload says that people can remember only so much at one time; therefore, you should not offer too much or be too technical. The principle of depth maintains that people will learn very little if they are offered very little. You know from your own experiences that, once you decide that material you are listening to is inconsequential and trivial, you cease to pay attention—and learning stops. In planning the depth level of your speech, you need to be especially sensitive to the makeup of your audience. Some key questions you should ask are, Who are they? What do they already know about the topic? What do they expect of me? Will they be able to understand all that I have to say in the amount of time I am allotted?

Learning is facilitated when the learner is provided with a central focus. Put another way, we tend to learn more when we know what we are expected to learn. Although your audience is likely to remember any number of things about your speech, you want them to be especially aware of your main idea and main purpose. If your purpose is clear, and you stay with that single purpose, it can serve as a unifying thread that holds everything else together. All the details you introduce will make more sense if they can be placed into a single context. Having a central focus helps you as well as your audience. It reminds you that every piece of information in your speech should relate directly to the central purpose. As Benjamin Disraeli wrote, "The secret of success is constancy to purpose."

Types of Informative Speeches

As you recall, *all informative speeches have a common goal—to increase the fund of knowledge of the audience.* Nonetheless, those speeches take different forms as they pursue that common goal. Speech teachers have attempted to classify informative discourse into four basic types. Although in some instances the categories may overlap, it is useful for speakers to be aware of the distinguishing characteristics of each type.

Instructions

The most frequently occurring type of informative talk is the one that provides an audience with instructions or directions. This type of speaking is often called the "how to" speech or the speech of demonstration. In these instances, the speaker is telling others how to perform a task, such as how to replace a sealed-beam headlight on an automobile or how to administer first aid to a burn victim. Employers use instructional speeches to show new employees how to perform their job assignments.

Some sample "how to" subjects might be

1. How to stock supplies for an earthquake emergency
2. How to compose an effective job résumé
3. How to organize a Neighborhood Watch program
4. How to construct overhead transparencies
5. How to administer CPR to someone who is having breathing problems
6. How to draw cartoon faces

Descriptions

Another common type of informative discourse offers a description of something. Engineers, teachers, sales managers, and supervisors are often called on to describe a new model, layout, display, location, event, or even an attitude. If you want your listeners to have a greater insight into the life of Buddha, you might describe his family, education, and his early interest in religion.

Some sample topics that would use description would be

1. The effects of sleep deprivation
2. A horseback riding tour on the floor of the Grand Canyon
3. Food markets in rural India
4. The floor plan of the White House
5. The underwater sea animals off the coast of San Diego
6. A typical day for an ambulance paramedic

Explanations

The third general type of informative speech is explanation—sometimes called exposition. Speeches that attempt to explain how and why an object, a process, or a procedure operates as it does fit into this category of information sharing. A speech that discusses the principles involved in the manufacture of soft bifocal contact lenses is an example of explanation.

Some sample speeches of explanation are

1. To explain the action of acid rain on ancient marble statuary
2. To explain how a hurricane forms
3. To explain how the federal deficit is calculated
4. To explain how seawater is converted into drinking water
5. To explain how electric cars differ from gasoline-powered cars
6. To explain how fax machines work

Reports

Most college students have been asked to present a report at some point in their schooling. Perhaps it was a book report, a committee report, or a report on a survey or project. At any rate, you were faced with the responsibility of transmitting to others the substance of what you had read, discovered, or deliberated on.

Some sample report speeches are

1. To report on efforts to overcome community resistance to a proposed landfill site
2. To report on plans for your city's participation in a cultural exchange program with a Japanese city
3. To report on Larry McMurtry's latest novel
4. To report on the new requirements in the General Education program at school
5. To report on efforts to secure legislative approval of a budgetary increase for a campus building program
6. To report on the early history of the Olympic games

Preparing a Speech to Inform

There is a Spanish proverb that offers the following advice: "A forward person is worth two." The message is sound, simple, and consistent with what we have said throughout this book—being prepared is a useful trait for any effective communicator. Before any behavior can be changed or any response secured, there must be both analysis and preparation. Several general principles of preparing informative speeches bear closer examination.

Determining a Purpose and Selecting a Topic

If your goal is to make ideas clear to others, you must first determine what you want them to know about those ideas at the conclusion of your talk. The specific purpose of any given informative speech is a statement of *exactly* what the speaker wants the audience to understand—for example,

1. To have the audience understand how high-definition television differs from ordinary television
2. To have the audience understand the role of a medical transcriptionist
3. To have the audience understand how to select drought-resistant ornamental plants
4. To have the audience understand how Hispanic cultures view the role of the elderly in a family
5. To have the audience understand how to reduce grocery bills by using free coupons
6. To have the audience understand how to find bargain air fares

7. To have the audience understand how to request documents under the Freedom of Information Act
8. To have the audience understand the best methods to begin a meditation program

Please notice that *all these specific purposes tell precisely what the speaker wants the audience to understand.*

In choosing and narrowing a topic for an informative speech, you should look to many of the criteria presented earlier in the book. Let us briefly review some of them as they apply to the speech to inform.

First, in most instances, *you should know more about the topic than do the members of the audience.* During the course of the speech, and in a manner that does not border on boasting, you should tell them how you came to know as much as you do about your subject. For example, you might say, "Having worked as a page in the United States Senate, I was able to learn a great deal about the evolution of a new law, and today I would like to share some of those experiences with you." You might say, "Having been born and raised in China, I feel I can offer you some interesting insights into the political structure of that country."

Second, *the topic should be relevant.* Intelligent people would not like to hear you talk about how to put frosting on cookies or your favorite ride at the amusement park. A comprehensive audience analysis (coupled with common sense) is perhaps your best guide to determining relevance. As always, try to view the topic from the position of your receivers. This listener-centered approach will help you avoid trite and uninteresting subjects.

Third, *the topic should be stimulating as well as timely.* Remember, in most instances you have selected the topic because it interests you. Therefore, it must be a topic that also arouses curiosity at the same time that it holds attention. It is an exciting challenge to take what appears to be a dull subject and give it life and vitality.

Finally, *locating sufficient material is yet another consideration in selecting and narrowing a topic.* Think how frustrating it would be if you wanted to discuss the types of wildflowers found in your region but could not find any information. Be assured that your frustrations would be shared by your audience, for they would not hear anything new.

Gathering and Selecting Materials

If you are to secure understanding, your speech must contain materials that are *interesting*, *clear*, and *comprehensible*. In order to accomplish this objective, you should begin by making an inventory of what you already know and the material you have available to you. You will then be in a position to determine what additional materials you need. If you are going to talk about how to manage stocks and bonds, and you have been a stockbroker, you already have a starting point. After the inventory, you are ready to locate and gather the necessary information. By realizing your aims, personal resources, and limitations, you can select the illustrations, examples, comparisons, definitions, statistical data, interest factors, forms of restatement, and visual aids that will accomplish your specific purpose.

Select material that will encourage the audience to interact mentally with your material. Think, for example, of how a rhetorical question requires the listeners to respond to the question even if they do not want to. Imagine your own mental reaction when someone says to you, "How many times have you started to open the hood of your car, only to realize you don't know the difference between a spark plug and a fire plug?" The speaker can then move to material that answers this question. You cannot help but become involved with the material if someone says, "What would you do if a person you love came running into the house, screaming, 'I've just been bitten by a black widow spider'?" In each of these examples, you are forced to take part in the communication process, because the speaker selected material and rhetorical questions to encourage your interaction.

Be sure to keep the knowledge level and cultural backgrounds of your audience in mind when you select material. The main reason audience analysis is crucial to informative speaking is that the speaker knows something that the audience does not and, therefore, must constantly adjust to this fact. However, that adjustment can take place only if the speaker knows the makeup of the audience. Remember, you are the expert and, therefore, know the distinctive vocabulary of the subject and all other specialized aspects. Many beginning speakers mistakenly assume that, since they know about the subject, their listeners do also. Try to overcome this shortcoming by selecting material that is aimed at your specific audience.

In these days of culturally mixed audiences, the importance of doing a thorough investigation of your listeners takes on added meaning. Think of how embarrassing it would be, and the wasted time involved, if you were to spend ten minutes talking about the life of Muhammad to a group composed of a large number of Muslims. What about the folly of talking about how to dress for success to people who believe they should always wear the traditional attire of their country? In short, remember the cultural makeup of your audience when selecting material.

Select materials to allow your audience to see as well as hear your main points. Chapter 7 listed a number of visual aids that you could use to make your material clearer and more interesting. As we have said earlier in this chapter, it would be helpful to return to chapter 7 to review those devices. All visual aids contribute to increased understanding and retention. Therefore, some of them should be integrated into your speech. Imagine what a good idea it would be if, for a speech dealing with acupuncture, you could show the actual needles used in acupuncture and a poster indicating where the needles are inserted into the body.

Your material should be reliable and accurate. Objectivity is important. Remember, you are telling your listeners something they do not know. Therefore, what you are discussing should be free from errors and distortions. Your credibility will be tarnished should your listeners discover that what you told them was inaccurate.

Select material that is varied. By using a variety of material, you can accomplish two important goals of informative speaking at the same time. First, you increase the chances that you will be understood. If your statistics fail to explain your point, then perhaps your quotation or example will. Second, by using various kinds of data, you can keep the audience's attention. As we discussed in the listening chapter, people have short listening spans; hence, they need to be able to transfer their focus while still understanding the point you are trying to make. Examples that are mixed with visual aids and definitions can both arouse and maintain interest.

Materials of Informative Speaking

Although increased understanding is the foremost concern of informative discourse, speakers must realize that information alone does not necessarily capture or hold attention. As we mentioned in the last paragraph, the mind constantly seeks new stimuli and quickly darts from idea to idea. Hence, listeners need a reason for listening—they must be motivated throughout the speech. Therefore, *the materials of an informative speech must serve a dual purpose; they must increase comprehension while holding attention.*

The features of a speech that hold attention overlap those that contribute to learning. What we might label an attention factor might also help explain a key point. For purposes of analysis, however, we are going to separate informative materials into two categories. First, we will begin by examining the kinds of content you can use to *facilitate understanding.* Next, we will explore some techniques that can help you *gain and hold the attention of your listeners.*

Contributing to Clarity

Materials that contribute to learning are as varied as the people who engage in the act of sharing ideas and information. However, scholars in the fields of education, psychology, and speech communication have isolated a number of devices that promote clarity. You will notice that all of these eight devices are linked directly to the *basic assumptions of learning* we examined earlier in the chapter.

Definition

Many mistakes are made when listeners are confused about meanings. A speaker may neglect to **define** some of the basic and important terms, phrases, or concepts of the subject because they are so much a part of the speaker's everyday thinking. We must always be mindful of the fact that words are symbols and are usually interpreted differently by different persons. Thus, a listener may attach meanings to words or phrases that are unintended by the speaker.

This entire problem of offering definitions takes on added significance in this age of cultural diversity. As noted in the chapter on language, we learn our meanings from our cultural experiences. If a particular culture does not have a specific experience, the people of that culture do not have a word for it. For example, imagine if you were from a small non-Western culture and were asked to define (understand) the words and phrases for "skywriting," "bungee-jumping," "affirmative action," "sexual dysfunctions," or "low-cholesterol cooking." Although all of these words have meaning to members of the North American culture, they may not be phrases that are used in other cultures. Therefore, you need to give special attention to definitions when your audience is composed of people from different cultures.

When trying to decide which words need definition, begin by examining those that are *abstract* or *unfamiliar.* If you are talking about *multiculturalism, educational dropout, welfare, liberals,* and *conservatives,* you should define what you mean by these abstract terms. These words, because they are often misused, are so abstract that they may evoke any number of meanings. Simply put, by defining such words, we tell our listeners exactly what we mean when we use them.

Confusion also results when we use unfamiliar words or phrases. If you were talking about alternative fuel sources for automobiles and you mentioned methanol, compressed natural gas, and ethanol without defining these terms, the audience might become confused. A speaker might also add to confusion if, in talking to a lay audience, she were to say, "The congruity theory of persuasion is an effective tool for advertisers." However, if she were to define *congruity*, the unfamiliar might become clear.

In defining words or phrases, speakers should observe the following rules:

1. *Define the unknown in terms of the known.* Using language that is simpler than the original expression is an application of this principle. Going from the known to the unknown establishes a common frame of reference and allows the audience to see what you mean. For example, a veteran Navy radar operator defined radar by comparing it to the action of a tennis ball being bounced off a garage door.

2. *Define a word by placing it in the context in which it will be used.* For example, you might say, "In discussing the problem of school dropouts, we shall concern ourselves with the student who leaves school, for whatever reason, before graduation or before the age of eighteen." In this way, the audience knows who you are talking about when you use the term *dropout*.

3. *Anticipate the knowledge level of your audience on the topic so that you will be in a position to decide which words need defining.* If you were talking to a group of electronics experts and used the simple radar analogy just cited, you might insult them, yet the same radar analogy might be very effective for a group of liberal arts majors.

4. *When defining terms or phrases, try to combine formal definitions with informal definitions.* By combining a formal definition with one of your own, you give the audience a clearer idea of what you are talking about. Notice in the following example how the formal and informal definitions contribute to increased understanding:

> Archaeology is the systematic recovery and study of material evidence of human life and culture in past ages. That is to say, an archaeologist tries to locate any type of material, be it animal fossils or clay pots, that will give some insight into how our culture has evolved through the ages.

5. *Define entire concepts as well as single words.* Definitions can be lengthy. If, for example, a speaker were discussing "holistic gardening," he or she might want to explain holistic philosophy as a means of defining this unique approach.

6. *Defining by synonyms is one of the most common forms of definition.* A synonym is a word that has about the same meaning as another word. When defining by synonym, you are actually incorporating many learning techniques into one device. You are using comparison and linking the unknown to the known. It is important to select synonyms that are familiar to the listeners. It does not make much sense to define one word with a word that is even more confusing. A speaker would be using synonyms if he or she were talking about primitive cultures and used words such as *instruments*, *tools*, *implements*, *utensils*, and *appliances* to help explain what primitive kitchens were like. Also, the notion of *dogmatism* would be easier to understand if a speaker used synonyms such as *opinionated*, *arrogant*, *bigotry*, and *closed-minded* to supplement the definition.

7. *Anticipate cultural differences in the way certain terms are understood.* In a multicultural society such as in the United States, there is always a possibility that certain words or expressions common to one cultural group may have no equivalent words or expressions in the culture of another group. This is particularly true of colloquial expressions and technical terms. If you were giving a speech about skiing and used the expression *hot dogging,* it might perplex a listener from Belize or Malaysia, who might be familiar with the usual meaning of *hot* and *dog.* If you were to refer to a tachometer when talking about automobiles, a person from an area where bicycles are the most common form of transportation might not have the slightest idea of that word's meaning. If you must use such words, show consideration to those of other cultures by offering definitions that fit within their frame of reference.

8. *Definitions can explain a concept or word by telling how it is used or how it functions.* When trying to explain mime theater, a speaker defined by function when she said, "A mime is a form of acting with only gestures and facial expressions. A mime performs without the use of words."

Examples and Illustrations

The value of **examples** and **illustrations** as means of clarification cannot be overemphasized. Examples are the simplest and most common of all the devices, and they are the easiest to use. Examples allow you to say, "This is what I mean." A speaker using examples to clarify an assertion might proceed as follows:

	I.	This university has a number of programs to help individuals with disabilities secure a college education.
Example:	A.	It has an "outreach" program that goes into various special education classes and explains admission requirements.
Example:	B.	It offers numerous scholarships to individuals with disabilities.

Thus far, we have talked only about brief examples. However, you should remember that many examples can become detailed narratives and, as such, these illustrations can also clarify. If you were talking about the plight of our national park system, you might use what is happening to Yosemite as an illustration:

Although Yosemite National Park is one of our most magnificent parks, with its sheer granite peaks, lush Sequoia groves, and magnificent waterfalls, it is also one that is experiencing the effects of too many people trying to live in harmony with nature. For example, an exposed sewer line feeds into the park's drinking water, the historic Ahwahnee Hotel is a potential fire hazard, and three bridges in the park have cracks in their foundations from the increased traffic.

The most important criterion for using examples is that they prove or clarify the generalization being made. For instance, if you were speaking of the roles played by contemporary first ladies, you could give explicit examples of the activities of Pat Nixon, Betty Ford, Rosalyn Carter, Nancy Reagan, Barbara Bush, and Hillary Rodham Clinton. These examples would explain your point in a vivid and concrete form while holding the attention of your listeners. Your illustrations do not always have to come from first-hand experience. Being able to read about first ladies can supply you with the examples you need. In short, membership in a street gang is not the only way you can gather illustrations on gang graffiti.

You should try to follow a few simple guidelines when using examples and illustrations in a speech to inform. First, your illustration should be an integral part of the speech, not added merely to gain interest. Many people try to put in their favorite story whether it fits or not. This only confuses the audience and wastes time that could be better spent in talking about matters that are more relevant to the topic.

Second, keep your illustrations brief. We all know from experience that a story can easily get out of hand. When this happens, we keep adding to the illustration until it finally becomes an entire speech in itself.

Third, it is best not to rely solely on illustrations and examples to help clarify an idea or a concept. Instead, combine them with other forms of clarification. You might start with an illustration as a means of explaining how a specific case reaches the Supreme Court, but you would want to follow that illustration with a different clarifying technique.

You can improve clarity through the use of **comparison** and **contrast.** Comparison shows how two things are alike; contrast shows how they differ. These devices are useful in leading listeners from the known to the unknown. In explaining the functions of the United States Senate, you might use comparison to explain the similarities between the Senate and your student council. By pointing out the duties and functions of the council (known), you would show the likeness in the Senate (unknown). **Analogy** is a good form of comparison because it also compares the known with the unknown. For example, a speaker trying to explain why digital systems are more accurate than analog systems begins with a simple yet clear analogy, using a concept that everyone is familiar with—watches:

Comparison and Contrast

> Consider watches: an analog watch uses a big hand and a little hand to represent information, while a digital watch uses numbers to convey the same information. Look at an analog watch and it will say that it's about 20 minutes to 11, while a digital watch tells you it's exactly 10:42.

Analogies and comparisons also have the added advantage of being interesting at the same time they contribute to comprehension. Imagine how attention would be heightened if you were talking about the problems related to drunk driving and said:

> Every year, more than 345,000 people are injured in alcohol-related crashes. Spread over each of our lifetimes, this translates into two out of every five people in the United States. Put into slightly different terms, this can be compared to seeing four of the people seated here in the front row being involved with a drunk driver.

When using comparison, it is important to remember that the items being compared should be similar. Think of how confusing it would be if you were to compare New York City to Billings, Montana, in a speech concerned with subway travel or ethnic restaurants.

In some cases, contrast may be more helpful than comparison. If the audience knows the point from which the contrast originates, the contrast will be particularly meaningful. A famous newsman discussing the relative freedom of speech enjoyed by journalists today noted that, when he started out as a reporter in the late 1950s, the newspaper would not print the words *rape, abortion,* and *condom.* Another speaker, discussing the financial woes of a nationally prominent banking company, pointed out that "shares sold today at forty-eight dollars sold at eighty-seven dollars just a year ago." This stark differentiation helped the speaker underscore the magnitude of the company's difficulties.

Statistics

Statistics are frequently useful to explain an idea in terms of quantity or size. For example, if you were talking about income tax in the United States, it would be useful to offer statistics on how much money is generated by this tax form and what percentage of the total budget this figure represents. If you were trying to explain the increased visitor population of the national park system, you might say, "Use of the parks has steadily increased, from 80 million visitors in 1960 to over 350 million last year." You could highlight the size of Central Park by noting that it occupies 840 acres, or about $1\frac{1}{3}$ square miles. The statistics could take on added meaning if you would say, "This is about the size of our entire campus—from the parking structure to the football field."

A few guidelines should be kept in mind. By themselves, statistics are abstract and meaningless. To be useful, they must be compared or contrasted with something else to show how many, how few, how large, or how small an idea or a thing really is. If you were offering statistics on the number of light-years to the nearest star, you might make such figures meaningful by explaining a light-year in terms of how many trips that would involve between campus and the downtown area. Second, a large list of numbers is hard to comprehend. Whenever possible, use round numbers. Third, it is important that you are very selective in citing statistics, for a listener will tire of a lengthy discussion of facts and figures. Fourth, try to make your statistics as interesting as possible. For example, a speaker discussing how much money North Americans spend on taxes made the numbers interesting by saying, "The average North American spends 2 hours and 45 minutes of every 8-hour workday earning enough to pay taxes."

Fifth, see that your statistics meet the tests advanced in chapter 6. Whether your aim is informative or persuasive, your material should be authentic, complete, and clear.

Sixth, by documenting the source of your statistics, you make them more believable. Studies have shown that people tend to place greater credence in information if it is from a highly credible source. Saying, "The National Institute of Mental Health reported last year . . . ," certainly demands more attention than your asserting, "I read last week . . ."

Finally, in a speech to inform, you must be careful not to use too many statistics at one time or statistics that are not clear. You want people to remember the key elements of your speech, not minor subpoints. If you assault them with too many numbers, they will not absorb anything. What would you remember from the following statistics dealing with the relationship of modes of travel and death? "Your chance of dying in a bicycle crash is one in ninety-six thousand. In an automobile, it is one chance in only fifty-three hundred. And in drowning it is one chance in thirty-seven thousand." Here we see not only too many numbers but also numbers that do not make much sense.

Some concepts can best be clarified and explained by means of a **description.** Description enables you to picture, or portray, an object, an event, or a person by stimulating the listeners' sense of sight, sound, smell, taste, or touch. A listener's mind is focused on the object by means of vivid word pictures. A speech on an ethnic neighborhood might describe homes, markets, children at play, musical sounds, traffic noises, overheard conversations, food aromas, and so on. For instance, an audience might be made to "see" a food market by including details such as these: "Strung like Christmas garlands are strands of chili peppers, some bright red, others green or yellow, and even some that are black. Hanging over the meat counter are long chains of plump chorizo, the spicy Mexican sausage—as many as eight or ten different varieties."

At times, descriptions are much longer than a sentence or two. When describing what a meteor looks like, a speaker noted the following:

> The luminous streak appeared in the sky all at once. It seemed to be about half the diameter of the full moon and much like a street arc light. Its tail, of brilliant orange, with a sharp blue flame fading out at the extreme end, looked to be ten or twelve times as long and fully as broad as the body. The downward course was leisurely, as if in slow motion.

Another speaker used description when trying to inform her audience about the various clues that can be used when trying to select the winning racehorse by examining them in the paddock (walking ring) before the race. She noted

> Watch the way the horses look in the paddock and how they are behaving. They should be prancing and alert. Their skin should have a bright shine to it. If they are feeling well the coat should actually glow. They should get very excited as the jockey mounts them. And as they leave the walking arena they should have a spring and bounce to their gait. They are saying they want to run!

It is important when using description to include as many details as possible so that the image or thing being discussed is clear. Discuss the event, person, place, or thing with vivid language. It is through these details that listeners visualize purpose, function, size, shape, and color. You should have noted in all our examples that the speakers sought to incorporate size, weight, amount density, color, form, arrangement, texture, and composition. All these verbal characteristics add to the picture the audience "sees."

Clarity can also be enhanced through **demonstrations** of an act or a process while you are discussing it. Showing the correct arm and shoulder movements for jogging would enable your audience to see and hear the point you are trying to make. You can also demonstrate with an object. Imagine how clear your lesson would be if you were assembling an aquarium at the same time you were giving a speech on that topic.

Demonstrations can be quite useful when many members of your audience are from cultures that might not be familiar with the point you are trying to make. Seeing what you are talking about would help clarify your words. For instance, if you were trying to explain some of the differences between football and soccer to a group of people who were from a culture in which only soccer is played, you could show one major difference by demonstrating how each sport kicks the ball. You would be enacting the words of the English poet George Herbert, when he wrote, "The eyes have one language everywhere."

Description

Demonstrations

In most instances, it takes time to display and exhibit while you are talking. Therefore, allow a few extra minutes when you are practicing for a speech that uses demonstrations. Also, as stressed elsewhere in this book, do not let your demonstration or visual aid get in the way of your eye contact. Your audience must remain your focus, not your demonstration or the object in front of you.

Reinforcement and Emphasis

We can never retain all that we hear. Therefore, by means of **reinforcement** and **emphasis,** a successful speaker underscores the materials he or she deems most important and compelling. Reinforcement and emphasis take on added significance when you are speaking to culturally diverse audiences that may not be familiar with some of your content. By reinforcing and stressing specific points, you are making it clear to your audience what ideas are most important. Four of the most common reinforcement techniques will now be discussed.

Restatement is more than simple repetition; restatement uses new words to convey and echo an idea already discussed in a speech. After speaking on the dangers of cigarette smoking, you might want to restate your main thesis as "cigarette smoking can cause you great physical harm." In this way, the listeners hear the idea again but expressed differently.

Repetition is the use of identical wording in presenting an idea again. Through repetition, the main point is better remembered. You might say, "Cigarette smoke is responsible for 150,000 to 300,000 cases of bronchitis and pneumonia; just think about it, 150,000 to 300,000 cases of bronchitis and pneumonia."

Both restatement and repetition have their roots in learning theory and should be used frequently in communication. Perhaps the author H. G. Wells was correct when he noted, "After people have repeated a phrase a great number of times, others begin to realize its meaning."

Calling attention directly to an idea you wish to stress is yet another device available to speakers. Simply saying "this is important" or "please listen to this" can focus attention on the point you wish to emphasize. These two phrases tell the audience that they are about to receive some significant information. Imagine how your attention would be arrested if, while you were daydreaming, someone looked directly at you and said, "It is important that you understand this issue."

The way you use your voice and body can also help reinforce and emphasize the aspects of your speech you would like listeners to retain. For example, you can reinforce an important idea by changing the loudness of your voice or by pausing. You can also add emphasis by moving toward your listeners. This activity accents the verbal elements of your talk. Even gestures, such as pointing, can stress an important aspect of the message.

Partition, Enumeration, and Summaries

As a speaker moves through a speech, the listeners can lose track of the main thesis unless their memories are refreshed occasionally. Therefore, it is of prime importance for the speaker to enlist devices that help the audience remember the main ideas as they are developed throughout the speech. In chapter 6, we talked about using transitions as a way of encouraging clarity and retention. We examined bridging and signposting as two such transitional devices. Now we will add four other techniques: partition, enumeration, internal summary, and final summary.

A **partition** (often referred to as an initial summary or preview) is a list offered early in a speech of the points that will be covered. You simply tell your audience what main ideas you plan to treat in the body of your speech—for example, "In talking about the special vocabulary associated with computers, I want to talk about bits, bytes, and chips." Having highlighted what you plan to cover, you are now ready to move to the body of your talk.

Enumeration, which occurs during the body of your speech, is the numbering of each point as it is introduced: "First . . . , second . . . , and third. . . ." This technique is helpful in increasing clarity by alerting the audience to movements from one idea to another.

An **internal summary** can appear periodically during the body of the speech. It is a summary that reminds your listeners of the main points or subordinate points that you presented earlier. An internal summary not only underscores key ideas, but it also is an excellent transitional device. Notice the twin uses of summary and transition in the following speech on satellite broadcasting:

> Thus far, we have examined the launching and positioning of the satellite, the transmission process, and the role of the transponders. Let us now turn our attention to the final phase—reception.

Final summary is the reiteration of main items at the close of the speech—for example, "In trying to explain computers, I looked at bits, bytes, and chips."

The English author Wilmot once wrote that "Attention makes the genius; all learning, fancy, science, and skill depends on it." Wilmot is saying that, without attention, concentration, and focus, the mind fails to completely grasp what is transpiring at the moment. The late James Winans of Cornell University built a theory of persuasion around "inducing others to give fair, favorable, or undivided attention to propositions." You will recall that we started this chapter by mentioning that persons learn more when the material is relevant. Interest and attention are simply corollaries of that relevance.

Contributing to Interest and Attention

For our analysis, think of attention and interest as interchangeable; they have interlocking and overlapping meanings. Human behavior proves that what interests us commands our attention; likewise, what we attend to interests us. In this approach to attention and interest, our awareness of a stimulus is greatly heightened. All competing stimuli are secondary as the main message goes directly to what psychologist William James called the "focus of consciousness." As you should suspect, however, gaining control of that consciousness is no simple matter. The brain must attend to something, but a little self-reflection reveals that this attention darts from idea to idea. Attention rises and falls and is always changing in both intensity and direction. As a speaker, you must gain some control over audience attention so that you can focus it on yourself and your topic. In the next few pages, we will examine some suggestions to help you steer your listeners' attention toward you and your message.

There is no magic formula that will transform a dull message into a scintillating experience for an audience. Each speaking situation makes unique demands. However, we can profit from the findings of psychologists who have probed the nature of attention and interest. These findings have yielded guidelines for minimizing the effort our listeners must exert in order to stay attentive to our ideas.

Each speaking
situation makes unique
demands.

Noting That Which Is Upcoming

Not only are we interested in that which has just happened but also in that which is soon to happen: the impending. We all find the future exciting. The American essayist Joseph Krutch said, "The most prevalent opinion among all of us seems to be that tomorrow will be wonderful." Appealing to the notion of "tomorrow," a speaker, wanting to discuss recent improvements in the safety features of automobiles, said, "I heard on the radio this morning that the first of the new model cars are due to arrive at dealers' showrooms within the next ten days. It will be interesting to see how they measure up to the safety standards that I'd like to discuss with you today." Yet another speaker, talking about new communication systems, aroused interest by saying, "People in the twenty-first century will wear their telephones like jewelry, with microphones hidden in necklaces or lapel pins and miniature speakers tucked behind each ear." A speaker, giving a talk on a ballot proposition, used "the impending" to arouse and maintain attention:

> In just two weeks, we shall be asked to decide the fate of this city's hiking trails. On Tuesday, November 7, the voters of this community are going to have an opportunity, by means of a ballot proposition, to decide if the State of California should use tax money to purchase several wilderness areas from the federal government. This issue has been debated for years, and now it appears that the time for action has arrived. Because you will be affected by the outcome, and because you will help determine that outcome, it might be helpful if I take a few minutes today and explain the proposition in detail.

> You have probably noticed how much more interested in college registration students become on the eve of the opening term or how prognostications about conference football standings take on greater interest closer to the start of the football season. Look for ways of linking your subject to the future.

Just as ideas involving temporal nearness catch interest more readily than those in the distant past or distant future, so are ideas involving physical proximity more compelling than those that are remote. A news item involving your neighborhood will probably capture your attention faster than one concerned with another city.

The immediate physical surroundings in which the communication act takes place also offer possibilities for applying this interest factor. For example, if you are trying to give your audience a conception of the size of a cantina in which you had worked during a summer in Baja California, you might compare its dimensions with the size of the room (or building) in which the audience is situated. If you are describing a pagoda in Formosa, you might say, "See that carillon tower on the old library building? The pagoda I'm describing was about that height." A speaker who wishes to use a hypothetical illustration to explain a principle of boating safety might say, "This weekend, two of your colleagues here—Nancy and Sara—are going out to Mission Bay to rent one of those small sailboats for a cruise around the bay." Give your listeners someone close to identify with and they will likely be more interested in following the illustration. Every teacher has learned the attention value of a student's name in promoting the student's interest in what is being said.

A female student whose hobby is skydiving used this analogy: "Jumping out of a plane gives you somewhat the same sensation you experience when you unexpectedly reach the top step of a dark stairway. You raise your foot for another step, then discover it isn't there." By relating the unfamiliar (jumping out of a plane) to the familiar (reaching for a step that is not there), she enabled her listeners to experience vicariously a small part of her favorite pastime.

This technique of relating the unfamiliar to the familiar is basic to effective speaking, whether persuasive or informative. The listeners' frame of reference must always be considered when attempting to explain a new idea or concept. Reference to the familiar, however, does not mean simply telling the audience what it already knows. Instead, tell the audience what it does not know in terms of what it does know. If you were attempting to explain to a college audience the game of jai alai, you might liken it to handball played on a larger court, with scooplike baskets substituting for the gloves worn by handball players. Describing the bureaucratic levels through which a welfare payment application must travel by referring to the steps and complexities of registering for classes would be another application of the principle of familiarity. You could also use familiarity if you were talking about anxiety to a speech class and asked them to remember the nervousness they felt in the hours and minutes preceding their first presentation to the class.

When creating interest by means of a reference to what is familiar, always make sure that all members of the audience are familiar with your reference. For example, in the case we used earlier involving handball, if there were people who, because of their culture, were not familiar with handball, your attempt at securing interest would be wasted.

Who is the most important person in the world to a listener? Without being critical to any of us, you would have to agree that it is probably the listener, as well as the things that directly affect him or her. Always ask yourself if your message has any bearing on the listeners' self-interest. Does it concern, directly or indirectly, the listeners' health, safety, family pocketbook, status, personal comforts, or any of a long list of needs and wants? Subconsciously, every listener may be asking the speaker, "How does this concern me?" One speaker capitalized on the audience's personal needs when he tried to interest a group of college students in a speech on "making effective use of our study time":

> Each one of us in this room has given up something to be here. We have given up activities ranging from making money on a job to playing tennis during this lovely sunny day. So why are we here in college instead of doing something else with these four years? If we reflect on it, the answer is very simple—we came here because we believe that a college education has both immediate and long-range rewards that we deem important. However, to be the recipient of these rewards, we not only give up certain things, but we have to attend classes and spend a great many hours studying. This study time comes from time when we could be socializing or engaging in other leisure activities. Knowing that we all want more time for various occasions, I would like to talk to you today about how you can improve your grades and, at the same time, have more freedom to have fun— specifically, how to make more effective use of your existing study time.

A speech concerning a nuclear power plant might be prefaced by remarks concerning possible cuts in the listeners' light bills or new conveniences to enjoy as a result of cheaper electricity. Allusions to new food additives that will cut cooking time drastically might enhance listener interest in an explanation of chemical compounds. A discussion of a proposed state budget takes on added impact when the speaker suggests that the listeners' children might not enjoy "free" public education if certain amendments are adopted. In short, never overlook the possibility of relating your message to the personal concerns of the audience.

Imparting Activity

In chapter 4, we discussed how a speaker who uses meaningful bodily action and vocal variety holds attention more readily than a speaker who does not. The content of a speech can also be infused with activity. If a speaker arranges ideas in a logical, easy-to-follow sequence, those ideas seem to move for the listener. A jumbled, helter-skelter lack of arrangement is one of the surest ways to lose audience interest.

Speakers should use words that suggest action. "He staggered out of the woods" is more compelling than "He walked home." "The old pickup truck was doing seventy-five when it drifted over the divider strip into the oncoming lane" is more meaningful and interesting than "She was going too fast in that truck."

During a classroom speech on memory improvement, one speaker demonstrated a technique for memorizing a list of items. Among other things, the speaker asked the audience to visualize each item in motion—the more absurd and exaggerated the motion, the better. He explained that we tend to remember moving objects more readily than stationary ones.

Varying your supporting materials also imparts a feeling of activity to your message. We all like action. Blaise Pascal wrote, "Our nature consists of motions." Give your listeners that motion. Rather than dwelling at length on sets of statistics, add variety by inserting appropriate examples, analogies, and quotations from authorities. In the following example from a speech dealing with federal aid to college students, notice how the speaker aroused interest by varying her materials:

The role of the federal government in helping college students meet their financial obligations is quite significant. One out of every three students, more than 4 million in all, receives federal assistance. Cindy Williamson, of Missouri Valley College, is a typical student who uses federal aid to help with her education. This coming summer, she will complete her sophomore year thanks to work, ingenuity, helpful college officials, a bank, and the federal government. Cindy has earned 1,000 dollars working for minimum wage in the admissions office, she won a 1,000-dollar merit scholarship for good grades, she received a 1,000-dollar scholarship for need, and she took out a federally guaranteed student loan for 1,700 dollars. Just as the Chrysler Corporation needed some government aid, so did Cindy, yet Cindy, and the other students who depend on these loans, may now be facing some difficult times. Perhaps you know that Congress, responding to the president, is in the process of slashing federal aid—not to Chrysler, but to the 4 million Cindys. The cut, which could go as high as $1 billion, will influence higher education in the United States. Let us see how.

If you happen to be discussing a serious topic, avoid falling into a pattern of unrelieved sobriety. Insert a light note here and there (consistent with your purpose, of course) to lend refreshing variety. *Remember, too, that you should use the attention and interest factors throughout the speech.* They not only secure attention at the start of your presentation, but, when used at the right times, they sustain audience interest throughout your entire speech.

A student speaker was discussing how free enterprise was now being practiced in Moscow by small entrepreneurs. "I bought this T-shirt I'm wearing from a sidewalk vendor who was operating right under the noses of the authorities," she said. "I can't translate the Russian lettering on it, but I think it's fun to keep people guessing," she continued. In another, more somber speech, the sister of a North American student being held prisoner in Turkey for alleged possession of illegal drugs recounted the anguish of her brother's confinement. "This envelope brought the first letter he was allowed to write from prison." Still another speaker, discussing the famous ocean liner the *Queen Mary,* held up a soiled logbook from the engine room of that vessel. "This is the chief engineer's log of the last transatlantic voyage of the *Queen Mary,*" he said. The first student did not need to wear the T-shirt with Russian lettering in order to discuss free enterprise in Moscow. The sister of the jailed student did not need to hold up the envelope from her brother to make clear his ordeal. The man talking about the *Queen Mary* did not have to use the logbook to recount the ship's history. In all three cases, however, a striking heightening of interest resulted from the use of an actual object. The real item is almost always more compelling than the best verbal description, pictorial representation, or mock-up that can be devised. By the same token, a reference to an actual example tends to be more compelling than a reference to a hypothetical example.

Naturally, it is not always possible or practical to produce "the real thing," whether it is an object or an example. In such cases, you have to substitute that which is realistic for that which is real. For example, if you are trying to get an audience to visualize a circumstance in the future, you obviously cannot produce the actual circumstance, but you can provide lifelike details that will cause the listener to respond, "Yes,

Using Reality

that could very well happen." Putting real persons in hypothetical circumstances or hypothetical people into an actual setting lends credibility and interest to such examples. You will recall our example in which a speaker said, "This weekend, two of your colleagues here—Nancy and Sara—are going out to Mission Bay to rent one of those small sailboats for a cruise around the bay." Although the event depicted was hypothetical, the persons and places were real. Thus, the event bore a resemblance to reality.

Pointing Out Conflict

From soap operas to sporting events, we are all drawn into examples of conflict. There is something captivating about disagreements, be they major or minor. Therefore, a speaker should be aware of the value of conflict in examples, illustrations, and the like as a means of holding audience interest on a subject.

Perhaps conflict is implicit in the subject itself. A speech opposing a proposed course of action has built-in conflict, as does a problem-solving speech. On the other hand, subjects in which conflict is not implicit require that the speaker superimpose it. A speech explaining what happens to a letter from the time it is mailed to the time it reaches its destination does not seem to have a built-in element of conflict, but, by the skillful use of a hypothetical illustration, a postal worker did introduce conflict into that subject. He asked the audience to imagine that a listener in the front row was carrying in his suit pocket an insurance premium he had forgotten to mail. To keep his insurance in effect, he would have to see that the premium reached the home office twelve hundred miles away within thirty-six hours. Would mailing the premium at this moment enable it to reach the company in time? For the remainder of the speech, he followed the progress of that particular piece of mail until it reached its destination in the nick of time. The twin ingredients of conflict and suspense kept the audience interested throughout the speech.

Although it was part of a lengthy introduction, conflict was used by a speaker to direct attention while discussing the issue of a clean environment:

> For the past ten years, our nation has developed a towering environmental ethic—a recognition that people must learn to live in harmony with nature rather than to exercise a professed inalienable right to use and misuse limited resources, to poison and pollute, to ruin our landscape, and to run from the consequences. Yet there is another view that argues that runaway inflation, unemployment, and a sluggish economy have been brought about by environmental regulations. Who is right? Do we need government mandates and environmental regulations to keep from having polluted water, fouled air, and scarred land? Or do these regulations harm us? And what are these regulations?

Using Humor

The English poet, essayist, and critic Joseph Addison wrote in *The Spectator*, "I shall endeavor to enliven morality with wit, and to temper wit with morality." Although Addison was referring to his journalistic intention, his declaration might serve as a guide for speakers. Throughout this book, we have made a case for the use of humor, and in chapter 15 we will develop the topic in great detail. We have observed that, unless the subject you are talking about is extremely serious, the judicious use of humor can be an effective means of securing and holding audience interest. However, using humor requires skill. Because the audience response to a speaker's use of humor is so unpredictable, it is best to use it sparingly and with propriety. Sometimes it succeeds too well, so that the audience's attention becomes focused on the humor as an end in itself rather than as a means of making the larger message more interesting.

Remember that the audience's reactions to your attempts at humor are apt to take a variety of forms. Humor can be successful without your listeners falling off their chairs in wild abandon. They may simply smile or take inward pleasure from your statements. Because humor can aid you in making your informative presentation more interesting, we will explore a few positive suggestions and possible dangers inherent in using humor.

When using humor as an attention device, think of something novel and original. Look to the possibilities offered by exaggeration, incongruity, and sarcasm. A student, informing his listeners how they could improve the value of their automobiles, used *exaggeration* as a form of humor when he told the following joke:

> I had a friend whose car looked so bad that, when a toll bridge operator said, "Three dollars," my friend responded, "Sold."

Likewise, *incongruity*, presenting the familiar in an unfamiliar manner, has humorous overtones. Speaking on the topic "What is the P.T.A.?" a student offered the following bit of humor: "My mother used to visit my teacher so often that the other kids elected her class president."

Sarcasm, if used carefully, can also be an effective humorous technique. While informing a class about the Women's Rights Movement, a speaker told the following story as a means of recapturing attention:

> A feminist who was giving a speech in support of the Equal Rights Amendment was interrupted by the deep voice of a heckler from the crowd: "Don't you wish you were a man?" "No," she replied without missing a beat. "How about you?"

When using humor in an informative speech, it is important to remember that your main purpose is still increased understanding. Stringing a series of unrelated jokes together would be highly inappropriate. In addition, an analysis of both your audience and your occasion are crucial. Because humor can be offensive, you must carefully consider how your efforts will be received. As Aesop wrote almost two thousand years ago, "Clumsy jesting is no joke."

Using Illustrations

Illustrations, stories, and anecdotes represent yet another technique of speech making that we have discussed in this book. In chapter 6, we saw how factual and hypothetical illustrations can be used to prove or clarify a point. In chapter 11 we also noted how useful illustrations can be in introductions and conclusions of a speech. Earlier in this chapter, we discussed how illustrations and examples increase understanding and aid retention. In each instance, we noted that all people, regardless of their culture, enjoy listening to stories. Now we will examine illustrations as a way of stimulating audience interest.

A speaker gave a speech on the topic of the history of manners. To demonstrate the various ways people respond to correct manners, she offered the following humorous illustration:

> Mark Twain, often careless about his dress and manners, one day called on
> Harriet Beecher Stowe without his necktie. On his return, Twain's wife noticed

the omission and scolded him. A little later, a messenger turned up on Mrs. Stowe's doorstep and handed her a small package. Inside was a black necktie and a note that read, "Here is a necktie. Take it out and look at it. I think I stayed half an hour this morning without this necktie. At the end of that time, will you kindly return it, as it is the only one I have. Sincerely, Mark Twain."

Keep in mind that listeners not only enjoy illustrations and stories, but they expect them. Notice how the evening television news, which is basically informative speaking, uses human interest stories to hold audience attention. Statistics on unemployment are more meaningful and vivid when the newscaster presents them in combination with an illustration of how one family is experiencing the effects of unemployment. Notice in the following example how Bruce Barton, a famous advertising agency executive, made the rationale for advertising both clear and interesting when he told the story of an advertising agent:

> Coming one day to a crossroads town, our friend found that there was only one store. The proprietor did not receive him enthusiastically. "Why should I advertise?" he demanded. "I have been here for twenty years. There isn't a man, woman, or child around these parts that doesn't know where I am and what I sell." The advertising man answered very promptly (because, in our business, if we hesitate we are lost), and he said to the proprietor, pointing across the street, "What is that building over there?" The proprietor answered, "That is the Methodist Episcopal Church." The advertising man said, "How long has that been there?" The proprietor said, "Oh, I don't know, seventy-five years probably." "And yet," exclaimed the advertising man, "they ring the church bell every Sunday morning."

In another informative speech, dealing with some of the little known facts about the life of the Greek philosopher Socrates, a student offered the following illustration to demonstrate how much the philosopher attempted to live a spartan life:

> Knowing the frugality of Socrates' way of life, a friend was surprised to discover the philosopher studying with rapt attention some flashy wares on display in the marketplace. He inquired why Socrates came to the market since he never bought anything. "I am always amazed to see just how many things there are that I don't need," replied Socrates.

Physically Involving Your Audience

Attention and interest can also be aroused and sustained by securing the audience's physical involvement in your speech. We have already discussed the need to secure the listeners' mental involvement; there might be occasions when your purpose can be served by having the audience perform an action. Think of how interesting a speech on meditation techniques would be if you actually had the audience practice some of these techniques. Or think of the interest created if your topic was how to draw human faces and you had the audience practice drawing human faces while you discussed various stages of the artwork.

This approach must be handled with great care, lest the audience allow the action to become more important than your verbal message. Therefore, use the three following recommendations only in special circumstances. First, *there might be occasions when you ask your audience to take notes or engage in another writing exercise.* Your listeners actively participate in the communication process. The specific action can range from taking notes to filling out forms. Second, *you can physically involve your listeners by asking them questions that they should answer aloud or by raising their hands.* Here again, personalizing your speech will give listeners the feeling that they are part of the communication experience. It is hard not to think that the speaker is interested in you when he or she says, "Please raise your hand when I point to one of the national parks on this map that you would like to visit." Finally, *there are certain subjects that literally demand the audience to participate.* How could you teach golf, dance, drawing, or swimming without having people engage in some activity? Even a speech on the problems of blindness would be aided by asking the audience to close their eyes and try to walk around the room. In all these examples, audience participation and interest work together.

Organizing a Speech to Inform

Almost two hundred years ago, Napoleon Bonaparte wrote what might well serve as both an introduction and a metaphor for this section, when he observed, "Unhappy the general who comes on the field of battle without a system." The same is true for public speakers. They must speak with a plan. The systematic arrangement of material is crucial in informative speaking if the listeners are to retain the presented information. Listen carefully the next time you hear an informative talk, and you will discover that there are occasions when the educated, as well as the uneducated, forget the importance of organization and clarity. Speeches that seem to bound from point to point without offering internal or external clues seldom leave the listeners with anything meaningful. Therefore, in this next section, we shall examine the basic step of organizing a speech to inform.

Introduction

The introduction to a speech to inform has four interrelated purposes: (1) *to arouse attention*, (2) *to create a desire for the detailed information contained in the body of the speech*, (3) *to establish your right to inform*, and (4) *to preview the main points of the speech*.

Arouse Attention

Chapter 11 discussed in detail the methods of starting a speech. We would urge you to return to that chapter as you think about starting your speech to inform. Also, keep in mind that you should select a method by reviewing your topic, the audience's interest, the audience's knowledge level, the speaking time available, and the speaking occasion. When listeners are not vitally concerned with a topic, it is often profitable to begin with a rhetorical question, a startling statement, or an unusual illustration. These devices arouse apathetic and disinterested listeners. For example, to stimulate audience interest in a speech on hang gliding, a speaker used the following introduction:

> The other day, while I was driving home from school, I noticed an extremely large bird gliding gracefully through the sky. As I looked again, I realized that this was truly the largest bird I had ever seen. I pulled my car over to the side of the road so that I could get a closer look. As I gazed into the sky this third time, I thought I must be dreaming, for what was flying over my head was not a bird, but a person—a person with wings.

Recently a student, whose specific purpose was to inform the audience about the personality of H. Ross Perot, offered the following story as a means of capturing attention:

> H. Ross Perot once decided that he would give a Christmas present to every American prisoner of war in Vietnam. Accordingly, thousands of parcels were wrapped and packed, and a fleet of Boeing 707's was chartered for the trip to Vietnam. Then the message came from the government of Vietnam—no such gesture could be considered during the time of war. Perot continued the correspondence. The Vietnamese replied each time saying any charity was impossible as long as Americans were devastating Vietnamese villages. As Christmas drew closer, the parcels remained undelivered. Finally, Perot had an idea. He took off in a chartered fleet of aircraft and headed for Moscow. The Russians were not at war with Vietnam. In Moscow, Perot and his associates posted each parcel one at a time at the Moscow main post office. The packages were delivered to Vietnam intact.

Another speaker, talking about solid waste disposal, began by trying to secure attention with a series of startling statistics:

> In the next year, we have to decide what to do with two million tons of major appliances; twenty-two million tons of food; ten million tons of newspapers; three million tons of paper plates, towels, and napkins; and fifty-two million tons of bottles and containers. Do you have any ideas where we can put all this? Suggestions now range from putting it all in satellites and sending it into outer space to making a large island out of it and calling it Son of Big Mac.

Attention is also aroused by using interesting quotations. A speaker who was about to discuss some of the features of the Mohave Desert opened his speech this way:

> J. B. Priestley said of the desert, "This country is geology by day and astronomy by night." I suspect that most people who try to cross the desert as quickly as possible would agree with Priestley's observation.

One speaker used the following quotation as a means of starting a speech dealing with the plight of the inner cities: "Author James Baldwin wrote that 'a ghetto can be improved in one way only: out of existence.'"

In selecting any introductory device, it is important to remember that, if you fail to arouse interest at the outset, you are apt to deliver the entire speech to an audience whose attention is focused elsewhere.

Create Interest

In all communication situations, it is to your advantage to stimulate a desire in the audience to want to listen to your presentation. In the introduction of an informative speech, make it clear to your audience that your topic holds significance for them and that they will benefit by listening. For instance, a speaker used an introduction to demonstrate that paying attention to her speech could save the listeners a great deal of money. The topic was gasoline conservation, and the speaker said, "By following the few simple suggestions I will discuss today, you should be able to save enough money on your gas bill each month to treat yourself to a nice dinner at an elegant restaurant."

In all communication situations, it is to your advantage to stimulate a desire in the audience to want to listen to your presentation.

There are many informative situations when "the reason to listen" is even more compelling. Shortly after a major earthquake in the region, a student pointed the material toward the audience:

Where were you when the earthquake hit last month? Did you panic? Did you stay calm? Did you know what to do? Well, regardless of your answer, experts say you will most likely get another chance to think about the rhetorical questions I just asked, for it is very probable that our city will experience another quake before too long. Today, I think I can offer you some information that will assist you in coping with that experience.

Other methods of stimulating interest in your topic can be much more elaborate. A student, trying to explain how to take better photographs, showed the audience some prints that were obviously examples of poor photography. While thumbing through the enlarged photos, she asked her listeners, "How many of you take photographs that turn out like these?" The audience laughed. She then said, "How many of you would like to take photos that look like this?" Then she displayed some beautiful specimens of outstanding photography. She added, "You can all take photographs similar to these if you follow a few simple steps. I have been an amateur photographer for six years and would like to share some of these steps with you now."

There are also occasions when the listeners' curiosity is appealed to as a way of arousing interest in what is to follow. Notice how intrigued we become if a speaker tells us a story of how the Masai dispose of their dead in ways that are very different from Western methods. Our interest would also be aroused by a speaker who asked us if we know where and how the AIDS epidemic began. When speaking on the philosophy of Francis Bacon, a student read the following paragraph as a way of pointing the audience to the body of the speech:

> Reading maketh a full man, conference a ready man, and writing an exact man; and, therefore, if a man write little, he had need have a great memory; if he confer little he had need have a present wit; and if he read little he had need have much cunning, to seem to know that he doth not. Histories make men wise; poems witty; the mathematics subtle; natural philosophy deep; moral grave; logic and rhetoric, able to contend.

He then added, in his own words, "What does this mean for us three hundred fifty years later?" You can better hold attention during the body of your speech if you have already created an atmosphere where the audience wants the information you are going to offer because you have created curiosity, awakened interest, or convinced them that they need the material. By motivating the audience early in the speech, you also increase the probability that they will learn something by the conclusion.

On some occasions, you can combine arousing attention and creating interest within a single example. For instance, a speaker, talking about the great white shark, combined attention and interest with the following introduction:

> What animal can you think of that is 21 feet long, has eyes seven times more powerful than humans, has a sixth sense that enables it to detect even the slightest of muscle movements produced by other animals, and has jaws that open to three feet? If you said the great white shark you are right.

Establish Right to Inform

The third task of the introduction is to establish your personal credibility on the subject you will be addressing. The objective of an informative speech is to increase listeners' knowledge of a particular topic. The assumption is that you know something they do not and that, by listening to you, they will learn more about this subject. In some cases, the audience will know about your expertise in the area and readily accept you as an authority. The chief of campus security talking about an escort service for women who are on campus late at night would be just such an example. However, there will be many occasions when the audience will not be aware of your knowledge of a topic. When this happens, *you should offer some information to help establish your credibility.*

If your specific purpose is to inform the audience of how to stop a victim's bleeding at the scene of an accident, you might mention your experiences as a paramedic. One student from Haiti established her "right to inform" by telling her audience that she had recently left that country and wanted to offer a first-hand report of what the new government was trying to accomplish. Yet another speaker, wanting to explain the inner workings of a mental institution, established her credibility in the following manner:

> As a psychology major, I have had three courses in abnormal psychology. This past summer, I also served as an intern at the Union Hill mental hospital.

Recently another student, whose specific purpose was to have the audience understand the difference between purchasing a single stock and investing in mutual funds, told the class that, before returning to college, she had a ten-year career as a stockbroker.

When you are demonstrating your expertise, make sure you do not sound boastful. For instance, you can tell your audience that you have been taking pictures and studying photography for eight years without implying that you are the greatest outdoor photographer since Ansel Adams.

Early in this chapter, we saw that people learn more when they know what they are being asked to learn. Therefore, the final part of your introduction should provide a brief initial summary (preview) of the main points to be taken up in the body of your speech. The speaker mentioned earlier who was interested in the topic of AIDS used the following preview to tell the audience what the speech would focus on: "Today, to better understand the issue of AIDS, I would like to begin by talking about the early cases of AIDS, then discuss the location of these early instances, and finally mention how AIDS has traveled throughout the world." By giving the audience a glimpse of the speech's organizational pattern, the speaker let the listeners know what to look for as the speech progressed. If you prepare the listeners for what is coming, they will find it much simpler to locate your main ideas. In the example of the amateur photographer, the speaker previewed her speech with, "In looking at these simple steps for improved photography, I will talk about composition, lighting, and equipment." On some occasions, it might even be useful to say the numbers "first, second, and third" as you offer your initial summary. For example, the speaker talking about photography could have said, "I will talk first about composition, second about lighting, and third about the necessary equipment."

Initial summaries can also be lengthy. Some speakers use their previews as a bridge to link what they have been talking about to what they will talk about. Notice how these two purposes are served in the following example:

> We all seem to agree that we want good grades but have very little time to study. How do we resolve this dilemma? Let me suggest a solution called "time management," but also let me warn you that time management is no simple matter. It takes goal setting, motivation, and evaluation. Let's look at these three in detail and try to figure out how we can accomplish more in the same amount of time.

Previews are also useful in that they lay the foundation for reinforcement and repetition—two processes that are important to learning. The preview is the initial step in that process. It is the first time you introduce your audience to your main points. As you move through the body of your speech and signpost each main idea, the audience will hear the key points for a second time. Finally, at the conclusion, you will once again tell the listeners what you have tried to do during your allotted time. Hence, on three occasions, you will highlight your main points.

You should follow the same order in presenting information in the introduction, body, and conclusion of the speech. That is to say, if you tell the audience in the preview that you plan to look at the advantages and then the disadvantages of contact lenses, you must not reverse the order in either the body or the conclusion. This change, while seeming insignificant, can confuse your listeners.

Preview Main Points

Body

As a speaker, once you have (1) *captured the listeners' attention*, (2) *aroused their interest in the information to come*, (3) *established your expertise, or right to inform*, and (4) *previewed your main points*, you are ready to present the information itself. To promote the listeners' comprehension of your ideas and to maintain their attention at a high level, you should organize the body of your speech into meaningful groupings. The division of the whole into its parts is an essential step in explaining any complex concept. No one, for example, can understand all the aspects of public welfare, but most persons could assimilate certain features if they were presented and explained separately. In most instances, the division of a speech is inevitable in light of the subject matter. Such groupings are more easily remembered if they can be worded in a logical pattern. Reexamine some of the patterns of arrangement discussed in chapter 10 in light of their application to informative speaking.

Chronological Pattern

The chronological pattern has its greatest utility in presenting historical events, explaining processes, and relating personal experiences. To discuss the history of phonograph recording, you might develop your material under these headings:

I.   Cylinder recordings of the late nineteenth century
II. Disk recordings of the early twentieth century
III. Long-play recordings of the mid-twentieth century
IV. Compact disc recordings of today

To discuss a medical procedure, you might use these headings:

I.   Preoperative procedures
II. The operation
III. Postoperative procedures

The speaker mentioned earlier, who talked about earthquakes, used time as an organizational scheme:

I.   How to prepare for an earthquake
II. What to do once an earthquake occurs
III. What to do after an earthquake

Spatial Pattern

Spatial order is especially effective in speeches describing a scene, location, or geographical distribution. For instance, your material could be arranged directionally from north to south, top to bottom, or center to outside. Weather patterns could be described according to East Coast, Midwest, and West Coast.

For a speech on sea life, you might select the following order:

I.   Surface sea life
II. Sea life twenty feet below the ocean surface
III. Sea life on the ocean floor

If your topic is how to enjoy the local zoo, you could use the following sequence:

I.   Animal exhibits when you first enter the zoo
II. The enclosures in the middle of the zoo
III. The displays that ring the outer perimeter of the zoo

If your topic is how to avoid serious hazards in the home, you could use the following pattern:

I.   Hazards found in the garage
II. Hazards found in the kitchen
III. Hazards found in the bathroom

The problem-solution sequence is a common organizational pattern for speeches to inform. It moves the listeners from an obstacle (problem) to a remedy (solution). If you are dealing with the topic of first aid, you could organize your presentation around two serious problems (bleeding and shock) and then discuss the solution to these problems (treating bleeding and shock):

Problem-Solution Pattern

I.   The problem of excessive bleeding
II. The victim in shock
III. Treating bleeding and shock

If your topic is carjacking, you might use the problem-solution pattern in the following manner:

I.   The rise in carjacking instances
II. Methods to avoid being a casualty of carjacking

Another speaker used the problem-solution sequence to inform on the subject of illegal immigration:

I.   What happens when people enter the United States illegally
II. What is being done to deal with the problem of illegal immigration

The ascending-descending sequence takes listeners from the simple to the complex or from the less important to the more important. A speech about how to execute a series of dives from the high platform could effectively use an ascending-descending order (less complex–more complex).

Ascending-Descending Pattern

I.   The basic platform dive
II. The swan dive
III. The pike dive
IV. The somersault dive

A speaker trying to teach the audience how to meditate used the ascending-descending order:

I.   Novice meditation techniques
II. Moderate meditation techniques
III. Advanced meditation techniques

Causal order tells of the causes of certain effects or tells of the effects resulting from various causes. In giving a talk entitled "The Sun and the Individual," your pattern might appear

Causal Pattern

I.   The effects of the sun on the skin

 II. The effects of the sun on the eyes

 III. The effects of the sun on the hair

When treating the topic "Why World War II?" you might select the following arrangement:

 I. United States and German relations before 1941

 II. United States and Italian relations before 1941

 III. United States and Japanese relations before 1941

By examining the relationship of the United States to each of these countries, you would be able to point out some possible causes of World War II.

Topical Pattern

The topical pattern is probably the most frequently used of all patterns. This arrangement sets out several facets of a topic that are obviously related and consistent. If you are talking about the financial structure of your university, your pattern might include

 I. The university's assets

 II. The university's liabilities

 III. The university's endowments

In speaking on the subject of giant pandas, you could use the following topical sequence:

 I. The pandas' diet

 II. The pandas' breeding patterns

 III. The pandas' natural habitat

In speaking on the subject of the Islamic religion, you could use the following topical pattern:

 I. The history of Islam

 II. The role of the prophet Muhammad in Islam

 III. The Five Pillars of Islam

The key to the topical pattern is that the arrangement is rather apparent and the one an audience most likely expects. For example, if you were going to talk about the mechanics of sight, the audience would expect your topics to include the optic nerve, retina, cornea, pupil, iris, and lens. You may wish to order the material so that it moves from the simplest to the most complex, the most familiar to the least familiar, the least important to the most important, or the most acceptable to the least acceptable. When deciding on an organizational pattern, review the suggestions offered in chapter 10.

Conclusion

The methods of concluding a speech were explained in some detail in chapter 11. However, certain concluding techniques are especially valuable for speeches to inform. For example, it may be helpful to restate your message and summarize its main points: "Today, we have seen that your grades can be improved if you select the correct location to study, learn how to determine the key points in your textbooks, and know how to prepare for objective examinations."

The most popular concluding technique is a final summary (or reiteration). Listeners tend to pay close attention when they feel the end of the speech is near. The final summary takes advantage of this captured attention by reviewing the main ideas in the same order they were presented in the initial summary and in the body of the speech. In speaking on the topic of college registration, you might conclude by saying, "We have seen that you can register for classes in three ways. First, you can register by mail; second, you can make special arrangements with each instructor; and, finally, you can sign up in the registration office on the first day of classes."

Another speaker, when talking about handicapping the horse races, ended her speech with two types of conclusion—a quotation and a summary:

> Knowing how difficult it is to make money at the races, most of us can agree with George Gissing's observation that "horse racing is carried on mainly for the delight and profit of fools, ruffians, and thieves." Yet, we also know that horse racing is fun, and we continue to go, so, to feel less like a fool, I urge you to follow the four steps of handicapping that I presented in my talk. First, examine the type of race you will be betting; second, the "class" of each horse in the race; third, the potential pace of the race; and, finally, the speed rating of each horse. Good luck—it's only money.

Once again, remember that your final summary should simply repeat your introduction and the main points of the body of your speech. If your initial summary said that you would teach the audience (1) how to prepare for an earthquake, (2) how to deal with the quake while it is going on, and (3) what to do once the quake is over, you should simply repeat these three ideas in your conclusion: "We should now know what to do before, during, and after an earthquake."

Sample Outline

Now that we have discussed the parts of an informative speech, we can look at a sample outline to review the relationship among those parts.

Title:	Who Pays?
General Purpose:	To inform
Specific Purpose:	To have the audience understand the major arguments for and against state aid to parochial schools

Introduction

(Rhetorical Question)

I. How many of you realize that one of the crucial battles that raged during the founding of this country remains an unresolved issue today?
   A. The early colonists were determined to separate church and state.
   B. Yet compulsory school attendance laws meant that some parents, who desired private schools, were forced to finance two separate institutions.

(Motivation Toward Topic)

II. This highly emotional issue affects us today as much as it did over two hundred years ago.
   A. If the state were to pay tuition fees for private schools, millions of additional dollars would have to be found.

        1. Some of the money would come from our taxes.

        2. Money now being used to pay for public education would be rechanneled into parochial schools.

    B. If the state were to support parochial schools, some say it would bring church and state closer together.

    C. Yet what about the people who believe that, under the First Amendment, we can educate a child in any way we deem appropriate?

        1. Is it not a denial of our freedom to be forced to pay dual taxation?

        2. What if you believe that our public schools are "Godless"?

(Right to Inform)

III. I have just completed a major research paper for my senior project in history on this topic.

    A. This paper focused on the specific issues involved in the separation of church and state.

    B. I plan to continue working on this project while attending graduate school.

(Preview)

IV. To better understand this important issue of state aid to parochial schools, I will examine the arguments frequently made in favor of tax support for these schools and then examine the arguments advanced by those who oppose such aid.

Core Statement: Opinion is strongly divided on the issue of state aid to parochial schools.

Body

I. Arguments that support tax aid for parochial schools are twofold.

    A. Denominational schools offer an important religious, spiritual, and ethical element not found in public schools.

        1. Only religious schools can teach Christian values.

        2. Public schools are Godless.

    B. The right of parents to determine the education and religious instruction of their children is a fundamental one.

        1. Failure to provide public funds for denominational schools is a partial denial of that right.

        2. This denial may well make some families second-class citizens who are not benefiting from their taxes.

II. Arguments advanced by those who oppose tax support for parochial schools are threefold.

    A. It is urged that the appropriation of public funds for denominational schools would be a long step toward breaking down the unique North American policy of separation of church and state.

        1. It was part of an early colonial policy.

        2. It was an idea contained in the First Amendment to the Constitution.

    B. It is contended that the organization of North American public schools along denominational lines would make education a divisive rather than a unifying factor in our lives.

     1. Schools now teach a variety of opinions and views.
     2. Denominational schools would tend to teach dogma and one-
       dimensional attitudes.
  C. It is argued that the present arrangements promote healthy growth among
    various religions.

Conclusion

(Summary)
  I. Today, by looking at both sides of an important issue, we have gained some in-
    sight into the pros and cons of tax support for parochial schools.
    A. Those in favor of tax support suggest the following:
      1. Denominational schools can do a better job of teaching values and
       ethics.
      2. It is unfair to deny a basic right to persons who select parochial schools.
    B. Those opposed counter by saying the following:
      1. Granting funds for these schools would bring church and state closer
       together.
      2. Denominational education is divisive.
      3. The status quo is beneficial to both church and state.
  II. In the final analysis, you must seek additional information before deciding how
    you feel about this important historical and religious problem.

Summary

This chapter examined speeches to inform, which are intended to increase an audience's knowledge of a subject. To achieve that end, you should be aware of some basic
characteristics of learning—motivation, coupling, organization, frequency, multisensory stimulation, overload, depth, and central focus.

There are basically four types of speeches to inform: instructions, descriptions, explanations, and reports. In preparing a speech to inform, make sure that your specific
purpose focuses on a worthwhile topic. You can then gather and select the materials of
your speech. To help the audience learn and retain that material, you should use some
of the following techniques: definitions; examples and illustrations; comparison and
contrast; statistics; description; demonstration; reinforcement and emphasis; and partition, enumeration, and summaries.

To make your material more interesting, use some of the following attention-getting devices: (1) noting that which is impending, (2) alluding to that which is physically near, (3) referring to the familiar, (4) invoking personal needs, and (5) imparting
activity, reality, conflict, humor, and illustrations.

When organizing a speech to inform, you should prepare an introduction that
arouses attention, creates interest, establishes your expertise or right to inform, and previews your main points.

In selecting an organizational sequence, you can select from a number of patterns:
chronological, spatial, problem-solution, ascending-descending, causal, and topical.

The most effective way to close an informative speech is to conclude with a
summary.

Chapter 14

Persuasive Speaking

Changing Beliefs, Attitudes, Values, and Behavior

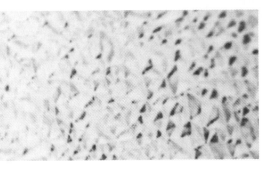

Change is scientific, progress is ethical; change is indubitable, whereas progress is a matter of controversy.

Bertrand Russell

It is a fact of life that people are always asking us to change our minds regarding various topics. Have we not all heard some of the following appeals? "Our elementary school should adopt a multicultural curriculum." "Casino gambling on Indian reservations should be made legal." "You should volunteer your services to the Big Brother or Big Sister program." "Affirmative Action laws are poorly administered." "You should try a vegetarian diet." "The president's new medical program should be supported." "The campus bookstore should be student run." "Let's start enforcing existing gun laws." "Drinking alcohol during pregnancy should be made a felony." "Three new trauma centers should be built in our county." "Prohibit the sale of disposable diapers." "Boycott sponsors of all television shows that implicitly or explicitly sanction premarital sex among teenagers." "Buy only foods that are organically grown." "Stop the developers from ruining our coastline." "Ban boom boxes at the beach!" "Reading proficiency in two foreign languages should be required for graduation."

The Importance of Persuasion

Whether we are the receiver or the sender, messages such as those in the last paragraph are part of daily life. From every side, we are asking others or they are asking us to agree with a particular point of view, feel a certain way, or carry out an action. As much as we may tire of hearing persuasive appeals, think of the alternative. Errors might go uncorrected if no one were allowed to convince us that errors exist. The misfortunes of others might go unheeded if no one were allowed to touch our social conscience. Actions needed to preserve our society might not be taken if calls for action were not permitted.

Examples of the utility of persuasion abound. You can see it at all levels of human communication, from the dialogues of high-level diplomats to the simple pleas of children seeking favors from their parents. Advertisers urge us to buy their products; politicians solicit our votes; friends try to get us to stop smoking; medical experts advise us to limit our intake of fat; parents try to win our cooperation in keeping the phone bill within reason. In short, whenever change is desired, people tend to choose persuasion as the means of bringing about that change.

In chapter 13, we observed that the purpose of informative speaking is to increase the listeners' understanding of a particular topic by being clear and interesting. And although people may act in a different manner because of the information that the speaker provided, the goal of the informative speech is learning. This is not the case with persuasion. In persuasive speaking, the speaker is not satisfied with offering options, but rather, *when persuading, the speaker seeks to modify and/or change the beliefs, attitudes, values, and behavior of their audience by asking for commitment.* Such commitment is brought about through logical and emotional appeals. A wise persuader knows that changes induced by coercive tactics—threats and the like—are apt to be short-lived and grudgingly endured, while changes that are willingly undertaken may last indefinitely.

Our aim in this chapter, then, is to examine some of the ways in which you, as a persuader, can ethically influence changes in the beliefs, attitudes, values, and behavior of your listeners.

Types of Persuasive Speeches

Persuasive speeches can be classified according to the kinds of audience response being sought. If your aim is to secure audience *agreement* with your position, then you are making a **speech to convince.** You might want the audience to agree that there is too much violence in children's cartoons, or that the library charges too high a fee for overdue books. Another example of a speech to convince would be the argument that term limits should be imposed on all publicly elected officials. In all three cases, you are trying to convince your audience of the validity of your assertion.

If your aim is to get audience *action* on a matter, then you are making a **speech to actuate.** Your emphasis is on an overt activity. Notice the action dimension if you urge your audience to donate to a charity, write to a legislator, buy an insurance policy, take a specific college course, get a pet from an animal shelter, or to sign an organ donor card.

If your aim is to *reinforce, intensify,* or *rejuvenate* listeners' existing attitudes or beliefs, then you are making a **speech to stimulate.** You are giving inspirational messages, arousing emotions, and inciting pride. Telling a group of college freshman to study hard or asking an audience to value the life of all animals represents speeches that try to arouse basic beliefs. Occasions for stimulating speeches range from sermons to company pep talks to commencement addresses.

The Goals of Persuasive Speaking

Persuasive speaking, like all of the forms of communication discussed in this book, is not a random and aimless activity. Rather, it is motivated by a speaker having a conscious set of goals. More specifically, *in persuasive discourse, a speaker seeks to accomplish a specific, predetermined purpose by bringing about changes in belief, attitudes, values, and behavior.* Therefore, as a persuasive speaker, you need to be concerned with these four variables if you are to accomplish your persuasive purpose. You need to ask yourself this simple yet complex question: How must my audience change or modify their beliefs, attitudes, values, or behaviors if they are going to respond favorably to my recommendations? To help you answer this question, let us pause and examine the key components of these four persuasive variables.

Beliefs

A **belief** is commonly defined as a personally held conviction in the truth of a statement or in the existence of something. In a sense, it is a way for people to structure their reality. Such convictions can be held with or without proof. We have beliefs about religion ("Muhammad was a messenger from Allah"), events ("NATO troops intervening in Bosnia was necessary"), other people ("Senator Smith would make an excellent president"), actions ("It is beneficial to take one aspirin each day"), and even ourselves ("I am very witty").

Beliefs may be founded on direct experience, on the word of someone you trust, or on your own reasoning. You might believe that aspirin alleviates headache pain, because you have experienced relief after taking aspirin. You might believe that a certain treatment will arrest the spread of a malignant growth because a physician you respect claims it has done so in the past. You might believe that a particular restaurant poses health hazards because you saw a dead cat next to the restaurant's garbage cans.

Beliefs are also strongly affected by culture. The reason is rather obvious: we are not born with our beliefs; they are learned, and culture is the teacher. We might acknowledge that "CBS Evening News" or the *New York Times* is a good place to learn about what we should believe. In the Islamic tradition, however, there is a belief that the writings in the Koran are an infallible source of what to believe in. Whether we trust the *Times*, the Bible, the Koran, the entrails of a goat, tea leaves, the visions induced by peyote, or the Taoist I Ching depends on our cultural background—and any successful speaker needs to remember that. People who have grown up in China, part of the African plain, or Cuba may believe that business and the means of production should belong to the state or to the people collectively. On the other hand, someone born in the United States or Canada most likely grew up believing that an individual "deserves what he or she earns" and is reluctant to share profits.

If you plan to persuade another person, you need to know his or her beliefs on the topic in question. This information will help you select your arguments and emotional appeals. If, for example, you predict that your audience believes that exercise is crucial for good health, you could appeal to this belief as you ask your listeners to support a new bike trail in the park.

Attitudes

An **attitude** can be defined as a state of mind or an emotion toward a person or situation. They are usually easier to change than are beliefs. You may feel a certain way about youth gangs, the police, military service, talk shows on television, labor unions, beauty pageants, and the use of animals in medical research. Your attitudes tend to guide you in your responses to these and countless other subjects and orientations. These predispositions to act one way or another are learned from our family, the media, schools, religious affiliations, and the like. They are important to persuasion in that most persuasive efforts seek to change or reinforce existing attitudes. As a speaker, you need to predict your audience's attitudes because they determine whether your listeners will respond favorably or unfavorably to your specific purpose. For example, if they have a positive attitude toward the German culture, they might support a plan to put a German car company in their city. In this case, your arguments are simple. However, if their attitude is that the Germans are already too influential in the economy of the United States, you would have to muster an entirely different set of arguments so that your position is consistent with some positive attitudes they do hold. Attitudes are so powerful that they can sway many decisions and actions.

When thinking about your audience, it is important to remember the role of culture in shaping and maintaining attitudes. As we noted in chapter 3, cultures have varying attitudes on a host of subjects. These cultural attitudes, whether about the elderly, gays, guns, individualism, work, women, or the future, need to be taken into account.

Values

Values represent yet another variable that influences what people are apt to think or feel about a particular subject. Many of our most important beliefs and attitudes are grounded in our basic value system. **Values** have been called the evaluative components of our beliefs and attitudes. Evaluative qualities include what is good, bad, right, or wrong; what ought to be or ought not to be; and what is useful, useless, appropriate, or inappropriate. *Values serve as a sort of "guiding light" that assists us in making choices and resolving conflicts.*

As indicated, what is important about values is that they underpin most of our attitudes, beliefs, and actions. The value placed on a woman's right to choose influences an attitude toward abortion. If we highly value education, we might find it easier to support a plan to increase taxes for a new university. If we value the sanctity of all life, we might support a suggestion to stop using animals for medical experiments. Should we place a high priority on physical appearance, we might find it easier to stop smoking if someone were to tell us that prolonged smoking will cause our lips to wrinkle badly as we get older.

Although each of us has a unique set of values, some values tend to permeate a culture and are called cultural values. Most cultural values are derived from the larger philosophical issues that are part of a culture's milieu. Cultural values define what is worthwhile for members of a culture to die for, what is worth protecting, what frightens people, what are proper subjects for study and for ridicule, and what types of circumstances lead to happiness. Cultural values include views of such topics as age, privacy, time, responsibility, change, equality, honesty, status, and work.

Behavior

Behavior refers to an audience's observable activity. You are asking people to do something that can be observed. That observable state ranges from total inactivity to hyperactivity. Changes in behavior can take one from action to inaction or the reverse; the change may involve an increase or decrease in the intensity, duration, or magnitude of an action. For example, if you were to urge your best friend to discontinue jogging as a form of exercise, you might observe one of these changes in behavior: your friend might jog more than ever out of defiance, might ignore your advice and continue to jog as usual, might cut down on the amount of time spent jogging, or might choose walking or another form of exercise. Behavior changes are sometimes immediate (persuading people to sign a petition that you circulate after your talk), sometimes delayed (persuading people to buy healthier foods next time they go to the market), and sometimes lasting (persuading people to stop eating meat). The acid test for the speech that stresses behavior change is that you are asking the audience to act (behave) differently than they did *before* you started speaking.

Concerns of Persuasion

Persuasive speeches, whether they seek to bring about changes in belief, attitude, value, or behavior, deal with questions related to facts, values, and/or policies. Before we examine these three types of questions, it is important to realize that a single speech might contain one, two, or all three of these questions.

Questions of Fact

When a speaker and a listener hold opposing views about whether something actually exists or is true, the issue involved is a question of fact, and the speaker's central point is termed a proposition of fact; he or she is attempting to prove or disprove the existence of something. The goal of the speaker is to persuade the audience that the proposition being asserted is true. Following are a few examples of propositions of fact:

"Overworked traffic controllers present serious risks to airline travelers."

"Tap water in our town contains many impurities."

"The county's landfill facilities are now at capacity."

"Boxing causes brain damage."

"A National Health insurance program will greatly increase taxes."

"A vegetarian diet reduces the risk of colon cancer."

Notice that, in each of the above examples, the speakers will have to offer evidence and sound reasoning to persuade their audiences that the assertion is a fact. Three additional observations regarding issues of fact are in order before we move on. First, it is important to note that propositions of fact deal with alleged facts—matters whose reality can be disputed. Second, they may deal with past, present, or future circumstances. "Last year's tax bill undermined voter confidence in the administration" alleges the existence of a circumstance in the past. "Water rationing is causing an increase in the insect population of the Central Valley" asserts a present condition. "Most Americans will be unable to afford a home by 2000" alleges a future condition. Finally, remember that propositions of fact set the stage for the other two propositions. Proving that overexposure to the sun can cause skin cancer (fact) allows you to then persuade your audience to use sunscreen lotions when going into the sun (policy).

If a speaker and a listener differ over the merit of a value judgment, the issue involved is a question of value, and the speaker's central point is termed a proposition of value. In other words, the speaker is placing an estimate of worth on something, alleging that it is good or bad, better or worse than something else, right or wrong, justified or unjustified. Most questions of value deal with propositions that tend to be subjective, personal, and even private. The following are examples of propositions of value:

Questions of Value

"State prisons are inhuman."

"Abortion is immoral."

"Capital punishment is incongruous with Christian values."

"Sex education has a place in health classes."

"Helping the homeless is our moral responsibility."

"Our culture puts too much emphasis on physical appearance."

Like propositions of fact, propositions of value may deal with matters in the past (the United States mistreated Native Americans), present (elderly people are ridiculed on most television programs), or future (our university does not care about affirmative action admissions).

Questions of Policy

Differences between a speaker and a listener over the advisability of pursuing a proposed course of action call for the speaker to defend a proposition of policy. The speaker argues that something should or should not be done. That is to say, questions of policy ask for a specific action and/or a new policy to be taken. Thus, one might recommend or oppose the following proposals:

"Films rated X should not be shown on campus."

"A lifeguard station should be installed at South Beach."

"The cigarette tax should be raised by fifty cents a pack."

"The insurance industry should be regulated."

"The proposed student center should not be built with student funds."

"Our college should provide a free child-care center for students with young children."

"The death penalty should be abolished."

As noted elsewhere, it is not unusual for a speaker to defend all three kinds of propositions (fact, value, and policy) within a single speech. For example, a speaker trying to win support for a proposed policy usually has to prove several propositions:

Something is wrong with the current system—proposition of fact: "There is too much violence on prime-time television."

The proposed plan will help solve the problem—proposition of policy: "Prime-time television needs to enact a stricter rating system."

The proposed policy is better than other proposals advanced—proposition of value: "Our children will not be exposed to harmful messages."

We have talked about changes in listener beliefs, attitudes, values, and actions as the aim of a persuader advocating propositions of fact, value, and policy. However, remember that it is not the persuader or the persuasive speech that changes those beliefs, attitudes, or actions—it is the listener who changes them. The persuader's job is to present the listener with a choice between an existing belief, attitude, or action and one that the speaker recommends. Then it is up to the listener to make a choice. If the speaker's recommendations prove to be sufficiently attractive, the listener will choose to make the desired change. Devising an attractive alternative, then, lies at the heart of persuasion.

Preparing a Persuasive Speech

Preparing a persuasive speech involves a process similar to that used in preparing an informative speech. A speaker (1) chooses a topic, (2) analyzes the audience, (3) formulates a specific purpose, (4) finds the materials for achieving that purpose, (5) organizes the speech, and then (6) practices it. Although all six of these steps have been discussed in great detail elsewhere in this book, their application to persuasion requires certain unique procedures.

Ideally, the choice of a topic for a persuasive speech should arise from the speaker's recognition of a condition that requires change. That change can take the form of individual change ("*You* should never drink and drive"), or it can be a change that cannot be effected without the help of others ("*We* all need to support House Bill #253, which requires an automatic jail term for anyone driving under the influence of alcohol"). Occasions that require persuasive action are nearly endless. Perhaps you feel that student activity fees at your school are too high, but you may never see a reduction until students get together to put pressure on those responsible for setting the fees. Such a situation calls for a persuasive speech. Perhaps you live near a pulp mill and suffer from the odor of its operation. You want the odor reduced but know that such a reduction will not take place until people unite to put pressure on the management. Again, the need for a persuasive speech arises. In each case, you become aware of a disturbing element. Then you take a stance with regard to the correction of that disturbing element.

There may be times when the topic and position are chosen for you. Perhaps a friend asks you to solicit for a worthy cause. Perhaps you become a salesperson and are told what to sell. Regardless of whether you originate the subject or someone else does, you should not undertake a persuasive task unless you are interested in the topic and are motivated to persuade.

Although we have already spent an entire chapter on the topic of audience analysis (chapter 3), once again we need to return to this crucial phase of communication. The reason is simple—*the majority of failures in persuasive attempts can probably be traced to an insufficient or inaccurate analysis of those whom the speaker wishes to influence*. Perhaps the speaker has taken pains to find out about the listeners as individuals but has failed to take into account what they are like when they become members of a group. The group imposes codes of behavior that do not necessarily operate on individuals removed from the group. A salesperson accustomed to dealing with one person at a time sometimes finds it difficult to deal with a group, so different are persons in their public and private behaviors. On the other hand, some speakers find it easier to deal with a group than with an individual because most people tend to think less critically as members of a group. Whatever the case, a speaker should become familiar with what motivates each listener as an individual and as a member of a group.

In analyzing your listeners, you should seek answers to the following questions: (1) What attitudes, beliefs, and values do they hold about my topic? (2) What has influenced them to take their present position on the topic? (3) What is their attitude toward me as a spokesperson? Let us examine each of these questions in detail so that you will have a greater appreciation of the link between audience analysis and persuasive speaking.

You may discover that there are many different individual and group attitudes toward your topic and your position on that topic. Generally, those attitudes may be clustered under the following heads: apathetic, hostile, interested but undecided, and favorable. It is important that you make an effort to determine which attitude is most representative of your audience. This will let you select the arguments and appeals that directly relate to the audience's beliefs, attitudes, and values.

Choosing a Topic

Analyzing an Audience

Determine Attitudes, Beliefs, and Values Toward the Subject

1. *Apathetic.* Individual listeners, or perhaps the entire audience, may have a "don't care" attitude. For example, if you are trying to enlist the support of a group of white-collar workers for legislation governing the wages and hours of farm workers, their attitude might be, What do the wages and hours of farm workers have to do with us? To help your listeners overcome their apathy, you might decide to place particular stress on the link between your proposal and the listeners' self-interests. If you are trying to persuade a group of land developers that a specific project should not be supported, you might use the argument that the new project would lower the property value of vacant and undeveloped land in the area.

2. *Hostile.* There may be individual listeners, or the audience as a whole, who are strongly opposed to the point of view you wish to urge. For example, imagine the attitude of a group of produce truckers toward your proposal to reduce the speed limit of all commercial vehicles to fifty miles per hour. In such a situation, you might commence with ideas on which you and the truckers agree before you turn to those areas in which you disagree. Maybe you would point out that you can understand their concern about possible produce spoilage if transit time is prolonged, but then you could show them that lower vehicle insurance premiums, occasioned by a safer speed limit, would enable them to purchase refrigeration units for their trucks. When dealing with hostile audiences, you can approach the topic indirectly and/or demonstrate to the audience that they already agree with the basic assumption behind your position.

3. *Interested but undecided.* If your audience analysis shows that some or all of your listeners are interested in but undecided about what you are advocating, you might decide to emphasize the use of factual evidence supporting your position. No doubt you have noticed that salespeople are quick to offer information about their products when they detect a sign of customer interest. In such cases, persuasion may be effected through information.

4. *Favorable.* If you know that your audience favors the point of view you intend to uphold, you might want to reaffirm your listeners' basis for agreeing with your position. This is especially the case in situations calling for a "pep talk." Sometimes beliefs have to be rejuvenated; listeners have to be reminded of the merits of their grounds for belief. There is nothing wrong with trying to persuade people of what often appears to be common knowledge. We all know that smoking is harmful to one's health, that drinking and driving is dangerous, and that seat belts should be worn at all times, yet think of the millions of people who need to be reminded of these three "facts."

Once you have thought about the type of audience you will be addressing, you can begin to ask some very precise questions. If you are planning to urge the adoption of a policy, you should try to obtain answers to the following questions:

- Does the audience know that a problem exists? Do they doubt or deny that a problem exists?

- Are they aware of the seriousness of the problem? Do they doubt or deny the seriousness of the problem?

- Are they aware of the causes of the problem? Are they likely to doubt my interpretation of the causes?

- Are they aware of the possibility of solving the problem? Do they doubt or deny that a solution can be found?

- Are they aware of the various solutions that have been advanced? Are they aware of the advantages and disadvantages of some or all of the proposed solutions?

- Do they doubt the workability of my proposed solution?

- Do they doubt the superiority of my proposed solution over other proposed solutions?

- Are there cultural differences that will influence how they perceive the problem and the solution?

It should be evident that persuasion should not be attempted until you have tried to secure answers to the foregoing questions. It would be folly to try to convince an audience that you have the best solution when they do not even believe that a problem exists. Finding out what an audience is thinking will also tell you the point at which you should launch your argument and will enable you to make a more reliable prediction of just how far you can move the audience from their present position.

If you are planning to limit your purpose to winning audience agreement on a proposition of fact or value, you should try to find answers to these questions:

- By what criteria does the audience measure the truth of the fact in question (or the value judgment in question)?

- Is each criterion valid?

- Are there criteria that the audience has overlooked?

- Are there better criteria available?

For example, if you want to convince an audience that aluminum siding is a better exterior house covering than stucco, you would be well advised to find out by what standards your audience judges the merits of exterior house covering. By its insulating capability? By its durability? By its appearance? By its initial cost? By its social acceptability? Unless you discover the criteria (and the priority of the criteria) that the audience uses, you may be wasting your time. You need not use the audience's own criteria, however; you can try to convince the listeners that other criteria are even more important. For example, you might try to convince them that a product's durability is a more significant criterion of superiority than its appearance.

Thus, you should attempt to discover whether your audience has criteria to measure the truth of the fact you are alleging or the value judgment you are urging. Then you will be in a much better position to offer convincing reasons your listeners should agree with you.

Important as it is to discover what your audience feels and believes about your subject and the position you are taking, it is equally important to try to determine the principal sources of influence operating on the audience. We are suggesting that the roots and deep structure of our beliefs, attitudes, and values often say more about us than the outward signs of these three variables. These are the *why* questions—the forces behind our belief system. We are urging you to ask, Why does the listener believe and feel a certain way? Any number of factors may be influential, but they can be grouped under two principal

Forces Influencing Audience Beliefs, Attitudes, and Values

categories. Both of these categories help us understand and appreciate human behavior. One category deals with influences that are placed on the listener by (1) **external factors,** and the other, by factors that (2) lie within the individual (**internal factors**).

External Factors   Much interest has been shown in the social pressures influencing the adoption, retention, modification, and abandonment of beliefs, attitudes, and values: (1) our cultural heritage, (2) the reference groups with which we identify, (3) the small groups with which we interact directly, and (4) the leaders to whom we look for guidance, who exert pressures on us to believe, feel, and act in certain ways.

As we have seen elsewhere, our **cultural heritage** influences our attitudes, beliefs, and values. For example, what makes us regard a source as authoritative is often dependent on what our culture has taught us. What one culture may regard as an authoritative source of information (for example, the visions of a seer) another culture might regard as devoid of credibility. If a listener, because of his or her cultural background and experience, believes a seer's earthquake prediction, no amount of contradictory information from *Scientific American* or Cal-Tech seismologists is likely to shake that belief. A persuader, then, should take into account the possibility that cultural influences have shaped at least some of the beliefs held by listeners.

The listeners' values—the standards by which the worth or desirability of something is measured—are also partially the product of their cultural background. Whether something is seen as good or bad, helpful or harmful, right or wrong, useful or useless, pleasant or unpleasant often depends on what one's culture endorses. Accordingly, there can be differences in the cultural values held by various members of an audience. For example, audience members from Eastern, African, and Muslim cultures tend to have greater respect for elders than do audience members from Western cultures. Being "number one" is more important to those from Western cultures than it is to those of Eastern and Latin cultures. Privacy is valued by the Japanese, Germans, and Chinese, openness by North Americans. Cultural values, then, provide guidelines for determining how one should behave in a society. Familiarity with the value structure of the various segments of your audience enables you to discover the points of commonality and, thus, minimizes the confusion and conflict that a clash of values might produce.

Each of us probably identifies with numerous **reference groups.** Maybe we identify with a given ethnic group, with a certain religious group, with one of the major political parties, with a certain age group, with a particular income group, with blue-collar or white-collar workers, with people from a certain geographic area, with idealists or pragmatists, to cite a few of the many possibilities. Some groups have no formal structure or goal, such as an age group, economic class, or ethnic group. Others have varying degrees of organization and orientation. Our "membership" in a given group may result from our parentage—religious and political affiliations are often inherited; our membership in others may result from voluntary actions that place us within the group. Whatever the circumstances of our becoming affiliated, a feeling of kinship with the group (but not necessarily the individuals within the group) develops, in some instances resulting in a kind of blind loyalty. Fan loyalty to a professional football team is a good illustration of this phenomenon. Typically, an ardent fan "hates" the rival team and its supporters.

We also belong to **small groups** that involve us in direct interaction with other members of that group. Our families, our circle of friends, our associates at work, our fellow club members, and our church congregation are representative examples of such groups. In varying degrees, these small groups bring to bear direct pressure on our behavior. Family influence, for example, can shape our attitudes toward work, study, recreation, food, politics, morality, and countless other things, thus causing us to behave in a manner consistent with those attitudes.

Since the moment of birth, we have all been influenced by a **leader** or **authority figure**. In some instances, the leader has been the one described by author Bergen Evans: "For the most part our leaders are merely following out in front; they do but marshal us the way that we are going." However, on countless occasions, we have confronted leaders who have been more direct and actually spelled out specific beliefs, attitudes, and values. The greater the confidence we place in a leader, the greater is our tendency to emulate that person's behavior and accept his or her attitudes and beliefs on certain matters as our own. It behooves any persuasive speaker to discover the leaders in a particular culture that have influenced the thinking of the members in that culture. While some cultures see religious leaders as being important (Islam for example), other cultures find leaders among government officials. Regardless of the source of leadership, other powerful and respected people help form our beliefs, attitudes, and values. Know some of these people and you know something about your audience.

What are the implications for persuasion in the social pressures exerted by one's culture, reference groups, small groups, and leaders? Depending on the circumstances, a speaker may find that a listener's consciousness of these external pressures either is an asset that can be used or is a detriment that must be offset. In some situations, an individual may consent to believe, feel, or act in a particular way if informed that a respected leader or others of his or her culture, reference group, or small group are doing likewise or endorse such behavior. The "bandwagon technique" of a propagandist exemplifies this principle. It attempts to intensify the listener's awareness of membership in the group. When the speaker finds that the social pressures operating on the audience are a roadblock to acceptance of the speaker's proposal, then he or she must look for ways to minimize those pressures.

Internal Influences   We have been discussing some of the external pressures that help determine a listener's position on issues. Equally important are the pressures from within, which each of us experiences. Several decades ago, Muzafer Sherif and his associates conducted extensive investigations into the relationship between our ego-involvement with an issue and our willingness to modify our position on that issue. The investigations led Sherif to suggest that the more ego-involved we are with an issue, the narrower are our "latitudes of acceptance," and thus the less likely we are to change our existing opinions on the issue.

For example, if you are a homeowner in a quiet neighborhood, and someone tries to convince you that a building permit should be granted for the construction of a fast-food restaurant on the lot adjacent to your property, you would resist the plea because of your personal stake, or ego-involvement, in the matter. Your "latitude of acceptance" would be very narrow. Sherif also studied the relationship between a person's degree of familiarity with an issue and that person's willingness to alter his or her position on the issue. His findings suggest that, the less familiar a person is with an issue, the more amenable he or she is to changing positions on that issue, if, indeed, he or she held a position to start with.

Extreme devotion to a position, Sherif maintains, virtually blinds one to any suggestion of change. To a fierce believer, even a moderate point of view is perceived with some hostility because "it falls squarely within his latitude of rejection." It is to a speaker's advantage to discover what "vested interest" the audience might have in the issue under consideration. This information will enable the speaker to set a more realistic persuasive goal.

Audience Attitude Toward the Speaker

Any analysis of the audience must include an evaluation of their perception of you as a speaker. The topic of credibility is so very important to the persuasive speaker that we will discuss it in great detail later in the chapter. We will offer some ways to assist you in having the audience perceive you as a highly credible source. But for now you must remember to involve all dimensions of credibility early in your preparation. For example, discover if the audience perceives you as having a good reputation before you give your speech. If your prespeech image is negative, you will have to exert great effort during your speech to supplant it with a favorable reputation. If the audience has no prior opinion of you, your job will be to create a good impression through the speech itself.

Formulating a Specific Purpose

In a persuasive speech, the statement of your specific purpose indicates exactly what you want the audience to believe, feel, or do:

"For my audience to believe that the act of poaching in parts of Africa is endangering many rare animals."

"For my audience to volunteer one hour each weekend to help clear a firebreak around the campus."

"For my audience to believe that all employees working in the transportation industry should be tested for drugs."

"For my audience to support a boycott of the campus bookstore."

"For my audience to believe that tanning booths are dangerous."

When you have formulated your specific purpose, you can begin to select materials that will best enable you to accomplish that purpose.

Finding Material

Theories of persuasion date back to the times of the ancient Greeks. Perhaps the definitive statement of the principal ways in which persuasion occurs was made by Aristotle twenty-four centuries ago, when he wrote in his *Rhetoric:* "Persuasion is effected by the arguments, when we demonstrate the truth, real or apparent, by such means as inhere in particular cases. . . . Persuasion is effected through the audience, when they are brought by the speech into a state of emotion. . . . The character of the speaker is a cause of persuasion when the speech is so uttered as to make him worthy of belief. . . ." A glance at the various treatments of persuasion since that time demonstrates the durability of Aristotle's classification of the modes of persuasion. That is to say, current research in the field of persuasion supports Aristotle's conclusion that, *to change the mind or behavior of other people, we must have a sound argument, appeal to their emotions, and be perceived as a highly credible source.* Therefore, in this section, we shall explore (1) convincing arguments, (2) impelling psychological appeals, and (3) personal credibility.

Factual evidence is a crucial part of any speech to persuade.

In *Henry V*, Shakespeare wrote "There is occasion and causes for the why and where-fore of all things." He is saying that, from the simplest to the most complex of acts, whenever we take an action or entertain a given belief or attitude, we like to think we have good reasons for doing so. In fact, we search for reasons to justify our behavior, whether it is past behavior ("I voted for Nancy because I was tired of student fees going up each semester"), present behavior ("I wear seat belts because I am concerned about automobile safety"), or intended behavior ("When I graduate, I plan to work for the Sierra Club so that I can concentrate on environmental issues"). You will notice that, in all three of our examples, the person has a reason for his or her action (a dislike of higher fees, a concern about safety, a desire for a certain type of career).

Convincing Arguments

What are some of the possible requirements for a reasonable argument? Perhaps we can begin to answer that question by examining the two principal ingredients of an argument—(1) *evidence* and (2) *reasoning*. In a sense, we have touched on these ingredients in other contexts, when we dealt with verbal and visual supports in chapter 6 and with critical judgment in chapter 9. However, let us now examine that information from a persuasive speaking perspective.

You will recall that, in chapter 6, we dealt with forms of support such as examples, instances, illustrations, statistics, and testimony. Another way of looking at them is as (1) *evidence of fact* and (2) *evidence of opinion*.

Factual evidence is a crucial part of any speech to persuade. Remember, in persua-sive speaking you are usually asking people to change their beliefs. Factual evidence may be drawn from your personal observations or from external sources. On many occasions, you have witnessed an event and then reported to others what you saw. Perhaps you saw an automobile accident at an intersection and then recounted the details to an investigating officer. Maybe you argued with a friend over which subcompact car gets the best gas mileage and cited figures compiled from your own driving experience in one of the cars.

The validity of factual evidence drawn from your own personal observation is dependent on two factors. First, how well equipped are you to be a good witness of the "facts" you report? Do you have the necessary physical capacities, such as keen eyesight and acute hearing? Is your perception colored by the emotional state you were experiencing at the time? Do you see only what you want to see? In short, are you an objective observer? Second, how well equipped are you to report what you have seen? Do you alter the story from telling to telling to make it more interesting? Do you relish the lurid details out of proportion to their importance? Do you possess the vocabulary necessary for relatively objective reporting?

Factual evidence (examples, illustrations, and statistics) that you draw from outside sources must meet these same tests plus some additional tests of validity. Is the fact being reported by the person who observed it? If so, that observer should be judged by the same questions you ask yourself when you are the primary observer. Is the fact being reported by a secondary source? If so, what is the secondary source's reputation for reliability? When was the fact observed, and when was it reported? What is fact today may not be fact tomorrow (witness how population figures change constantly). Is the fact represented out of context? Do other sources report the same fact?

Persuasive arguments need factual evidence if listeners are to believe your assertions and observations. For example, if you were trying to prove the extent of "downsizing" in the military, you might use the following facts to support your point:

> The cutting ax has been deep. According to the Department of Defense, one hundred sixty-five facilities are to be shut or slimmed down, forty-three of them major bases. More than sixty thousand civilian jobs will be eliminated.

If you are persuading an audience that waste disposal is a serious problem in the United States, you could offer the following fact: "Half of our six thousand landfills will be full or closed by the year 2000." In both of the previous examples, you can see how the persuasive speaker used facts to help convince the listeners that they should believe the validity of the assertion being advanced.

Opinion evidence has two sources also—your own personal opinions based on your direct experience and the opinions of others who, presumably, are experts. The acceptability of an "educated guess" is, of course, dependent on whether the audience views you as a person qualified to express an informed opinion. If, by reason of your occupation or your major field of study, you do possess the necessary qualifications for expertise—and if your audience recognizes these qualifications as adequate—you may use yourself as a source of opinion. By and large, however, student speakers should use the testimony of a recognized authority. Your arguments would have a persuasive tone if you were to say, "The Surgeon General of the United States recently said that secondhand smoke represents a serious health hazard for nonsmokers." Think of the added weight of your position on the destruction of the world's forests if you were to offer the following testimony: "Professor Daniel Wilson of the University of California Environmental Biology Department said that three plants that might help cure AIDS are currently being bulldozed over in the forests of Panama, Brazil, and Costa Rica."

William Shakespeare wrote, "Strong reasons make strong actions." What he was saying applies directly to persuasive speaking. In most instances, evidence alone is insufficient to change someone's mind or behavior. If people are going to act and think differently in the future, they also want the new positions and conclusions to be logical and reasonable. Careful and thoughtful reasoning demonstrates to an audience that the position one is advocating is worthy and makes sense. Convincing others that a position makes sense is called the **reasoning process.**

Traditionally, scholars concerned with the study of argumentation and reasoning have isolated four basic approaches to reasoning that can aid persuasive speakers: (1) applying a general rule (or axiom) to a particular case (*deduction*), (2) examining a series of items and then generalizing about the class of items to which they belong (*induction*), (3) drawing comparisons between things well known and those less well known—or unknown—(*analogical*), and (4) detecting what appears to be a causal relationship between events (*causal*).

When we ask an audience to use **deductive reasoning** to believe in our position, we are suggesting that what is true of a general class can be applied to specific cases. This is a powerful form of reasoning in persuasive speaking because, if you can convince an audience to accept your general premise (general class), your conclusion should follow. Quite a bit of our everyday reasoning is deductive. All of us have a stock of rules, or axioms, that we apply when we have to make decisions. We have axioms to guide us in choosing which videotapes to rent—"Movies starring Robert DeNiro are interesting. Here's one of his movies on videotape. I'll bet it is interesting. I'll rent it for tonight." Other axioms guide us in selecting places to dine—"The food at Bayou Belle is always good. This ad in the paper says they are featuring a new lobster and shrimp casserole. I'll bet it will be good. I'll make reservations for us." Still others guide us in choosing what classes to take—"Classes involving lots of math are hard for me. The catalog description of this class specifies calculus and trigonometry as prerequisites. The class must involve a lot of math work. I think I'll choose something else." In each of these instances, we have applied a general rule to a particular case and have drawn a conclusion about the relationship. We can diagram the first example as follows:

- Movies starring Robert DeNiro are interesting. (General rule or axiom)
- This is a videotape of a Robert DeNiro movie. (Case at hand)
- Therefore, it will be interesting. (Conclusion)

In persuasive speaking, it is usually wise to begin with an assertion that most people will accept, for, later in the speech, you will ask the audience to believe that what is true with regard to one case is true of an entire case (as the previous examples demonstrated). For instance, if your speech deals with the treatment of women in the Armed Forces, the first leg of your argument could state that all members of the military forces should be treated equally. Second, you would say that Sally Jones is in the military; therefore (conclusion), she should be treated as the men are treated. Although our example is somewhat stilted, it nevertheless shows the need to have a believable general rule so that you can support the remainder of the argument.

Deductive arguments are seldom presented in the formal style used in our examples. Normally, one of the premises or the conclusion is obvious and can therefore be omitted to give the speech a smoother flow. Hence, you might say, "The Armed Services always sought to promote equality; this is not the case in the career of Captain Sally Jones."

How do you know if your deduction is reliable? There are several tests that help us detect the existence of any weaknesses in our reasoning. First of all, is the general rule really true? Are Robert DeNiro movies usually interesting? Why do we say so? How many of his movies have we seen? Is our generalization about his movies based on our own personal viewing or on the judgment of a friend or a couple of movie critics who review films on television every week?

We should also ask ourselves whether the case at hand is really within the scope of the general rule. Does this movie really star Robert DeNiro, or does he appear only in a cameo role? Is it a picture he made recently or one he made before achieving stardom? Unless the case at hand falls entirely within the scope of the general rule, we cannot reasonably conclude that the videotape will be interesting.

As speakers, we also use deductive reasoning in many of our arguments. To be sure, we may imply rather than state our axioms or conclusions, but we do so when we fully expect the listener to supply the missing parts. For example, when we urge others to defeat a tax reform measure "because it is reactionary," we are implying both an axiom and a conclusion. We can diagram the reasoning as follows:

- Things reactionary are bad. (Implied axiom)
- This tax reform measure is reactionary. (Stated case in point)
- Therefore, it is bad. (Implied conclusion)

The success of such reasoning hinges on the listeners' ability to detect and agree with the implied axiom, to agree that the case in point falls within the scope of the axiom, and to add and agree with the implied conclusion.

Inductive reasoning is the opposite of deductive reasoning; with induction, the analysis moves from the specific to the general. It is also called reasoning from examples and reasoning from the particular to the general. To say that violence against teachers has increased in New York, Los Angeles, Washington, DC, and Cleveland and, therefore, is a serious problem in many major cities is an example of reasoning by means of the inductive process.

When a speaker uses induction in persuasive speaking, often he or she offers a number of pieces of specific evidence and then draws a conclusion from the audience:

> Tobacco smoke causes a build-up of fluid in the middle ear of young children. Cigarette smoke is responsible for 150,000 to 300,000 cases of bronchitis and pneumonia and other lower respiratory infections in children up to 18 months of age. Cigarette smoke increases the frequency and severity of symptoms in 200,000 to 1 million children with asthma and increases the risk of new cases. From these facts, it seems obvious that secondhand cigarette smoke is harmful to young children.

As you can tell from this example, inductive reasoning works well when your goal is persuasion. It is perhaps most useful when your audience is skeptical or even hostile to what you are going to propose. You can build a very powerful case for your cause if you start by offering solid evidence that is hard to refute and then draw a conclusion from that evidence. Observe this technique in the following speech on polluted water systems:

Last month, Banner Beach was closed because of contamination from the city sewer system. Three weeks ago, Paradise Cove had to be closed when poisonous chemicals were found in the fish that people were catching. And, just today, lifeguards told swimmers to stay out of the water at North Beach because of an oily substance floating near the surface. I think we can all agree that something needs to done at once about the amount of pollution contaminating the beaches in our city.

You must be careful when using induction. Notice the errors in reasoning found in the following examples. A magazine pollster interviews five hundred voters and concludes that "the American voter is more conservative today than ten years ago." A TV reviewer sees the pilot episode of a new mystery series and predicts that the series will be the "hottest thing on television." You read that two local restaurants have been shut down by health officials because of the incidence of hepatitis among some of their employees, and you conclude that "it's unsafe to eat out in this town." All these examples are imperfect inductions because the generalization, or conclusion, that is drawn in each case is based on a limited number of examples. However, it is usually impossible for a person to investigate every single part of the whole: the pollster could hardly interview every American voter, the TV reviewer could hardly preview the entire season's episodes, and you could hardly eat at all the restaurants all the time. Consequently, we have to rely on what we feel is a representative sample.

Since we all use inductive reasoning, we should remember that the examples from which we draw generalizations must meet certain tests. Chapter 6 mentioned those tests: (1) Are there enough examples to justify the generalization? To sample two peaches from an entire truckload and then generalize about the whole truckload is to trust to luck rather than to logical reasoning. (2) Are the examples representative of the class of things about which we are generalizing? While the first test relates to the quantity of examples, the second test relates to their quality.

We should also ask ourselves, Have we confined our generalization to the class of things from which our examples were drawn? To generalize about all fraternities on the basis of the misdeeds of one local chapter is hardly warranted. At best, one could safely generalize only about the behavior of that chapter.

Analogical reasoning, or reasoning from comparison, is a type of inductive reasoning. The premise behind this classification compares one circumstance, process, thing, or person to another. The speaker says that what is true of A is also true of B. Reasoning by analogy may be illustrated by such arguments as the following: "Gun control will work here. It works in England." "This stuff will make your stomach feel better. It sure helped mine." "I don't know why I can't have a motorcycle. Carol's parents bought her one." In each of the examples, the speaker is drawing on certain perceived similarities to argue that there will be a further similarity not yet perceived. In the first example, the speaker is assuming that "here" and "England" are already similar in many respects and, hence, will be similar with respect to the workability of gun control measures. In the second example, there is an assumed similarity between two persons and their stomach conditions, leading the speaker to conclude that treatment measures that were successful for one will be successful for the other. In the final example, "Carol" and "I" or "Carol's parents" and "my parents" are the things perceived to be similar and, thus, ought to be similar with respect to owning a motorcycle.

Of all the forms of reasoning, analogical reasoning is perhaps the one most subject to error—and for a very simple reason. The validity of any argument based on comparison is dependent on a high degree of similarity between the circumstances compared. In focusing on similarities, it is very easy to overlook pertinent points of dissimilarity that might invalidate any conclusions based on the similarities. It is extremely important, then, to make certain that relevant points of similarity outweigh the dissimilarities.

What are the relevant points of similarity that should exist in the items compared? A physician is trained to recognize relevant points of similarity between the patient at hand and a patient already treated. Thus, Dr. Evans can reason that "Joe has the same symptoms as Harry; penicillin treatment worked for Harry, so I'll prescribe it for Joe." Too often, however, speakers do not take the time to analyze the constituents of relevance. Noting that a great number of similarities exist between two situations, they do not take the time to ask if the similarities are pertinent.

It might be helpful to return to chapter 6 and reread about the three ways you can test the validity of your analogies. Even though we were discussing the forms of support, the tests also apply to reasoning by analogy.

Reasoning by causation is based on the concept that nothing happens without a cause. Every effect has a cause, and every cause produces an effect. We see this type of reasoning all day long. For example, we are told that, if additional safety features are added to automobiles (cause), the price of cars will rise (effect).

Reasoning from causation can appear in at least three forms. We can reason from a known set of circumstances to a probable set of consequences—that is, from known cause to predicted effect. We can reason in just the reverse order, from known effect back to probable cause. We can also reason from one set of circumstances to another set of circumstances, effect to effect.

Cause-to-effect reasoning can be readily illustrated. We read in the newspaper that home mortgage rates are declining, so we predict that more people will start buying homes. In election years, we hear Democrats saying things like, "Don't elect a Republican Congress unless you want big business to get all the breaks." The Republicans, in turn, may say, "Don't elect a Democratic Congress unless you want the most massive national debt in history."

Effect-to-cause reasoning is just as common. Shortly after the election of a new president, the stock market climbs sharply and we reason that the new administration must have done something to inspire confidence. Our usually impoverished neighbor parks a brand new sports car in his driveway, so we figure he must have received a financial windfall. We see a sad-faced person exiting from a theater that features a comedy bill, so we have second thoughts about buying a ticket to the next performance.

Effect-to-effect reasoning is a special form of reasoning from analogy. It says that, because two sets of circumstances are similar (similar causes), their consequences will be similar. Dr. Evans, who prescribed penicillin for Joe because it worked for Harry (who exhibited the same symptoms) was using both analogical and causal reasoning.

Reasoning from causation should be subjected to the following tests: (1) Does the alleged cause always produce the same effect? (2) Can the effect result from more than one cause? (3) Are there any conditions that can interfere with causal connection? (4) Are minor causes being confused with major causes?

We have sketched some of the ways individuals of Western culture reason, and we have examined the kinds of evidence they use. As you construct arguments, then, bear in mind the tests of reasonableness that Western audiences may require you to meet. Later in this chapter, we will discuss some of the differences in reasoning as they apply to various cultures.

French writer Joseph Roux observed, "Reason guides but a small part of us, and that the least interesting. The rest obeys feeling, true or false, and passion, good or bad." Placed into the context of this portion of the chapter, what he is saying is that people are not computers or machines, that on most occasions reasonable arguments alone are not sufficient to induce the desired response from an audience. This is particularly true when that response calls for behavioral change, such as taking (or refraining from taking) an action. You can probably think of a time when someone convinced you that you ought to take a certain action, but you never got around to doing so. Perhaps the person used faultless reasoning and unimpeachable evidence to convince you that a problem existed and that there was an ideal solution to that problem, yet you failed to take the steps necessary to implement that solution. Why? Because they failed to touch you on a personal and intimate level.

What are the forces that motivate and impel us to act? As you would suspect, these forces are complex and multiple. Therefore, we would be the first to admit that people are much too complex to be analyzed in a few pages of a textbook, yet philosophers, pastors, and psychologists seem to have agreed on at least three general forces that tend to exert an influence on actions: (1) *our desire to satisfy a personal need*, (2) *our desire to maintain consistency*, and (3) *our susceptibility to suggestion*. What is interesting about these three characteristics is that they are found in all cultures. Let us look at each and see how it can be used by a persuasive speaker to accomplish a purpose.

Our Desire to Satisfy a Personal Need   In his renowned study of human needs and motivations, A. H. Maslow supplied a classification system that lists human needs in their order of urgency. Knowing something about these needs will enable you to link them to your specific purpose and to your material.

Of first importance, says Maslow, are our *physiological needs*, such as our needs for food, water, air, and rest. These biological needs have to be met before we are inclined to attend to other less urgent needs. If your audience is in a hot, stuffy room, they might be receptive to signing a petition that would urge the college administration to add a new air conditioning system to the campus classroom building.

Second in importance, according to Maslow, are our *safety needs*. A strong need in all of us is the desire to feel free from harm in the present and future: safe and secure in our homes, jobs, and play. Speeches dealing with seat belts, drunk driving, smoking, health, crime, and the like can make effective use of this important need. One speaker appealed to this need in a talk on the advantages of a vegetarian diet. Among other things, she told her audience that, when compared to nonvegetarians, people who do not eat any animal products have a lower incidence of heart attack and colon cancer. Another speaker, who was urging the city to add additional police officers to the local parks, used the need for safety when he talked about the increased number of violent crimes against children taking place in the parks. He not only offered statistics, but he also told the story of a little boy attacked by two other youths who wanted his money.

Impelling Psychological Appeals

Third, once physiological and safety needs have been met, we are ready to confront less urgent needs. Therefore, Maslow maintains, we are then ready to turn to *love needs*. We all need a sense of belonging to or being a part of someone else's life. Families, friends, and lovers help us satisfy this need. A speaker who appeals to the love needs may show an audience how his or her proposal will offer their parents a complete health plan without depleting their parents' savings accounts. A speaker appealing to college spirit, love of country, or the welfare of loved ones is also tapping into this basic need.

Fourth among our needs are *esteem needs*. Maslow suggests that each of us wants to experience a feeling of self-respect as well as recognition from others; thus, we take many paths to satisfy these yearnings. Telling listeners how, by adhering to your message, they can achieve a specific goal, gain respect, be accepted, or raise their status and credibility are all examples of appealing to this need. As you would suspect, this is a very popular allure if your topic deals with having your listeners purchase a product. To tell a group of students that, by purchasing a study guide, their grades will go up and their professors will think better of them is an example of using the esteem need.

Finally, *self-actualization needs* center on our desire to realize the full potential within us. Thus, we turn to creative acts in whatever areas our interests dictate. You are appealing to this highest of motives when you show your audience that, by adopting your proposal, they will "enrich their lives and reach their full potential."

Again, what are the implications for persuasion in Maslow's classification of needs? For one thing, a person with an unfulfilled need would probably be amenable to recommendations about how to fulfill that need. Consequently, a persuader is well advised to discover the listeners' needs and then plan a strategy of persuasion based on fulfilling those needs. By showing listeners that the speaker's proposal will satisfy a felt need, he or she increases the chances of achieving a specific purpose.

How does a speaker invoke the listeners' needs? Perhaps an examination of some motivational appeals used by persuaders over the years can help us answer that question.

1. *Self-preservation.* Safety devices, physical fitness courses, and life-prolonging medications are examples of goods and services that provide a partial answer to our need to stay alive and enjoy physical well-being. Construction workers who wear hard hats and buy shoes with steel-reinforced toes are acting out of a desire for self-preservation. We buy smoke alarms for our homes in response to that desire. The familiar tactic of those soliciting support for an increase in military expenditures is to use self-preservation as the appeal: "With more and more small countries developing nuclear weapons, we'd better move fast in our own program of weapons development if we want to avoid a war in a remote area of the world." Self-preservation is also the obvious motive when a speaker asks for added campus security by telling the story of a couple "mugged" and seriously injured after a college basketball game. By simply adding the phrase, "Just think about it, you could have been the one that was sent to the hospital," the speaker points the example directly at the audience.

2. *Sex attraction.* A quick glance at almost any magazine, newspaper, billboard, or television advertisement confirms the power of sex attraction as a motive to buy an astonishingly wide range of goods and services. Advertisements that urge you to buy an airline ticket to Cancun conjure up images of a sun-bronzed lover. Even the purchase of a microwave oven is supposed to leave you more time for the one you love. While an advertiser can flaunt sex appeal freely, a public speaker is well advised to use this motive more discreetly.

3. *Acquisition of property.* In the dominant North American culture, the acquisition of material goods is a basic value. We even see bumper stickers that proclaim, "The person with the most toys wins." Advertisers and public speakers know of this value and make great use of appeals to our wallets and purses. Bargain sales, "giant economy sizes," higher rates of return on investments, and various speculative ventures are manifestations of the nearly universal desire of persons to acquire property. For instance, a spokesperson for a school bond drive points out that a better-educated citizenry will be a more prosperous citizenry, suggesting that money spent now will be returned many times over as a result of a healthier economy.

4. *Self-esteem.* At times, we will sacrifice personal safety, sublimate sex attraction, and disdain the acquisition of property if it means that our self-esteem can be increased. The desire to be "looked up to," to be well regarded by our peers or superiors, to be perceived as responsible and reliable is a powerful motivating force. It may show up in such diverse actions as donating a large sum to charity, enrolling in night school, climbing the Matterhorn, skydiving, "standing up for our rights," or driving an expensive sports car. Extended to groups, self-esteem takes the form of civic pride, a desire to be "number one," a wish to be the host of the Super Bowl, or a desire to have the world's finest medical research laboratory.

5. *Personal enjoyment.* Our love of cars containing all the options, of exotic food and drink, of luxurious accommodations, of remote-controlled appliances, of all the so-called good things in life becomes a more dominant motive once our basic needs for food, clothing, and shelter have been satisfied. We do not buy cream cheese for its life-sustaining qualities but for its power to bring pleasure to our taste buds. We do not buy a $200,000 home just to keep out the elements but to satisfy our love of the good things. Portable compact disc players, holographic art, catamarans, hang gliders, and motor homes are acquired primarily to satisfy our need for personal enjoyment.

6. *Loyalty.* Whether our allegiance and loyalty be directed at country, state, community, or campus, we are all proud of our affiliations. A speaker who is aware of this devotion to country or club can effectively use it to motivate an audience. An example of using loyalty as a motive appeal is telling a group of students that, unless we get the money for the new library, our university will become a second-rate institution.

7. *Individualism.* Although it is a very Western trait, a call to individualism is an effective motive appeal. In the North American culture, individualism is the belief that the interest and welfare of the individual is paramount. It stresses individual initiative and encourages free expression. If speakers can link their central themes to these characteristics, they can greatly improve the chances of accomplishing their persuasive purposes. Recently, we heard a speaker justify the need to spend more money on police protection by suggesting that, when burglars enter your home illegally, they are violating your private domain.

8. *Curiosity.* We undertake many things not simply for tangible benefit but to satisfy our sense of curiosity. We flock to a balloon-launching event, patronize a wax museum, buy a paperback book with an enticing cover, or try a "new taste sensation" because we find the unusual and the novel so alluring.

9. *Imitation.* The desire to "be just like" a person we admire may prompt us to buy the breakfast food recommended by an Olympic gold medalist, to acquire the same kind of large screen color television set as our neighbor, or to vote for the political candidate recommended by our favorite movie actor. A speaker must be cautious, however, in appealing to imitative instincts. Pains should be taken to discover whether or not the listeners really admire the model. If the listeners envy the model instead, they may go to great lengths to avoid imitation.

10. *Altruism.* We like to think that we are compassionate and that most of our actions are not selfishly motivated. We make anonymous donations to charity, we send CARE packages abroad, and we volunteer to read to the blind. A successful persuasive speaker is well aware of altruism in all of us and uses this appeal when asking help for subjects as diverse as abandoned animals and neglected children. Notice in the example that follows (on the subject of the laboratory testing of animals) how the speaker connects compassion to her topic while describing a cosmetic testing laboratory.

> They had over one hundred rabbits in a large crate. They then shot the rabbits with a chemical. Regardless of whether or not the rabbit was dead they would throw it ten feet onto a pile in the middle of the floor. Many rabbits would still be crawling around on the floor and on top of the other dead and dying rabbits. I could tell that the main objective in the laboratory was not killing the rabbits humanely and painlessly, it was speed and efficiency. Many of the rabbits had blood coming out of their mouths, others were convulsing and having spasms. It got to the point where I could no longer stand to watch their suffering. I literally became ill and had to leave the laboratory.

A speaker needs to keep a number of ideas in mind when using motive appeals. First, *try to consider using as many appropriate appeals as possible, because not all members of an audience are motivated by the same appeal.* Needs and wants differ from individual to individual and from culture to culture. For example, if you oppose the construction of a new state prison near a residential area, you might be addressing citizens who live in the affected area, others who live in the same city but not close to the affected area, and still others who are residents of other cities hundreds of miles away from the prison. Moreover, you might find them to be of diverse ages, financial means, social classes, and value systems. With such a heterogeneous audience, it would be folly to rely on a single type of motive appeal. Although a fear appeal (threat to self-preservation) might motivate those who live in the affected area, it would hardly be applicable to those from another city. You might have to inform those people of the threat to their pocketbooks (acquisition of property) posed by expenditures of tax dollars for the building and operation of the proposed prison. Pointing out to other segments of the audience that their personal enjoyment of the natural beauty of the area is threatened by the construction of a new prison might be appropriate. Conceivably, you might use the "fight city hall" appeal (destructiveness) if some of your listeners believe that government has too much power and is forcing an unwanted prison on the community.

Second, remember *there are many more categories and appeals available to creative speakers than the ten we highlighted* earlier in the chapter. You might want to attract interest in your topic by using fear, hope, power, control, independence, and conformity. You must remember to always consult your audience analysis when considering which appeal may have the best results.

Third, *try to predict conflicting appeals.* If you are talking about financial investments, you must realize that you are dealing with our desire to make money along with our reluctance to risk losing our money.

Fourth, *always combine emotional appeals with logical appeals.* This blending allows an audience to see the wisdom of your proposal at the same time they are "moved" by it. Notice in the following example, dealing with stricter drunk driving laws, how a motive appeal (in the form of a factual illustration) is fused with statistics.

> The holiday season was special to nine-year-old Carla and her family. Carla's birthday was five days before Christmas, and her grandmother's birthday was Christmas Eve. The family was going to celebrate both birthdays and Christmas that night. So, for this young girl, as the family headed down the highway, a very special night was awaiting her. However, one thing went dreadfully wrong. On the way to the family gathering, a drunk driver, with three times the legal limit of alcohol in his blood, crashed into the side of the car where Carla's head was resting. The bright, cheerful, loving child was killed instantly. Carla would not get to open presents on Christmas morning with her family. In fact, like the other 2,000 people killed by alcohol-related crashes between Thanksgiving and New Year's Eve, Carla would never get to celebrate another Christmas. Instead, Christmas will always remain for Carla's family a tragic remembrance of the cruelty of drinking and driving.

Finally, as the above example demonstrated, *use specific and personal examples when employing motive appeals.* It is easier for all of us to visualize a single case than an abstract number. As professor Clifford Orwin once noted, "compassion depends on imagination." Think about the hurt and impact we feel if one of our best friends dies of AIDS as compared to how we would respond to statistics that tell us that over 200,000 deaths have been reported from AIDS in the last ten years. Again, we urge you to personalize your motive appeals.

Our Desire to Maintain Consistency   There are a number of theories of attitude change based on the hypothesis that people attempt to be consistent with their existing thoughts and actions. Although there are some minor variations among their approaches, scholars such as Fritz Heider (balance theory), Leon Festinger (cognitive dissonance), and Charles Osgood and Percy Tannenbaum (congruity theory) are all concerned essentially with our apparent need to maintain consistency and balance within our beliefs, attitudes, and knowledge—cognitions. If something introduces an element of inconsistency (imbalance, incongruity, or dissonance), according to these theories, we make adjustments necessary to restore a state of consistency.

When applied to human communication, the balance theories tell us that, if we receive information that causes us discomfort ("We need to raise taxes"), we lose our sense of balance and harmony. If we believe, for example, that a secret organization is a "hate" group that preaches one ethnic group's supremacy over all others and then we are told that our childhood idol, our late grandfather, was a member of that organization, an element of inconsistency has been introduced into our cognitions. We have warm memories of our grandfather's gentle, caring ways, his efforts in charitable drives, his friendliness to everyone, and his staunch defense of anyone who was considered an underdog. How do we resolve this inconsistency? Perhaps we will resolve it by changing our belief about the secret organization or our attitude toward its members. We might transform our unfavorable predisposition toward them into a neutral or (conceivably) favorable one. Perhaps we will resolve it by telling ourselves that the organization was not a hate group at the time our grandfather was one of its members. Maybe we will speculate that our grandfather was a "double agent" who had infiltrated the organization in order to keep authorities informed of the group's activities. We might resolve the inconsistency by simply refusing to believe the news of his alleged membership. We might say to our informant, "You are mistaken," or "You are lying!" Conceivably, we might try to banish the memory of our grandfather or be filled with disgust or hatred for him or a deep sense of betrayal.

The application of the consistency principle to persuasion can readily be seen in selling. Much selling is rooted in the introduction of a dissonant note to a prospective buyer. Let us say that Susan is happy with the set of tires on her car because she believes them to be safe. Into this picture of contentment intrudes a salesperson who raises serious questions about the durability of the tires. Susan's cognitions, thus, are thrown out of balance. The salesperson has the answer that will restore the balance (or at least hopes so).

Sometimes a persuader's job is to help listeners live with an existing inconsistency by offering a means of reducing its intensity or rationalizing its existence. Wartime propaganda furnishes an example. The people of a peace-loving nation are besieged with a sense of guilt at becoming involved in a war. They are offered the palliatives, "This is the war to end all wars," "We must not desert the cause for which so many of our people have died," "We must fight so that our children can live in peace," and "If we don't stop them here, we'll have to stop them somewhere else." In these instances, the persuaders have attempted to offset the severity of the listeners' cognitive dissonance—"I don't believe in war, but here I am supporting a war"—by reminding the listeners of other beliefs or attitudes they hold that are consistent with supporting the war—"I believe in safeguarding our children," "I believe in honoring our dead," "I believe that the achievement of peace is worth any price," and "A stitch in time saves nine."

Our apparent need to maintain consistency offers a wellspring of opportunities for a person engaged in persuasive speaking. Let us look at some of those opportunities and some guidelines in the use of dissonance theory. First, remember that people hold several attitudes on the same topic. We might believe in the separation of church and state but accept the idea that young children need to learn spiritual values while attending school. Knowing that attitudes are diverse enables persuasive speakers to select from a host of appeals instead of feeling that they are tied to only one argument.

Second, realizing that the existence of dissonance makes people psychologically uncomfortable should allow you to seek ways within your speech to abate that frustration. For example, if you are asking an audience of hunters to reduce the number of deer they can hunt in a single season (creating dissonance), you might lessen that dissonance by telling them that, if they do not curtail their activity, they will deplete the deer population within the next two years.

Third, there might be competing values and attitudes at work within the same individual. That is to say, attitudes are situational and contextual. Someone might believe that spotted owls should be protected in the redwoods but, because he or she dislikes the petition process, might balk when you ask him or her to sign a petition putting the issue on the state ballot.

Our Susceptibility to Suggestion   Our final inducement to action centers on our vulnerability to suggestion. Do you find yourself wanting to yawn when you see another person doing so? Do you develop a sudden yearning for a bag of peanuts when you see someone at the ballpark eating peanuts? Are you tempted to join a growing crowd around a sidewalk musician? If so, you are probably yielding to the power of suggestion.

Suggestion is the arousal of a response by either indirect or direct means. In the public-speaking arena, it may operate through channels external to a speech's message, such as the decor of the surroundings, flags, paintings, posters, comfortable seating arrangements, proper lighting, giant photographs, acts of ritual music, and prominently displayed collection plates or canisters. These factors may condition listeners to respond positively to a speaker's message. When your goal is persuasion, you should be aware of these external contingencies. Creating the proper atmosphere is often as powerful as the words you utter.

Suggestion also operates through your message. If you stress positive ideas, if you are fair when mentioning ideas contrary to your position, if you avoid name calling, and if you acknowledge controversy when it exists, you condition the audience to respond favorably to your point of view (or at least you condition them against a negative response).

There is also a power of suggestion audience members exercise on one another. If we see others laughing, we often find it easier to do so. If others' nonverbal behavior signals apathy or interest, disagreement or agreement, hostility or enthusiastic support, we may be affected in surprising ways. Carnival "barkers" recognize the influence of decoys to draw customers to their sideshows and concession stands.

You hear two speakers arguing the same cause but on separate occasions. Both use essentially the same lines of reasoning and similar evidence. Nevertheless, you want to agree with one speaker, while the other fails to budge your convictions. Something about that one speaker inspires believability. What is the difference? There are many words that might describe this phenomena. We hear words such as "image," "credibility," "charisma," and "character." Regardless of the words we use, the point is that often, despite the compelling arguments and evidence you cite, all your efforts will be wasted if the audience does not perceive you in a positive light. Your character touches the audience as much as your content. The American author Josiah Holland wrote, "Character must stand behind and back up everything—the sermon, the poem, the picture, the play. None of them is worth a straw without it."

In human communication, the word *credibility* is most often used to discuss this important and complex personality trait. It is generally how the audience perceives *you* and the causes *you* represent. Before we discuss the constituents of personal credibility, and ways to increase credibility, it might be useful to pause and offer a few introductory observations.

Personal Credibility

First, *judgments about your credibility are made rather quickly*. This, of course, means that you must start demonstrating your character the moment you begin to talk. Second, although the audience is swift in deciding on your character, they nevertheless *construct the image of credibility in four stages*. They (1) may know something about you *before you talk,* (2) will have an *initial impression,* (3) make alterations *as you speak,* and (4) have *a final impression.* Finally, *the components of credibility are multidimensional.* This simply means that the data the audience uses to decide if you are a credible source is varied and detailed. It is seldom a single factor but rather a combination of factors. As you will see later in this section, we will offer a long list of techniques that can enhance your credibility.

Thus far we have been referring to credibility in rather general terms. Let us now be a little more specific and ask this question: What are the constituents of personal credibility—that "something special about the speaker" that affects us so profoundly? Ever since Aristotle, speech theorists have attempted to isolate those elements. Aristotle maintained that, if a listener perceives a speaker to have good character, good sense, and goodwill, then the speaker's arguments are more apt to be believed. Aristotle treated personal **credibility,** or **ethos,** in terms of how it derives from a speaker's verbal message. Contemporary theorists now also take into account a speaker's nonverbal behavior in discussing personal credibility. In addition, they point out that credibility is partially a product of a speaker's reputation. They use terms such as (1) competence (being knowledgeable), (2) trustworthiness (integrity), and (3) dynamism (attractiveness) in discussing personal credibility. **Competence** seems to be somewhat like Aristotle's *good sense,* since both deal with the speaker's apparent level of knowledge and fitness to speak on a topic. **Trustworthiness** and Aristotle's *good character* seem to be closely akin, since both treat evincing traits of character, which the audience finds reassuring. **Dynamism** is closely related to a speaker's presentational traits—those nonverbal signals of competence, trustworthiness, and amiability or goodwill. The popular term, *image,* is a composite of all these factors.

Let us examine the three components of credibility more closely. The following list, which is by no means exhaustive, suggests some of the facets of speaker behavior to which North American audiences respond favorably. As we shall point out later, people from other cultures may not use the same traits to access credibility as do members of the dominant culture of North America.

Competence is a shorthand word that represents a number of different aspects of credibility. Our demonstrating competence also takes a number of forms. For example, a speaker can manifest competence through intelligence. The extent to which a speaker seems to have mastery of the subject matter is a determinant of our response. In general, the speaker's credibility is enhanced if he or she has conducted extensive research and marshals an impressive amount of diverse evidence, shows insight into all aspects of the question, uses reasoning that meets the tests of logical validity, and displays "common sense."

There are some very specific behaviors that can contribute to a speaker's level of competence:

1. *Use proper language.* Nothing lowers credibility faster than a poor vocabulary, mispronunciation, and the misuse of language. It might be helpful if you were to return briefly to chapter 12 and reexamine language distractions.

An image of
competence can be
projected by appearing
to be poised.

2. *Creating clear and original visual aids also helps establish a high level of competence.* The audience will feel that you are serious about your topic if they perceive that you have taken the time to prepare audiovisual aids.

3. *There is some research that suggests credibility is enhanced when a speaker uses credible sources and cites those sources.* If the audience knows that you have contacted responsible and reliable sources, they will often link the high-credibility source to your credibility.

4. *You should arrive on time and start your speech on time.* You know from your own experiences that all of us assign meaning to the way in which someone uses the clock. The assumption is that a person is not very conscientious if he or she is tardy.

5. *An image of competence can be projected by appearing to be poised.* A speaker who is in command of himself or herself inspires confidence. Not becoming unsettled by distractions, handling interruptions gracefully, and coping with hostile questions calmly are all signs of a temperament that inspires confidence.

6. *Using a number of different forms of support would assist the audience in believing you are competent.* Remember that this component of credibility is the one that shows the audience that you know what you are talking about. Admittedly, you cannot be an expert on all subjects, but you can show the audience that, by your supporting evidence, you are at least knowledgeable on the subject being discussed.

7. *Finally, you are often judged even before the audience sees or hears you.* Therefore, if you are going to be introduced to the audience by another speaker, make sure he or she imparts information that clearly demonstrates your qualifications. The person introducing you should have access to all the data pertaining to your accomplishments, training, background, expertise, and the like.

If done with good taste, you can promote your own competence. You will recall that you can tell the audience why you are qualified to speak on a particular topic, thereby helping the audience perceive you as competent (a high-credibility source). If you are trying to persuade a group of people to sign up for a first aid class, and tell them you have taught first aid for the past ten years, you are contributing to the audience's perception of you as a knowledgeable person.

As was the case with competence, the second component of credibility, *trustworthiness*, goes by many names. It is often referred to as integrity, altruism, goodwill, and ethical character. Benjamin Franklin even referred to it as "heart" when he wrote, "The heart of a fool is in his mouth, but the mouth of a wise man is in his heart." Regardless of its label, an audience's perception of you as a sincere, honest person is one of the most important aspects of successful public speaking. What makes this component so engrossing is that we tend to show our character in many different ways. Ralph Waldo Emerson noted that "if you act, you show character; if you sit still, you show it; if you sleep, you show it." The question for us is to show it in your speech. Let us examine some actions that often convey integrity:

1. *Moderation is usually equated with reasonableness.* Although intellectual enthusiasm and commitment are admirable traits, most people are fearful of an extremist. Hence, moderation should be your guide. People tend to be wary of those who indulge in overstatement, in personal abuse, or in unseemly emotional displays.

2. *Closely associated with moderation is tact.* Tact is the ability to deal with others without giving offense. In application to persuasion, it means such things as disagreeing without being disagreeable, admonishing without scolding, and enlightening without insulting the audience's intelligence.

3. *Goodwill is contagious.* A speaker who shows a good disposition toward the listeners, even though there may be matters on which they disagree, clears one of the obstacles to persuasion.

4. *Sincerity is greatly admired in all cultures.* A used car salesperson tells a customer, "I'd like to sell you this car because, quite frankly, I stand to earn a good commission. Furthermore, you are going to get a good car in the process." The salesperson's sincerity and candid disclosure of her real motives may have a disarming effect on the customer because most of us place credence in the remarks of those we regard as sincere and open in their dealings with others. None of us likes being duped; hence, of all the traits of character, sincerity may be the most important in persuasion.

5. *People tend to trust speakers who they believe share many of their own traits and attributes.* In the study of credibility, this concept is called homophily. It means the degree to which the individuals involved in the communication act believe they are similar. As a persuasive speaker, you need to convince your audience that you share some of their concerns, values, attitudes, and beliefs. If possible, you should also indicate how your backgrounds might be comparable. For example, if you are an honor student talking to a group of potential high school dropouts about the need for them to stay in school, your credibility would be aided if you were to mention that, at one time, you were a poor student and had even thought about leaving high school.

6. *Credibility is also linked to reliability.* Someone who "stands by their convictions," even if such a position is unpopular, is admired by most audiences. We admire the person who is not swayed by public opinion and fads, but instead can be counted on to follow their beliefs. Such a person is reliable and is thus appreciated.

7. *Honesty contributes to an image of being trustworthy.* Honesty can be reflected by such things as granting the existence of opposing views, not withholding evidence that the audience should have, and admitting that there might be some legitimate drawbacks to your proposal that need to be examined. Your audience will respect such actions on your part. Remember the good advice regarding honesty supplied by Shakespeare: "No legacy is so rich as honesty."

Our final ingredient of credibility is harder to describe than were the first two. *Dynamism* is a rather abstract term referring to such things as how we present ourselves and how attractive the audience perceives us to be. Research has isolated specific behaviors that help a speaker project an image of dynamism:

1. *Eye contact is crucial if you plan to "tell" the audience you are interested in them.* By looking at your listeners, you are making an effort to "connect" with them. This combining of personalities through gaze is part of dynamism.

2. *We all tend to like people whose appearance is suited to the occasion.* We would not have much confidence in a doctor whose lab coat is covered with grime and whose hands are dirty. In the same vein, although wearing jeans, an untucked shirt, and sandals might be appropriate in many places, it is impertinent to wear such attire in a formal situation. In most public-speaking situations, credibility is directly linked to a neatly dressed and well-groomed speaker.

3. *Facial expressions are yet another important measure of credibility.* A great deal of research indicates that a smile is a powerful communication tool. Ask yourself how much more comfortable you feel when someone is wearing a pleasant face instead of a frown.

4. *Enthusiasm in voice and body is perhaps one of the most vivid signs of a speaker who is dynamic.* If your outward expressions are passive, dull, indifferent, and listless, the audience might assume that you are not interested in them or the topic you are discussing. If this is the case, they ask themselves, If you do not believe in yourself or in your arguments, why should I? Enthusiasm also tends to be contagious. If you feel good about yourself, you might even make the audience experience similar feelings about themselves. The appreciation of this sensation could add yet another dimension to your credibility.

5. *Appearing relaxed also helps create a favorable impression.* If you are tense and nervous, the audience is apt to infer that you are not comfortable with your arguments or are not well prepared. As you recall, mannerisms tend to be contagious. If you are uncomfortable, you might make your audience uncomfortable.

Organizing a Persuasive Speech

As far back as the eighth century B.C., the Greek poet Hesiod offered the advice that "it is best to do things systematically, since we are only human, and disorder is our worst enemy."

Because every communication situation is unique, the organizational requirements of one persuasive speech may differ radically from those of another. One may be organized as if it were an informational speech, while another may be an extended narrative. Your good judgment will tell you if a given plan of organization is applicable to the persuasive situation you face.

Most speeches have one structural characteristic in common—they are divided into three parts. Let us explore briefly the principal functions of the introduction, body, and conclusion as they apply to a persuasive speech.

As you know from previous chapters, the basic functions of an *introduction* are to get attention and to prepare the audience for what is to follow. In a persuasive speech, these two functions have to be accomplished in a way that creates a climate of acceptance. If you are going to ask an audience to change or alter a belief ("Dumping of nuclear waste is a serious problem for our city"), or to behave in a different manner ("You should carry a donor card in your wallet"), you must make sure that you establish rapport with the audience at the same time you are arousing interest. It is also wise for a speaker to refrain from assertiveness in the early stages of a persuasive speech, because such behavior may generate suspicion and hostility. Opening in a spirit of inquiry is much less likely to erect barriers. As we indicated, it is also important to affirm your credibility early in your speech, so that you can begin to establish some common ground. If you decide to announce your central point, or core statement, sometime during the introduction, you should consider phrasing it in the form of a question. Compare these two ways of orienting your audience to the nature of your talk:

> "Today, I would like to discuss with you the question, Are prisons justified in a modern society?"

> "Today I will attempt to demonstrate that prisons are not justified in a modern society."

Many experienced speakers find that illustrations (hypothetical or factual), rhetorical questions, and/or startling statements are effective when giving a persuasive speech. Before deciding on an introduction, we would urge you to return to chapter 11 and review some of the techniques we discussed in that chapter.

The *body* of a persuasive speech contains the defense of the persuasive proposition, or core statement. For example, if you are defending a proposition of policy, you will probably offer arguments to show the need for a policy and demonstrate the capacity of your policy to satisfy that need. If you are defending a proposition of fact or value, you will probably offer criteria to measure the truth of the fact or value judgment in question and then apply those criteria.

The *conclusion* of a persuasive speech should place the audience in the state of mind most conducive to the accomplishment of the speaker's purpose. For example, if your purpose is to actuate, the audience should be ready to act. If your purpose is to convince, the audience should be ready to assent. As was the case with the introduction, it would behoove you to return to chapter 11 and review some of the suggestions we offered regarding conclusions.

With these general considerations before us, let us now turn to some specific strategies of design.

In chapter 10, we discussed a number of organizational patterns that can be used when preparing a speech. Let us return to some of these sequences and place them in the context of this chapter.

If you are interested in persuading an audience to implement a specific policy, the problem-solution pattern is very useful. This pattern is one of the simplest outline forms and is based on dividing the body of a speech into three parts. After an introduction designed to gain attention and orient the listeners, the speaker moves into the body of the speech, where he or she (1) presents the problem area, (2) explains the solution to the problem, and (3) defends the solution. The speech concludes with a call for the appropriate belief or action. An example of a proposition of policy structured around the problem-solution order follows:

Problem-Solution Pattern

INTRODUCTION

I.   While driving home from work last Tuesday, I saw a Lincoln Continental plow into a Ford, which spun into a BMW, which ended up halfway underneath a garbage truck.
   A. I stopped my car and went over to help the injured people.
   B. One of those hurt in the accident was our classmate Brenda.
II. The locale of that pileup was Grand and Main, an intersection that has experienced many such accidents.

Core Statement: A left-turn traffic light should be installed at the intersection of Grand and Main.

Body

Problem: I.   The intersection presents the worst traffic problem in town.
Support: A. It is the scene of numerous collisions.
                          1. Evidence.
                          2. Evidence.
Support: B. It is a bottleneck during morning and afternoon rush hours.
                          1. Evidence.
                          2. Evidence.
Cause: II. The cause of this problem is the lack of a left-turn traffic light at the intersection.
Support: A. Cars attempting left turns from Grand onto westbound Main are targets of cars southbound on Grand.
Support: B. Cars waiting to turn left produce a backup of homebound traffic on Grand.

Solution:	III.	A left-turn traffic light would correct the existing problem.
Support:		A. It would minimize collisions.
Support:		B. It would speed northbound traffic on Grand.
Defense:	IV.	A left-turn traffic light would be practical to install.
Support:		A. It would be practical from an engineering standpoint.
		1. Evidence.
		2. Evidence.
Support:		B. It would be practical from a financial standpoint.
		1. Evidence.
		2. Evidence.
Defense:	V.	A left-turn light would not introduce disadvantages.
Support:		A. It would not introduce hazards.
Support:		B. It would not be aesthetically unpleasing.
Defense:	VI.	A left-turn light is the best solution to the problem.
Support:		A. It would be less costly than an overpass.
Support:		B. It would be more convenient than rerouting northbound traffic onto Cisco Avenue.

Conclusion

I. I have attempted to show that a solution to this dangerous traffic condition does exist.

II. You can help this proposal become a reality by signing the petition that I am about to circulate.

III. Perhaps if we had this light a month ago, Brenda might be in class today.

Monroe's Motivated Sequence

This organizational strategy is a variant of the problem-solution order, and as such is useful for speeches that ask the audience to take a specific action. As its name suggests, the motivated sequence has a psychological orientation. That is to say, the motivated sequence seeks to move listeners through a succession of psychological steps. Let us look at the five steps in the sequence (attention, need, satisfaction, visualization, action) to examine the natural progression.

Attention must be a speaker's first concern. Unless the speaker can get the listeners to focus their attention on the speech, all other attempts at persuasion will fail. It is important to remember the audience is most likely thinking about other matters before you begin, so it is crucial to create interest and arouse

General End: To Persuade

Specific Purpose: To encourage people to reduce the size of their lawns.

I. What is it that we enjoy looking at and sitting on that also causes all of us serious problems? Lawns!

attention. Attention can be awakened by using any of the techniques discussed throughout this book (illustration, startling statement, rhetorical question, quotation, etc.)

    A. Lawns occupy more land than any other single crop.
    B. They also use 60 percent of the water in most cities.
    C. And most importantly, we cover them with dangerous chemicals.

The main purpose of the *need* step is to have the audience see that there is a problem that concerns them. There is something wrong with the status quo. In the speech we are analyzing, the speaker will make the listeners aware of the serious health problems associated with pesticides used on lawns. It is here that you employ evidence, arguments, and the motive appeals we discussed earlier. By pointing out that a problem exists, you build a case for the solution you will offer in the next step of the sequence. Again, notice that the need step also illustrates how the problem relates directly to the audience.

II. The abundance of lawns in our city creates serious health problems that affect us all.

    A. Homeowners use ten times more chemical pesticides per acre than farmers.
    B. Some of these pesticides contain poisons that can have harmful effects on humans and pets.

      1. Evidence.
      2. Evidence.

In the *satisfaction* step, you offer, explain, and defend your solution to the problem. You offer support to show it is workable. In this step, you also respond to any objections the audience might have.

III. To deal with this problem, we should limit the area we use for decorative lawns.
    A. This would reduce pesticides.
    B. This would save water.

The *visualization* step projects the listeners into the future, where they are

VI. If we reduce the size of our lawns, our pets and children will not be exposed to enormous amounts of pesticides.

made to picture the solution in operation, especially as the solution personally concerns them. You paint either a positive or negative picture of the future.

The *action* step (your conclusion) calls on the listeners to implement the solution. It should be brief and specific so that the audience will remember the action you want them to take.

A. Imagine looking out the window not worrying if your little boy or girl put their hand in their mouth shortly after playing on the lawn.
B. Also imagine how less stressful it will be if you see your dog licking his or her paw after playing on the lawn.

V. In the coming years, when you design your yards, please try to think small.

Deduction

Earlier in this chapter, we discussed deduction and induction as forms of reasoning. It is not by accident, then, that the two patterns are commonly used in the development of propositions of fact and value.

In *deduction*, the proposition is disclosed prior to the presentation of the materials that support the proposition. For example, if a speaker wishes the audience to agree with the proposition "Our selling used books would be a better fundraiser for our club than a car wash," the speech might be organized in this order:

Introduction

I. By the end of this month, we have to make a decision about our annual fundraiser.
II. There are two alternative fundraisers that are available to us, a used book sale and a car wash.

Body

Core Statement: A used book sale would be a better fundraiser than a car wash.
I. It would involve very little expense because we can all donate books.
II. It would be easier to prepare because we would only have to display the books in front of the fraternity house.
III. It would yield a great profit because both the product and the labor would be free.

Conclusion

I. I hope you will give careful consideration to a used book sale.

Induction

When using *induction* as a mode of organization, a speaker withholds disclosure of the proposition (core statement) until after presenting the materials supporting the proposition. Using the same proposition that we just used, "A used book sale would be a better fundraiser than a car wash," the inductive order of presentation might appear this way:

Introduction

I. By the end of this month, we have to make a decision about our annual fundraiser.

Body

I. The fundraiser we choose should have these qualities:
   A. It should involve minimal expense.
   B. It should be easy to prepare.
   C. It should yield a profit.
II. We have two alternatives from which to choose.
   A. A used book sale.
   B. A car wash.
III. A used book sale has these merits:
   A. It involves less expense.
   B. It is easier to prepare.
   C. It yields a greater profit.

Core Statement: A used book sale would be a better fundraiser than a car wash.

Conclusion

I. I hope you will give careful consideration to a used book sale.

When choosing between deductive order and inductive order, a speaker should be guided by his or her knowledge of the audience's predispositions. If the speaker feels the direct approach exemplified by the deductive order would make the audience defensive, then the speaker should choose the inductive order. However, there are occasions when the direct approach is preferred. For example, if two speakers are debating a proposition of fact or value, the audience might view a late disclosure of position as ridiculous.

Behavioral scientists have attempted to answer the persistent questions of organization strategy. Of particular interest to students of persuasion are scientists' tentative answers to the following questions.

Considerations for Idea Placement

Does an argument exert a more lasting influence if it is heard first or heard last in a series of arguments? If the audience is familiar with the issue or if it is involved in the controversy, say scientists, it is influenced more by the argument heard first. If the audience is disinterested or if it is relatively uninformed about the issue prior to hearing the arguments, it is influenced more by the argument heard last. Regardless of where you place your strongest arguments, it is absolutely essential that you conclude your speech by reminding your audience of the specific action you wish it to take.

When both sides of a controversy are presented in succession, will the side presented first or the side presented last be in the more advantageous position? Some studies have concluded that the side presented first has the "natural" advantage. Other studies, however, have been inconclusive. Therefore, what is needed, as always, is detailed audience analysis.

Are attempts to persuade helped or hindered when "the other side" is presented as well as the speaker's own side? It is usually a good idea to discuss opposing views. In most instances, the listeners will have these assessments in their minds and you might as well treat them as part of your approach. In addition, if the listeners are initially opposed to the speaker's position, the stratagem exerts a persuasive effect.

Is it more effective to imply the conclusion one wishes the audience to accept or to state it explicitly? Research indicates that an explicit statement exerts a more persuasive effect on the majority of listeners. In short, you should not keep the audience guessing about your solution to the problem you have outlined.

Remember that the foregoing answers are tentative. Many variables operate in any communication situation; it is virtually impossible to design an experiment that will take them all into account.

Culture and Persuasion

Although we have alluded to the issue of culture throughout this chapter, it is now time for us to examine this important topic in more detail. Specifically, let us explore the ways in which culture influences the three dimensions of persuasion that we discussed earlier in the chapter: (1) convincing arguments, (2) impelling psychological appeals, and (3) personal credibility.

Culture and Convincing Arguments

There has, for centuries, been in the West a long history of public debate. Many of the early democracies of Greece and Rome were built on the traditions of argumentation and persuasion. Even today, Western cultures believe that the best methods for persuasion demand the use of sound arguments and the application of reliable evidence. Both of these areas (reasoning and evidence) have an intercultural element. In chapter 6, when we examined the forms of support, we noted that there were no culturally agreed upon standards for what was considered concrete evidence. You will recall that some cultures favor stories, allegories, analogies, and parables (Latin American, Arab, Native American). Members of these cultures have long believed that stories are a powerful form of evidence. In other cultures, the people prefer concrete data (German, English, North American). We also explored cultural idiosyncrasies with regard to what constitutes a reliable source. In one culture, an authority is someone associated with religion, while in another the authority is the oldest person or the one with the most education. In cultures that do not have a long tradition of a free and open press (Chinese, African, Russian), even the citing of so-called reliable sources does not have the impact it does with an audience composed of only members of the North American culture.

There are also cultural differences in the amount of evidence that people from various cultures expect. Cultures that emphasize logic (European, North American), and deemphasize feelings and emotions, anticipate that a persuasive speaker will offer a great deal of evidence to support his or her claims. In cultures that show feelings and are more emotional (Latin, African, Arab), less evidence and more motive appeals might be the rule.

The mental processes of reasoning prevalent in a community is another major characteristic of culture that often influences the persuasive process. If you are a North American speaker, and you use the deductive method of reasoning to make your case, and you are interacting with someone who usually uses the inductive method (as in the case of the Korean culture), you are apt to have a major misunderstanding when you finally reach your conclusion. You are moving from broad categories to specific examples that most likely rely on "facts," while many people from Korea start with specific observations and eventually extract generalizations.

There are also differences when we compare the use of deduction and induction in North America with the methods found in much of the Arab world. Because the Arab language tends to combine ideas with the use of conjunctions, speakers using this language do not always place their main points where non-Arabs would expect them. And conversely, Arabs often have difficulty with Western forms of linear thinking.

Western thought and reasoning patterns are often difficult for other cultures in that they also assume a direct relationship between mental concepts and the concrete world of reality. This orientation places great stock on logic and rationality. Most Westerners believe that truth is "out there" and that it can be discovered by following scientific methods and engaging in logical, linear calculations. The Eastern view, best illustrated by Taoist, Buddhist, and Zen thought, holds that reasoning works quite differently. To begin with, people are not granted instant rationality. In fact, there is even a strong belief that intuition transcends the data of the senses. People that hold this view do not believe that one finds truth through active searching, talk, and the application of Aristotelian modes of reasoning. On the contrary, one had best wait and be patient, and if truth is to be known, it will make itself apparent.

Cultures differ in both the amount of emotional appeals they find appropriate and the content of those appeals. We just finished reminding you that some cultures rely on linear logic and "facts," while others are more comfortable focusing on people and their feelings. Italians, Portuguese, Arabs, and Mexicans believe that sincere and emotional feelings transcend rigid syllogisms and tangible facts. Conversely, some people in the Western culture believe that persuasion rooted in emotional appeals alone should be avoided. In fact, since the time of the early Greek and Roman philosophers, people have been warned to be leery of the sophist. This view often clashes with cultures that appreciate a speaker with a rhetorical flair. Therefore, in selecting your specific motive appeals, you must analyze your audience to discover its cultural composition.

As you saw when we discussed attitudes, beliefs, and values earlier in this chapter, not all cultures perceive the world in the same manner. As such, what appeals to one culture may not inspire another. For one culture, appeals that center on material possessions might be effective, yet that same plea would not work with cultures that value a spiritual life over the acquisition of property. Some cultures value modesty (Japan, China, etc.) and would find your resorting to sexual appeals somewhat offensive. Even linking your message to fear should be carefully analyzed if your audience is culturally mixed. Some cultures tend to be apprehensive about the future and the uncertainty of life (Japanese, Greek, French), while others usually do not find the ambiguity of life the least bit frightening (North American, Danish, Swedish, English). You need to learn all you can about the cultural characteristics of the members of your audience when deciding if you should use motive appeals and how to make those you select compelling and forceful.

Culture and Psychological Appeals

As we have seen, the traits of credibility we have discussed are from the perspective of North American listeners. Other types of behavior are prized by listeners of other cultures. The people of Japan, China, and other Asian cultures tend to look favorably on the speaker of few words, since such behavior is taken to indicate that the speaker is reflective. There is even a Japanese proverb that says, "He who speaks has no knowledge and he who has knowledge does not speak." Most Asian listeners are leery of speakers

Culture and Personal Credibility

who are wordy, impulsive, or assertive. Although self-disclosure is regarded favorably by North American listeners, it is viewed as a breach of good taste by German and Japanese audiences. Jewish, Mexican, and Greek cultures expect speakers to be very animated and emotional in their visual and vocal mannerisms. To be otherwise is to be suspected of lack of conviction. As we pointed out in chapter 12, Arab cultures deem it important for speakers to use a great deal of embellishment in their language, so a speaker addressing an Arab audience would probably make greater use of metaphors and similes than would a speaker addressing an American audience. In many cultures (Latin America, Asia, Germany, etc.), a speaker's status and reputation influence the development of credibility.

Persuasion and Ethics

We have attempted throughout this book to weave the topic of ethics in and out of every chapter. The subject of persuasion is no exception, because the very core of persuasion is change—you are asking someone to think and act differently. Let us suggest five questions you should ask yourself as a way of determining if you are being ethical in your treatment of your material.

1. *Who will benefit from my persuasive speech?* The implications to this question are obvious. Are *you* the only one who will profit from the changes you are asking of your listeners, or will they also benefit if you accomplish your specific purpose? Asking someone to buy a product that they do not need, but will make you a great deal of money, is an example of persuasion with selfish ends. Consider how much you would resent a speaker who led you to think that you would benefit from signing a petition against a new walking trail, when in reality the speaker only wanted your signature because the public trail would pass directly in front of his or her house. Concealing your persuasive intent is both insulting and unethical. The ethical speaker makes his or her motives very clear. They will even tell their audience that there might be a second side to the issues being discussed.

2. *Am I using inflammatory language to help accomplish my purpose?* We defined what we meant by inflammatory language in chapter 12. We now simply remind you that language is a powerful tool that can be used for good or for evil. So ask yourself if you are avoiding the real issues in the case and appealing to a lower level of reasoning by using emotional words and phrases such as "male chauvinist pig," "right winger," "red-neck racist," or "practicing feminist." We should never, as the French essayist Voltaire advised us, "use words to hide our thoughts."

3. *Am I misusing fear appeals?* The improper use of fear appeals can take a variety of forms. In many persuasive situations, speakers use fear appeals to replace rather than augment concrete evidence. There is nothing inherently wrong with legitimately using fear to accomplish your purpose. Showing people, through the use of vivid word pictures, the dangers of smoking, the hazards of drinking and driving, or the results of unsafe sex, is not an unethical act if such fear appeals were accompanied by other material (statistics, expert testimony, and the like). In addition, you must be careful that your fear appeals do not involve exaggerated claims. For example, to tell people that *everyone* who smokes dies a horrible and painful death would be a major exaggeration.

4. *Am I cognizant of the specific composition of my audience?* This means that a speaker knows the makeup of the audience, but ignores the information and chooses to be unethical. For example, if you are talking to very young children, who might be impressionable, it would be unethical to ask them to make decisions that demand maturity beyond their years. Every Christmas, dishonest advertisers encourage children, when their parents are not at home, to call a 900 number and "talk to Santa Claus." Such persuasion attempts are both dishonest and unethical.

5. Perhaps in deciding on your ethical stance you might ask yourself this final question: *Would I like to be treated in the same manner I am going to treat my audience?* For most of us that sentence has a familiar ring to it. It is a paraphrase of one of the most quoted passages from the Bible. Actually, the admonition is "Do to others what you would have them do to you." What is so intriguing about this ethical decree is that it is found in every religious tradition. Whether it be Hinduism, Buddhism, Islam, Judaism, or Christianity, the message is the same, and one worth repeating as we conclude our section on ethics—**regard others as you would like to be regarded.**

Summary

Persuasion is the process of inducing willing changes in a listener's beliefs, attitudes, values, and behavior. Successful persuasion rests on a thorough knowledge of the audience and its attitudes toward the speech topic, the speech purpose, and the speaker. The objects of change are the listeners' learned predispositions, convictions, and manifest behavior—particularly with respect to issues of policy, fact, and value. A speaker's position should rest on a knowledge of the audience's thinking about the subject.

The means of persuasion, according to rhetorical tradition and modern social psychology, lies in logical appeals, psychological appeals, and the listeners' perception of the speaker's personal credibility. The constituents of logical persuasion are evidence and reasoning. Evidence should be derived from an authoritative source, fairly presented, recent, and capable of corroboration. Reasoning takes four forms, according to the traditional view. Deductive reasoning moves from a general rule, or axiom, to the specific case at hand. Inductive reasoning proceeds from particular cases to a generalization about all cases. Reasoning from analogy is based on the supposition that, because two things are alike in certain known respects, they will also be alike in the point at issue. Causal reasoning may appear in at least three forms—cause to effect, effect to cause, and effect to effect.

Persuasion through psychological appeals traditionally is thought to involve the use of motivation and suggestion. The needs and wants to which the speaker may link the message include self-preservation, sex attraction, acquisition of property, self-esteem, personal enjoyment, loyalty, individualism, curiosity, imitation, and altruism. Suggestion is the arousal of a response by indirect means. It may operate through channels external to the speaker, through the speaker's delivery, and through the verbal message.

Persuasion through personal credibility is possible when a speaker manifests poise, modesty, moderation, tact, goodwill, common sense, reliability, honesty, friendliness, sincerity, enthusiasm, and genuine concern for the listeners' welfare—provided they perceive these factors.

Although a persuasive speech can be organized in a variety of ways, certain methods seem to enjoy high popularity. The problem-solution order and the motivated sequence are particularly appropriate for developing propositions of policy. Deductive order and inductive order are among the patterns well suited to developing propositions of fact and value.

To be successful as a persuasive speaker, it is essential for you to understand the role of culture in persuasion. Culture will influence the arguments you use, your selection of motive appeals, and how the audience perceives your credibility.

Finally, you must consider the ethical ramifications each time you appeal to an audience to change their belief system and/or the way they behave. The best, and in some ways the simplest, ethical rule to apply is the one that asks you to put yourself in the place of the audience. Would you be willing to have someone persuade you by using the same techniques you are applying to your audience?

Part IV
CHANGING ENVIRONMENTS

Circumstances alter cases.

T. C. Haliburton

Chapter 15

Special Occasions
The Unique Communication Situation

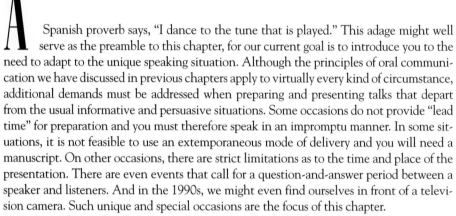

All things good which exist are the fruits of originality.

John Stuart Mill

Spanish proverb says, "I dance to the tune that is played." This adage might well serve as the preamble to this chapter, for our current goal is to introduce you to the need to adapt to the unique speaking situation. Although the principles of oral communication we have discussed in previous chapters apply to virtually every kind of circumstance, additional demands must be addressed when preparing and presenting talks that depart from the usual informative and persuasive situations. Some occasions do not provide "lead time" for preparation and you must therefore speak in an impromptu manner. In some situations, it is not feasible to use an extemporaneous mode of delivery and you will need a manuscript. On other occasions, there are strict limitations as to the time and place of the presentation. There are even events that call for a question-and-answer period between a speaker and listeners. And in the 1990s, we might even find ourselves in front of a television camera. Such unique and special occasions are the focus of this chapter.

As we begin this chapter, it is important to keep in mind that one of the attributes of a highly successful public speaker is an ability to adjust to any predicament. There is a story of how Teddy Roosevelt was shot in the chest in an assassination attempt and uttered the words, "I will deliver this speech or die, one or the other." This story, although somewhat theatrical, does make the point that adapting and modifying your message is important. Any successful communicator must be prepared when called upon to deal with the following six speaking occasions: (1) *impromptu speeches*, (2) *manuscript speeches*, (3) *entertaining speeches*, (4) *speeches before television cameras*, (5) *speeches of introduction*, and (6) *occasions when they are asked questions from the audience during or after a speech*. We shall examine each of these unique communication situations.

Impromptu Speech

One of the questions that students tend to ask on the first day of speech class is, "Will there be any impromptu speeches?" While there are probably some students who actually hope for impromptu speeches because virtually no preparation is involved, there are more who fear being called on suddenly to "make a few remarks." To be asked to give a speech on the spur of the moment is often unnerving, in spite of the fact that we do a lot of impromptu talking every day and are not troubled about it. If you were to analyze your normal conversations, you would probably find that they are spontaneous responses to another person's equally spontaneous remarks. Why is it that we fear making an impromptu speech? Probably because we think people expect more from a public speaker than they do from a private conversation. How, then, do we cope with that dreaded "Why don't you come up here and say a few words to our audience?" The answer to that question will be the focus of the next section of this chapter.

Someone once said that the great orator Winston Churchill had devoted the best years of his life to preparing his impromptu speeches. This simply means that, like all good speakers, he knew that his past experiences had prepared him to talk on almost any topic. Hence, the first thing that should cross your mind when confronted with an impromptu event is that *your memory contains countless pieces of knowledge and millions of experiences that can serve as the keystone of an impromptu talk.* You are your own private encyclopedia; open up the "pages" and you are apt to be surprised and pleased with what you find. As Ralph Waldo Emerson wrote, "Wherever we go, whatever we do, self is the sole subject we study and learn."

The second step in preparing for an impromptu situation is to *adopt a positive mental attitude toward the impromptu event.* Keep in mind that those who ask you to speak impromptu do not really expect a polished oration; your listeners' expectations are not as demanding as they would be under different circumstances. Your listeners are probably more concerned with hearing your off-the-cuff remarks about the subject than they are about watching a display of oratorical brilliance.

Consider, too, that, when someone asks you to speak on the spur of the moment, that person feels you are knowledgeable about the topic. Otherwise, why would your impromptu remarks be solicited?

Try to anticipate an "unexpected" request. Pay close attention to what is going on at a conference, dinner, or meeting you are attending. Listen to what is being said by others. Often, you can build on their remarks when you are called on to speak. Avoid daydreaming so that you can spare yourself the embarrassment that can occur when you are unexpectedly asked to speak. Listening is a part of the preparation for any speech and especially so for an impromptu speech.

Once you are called on to speak, *make good use of the time interval prior to your first words.* Although this time may range only from a few seconds to a minute or so, it can still be put to good use.

Try to formulate a central point around which you can build your remarks. Perhaps you can build on what a previous speaker has said—for instance, "Tom is absolutely right, and I'd like to add a few observations of my own." Perhaps you disagree with remarks that have been made and can build your speech around the reasons for disagreement: "I'm afraid I'm going to have to take issue with my friend's arguments on at least three counts." If you happen to be the first speaker (or the only speaker), then you might design a speech that answers one or more of the following questions about the topic you have been given: *What* is it? *Who* is connected with it? *Where* can it be found? *When* did it come into being? *Why* should I be concerned about it? *How* can I deal with it? Needless to say, many other questions might apply, each of which could provide a central point around which to build your speech. *The important thing is to try to find a unifying theme and then stick to it.*

Once you have arrived at a central point for your speech, *select an organizational pattern that will let you develop that central point.* Following are six commonly used patterns:

1. Refer to what has been said by a previous speaker. State your position on the issue. Develop your position by an illustration, an analogy, or any appropriate form of support. Summarize what you have said and sit down.

   I. John said that there is no solution to the high cost of medical bills in our country.

      II. I believe he is wrong.

        A. We need only look at what Hawaii, Oregon, and California have done to control cost.

          1. Hawaii

          2. Oregon

          3. California

     III. In short, although I respect John's views, we have seen that there are some possible solutions to the health-care problem if we just turn to what some of the states have done.

2. Start with an illustration. Draw a central point out of that illustration. Add additional support to your central point and conclude.

       I. Last week, I drove home in the rain.

        A. A car came directly at me.

        B. As I started to move out of the way, my brakes locked.

        C. I started to skid out of control.

        D. Luckily, I hit a soft embankment.

      II. As I started to talk to people, I discovered that skidding is a common problem.

     III. I also discovered that skidding in the rain can be avoided with an antilock braking system.

3. State a proposal. Tell your audience why it is important. Then explain the proposal.

       I. I believe body transplants are important.

      II. They give people who are still living a chance for life.

     III. One dead body can produce many essential body parts.

        A. One heart

        B. Two lungs

        C. Two kidneys

        D. One pancreas

4. Develop your theme chronologically.

       I. Glycol ether exposure on the job first became a serious problem in 1996, when a study of nine hundred painters at a plant in Connecticut developed serious blood disorders.

      II. A recent three-year study showed a 40 percent increase in miscarriages among women exposed to glycol ether on the job.

5. Develop your theme according to spatial or geographical considerations.

       I. The war in the gulf had an impact on Europe.

      II. The war in the gulf had an impact on the Middle East.

     III. The war in the gulf had an impact on the United States.

6. Divide the topic into components, such as economic, social, and political aspects or mental, moral, and physical aspects.

       I. What are the implications of breast implants?

        A. Emotional implications

        B. Physical implications

        C. Cultural implications

    A review of the organizational patterns presented in chapter 10, as well as the informative and persuasive patterns discussed in chapters 13 and 14, will suggest a variety of ways to put together a coherent message.

Be brief! Your listeners realize you did not have long to prepare, and are therefore not expecting a long dissertation. Remember the sound advice offered by a French philosopher over two hundred years ago: "All pleasantry should be short; and it might even be as well were the serious short as well."

Try to have an introduction so you do not have to hurry into the main part of your presentation. This will give you valuable time to think of what to say and will help you relax and gain your composure.

Do not apologize. Although an apology might be appropriate in the Japanese culture, in the North American culture it often seems insincere and lowers a speaker's credibility.

Do not prolong your conclusion. Too many impromptu speeches end on a note of apology or embarrassment. Why not simply summarize what you have said, restate your central point, and sit down? You might even find it helpful to plan your last line before you start talking. This will keep you from having an awkward moment as you attempt to end your remarks.

Practice making impromptu speeches. The ability to cope with an impromptu speaking situation can be greatly improved if you are willing to practice. One good method is to read the editorial page of your local paper and frame a reaction to each editorial or letter to the editor dealing with subjects about which you feel strongly. Valuable, too, are speeches you can build around a word or phrase such as sexism, integrity in public office, consumerism, business ethics, global economy, and military alliances.

Other tools of improvement are books of quotations and anecdotes. Try to master a few interesting and generic citations and stories that can be used on almost any occasion. Having a storehouse of engrossing material will not only help your speech, but knowing that you tucked away some good information will help you relax when you are called on to give an impromptu talk.

Manuscript Speech

In chapter 2, we discussed speaking from a manuscript and examined some of the disadvantages of this form of public speaking. There are many cases, however, in which a manuscript speech is highly useful. If you watch the president delivering the annual "State of the Union" address, you will be aware that the speech is being read. If you attend a professional convention, you will witness speeches being presented from manuscript. At important business meetings, reports are frequently read aloud. If you have observed the proceedings of a local government agency, you have seen people read their written responses to an important issue being considered by the elected officials. Manuscript speeches are also useful when the exact timing of the speech is important. In fact, there are many occasions when a speaker can benefit from a "polished" speech, in which every word is carefully crafted and selected for accuracy and effect. In addition, many people who have English as a second language often feel more comfortable reading their speeches instead of having to think about selecting the right word on the spur of the moment. To derive the optimal benefit from a manuscript speech, certain considerations of preparation and presentation need to be taken into account.

Preparing a Manuscript Speech

An occasion that calls for a manuscript speech is usually a very special one. Accordingly, most speakers are willing to put a great deal of energy into the preparation of their manuscripts. The following sequence, although somewhat time consuming, is helpful in preparing a manuscript.

Begin by going through many of the same steps we discussed in chapter 1, in the section titled "Organizing Ideas." After addressing questions of purpose, audience analysis, and analysis of the occasion, begin developing an outline. An outline for a manuscript, like an outline for an extemporaneous speech, should be concerned with matters such as the introduction, body, and conclusion.

Once you have researched and completed an outline, you are ready to write your first draft of the manuscript. Because written language is somewhat different from spoken language, you should try to keep some of the following ideas in mind so that your manuscript will sound more like spoken language than written. First, *use short and simple words and sentences*. Most of our conversations use natural, comfortable language. The same should be true of a manuscript speech, even though it is in written form. This does not mean that you should avoid eloquent vocabulary. It means that you must keep in mind that you are writing a speech, not an essay. Second, as we have seen throughout this book, transitions are important in oral discourse. Therefore, when writing a speech, *use many transitions, internal summaries, and other techniques that contribute to clarity.* Finally, *use personal pronouns to draw your listeners into the speech.* In writing, we often remove the personal aspect of the communication event. Don't let this happen. Again, you need to realize you are engaged in an oral exchange, even though you are reading.

After reading the first draft aloud, you will want to make changes. Many sections that would be acceptable in an essay are ineffective when read aloud. Recording your talk or having a friend listen to an early draft of the speech is also valuable.

Once you have made the necessary corrections and additions, you should have a well-written and highly polished speech. The manuscript from which you read can be made even more useful by following a few simple guidelines: (1) use stiff paper; (2) write on only one side of the paper; (3) number the pages; (4) type the manuscript, using triple spacing; (5) use short paragraphs—they are easier to locate when you return to the manuscript after establishing and maintaining eye contact; and (6) use a fresh ribbon in your typewriter or computer printer—dull or faded print is difficult to read.

Practice speaking from the final draft a number of times so that you become familiar with the material and develop dexterity in handling the paper. You might also find it helpful to mark the manuscript where you want to pause or add vocal emphasis and variety. You should also add a note or two on the manuscript that simply says EYE CONTACT. This will remind you to look at the audience as well as your manuscript.

Delivering a Manuscript Speech

The principles of good delivery discussed in chapter 4 also apply to manuscript delivery, as well as these practices unique to manuscript delivery:

1. *Do not try to conceal the manuscript.* Many speakers have tried to feign total spontaneity, only to discover that such deception works against them. In addition to having trouble locating their places in the speech, they incur audience displeasure at being deceived.

2. *Establish and maintain eye contact.* The fact that you are speaking from a manuscript should in no way detract from your initiating and maintaining rapport with the audience. Eye contact can be fostered by becoming very familiar with your speech.

3. *Concentrate on ideas rather than words.* Keep in mind that it is a speech you are delivering. If you start to read every word and forget the influence of ideas, you will no longer have the unique effect of speech communication.

4. *Be animated in both voice and body.* There is nothing inherent in a manuscript that stifles delivery. From correct posture, to vocal variety, to sincere and enthusiastic gestures, the manuscript speech demands good delivery.

Entertaining Speech

We need only look at the TV evening news or the daily newspaper to know that life is full of troubling and complex issues. Our personal life can also offer countless examples of the often difficult nature of modern existence. It is no wonder that all of us like entertainment and humor to relieve some of the tensions of life and to add pleasure to daily activity. This was true even in ancient Greece, as Plato once noted, "Even the gods love their jokes." It is often a public speaker who supplies the jokes and the entertainment.

Many occasions call for a speech to entertain. You may be familiar with after-dinner speeches (although they are often after breakfast or lunch), in which the objective is to help the audience relax in a lighthearted mood. Possibly, you belong to a club or an organization that will have occasional meetings of a purely social nature, where speeches will provide part of the entertainment. Maybe you will be asked to talk about an interesting experience you have had, to tell about a celebrity you have met, or to take part in "roasting" a fellow club member. Perhaps you will be allowed to choose your own entertaining topic, or you might decide that your speech to persuade or inform would be more effective if you were to incorporate some entertaining aspects. Regardless of the specific circumstance, the speech to entertain is a common form of public and private address.

Characteristics of Entertaining

A speech to entertain can be humorous, but not all speeches to entertain need to be funny. The one basic requirement for all speeches of entertainment is that they must hold attention and interest in themselves. A speaker can best accomplish this objective by incorporating into the speech many of the factors of attention and interest discussed in chapter 13. Attention can be gained and held by imparting action and using illustrations and humor. Some additional characteristics of a speech to entertain are as follows:

1. *The delivery should be lively, enthusiastic, and animated.* If the speech is delivered in an extemporaneous manner, it will sound more natural.

2. *As we have already seen, stories, illustrations, and humorous anecdotes are liberally used.* A fully developed example is often so vivid that it captures and maintains attention. Remember, these illustrations should be fresh and free from triteness.

3. *Like all speeches, a speech to entertain is well organized, easy to follow, and usually constructed around a central theme or idea.* The theme often deals with a common topic in a novel manner. For example, the problems of eating three meals a day while orbiting the earth in a space shuttle would make a good entertaining speech.

4. *The response sought is usually immediate and momentary.* The audience may remember some of the information long after the speech, but the speaker's primary concern is the audience's response at the time of the talk.

5. *The audience needs to be considered during all phases of an entertaining speech.* It is easy when using humor to forget that not all people see a situation in exactly the same way. Hence, audience analysis takes on special meaning when you are preparing and delivering an entertaining talk. Try to remember the importance of being tactful. Don't embarrass or ridicule any segment of the audience.

6. *The general mood of an entertaining speech should be "upbeat" and genial.* Pessimism, bitterness, gloom, and denunciation are out of place in a speech to entertain.

7. *In selecting a topic, try to avoid subjects that are too controversial or weighty.* People do not want to hear serious talk about your religious beliefs or your view of capital punishment if they have come to be entertained.

Using Humor

The French philosopher Sébastien Roch Nicolas Chamfort wrote that "the most wasted day of all is that on which we have not laughed." Although this counsel might be slightly overstated, it nevertheless reminds us of the important role humor and laughter play in our lives. Although this section of the book examines speeches to entertain, much of the advice about using humor can be applied to all forms of speech making. That is to say, *regardless of the type of speech you are giving, humor can be very useful.*

Elements of Humor

As we noted elsewhere, humor is universal—it is a common language; the whole world likes to laugh. Humor is the mainstay of the majority of entertaining speeches. It holds our attention and, if properly used, creates an enjoyable and friendly atmosphere. In some respects, however, it is one of the most unpredictable devices a speaker can use, because a favorable audience response depends on so many variables. If the humor is dependent on adroit timing, then woe to a speaker whose timing is off. If the humor is topical and the audience is not up-to-date in its knowledge of current happenings, then the humor backfires. All of us have had experience with telling a joke that "went over like a lead balloon." We are confronted with the same problem that has faced speakers for centuries: what makes audiences laugh?

Exaggeration (overstatement)   A circumstance deliberately overstated is a potentially humorous situation. As long as the exaggeration maintains a semblance of reality, then the audience can enjoy what it knows is an obvious, intentional distortion. To describe an egg fight in terms usually reserved for describing an epic battle between mighty nations would be perceived as obvious exaggeration (and, if all goes well, as something humorous). Whole speeches have been devoted to recounting a mundane event as though it were a major moment in history. You can even take a common occurrence, such as automobile traffic, and make it humorous. Think for a moment of the potential for exaggeration as you talk about, in detail, the traffic congestion in your town by noting that the situation is so bad that most people not only have car phones, but also cooking and toilet facilities in their cars. Exaggeration as humor can even be concise. One speaker, talking about people being bored during his speech, said: "I do not object to people looking at their watches when I am speaking— but I strongly object when they all start shaking them to make certain they are still running." Another speaker used exaggeration when she remarked that "Lottery prizes were getting out of sight. First prize in the California lottery is now Arizona." If you have ever watched any of the celebrity "roasts" on television, you probably recall that one of the tactics used by the roasters is to embellish a minor failing of the roastee and make it sound downright calamitous.

Incongruity   A piece of chocolate cake topped with anchovies makes a ludicrous combination; the two foods are hardly "right for one another." In a literal sense, incongruity is present in any situation in which the parts do not fit together. The unusual, the sudden, an unexpected twist, and the inconsistent are all potential sources of humor. The notion that England's Queen Mother might say to a royal gathering, "Hey, let's party!" strikes one as incongruous. Similarly, a speaker would use incongruity if he or she were to describe the courtship of a buzzard and a bird of paradise. The casual mixing of the exotic and the ordinary, the timid and the boisterous, the vulgar and the refined is always incongruous and usually amusing.

Offending Authority   All of us seem to enjoy seeing figures of authority made the targets of jokes. A boss, political leader, bureaucrat, or teacher are popular choices for a good-natured "assault." Think for a moment of the subtle humor contained in the simple line "It is good we have four years between elections; it takes us that long to forget the promises the politicians made and forgot to keep." Even good-natured jokes about ministers and priests are examples of having fun at the expense of someone or something normally regarded with respect and reverence. Most of your audience could relate to the following joke because it has fun at the expense of an authority figure:

> A preacher observed a young boy sleeping during his sermon, so he asked the boy's mother to please wake him. The boy's mother replied, "Sir, it would be fitting if you were to wake him up yourself; you put him to sleep."

Sarcasm   Following is a joke that some say was first told in 413 B.C.:

> A barber, talkative like the rest of his profession, asked King Archelaus how he would like his hair cut. "In silence," replied the king.

One reason this joke might have lasted so long is because, if handled with tact, sarcasm is an excellent source of humor. Think of the wit and sarcasm if someone was to offer the following story of one of their professors:

> My history professor really trusted us not to cheat on examinations. Once he came into class and announced that the exam would be conducted on the honor system so we should all take seats five seats apart from each other and in alternate rows.

Sarcasm has the added advantage of being able to make a point while it entertains. Notice in the following example how a speaker, talking to a women's group, used humor and sarcasm to deal with a common misconception:

Famous British actress Beatrice Campbell was once asked by a rather pompous gentleman why some women were so devoid of any sense of humor. She replied, without skipping a beat, "God did it on purpose so that we may try to love men instead of spending our life laughing at them."

Yet another speaker made effective use of sarcasm when called on to introduce a friend at the end of his after-dinner speech. He told the audience, "We have been eating and giving our full attention to a turkey stuffed with sage; now it is time to listen to a sage stuffed with turkey."

Again, although sarcasm is often a good source of humor, be sure that it is gentle, not cruel.

Human Predicaments   Experiences that are common to all of us can also be a reference point for humor. A speaker gave an entertaining speech with the theme of how poor service has become in the United States. To make one of her points, she told the following joke:

> Good service is so hard to get now that a friend of mine sent a collection agency only half of a ripped check for payment on his newspaper subscription renewal. He also included a note that said, "The other half of this check is somewhere in the bushes in my yard, where half of my papers end up each month."

Another speaker used common predicaments in a speech to stress how we are all becoming victims of the electronic age. Specifically, she told the following story to demonstrate one of the curses of electronic phone systems:

> Recently, I was on the phone for what seemed like an eternity, while this electronic voice moved me through countless recordings and numerous push-button assignments. I became so frustrated with the entire procedure that, when a real voice finally arrived on the phone and asked for my account number, I responded by saying, "please press one." I hope they got my message.

Don't be afraid to laugh at yourself. Using ourselves as the point of humor often establishes rapport with the audience.

Humor and Culture

As we have noted elsewhere, a careful analysis of your listeners is necessary before you launch a humorous attack against one of their authority figures. You do not want to trespass their boundaries of good taste or offend their morals or standards in any way. You are not a nightclub performer or a professional comedian. Therefore, there is no need for vulgarity or obscenity.

The author Virginia Woolf wrote, "Humor is the first of the gifts to perish in a foreign tongue." Her astute observation might well serve as a warning to all of us who attempt humor when speaking to a culturally diverse audience. We have already seen that laughter is universal, so do not avoid using humor when your listeners come from dissimilar backgrounds; *however, do become aware of two cultural issues that can affect your attempts at being entertaining.*

First, as we have discussed elsewhere, there might be language problems that affect the impact of your joke. For example, much of North American humor uses idioms. Imagine what would happen if you were speaking to an audience in which most of the members had English as a second language and, at the end of your joke, you were to say, "So you can see he was a real couch potato." What do you think would be the reaction if, as part of your humor, you were to say, "They just didn't stop bugging me"?

A second potential problem in cross-cultural humor relates to our earlier discussion of what is deemed an appropriate topic for humor in each culture. In one culture, jokes about the elderly, status differences, and religion might not be offensive, yet to many cultures these are sacred subjects. Even using animals as sources of humor shifts from culture to culture. What is most important is that you do a thorough audience analysis before you select your jokes or humorous examples.

As we have noted, the primary consideration in developing an entertaining speech is knowing the exact makeup of the audience. In addition, your audience analysis should include some information on the occasion. It is important to know if the audience came only to listen to you, if they came to laugh, or if they expect some concrete information to take home. Once these questions have been answered, you are ready to determine the central theme and to decide on an introduction, an organizational pattern for the body, and a conclusion.

Developing an Entertaining Speech

Introduction

Your opening remarks in an entertaining speech have the task of arousing attention, setting the mood, and establishing the main point. In a speech to entertain, you must make it clear that you do not plan to develop any profound concepts, for, if the audience expects you to "get somewhere," they will be confused as you continue to provide only entertainment.

The rhetorical question is often a good technique to start a speech that seeks to entertain. If it is startling enough, it can readily capture attention. Imagine how your attention would be aroused if you heard an introduction that asked this rhetorical question: "How many realize that someone has been following your every move this week and recording it with a video camera?"

Body

When choosing your speech plan, or approach, you must keep in mind the nature of the audience, the occasion, and your speaking talent and limitations. There are endless varieties in the organization of a speech to entertain. A topical order or a chronological order is especially appropriate.

A single, long narrative is a popular device in entertaining. As we noted in chapter 6, a narrative, when presented as an illustration, holds attention, makes a point, and is interesting. A good narrative tells a story; for an entertaining speech, the story should be humorous. One student told the story of how her wedding was plagued by one unforeseen disaster after another.

You can use a series of short narratives developed around a central theme. A series illustrating registration problems in college is an example of this approach. In any case, a speech to entertain should not lead in many different directions but should be built around a central theme. Remember also that interest may be derived from associating your ideas with things that are recent, impending, physically near, familiar, vital, active, unusual, suspenseful, concrete, real, humorous, or conflicting.

Descriptions also can be used in the body of the speech to entertain. A student who had worked as a chef at a famous restaurant described, in rather humorous terms, what went on "behind the scenes" in the kitchen.

Conclusion   The conclusion is usually very brief and continues to carry the robust and cheerful mood that was maintained throughout the speech. Specific devices for concluding were discussed in chapter 11 and should be reviewed as a means of determining which technique best applies to the specific communication situation you face.

Television Speech

The Wall Street Journal noted that "if you are thirty years in business or the professions, the chances of your avoiding an appearance on television are nearly zero." Appearing on television is no longer the exclusive domain of professional broadcasters. For a long time, we tended to think of ourselves primarily as receivers of televised messages. We used to believe that we simply would sit and have television do something to us. However, the role and use of television in our culture have changed drastically. We are becoming senders as well as receivers. In short, in the 1990s, regardless of our professions, we are becoming users of television as well as its consumers. In both our private and professional lives, we are finding ourselves in front of television cameras. We will all engage in mediated events sooner or later, such as videotaped events in classrooms or courtrooms, or perhaps a videoconference that is televised to twenty campuses.

In part, technological advances in the medium of television are responsible for the increased likelihood that you will appear on camera. With the invention of cable and satellite systems, the number of people needed to fill the added stations and channels began to grow at a rapid rate. With the advent of fiber optics, channel capacity will continue to grow, as will the need for people to fill these channels. In a brief period of time, the number of TV channels in the United States increased from 1,000 to a potential of 350,000. In short, cable systems have accelerated the need for people in the professions to be effective communicators in front of television cameras. It is not only Dan Rather, Larry King, and Barbara Walters doing the talking; it is now all of us.

Television's new impact on our daily interactions does not stop with commercial, educational, and cable television. Inexpensive, portable video equipment makes it possible for people to produce and play back their own television programs. We can all produce, direct, and even "star in" our own shows.

Teleconferencing, both in the United States and internationally, is yet another example of how more and more people are using television in noncommercial ways. People in New York can now interact with people in Iowa, Tokyo, Moscow, and Indiana at the same time.

As we indicated at the outset of this section, appearing before a camera is no longer the sole domain of professional broadcasters. Business executives are now finding numerous uses for television. A full page advertisement showing executives on television appeared in *Time* and *Newsweek* with the following caption: "Getting together by satellite—the world's largest privately owned earth station network lets you hold videoconference meetings at hundreds of Holiday Inn hotels at the same time." In addition, most large corporations now have their own in-house "mini-private networks."

If you are going to be an educator, you will also be using television, because "distance learning" will be used more frequently in the near future. Educators are now using closed-circuit systems, some with interactive units, to teach many of their classes. Other teachers are supplementing their instruction by making specific tapes tailored to various topics.

Inexpensive, portable video equipment makes it possible for people to produce, direct, and even "star in" their own "shows."

The medical field, at all levels, is finding countless uses for television. Health care professionals are appearing before the camera for situations such as giving information on the Hospital Satellite Network and diagnosing patients thousands of miles away.

Judges, lawyers, and defendants are also seeing the need to understand this important media. They must learn to present themselves in the best possible manner.

Politics is a field whose participants are already aware of the power of television. The politician who knows how to manipulate the television audience is usually elected.

As pervasive and widespread as television is, however, most people are still horrified at the thought of appearing before a camera. Why do they become extremely self-conscious and nervous when the camera is turned on? The answer is quite simple—most people do not understand the medium. A lack of understanding regarding television's uniqueness contributes to preperformance anxiety and on-camera failure. Hence, it is the purpose of this section of the chapter to dispel some of the myths of television and to assist you in overcoming the feelings of apprehension associated with this medium. Try to remember the advice of Antoine de Saint Exupéry: "Only the unknown frightens us."

We can begin to feel comfortable with television and overcome our dread of it if we keep two basic ideas in mind. First, *speaking on television is fundamentally an act of communication*. Therefore, everything we have discussed in preceding chapters applies to television speaking—with some minor modifications. For example, regardless of the medium or the setting, you should strive to be prepared, organized, logical, and interesting. Second, *although television is basically a communication activity, it possesses certain unique characteristics that set it apart from face-to-face interaction*. Once these features are identified and understood, they can help rather than hinder you. In the pages that follow, we will (1) discuss some of the special features of television that need to be taken into consideration, (2) examine how speech preparation is slightly altered by television, (3) offer some suggestions that apply to your television performance, and (4) consider some ethical considerations when using television as a communication medium.

Television's Unique Features

As we have just suggested, your first step toward improving your communication skills on television, whether you produce your own program or are interviewed on a professionally produced program, requires you to understand how television differs from face-to-face interaction. Let us begin our analysis by looking at eight features that are unique to television speaking. By comparing these to nontelevised events, you can learn to adapt your preparation and presentation to this special medium.

Feedback

First, appearing on television, in most instances, differs from face-to-face interaction in terms of *feedback*. Throughout this book, we have stressed that you should be sensitive to how your listeners are responding to you and your messages. We urged you to notice if they seemed interested, confused, or irritable, and suggested that you make adjustments to your delivery and content as audience feedback dictates. As you would suspect, speaking before a camera, whether it is a personal hand-held unit or a large expensive studio camera, does not allow for the same levels of feedback. To begin with, the people who will receive your message are not in front of you, and will most likely see and hear you at a later date. Therefore, you must anticipate and speculate about the responses you are apt to produce. In this sense, audience analysis takes on added significance when using mediated devices.

Distractions

Second, although public speakers can face occasional hecklers or people walking in late while they are talking, they seldom are confronted with the host of *distractions* that the television speaker encounters. Try to imagine how hard it would be to concentrate on your presentation during the hustle and bustle that takes place in a television studio. While you are trying your best to look relaxed and at ease, camera crews are adjusting microphones and cameras, technicians are working with equipment, and producers and directors are giving cues and signals. Even the simplest home video has activity and movement that is not found in most public-speaking situations. Being able to cope with all this activity is yet another ability that separates the advanced television speaker from the novice. The key, of course, is concentration.

Heterogeneous

Third, although there might be some occasions when your audience is composed of coworkers or classmates, in most instances television viewers, because of the "mass media" dimension of the medium, are *more heterogeneous*. This diversity of backgrounds and interests places special demands on each phase of the communication process. When the event is an international teleconference, the necessity for insightful adaptation is even more significant. Your preparation, content, and presentation must all be altered to meet the cosmopolitan makeup of your audience. Throughout this book, we have emphasized the importance of adaptation. We can all learn to adapt if we remember the words of the English novelist George Gissing, "Human creatures have a marvellous power of adapting themselves to necessity."

Fourth, *the size of the television screen* is yet another variable that must be taken into account. The ramifications of the small screen are numerous. For example, although it is obvious, people often overlook the idea that you do not look the same on television as you do in person. Even your movements look different on a screen than they do in "real life." In addition, the television camera can focus on certain parts of the body while avoiding others. The public speaker is in full view of his or her audience, while the televised speaker may be only partially in view. Even when you are in front of the simplest home video unit, you may not be aware of what part of your body is going to be captured on the screen. You can regulate your delivery if you know the impact of the small screen and the "selective process" of the camera. Later in this section, we shall discuss television delivery in more detail.

Television Screen

Fifth, television places *specific time restraints on the speaker*. There are, of course, a number of reasons why the clock holds sway over television. Speakers and programs are assigned specific time slots in all commercial, educational, and private facilities. The "show" is over when the time allowed for the program has expired. If you are being videotaped and the tape runs out, you are off the screen, whether you like it or not. Contrast this with the public speaker who simply smiles and announces that he or she has a few more things to say. You can clearly see how time restraints would influence your preparation, practice, organization, and content.

Time Restraints

Sixth, the public speaker in face-to-face situations requires no intervening parties to establish a bond of communication with the audience—he or she is usually a free agent. Using television for simple or elaborate productions is a *collaborative effort*. You must use the time and energy of other people in order to be seen and heard. You cannot get on the screen or on the air by yourself. You need other people, who are cooperating with each other, in order to have a successful "program." Just as the Malay proverb tells us that "clapping with one hand will not produce noise," so too, working alone will not produce good television. You cannot simply talk and in some magic way appear on the screen; at least one other person must be involved to operate the camera.

Collaborative Effort

Seventh, although we encourage you to be relaxed and conversational while on television, we must also point out that television *thrives on action*. Viewers can be easily distracted because of the size and privacy of the screen. In addition, people are conditioned to expect activity when they watch either a movie or a television screen. You must be prepared to deal with these expectations. Your speech material must be interesting and tightly organized. We even recommend that you talk a little faster than usual in order to blend with the speed of the medium. Some studies suggest that people comprehend more words per minute watching television than they do in face-to-face encounters. Visual aids must be used whenever possible, because they involve activity and movement. Refer to chapter 7 for more information on visual aids.

Action

Control

Eighth, when you deliver a speech in person, what you say and what you do at that moment are what the "live" audience sees and hears. The cliche, "what you see is what you get," certainly applies to public speaking. This is not the case with television speaking. In television, you have a much *greater degree of control* over the program that the audience eventually receives. Camera angles, videotaping procedures, editing devices, and the like enable the speaker, either working alone or with technicians, to manipulate and control what the audience sees. Learning how to use this control is one of the attributes of a successful television speaker.

Preparing for Television

Teachers, business executives, doctors, lawyers, political leaders, and laypeople have all had problems with television that can be clearly traced to their lack of preparation. Regardless of the situation or type of speech, thorough preparation enables you to anticipate potential problems and to adapt your material to your specific audience.

Analyzing the Television Audience and Occasion

In chapter 3, we devoted a considerable amount of time to the important topic of audience analysis. You might want to reread that chapter whenever you need to analyze your television audience. However, some of the distinct characteristics of television that we just finished discussing demand special consideration. Let us return to some of these features and see how they affect your audience analysis.

1. *When speaking to a "mass audience," your supporting material and emotional appeals should be kept somewhat general.* Imagine the countless backgrounds and value systems you face when you talk to thousands, or even millions, of people at the same time. Appealing to only one segment of this audience does not usually attract support from all the others. Telling a mass audience that they should donate funds to your college tennis team so that it can attend the national championships does not have the same appeal as a request for donations to the Red Cross right after a national disaster.

2. *Your organizational pattern should also consider the general nature of the audience.* This means you should use a simple, clear pattern. If you believe that those who might be viewing your presentation are from diverse educational and cultural backgrounds, you need to make abundant use of transitions, previews, and summaries.

3. *Because the audience is going to represent a variety of interests, you should arouse attention quickly, then maintain that attention level.* Notice how many television programs use techniques such as color and motion to capture your interest. Producers and directors are well aware of the short attention span most of us have. When you find yourself preparing for a television appearance, try to work with the technical staff so that they can offer you some help in this area. For your part, you should use the factors of attention discussed in chapter 13 and the types of visual aids highlighted in chapter 7.

4. *The fact that your presentation is designed for a mass medium should be considered as you choose your language.* While a group of classmates might understand the words *immune system*, a multicultural audience might contain people who do not even have those words in their language. When addressing a heterogeneous audience where some of the listeners might have English as a second language, your language should be simple, clear, direct, free of jargon, and devoid of confusing idioms.

Although the delivery requirements of a televised speech are in many respects identical to those of any other public speech, the acuity of the camera's eye requires that certain modifications be made. The following is a discussion of the factors that must be modified when you appear on television.

Over two hundred years ago, the philosopher Thomas Fuller wrote, "By the husk you may guess at the nut." He was, of course, alluding to the importance of appearance. Your own experiences tell you that looking good on television is not only important but expected. However, for a host of reasons, dressing appropriately for television is more complicated than selecting clothes and accessories for face-to-face speech making. Not only must you be guided by good taste and cultural constraints, but you must also consider the impact of the camera, microphone, and screen. Your attire must be pleasing and yet free of distractions. To help accomplish these goals, study the guidelines in the following discussion.

First, *the resolution limitations of the camera tend to distort certain colors and patterns.* For example, thin stripes, pronounced checks, and sharply contrasting patterns tend to jump around the screen. Even clashing or loud colors, such as reds, cause distortion. Thus, in addition to wearing comfortable and attractive clothing, try to wear medium tones of gray, brown, and blue. Never wear just black and white on camera—the combination tends to photograph in a rather strange manner.

Second, *avoid wearing baggy blouses, shirts, suits, and dresses.* On television, these loosely fitting and hanging clothes will make you look ten pounds heavier.

Third, *although jewelry and other accoutrements can lend variety and even enhance your wardrobe, beware of their impact on your televised appearance.* Highly polished gold and silver and large diamonds or rhinestones reflect studio lights and tend to "flare" and distort the picture. These items will also attract attention and take the focus away from you. Glasses can also cause glare and should be worn only when necessary. This does not mean that you should deprive yourself of the means to read the TelePrompTer, but you and the lighting crew may have to make some minor readjustments in the placement of the lights.

Fourth, *avoid wearing clothing and accessories that make noise.* Microphones are highly sensitive and will broadcast the rattle of jewelry and the squeak of shoes.

Fifth, *do not smoke on television.* Your image can suffer from the effect of this somewhat messy and unhealthy activity. In addition, viewers find it very distracting to see wisps of smoke floating across the screen while someone is talking.

Sixth, *some skin colors look washed out and "ghostly" on television.* Therefore, makeup is almost invariably used to enhance the video image. One way to determine how much and what kind of makeup you need is to do a video test. Seek some help in determining the results of that test. You might not be your own best critic. While a bald Caucasian may need his head "touched up" or darkened a little, a dark-complexioned speaker may need the skin lightened somewhat. These applications of makeup are for technical reasons; they are not intended to have you appear to be something other than what you are.

Eye contact seems to be an aspect of television delivery that causes people the greatest amount of apprehension. However, by following a few simple suggestions, your visual rapport with the audience can be improved.

Presenting Yourself on Television

General Appearance

Eye Contact

In a pamphlet called "So You're Going on TV," published by the National Association of Broadcasters, the following advice is offered: "Remember that although you are talking to a large audience, you should pretend you are speaking to a few friends who are comfortably seated in their homes." Although this suggestion seems somewhat self-evident, it is often ignored. Most beginning television performers do not know what to do with their eyes. Some look down at the ground or seem to enjoy viewing themselves on a monitor situated off-camera.

When to look at the camera, or how often to look, is yet another issue facing novices. The answer to this question is contingent on a number of factors. For example, if you are speaking to a live audience (people in front of you), you should treat the camera as if it were simply another pair of eyes watching you. This means the camera is no more or no less important than the rest of the audience. If, on the other hand, you are aiming your message to television viewers only, you should speak directly to the camera and disregard the studio audience. If you are being interviewed on television, you should look at the interviewer as if he or she were the camera. This will give your presentation a much more natural look.

Remember, the camera that is "seeing" you at any given moment is the one whose red light is lit. With practice and experience, you will be able to transfer your gaze as the red light shifts from camera to camera. In addition, your floor director will signal you when a camera change is imminent. This will help you avoid sudden and jerky movements as you alter your eye contact.

The use of notes is yet another matter that faces most television speakers. If you need notes in order to remember certain main points or exact wording you do not want to forget, you will find that television usually allows you three options. First, *you can use notecards just as you would for a public speech.* Do not try to conceal your cards from the audience. Some people believe that these cards even add to your professional look. In using your cards, remember to refer to them only as you need them; do not let them become more important than the television audience. Make sure you can see them easily. Using stiff paper, double-spacing your copy, and numbering your pages will aid you in your efforts.

Second, *you can put your notes on large poster board cards and ask a member of the studio crew to hold them next to the camera.* With this method, make sure the printing on the cards is large and clear enough so that you find them easy to read from a distance.

Finally, *you can use a TelePrompTer to help you remember your message.* This device, which is positioned next to the camera, shows either your entire speech or brief notes as you look toward the camera. Like the other two forms of using notes, this one also has some potential problems. Many TelePrompTer users can be identified by their obvious left-to-right eye movement as they read their speech from the screen. In a personal conversation, such eye movement would be taken as an indication of a malady. You should learn the material on the TelePrompTer so that you will be able to read the contents in a natural manner. Once you learn how to use the TelePrompTer, you will find it quite useful.

Having talked about a number of factors that influence eye contact, we are now ready to examine a few specific suggestions:

1. *Look directly at the camera that has the red tally light turned on.* Look at the activated camera 100 percent of the time you are talking. Breaking your gaze, at least on television, gives the impression that you have lost your place or are being shifty or dishonest. If the red "tally light" changes or if the floor manager points to another camera, simply redirect your eyes to the other camera as smoothly as possible. With practice, these transitions will become graceful. For now, remember to imagine that the person you are talking to is inside the camera.

2. *Try not to yield to the distractions that draw your eyes away from the camera.* These distractions range from looking at yourself on the studio monitors to watching the stage crew move from job to job.

3. *Do not stare at the camera as if you have been hypnotized.* Countless performers have become transfixed by the camera; they gape, unblinking, at it. You would not do this in face-to-face conversation, and you should not do it on television.

The advice with regard to facial expressions while appearing on television is similar to that offered for nontelevised speeches: *be yourself.* Remember, you are not acting but are trying to appear natural and spontaneous. Of course, you should try to avoid looking deadpan or too serious. Our experiences tell us the obvious—that people enjoy seeing a smile. This does not mean you grin while talking about a major earthquake, but it does mean that, whenever possible, you smile at the people you are trying to relate to.

Facial Expressions

Because you can never know for certain when a close-up shot is being broadcast, you should act as if the camera were on your face at all times. This means that you should be concerned with how you look for as long as the red tally light is on, even if the camera is not pointed directly at you. Many first-time performers have been caught off guard because they thought the camera was focused elsewhere.

The requirements of movement, posture, and gestures on television are somewhat different from those for traditional public speaking. Let us explore a few of the differences that might affect your overall performance.

Movement

Ordinarily, the camera moves more frequently than you do. It not only moves from side to side and back and forth but the lens zooms in and out on you, making you appear close up even when the camera is some distance away. This means that there are many shots of which you are not aware. During the broadcast itself, angles and distances are always changing. Because you do not always know what is on the air, your gestures should be limited and controlled. You should avoid sweeping and rapid gestures so that the camera does not lose you or get out of focus. Gesturing directly toward the camera can also cause considerable distortion on the screen. Crossing your legs is yet another movement that can photograph awkwardly.

When you are using props or referring to maps or other graphics, you may need to move around and to point. If this is the case, arrive at the studio early enough to rehearse these movements before the taping of the program.

Even the most subtle of mannerisms become greatly magnified on camera. Scratching the top of your head, rubbing your arm, or playing with your glasses appears to be an irritating habit when performed on screen.

Try to adapt your posture and movement to the constraints imposed by the studio or setting. Your physical distance from other people, the social conventions that are operative, the number of people on the set, and the props (or lack of them) all influence your posture and movement.

Finally, be prepared to change posture quickly if the need should arise. Camera movements, microphone placement, and signals from your director may force you to shift positions on very short notice. You may have to move from giving a speech to being a member of a panel discussion. The first is likely to be formal, the latter informal. In addition, the equipment you use in the studio will demand that you adapt to or make changes in the environment. For example, a microphone on a table should not cause you to lean forward in an awkward position, an overhead boom should not make you look up, and a friend carrying a small portable camera with a built-in microphone should not force you to chase after him or her.

Vocal Aspects

An interesting phenomenon of television technology is its ability to alter the human voice. It can, for example, control volume, rate, and tone, but this electronic manipulation does not exonerate you from being aware of these and other aspects of vocal delivery. The same electronic systems that can help you sound better also have the capacity to hamper your delivery. For instance, a microphone tends to attract more attention to pauses and unpleasant qualities than does unmediated speech. Microphones are so sensitive that they can pick up and broadcast poor inflection, incorrect pronunciation, sound omissions, slurred sounds, and misplaced accents. Therefore, when speaking on television, be aware of your voice: be natural, enthusiastic, relaxed, and conversational.

You might also consider increasing your rate slightly when speaking before the camera. What often appears to be reasonably paced discourse in face-to-face situations seems dull and slow on television. You might want to move from 120 to 130 words per minute, the normal rate, to 130 to 140 words per minute. A fast rate connotes action, and television thrives on action.

Using Microphones

The presence of a microphone is one of the differences between electronic presentations and face-to-face communication. We will pause at this point to look at some of the general do's and don'ts concerning the use of microphones, whether you are speaking on television, radio, in an auditorium, or at an outdoor rally.

1. *When taking your sound check, use a normal voice.* Do not mumble, yell, or try to imitate a professional newscaster—be yourself. Do not take your sound check by saying, "Testing one, two, three." That is the way you count, not the way you talk. Finally, when taking a check, sit or stand in the same place you will occupy during the actual performance. Taking the check sitting down and then giving your talk standing up will not provide an accurate voice-level reading.

2. *Do not alter your pitch or volume range too much from the original volume check.* Distortion may occur if you increase or decrease your volume, pitch, or rate without the control room knowing about it, although a good sound technician can usually compensate for such variations.

3. *Remember to stay within microphone range so that your voice can be broadcast to your audience.* The correct range is usually determined by the audio engineer. Your responsibility is to make sure you do not walk or turn away from the microphone unless you know for certain you can be heard. This means knowing the range of a boom or how much cord you have left on your lavaliere microphone. If you run out of cord, do not pull on the cord out of frustration—you might unplug your microphone.

A microphone is a highly sensitive instrument.

4. *Do not place the microphone too close to your mouth.* A good distance for a hand-held microphone is approximately one foot below and slightly in front of your mouth. A lavaliere microphone goes approximately six inches below the chin.

5. *Do not speak directly into the microphone.* Try to visualize yourself speaking across it instead of into it. This will give your voice a more natural sound.

6. *Be careful with "s," "ch," and "sh" sounds.* A microphone exaggerates these sibilant (hissing) sounds. Spend some time learning to "swallow" these sounds and concentrating on the sound that precedes or follows them. For example, focus on *ga* in *gas*, and *ould* in *should*. You might also be wary of "p," "v," "t," and "b" sounds. If they are stressed, they create a "popping" sound. Also, microphones magnify asthmatic or heavy breathing, so be careful not to breathe directly into them.

7. *Remember that a microphone is a highly sensitive instrument, engineered to pick up all sound, not just your voice.* The rattling of your jewelry can sound like a full orchestra if it is broadcast. You should also refrain from moving paper too near a microphone or tapping a microphone with your finger or pencil.

In chapter 4, we talked about speech fright and some ways to overcome it. As you might suspect, speech fright is often more serious when you visualize yourself in front of a

Controlling Nervousness

camera. Although some nervousness and apprehension can be beneficial, most of it impedes your delivery. The following are a few simple techniques that can reduce some of the harmful effects of too much nervousness:

1. *Yawn excessively before you go on camera.* This not only gives you more oxygen, but it relaxes your throat muscles.

2. *Stretch as many parts of your body as you can without calling attention to your strange preperformance acrobatics.* Stretching relaxes the muscles that are apt to tense up as you wait for the program to begin.

3. *Have some water available so you can avoid the dry mouth feeling that makes talking seem impossible.* Be careful of too much water, however; you need to be on television, not in the restroom.

4. *Develop a good mental attitude.* This means being prepared and actually looking forward to your television appearance. The experience will not hurt; in fact, you might actually enjoy being "a television star." This positive attitude will help you accomplish your purpose while adding to your self-confidence.

Practicing Your Television Presentation

Throughout this book, we have stressed the importance of practice for successful speech making. This advice also applies to television. Let us therefore suggest three steps you should follow as you try to make your television appearance as productive as possible.

Practice Aloud

First, *practice your presentation aloud and, during these practice sessions, make sure you time your speech.* If your talk is too long, you are apt to find yourself offering your conclusion to the stage crew but not to the people viewing their televisions. If you are making your own tape and you fail to time your talk, you might discover that you will run out of tape before you run out of words.

The availability of television equipment should offer you the opportunity to practice your speech before a camera. By using a playback system, you can see and hear your speech in about the same way your audience will be receiving it. Hence, you will be able to make the necessary adjustments in both delivery and content. As you view your tape, you should ask yourself some of the following questions:

- Did I have enough vocal variety to hold attention?
- Was my eye contact focused in the right direction? At the correct camera?
- Did my wardrobe and accessories detract from my message?
- Did my voice add to or detract from my presentation?
- Did I engage in any distracting mannerisms?
- Will I need makeup?
- Did I appear nervous?
- Were my movements (gesturing, walking) natural?
- What overall impression did I give?

The second part of your practice session should include the *soliciting of advice* from people who have successfully used the media. For example, someone who has been on many interview programs can tell you whether to use a clipboard for your notes or have them printed on cards. You might also have some of your friends view your videotape and ask them what they think of your presentation. Keep in mind that this entire book has been about advice. We are now simply asking you to look to other places for that assistance. As Shakespeare once wrote, "Friendly counsel cuts off many foes." Or put another way, good advice can eliminate some potential problems.

Solicit Advice

Third, locate and develop models. In ancient Rome, students had to memorize great speeches and deliver them as they were said to have been delivered originally. While we are not suggesting you mimic people you have seen on television, we are suggesting you observe people who use the medium well to discover some reasons for their success. By isolating what makes them effective, you can evaluate your own television personality. Again, we are not advocating the cloning of television performers, but rather the finding of models that can offer you some specific clues as to what works and what does not work on television.

Locate and Develop Models

Throughout this book, we have directly and indirectly discussed the ethical responsibilities facing anyone who sends a message to another human being. We have said that it is an undeniable truism that, when someone receives a message from us, we are, in one degree or another, changing them. While some changes might be significant and others subtle, it is change nevertheless. Nowhere is the import of this notion more meaningful than in our use of television. For there is power and influence associated with television that is not found in most other communication environments. This point was clearly made by the Pilkington Report on television when it concluded that "Unless and until there is unmistakable proof to the contrary, the presumption must be that television is and will be a main factor in influencing the values and moral standards of our society."

Ethical Considerations and Television

Your own experiences will also verify the power of television and the influence of the people who appear on this medium. Notice how many times you listen to a person on a talk show and find yourself responding differently than if you were talking to that person informally. A guest on a national talk show suggested that powdered vitamin C was healthier than the tablet form. In three days, most health food stores were completely sold out of powdered vitamin C.

We have been trying to suggest that the personal use of television involves personal responsibility. That responsibility can best be examined by looking at how you deal with (1) objectives and (2) values.

Having objectives is one of the more distinctly human characteristics of television communication. Electronic hardware does not have objectives beyond those imbued by its human masters. It is simply a conduit delivering your ideas and values. Therefore, when we talk about objectives in television communication, we are talking about *your* objectives. Make sure you identify and understand them so that you can prepare and participate in an intelligent, ethical, and effective manner. A course that you might be teaching via a closed-circuit system has a different set of objectives than does a group of your friends

Objectives

making a home video to be played back at a birthday party. How well you identify your own objectives—be they to inform, persuade, or entertain—and how well you take the audience's objectives into account, will determine how successful you are when using television to communicate. As the American author Norbert Wiener reminds us, "We need to determine not only how to accomplish our purposes, but what our purposes are to be."

Values   As you attempt to accomplish your objectives, you must develop a code of ethics. All individuals who step in front of a camera must be aware of the potential impact they are having on other people. The corporate executive videotaping a message for employees regarding the treatment of clients, as well as the person being interviewed on a talk show, must accept their ethical responsibility. Questions such as Am I being truthful? Am I withholding information? Am I bowing to popular tastes? Do my objectives reflect the best interests of my receivers? These and other ethical questions must be confronted *before* you appear on television. As we have said repeatedly, whether you want to acknowledge the responsibility or not, what people see and hear on television can reshape the way they perceive reality. The communication scholar Richard Weaver made much the same point when he observed, "We are all of us preachers in private and public capacities. We have no sooner uttered words than we have given impulse to other people to look at the world, or some part of it, in our way."

As we have said elsewhere, because television is a mass medium, being on television often can give you power, influence, and stature that may not have ever been available in face-to-face encounters. Therefore, you can see why we recommend that you ponder your ethical responsibilities when appearing on television. In short, ask yourself these two crucial questions: First, have the ideas and values you discussed diminished the individual and human potential of your viewers? Second, have you contributed to your viewers' emotional, spiritual, intellectual, or mental well-being?

Speech of Introduction

A common practice in most public-speaking occasions is for someone to introduce the principal speaker. However, such speeches of introduction are often poorly done. The person making the introduction either fails to take the assignment seriously or uses the occasion to demonstrate his or her cleverness or "superior knowledge." Regardless of the reason, the introducer fails to tie the topic, guest speaker, and audience together.

A speech of introduction has three main purposes: (1) to get the audience interested in the guest speaker, (2) to arouse audience interest in the speaker's subject, and (3) to establish a warm and friendly climate. To see that a speaker and a speech secure a favorable reception, a person giving a speech of introduction can follow seven simple rules:

1. *Be brief.* An introducer subordinates his or her own speech for the sake of the main talk; he or she is only an emissary linking the speaker to the audience. In most instances, one to five minutes is the time allotted to a person making an introduction. This should allow ample time to get attention, point the audience toward the topic, and establish the speaker's credibility.

2. *In making an introduction, make sure your information concerning the speaker and his or her background and topic is accurate.* Errors in pronunciation should always be avoided. Contact the speaker in advance if you have any doubts regarding how the speaker pronounces his or her name. The issue of correct pronunciation is even more crucial in this age of cultural diversity. Often you will be asked to introduce someone whose foreign name is one you have never seen before. You should also have accurate information about the speaker's personal and professional background. Inaccurate information can cause a great deal of embarrassment to you, the speaker, and the audience. Secure the essential and personal information from the speaker well in advance of your formal introduction.

3. *It is often effective to begin an introduction with a brief reference to the nature of the occasion.* This may serve as a bond between the speaker and the listeners. Also, there may be occasions when it will be valuable to emphasize the importance of the subject.

4. *Once you have established rapport with the audience by humor, a reference to the occasion, or any other form of motivation, you are ready to give the biographical data necessary to identify the speaker and to make that person sound interesting and authoritative.* In most cases, the biography should include (a) the speaker's place of residence, (b) his or her achievements (publications, honors, and awards), (c) the speaker's background on the topic (professional and educational), (d) the speaker's relationship to the audience, and (e) the reason this person was selected to deliver the talk. It is very important that all the data contained in the introduction be completely accurate.

5. *If the occasion allows, hold the speaker's full name and subject until the end.* In this way, the speaker's name and topic can be presented as a climax: "Now that we know just how important it is to talk to someone who has actually done business in Japan, let me introduce Mr. James Ray, who will speak to us today on the topic of how to make contact with Japanese corporations."

6. *Refrain from excessive exaggeration.* On many occasions, we have seen introductions that embarrassed the person being introduced because of the amount of extreme veneration and admiration heaped on the speaker. In short, be flattering but not artificial.

7. *Avoid hackneyed words and phrases.* Introductions such as "Our speaker needs no introduction," "I am indeed honored," "I consider it a rare privilege," and "without further ado" are too common.

8. *Pay close attention to the speech so that, at its close, you can refer to the ideas and their value to the audience as you thank the speaker.*

Question-and-Answer Sessions

Student Cynthia Connors has just completed a classroom speech about half-human, half-beast legends. Someone in the audience poses this question to her: "Why do you say it is biologically impossible for such creatures to exist?"

Tom Fernandez is urging the city council to approve plans for the construction of a 160-unit condominium project adjacent to the municipal stadium. A councilman interrupts Tom to ask, "Have you considered the impact that stadium traffic on game days is going to have on the residents' access to their homes?"

George Thurmond is demonstrating the features of a food processor to a group of interested spectators in a department store. One of the spectators asks, "Why is this product so very expensive?"

Answering both general and specific questions from the audience is a routine part of most communication encounters. A speaker seeking to instruct often invites the audience to pose questions whenever appropriate as a way of clarifying points that might not be self-evident when they were first explained. A speaker attempting to persuade is likely to be questioned or challenged by some listeners who disagree with the speaker's arguments or conclusions. A speaker who stimulates the audience's curiosity with unusual subject matter may be bombarded by questions after the address. A politician who takes part in a town meeting expects questions from the floor. With interactive television systems, people can ask each other questions even if they find themselves at different locations. In short, almost all speech situations lend themselves to a question-and-answer session. Because the audience's impression of a speaker is based not only on what happens during the speech but also on the speaker's prespeech and postspeech behavior, it is important to examine the ways in which a question-and-answer session can promote a favorable impression of the speaker.

Characteristics of an Effective Reply

In a question-and-answer session, remember that the people who ask the questions may not all have the same motives. That is to say, some members of the audience might be very sincere when they state their questions. However, you might also be faced with people who want to give their own speeches and use the question-and-answer period as an opportunity to do so. You are even apt to hear a question from an individual who enjoys verbal confrontation. Regardless of a questioner's motive, you need to learn the characteristics of an effective reply, for as the journalist Sydney J. Harris noted, "More trouble is caused in this world by indiscreet answers than by indiscreet questions."

Calmness

It is easy to find yourself nervous or believing you will get caught off guard when you face questions from your audience. Nevertheless, it is important that you remain calm so that you can think of an intelligent response to the questions you are asked. Part of staying calm is making sure you start listening from the outset. You will recall that, when we discussed listening in chapter 5, we told you that one of the most common errors in listening is not being prepared to listen. Remember, just a few words can alter the entire idea behind the question. Being asked about a specific 1995 court ruling on capital punishment is not the same as being asked to comment on capital punishment in general.

Listening and staying calm is complicated if the question is a hostile one, yet, even in these situations, it is crucial that you keep your senses about you. In fact, remaining composed when facing a difficult predicament can aid your credibility and even astonish the person asking the unfair question. A classic example of disarming an aggressive skeptic is found in the following story concerning Buddha:

> A man interrupted Buddha's preaching with a flood of abusive questions.
> Buddha stayed calm and waited until the man had finished. He then asked him,
> "If a man offered a gift to another but the gift was declined, to whom would the

gift belong?" "To the one who offered it," said the man. "Then," said Buddha, "I decline to accept your abuse and request you keep it for yourself."

Buddha's advice is valid today. Be patient and stay calm when you are asked a question.

Repeating or rephrasing a question from the floor is one of the chief characteristics of an effective response: "You asked which animals are most endangered by the logging industry in the Pacific Northwest. It is the spotted owl." This technique is useful with both large and small audiences. **Repetition**

There are a number of reasons why your repeating the question is a good idea. First, there might be people in the audience who failed to hear the question you are being asked. This could be caused by room noise, or the person asking the question may be using a soft voice. Second, the question may be poorly phrased, too wordy, ambiguous, or one-sided. By repeating or rewording the question, you are in a much better position to answer it. Third, the time it takes to repeat the question may afford you valuable time in which to formulate an answer. Finally, repeating the question allows you and the person asking the question to make sure that you have identified the main point of the question.

Put yourself in the role of a questioner for a moment and think about the kind of reply you would appreciate from a speaker—probably one that is polite. Politeness is taught in every culture, and people have come to expect certain rules of politeness to be followed when they interact with other people, including when they ask a question. Usually, when someone asks a question, it is because he or she believes that question is important. Regardless of how naive, irrelevant, or poorly worded a question seems, the speaker should treat the questioner with dignity. If members of the audience laugh in derision at a poor question, it is wise for the speaker to refrain from joining in that laughter. A speaker who shows respect for a questioner's feelings deserves the goodwill that almost inevitably follows from such a gesture. As indicated earlier, even hostile questions should be answered without rancor. There is great wisdom in the proverb "A soft answer turneth away wrath." One can disagree politely with a questioner, especially if the focus of the reply is on issues, not personalities. Moreover, meeting hostility with politeness can disarm a hostile questioner while minimizing that person's influence on the other listeners. Let your answer be logical enough to satisfy a cynic and congenial enough to satisfy a friend. **Politeness**

Straightforwardness is another desirable feature in answering questions. Audiences are usually quick to sense evasiveness; sometimes, the favorable impression left by a speech can be negated by a shifty answer to a question asked afterward. If you do not know the answer to a question, it is better to say so than to try to divert the issue elsewhere. Likewise, if you do not wish to answer a question, then say so, adding an explanation for declining. When a question is asked, come directly to grips with it and avoid diversionary tactics. If you do not know the answer, simply say so. If you bluff, the audience will know it and will resent you for trying to deceive them. **Straightforwardness**

We should mention here that eye contact and speaking directly to the person asking the question can also manifest a straightforward and candid image. By looking at the person posing the question, you are nonverbally saying, Here is my sincere and honest response to your question.

Brevity

William Shakespeare remarked that "brevity is the soul of wit." Brevity should also characterize your answers—that is, brevity consistent with completeness. Some speakers are guilty of overkill in their answers. Not only do they use a question as an excuse to give another long speech, but they get sidetracked, answering questions that have not even been asked. In addition, taking a long time to answer a question often leads to vocal fillers such as "well . . . ," "um . . . ," and "er. . . ." If there appears to be a number of questions forthcoming from the audience, brevity is a necessity.

Preparation

An answer that reflects preparation is another hallmark of a competent reply. Put yourself in the listeners' place and try to imagine what they might ask. Preparation also means researching the material for your reply and practicing it aloud. This rehearsal period is very common among public figures who find themselves facing press conferences. Being prepared not only makes your response more acceptable, but it also adds to your credibility. It is yet another way to show the audience that you know the material.

Organizing a Reply

The organizational format most appropriate for a reply is dictated by the nature and scope of the question itself and the amount of time allowed for the question-and-answer period. However, some organizational schemes seem to fit most occasions. Next, we will examine four of those formats.

Request for Clarification

1. Refer to the section of your speech requiring clarification.
2. Use the appropriate clarifying devices—such as definition, restatement, example, illustration, analogy, diagram, and demonstration.
3. Ask the questioner if the point is sufficiently clarified.
   An example of clarification might appear as the following:

   I've been asked to define the word *resistor*, which I used earlier in telling you about controlling power surges that can impede the electrical outlets in your home. In simple terms, a resistor is something that resists. In the case of electrical circuitry, it resists the flow of electricity. It enables just the right amount of voltage to be supplied to other components in the circuit. In a sense, a resistor acts somewhat like a water faucet valve that resists, or controls, the flow of water coming from the supply line. Does that explain it clearly enough?

Request for More Information

1. Refer to the point on which you have been requested to offer further information.
2. Relate the information using an appropriate sequence—such as chronological, spatial, topical, or logical order.
3. Ask the questioner if you have answered the request sufficiently.

Consider the following example: Sarah asked where the blood bank is located in relation to the park. As you know, Sarah, the western boundary of the park is along Sixth Avenue, from about Fir Street on the south to Upas Street on the north. Using the northern-most intersection—Sixth and Upas—as our reference point, the blood bank is located one block west at 440 Upas Street. Can you visualize that location now?"

Challenge to Your Position

1. Refer to the point that has been challenged.

2. State the nature of the challenge.

3. Answer the challenge by offering additional evidence in support of your position and by showing the fallacious character of the questioner's objections.

Following is an example and a challenge: The source of my data relating to the high prison population of California has been challenged by the gentleman in the front row. If he questions the syndicated columnist I quoted, let me refer him to the latest publication of the Bureau of Justice Statistics, United States Justice Department. He will find, and I am now reading from that publication, that California has more prison inmates than either New York or Texas. In fact, it has more prisoners than the combined prison populations of Washington, Oregon, Idaho, Montana, Colorado, Utah, Arizona, New Mexico, Nevada, Wyoming, Alaska, and Hawaii.

Redirect the Question

1. Repeat the question so that the person knows you heard the request.

2. Refer the question back to the person asking the question.

3. Ask the questioner for a specific response.

Consider the following example of redirect: You are wondering why I am asking the paint company to remove the residue of their product. That is a very good question. I am curious as to what you would do with the waste material coming from the new paint factory.

Summary

In this chapter, we dealt with special communication situations. Although, in a sense, all communication is special and, therefore, has similarities in form and style, certain situations demand a different degree of proficiency if a speaker is to accomplish a specific purpose. The situations dealt with were those calling for impromptu speeches, manuscript speeches, entertaining speeches, television speeches, speeches of introduction, and question-and-answer sessions.

An impromptu speech is given on the spur of the moment or when a speaker has little time to prepare. To keep from being completely overwhelmed, a speaker can call forth a few simple techniques such as remembering what was said just before being asked to speak, thinking about past reading and speaking experiences, and working out a suitable organizational pattern.

A manuscript speech is unique in offering a speaker an opportunity to write out a speech in detail before delivering it. In preparing this type of speech, it is important to remember that it is a speech and not an essay. Once an outline is completed, the speaker is in a position to start the manuscript. Rewriting is always beneficial. The final draft should be highly polished. In presenting a speech, the essentials of good delivery must be kept in mind. Eye contact, vocal variety, and gestures are as important to good manuscript speaking as they are to good extemporaneous speaking.

The major purpose of a speech to entertain is to have the listeners enjoy themselves. A speaker, by using the concepts of attention and interest, has the audience relax in an enjoyable atmosphere. Humor is often a trademark of entertaining; a successful speaker must learn to use humorous illustrations, exaggeration, incongruity, attacks on authority, sarcasm, and human predicaments.

Changes in commercial and public television, new cable systems, and low-cost portable sending units have created a situation in which more and more people are finding themselves in front of a television camera. For these appearances to be successful, a television speaker should understand some of the unique features of television, conduct an audience analysis, adapt his or her delivery to the medium of television, and accept the ethical responsibilities associated with television speaking.

The main task of a speech of introduction is to create a rapport among the speaker, subject, and audience. By stimulating interest in both the speaker and the topic, you create a friendly climate, in which the audience is interested in hearing what the guest speaker has to say.

A question-and-answer session is a common part of communication encounters. Calmness, repetition, politeness, straightforwardness, and brevity are desirable qualities in replying to questions. The nature and specificity of the question, as well as the perceived motive of the questioner, affect the speaker's strategy for reply.

Light is the task
where many
share the toil.

Homer

Chapter 16

Discussion

Group Communication

389

We are never so likely to settle a question rightly, as when we discuss it freely.

Dame Rose Macaulay

Each one of us is very special, unique, and one-of-a-kind. Yet, while we live our lives as individuals, we spend great amounts of time communicating as a member of a group. Whether at work, school, or social functions, we constantly meet with others to discuss items of business or to solve mutual problems. Although, at times, these meetings are frustrating, numerous rewards can grow out of working with others. As an Ethiopian proverb says, "When spider webs unite they can tie up a lion." We all know the feelings of cohesiveness and solidarity associated with being part of a group that has successfully shared a web and resolved a mutual problem.

Importance of Group Communication

Being a member of a group is an essential part of life. We are born into a group called "our family." This primary group teaches us everything from language to manners to what goals to pursue. Our success in life is often directly linked to how well we function in this group.

The concept of group involvement is also fundamental to the democratic process. In a democratic society, it is only natural that decisions should be made after considerable deliberation and discussion. We pride ourselves on being fair—that various points of view are presented and considered before a judgment is given or a decision rendered. As part of our democratic philosophy, each person counts and has the right and responsibility to contribute to the resolution of both individual and public problems through group discussion. Involving interested citizens in this democratic process was one of the motivating factors behind candidate Bill Clinton's use of town meetings during his two presidential campaigns. President Clinton realized that now, more than ever, we are using groups as a mechanism to get things done.

The uses of discussion are obvious when we reflect on the occasions and situations when we are in a position to exchange ideas and information with others. Group contacts are so common in our culture that an estimated 20 million meetings a day are held in the United States. The average manager and technical professional, for example, spends nearly one-fourth of his or her total work week in meetings. Most professionals attend eight to eleven meetings per week. How well people function in these meetings help determine both the accomplishments of the group and the success of the individual within the organization. That is to say, if you are a skillful member of a group, you and the group will benefit.

The importance of group activity is not unique to North American culture. Group interaction is found in nearly all cultures. In fact, in many cultures, it is the preferred method of conducting life and business. In Japan, for example, it is very common for major decisions to be made by the people involved instead of by one individual called "the boss." For centuries, Native Americans have used tribal councils and meetings to make most of their major decisions. Improving your discussion skills should enable you to be more competent when you are with members of these and other cultures that stress collective communication.

In education, many classes function by means of the discussion process. In countless educational situations, we meet with others to resolve problems, share feelings, and gather information. In most Latin American cultures, nearly all classroom activities are conducted in groups.

Speech Communication and Group Communication

Before embarking on a detailed exploration of group communication, it will be valuable to examine the relationship between speech communication and group communication. The following definition of group discussion shows the link between speech communication and being a member of a group: *Group communication is the systematic and objective sharing of ideas and information by two or more persons who work together in an effort to solve a problem or to gain a better understanding of a problem.*

Although the units of speech presented by any discussant might, by necessity, be shorter and more fragmented than in solitary public speaking, much of what is being done still uses the skills, principles, and techniques of oral communication. On the platform or sitting with others in a group, one must pay attention to such matters as audience adaptation, feedback, preparation and research, the expression of concrete ideas and their support in an organized manner, and language usage. Let us now return to these communication principles and see how they can be applied to the group situation.

Types of Group Discussion

We have seen the importance of group communication, or discussion, and that it is an extension of speech communication. Besides understanding these two ideas, it would be useful for you to appreciate some of the forms of small-group communication. By knowing some of the types of groups you may be affiliated with, you will be able to make the minor adjustments needed to be an effective speaker.

Although most classifications are not hard and fast, discussion groups are normally categorized as either public or private—with subclassifications within each of these two major categories.

Public Discussion

Public discussions are group experiences held before an audience. They are often formal and generally very structured. Public discussions usually follow one of the following three patterns:

1. **Symposium.** In a symposium, each of several speakers, generally two to five, is introduced by a moderator and then delivers a talk. These speeches center around one topic, theme, or issue. Each speaker may explain his or her position and thoughts on the subject as a whole or be limited to one phase of the subject. Frequently, the audience is allowed to ask questions at the conclusion of all the talks.

2. Panel. A panel is a discussion within a discussion. In this arrangement, a limited number of persons, usually four to seven, sit before an audience and discuss a topic. There are no planned speeches; all the remarks are short and spontaneous. When the panel finishes its discussion, the members answer questions from the audience. During the past few years, the panel has become a very popular method of group discussion. Advancements in electronic media have allowed panel discussions to take place before a television camera, and the viewing audience can call in questions and comments.

3. Informal group discussion (round table). This is the most common form of discussion. It is frequently a nonaudience discussion and tends to be more informal than the other methods. It consists of a small group seated around a table. In this setting, group members exchange their views and information freely and spontaneously. The stimulus-response pattern constantly changes as attention shifts from one person to another. This pattern is well suited for either decision making or information sharing.

You will notice that some public discussions demand interaction among the members of the group and the members of the audience. Often, oral reports or short speeches are given as part of the format. Thus, many group discussions have a public-speaking component.

Private Discussion

We also engage in many, more personal exchanges, called **private discussions**. These may have overlapping purposes, but, as a means of classification, we will examine three of the most common types:

1. Therapy groups. This form of group discussion has many different names—support groups, encounter groups, sensitivity sessions, experiential groups, consciousness-raising groups, and T-group training. Therapy groups are composed of persons who meet to gain personal insights from the advice and feedback provided by the other members of the group. These groups examine issues ranging from drug rehabilitation to management training problems. No group solution is sought; rather, the aim is to learn about oneself and to offer encouragement and support to others.

2. Educational groups. Educational groups have one basic purpose—to help group members learn more about a subject by allowing them to pool their thoughts and information. The content of such knowledge shifts from group to group. A group of teachers might want to learn the best ways to teach their students the metric system, tax accountants might be interested in knowing the ramifications of new federal tax laws, and executives about to be sent overseas might get together to learn about the German culture and language.

3. Problem-solving groups (often called **task-oriented groups**). This is by far the most common of all group discussions. People participate in order to get something done. Problem-solving groups can take the form of a committee, a conference, or simply a group of individuals who share a problem and join together as a means of solving it. One group of business managers, facing lower profits, might meet to decide on the best ways to generate income for their company, while other people might gather to discover how they can keep a landfill from coming to their town.

Cooperation is stressed
in group discussion.

Because of the widespread nature of problem-solving groups, we shall make this
group activity the focus of the remainder of the chapter.

Characteristics of Group Discussion

Although problem-solving groups share many features
with other kinds of groups, they have several distinguish-
ing characteristics, which can be translated into guidelines for participating in a group.
That is to say, knowing these features enables you to have a clearer picture of what discussion is, how discussion operates, and what your role is within the group.

Cooperation is stressed in group discussion. It is important to remember that members of
any problem-solving group have come together because they share a common purpose and
have the same goals—the resolution of a mutual problem. Therefore, cooperation, not competition, is an important attribute of a good problem-solving discussion. Although arguments and disagreement occur, they focus on ideas and content, not on personalities.

Striking a balance between the goals of the individual and the goals of the group
is often a difficult assignment. For example, there are apt to be occasions when the
group's goals differ from individual members' goals. When this happens, there is often
antagonism and resentment. The key to overcoming this problem is to remember that
it is a common goal that has brought the group together. By keeping this essential idea
in mind, the group can often discover complementary goals that can satisfy both the individual and the group. Once members realize they can reach their individual objectives
within the group, they are more likely to seek cooperation over competition.

Analysis and investigation are part of the discussion process. As we have seen, group
members join together because they are vexed by the same problem. To find the best solution to that problem, they must be willing to analyze and investigate all sides of the

issues involved. Members should be open-minded and not fearful of giving all points a fair hearing. A person who already has all the answers does not help the group, for it is the analytic, systematic search for those answers that gives a problem-solving group its investigative spirit. The philosopher John Stuart Mill wrote, "He who knows only his own side of the case, knows little of that." Problem-solving discussion demands that the group examines all sides.

Discussion is a method of reflective thinking. Think for a moment of all the discussions that you have been a part of that ended with nothing being accomplished. How frustrated you felt as the group leaped from point to point in a random and aimless fashion. This should not have happened. Purposeful problem-solving groups follow a thoughtful process that is structured, systematic, and organized. The most common pattern of group reflective thinking is one developed from the phases of reflective thought described by the American educator and philosopher John Dewey. These phases, which will be discussed in detail later in the chapter, consist of (a) defining and limiting the problem, (b) analyzing evidence for the causes and effects of the problem, (c) proposing solutions for the problem, (d) evaluating and analyzing all the solutions, and (e) deciding on ways to put the chosen solution into operation. Even a simple reading of the above five steps reveals a structure that seeks to resolve a problem.

Discussion groups attempt to strike a balance between the emotional and the rational. This balancing of emotional and personal feelings with logical arguments is essential if a group is working toward the resolution of real-life problems. Imagine how difficult it would be to talk about a problem such as capital punishment, birth control, abortion, gays in the military, or censorship without having personal feelings fuse with rational research. This blending of what you feel and what the research reveals is one of the essential components of successful problem solving.

Sincere skepticism is encouraged. Although a group strives for a high degree of solidarity, individuals should feel free to question and criticize ideas they believe are weak or insubstantial. Communication must be open and honest. A group that spends all its time simply nodding heads in agreement produces rather shallow conclusions. Therefore, phrases such as "I'm not sure that is a very good plan" and "Are you certain of that?" should be encouraged by all members. Later in this chapter, when we examine cultural variations in group participation, we will discuss the need to adapt attempts at skepticism to fit with cultural norms. For example, the Japanese tend to value group harmony over the final product and may say yes even when they mean no. For now, it is important to remember the excellent advice offered by the French philosopher Denis Diderot: "What has not been examined impartially has not been well examined. Skepticism is therefore the first step toward truth."

Group cohesion is an important element of group discussion. Although group cohesion may appear to be only an extension of cooperation, it is much more complicated than simply trying to cooperate. Cohesion is the special ingredient that molds a group of individuals into a unit. Group cohesion, once it is established, offers each member a sense of belonging and feeling pride that they affiliated with the group. It tends to be contagious, and, once trust is established, cohesiveness permeates all the group's activities. This bond, which is so important to the group, is encouraged when members share a concern. Reflect on your own motivations in a group, and you will realize that you feel enthusiastic when you believe that other persons share your concerns and your involvement. It is on those occasions when cohesiveness is strongest and when openness and high productivity characterize the group.

Because our culture stresses the individual over the group, it is often difficult to develop feelings of group solidarity and loyalty. In "collective cultures," such as Mexico, Japan, Venezuela, Thailand, Pakistan, and Peru, people are raised to value the group before the individual. For them, cohesiveness is a way of life. If you are from North America, you must learn to appreciate the advantages and rewards of working for a common goal. A willingness to stick together, instead of asking "what is in it for me?" can benefit both you and your colleagues.

Group norms form the basic standards of behavior for the group. Norms tell the participants how to act. As communication patterns evolve, each group establishes various rules of conduct. These guidelines are both formal (a specific person to start the meeting) and informal (people talk whenever they have something to say). Norms are parameters that all group members should clearly perceive and follow as a means of reducing uncertainty. Norms also contribute to cohesiveness and increased productivity. However, norms are not always as transparent as they should be; when this happens, frustration, tension, and anxiety become part of the group's experience. Hence, it is important to work toward realistic norms and to see that all members recognize them.

Most group norms grow out of our cultural experiences with groups, and, as cultures differ, so do norms. For example, in North American culture, we have been raised to say what is on our mind. The proverb "the squeaky wheel gets the grease" tells us to be assertive. However, in many other cultures, the message is quite the opposite. In Japan, for example, there is an adage that "the nail that sticks up is the first to feel the blow of the hammer." In Chinese culture, people learn the proverb "he who has wisdom does not speak, he who speaks does not have wisdom." Hence, in these, and other Asian cultures, group norms call for a different level of participation than do norms in North America.

Problem-solving discussion stresses the democratic process. One point that should be clear by now is the idea that group discussion is a highly democratic process. In a variety of forms, we have stressed the notion that, in a problem-solving group, each person has mutual influence. Each individual member is offering their time and energy because they are disturbed by something in the status quo. Whether it is a parking problem or worldwide pollution, everyone is seeking a solution and therefore has a right to be heard. In this sense, discussion is acting out the words of the Swiss novelist Friedrich Dürrenmatt: "What concerns everyone can only be resolved by everyone."

Limitations of Group Discussion

Having made a case for the discussion process and highlighted the positive characteristics of group discussion, perhaps it is only proper that we pause for a moment to mention some of the conditions and topics that do not lend themselves to group deliberation.

First, there are occasions and topics when only one person, rather than an entire group, is needed to solve a problem or answer a question. It would be a waste of everyone's time to have a group look into how many parking places exist on a college campus. A simple phone call to the security office would answer such an inquiry. Or think of how foolish and humiliating it would be if the "boss" has decided on the new communication system for the office yet you are asked to be a member of a group working on that same topic.

Second, as you shall see, when we examine the steps used by problem-solving groups, good group discussion takes time. Listening to all sides and evaluating a host of options can be a slow, deliberate process. In North American culture, unlike most Latin American and Asian cultures, there is a tendency to value and admire people who can make quick decisions. We often frown on individuals who appear to be moving too slowly. If a group is composed of individuals who are compulsive instead of reflective, the discussion process will not work. In addition, if an immediate decision is needed, group discussion may not be the most efficient method.

Third, because the human personality is individualistic, cohesion and harmony are not always the rule. People often bring personal agendas to the group that create hostility and ill will. Not everyone in a group will become "great friends," and there are situations when personality clashes foster hostility and ill feelings. On these occasions, withdrawal from the group might be a better solution than trying to act out the myth that talking makes everything right. The course of conversation can also be impeded by the fact that most discussion groups are composed of individuals with diverse communication styles. A single group might have someone who is dogmatic, someone who is cautious, and a person who is impetuous. These personality traits, all trying to work together, could greatly limit the productivity of the group.

Fourth, many people believe that group discussion is much like the Yiddish proverb that states, "What use is a good head if the legs won't carry it?" Put in less poetic terms, group discussion can encourage laziness. It can be the head without the legs. The argument is that having a number of people work on the same problem provides some members of the group a means to avoid contributing. Having others to depend on allows them to become lazy and shun their personal responsibility. When deciding if you and your associates should use the discussion process, you need to determine the level of motivation of all the concerned individuals.

Fifth, there are times when the environment itself can limit the effectiveness of the discussion process. We have all seen groups that are influenced by the setting or location of the meeting. For example, think about some occasions in which the setting was so ceremonial and formal that you could not feel comfortable. In those instances, communication behavior was controlled by the environment, and the entire group suffered.

Sixth, if a group is not careful, it can be influenced by the strong pull of conformity. Although we all like to believe that we are highly autonomous and independent, there is nevertheless a part of us that seeks to be accepted. At times, the desire for acceptance contributes to conformity. When this happens, creativity and skepticism suffer. Later in this chapter, we will talk about how participants can cooperate and work for a common goal without sacrificing their uniqueness.

Finally, the success of any group is affected by how much the participants know about the skills and techniques of group discussion. Groups are limited in what they can accomplish by the characteristics of their members. If group members do not understand research techniques, the reflective process, or have not learned how to participate in a group, the final product of the group suffers. To overcome this problem, we will discuss material in this chapter that is intended to help you develop the necessary skills to be an effective group member.

Even with the above limitations, we would suggest that group discussion is an effective problem-solving method. It enables the members of the group to pool their information and ideas while at the same time strengthens their commitment to the final solution because they were part of the solution.

The philosopher Sir Thomas Buxton wrote, "In life, as in chess, fore-thought wins." This notion of forethought has been one of the major themes of this book. In each and every chapter, we have stressed the importance of preparation. Unless you prepare in advance, discussion will be an aimless, purposeless activity. Preparing for discussion involves three closely related activities—(1) selecting a subject, (2) wording the subject, and (3) gathering material.

Preparing for Discussion

On most occasions, members of a private discussion group are in a position to select their own subjects ("How can we control excessive noise in the dormitory?") or at least have a major influence over what aspects of the subject should be examined ("How can we help the college administration recruit more minorities?"). In deciding what to talk about and what problem to investigate, participants will find it helpful to follow a few guidelines:

Selecting a Subject

1. *Decide early if you will be dealing with a proposition of fact, value, or policy.* In chapter 14, when we examined the issue of persuasion, we introduced you to questions of fact, value, and policy. Propositions of *fact* are those that are concerned with the truth of a question or statement. Such questions are concerned with the existence of things, the occurrence of acts, the classification of data, and the sequence of events. A group asking "What is the current status of the world's rain forests?" would be investigating a question of fact. If the question centers around a proposition of *value*, the group would be discussing an issue that involves a subjective judgment: "What is the best community college in our city?" It is probably safe to say that most discussions focus on questions of *policy*. These are issues that are concerned with future actions and solutions. The word "should" is the key to these questions. "What should our university do about recent affirmative action rulings?"

2. *Select problems in which the participants are interested.* If the members of the group feel personally involved and are committed to the subject, they will be active in both research and participation. If you were living in a dormitory and found that the noise kept you from studying, which in turn was lowering your grades, you would want the problem resolved.

3. *The topic should be important and worth discussing.* Time is too precious and serious questions are too numerous to waste time on trivial matters. "What are the best rides at Disneyland?" might be an interesting topic but certainly not worthy of a group's time and research efforts.

4. *Select problems that can be investigated prior to the discussion and that can be discussed in the time allotted to the group.* A group that is rushed, both before and during the discussion, usually produces a solution that reflects just such a hasty analysis and lack of deliberation.

5. *The subject should present a problem.* If the group is going to be motivated in a problem-solving discussion, its members should feel a common need to find a solution. The topic should provide at least two sides for investigation. If the solution is obvious at the outset, there is no valid reason to engage in the time-consuming steps of the reflective process.

Wording the Subject

The correct statement of the problem area is as important as the problem itself, for, if the group formulates the problem in a way that distorts the issue, confusion and misunderstanding will result. A poorly worded subject can also cost the group valuable time. The group will thrash around, trying to decide what interests it. In addition, the general subject area must be worded into a workable topic if all group members are to deal with the same problem. Consider the following suggestions for wording the subject:

1. *Phrase the subject-problem as a question.* The question highlights a specific problem while it motivates persons to seek answers to the problem. Phrasing such as "price fixing," "how to be happy," and "war and peace" are so general that they cannot be discussed in a specific manner. On the other hand, a question such as "What should be the role of the federal government in regulating children's television?" or "What can our college do to improve the registration process for entering freshmen?" calls for an answer; hence, discussion can take place.

2. *Phrase the question clearly.* If the wording is ambiguous, the group may have to spend long periods of time trying to decide what to talk about. A question such as "What should be the current status of business?" is an example of ambiguity. The group must stop and decide what "business" and "current status" mean before it can even start working on the problem. Careful wording of the problem, even before the group begins discussion, also serves the dual functions of limiting and restricting the scope of the problem. A topic worded "How can we best secure an additional one hundred thousand dollars for graduate fellowships at our university?" indicates precisely what the group will talk about.

3. *Whenever possible, avoid wording the problem-question in a yes-or-no form.* A yes-or-no response limits the available solutions and leads to debate instead of cooperation. Questions such as "Should our school adopt a year-round session?" place restrictions on the group and limit the responses participants can make. To provide the group with more than two answers, the question could have been phrased "What is the most effective way to use the resources and facilities of the university?" This wording allows the group to examine a host of options, including year-round sessions.

4. *Word the topic impartially.* We all know that one can state a topic in such a way that it favors one side. One can also word a topic so that the conclusion appears obvious at the start. Both of these evils should be avoided. "Since all students would like a Democrat to be elected president, how can we raise money for the campaign of our Democratic governor?" This example reflects partiality, states the conclusion at the start, and therefore greatly limits the group's latitude.

Gathering Material

Depth of preparation is as vital in a discussion as in a speech. Each member of a group depends on the other members for fresh ideas; if one member fails to gather concrete data, the entire group suffers.

In chapter 8, we discussed the steps and techniques of gathering and preparing material for a speech. Because these procedures are also essential for successful group discussion, they are worth reviewing.

First, *think carefully about the subject before you begin your research.* To start researching a topic before you know specifically what problem you are trying to solve wastes a great deal of time and contributes to a high degree of frustration. For example,

It is important to
gather information
before the group
begins.

knowing that you are concerned with prison reforms, and not the entire criminal justice system in the United States, could save you both time and energy.

Second, *decide what you already know about the subject and what areas you should investigate in more detail*. If you have a part-time position in a maximum security prison,
you would likely have some excellent firsthand knowledge of the inmates' daily activities. However, you might find that you need more research on areas such as prison bud-
gets, training programs for the guards, and visitation rights.

Third, *after you have identified your research strengths and weaknesses, gather your information*. As you recall, this information can take the form of illustrations, examples, expert
testimony, or statistics drawn from interviews, printed material, and electronic media.

Finally, *record and organize your material in a purposeful and meaningful pattern*. For
a group to be successful, its planning must be as organized as a speech. Hence, your material and your group must be organized around a sequence that will make sense to all
the members. This means that you should arrange your materials in the same general
order that the group deliberations will follow. You would not start with the solution;
therefore, your notes should not begin with the solution. Most problem-solving groups
use the **reflective pattern** as their organizational scheme. If you are going to be in a
group whose basic aim is problem solving, it will be helpful to organize your research
into the following general categories:

I. Define and limit the problem.
   A. Define important words and phrases found in the problem.
   B. Find materials that help limit the scope and range of the problem area.

  II. Analyze the problem.
    A. Research material related to the history of the problem and place it next in your outline.
    B. Provide information and evidence to highlight specific incidents of the problem. (These are usually called effects or symptoms of the problem.)
    C. Gather evidence that reveals and explains the causes of the problem.
  III. List all possible solutions.
  IV. Evaluate and analyze the solutions.
    A. Exploring the advantages and disadvantages is often helpful.
    B. Evidence that examines the effects of all the solutions is normally treated in this portion of the outline.
  V. Treat evidence and research that discusses the best method of putting the solution into practice.

Organizing a Discussion

The famous British orator Edmund Burke once remarked, "Good order is the foundation of all good things." With regard to group problem solving, organization is essential. As we have seen, successful groups and the individuals within those groups do not simply jump from point to point as they attempt to solve their problem. Rather, if a group and its members are to accomplish a specific purpose, a sense of organization is crucial.

Although there have been many modifications to John Dewey's original pattern, in most instances group discussion follows the steps he developed over fifty years ago. Dewey advanced a simple pattern allowing discussants to adapt the steps of problem solving to group deliberation: (1) recognition of a problem, (2) description of the problem, (3) discovery of possible solutions, (4) evaluation of solutions and acceptance of the best solution, and (5) planning action for the preferred solution.

Most problem-solving groups can derive numerous benefits from using the steps of reflective thinking. Two of the more common advantages are worth mentioning. First, it is assumed that, by performing the five steps systematically, a group will progress logically from a problem to a solution. By analyzing the key issues step-by-step, reflective thinking seeks to eliminate the haphazard decision-making processes characteristic of many deliberations. Think of all the occasions in which you were in a group that chose the first solution proposed, only to find later that the decision would have been much better if judgment had been suspended until all alternatives had been examined.

A second advantage of Dewey's five steps is manifest within the group itself. If the entire group is concerned with the same step of the reflective thinking process at any given moment, then all the participants are talking about the same issues at the same time. We hope to be spared the person who begins a discussion by saying, "Now, the best way to solve this problem is . . ." Because each person knows what phase the group is in at every instance, it is a simple matter to tell a person who is out of order that he or she has bypassed the first step of the problem-solving process, the defining of terms.

Recognizing and Defining the Problem

Before we can solve a problem, we must be aware that one exists. Therefore, the first step in trying to resolve or understand a problem is *defining and limiting it.* By defining the problem early in the discussion, the group can set limits if the topic is too broad for the amount of time allotted. Defining terms early also lets the group make sure that they are all talking about the same issues. If a group were examining the issue of overpopulation, it would be beneficial to decide if they were talking about global, third-world, or United States population problems. By analyzing crucial terms and key concepts early in a discussion, a group is in a better position to comprehend the problem's scope and seriousness. For example, if a group were to discuss the topic of high school dropouts, it should use the initial period of its discussion to define "high school dropout." Is it anyone under sixteen years old, or is the age to be eighteen and younger? Deciding issues such as these early in a discussion helps a group avoid the all-too-common problem of nearing the end of a discussion only to discover that no common definition was agreed on.

After group members have recognized, stated, defined, and limited the problem, they are ready to *analyze the nature of the problem*. Such analysis and evaluation normally demand that the participants exchange ideas and information on three topics: (1) the history of the problem, (2) the effects of the problem, and (3) the causes of the problem.

Description of the Problem

1. History. Adlai Stevenson offered sound advice when he wrote, "We can chart our future clearly and wisely only when we know the path which has led to the present." *What has led to a problem situation may offer insight into how that situation can be remedied.* For instance, if a group is discussing increases in student tuition, it might be helpful to explore the history of these fees to find out when they were first initiated and the rationale behind the proposed increase. If the topic is the worldwide dwindling elephant population, the group would want to look at facts and figures that demonstrate historically that the elephant population was 1.3 million in 1979, 650,000 in 1991, 600,000 in 1993, and 555,000 in 1995. A group discussing television censorship would be aided if they could historically trace how censorship was applied with this medium in the past.

On occasion, the history phase must be omitted. Problems that call for immediate action may not offer a group the luxury of historical review. In addition, very new problems do not have much history. However, in most instances the history phase of the discussion is an important one.

2. Effects. Using the various forms of support mentioned in chapter 6, *the group should discuss how serious the problem is, who is being affected, and how large the problem is.* By reporting observed effects (what is happening?), the members can see the outward manifestations of the problem and how widespread it is. For example, if the group is discussing "What can be done about the increased crime rate among teenagers?" someone might ask if the problem is serious; in response, another participant might attempt to substantiate the seriousness of the problem by stating that "the governor indicated the crime rate among teenagers has doubled in the past ten years." A group trying to solve a problem related to AIDS would benefit by knowing the number of current AIDS cases and who is affected by AIDS. By knowing these facts the group can see what is transpiring at this time. If the problem is rain forest depletion, someone in the group could look at the effects by pointing out, "As of July 1994, rain forests were being burned and cleared at a rate of 42 million acres a year." By knowing what is happening (amount of rain forest being destroyed) and how widespread it is (effects of the problem), the group can later decide how to remedy the situation.

3. Causes. The group, having investigated and verified the effects of the problem, then turns its attention to an examination of the conditions that produced the effects identified earlier (why are things happening?). For example, in deciding what caused the increased crime rate (effect), someone might offer support to establish teenage unemployment as a possible cause. A group studying highway safety could examine the causes of the problem by noting that "well over 50 percent of all traffic deaths and injuries have been caused by people not wearing their seat belts." They could offer yet another cause by looking at the evidence that says "five hundred people are killed each week in alcohol-related crashes." By knowing what created the problem (not wearing seat belts, alcohol), the group can later propose solutions that directly relate to the problem.

Discovery of Possible Solutions

Before a group recommends any solutions to a problem, the members should *decide what criteria are most appropriate in judging these solutions*. Criteria are the standards that the group applies to any solution they might propose. For example, a group might decide that any solution to teenage crime should (1) not violate the constitutional rights of the person arrested, (2) not be too costly, and (3) not add to the overcrowded conditions now facing most juvenile detention facilities. A group deciding on which fast-food outlets should be allowed on campus might establish that any solution should (1) ensure fair hiring practices, (2) not violate existing campus laws, and (3) not result in increased food costs. If a group were focusing on alternative fuel sources, it could say that any solution should (1) not be costly, (2) not create serious pollution problems, and (3) not make us dependent on other countries for fuel.

After the group has determined the specific problem to be solved, examined the effects and causes of the problem, and listed the criteria the solution(s) must meet, the group is ready to suggest possible solutions.

Groups can suggest either singular solutions ("The courts should be stricter with teenage offenders") or multiple solutions ("Stricter courts, better probation procedures, and parent counseling programs are needed"). At this stage of the discussion, it is important to *list as many solutions as possible*—if they meet the criteria. If the topic is alternative fuel sources for automobiles, the group might list and consider methanol gases (natural gas, coal, wood), compressed natural gas, ethanol (corn, sugar), and electricity (solar, nuclear, fossil fuel).

Evaluation of Solutions and Acceptance of the Best Solution

One of the most important characteristics of reflective thinking is the practice of withholding judgment until all possible solutions can be objectively and completely considered (a concept often referred to in the literature of group processes as "suspended conclusions"). The participants should *talk about each solution in detail*, testing their remarks with concrete evidence and analyzing their conclusions in light of logical reasoning. In this deliberation, the advantages and disadvantages of each solution should be discussed and evaluated. For example, the group dealing with alternative fuel sources might present evidence and discuss how methanol has fewer hydrocarbons than petroleum but, on the negative side, has only half the energy content of gasoline and is fatal if ingested or absorbed. They could note how electricity has almost no emission but has a range limited to about one hundred miles per charging period.

In this phase of the discussion, some of the following questions should be asked:

- How will the solution solve the problem?
- What will the solution do to the causes and effects mentioned earlier in the discussion?
- What will the solution do to the status quo?
- How does the solution meet the criteria?

Once these questions have been answered, and all the advantages and disadvantages have been discussed, the group is ready to decide which of the solutions will best solve, or at least minimize, the problem. The acceptance of the best solution is tentative and related only to the problem mentioned in the discussion.

As a final step, the group must decide whether or not its preferred solution can be put into effect. If the solution seems workable, desirable, and practical, the group should determine the most effective means of implementing its findings and conclusions.

Plan of Action

Specific plans for implementation are influenced by factors such as the topic, the time, and the power of the group. For example, a group discussing a local campus problem might present its solution to the college administration or to the student council. By contrast, a group dealing with an international topic might write a letter to representatives in Washington.

Often, solutions are presented in a symposium format. On these occasions, each member of the group gives a five- or ten-minute speech that summarizes the conclusions reached during the discussion process.

As indicated earlier, the reflective process, although it is the most widely used discussion pattern, is by no means the only organizational scheme available to group participants. Two additional patterns may increase your ability to practice successful small-group communication in a variety of settings: the creative problem-solving pattern and brainstorming.

Other Discussion Patterns

A variation of Dewey's reflective process is one developed by Osborn and Parnes. This sequence seems most suited to situations with many possible solutions. Like Dewey's pattern, this organizational scheme uses five steps. *Each step takes the form of a question.* The following outline illustrates the steps:

Creative Problem-Solving Pattern

I. What is the nature of the problem—what are we here to talk about?
   A. Do we need to define any terms?
   B. How much freedom do we have?
   C. What has been happening that is unsatisfactory?
      1. What are the manifestations and effects of the problem?
      2. What has been tried in the past to correct the problem?
      3. What additional information do we need to assess the problem?
   D. What goal would we like to achieve?
   E. What factors (causes) have brought about this problem?
   F. What is the best summary of the problem we can offer?
      1. Do we all agree on this summary?
      2. Should we divide the problem into subareas and subproblems?

II. What should be done to solve the problem? (A brainstorming session is often used at this juncture.)

III. What standards and criteria shall we use to judge the merits of our possible solutions?

IV. What are the merits of each solution?
   A. What solutions can be eliminated?
   B. Can we combine any of our solutions?
   C. How do our solutions match our criteria?

V. How do we put our solution into operation?
   A. Who will do what, when, and how?
   B. Shall we follow up on our procedures?

Brainstorming

In its simplest form, **brainstorming** is a technique that generates the free expression of ideas within a group setting. Those who favor this discussion style maintain it has two major advantages over some of the other discussion formats. First, it fosters creativity because it is not as rigid and structured as the other patterns. Group members are urged to string their ideas onto the ideas of others. Members are encouraged to make contributions as rapidly as possible, and no ideas are barred. In fact, there are certain "brainstorming rules" that a group adopts as a way of supporting this open and loosely structured orientation. The second advantage of brainstorming is that it advocates equal participation. Since the goal is to produce as many ideas as possible—no matter how bizarre they may seem—people feel free to take an active role.

The two benefits of brainstorming can be translated into the following five "rules":

1. All adverse criticism is prohibited during the early stages of the brainstorming session. One is not to criticize ideas or personalities until *all* ideas have been suggested.

2. "Freewheeling" is welcomed. Members are urged to submit even the most bizarre and remote ideas and suggestions. The assumption is that it is better to reject an idea than to not even hear that idea.

3. Quantity of ideas is encouraged. Members are asked to submit long lists of ideas, the theory being "the more the better."

4. Combination and improvement of ideas is one of the chief goals of brainstorming; therefore, each member feels free to add to any idea being discussed for one idea can trigger another.

5. All ideas should be recorded so that they can be evaluated. The cataloging of ideas means the group will be able to eventually slow down and talk about those ideas that, at first glance, were generated with great dispatch.

Although brainstorming is loosely structured, and at times appears chaotic, it often has the effect of getting the group moving at the same time the group is generating ideas. As noted for the previous pattern, some groups insert a brief brainstorming session into their regular discussion.

Although to this point we have been talking about organization, structure and procedure, *this book is about all forms of human communication*. It is about the ways we send and receive messages. Therefore, the remainder of this chapter will be concerned with how you can become a competent communicator whenever you find yourself in a group.

Participating in Small Groups

Group interaction and interpersonal relations are highly complex concepts and cannot be taught effectively in a single session or by reading a few pages of techniques. However, most writers in the area of small-group communication agree that there are certain communication requirements for successful small-group communication and that these behaviors *can be learned and practiced by motivated participants*. These behaviors are usually divided into two interrelated categories: (1) *functional and task roles* and (2) *maintenance and supportive roles*. The first set of roles, or behaviors, centers around the communication functions that must be performed if the group is to achieve its desired purpose and accomplish its goals. These roles primarily concentrate on the "duties and responsibilities" of group members to get a discussion started and keep it moving toward its goal. The second set, the maintenance and supportive roles, has a more personal dimension associated with it. These are the roles we play in an attempt to establish and preserve group and individual harmony; they are intended to build group cohesiveness and solidarity.

Placing communicative behavior into two categories is a very subjective assignment. Inevitably, categories overlap, and in some instances a single sentence might serve in both functional and supportive roles. For example, you might be performing both kinds of roles if you were to say, "John, your ideas always help us over difficult periods (supportive role). What do you think we should do about the amount of money this plan will cost (task role)?"

Performing the following functional and task roles, whenever they are needed, will profit both you and the group:

Functional and Task Roles

1. *Your participation should adhere to the logical pattern the group selects.* If the group chooses Dewey's reflective pattern, see to it that the group stays on track. Jumping from effects to solutions and back to definitions of terms not only wastes time but frustrates the participants.

2. *Make your presence known throughout the discussion.* Take it upon yourself to be an active member of the group. The amount of time the group has and the number of participants obviously influence the frequency and length of your contributions, but you should feel free to participate as often as you have something to say. However, when possible, you should keep your contributions and exchanges brief and precise. Long and detailed contributions, although sometimes needed, frequently bore the other participants and keep others from getting their turn to talk.

3. *Ask questions of the other participants.* A lack of understanding about what is said by any of the participants hampers the reflective process. By asking questions of one another whenever there is a basic misunderstanding or need for information, the group can overcome many obstacles. Many times, groups move ahead in a discussion only to discover later that they did not understand the earlier premises that led to the current stage of the discussion. By raising questions, the group can locate errors in reasoning. For example, someone might say, "Roger, my readings made it look as if the administration was completely at fault. Is that what you found out?" Asking Roger this question encourages further deliberation on the topic before the group moves on.

Even when you have objections, they should be formed as questions. It gives the group something to work for, and keeps hostility at a lower level, if you say "Why do you think that will work?" instead of "That is not going to work."

4. *Supply leadership for the group whenever needed.* Many participants rely solely on the judgment of the leader for decisions that should be the responsibility of all participants. Many leadership functions can be performed easily by any alert member of the group. For example, any participant can offer summaries whenever he or she feels they are appropriate and would aid the group. Do not make the mistake of assuming that the leader, because of the title, has all the answers. If you perceive that there is a task that needs to be performed, you should perform it. If the group appears fatigued, you should feel free to say, "Why don't we think about stopping for tonight?"

5. *Speak to the point being discussed and stay on that point when you speak.* One of the most common errors made by participants in a group is that they stray off the subject being discussed. During that fraction of a second before you get ready to speak, ask yourself if what you plan to say is directly related to the topic currently on the table.

Maintenance and Supportive Roles

Having discussed functional and task roles, we will examine six maintenance and supportive roles that also contribute to successful group discussion:

1. *Be tolerant of individual and cultural differences that will appear in the group.* Each of us is unique; we come from different backgrounds and, therefore, bring different personal histories to a group. These individual and cultural differences will be manifest in countless ways. What one person finds humorous, another may consider offensive. What is "planned growth" to you may appear to be "stifling free enterprise" to the person sitting next to you. From judgments of beauty to issues of truth, our decisions are influenced by our experiences, and, thus, having had different experiences, we often reach different conclusions. Effective participants are aware that perceptual differences are a natural outgrowth of individual and cultural diversity and that, in most cases, this diversity can benefit the group.

2. *A watchful participant is aware of the total communication situation and is cognizant that symbols other than words can send messages.* It is important to be alert to all aspects of nonverbal communication—facial expressions, body movements, eye contact, spatial relationships, and seating arrangements. For example, some members in the group might be "talking" with their bodies as they become upset with the group and slowly edge their chairs from the inner circle. Your own use of nonverbal communication should be considered. Avoid such actions as poor eye contact or slumping in your chair. Both of these behaviors often convey boredom and disrespect.

3. *All participants should provide clear, concise feedback.* Respond directly, verbally and nonverbally, to the remarks of others. We all know how frustrating it is when we make a statement to someone and receive only silence. In a group, the problem is compounded, for there are eight or ten persons who are not responding to what is being said. By nodding, smiling, or talking, we let our colleagues know our reactions to what they present. Feedback not only keeps the group moving, but it allows other persons to know we are interested in them and their ideas.

4. *Create an atmosphere conducive to constructive and purposeful discussion.* This means supporting and rewarding the contributions of others—even if they represent dissenting views. Remember that a relaxed, friendly atmosphere is far more productive than a tense one. Simply ask yourself this question: "Is it not true that I am at ease and do my best work when I am treated fairly and in a situation that is free from hostility and anxiety?" If the answer is yes, then do your part to make the communication environment a pleasant one. Discussion should not be conducted in an authoritarian atmosphere but in a climate in which each person is honest and speaks freely. It is a healthy atmosphere in which each person can say, "The discussion belongs to all of us—it is a chance to say what we think and feel."

5. *Communication is a two-way process; listeners also play a key role in discussion.* It is unfair to place the burden for understanding completely on the speaker. Participants in a discussion cannot sit back and contentedly assume they have nothing to do but wait for their turns to talk. Each listener must pay close attention to what is being said. Participants must ask questions and attempt to narrow and define all ambiguous concepts.

Listening to the feelings and remarks of others means that the deviant is respected as much as the person who conforms. Not only is it philosophically consistent with democratic principles to accept the deviant, but it also proves beneficial to the group. The deviant is often the one who challenges inconsistent evidence and faulty reasoning. He or she is often the one who makes us reevaluate our assumptions and values, and this deviance can, on occasion, force us from apathy and complacency. Welcome and encourage the "oddball"—he or she could be you.

6. *Be prepared to play a variety of roles.* A competent group member is not tied to a single mode of behavior but, rather, can adapt to people and events. Gerald L. Wilson and Michael S. Hanna, in their book *Groups in Context: Leadership and Participation in Small Groups*, recommend some roles that can have a positive influence on the group. Perform some of these roles if it will help the group accomplish its purpose:

    a. *Evaluator role:* "I am not sure we have spent enough time looking at this issue. I suggest we don't move on until we have examined this idea in a little more detail."

    b. *Initiator role:* "I think the time might be right for us to establish some standards by which we can judge our solutions. What do the rest of you think?"

    c. *Opinion seeker role:* "Do any of you have some evidence that would tell us how long this has been a problem?"

d. *Coordinator role:* "It seems that Robert and Susan are saying about the same thing. Perhaps we now have some agreement on this idea."

e. *Energizer role:* "We have accomplished a great deal so far. Why don't we keep going so we can finish this project by tonight."

Presenting Your Ideas

Regardless of the role you play or the contributions you make in a small-group discussion, it is important that your comments be timely and presented clearly and concisely. If you do not speak well, you damage your chances for accomplishing your purpose. Therefore, as we conclude this section on participation, we need to remind you that your remarks should (a) relate, (b) state, (c) support, and (d) integrate.

First, *when offering an idea, you should relate it to what is being discussed at that moment or to something that has been talked about earlier.* Remarks that are simply submitted to the group without being placed into a context often result in confusion or force the group to depart from the established agenda. Think of how frustrating it is for the entire group when someone begins to recount a personal experience related to the causes of the problem while the group is trying to work on specific solutions to a problem. Therefore, try to begin your contribution by linking it to what is going on at the moment: "Pat, you are right about the administration not facing the problem, but I think there are other reasons for the lack of support for this proposed clinic."

Second, *once you have used what was being discussed as a transition to your comments, you are ready to state your position or offer some new information.* "My research revealed that there was also a lack of interest among the students for this new clinic." It is important that you make your statements clearly and concisely.

Third, *once you have tied your comments to what is going on and have stated your position clearly, you should offer support for your assertion.* "A recent poll in the school paper showed that only 13 percent of the student body wanted the new clinic. Most felt they did not want their funds used on a project that would not be completed until after they had graduated."

Fourth, *you should conclude your comments by integrating them into the flow of the meeting.* This can be done by ending your contribution with a question: "Do the rest of you feel that the lack of progress is caused by both the administration and the students?"

Leadership in Small Groups

Having examined the characteristics of participation, we are now ready to move to the topic of leadership. *Leadership is exercising influence over a group to help it achieve its goal.* What is interesting about our definition of leadership is that *it can apply to all the members of a group.* In most instances, the person called "the leader" is also a participant. Therefore, our division of skills and techniques is not as inflexible as it first appears. What is important is that you learn both roles—leader and participant—to become an effective group member. By knowing the characteristics of participants and leaders, you can function in either role whenever necessary.

Styles of Leadership

Learning how to lead a group is much more complex than simply memorizing a series of techniques. Each group, because of its unique personality and choice of topic, requires leadership specifically suited to its needs. While one group may work best with a strong leader, another group might be hampered by such control. Therefore, various styles of leadership have evolved. Most treatments of approaches to leadership have identified five styles found in discussion groups. Let us briefly examine these five approaches so that you will be able to decide which style is most appropriate for your particular group. We shall begin with leadership that seeks control of its members and move gradually to a leadership that permits complete and total freedom.

At one end of the continuum is the pattern called **authoritarian** or **autocratic leadership.** As the name implies, nearly absolute power rests with the leader, who not only conducts the meeting and leads the group but also makes most of the important decisions concerning content and participation. As the leader, this person normally assigns specific tasks to certain people. If someone exercises this much control over the group, it is usually because he or she has a power position before the group ever gets together. He or she is the "boss" prior to the meeting and remains the "boss" during the meeting.

When time is short and group efficiency crucial, **strong supervisory leadership** is often used. Although this type of leadership is not as radical as the authoritarian approach, it is based on the premise that groups need a strong and aggressive leader. The leader usually asks specific questions and directs the flow of the meeting in a direction that has been personally predetermined. In essence, the leader is concerned with procedure and solutions and spends little or no time treating issues of group maintenance, member satisfaction, and interpersonal relationships.

The **democratic style** of leadership is most often found in group discussion. The leader plays an active role but sees to it that a democratic atmosphere prevails in the group. The leader is objective and attempts not to pass judgment on ideas or people. This leader encourages participation, stresses individual initiative, and shares control by allowing members to decide how tasks will be divided. Unlike an authoritarian or supervisory leader, a democratic leader is concerned with personalities as well as procedure.

Group-centered leadership offers the participants the freedom to make procedural as well as policy decisions. This style of leadership is predicated on two premises: (1) each person has the capacity to lead and, therefore, the ability to determine goals; (2) people will support most readily the policies they have helped create. Hence, leadership duties are not vested in any individual but are shared by all members. For example, if the group would be aided by a running summary, any of the group's members could offer that summary.

The most permissive of all is the **leaderless style.** When this style prevails, there is a total absence of leadership. Leaderless discussions are often characterized by a high degree of member satisfaction but a low degree of productivity. It takes skilled participants to function in such anarchy.

In summary, we believe that *a leader is a person who leads only when leadership is needed, a group member who positively influences and assists the other members to achieve the group's goals.*

Leadership Tasks

Research in group discussion and group dynamics has revealed that the so-called born leader is a myth. Leadership is composed of traits and characteristics that can be learned and cultivated. In an ideal group, everyone possesses those traits, and we would not have to worry about appointing someone to serve as the leader. In this model situation, all the participants would monitor the group's behavior as well as their own, the roles of leadership would be diffused throughout the group, and the leadership tasks would be performed by any person who believed that a particular task would benefit the group.

There are, however, occasions when shared leadership does not work or is inappropriate. For example, the principal of a school would most likely lead a faculty meeting. In such instances, the group must rely on a single leader to guide it and to stimulate participation. Even in these cases, though, numerous leadership functions can be shared.

Because leadership duties can be shared by all members or can be vested in one person, the suggestions that follow apply both to an appointed leader and to any participant who perceives a need for leadership in the group and attempts to fulfill that need.

The leader has the responsibility to see that the discussion gets started. This assignment actually has a number of components. First, the phrase "getting started" often involves having group members get acquainted. We have all experienced an uneasy silence when forced to interact with strangers. The leader should help us over these periods by making sure there are some introductions and social conversation before the group begins its serious deliberations. Second, part of getting started means setting the tentative agenda for the meeting. This might mean everything from explaining what the group hopes to accomplish down to a discussion for the meeting to end. Third, the leader should also state the purpose of the meeting and mention the problem to be discussed. As the philosopher Irving Kristol has noted, "Part of every solution is to state the problem correctly." Fourth, the leader needs to make arrangements for the proceedings to be recorded. Having someone take notes during the discussion is beneficial for the entire group. For example, there will be many occasions when the members will want to know what they accomplished earlier in the discussion. Reviewing the group's notes can provide that summary. By having previous decisions at their disposal, the group can avoid needless duplication. Finally, these early duties should also include taking care of some mechanical and personal chores such as making sure that there is a place for the group to meet, that the necessary furniture is available (arranged in a circle if possible), and that the participants will be made to feel comfortable in the setting.

The leader should create a cooperative, democratic climate. A group atmosphere characterized by demagoguery is not very creative and is often filled with discontent. You know from your own experience that, if you feel uncomfortable due to the actions of an authoritarian leader, you do not do your best work. On the other hand, imagine how you would be encouraged to talk if a leader were to say to you, "Peter, you seem to understand what happened last year. What do you think we should do?" Part of being a democratic leader means getting participation among all members. This includes changing the communication behavior of the monopolist as well as the shy member of the group.

The leader should try to remain impartial whenever possible. Among group members, a tendency exists to view the leader as a boss or someone of superior rank. Viewed in this way, a leader who states his or her personal conclusions at the beginning of a discussion tends to close the door on free and open deliberation. This does not mean that, as leader, you cannot take part, simply that you must see that all sides are presented and that you do not become a spokesperson for one point of view too early in the discussion.

The leader should see that a plan, an agenda, or an organizational pattern is followed and that the main phases of the problem are considered. If the group uses an agenda, the leader should become its guardian. The leader must always be asking, "Where have we been?" "Where are we now?" and "Where are we going?" By using these phrases, the leader can keep the discussion organized and also keep everyone informed of the group's progress. Imagine how helpful it would be to have someone say, "Now that we have seen the effects of overpopulation, it might be to our advantage to examine some of the causes of this problem." Although personal stories can be interesting, they often take the group away from its task. When this happens, the leader should help the group return to the issue being discussed before the irrelevant comment was made ("Mary, that was helpful, but I think we should be talking about what has caused this problem").

The leader should try to clarify details and contributions whenever possible. If necessary, contributions should be rephrased. Asking appropriate questions is one of the most effective ways of clarifying ideas and information. These questions can take a variety of forms. First, a question can probe for additional information to clarify the point being made: "That idea seems unique. Did any of the rest of you come across a similar plan?" Second, a question can refocus the conversation on the topic: "Mary, how do you think those statistics relate to the idea Tom was making?" Third, a question can help clarify the issue to move the group forward: "Okay, we seem to know what caused the fee increase; what can we do about it?" Finally, a question can deal with an interpersonal problem: "Tom, you and Susan seem to have conflicting interpretations of this event. Why do you think that is the case?"

A leader should know the appropriate times to intervene. As we have said elsewhere, personal hostilities and pettiness have no place in a problem-solving group discussion. A group of this kind cannot waste its time on therapy; it has too much to do. Therefore, the leader must set a tone that does not allow destructive behavior to develop. If, by chance, conflicts do emerge, the leader must resolve them. The leader may have to change the behavior of a troublesome participant, settle an argument, and at times even offer friendly reprimands.

Part of intervening might take the form of the leader discouraging side conversations between some members of the group. It is rude and disconcerting to have two or more participants engaging in a private conversation while the group is conducting its business. On these occasions, the leader might very tactfully ask the discourteous members to direct their comments to the entire group.

The leader should offer periodic summaries throughout the proceedings and also bring the discussion to a satisfactory conclusion. Internal summaries allow the group to see what they have accomplished during various phases of the deliberations. The solution can also be summarized if one has been reached, or a summary can highlight the points of agreement. The discussion can also be concluded by reviewing the questions and problems that still remain unanswered.

If the group plans to meet again, it is important that the meeting end on a positive note. Creating this friendly tone as the members leave is yet another task an effective leader must perform.

Later in this chapter, we will examine the role of culture in group communication in some detail. However, for now let us mention just a few cultural variations in how people perceive and respond to leadership.

First, as part of our culture, each of us has learned how to define, perceive, and respond to status. We have also learned how close or far away we are from power. This idea is called *power distance*. It basically refers to whether or not status differences among people are minimized or maximized. People who are from high power distance cultures

Culture and Leadership

(India, China, Mexico, Philippines) have learned to live with rigid status differences, hierarchical definitions of assigned roles, and a strong line of authority. People from these cultures often find it easier to work with leaders who are domineering and arbitrary. In the North American and many Scandinavian cultures, people often oppose leadership that is too rigid and controlling. As you move in and out of various groups, you will find people who like autocratic leaders and those who do their best work with a democratic leader.

Second, there are also cultural differences in what is called *"participatory decision making,"* which can influence the variable of leadership. For example, in Japan, where quality circles are popular, workers and managers work jointly on many projects. Ideas and information flow freely during meetings and discussions. However, this style of leadership would not work in Latin America, India, or most Arab cultures. Most members of these cultures expect "the boss" to decide and are not prepared to function as leader.

Third, there are even cultural disparities in the amount of comfort people experience both with leaders who ask for an abundance of *rules and regulations* and with those who have a minimum of guidelines. In the Chinese culture, in which the ordering of relationships goes back to the time of Confucius, most people feel comfortable with dictums and canons of behavior. Such is not the case in most Western cultures. Individuality is so strong that most North Americans dislike having to follow rules and challenge all attempts to regulate their actions.

Fourth, as we have seen, cultures also vary in what they *expect from their leaders*. In cultures that have a strong work ethic, such as the German culture, group accomplishments are more important than group satisfaction. Hence, people in those cultures expect their leaders to get things done. Your personal experiences tell you that, in North America, it is also important for people to feel good about their group affiliations. Leaders are counted on to create an atmosphere that contributes to those feelings of satisfaction.

Fifth, *perceptions of formality* is yet another approach to leadership that is reflected in culture. The Western notion of informality is in sharp contrast with the formality found in much of the world. In the cultures of Germany, Japan, Egypt, Turkey, Korea, Mexico, and Iran, people have been raised to respect rank and status. When members of these cultures are in groups, they will treat the leader as a very high status person. They will not contradict the leader and, in most instances, will not take an active role unless the leader urges them to do so.

Finally, there are cultural differences in the *perception of gender*, which can influence leadership. In cultures that highly value masculine traits (Indian, Japanese, German, Mediterranean), it is very difficult for a woman to function as leader. However, in cultures with a more fluid distribution of sex roles (North American, Norwegian, Swedish), gender is less of a consideration.

Dealing with Conflict

On many occasions, the behaviors described in the previous section do not resolve every problem that a group encounters. Human nature being what it is, most groups face some conflict during their existence. In spite of our best intentions, the potential for interpersonal controversy seems to shadow most of our relationships. Because we are all unique, we bring our originality to every group. When we add the influence of culture to this mix, these differences are bound to create some tension and even conflict. Because conflict is so common, it is important that we understand it and learn to treat it in ways that are constructive instead of destructive. If we let animosity and anger fester, the group will suffer. A Chinese proverb says it even better: "The fire you kindle for your enemies often burns yourself." Why is it that interpersonal and group conflicts flare with such regularity? What can we do about them when they arise?

In its simplest form, **conflict** is a disagreement over an opinion or a course of action facing members of a group. This normally happens when two or more participants perceive obstacles interfering with their own or the group's goals. What is interesting about conflict is that it can revolve around trivial matters ("Why does Ann always get the chair at the head of the table?"), or it can have its roots in more significant issues ("I don't want to be around people who believe the way you do about abortion").

Definition of Conflict

Not all conflict is bad, however; on many occasions, rewards can be gained from group conflict. For example, conflict can defuse more serious problems if the conflict is dealt with when it first arises. In this sense, conflict is used to stimulate rather than stifle discussion. Conflict can also lead to the acquisition of concealed information if the conflict encourages people to expose their hidden agendas. We feel better when things are out in the open. If handled effectively, conflict can even give us a better understanding of the problem because it often forces us to look at new information. Finally, group solidarity can be strengthened as members realize that they have overcome a serious problem.

As we have seen, in most instances conflicts appear because we perceive incompatible goals or threats to our ego. In short, we are frustrated or believe we are about to be frustrated by the behavior of someone in the group. Conflicts can usually be traced to four interrelated causes.

Causes of Conflict

First, *our individual personality (introvert, extrovert, aggressive, passive, and so on) has conditioned us to respond to events in ways that often appear to be habitual.* Without much forethought, we seem to gravitate to our basic personality. Often that personality creates behavior that is negatively perceived by other people. Ask yourself if *you* are creating the conflict because you are acting in an attacking, boasting, or dominating manner. In short, be careful that you do not become a cause of the conflict. As the great philosopher Pogo once remarked in the comic strip, "We have met the enemy, and he is us."

Second, *our perceived, and often rigid, relationships with the other group members can also cause controversy.* If we respond to someone in reference to only the role he or she occupies (boss, leader, fellow student), we limit our options when disagreements arise. A narrowing of behavioral choices is frustrating and can produce conflict.

Third, *the meanings people attach to words during the group's deliberations can be a primary cause of conflict.* We can never fully know someone else's meaning for a particular word. The simple word *gay* may cause some group members to react emotionally. Be aware of the power of words.

Fourth, *conflicts often occur because certain people mentally withdraw from the group.* When someone in the group, regardless of the reason, draws away from the group it can make the other members very angry. They infer that the "departed" person is disloyal because he or she has abandoned the group.

Finally, *conflict can be created because someone in the group actually enjoys arguing and controlling other people.* Someone in your group, because of his or her self-image or perception of power within the group, might attempt to control, dominate, and manipulate the group into situations in which conflict is inevitable.

For anyone who has been involved in a group, the five causes of conflict are obvious. They can keep a group from accomplishing its purpose, produce tension that interferes with the quality of the discussion, and even destroy the group by pushing it to its extreme. Therefore, it behooves you to know the signs of group conflict and how to manage it when it appears. Let us examine a few strategies you might find helpful as you attempt to guide a group over these difficult periods.

Managing Conflict

First, *try to get everyone to agree that, although the conflict might begin in what appears to be an irrational manner, it can be settled responsibly and intelligently.* This sets a tone that can disarm even the most antagonistic members of a group. What you are getting people to say is "perhaps we can work things out." It is the "perhaps" that is often the first step in dealing with conflict. This approach is far more effective than saying the conflict cannot be resolved or pretending that the conflict does not exist.

Second, *define the conflict.* Be as specific as possible as you urge the participants, including yourself, to focus on the issue—whether it is an issue of content ("I know from my reading that approximately 25 percent of all babies born in the United States are born to unwed mothers") or an issue of personality ("John, like all men, you don't care about unwed mothers"). To help mediate the conflict, you could say, "It seems to me, Tom, that you and Mary are arguing over two issues: first, the exact number of people who are affected by this problem and, second, Mary's comments regarding your attitude about the consequences of the problem. Would you both agree?"

Once you have clarified the issues of the conflict, all parties can begin to focus on solutions to the controversy. If you are too vague, the conflict may never be identified or resolved. By being specific, you let all parties check their perceptions and give them a place to begin.

Third, *avoid putting the participants into a win or lose position.* The solution to a conflict need not mean that someone wins and someone loses. If you were to say, "Mary, you are wrong when you say Tom is not interested in the problems facing unwed mothers," you would be placing Mary in a losing situation. The key is to have people focus on the common interest that brought them together rather than individual positions. The notion of separating people from problems and issues is at the heart of successful conflict resolution.

Fourth, *try to mediate the direction and tone of the conversation.* You could say, "Mary, why don't you give Tom a chance to explain his point again, and then we can see if the two of you are disagreeing or just expressing the same idea with different words."

Fifth, *slow down the discussion during the conflict.* Conflict episodes often move so fast that they can get out of control before anyone realizes what is happening.

Sixth, *you need to respect people who do not like confrontations or any form of conflict.* Many people avoid conflict at any cost. These people tend to withdraw from the group when conflict occurs. Once they mentally leave, it is hard to recapture their interest. Therefore, work to establish an atmosphere that keeps people focused on issues, not personalities.

Seventh, *although at times you may have to refer to people by name, you should try to develop the practice of using group pronouns as a way of centering on content instead of people.* Notice how words such as "we" and "our" focus the discussion on the group, while pronouns such as "I," " me," and "you" and specific names (Tom and Ann) can pit members against each other. This technique has all parties seeing themselves as attacking the problem instead of each other.

Eighth, *seek a position of compromise whenever possible*. We already noted the importance of avoiding a win-or-lose position; getting members to give a little is often a good way out of the either/or dilemma. Notice how compromise is used in the following example:

> There seems to be two different proposals on the floor. Some believe that we should give the men's golf team one thousand dollars, while others would like the money to go to the debate team. Perhaps we might give each team five hundred dollars. What do you think of that idea?

We all need to get over the notion that compromise is a form of appeasement. A healthier view is the one expressed by the British statesman Edmund Burke: "Every human benefit and enjoyment, every virtue and every prudent act, is founded on compromise and barter."

Ninth, *be willing to admit it when you are wrong*. On many occasions, conflict can be managed and kept under control if we are willing to take the difficult stance and grant that we made a mistake.

Finally, *if you are the target of the conflict, it is important that you try to stay calm*. This advice, of course, falls into the category of counsel that is easier to state than to act out. We all know how hard it is to remain composed when we feel we are under siege. Yet, by remaining patient, we can calm the entire group and perhaps get them to resolve the conflict.

Conflict and Culture

Although interpersonal conflict is part of every culture, each culture's ways of perceiving and dealing with conflict are influenced by its values. More specifically, our culture helps us define conflict and determine how it can be managed.

Not all cultures agree on what constitutes discord and conflict. In North America, there is a general belief that we can experience controversy over issues and not perceive the debate in personal terms. That is to say, most people are able to distinguish between conflicts based on tasks and those related to personalities. This is not the case with many East Asian and Latin cultures. Members of these cultures believe people, ideas, and issues cannot be separated; they are one and the same. Hence, members of these cultures are not likely to engage in direct hostility, even over tasks or assignments. Interpersonal harmony is highly valued, so people in these cultures seek to "save face" for themselves, as well as for others.

In many Mediterranean cultures, the view of conflict is very different from the one found in East Asia and Latin America. People in the Mediterranean area perceive conflict as a natural way of life. They expect people to have intense feelings on many issues. In a group, the expectation is one of debate, argument, direct confrontation, and controversy. It is also anticipated that the combatants will be extremely animated and boisterous when dealing with conflict. To the English and Japanese, however, who value a calm and reserved demeanor, this vigorous approach to group conflict would be considered rude and even vulgar. For them, a more indirect approach to conflict would be the proper method.

Finally, there are cultural differences regarding the conflicting participants. In cultures that stress the equality of all people and seek to avoid distinctions based on class, caste, rank, and superior and subordinate roles, there is apt to be more group and interpersonal conflict. These cultures encourage people to speak up and have their say in the matter ("The squeaky wheel gets the grease"). However, in cultures in which roles and status are clearly defined (Japan, Mexico), people are less likely to challenge the thinking of someone of higher standing.

Barriers to Discussion

The most common barriers to successful group discussion are violations of the guidelines we offered for participation and leadership. There are, however, some additional barriers worth noting. Because they affect everyone in a group, a common effort must be made to overcome these seven barriers whenever they surface.

Apathy among group members is perhaps the most common barrier to successful group discussion. Apathy is a complex phenomenon. It can be brought to the group by a single member or it can be generated during the life of the group. Apathy can be reflected in a variety of ways. A member might withdraw from the group, or the entire group could surrender any vitality or spirit it had at the outset of the meeting. In any case, apathy, and all of its external and internal manifestations, can destroy a group. When a group appears apathetic, you should not be reluctant to ask the participants to pause and examine their indifference. Although the following quotation is from an anonymous source, we would nevertheless exhort you to remember the wisdom of these words the next time you drift toward being apathetic or see it in your group:

> Indifference never wrote great works, nor thought out striking inventions, nor reared the solemn architecture that awes the soul, nor breathed sublime music, nor painted glorious pictures, nor undertook heroic philanthropies. All these grandeurs are born of enthusiasms, and done heartily.

Although some cultures are comfortable with high levels of formality (German, Mexico, English, Japanese), in most instances people from Western cultures do not like **excessive formality.** Whether through rules or attitudes, an inordinate amount of formality hampers participation and increases tension. Whereas some rules might be helpful, too many rules appear restrictive and can keep the members stiff in both mind and communication.

Closely related to formality is the problem of **control.** A lack of freedom and spontaneity destroys the free flow of ideas, feelings, and information. Control, like apathy, can take many forms. One person may try to monopolize a conversation as a means of control, while another may exercise control by only calling on certain people to talk. Regardless of how control shows itself, it is a barrier to successful group communication.

Dogmatism, although a corollary to the idea of control, is also a barrier that plagues many discussion groups. If a group or any of its members is dogmatic and asserts principles and opinions as if they were gospel, the entire discussion suffers. Dogmatism is characterized by narrow-mindedness and authoritarianism, both of which have no place in group discussion.

A **lack of patience** is another communication barrier that must be overcome if a group is to reach its full potential. In our culture, dispatch is valued, yet, as we have seen, the group process takes time. Sharing opinion and research is often tedious. Without patience, the group process is rushed and characterized by jumping to conclusions. Do not let this happen to your group. Remember the words of the Persian poet Saadi, "Whoever has no patience has no wisdom."

Our sixth barrier has been alluded to elsewhere in this chapter. However, because of its negative impact on group communication, we have decided to examine the topic one more time. Simply put, a **nonsupportive atmosphere** can be a major barrier to successful group discussion. This lack of support can take a number of forms. Our words can be harsh if we abruptly and bluntly say to someone, "Your lack of insight into this problem is hurting the entire group." A nonsupportive atmosphere can also be created by our actions. Think of the negative messages being sent to someone if we fail to look at them, lean back in our chair with our arms folded, seldom smile, or remain silent after they offer a personal opinion. All of nonverbal acts fail to extend support to our communication partners.

The final barrier, **groupthink,** is a concept that grew out of the work of Irving L. Janis. Groupthink is a type of conformity that is directed at ideas as well as people. Group members perceive that cooperation is crucial and that everyone must work together toward a common goal. However, some groups, because of peer pressure and a desire to appear confident, take this position to the extreme. They become closed-minded and refuse even to look at contrary views and opinions. People and ideas that fail to conform are discouraged and even ignored. Groups can overcome groupthink if they grant that it is a potential barrier and work to eliminate the causes of individual and group conformity. There are a number of steps that can be taken to overcome the barrier of groupthink. First, the group must encourage free and open discussion of all issues. Second, alternatives must be welcomed during the entire course of the discussion. Third, the consequences of all decisions must be considered, even if they may be negative. Finally, what has been decided should be periodically reviewed to determine if earlier decisions are still valid in light of newer findings. Perhaps the best way of survive groupthink is to heed the good advice of the humorist Thomas Haliburton, "Hear one side and you will be in the dark; hear both sides, and all will be clear."

The Role of Culture in Group Communication

It seems only fitting that we move from a discussion of communication barriers to an examination of the role of culture on group discussion. For if the group members fail to have an appreciation of how culture might influence group communication, a group might experience some serious interpersonal problems. Small-group communication settings involve intercultural communication when a group is composed of people from diverse cultural backgrounds. This occurs in international settings, when people from various countries and cultures meet to discuss international politics, economics, or business and in domestic areas, when civic bodies attempt to solve problems within the community or when students representing numerous ethnic backgrounds meet to recommend school policies and actions. We will look at some of the ways culture is apt to manifest during the course of the discussion process.

First, *culture influences whether or not we value a group or an individual.* In cultures that have a strong group orientation (East Asian, Latin American), collectivism rather than individualism is stressed; cooperation is emphasized over competition. People raised in these cultures find it natural to work for a common goal. However, people from cultures that place the individual ahead of the group (North American, French, Danish) usually find it difficult to adapt individual goals to collective goals. Think of the strong message of individualism in the phrase "God helps those who help themselves." This type of orientation stresses a "I'll do it myself" attitude instead of a cooperative set of values. The individual is also expected to accept blame for decisions that lead to bad consequences ("You made your bed; now lie in it"). In a sense, North Americans want to know who to castigate when things go wrong. Asian and Latin cultures, however, have a strong group orientation rather than an individual orientation; decisions result from group interaction and group loyalty. The group, not the individual, is responsible for the consequences of its action, and when something goes wrong the group, not the individual, is held responsible.

A second difference can be found in how cultures perceive and value *conformity*— a topic we discussed in our section on barriers. This aspect of group behavior is somewhat related to the idea of collective versus individualistic cultures. Cultures that place a high value on individualism (North American, Australian, English, Israeli) encourage and tolerate independence, initiative, and self-reliance. These traits nourish nonconformity. On the other hand, people from collective cultures (Latin American, East Asian) seldom violate group norms. This desire to agree with others and conform shows itself in a number of ways that directly affect group interaction. For example, people from cultures that stress accord and harmony over deviation usually do not express their feelings if they sense it will offend another person. They remain silent and use indirect speech. For example, Native Americans do not like to humiliate or embarrass other people, hence they are apt to agree with what is being discussed, even if they internally hold the opposite view. Asian and Filipino members of a group might even smile and nod politely to show they are conforming, when in reality they may disagree with what is transpiring. Being aware of cultural differences as they apply to conformity will help you understand the messages, or lack of them, you get from other people.

Third, the influence of culture in groups can be seen in how participants *use language*. In cultures that have a strong verbal tradition (North American, Arab, Jewish), many people use words with great ease. Members of these cultures value talk, rely heavily on verbal language to express their feelings, and tend to be very direct. However, in many Asian cultures, where politeness is highly valued, people are less direct. They also hold the view that in many instances the strongest and most important emotions and feelings cannot be expressed with words. There is even a Chinese proverb that states "Fear the dog that is not barking." Because verbal language is often held in check, people from these cultures "read" other people by their nonverbal actions. Individuals from these cultures believe that people often understand each other without words. In fact, in the writings of Buddhism, one line notes that "there is a supreme truth that words can neither reach nor express." When in a group, people with this point of view might not talk as much as others would like them to. You need to appreciate the role of silence in certain cultures and not push too hard when people from Asian cultures wish to remain silent. They are taking part in their own way. *For them, silence speaks*. Not only do these cultures value silence and deliberation, but they also value process over product. These Eastern cultures want the participants to enjoy the group. For them, the final product is less important than harmony among the group members. According to this orientation, silence contributes to that sense of harmony.

Fourth, a culture's perception of *time* can also be revealed during group discussion. In our culture, we learn that "time is money" and should not be wasted. Like the Germans and Swiss, we value time and try not to squander it. This often forces us to rush, be impulsive, and make quick decisions when we are in a group. People from Mexico, Japan, China, and Korea have an entirely different view of time. They believe one should give full attention to the moment and not act as if one is just "passing through." In a group, they tend to be more reflective and resist moving too quickly. A Korean proverb says, "Even if a bridge is made of stone it may not be safe." The meaning is obvious—proceed with caution. People with this outlook will often want to take time when considering all phases of a problem.

The desire to go slowly is also seen in the amount of time various cultures set aside to *establish relationships*. In North American culture, people are often valued because they are open and friendly. In North America, there is a belief that it does not take long to get to know someone. An outgrowth of this orientation is found in the speed with which a group of North Americans is ready to focus on the work at hand. Many cultures take an opposing view when it comes to developing social and working relationships. The Japanese and the Mexicans, for example, believe in establishing rapport with their associates before they conduct business. In a group situation, this value is translated into a slower pace and a desire to postpone focusing on the problem before the members of the group know each other.

Fifth, culture can also govern the processes by which the group *negotiates and reaches compromise*. For instance, in the Persian language, the word for "compromise" does not mean a midway solution that both sides can accept, as it does in English. Instead, it means surrendering one's principles. Also, a mediator is seen as a meddler, someone who is bargaining uninvited. In India, Mexico, and the Middle East, the process of negotiation is enjoyed. Bartering is seen as an act of bargaining, in which there is give and take. Each person sets out to obtain the best possible deal, and everyone enjoys the process. However, this sense of pleasure in negotiation is not found in most Asian cultures. Many people from these cultures find the entire act of direct negotiation rather awkward. They prefer compromise over conflict. To be an effective group member, you need to discover if the background of the other participants makes them either willing to compromise or delighted with the prospects of a good argument.

Sixth, you will find that there are also cultural differences with regard to *decision making*. Although some of these ideas might have been hinted at earlier, they are worth underscoring at this time. In the Japanese culture, where consensus is valued, decision making that does not have "winners" or "losers" is the norm rather than the exception. Not only is consent the rule, everyone is expected to support the decision even if they do not agree with the conclusion of the group. The Chinese, because they also value outward signs of harmony and consensus, hold much the same view as the Japanese toward decision making. In Latin America, decision making is often autocratic. People are socialized in these cultures to respect authority and not to question superiors. Hence, when working in groups, they will often look to the "leader" for all decisions. This same approach toward decision making is also found in Germany and France where authority means "top-down" decisions.

Decision making is also influenced by a culture's view toward *uncertainty*. That is to say, how do members of a particular culture cope with ambiguous and equivocal situations?

In many cultures (Japan, Greek, French), uncertainty and the unpredictable make people anxious. They function more effectively when there is structure and specific rules to follow. People who dislike uncertainty also avoid taking too many chances. Cultures who have socialized their members to be less apprehensive of the uncertainty of life (United States, Great Britain, Canada) have a higher tolerance for ambiguity, tend to dislike too many rules, and are willing to take risks. You can imagine the potential for communication problems when members from these two orientations are in the same group. The clash of cultural values would influence everything from the pace of the meeting to the amount of control given to the leader. Being aware of these differences can help *you* be a better group member when you are in a culturally diverse group.

Seventh, as a member of a group, you will observe cultural differences in *nonverbal communication*. For example, cultures have differing views toward *clothing and appearance*. An Arab wearing a robe called a *dishdasha* or *thobe* and a headpiece can cause some people to feel strange because he or she does not understand the significance of a person's appearance. If some members of a group are from cultures that value formality, such as Germany and Japan, they are apt to dress in what appears to be formal attire. On the other hand, in the North American culture, being relaxed is valued; hence, we usually attend meetings in casual clothing. Try to remember that one mode of dress is not superior to another, but, rather, it expresses a different attitude toward clothing and general appearance.

The use we make of our *body* is also a reflection of our culture. As we noted in chapter 4, most people from the Mediterranean cultures use large gestures and are more animated than most people from England and Southeast Asia. You should not allow the size or ferocity of another member's gestures to represent his or her level of interest or commitment to the group. Rather, you should realize that movement and gestures are but another cultural difference found in small-group behavior.

Because *emotional expressions* are culturally learned, the members of your group might use facial expressions in a unique way. The Chinese and Japanese, for example, do not readily show emotion in public. These cultures even use the face to conceal rather than reveal emotions. However, in Latin American and Mediterranean cultures, signs of emotion are not only shown but often exaggerated.

The amount and type of *eye contact* in a group are still other aspects of culture that you need to understand. In our culture, eye contact is used to show interest and to indicate that the channels of communication are open. However, in many Asian, Native American, and Latin cultures, too much direct eye contact creates feelings of discomfort. Exactly the opposite orientation toward gaze is found in Arab cultures, in which one expects to stare directly into the eyes of one's communication partners.

You should also be aware of cultural modifications with regard to *touch*. It might seem very natural in the group setting to reach over and touch someone as a way of making a point or offering comfort, yet cultural variations in this form of communication must be considered. For example, Muslims eat and do happy things with the right hand, but to touch another person with the left hand is a social insult; the left hand is reserved for toilet functions. People in cultures such as the Jewish, Italian, and French touch a great deal, but less touching is found among the English, Chinese, and Japanese. In short, be careful of using touch as a form of communication if you don't know all group members' views of physical contact.

Videoconferences now link people together.

Courtesy of MEANS Telcom Videoconferencing.

Smell is another nonverbal variable that is influenced by culture. Although in our culture we tend to cover up body odor with perfumes and lotions, many cultures believe that natural smells are very pleasing and don't use any artificial odors. This means you might sit next to someone in the group whose body odor is quite different from your own.

There are also cultural differences in the use of the *voice*. Be prepared for people who use a great deal of volume such as Italians, Greeks, and Arabs, as well as those who speak in hushed tones (Thai, Japanese).

There are also cultural variations in the use of *space*. Eastern European, Arab, and Latin cultures consider it normal for people to sit very close to each other. The North American culture regards this lack of space as a violation of its cultural norm toward privacy. There are also cultures, such as the Chinese, who prefer side-by-side seating rather than face-to-face arrangements. Be prepared for these disparities as you interact with people from different cultures.

Perhaps we should conclude our section on cultural differences within a group by mentioning *the role of gender* in small-group communication. When in a small-group situation, men tend to speak more frequently and for longer periods of time than do women because of the way they have been socialized in North America. It behooves all members of the group, regardless of gender, to overcome these differences so that participation can be equally shared. As we have said repeatedly, it is to everyone's advantage to pool ideas and information.

Taking Part in a Videoconference

In chapter 15, we talked about using television as a device for giving speeches. We now turn our attention to the use of television as it applies to group interaction, more specifically, videoconferencing. The videoconference, often referred to as an electronic meeting, electronically links people together who are physically separated. For people living and working in the electronic age, knowing how to participate in a teleconference is almost as much as a necessity as knowing how to use a computer or a fax machine.

The practice of holding videoconferences has grown so popular in the last few years that now many organizations, universities, and corporations own their equipment. The benefits of such meetings are obvious. Not only is the expense of travel eliminated, but also electronic meetings take less time and can be arranged quickly. They also foster cooperation among geographically separated employees; the office in Mexico City can know what the office in Madison is thinking. The videoconference also allows more people to participate. There is even some research that suggests that electronic meetings are more orderly and productive than traditional face-to-face discussions.

Educational uses of teleconferencing are also increasing. Basically, there is a need to reach learners who cannot travel to the classroom. The teleconference provides an effective way for the teacher and class to interact as if they were in a single setting.

As a professional, you will most likely be a member of a group that is using television to conduct your company's business. To assure that your appearance will be a successful one, let us offer you some information on (a) the characteristics of videoconferences, (b) preparing for a videoconference, and (c) participating in a videoconference.

The Characteristics of a Videoconference

As we have indicated, the videoconference is basically a group communication experience conducted via television. Therefore, much of what we proposed in chapter 15 concerning televised speech and the material on group discussion already presented in this chapter applies to the videoconference. However, there are two general characteristics of the videoconference that make it different from face-to-face exchanges. You should be aware of those differences so that you can make the necessary adjustments to your preparation and participation.

First, there is the obvious *physical separation* in electronic meetings and classes that is not found in face-to-face groups. This separation brings with it some specific needs to modify some of your communication behaviors. For example, you will not be able to touch your colleagues or even exchange objects. A certain amount of intimacy will be lost. The physical separation may also mean a separation in time, as the exchange crosses time zones both in the United States and abroad. One group could want a short break for morning coffee while another set of participants is ready for a long lunch. Because of these and other limitations, you need to develop a new outlook toward interpersonal distance. Simply stated, although you will be expected to talk to your video partner or television instructor, you will not be able to sit near him or her.

Even the premeeting chitchat that is so much a part of the classroom and group experience is influenced by the fact that the participants are at different locations. The imposed separation also has an impact on the kinds of feedback you will use. Later in this section we will talk to you about ways of adapting your feedback to the limitations brought about by physical separation.

Second, the *electronic components of television* (sight and sound) also control interaction. Who is on camera, the angle of the camera, volume control, and the like influence who and what is being seen and heard. Even the clock plays a unique role in this medium. Television time is expensive, valuable, and usually in short supply.

To be an active participant in a videoconference, you must be prepared. Many of the steps of preparation have been discussed throughout this book. However, as you learned in the last chapter, television does call for some additional planning.

Preparing for a Videoconference

First, make sure you and everyone concerned with the conference *knows the purpose of the meeting*. Because the participants most likely do not have daily contact, it becomes crucial that they know *exactly* what is going to be discussed. Whenever possible, the purpose, much like the specific purpose of a speech, should be stated in one clear, concise sentence. For example: "The purpose of the May 8th videoconference is to have all members of the sales force discuss what can be done to improve intercultural communication within the organization."

Second, *try to find out all you can about the other participants*—Who are they? Why have they been asked to participate in the conference? Who will the leader be? If it is an educational setting, who is the instructor? How much will they know about the topic? Will there be a guest? Will all the participants be of equal status? How much participation is expected of each member? Are there going to be people involved that use English as a second language? What countries and cultures will be represented?

Third, *prepare by analyzing the technical aspects of the meeting*. Here are a few questions you should ask in this category: Where will the participants be located? Hotels? Television studios? Classrooms? The company conference room? How many people will be at each site? How long will the conference last? How many cameras will be employed? What time zones will be involved?

Fourth, *arrange for your visuals long before the actual conference begins*. Participants are at different locations and therefore coordinating any visual aid will take careful preplanning.

Finally, while you cannot establish much rapport with the people at separate sites, *try to create a relaxed and friendly atmosphere* with the participants at your site. Getting to know each other and feeling at ease will help overcome some of the fear associated with appearing on television.

Participating in a Videoconference

Your effectiveness as a participant in a videoconference can be enhanced if you follow the advice we have offered in chapter 15 when we discussed television speaking. In addition, much of what we said about group processes earlier in this chapter directly relates to videoconferencing. However, there are a few other communication behaviors that will make your appearance much more rewarding. Let us offer a few of these at this time.

1. Follow the teleconference schedule and encourage others to do the same. This means that contributions should be brief and relevant so time is not wasted. We have seen some students dominate an instructor's time during a videoconference. When this happens, they tend to be on camera more than the professor. To make television more interesting, it is a good idea to change speakers as often as possible.

2. Emphasize good communication skills. People expect more of you if you are on television—this also includes the way you communicate. Therefore, eye contact, body language, vocal variety, appearance, and the like must be given special attention. It might be helpful to review the advice we offered in chapter 15 on television presentations so that you understand all the nonverbal actions from attire to posture.

3. In most instances, you should identify yourself each time you speak. For example, "This is Mike Smith in El Cajon." In hookups with only a few people, you might be able to suspend the identification once the meeting progresses. You can also disregard the self-introduction if you find yourself talking a great deal. People will find it offensive if you repeat your name too many times.

4. Most of your questions and comments should be aimed at specific people, and those people should be identified. "Susan, what is the reaction in your office to this new proposal?" Or, "Doctor Jones, could you please explain the point in a little more detail?" The reason for the verbal contact is that not everyone will be able to use eye contact to get the floor.

5. When you ask a question, wait a few seconds for the reply. People need time to think about their response. In addition, there is a split-second delay when using most telecommunications equipment.

6. Because you are not on camera all of the time, or even being seen by all the other participants, it is easy to lose concentration. Do not let this happen! Make yourself listen to all of the proceedings. In this way, you will be able to take an active role during all of the meeting.

7. Remember you must adapt your feedback to the electronic medium. This means using verbal feedback even though you are on television. You may not always know what is "on the screen," but your microphone, or one near you, will always be turned on. We have seen many participants embarrass themselves by talking to each other without realizing their microphones were transmitting every word they were saying to over fifty other people.

8. Emphasize social niceties and a relaxed atmosphere as a way of overcoming the formal nature of a television studio or a conference room. Using first names, smiling, and laughing are just a few things you can do to put people at ease. Try to keep a friendly and attentive expression on your face even when you are not "the star of the moment." You may not always know when the camera will focus on you, and it would indeed be embarrassing if you were caught yawning or doodling when the boss or professor was talking.

Evaluating a Discussion

For centuries, philosophers have told all who would listen, "Know thyself." You should also seek to "improve thyself." One way this can be accomplished is through group and self-evaluation. In fact, most groups find it useful to evaluate the process they use and the effectiveness of their techniques. An evaluation of a group's behavior and actions can take place at any time and can take a variety of forms. Evaluation allows a group time to measure and isolate its successes and failures, and it points out what happened and why.

Many groups find it helpful to evaluate periodically as they move through the discussion process. They simply stop and ask questions concerning what is happening, why it is happening, what the results are, and what should be done.

Evaluation can examine a host of variables. Members can evaluate group processes, participation, leadership, communication patterns and problems, interaction, tasks, and final products. These evaluations can be made by individual participants or by the group as a whole.

A large number of fill-in forms can be used in group and individual evaluations. Many groups enjoy developing their own evaluation forms.

Remember that, through evaluation and analysis, we are able to learn from the group experience. The insights gained from each discussion can contribute to more effective participation in the next group in which we find ourselves.

Summary

Whether to exchange information in a learning situation or to solve problems, we all find ourselves participating in group deliberations. As discussants, we may find ourselves participating in symposiums, panels, group discussions, support groups, educational groups, and problem-solving groups. Regardless of the context, it is important that we be well informed and follow an organizational scheme that leads us through the important phases of the problem. If the purpose of the group is to solve a problem, it is useful to observe the five steps of reflective thinking developed by John Dewey: (1) define the problem, (2) analyze the causes and effects, (3) identify all possible solutions, (4) select the best solution, and (5) put the solution into operation.

When participating in or leading a group, each person should adhere to a logical pattern, be prepared, take an active role, ask questions, supply leadership, be tolerant of diverse views, use feedback, create a friendly atmosphere, listen carefully, allow for deviant behavior, be willing to play a variety of roles, relate comments to what is transpiring at the moment, deal with conflict constructively, work to overcome barriers, adapt to cultural differences, and evaluate the group's progress.

Finally, if you find yourself in a group that is using videoconferencing, you should know some of the characteristics of this medium, how to prepare for videoconferencing, and some of the steps of successful participation.

Index